BACKGROUND AND DEVELOPMENT
OF
BRETHREN DOCTRINES
1650–1987

by
Dale R. Stoffer

Published by the
BRETHREN ENCYCLOPEDIA, INC.
Philadephia, Pennsylvania

1989

BRETHREN ENCYCLOPEDIA MONOGRAPH SERIES
William R. Eberly, editor

Number 2

BACKGROUND AND DEVELOPMENT OF BRETHREN DOCTRINES
1650–1987

Dale R. Stoffer

Availability of related materials: Related materials are available from The Brethren Encyclopedia, Inc.: *The Brethren Encyclopedia*, vols. I, II, and III (1983–1984); *The German Hymnody of the Brethren (1720–1903)* (1986); and a paperback book entitled *Meet the Brethren* (1984). Requests for information or orders may be sent to The Brethren Encyclopedia, Inc., 313 Fairview Ave., Ambler, PA 19002.

Explanation of logo: The logo used on the title pages of the volumes of this series is derived from a seal which has been attributed to Alexander Mack, Jr. (1712–1803), son of the first Brethren minister and himself an active elder in colonial America. The *Brethren Encyclopedia* article on this "Mack seal" states, referring to the religious symbols: "Central to these is the cross, on which is superimposed a heart, suggesting a strong emphasis on sacrifice and devotion. The importance of bearing spiritual fruit is represented graphically by a vine, laden with grapes, whose branches spring from the heart. All of these symbols express an understanding of discipleship that was significant in the early history of the Brethren" (p. 775). The "Mack seal" has often been used by Brethren congregations on stationary, artwork, and publications.

ISBN 0-936693-22-3

Typeset by Eisenbrauns, Winona Lake, Indiana
Printed in the U.S.A.

CONTENTS

FOREWORD

We continue to be blessed by M. R. Zigler's remarkable achievement in gathering 125 members of the five largest Brethren bodies at Tunker House in June 1973. Though they came together to "just shake hands," we are gratified they did more. In subsequent meetings, the historians implemented their mentor's counsel by successfully giving us the already treasured three volume BRETHREN ENCYCLOPEDIA. Soon after their indefatigable editor brought to fruition the monumental task, they inaugurated a monograph series in order to make available basic sources of our faith tradition. For the first volume, they chose the extensive research of their editor's spouse, Hedwig T. Durnbaugh's THE GERMAN HYMNODY OF THE BRETHREN (1986).

Consistent with their purpose, the second selection in the monograph series provides sources which will continue to be invaluable as long as people study and reflect on our heritage as Brethren. This reprint makes available the fruit of five years of extensive research by Dale Stoffer for his doctoral dissertation at Fuller Theological Seminary, THE BACKGROUND AND DEVELOPMENT OF THOUGHT AND PRACTICE IN THE GERMAN BAPTIST BRETHREN (DUNKER) AND THE BRETHREN (PROGRESSIVE) CHURCHES (c. 1650–1979).

As a teacher and interpreter of Brethren thought, I am gratified to have Stoffer's research available in something other than the printouts from University Microfilms International. Students who have read his dissertation have been enthusiastic. In checking out his references, I have been impressed with the thoroughness of his research. In this volume we have the first extensive systematic treatment of Brethren thought. Though rooted in the Progressive body, the author's fairness is revealed throughout as illustrated in his comprehensive treatment of the issues and the story of the major three-way schism.

Whereas some of us have concentrated more on discipleship and ecclesiological and ethical concerns, Stoffer adds doctrinal themes such as Christology, sin, soteriology, and eschatology. Though human limitations prevented him from completing the story of all five Brethren bodies, it is invaluable to have the life and thought of our common history related so thoroughly, from Brethren origins through the "great divide" of the 1880s. Then as frosting on an already tasty cake, we have a more complete story of the Ashland and Grace branches of the church, the part of the history concerning which I have been the most ignorant.

This monograph will serve well all who agree that historiography is intimately a part of seeking faithfulness to our present calling. For as we seek to understand who we were and what we believed, we are formulating visions of what God wants us to become.

Dale W. Brown
Professor, Christian Theology
Bethany Theological Seminary

ACKNOWLEDGMENTS

Though written for the most part nine years ago, the following acknowledgments are just as appropriate today as they were in 1980. Several of the people listed below are now deceased, but this fact makes the mention of their part in this work all the more significant. (A few minor revisions have been made to the original text and the last three paragraphs are newly added or revised.)

This work is the culmination of a refining process during which the writer was indebted to a number of individuals for their special insights and suggestions. Throughout the process Dr. Geoffrey Bromiley (of Fuller Theological Seminary) offered valuable guidance for theological, historical, and grammatical questions. All this was done in his usual warm and encouraging manner. At several stages of the program, Dr. Paul K. Jewett (also of Fuller) provided much appreciated counsel on a variety of theological issues. Of particular note are individuals from the major Brethren bodies who shared their understanding of the Brethren heritage and/or their firsthand accounts of the events and people who have shaped Brethren thought during this century. These people include Marcus Miller, M.D., and Fred Benedict from the Old German Baptist Brethren Church; L. W. Shultz and Dr. Vernard Eller from the Church of the Brethren; Dr. Herman Hoyt, Dr. Homer Kent, Sr., and Dr. Charles Mayes from the National Fellowship of Grace Brethren Churches; Dr. Delbert Flora, Dr. Jerry Flora, Dr. Joseph R. Shultz, Dr. Leslie Lindower, Dr. Frederick Burkey, Rev. J. Ray Klingensmith, Dr. Glenn L. Clayton, A. Glenn Carpenter, Rev. D. C. White, and Grace Ferre of The Brethren Church; and Dr. Kenneth Monroe, formerly of The Brethren Church. No small thanks also go to Dr. Donald Durnbaugh and Dr. Roger Sappington for their work in making primary resources accessible to the researcher in the Brethren Source Book Series.

Deserving of special mention for their generous assistance in making available rare source materials are the staffs of the Brethren Historical Library and Archives, Elgin, Illinois; Bethany Theological Seminary, Oak Brook, Illinois; Juniata College Library, Huntingdon, Pennsylvania; Grace Theological Seminary Library, Winona Lake, Indiana; Ashland College Library, Ashland, Ohio; and the Mennonite Historical Library, Goshen, Indiana. Separate recognition is to be accorded Bradley Weidenhamer, the librarian at Ashland Theological Seminary, whose liberal loaning of archival materials, to a large extent, made the writing of the section on The Brethren Church possible.

The support of Henk and Brenda Colijn has been particularly meaningful to the author. Not only have they made their computer system and technical expertise available for some of the more tedious aspects of the project over the last two years, but their friendship has been a constant source of encouragement as well.

The present form of this study is the fruit of the joint cooperation of all the major Brethren groups mentioned herein. Its appearance as the second work in the Brethren Encyclopedia Monograph Series is a tribute to the fact that we are still Brethren, brothers and sisters in the Lord.

Finally, it is with heartfelt gratitude that the writer acknowledges his debt to his wife, Marcia. Her unselfish support during nearly five years of research at Fuller Theological Seminary, climaxed by her typing of this manuscript twice, is the principal reason for the existence of this study.

INTRODUCTION

Overview, Purpose and Scope of the Study

In 1708 a group of eight men and women who had separated themselves from the established churches of Germany covenanted together to follow in humble obedience the footsteps of Jesus Christ. Asserting the fallible and limited nature of all human authorities, whether human reason, church creed, or papal dogma, they set out on a spiritual journey in which they sought to be guided by the outer Word of Scripture and the inner Word of the Spirit. Upon their removal to America, they and their spiritual heirs were faced with the vicissitudes wrought by a new and, at times, hostile culture and the anguish arising from internal dissension and schism. Inevitably, the cultural, political, and religious currents of American life have left their impression to varying degrees on each of the Brethren bodies.[1] Yet all groups that still bear the name "Brethren" would still profess fidelity to that original genius of a Spirit-led and Word-oriented community of believers committed to Jesus Christ.

The purpose of this study is basically fourfold. First, the European background and origins of the Brethren will be studied in order to (1) identify the interpretative tools and sources of authority used by the early Brethren to arrive at their distinctive beliefs and (2) characterize the basic features of Brethren thought and practice. In both cases an attempt will be made to suggest possible outside influences. Second, the impact of major American cultural and religious movements on Brethren thought and practice will be given special prominence.[2] Third, the thought of three men—Alexander Mack, Peter Nead, and J. Allen Miller—will be examined in depth. These men, who reached prominence during the eighteenth, nineteenth, and twentieth centuries respectively, were recognized by their peers as the leading exponents of the Brethren faith during their lifetimes.

Because of their influence, the writings of each of these men will be used as a "bench mark" for the thought of their respective periods. Fourth, on the basis of these three investigations, conclusions will be drawn about how the Brethren approach the theological task. Because of the Brethren claim to have no fixed theological standards other than Scripture and the resulting aversion to dogmatic theology, their theological method necessarily differs from that of Roman Catholics, Lutherans, and Reformed.

Due to the scope of this study, certain limitations must be set. No attempt will be made to detail the *historical* development of the church. This aspect of the church's life has already been well documented.[3] For the sake of background orientation, however, summaries of the historical progress of the church will be presented or, when possible, the historical and theological developments will be interwoven. In addition, this study will give primary attention to The Brethren Church (Progressives) following the 1882–1883 division and the Ashland Brethren following the 1939 split.

The Values of a Historical-Theological Study

The values of such a study as this are varied. First, a historical-theological method would seem to be the most logical approach to studying Brethren thought. Brethren doctrine cannot be studied in a "linear" fashion by assuming that the current emphases of the church are the same as those anywhere else on the time line (as has been done at times in the past). Because Brethren thought has undergone significant changes, an investigation of the significant emphases of each major period of Brethren history can reveal those elements of Brethren doctrine that have changed and those that have remained the same. On the basis of this investigation, definite conclusions can be made concerning the theological method of the

1

Brethren. A related benefit of such an approach is that possible cases in which interpreters of Brethren thought have misrepresented the heritage can be identified and evaluated.

Second, by tying the Brethren into the larger theological movements with which they were associated, it will be seen that Brethren thought did not evolve in a vacuum but actually represents a microcosm of European and American developments. A study of these developments may also aid in testing the hypotheses and conclusions advanced by other writers concerning phenomena of which the Brethren were a part, *e.g.*, Ernest Sandeen's thesis that "fundamentalism of the late nineteenth and early twentieth centuries in America was comprised of an alliance between dispensationalist and Princeton-oriented Calvinists."[4]

Third, this study can play a part in filling some of the gaps existing in the analysis of Brethren thought. The recent renaissance of research into Brethren heritage[5] has, for the most part, focused on Brethren history. Yet it is gratefully acknowledged that such a survey of Brethren thought as presented here would be difficult, if not impossible, were it not for the groundwork laid by this historical and source material research. It is hoped, however, that further analysis of the thought of the Brethren may be spurred by this work, especially into areas where only a summary treatment has been given.

Previous Work in the Field

Previous studies of Brethren thought have focused primarily on the origins and early development of Brethren theology in Germany and America. The first in-depth interpretation of Brethren thought was that made by Robert Porte who constructed a good case for the Pietistic indebtedness of the Brethren. However, he overlooks Anabaptist influence and makes use of few non-Brethren primary sources.[6] More recent studies have evaluated the relative importance of Anabaptism and Radical Pietism in shaping the Brethren mind. Though a consensus of opinion has evolved on this question (based on Eller's position below), the original working hypotheses might be characterized as follows: David Ensign stressed Radical Pietism and minimized Anabaptism, William Willoughby claimed about equal influence, Donald Durnbaugh stressed Anabaptism and minimized Radical Pietism, and Vernard Eller proposed a dialectical tension between the two elements.[7] These theses will be evaluated later in this work.

Very little attention has been given to Brethren thought between the late eighteenth and mid-

nineteenth centuries, due possibly to the inaccessibility of primary sources. However, a brief, but insightful, article has been written by Dale Brown on this period.[8] Likewise, only one major study, by Kerby Lauderdale, is available focusing on the crucial years of 1850–1883 which culminated in the division of the German Baptist Brethren Church.[9]

Though this study will limit itself to the course of the Brethren Church (Progressives) following the 1881–1883 division, it should be noted that an in-depth evaluation of the Church of the Brethren's interaction with twentieth century cultural, intellectual, and theological movements has been written by Herbert Hogan.[10] Dennis Martin has made a similar investigation of developments in the Brethren Church following the division. Martin's fine study has already covered most of the historical and some of the theological ground, but restudy of this field of research seems justified in light of the fact that Martin's use of primary source materials begins with 1914.[11] It is hoped that this paper will demonstrate that events in the teens, twenties, and thirties in the Brethren Church have their genesis in the years 1895 to 1910.

As can be seen from this brief review of studies interpreting the thought of the Brethren, there has been no work which has sought to present a comprehensive evaluation of the history of Brethren thought. This segmented approach to research on Brethren doctrine has resulted in the investigation of historical and theological events in isolation from preceding and succeeding phenomena. Thereby the possibility of misinterpreting Brethren thought and history is increased. This paper seeks to alleviate in some measure this need for a more comprehensive discussion of Brethren thought.

Strictures on the Use of the Term, "Theology"

Whenever the subject of theology comes up in Brethren circles, an apologetic must be offered for its consideration. The reason for this is not difficult to ascertain. One need only skim the minutes of German Baptist Brethren Annual Meetings or the periodical literature of any Brethren group to realize that the Brethren clearly emphasize the practical and devotional side of the Christian faith. Likewise, the aforementioned non-credal stance of the Brethren has created a general indifference or even antipathy toward closely reasoned dogmatic theology. This characteristic of the Brethren gave rise at the beginning of this century to the generalization:

The Dunker church has never been a theological church. All the theology it ever had it obtained from other denominations. Its contribution to Christianity has been a pietism of life and a devotion to certain Biblical practices which had been dropped in the history of Christianity.[12]

In another article in a similar vein, J. L. Gillin supported his contention that the Brethren have never been theological by appealing to the non-theological tradition of Pietism which the Brethren imbibed.[13] This theology/life style dichotomy has now found wide acceptance among interpreters of Brethren thought.[14]

Such a complete indifference to theology as suggested by Gillin is characteristic of neither Pietism nor the Brethren of the eighteenth and nineteenth centuries. The Pietists, to be sure, rejected entirely the theological method of Protestant Scholasticism. They deplored the subordinate position that was accorded Scripture when it was utilized as the source for proof texts to support the creeds or symbolical books. They reacted against the polemical style that was characteristic of many of the sermons and writings of the day. They criticized the priority which the study of dogmatic theology assumed over exegesis in the universities. They felt the legacy of these practices was a decline in personal piety and morality. The Pietists desired to replace the scholastic method with a *theologia practica*, a Biblical theology which was practical and devotional and whose guiding principles were *das Nützliche* (the edificatory), *Seligkeit* (the enjoyment of salvation), and *Gottseligkeit* (godliness). These criteria led to an evaluation of all aspects of traditional theology. Those doctrines whose emphasis would not foster piety and the edification of the believer were either not treated or given only peripheral attention.[15]

An investigation of Brethren literature of the eighteenth and nineteenth centuries reveals that the Brethren clearly followed the Pietistic penchant for devotional and edificatory writing. The majority (53%) of Brethren works published between 1713 and 1865 were devotional in nature (between 1866 and 1880 doctrinal writings predominate over devotional). Nevertheless, a significant percentage (33%) of Brethren materials published through 1865 were doctrinal in nature.[16] These doctrinal writings tend to reflect the Pietistic hermeneutical heritage. Though the Pietists would by no means have emphasized the ordinances to the extent the Brethren did, Brethren writers did, for the most part, omit discussion of the generally accepted evangelical truths concerning the doctrines of God, man, and sin while emphasizing their distinctive doctrinal views concerning salvation and the church, especially the ordinances. Likewise, the significant doctrinal writings of the period reveal the bias for Biblical theology as opposed to systematic theology. The influential writings of the spiritual leader of the early Brethren, Alexander Mack, Sr., and his son, Alexander Mack, Jr., are replete with studies of very practical doctrinal points (marriage, discipline, the ordinances) which begin with Old Testament thought on a particular subject and trace the development of the doctrine through to its fulfillment in the New Testament. Even the first and most influential Brethren theology of the nineteenth century, Peter Nead's *Theological Writings* (the title is significant for the use of the word "theological"), is not a true systematic theology. Nead simply arranges systematically various doctrinal themes (especially relating to salvation and the church) which he has investigated by tracing their development in Scripture. He allows the combined weight of a lengthy series of Scriptural quotations to demonstrate his doctrinal points. Little attempt is made to work out philosophically or rationally the implications of the relationships between these doctrines. What Vernard Eller has said concerning the early Brethren would apply to the Brethren generally up to the close of the nineteenth century. The Brethren "recognized the importance of a correct understanding of Christian doctrine." Among the Brethren there was no

hint of an "it doesn't matter what you believe" attitude. But on the other hand, . . . the Brethren saw doctrine as *correct* only insofar as it was *edifying*, relevant to one's immediate existence. The test of true doctrine is whether it edifies, not whether it is logically consistent. Just as soon as doctrine wandered toward the abstract and theoretical, . . . the Brethren lost all interest.

The position of . . . the Brethren surely can be described as antiintellectual [*sic*]; it accurately could be called nontheological if one confines the term "theology" to formal, speculative, systematic thought; it would be inaccurate to call the position doctrinally heedless or promiscuous; and it would be entirely out of order to term it irrational.[17]

Eller is entirely justified in attributing the term "non-theological" to the Brethren when theology is understood in a scholastic or dogmatic manner. However, the unqualified use of the term "non-theological," as Eller also points out, and the suggestion that theology and life style belong to mutually exclusive spheres (as noted in the writings of J. L. Gillin and others) do not find support from Brethren sources. Instead, investigation of Brethren literature reveals that these concepts have their source in the early twentieth century, initially among Brethren influenced by classical liberalism. The attack of Harnack and others against "dogma"[18] naturally struck a responsive chord among Brethren exposed to German liberalism in their pursuits of higher education.[19] When these men began to interpret the Brethren heritage on the basis of German liberalism, traits that were not characteristic of the Brethren—doctrinal indifference, the advocacy of theological pluralism—became a danger.[20] Though it must be pointed out that those who today refer to the pre-twentieth century Brethren as being "non-theological" have, for the most part, not been influenced by liberalism, yet their unqualified discarding of the term "theology" reflects a bias that is a legacy of a liberal view of the Brethren heritage.

This extended introductory discussion is included as a plea to recognize the legitimate use and domain of the term "theology" in Brethren studies. Traditionally, the Brethren saw an intimate connection between theology or doctrine and life style. Because of their commitment to the Bible "as it reads," Brethren practice was molded by doctrinal truths derived from a Biblically based exegetical method. Because of their commitment to that which edifies, their theological method was kept devotional and existential. In this work the words "doctrine" and "thought" will be used frequently to avoid the still regnant aversion to "theology." But when the word "theology" is utilized to describe Brethren thought, its use is meant to reflect the Pietistic approach to the Scriptures—an edifying and devotional Biblical theology.

Chapter 1

PIETISM

Introduction

Three basic elements were alloyed in shaping the mind of the early Brethren: Reformed thought, Pietism, and Anabaptism. Of these, Pietism and Anabaptism were the most significant. Our investigation will be organized on the basis of both the chronological order in which these elements influenced the early Brethren and their relative theological impact on the Brethren. Thus Reformed Pietism will be discussed first not merely because it antedated Spener-Halle Pietism but because most of the first Brethren were Reformed. Since Radical Pietism was of greater import for the Brethren than any other form of Pietism, the most attention will be focused on this movement. Finally, Anabaptism will be considered after Pietism in order to reflect the actual historical relationship between these two movements as they relate to the Brethren.

The Background of Pietism

With the Peace of Augsburg in 1555, a measure of peace was brought to Germany following nearly a decade of intermittent warfare involving the Lutherans and the Catholic imperial forces of Charles V. The compromise reached granted equal rights and recognition to only two faiths in Germany: Lutheranism and Catholicism. Each lay prince was to determine which of the two faiths should be professed in his territory; his choice determined the faith of all his subjects. Under this principle of *cuius regio, eius religio*, Lutheranism dominated the northern half of Germany while Catholicism was ascendant in the south.

During and following this struggle for political consolidation, Lutheranism was involved in another equally crucial conflict. At stake was the internal theological consolidation of Lutheranism. For some

time two antagonistic parties had been forming in Lutheranism. The first party, the self-designated Gnesio-Lutherans, was led by such men as Matthias Flacius, Nicholas von Amsdorf, John Wigand, and Heshusius. These men were uncompromising advocates of the theological views of Martin Luther. In opposition to this party were the Philippists, the followers of Melanchthon. They tended to be more moderate in their theological relationship with Calvinism and their political relationship with Catholicism. Major representatives of this party were George Major, Victorine Strigel, and Caspar Cruciger. The controversies engendered by these two theological perspectives lasted nearly thirty years (1548-1577).[1] They were brought to an end with the composition of the last great Lutheran creed, the Formula of Concord, in 1577. This creed represented the sentiments of the majority of Lutheran Germany. It takes a strict Lutheran stance and is noticeably more minute, technical, and scholastic than the earlier Augsburg Confession (1530).

Though Germany experienced relative political peace until the end of the century, a period of theological warfare among the Catholics, Lutherans, and Reformed ensued which proved more decisive for the final religious alignment of Germany than the several periods of open hostility during the sixteenth and seventeenth centuries. These three faiths began to vie for the allegiance of the approximately three hundred sovereign principalities and territories which honeycombed Germany. Following the Peace of Augsburg, Lutheranism made considerable headway into Bavaria, Bohemia, and Austria. However, the Lutheran advance reached its zenith about 1566.

The Reformed made significant inroads into northwest and southwest Germany at the expense of Lutheranism. In the early 1560s the Elector Palatine accepted Calvinism, though this religious change was contrary to the Peace of Augsburg. It was for him that

5

the Heidelberg Catechism, representing an experiential exposition of Calvinism, was prepared in 1562. In addition, the acceptance of the Formula of Concord by the majority of Lutherans caused the Philippists to turn increasingly to Calvinism. Between 1577 and 1613, Nassau, Bremen, Anhalt, part of Hesse, and the electoral house of Brandenburg became Calvinist.[2]

Even more significant were Catholic gains in Lutheran strongholds. During the mid-sixteenth century, a renewed and aggressive Catholicism emerged, spurred by several reform-minded popes, the Council of Trent, and the Jesuit Order. The Jesuit "weapons" of an efficient political and educational organization were primarily responsible for the Counter-Reformation's success in restoring lost territories. Bavaria, the dominion of the abbey of Fulda, Mainz, Trier, Cologne, Austria, and Bohemia were all brought under increasing Catholic domination between 1566 and 1618.

Tensions between Protestants and Catholics finally reached the breaking point in 1618. The resulting Thirty Years' War (1618–1648) saw Germany turned into the battleground for a war of aggrandizement involving German, Spanish, Danish, French, and Swedish armies. The ravaging of many parts of Germany, especially the Palatinate, was finally brought to a close in 1648 with the Peace of Westphalia. Under its provisions German Calvinists finally secured recognition and full rights. The year 1624 was taken as the norm for the religious settlement; whatever territories were in the possession of the Catholics or Protestants this year should remain so. The principle of *cuius regio, eius religio* was modified by the provision that where divided religious worship had existed in 1624, each party could continue in the same proportion as then existed.[3]

Though the effects of the war on Germany have been a source of some discussion throughout the present century,[4] there is no disputing that all areas of life—economic, intellectual, ethical, religious—suffered greatly. C. V. Wedgwood provides a fair assessment of the results of the hostilities: "The breakdown of social order, the perpetual changing of authority and religion in so many districts, contributed to that disintegration of society which was more fundamentally serious than the immediate damages of the war." In her concluding observations she emphasizes the futility of the hostilities:

> In Germany the war was an unmitigated catastrophe. In Europe it was equally, although in a different way, catastrophic. The peace, which had settled the disputes of Germany with comparative success because passions had cooled, was totally ineffectual in settling the problems of Europe. . . . The Peace of Westphalia was like most peace treaties, a rearrangement of the European map ready for the next war.
>
> . . . The war solved no problems. Its effects, both immediate and indirect, were either negative or disastrous. Morally subversive, economically destructive, socially degrading, confused in its causes, devious in its course, futile in its result, it is the outstanding example in European history of meaningless conflict.[5]

The foregoing catalog of internal theological and political disunity and of external pressures from both Reformed and Catholics helps to explain Lutheranism's defensive posture which lasted well into the seventeenth century. In an all too real sense, Lutheranism was fighting for survival. These realities are significant for understanding the bitter polemicism and rigid orthodoxy which characterized Lutheran theology during this period. An impregnable theological position became just as important as a sound political front.

The foundation for Lutheran orthodoxy was found in the symbolical books, especially the Augsburg Confession and Formula of Concord. The latter symbol, which was primarily the work of Martin Chemnitz, Jakob Andreae, and Nikolaus Selnecker, provided detailed elaboration of exactly what did and did not constitute acceptable interpretations of "sound doctrine." Around these symbols grew an arsenal of dogmatic and polemical works during the seventeenth century penned by such men as Johann Gerhard, J. F. Koenig, John Andrew Quenstedt, and Abraham Calovius and taught by centers of Lutheran orthodoxy like the Universities of Jena and Wittenberg.

The resulting Lutheran Scholasticism thus possessed a solid foundation for criticism of external adversaries—Reformed and Catholics—as well as internal ones—the syncretistic and ecumenical movement of the Philippist, George Calixtus, and an even more formidable movement, Pietism. Yet the reintroduction of Aristotelian thought and the use of Scripture as proof texts to support the credal dogmas gave an extremely objective, rigid, and formal character to orthodoxy. In both writings and sermons the emphasis was placed on correct belief rather than a vital, life-changing faith.

The Reformed by no means escaped the scholastic trend of the so-called Age of Orthodoxy. The same combination of forces that worked to shape Lutheran orthodoxy—external pressures and internal theological dissension—likewise wielded their influence on the Reformed. In the Netherlands the struggle for independence from Spain which lasted from 1567 to

1609 resulted in the weakening of the significant Lutheran and Anabaptist populations, especially during the reign of terror (1567–1573) by the Spanish forces under the Duke of Alva. The Calvinists, who had not even entered the religious scene in a prominent way until the 1550s, emerged from the war as the dominant religious faith. Spared the trauma and destruction of the Thirty Years' War, the Dutch Reformed provided the theological leadership for the Calvinistic lands.

By the second half of the seventeenth century, the Reformed territories in Germany formed a chain stretching south and east from the North Sea and Holland, along the Rhine, and towards the Weser River. The Reformed in these areas were not as fortunate as their Dutch counterparts during the Thirty Years' War. The Palatinate and Hesse-Cassel were among the areas most devastated by the war. With the inevitable disruption of ecclesiastical life and especially of ministerial training and recruitment during and after the war, the Reformed territories of Germany looked to the Netherlands for intellectual leadership and moral support. The sense of community felt by these two Reformed areas is significant for the rise and spread of Reformed Pietism.[6]

Unlike the Lutherans, the primary theological standard for Reformed Orthodoxy was not a confession. Rather, it was the *Institutes* of John Calvin. Nevertheless, a number of Reformed confessions and catechisms were of great importance for catechetical instruction. Of special note are the Belgic Confession (1561), written primarily by Guido de Bres, the Heidelberg Catechism (1563), co-authored by Zacharias Ursinus and Caspar Olevianus, and the Second Helvetic Confession (1566), written by Heinrich Bullinger.

Two theological controversies which raged in the Netherlands are reflective of and contributed to the scholastic development in Calvinism. A theological storm had been brewing for some time over the attack of Diryck Volckertszoon Coornhert (1522–1591) on the Calvinistic doctrines of double predestination, total depravity, irresistible grace, bondage of the will, and the forensic emphasis with regard to the work of Christ. Jacobus Arminius (1560–1609), a former student of the High Calvinist, Theodore Beza, was commissioned by the Amsterdam city fathers to refute the Coornhertian errors. However, during the course of his investigation, not only was he converted to Coornhert's position, but he became the leading advocate of a Reformed theology which placed greater emphasis on man's freedom and moral responsibility. The views of Arminius and the Armin-

ian party were stoutly opposed by orthodox Calvinists, notably Franciscus Gomarus. The ensuing controversy led to the calling of the Synod of Dort (1618–19). Here the Arminians were condemned, and the Canons of Dort set in credal form the five points of High Calvinism.

The second controversy centered upon Johannes Koch (1603–1669), better known as Coccejus. The unique slant which he gave to federal theology differed at key points from the emphases of orthodox Calvinism. He was far less emphatic on the doctrines of God's sovereignty and predestination than Gomarus and Gisbertus Voetius (see p. 9). His view that the *post legem* economy is the fulfillment of previous ages caused him to lay less stress on the Old Testament than did the Voetians. This view, combined with

> the related idea that the covenant of grace is based upon God's eternal promise which finds its culmination in the work of Christ, completely undercut the rigid legalism of the older Calvinism and substituted the principle of Christ-centeredness in the field of Christian interpretation.[7]

Likewise, his emphasis on contextual and Christ-centered hermeneutics resulted in a Biblical theology which was in marked contrast to the scholastic, proof-text approach of Orthodoxy.

The bitter earnestness with which the above theological battles were fought in both the Reformed and Lutheran churches is reflective of the premium placed on correctly formulated propositions. The subsequent pietistic reaction was viewed, especially by Lutheran Pietists, as an attempt to regain a balance between knowledge and piety and thereby to return to the ideals of the Reformers which were obscured by Protestant Orthodoxy.[8] It is against this backdrop of the polemics and scholasticism of Orthodoxy and the religious and moral decay that resulted from the Thirty Years' War that Pietism must be viewed.

Reformed Pietism

DEVELOPMENT IN THE NETHERLANDS

> . . . Calvinism was intrinsically oriented toward piety. It is understandable, therefore, that from the beginning the Reformed churches on the Continent provided at least the outward framework within which Protestant piety could find a home . . .[9]

Stoeffler proceeds to note that the Synod of Dort gave added support to the framework of piety— close supervision of the theological soundness of professors, preachers, and teachers; an emphasis on catechetical preaching and teaching; the advocacy of weekly meetings with adults for instruction in the contents of the catechism.[10]

In the Netherlands a long tradition of piety had remained vibrant. This tradition included the medieval mystic, Jan van Ruysbroeck; Gerhard Groote and Florentius Radewijns, who were instrumental in founding the Brethren of the Common Life, a movement whose mystical piety found expression in the *Imitation of Christ*; and the Anabaptists. Likewise, numerous Puritan devotional works, themselves dependent on Reformed piety, were translated into Dutch and had a decided influence on several leading Dutch Reformed Pietists.[11]

Stoeffler sees Reformed Pietism characterized by the confluence of two streams of Reformed piety originating in the sixteenth century. The embodiment of the first stream is the Huguenot, Jean de Taffin (1529?–1602). A devout Calvinist, he differed from many other orthodox Calvinists in his earnest practice of piety and his desire for political and theological conciliation rather than controversy.[12] Taffin's piety was characterized by an emphasis on inwardness, prayer, and *Gelucksaligheyt* (feelings of spiritual elation). His first tract, *The Marks of the Children of God*, was written against the background of the Dutch struggle for independence from Spain. In it he stresses the importance of assurance and the knowledge of being a child of God. This knowledge is the result of possessing certain outward and inward marks.

> The outward marks consist of the willingness to hear the Word of God "purely preached" and to receive the sacraments "purely administered." The inward marks consist of "the testimony of the Holy Ghost in our hearts, the peace and quietness of our consciences before God, feeling ourselves justified by faith."[13]

For Taffin, the "feeling" of the inner testimony of the Spirit has practical results, for the certainty which results from it allows one to deal with the temptation to doubt and with affliction.

The second stream of Reformed piety having its roots in the sixteenth century is exemplified in the writings of the Dutch pastor, Gottfried Cornelius Udemans (1580?–1649?). This type of piety became known as "'precicianism' [sic] because it conceived of the practice of piety as consisting mainly in the keeping of God's law revealed in Scripture."[14] This characteristic is discernible in three of his important writings. His *Christian Meditations* (1608) is a book of daily devotions which discusses a number of "cases of conscience" and recommends specific duties for the various classes of readers. In a later com-

panion volume, *Jacob's Ladder*, Udemans describes various steps involved in the development of the Christian life: humility and repentance, knowledge of Christ, true faith in God through Christ, true confession of faith, a godly life, Christian patience, spiritual joy through Christ, and perseverance of the saints. With his main work, *Practice* (1612), he sought to induce his readers to practice the basic Christian virtues of faith, hope, and love. He considers the exercise of these virtues as the "soul of the faith," which is good works. Their practice is reinforced both by noting certain outward marks by which one can determine whether faith, hope, and love are being exercised and by warning "mouth Christians" of the damning consequences of the failure to manifest these marks.[15]

The convergence of these two streams of piety occurs in four men who bring Reformed Pietism to maturity: William Teellinck, William Amesius (Ames), Gisbertus Voetius, and Jadocus van Lodensteyn. William Teellinck (1579–1629) is generally recognized as the father of Reformed Pietism. While studying in England he was profoundly influenced by the Pietistic Puritans. This influence is evidenced in Teellinck's ministry in the Netherlands as an effective preacher, caring pastor, and edifying writer. Though deeply loyal to the Reformed faith, Teellinck constantly contended, against the backdrop of Calvinistic scholasticism, that a new life of piety and godliness cannot be ignored in the struggle for sound doctrine. His frequent calls for moral and spiritual reformation brought upon him the suspicion of orthodox Calvinists. Pietistic themes are found throughout Teellinck's discussions of the Christian life. For him, faith involved more than trust in the merits of Christ's atoning work; it was commitment to Christ who will regenerate the believer's life progressively each day. Such faith becomes active in love. Through repentance and conversion, one enters into the new life. This new life consists of a thoroughgoing self-denial on the one hand and the devotional ordering of one's daily life according to the ethic of the Scriptures on the other. Teellinck did not view keeping the law as an end in itself but as a means of enjoying divinely intended temporal and eternal felicity. Here we find in Teellinck the harmonious merging of Taffin's emphasis on felicity and Udemans' stress on preciseness.[16]

William Ames (1576–1633) has been given the designation, the first theologian of Reformed Pietism.[17] He was born in Norfolk, England and studied under William Perkins. Ames' strict Puritanism aroused opposition in his homeland and caused him to seek refuge in Holland. His influential *Medulla Sacrae Theologiae* served as a theological foundation for Reformed piety. In this work he held that theology does not deal primarily with assertions about God but with the knowledge of how to live for Him. This knowledge is to be found only in God's self-revelation in Scripture wherein are to be found all the principles and rules according to which life is to be lived. Likewise, such knowledge is not the result of natural intelligence; it is gained only through the divine illumination of the regenerate man. Ames divides theology into two parts, faith and observance. In his view of faith there is a definite note of voluntarism. While the application of Christ's redemptive work is initiated by God through the external offer of His Word and the internal offer of illumination by the Holy Spirit, God's offer must be joined with man's will to receive it. Thus faith becomes not mere intellectual assent but an act of the will which involves the whole man. Predictably, conversion implies certain activities on man's part: humility, faith, repentance, and obedience. Conversion is the means by which one enters union with God. The benefits of union which God communicates to the sinner are justification, adoption, sanctification, and glorification. For Ames, the second part of theology, observance, involves the conformity of every detail of one's life to the law of God and the regular examination of one's life for any deviations. Though Ames does emphasize preciseness to a greater extent than Teellinck, he still evidences an element of felicity in his view of glorification as an experience beginning now through inner assurance and the sense of God's love but culminating hereafter in the enjoyment of eternal happiness.[18]

The most rigid advocates of preciseness are to be found in Gisbertus Voetius (1588–1676) and one of his pupils, Jadocus van Lodensteyn (1620–1677). Though one might question what relation a firm defender of Calvinistic Scholasticism like Voetius could have to Pietism,[19] yet his lifelong concern for both true godliness and right learning place him within the tradition of Reformed piety. While as a theologian he became internationally recognized as a defender and systematizer of orthodox Calvinism, in his personal religious life and his devotional writings he expressed a form of piety dependent upon Teellinck, Taffin, and Udemans as well as the English Puritans. The precisionism of Voetius and his followers was expressed negatively in scruples against worldly amusements and luxury, the continuation of Catholic customs, state control over the church, and the profanation of the sabbath and positively in the use of conventicles to cultivate an educated and spiritually edified membership.[20]

Though Lodensteyn shared Voetius' precisionism, he manifested none of Voetius' preoccupation with Scholasticism (his having studied under Coccejus as well as Voetius may have had some influence at this point). Lodensteyn represents the pietistic spirit in full bloom in the Reformed church. His greatness as a preacher of practical Christianity, his diligence as a pastor, his use of conventicles, his concern for edificatory tracts and poetry, his tireless efforts at reform and the reestablishment of discipline in connection with communion led to his recognition as the leader of the Pietists. Lodensteyn's theological emphases were typically Pietist. He believed that a radical difference existed between people in the natural state and those in the state of grace (this distinction, common to Pietists in general, is referred to as "the doctrine of the two states"). The great divide was found in conversion, which, he held, involved the illumination of the intellect (following Voetius) by the Holy Spirit. This divinely wrought illumination results in the understanding of Scripture, the losing of oneself in meditation upon God's attributes and will, and the stirring of a love for God which enables the Christian to live a life of complete self-denial and surrender. Lodensteyn stressed that the Christian must be committed to precise living by attempting to perform God's will as perfectly as possible. Though recognizing that perfection is not attainable in this life, he cautioned that the Reformed doctrine of the imperfection of believers must not blunt the desire for perfection.[21]

These men—Teellinck, Ames, Voetius, and Lodensteyn—through whom Reformed Pietism became a discernible movement, were followed by several capable leaders. Briefer consideration will be given to these men. In Theodore Gerardi à Brakel (1608–1669) a more mystical piety is discernible. For him the essence of personal Christianity was the feeling of felicity derived from daily communion with God. Even the living of a moral life according to the strictest code of Christian ethics became a means to this end.[22]

The sons of two men previously mentioned played important roles in the mid and later seventeenth century. John Teellinck (d. 1663) followed in the tradition of his father, William, in seeking a balance between preciseness and felicity. Likewise, he was similar to his father in his desire to remain faithful to the Reformed faith and in his interest in applying doctrine to life. William à Brakel (1635–1711), son of Theodore, was the main representative of Reformed

Pietism toward the close of the seventeenth century. Of special note is the fact that his *True Service of God* supplies Reformed Pietism with a theological work which, unlike Ames' *Medulla*, originated from a tradition which was wholly native to the Netherlands. In it he preserved the balance characteristic of Reformed Pietism between the mystical and ethical elements of the Christian life.[23]

Though Calvinism's openness to the pietistic spirit tended to neutralize the impulse for separatism, two movements with a critical attitude toward the established church did arise from Reformed roots. The first movement was the Collegiants. This Dutch religious association was formed in the wake of the controversies surrounding the Synod of Dort. With the ouster of some three hundred Remonstrant ministers by the Synod, many churches were left without pastors. At Warmond, near Leiden, a layman, Gijsbert van der Kodde, together with his two brothers, began leading such a congregation. The informal services were composed of Bible reading, prayer, and devotional addresses by any member who felt led to speak. These *collegia*, which probably go back historically to Zwingli's "prophesyings" and which were much used by the English Puritans under Elizabeth, soon spread, and by 1640 meetings had been established throughout the Netherlands.

The Collegiants were essentially an anti-ecclesiastical, lay movement. Though many pastors were active, they participated as private persons. Some Collegiants were members of a church (Reformed, Remonstrant, Mennonite) and remained so; others were members of no church. The leading principle of this spiritual movement was "the conviction that all churches had forsaken the principles and practices of the apostolic church, and that none of the existing churches could lay claim to be the true church of Jesus Christ."[24] They desired an evangelical renewal in both religious practices and principles without actually establishing a new church. Many of their distinctive ideas and practices resemble those of the Anabaptists: the priesthood of all believers, adult baptism (by immersion, however), rejection of military service, simplicity in life and dress, and the practical application of the Sermon on the Mount.

After 1640, Collegiants from throughout the Netherlands met at Rijnsberg twice a year to observe communion and baptize those who desired it. One group of Collegiants came under the rationalist influence of Descartes and Spinoza (who lived at Rijnsberg), a development which led to dissension within the movement. During the eighteenth century membership declined with many turning to Socinianism,

Deism, or joining the Mennonites. The last meeting was held in 1791.[25] Though Stoeffler is correct in differentiating the Collegiants from church-related Pietism, the Collegiants did hold a number of ideas that were "in the air" in Pietistic circles of a more radical and spiritualist nature.[26]

The second separatist group which arose from Reformed roots was begun by Jean de Labadie (1610–1674). Labadie had been a Roman Catholic priest in France before joining the Reformed communion about 1650 following his reading of Calvin's *Institutes*. He held Reformed pastorates at Geneva and Middleburg in the Netherlands between 1659 and 1670.

Labadie's piety is a mixture of Jansenism and Reformed Pietism. Jansenists held great appreciation for the mystics' desire for union with God and their insistence upon self-mortification. As a result, Jansenists gave special place to prescribed periods of prayer, fasting, silence, and sexual abstinence. They also stressed separation from the world and utilized conventicles for the discussion of personally meaningful religious topics. Labadie's indebtedness to Reformed Pietism is found in the gravity with which he viewed the doctrine of the two states. The new birth and subsequent holy life became the controlling factors for his thought and practice. Combining elements of Jansenist and Reformed piety, he held that the life of piety must have certain internal and external aspects. Internally, one must cultivate love for God through meditation and interior prayer. Externally, all conditions of life must be conformed as much as possible to the apostolic pattern.

These convictions were molded into a definite program of reform especially during his Middleburg pastorate. This program included communion only for those evidencing a regenerate life, a special emphasis on catechization and preaching, and the use of conventicles for spiritual edification. These efforts and his attempt to foster reform throughout the Reformed communion led to increasing tensions with his synod. In 1669 Labadie was suspended by his synod.

Following this action Labadie went to Amsterdam, taking along some of his most ardent supporters. Here they established a *huiskerk*, a kind of cloister composed of truly converted Christians whose activities were supervised by a house father. A concerted evangelistic program spread the Labadist movement to several west German cities and even to Maryland and New York. Due to the leadership of Pierre Dulignon, Pierre Yvon, and Anna Maria van Schurman, the movement showed considerable vitality for several decades following Labadie's death. By 1730, however, the movement was dead.[27]

DEVELOPMENT IN GERMANY

The fluid relationship between the Dutch and German Reformed has already been noted. This intercourse is manifested in the outstanding personality among German Reformed Pietists, Theodor Untereyck (1635-1693). He studied under both Voetius and Coccejus and sought to take the best from their competing theological systems. He utilized the characteristic Pietistic practices—conventicles, catechization of children, disciplined communion, deviation from the liturgy—during his pastorates at Mühlheim on the Ruhr and Bremen. In his *Bride of Christ*, a devotional guide, Untereyck reveals his indebtedness to various church fathers and mystics (including Johann Arndt). In the first part of the work, he emphasizes felicity, the inexpressibly sweet communion with God in Christ, though this comes only as the result of a God-centered love which separates itself from all worldly gods. The second part of the book is addressed to those who have not experienced such exalted or "emotional" states of feeling. He counsels that the final criterion for man's acceptance by God is not felicity but love for God and denial of worldly things. Untereyck reveals less rigorism in his view of Christian ethics than other Reformed Pietists. He allowed a degree of individual liberty in the performance of worldly duties and the possession of worldly goods under the principle that every Christian must be as wise as a serpent in knowing what God requires of him.[28]

Mention should also be made of Joachim Neander (1650-1680), one of the great hymn writers of Protestantism. His piety, as expressed in his hymns, bears the characteristic trademark of Reformed Pietism—a combination of mysticism and ethical sensitivity. His special emphasis was upon oneness with Christ and wholehearted devotion and service to Him.[29]

Just as Pietism found a receptive atmosphere among the Dutch Reformed, it also did among the German Reformed during the late seventeenth and early eighteenth centuries. This receptivity was occasioned by two factors. The first was the aforementioned natural proclivity of the Reformed for pietistic influences. The second factor arose from the political situation in which the German Reformed found themselves. Many of the German territories which had large Reformed populations were ruled by either Prussia or Roman Catholic sovereigns. Cleve, part of Geldern,

Moers, Mark, Ravensberg, Minden, and Tecklenburg were under Prussian sovereignty, and it was the inflexible policy of the Hohenzollern rulers to support the opponents of Orthodoxy. The Roman Catholic rulers of the Palatinate[30] held sovereignty over Sponheim, Jülich, and Berg. To be sure, these rulers had little interest in checking pietistic inroads into Reformed Orthodoxy.[31]

The above theological and political factors caused the Reformed synods generally to take a basically tolerant, though moderately critical, attitude toward Pietism. A good deal of latitude was given to pietistic practices. The holding of conventicles was approved as long as they became no occasion for separatistic activity; catechization was encouraged; more careful preparation of communicates was endorsed; preachers, parents, and governmental officials were reminded of their responsibilities to exemplify moral and religious values. These realities, combined with Reformed Pietism's historic openness for a mystical strain of piety, created fertile ground for the development of more enthusiastic and separatistic expressions of piety during the eighteenth century. The frequent appeals from representatives of the established order for Reformed synods to take steps at curbing pietistic excesses are made understandable against this background.

This overview of Dutch and German Reformed Pietism has brought out several noteworthy points. First, two identifiable streams of piety are present in Reformed Pietism from the start: precisionism and a more mystical, feeling-oriented strain. Reformed Pietism is at its best when these two streams are balanced. Second, the leading representatives of Reformed Pietism sought to combine their practice of piety with faithfulness to Reformed thought. They sought to be a reform party *within* the church. Inevitably though, points of departure in thought and practice do appear. Third, as the seventeenth century proceeds into the eighteenth, a progressively more critical attitude arises in and on the fringes of Reformed Pietism. The critical, reform-minded spirit of men like Lodensteyn and Untereyck, who remained firmly committed to the Reformed faith, gave way to separatism as early as the 1670s in Labadism. The partaking of communion by unworthy church members received bitter condemnation from men like Samuel Nethenus (1628-1700) and Reiner Copper (1645-1693). By the turn of the century, separatism, as an answer to the undisciplined and worldly conditions perceived in the church, was becoming more of a problem, particularly among the German Reformed. Henry Horche (1652-1729), who had studied under Untereyck, served as a link between German Reformed Pietism and Radical Pietism in the early eighteenth century,[32] while the Lutheran itinerant preacher, Ernst Christoph Hochmann von Hochenau (1670-1721), received some of his best response in Reformed areas (Wittgenstein, Lippe, and the lower Rhine). These developments, combined with the theological and political factors already noted, made German Reformed areas quite susceptible to a Radical Pietist message.[33]

Lutheran Pietism

THE RISE OF LUTHERAN PIETISM

Like Reformed Pietism, Lutheran Pietism drew upon a native tradition of mystical and practical piety. The medieval mystics like Tauler, à Kempis, and the author of the *German Theology* were widely read by sixteenth and seventeenth century Lutheran families and had even been held in high regard by the young Luther (though later in life he drew away from this mystical tradition).

The tradition of mystical piety within Lutheranism was embodied in a trio of Lutheran pastors during the sixteenth century: Stephan Praetorius, Philipp Nicolai, and Valentine Weigel. Of these men Praetorius (1536-1603) is the most important forerunner of Pietism, for he combines the evangelical mysticism and practical piety which is to be seen in Johann Arndt. Praetorius was completely committed to Luther, as his writings attest. He does exhibit some unique emphases, however. Noteworthy is his stress on oneness with Christ which he views as an important aspect of the righteousness of Christ imputed to the sinner in baptism. This oneness leads to blessedness in Christ which has begun even now and to the gift of the Holy Spirit who illuminates, consoles, and vivifies the believer. Praetorius further sees baptism imparting the divine nature. With an emphasis not characteristic of Lutheranism in general, however, he maintains that one who has become a partaker of the divine nature and who has received the indwelling Christ should walk according to Christ's will in holiness, righteousness, love, and service. He sought to cultivate this practical piety through edifying sermons and spiritual conversations with his people.[34]

In the writings of Philipp Nicolai (1556-1608) mystical union became the dominant emphasis. He gave it further Lutheran undergirdings by applying to it the Christological doctrine of *communicatio idiomatum*—man becomes one with the whole Christ in baptism. Like Praetorius, Nicolai saw the doctrine

of mystical union having definite ethical implications. The baptized Christian who is united with Christ should will nothing except what God wills. Man's highest duty and privilege becomes to love God and reflect God's love in his life. Nicolai also introduced the term "rebirth" into the vocabulary of seventeenth century Lutheranism. He held that the true Christian (as distinguished from children of the world and worldly Christians) lives in a higher state of existence through rebirth. Such a believer will follow the call of Christ, separate himself from his former nature and worldly intercourse, and desire to live a holy life.[35]

Though the theosophical[36] thought of Valentine Weigel (1533-1588) had little influence on the rise of Spener-Halle Pietism, it did have considerable impact on Jacob Boehme and the Radical Pietists. Weigel gave few hints about his heterodoxy during his lifetime, but when his writings were published after his death, they created quite a stir. His theosophical writings combined the theosophical speculations of Agrippa of Nettesheim and Paracelsus with the spiritualism of men like Sebastian Franck and Caspar Schwenckfeld. Stripped of its theosophical trappings, however, his view of the Christian life differs little from that of Praetorius or especially Nicolai. Emphasis is placed on mystical identification, wherein man shares God's spiritual eye; on the new birth, which involves a radical reorientation from love of self to love for God; and the new life, which consists of seeking God's will as it is mirrored in the historic Jesus. Weigel was also quite critical of the confessionalism and scholasticism of his day.[37]

The emphases of these three men on mystical union, rebirth, and ethical sensitivity helped to pave the way for Johann Arndt (1555-1621), who is now generally recognized as the father of Lutheran Pietism. His preaching, pastoring, and writing[38] breathe a warm, experiential Christianity which came to typify Pietism at its best. Besides the three men mentioned above, Arndt reveals indebtedness to the medieval mystics as well as to Luther (Arndt maintained his loyalty to Orthodoxy). Arndt's understanding of the Christian life can be considered under three headings: (1) spiritual renewal, (2) the new life, and (3) the means for the cultivation of the regenerate life. (1) Arndt emphasized the necessity of man's spiritual renewal through God's gracious work. Through His Word and Spirit, Christ works true faith within the individual who is thus renewed "from the inside out." Intimately involved in this renewal or regenerative process are true inward repentance and a faith which includes absolute trust of and commitment to Christ. Typical of later Lutheran Pietists who felt uneasy with the Lutheran doctrine of baptismal regeneration, Arndt downplayed the historic Lutheran view and put the emphasis on conversion and a holy life. Baptism thus was conceived as a once-for-all cleansing performed by God which becomes both the objective condition of and the incentive for a holy life. For Arndt, the immediate result of the new birth was identification with God. Identification with God means not only the believer's unity with Christ as a member of the body of Christ but, much more, his unity with Christ on a personal level. With Nicolai he held that the divine and human natures are conjoined in the believer as they were in Christ, with the result that he is now receptive to divine illumination through the Spirit and is enabled to live a holy life.

(2) It must be emphasized that the central theme for Arndt was not that of union; rather, it was the subject of the new life. He constantly reiterated that Christians are to continue to grow in faith and a virtuous life until they reach the stature of a perfect man in Christ. The new life meant existence on the highest ethical plane, a standard which necessitated, on the one hand, dying to the world and self and, on the other, total commitment to God in will and affection. Love for God and one's fellow man is an integral element of this ethic. (3) Though the life in Christ which expresses itself in ethical excellence is God's gift, there are certain spiritual exercises which the Christian must practice to ensure growth in the new life. Of foremost importance is the Christian's constant look toward Christ. Yet the believer must also engage in self-examination, separating himself from all worldly hindrances, meditating upon those things which enhance his spiritual welfare, and especially praying.[39]

Theologically, Arndt's chief contribution to Lutheran piety was his fusion of a dynamic kind of Christ mysticism with profound moral concern. Historically, both Spener-Halle Pietism and Radical Pietism draw directly from his insights. Likewise, he is a key figure in the phenomenon which has come to be known as the tradition of Lutheran self-criticism.

Within seventeenth century Orthodoxy there existed a reform party which sought the spiritual revitalization of Lutheranism. This party reacted to not only the moral and cultural degradation of the Thirty Years' War but also the failure of Orthodoxy to make Lutheranism practical and relevant to the people.[40] Identification of the key representatives of orthodox self-criticism together with some of their characteristic complaints helps to reveal the ethos of the party.

John V. Andreae (1586-1654) expressed his dissatisfaction with the power which the state exercised over church life (caesaropapism), the moral laxity and lack of discipline in the church, the contentiousness of theologians, and the seemingly vain education received at the schools. Balthasar Meisner (1587-1627), a professor at Wittenberg, wrote in his *Pia Desideria* (1626) that the scandalous life of many ministers was the great defect of the church with which any reform needed to begin.[41]

The University of Rostock was a key center for the reform party. An appreciation for the Reformed tradition, characteristic of Rostock, produced some predictable emphases. John Quistorp the younger (1624-1669), a professor at Rostock, emphasized the importance of personal piety. Theophilus Grossgebauer (1628-1661), a student of Quistorp and pastor at Rostock, called for the restoration of the presbyterial element in Lutheranism, a ministry that spoke from a personal experience of God, and the cultivation of a piety denoted by heartfelt repentance, conversion, and a holy life.

Another noteworthy characteristic of three of the leading reformers was a commitment to Arndtian Pietism (all were also connected with Rostock). Joachim Lütkemann (1608-1655) was a professor at Rostock and shared the reformatory perspective of the faculty. His special concern was a piety which expresses itself in a Biblically based, personal morality. Henry Müller (1631-1675), a preacher and professor at Rostock, gave to Pietism and especially Radical Pietism the satirical slogan of the "four dumb idols of Lutheranism": the baptismal font, the pulpit, the confessional chair, and the altar. For Müller the essence of Christianity was love for God and mystical union with Him. Though giving credence to the Lutheran conviction that such love is the result of a God-given faith and that baptism plays a role in its reception, he always placed the emphasis on the resulting love, not its causes. Müller is also known for his erotic Christ-mysticism with its love-play between the soul and Jesus based on the Song of Songs.[42] Possibly the greatest of this trio of Arndtian Pietists was Christian Scriver (1629-1693), who had imbibed the reform spirit while studying at Rostock. Though he maintained the divine agency in human redemption, he felt that what God has done for man must become a reality in him through the work of God's indwelling Spirit. He saw the essentials of this "realized" personal Christianity as conversion, repentance, forgiveness, adoption, betrothal to Christ, love for one's fellowman, and a holy life. His writings also focus attention on the cultivation of piety through prayer, reading and meditating on Scripture and edificatory books, and daily self-examination.[43]

Generally speaking (with the exception of the last three men), the reform-minded representatives of Orthodoxy did not place a special priority on the cultivation of piety, but saw it as only one of many facets of the church's life needing reformation. Yet these men created a climate within which Pietism could flourish. More importantly, this active tradition of self-criticism gave rise to the programmatic writing of Lutheran Pietism, Spener's *Pia Desideria*. "Spener consciously drew upon this backlog of concern for spiritual revitalization in Lutheran orthodoxy, quoting the complaints and suggestions of as many as possible in order to enlist the support of as wide a group as possible."[44]

THE FLOWERING OF
CLASSICAL PIETISM: SPENER AND HALLE

In Philipp Jakob Spener (1635–1705), a number of different theological and pietistic traditions converge. Spener was raised in an atmosphere imbued with Arndtian and Puritan piety. He read not only Arndt's *True Christianity* but also the English devotional works of Emmanuel Sonthom, Lewis Bayly, Daniel Dyke, and Richard Baxter. In his education at Strassburg under Johann Georg Dorsch, Johann Conrad Dannhauer (who introduced Spener to Luther's writings), Johann Schmidt, and Sebastian Schmidt, Spener received training in strict Lutheran orthodoxy. However, a traditional Reformed spirit at Strassburg tempered this orthodoxy with a concern for practical religious needs. While in Geneva on his academic pilgrimage, Spener became acquainted with the knowledgeable Waldensian preacher, Antonius Legerus. Even more importantly, however, here Spener was favorably impressed by the fiery preaching of Jean de Labadie. Spener came to appreciate the piety and warmth of the Reformed church at Geneva and was impressed by the freedom of the Geneva church from Caesaropapism. In his writings, Spener also shows an appreciation for the German mystical tradition of à Kempis, Tauler, and the *German Theology*.[45]

Spener held three pastorates during his lifetime. While serving at Frankfurt on Main (1666–1685) as pastor and senior of the ministerium, he began his controversial *collegia pietatis* and wrote his *Pia Desideria* (1675), which thrust him into the forefront of Pietism. In 1686 he was appointed court chaplain at Dresden. After relations with the Saxon ruling family became strained, in 1691 he accepted the invitation of the elector of Brandenburg to the pastorate of St. Nicholas Church at Berlin. In all of these pastorates, Spener left an indelible mark on the course of Pietism by his considerable influence on the men who surrounded him.

Though a more comprehensive discussion of the theological and practical emphases of Lutheran Pietism will follow, a brief discussion of the contents of Spener's *Pia Desideria* is warranted. In this work of about one hundred pages in length, Spener has outlined "the essence of what Pietism has meant and its basic program for reform."[46] In it he articulated in a simple, succinct way the feelings and thoughts of many and it soon become a rallying point for those who desired reform.

The work is divided into three parts of varying length. The first part deals with the corrupt conditions prevailing in the church and society in general, conditions for which clergy and laity are equally to blame. For added support, he cites the writings of various men in the tradition of Lutheran self-criticism. He gives special attention to the Caesaropapism of the Lutheran princes, the polemicism and sophistry of the Lutheran clergy and theologians, and the drunkenness and low ethical standards among the common people. Sharp criticism is leveled at *ex opere operato* interpretations of baptism, confession, absolution, and the Lord's Supper which undermine motivation for good works and a pious life. The practical result of these offenses is that Lutheranism loses any evangelistic appeal to the Jews, heretics, and Roman Catholics.[47]

The second and shortest section deals with the eschatological expectations of better times for the church which God Himself has promised. The pattern for these better conditions is to be found in the "early Christian church."[48]

The final section offers six concrete proposals for the reformation of conditions in the church. These proposals are: (1) There should be more extensive use of the Word of God. To accomplish this pastors should read and preach from the entire Bible rather than merely using the lectionary passages; private reading of the Scripture in the home preferably by the father of the house should be encouraged; more Bible studies need to be established. (2) There should be renewed emphasis upon the Lutheran doctrine of the priesthood of all believers. Depending upon Luther for support, Spener maintains that the difference between laity and clergy must be minimized. (3) The cultivation of the spiritual life of Christians should be stressed. Spener underscores his conviction that Christianity consists of practice with the plea that a concerted effort be made to inculcate love for God and man. (4) Care must be taken in the conduct of religious controversies with unbelievers and heretics. Truth can be lost in the course of disputation. True doctrine can be demonstrated more effectively through the use of earnest prayer, a good example, a modest but firm presentation of the truth, and heartfelt love for all unbelievers and heretics. (5) Candidates for the ministry should be "themselves true Christians." Spener urged that the theological curriculum should be practical as well as theological and that *collegia* be established at academic centers for mutual edification of professors and students. (6) The goal of preaching and worship should be edification, for Christianity consists of the creation of the inward and new man.[49]

The development of a self-conscious Pietist movement was greatly furthered by Spener's *Pia Desideria* (predictably, open opposition from Lutheran Orthodoxy also commenced). Another significant factor in this development was the establishment of a university at Halle by Frederick III, Elector of Brandenburg (Prussia). While the university was formally founded in 1694, its roots went back to the successful law lectures of Christian Thomasius, begun in 1690. The faculty positions of the new university were purposefully filled with leading Pietists: Joachim Justus Breithaupt, Paul Anton, Joachim Lange, Johann Heinrich Michaelis, and August Hermann Francke. At Halle, Spener's varied religious insights took on a more clearly defined theological perspective with the result that Halle became the main eighteenth century center of the Pietist movement begun by Spener.[50]

The most prominent figure at Halle was Francke (1663–1727). He had received his theological training at the University of Leipzig, a bastion of Lutheran Orthodoxy. While continuing his studies at Lüneburg, he experienced a decisive conversion in 1687. Soon afterward he came under Spener's influence. His pietistic activities as leader of a *collegium* at Leipzig (1689) and in a deaconate at Erfurt (1690) were both cut short by the determined Orthodox opposition of especially Johann B. Carpzov, professor of theology at Leipzig. Through Spener's influence (Spener had just recently come to Berlin), Francke became pastor at Glaucha and professor of oriental studies at Halle in 1692.

Francke's chief contributions to the history of Pietism were in theology and education. Stoeffler feels that Francke's synthesizing of the Arndt-Spener development helped to effect a shift in the religious emphasis of his entire age.

It was a shift from "true doctrine" to right action, from theological speculation to devotional earnestness, from ontological to psychological interest, from an intellectualized to an experiential approach to the Christian Faith, from systematic theology to biblical exposition, from that which God has done in history to that which he wants to do in every human being now, from passive reliance on God's initiative to human responsibility.[51]

Spener had hoped for reform to take place through the pastorate and as a means to this end had called for seminary training of a better type. Francke, however, sought reform primarily through a thorough revision of the educational system. Francke had a twofold goal at Halle: (1) to make it a model theological community and (2) to supply dedicated pastors and teachers who were imbued with the Halle spirit. In fact all the institutions connected with Halle—orphanages, schools, Bible society, Jewish evangelism, missionary program—were established in order to further the essential goal of the formation of Christian character.[52]

Halle Pietism came to dominate the ecclesiastical scene in northwest Germany during the first half of the eighteenth century. This ascendancy was assured by the power of appointment which Spener, Francke, and their successors had due to their intimate connection with the Prussian court. The gradual eclipse of Halle's influence resulted from the theological narrowness and less effective administration of the school by Francke's son, August Gotthilf Francke, and the increasing strength of Enlightenment views.

THEOLOGICAL AND PRACTICAL DISTINCTIVES OF LUTHERAN PIETISM

It is quite true that Lutheran Pietism (in the Arndt-Spener-Halle tradition) offered no recognized theological statement. Not only did Pietists in general leave many theological questions untouched, but on certain questions there were majority and minority opinions. Nevertheless, it does seem possible, especially when limited to one of the major subdivisions of Pietism, to speak of a consensus of thought on central Pietistic themes.[53]

Writers on Pietism tend to agree that the constitutive element of Pietism was *praxis pietatis* (the practice of piety). The difficulty arises when the attempt is made to discern the various components of this element.[54] However, most of these analyses list at least four central theological motifs (though of course the terminology various): (1) the new birth, (2) the new life, (3) emphasis on the Bible, and (4) an optimistic call for reform.

(1) The keystone of Lutheran Pietism was the new birth. This new state of being provided the basis for the call for a radical change of life. Both Spener and Francke[55] were true to the Reformation conviction that the salvation process must be divinely initiated. A divinely initiated faith is necessary because of original sin and man's inability to do good. Inborn evil for Spener was not merely a defect or corruption but was basic sin and guilt. However, he and other Pietists tended to emphasize the power of sin rather than the guilt of sin. This was done to underscore the conviction that the God who is good enough to pardon sins is powerful enough to transform the life of the sinner.[56]

With Lutheran Orthodoxy, Spener and Francke held that any righteousness we have is imputed or forensic and that Christ's own righteousness is obtained for us through the atonement. However, they stressed that Christ's work for us must be supplemented by the understanding of Christ's work in us and through us. In addition, they lived with the tension between God's absolute sovereignty in working salvation and man's responsibility for responding to God's initiative. Thus, repentance and faith are human responses to divinely offered grace. Repentance involves not only the penitent knowledge of sin but, for Francke especially, the putting off of the old man. Francke, much more than Spener, noted that this penitential change is frequently accompanied by a decided inner struggle, the *Busskampf*. Even though faith is a gift of God, man bears a responsibility for possessing and increasing this faith.[57]

The experience of repentance and faith leads to the new birth.[58] Spener saw the new birth as initially a gift but also a new creation. This new creation is effected by the Spirit (it is a spiritual birth) and the Word, in the form of both law and gospel. To a much greater extent than Luther, Spener and Francke saw both the law and gospel at work in the conversion process and throughout the life of the believer. The law makes known to the believer what the conditions of the new life are meant to be. The gospel provides the gracious means for fulfilling the divine command. Brown sees this relationship between law and gospel as producing

> a doctrine of redemption in which Christ was not only accepted as priest but honored as king. Christianity not only gives forgiveness of sin but also offers to work obedience in us. The view of obedience to Christ as king expands the domain of law to encompass his command, the law of love.[59]

The relation of the new birth to baptism caused Lutheran Pietists much trouble. Both Spener and Francke sought to avoid any *ex opere operato* concept of baptism. Therefore they spoke of faith and baptism together and stressed that the promise of salvation is not connected with baptism alone. They held that infant baptism does establish some sort of objective relationship between the infant and God. However, when the individual reached maturity, the baptismal covenant had to be confirmed through personal faith. As Stoeffler points out, two disparate views of salvation are present in this conception. "The one is based on sacramentally infused grace, or at least a sacramentally induced change in God's attitude, the other upon a personal faith commitment."[60]

The new birth effects a new state of being in the believer in which he is united with Christ in a psychological or volitional union. The stress on mystical union found in many Arndtian Pietists is not present in either Spener or Francke.[61] Instead, the emphasis is placed on the existential reorientation which the new birth brings about. The believer's sins are forgiven and the power of sin is broken. Though the old nature still clings on, the believer has the divinely bestowed power to deny himself and follow Christ in discipleship to Him. Thus the new birth is not a once-and-for-all event but issues in a process of daily renewal into the image of God.[62]

(2) Pietists in general held that the new birth must necessarily manifest itself in a new pattern of life. The theological shibboleth which most clearly distinguishes the perspective of Orthodoxy from that of Pietism with regard to the Christian life is their respective views of the relationship between justification and sanctification (or good works). Orthodoxy placed the emphasis on justification which it regarded as a divine act completed once-and-for-all and forensically valid. Thus the works which should follow are good but not so important. Spener and Francke placed the emphasis on sanctification as an actual transformation of character which God initiates and for which He provides the strength. Though denying that works are necessary to justification, they put a new stress on them as attributes which necessarily follow from an active, living, justifying faith. They saw an intimate connection and coordination between justification and sanctification due to the conviction that the faith which justifies is also the faith which sanctifies.[63]

Such a view has an inherent bias toward perfection. Spener saw human cooperation with the Holy Spirit's sanctifying work as necessary for the gradual eradication of sin and the steady growth in divine love.

He even held that one could reach perfection in the sense of no longer sinning intentionally (here he anticipates Wesley). Nevertheless, he recognized that, because sin remains within us, we can never completely achieve perfection in this life.[64] Pietists characteristically endorsed a number of devotional practices as means of enhancing one's growth in the virtues of faith, wisdom, good works, and love while at the same time fostering separation from the vices of the world and the flesh. Of special note are conventicles, ethical sensitivity, and such devotional exercises as the reading of the Bible and edifying literature, prayer, and divine worship.

Certain special marks of the life of faith receive constant emphasis in the writings of Spener and Francke. These marks include trials, cross bearing, obedience to God's law, trust in God, and joy. Francke speaks frequently of *Anfechtung* or trials, a concept found often in Luther and common to the more mystical Lutherans of the sixteenth century and the Reformed tradition. Francke viewed trials as an important facet of the Christian life. They were special occasions of testing sent by God in order to strengthen the believer's faith and commitment. Suffering and crossbearing served a purpose similar to that of trials. A necessary mark of the Christian life, suffering is a natural outgrowth of the Christian's denial of self and of worldly values and practices. As mentioned before, both Spener and Francke viewed obedience to God's law as an important facet of the new life. It confronted the believer with God's holy demands, especially His call for active love expressed both toward Himself and toward the neighbor. Yet true evangelical obedience should never need to be coerced from the individual by the tyrannical demands of the law; rather, it should be a free, loving response to one's heavenly Father, a response enabled by the indwelling Spirit. Implicit in such a relationship with God are the two other marks of faith—trust in God and joy. The experience of a new relationship with God brought about by the new birth fosters not only a loving psychological union with Him but also a sense of joy in the knowledge that one can trust his heavenly Father absolutely in all the vicissitudes of life.[65]

(3) The Pietistic approach to the Bible quite effectively freed the Scriptures from any formalistic methods of interpretation. Though the opposite problem of subjectivism became a danger in certain Pietistic circles, Spener and other Pietists felt a corrective was needed to Orthodoxy's mechanical, material view of Scripture, i.e., Scripture is efficacious because of its divine origin and intrinsic power.

Central to Pietism's approach to Scripture was the conviction that Scripture does not become effective mechanically but must be brought to life in the soul by the Holy Spirit. Thus Scripture can be savingly understood only with the aid of the Spirit and only by those who have been regenerated and illuminated by the Spirit. Such a view democratized the use of the Bible, freeing it from the domain of the professionals. Spener was careful to avoid an overly subjective conception of the Spirit's work, however, by insisting that the Holy Spirit does not work without the Bible or outside the Bible but in and through the Bible. It would seem that Spener was somewhat less successful in compensating for the related problem of private interpretations, though his urging that the Bible be studied in *collegia* under the guidance of pastors can be seen as an attempt to deal with this danger.[66]

Spener further sought to free Scripture from the limitations placed on it by the church symbols and by the dogmaticians. If Scripture was to be the supreme authority, one must not limit its voice by finding in the Bible only what was sanctioned by the creeds.[67] Likewise, Orthodoxy's scholastic, proof-text approach to Scripture undermined an exegetical, Biblical theological method.

Spener and Francke held that Scripture must be its own interpreter. The meaning of a passage must be considered in its broader context, while difficult passages should be interpreted by those which are clear. Both men likewise took progressive revelation seriously. Though he considered all Scripture as God's inspired Word, Spener held that the New Testament is a higher revelation than the Old because it fulfills the Old Testament. Thus the Christian experiences the New Testament more directly and it raises man to a higher level. Francke's use of a Christological hermeneutic led to a similar view of revelation.[68] The introductory discussion of Pietism's reading and interpreting Scripture through the principles of edification, godliness, and blessedness (see p. 3) should also be borne in mind.

The goal of all these emphases with respect to the common people was to familiarize them with the simple message of the Bible and to make it a book which they could read intelligently and by which they could order their lives. With respect to the educated, Spener and Francke sought to encourage the study of Biblical theology. To this end the scientific and philological study of the Bible to open its shell and get to the kernel became a hallmark of Halle as did an emphasis on reading the Scriptures in the original languages.

(4) It needs to be remembered that Pietism was born of a reform spirit within Lutheranism. It was the wide-spread conviction of Lutheran Pietists that the Reformation had not been completed. The reformation of doctrine never reached its culmination in the formation of a truly Christian life style.

> Because of this concern [for transformation of the lives of the mass of people in the churches] there was abroad within the whole Pietist movement a profoundly critical attitude toward ecclesiastical leaders whose teaching and preaching seemed to confirm religious superficiality and moral apathy, as well as toward institutional practices which were deemed to be inimical to the Pietist understanding of the Gospel and its demands.[69]

Given the enormity of the task of reform, one wonders what vision captured the mind of Spener-Halle Pietists to undertake such a challenge. Crucial here is Spener's optimistic hope, as expressed in his *Pia Desideria*, that God had promised better times for the church. This conviction was based on his study of Revelation 18 and 19 and Romans 11. On the basis of these passages, he not only proposed to work toward the conversion of the Jews and the final downfall of papal Rome, which he considered to be Babel, but he also was convinced that the Holy Spirit's power would again manifest itself to transform Christendom into the pristine character of the primitive church. This eschatological hope was caught by Spener's friends and became the driving force behind both Spener's manifold reform efforts and Francke's extensive charitable, educational, and evangelistic institutions at Halle as well.[70] Nor should it be overlooked that an even more critical attitude toward Lutheranism combined with an even more frenzied eschatological hope to fuel the separatistic and evangelistic activities of the Radical Pietists.

Chapter 2

RADICAL PIETISM

The Basic Character of Radical Pietism

The term, Radical Pietism, reveals two important facts about the movement: it emphasizes the uniqueness of this group (radical) as well as the group's continuity with the basic goals and emphases of the broader movement (Pietism). There has been some hesitancy, however, to apply the category "Pietism" to men like Gottfried Arnold, Ernst Christoph Hochmann von Hochenau, Johann Konrad Dippel, Johann Georg Gichtel, and Gerhard Tersteegen. This reservation seems to arise from a desire to legitimate the phenomenon of Pietism by limiting its use to intra-confessional developments. Stoeffler suggests two reasons why such a restriction is unjustified. First, Pietism represents the first truly inter-confessional movement of the modern world; to try to legitimate Pietism by depicting it as an intra-confessional development is a misrepresentation of the movement. Second, the men mentioned above shared with church-related Pietists an "overriding interest in the kind of Christian piety which concerned itself with practical, everyday matters, and which was based on a more or less literal interpretation of the New Testament ethic." These men were not primarily interested in mystical union, as some historians have intimated. Rather, their "mystical-spiritualistic theology was merely their rationale for such piety."[1] In short, Radical Pietism was a branch of the Pietist movement which expressed its piety through channels which were mystical, spiritualistic, Boehmist, and separatistic (for definitions of these terms, see below and especially footnote 9).

Though Radical Pietism shared many of the basic features of Reformed and Lutheran Pietism, the distinctive character of Radical Pietism derives from the convergence of three streams of mystical piety. The first stream flows from the thought of Johann Arndt. The Radical Pietists were indebted to Arndt

for his view of the Christian life, which has already been detailed, and his Christ-mysticism. Though Arndt's immediate followers such as Friedrich Dame (1567–1635) and Paulus Egardus (d. after 1643) followed Arndt's synthesis of mystical identification with Christ and moral concern, some later followers turned the focus of attention to mystical union. Their mode for expressing this union was a religious eroticism and excessive sweetness which mirrored medieval mysticism's fascination with the Song of Songs. Prominent representatives of this development were Josua Stegmann (1588–1632), Joachim Emden (1595–1650), and John Lassenius (1636–1692). The erotic mysticism of these and a number of other writers contributed to the religious atmosphere in which Radical Pietism was born.[2]

Of major importance to the character of Radical Pietism is the second source of Radical Pietism's mystical-spiritualistic piety: Jacob Boehme (1575–1624). The main legacies of Jacob Boehme to Radical Pietism consisted of his theosophical speculations concerning God, the creation, the fall, and redemption and his profoundly critical attitude toward accepted theological and ecclesiastical norms.

Boehme's theosophic system borrowed much of its terminology and many of its underlying concepts from the thought of Schwenckfeld, Paracelsus, and Weigel. Yet the finished product was clearly his own creation. Boehme maintains that there is an intimate connection between God and nature. A trinitarian structure underlies the being of both God and the universe. Boehme conceives of God as the eternal *Wesen* (essence) who reveals Himself not so much in terms of three persons but as three forms of will or energy.

As "abyss," God dwells in bitter darkness but reveals himself in the world as a consuming fire. The Son is within the Father as the light, heart, and mercy. In God there are wrath and love, hell and heaven, evil and good. In Christ we know that God is love while apart from Christ, God is a consuming fire. The Spirit proceeding from the Father and the Son is the gurgling, bubbling element in God. He is God in action.[3]

A further aspect of the divine essence is *Sophia* (Wisdom, Idea, the *Jungfrau*, the Maiden). Sophia, a term which is used quite enigmatically by Radical Pietists, is generally identified with the Son though occasionally also with the Spirit. Boehme views Wisdom as the mirror which reveals what is concealed in God.[4]

A trinity of principles underlies all nature: darkness, light, and the material world. In God all these principles and all aspects of the spiritual and natural realms are in perfect harmony or *temperature*. Unlike the material world, the angels and Lucifer, who was the mightiest of created things, possessed only the first two principles, darkness and light. However, Lucifer was tempted by pride and fell from light into the dark principles (also described as fire deprived of light or the wrath of God). As a result of Satan's fall, the harmony of all creation was dissolved so that the earth became waste and void.

Man was then created to replace Lucifer as the ruler of the external world described in the Genesis creation story. He could exist both in the heavenly realm and the external world and had within himself all three principles which were in *temperature*. He possessed a spiritual, translucent body like Christ's resurrection body. Such a body was androgynous, combining within itself the male and female principles, though in this state sex organs were missing. For Boehme, Adam first fell before the creation of Eve through his "imagination" or will. He succumbed to Lucifer's temptation to desire the material world and thereby lost his spiritual body and its divine image. In Boehme's depiction of this initial fall, Adam went to sleep in the heavenly realm and woke up in the external world. During Adam's sleep Jesus effected the separation of the male and female principles. The respective organs appeared in Adam and Eve as a sign of their animal, earthly nature. The formal act of eating the forbidden fruit was the inevitable outcome of the lust Adam had harbored in his desires and imagination.[5]

Sophia had been man's "bride" prior to the first fall. In order to effect the restoration of God's image in man, Sophia entered into the Virgin Mary and Christ was born.[6] Not only did Christ possess both a human and divine nature, but He also was androgynous (spiritually, not physically). He offered up His earthly, human body on the cross, quenched the "wrath," and restored the temperature in man.[7]

When discussing the appropriation of the salvation made available in Christ, Boehme offers a very critical evaluation of Lutheran Orthodoxy and its bias toward *ex opere operato* interpretations of the efficacy of the Word and sacraments. He felt that traditional formulations of the Christian faith were actually obscuring the Christian message. For him the essence of biblical faith was love for God as revealed in Christ. The foundation of this love is God's own saving love, a love which was made supremely visible in Christ, which goes out to all men, and which man can experience only through the humble, yet resolute, act of his will to devote himself fully to God. The Christian life which results from experiencing this divine love involves, first, "an affectively accomplished, existential union with God, and, second, the life of piety which may be expected to result from such union."[8]

Boehme's criticism of the established church was quite caustic. He distinguished between the Church of Abel, the invisible and universal church composed of those who are experientially united with God whether they may be living or dead, and the Church of Cain, the church visible in history. The visible church is cuttingly caricatured as being "stone churches" led by unregenerate pastors who are, in reality, the servants of Babel.[9]

Boehmist convictions were transmitted to the Radical Pietists of the late seventeenth century by a number of men. In two early followers of Boehme, Joachim Betkius (1601–1663) and Christian Hohburg (1607–1675), Arndtian thought forms continued to be prominent. Boehmist influence was noticeably strong, however, in Friedrich Breckling (1629–1711), who was a disciple of Hohburg, and Johann Georg Gichtel (1638–1710), who was awakened by Breckling. Both Breckling and Gichtel exerted a considerable influence on Gottfried Arnold and other German Radical Pietists. These men reveal Boehme's direct influence in insisting that all established churches were "Babel" and that the pastoral office should not be respected apart from the personal worthiness of its bearer.[10]

One other current of Boehmist thought came to have considerable influence on Radical Pietism—the English Philadelphian Movement.[11] This movement grew out of a small circle of Boehmists (Boehme's writings began to appear in English in 1645) whose principal leaders were John Pordage (1608–1688), Jane Leade (1623–1704), Thomas Bromley (1629–1729), and Dr. Francis Lee (1661–1719). The Philadelphian message was inspired above all by Jane

Leade, who combined Boehme's critical attitude toward established Christianity with the apocalypticism which had found its way into Puritanism.[12] Her understanding of the course of church history, as set forth in her tract, *The Heavenly Cloud Now Breaking* (1681), is derived from the messages to the seven churches of Asia in Revelation 2:1–3:13. She held that God's dealings with men are passing through seven stages. The fifth, or Sardic, period, during which true Christians are persecuted by the forces of Babylon (i.e., organized Christianity), is about to come to an end. The demonic forces which are rampant in Babylon will bring about its ruin. The Philadelphian period will then commence with the breaking in of the Spirit of Christ. The golden age of the Spirit will manifest itself in an open door which no man can shut. Following a brief "hour of temptation" during the Laodicean period, the Lord will come and usher in the millennium. The Philadelphians were vague about the final aspects of the scheme. Instead, their immediate expectation and emphasis related to the coming of Christ in the powerful demonstration of the Holy Spirit rather than His bodily return.[13]

In the development of this scheme, Mrs. Leade's chiliasm took on a more concrete nature than Boehme's spiritualized millennial expectations of the "Lily-Time" and the "Seven Branches of the Tree of Life."[14] She likewise felt moved by a "vision" in 1693 to depart from Boehme in another facet of eschatology: universal restoration.[15] This doctrine, having ancient roots in Origen, is founded on the conviction that God's love will ultimately reach all men. Among Radical Pietists it was held that even the devil and fallen angels would eventually be brought to a oneness with God's will. Such a doctrine found ample foundation in Boehme's emphasis on divine love and the Philadelphian expectation of an open door for spreading the message of God's love to all peoples.

Philadelphian ideas found ready acceptance by Radical Pietists in Germany due to the common heritage of Boehmism. The translation of the works of Pordage, Leade, and Bromley into German fostered the spirit of kinship.[16] Instrumental in spreading Philadelphianism in Germany were the former Lutheran pastor and superintendent, Dr. Johann W. Petersen (1649-1727), and his very capable wife, Johanna Eleonora of the house of Merlau. Dr. Petersen, trained at Rostock and a friend of Spener, had been dismissed from his church positions in 1692 for his chiliasm. They were converted to the Philadelphian cause around 1695 and in the following years became quite active in its promotion in Germany. Though at first Dr. Petersen was critical of Mrs.

Leade's restoration views, he came to accept this doctrine, being strongly impressed by the verse, "Behold, I make all things new" (Rev. 21:5).[17] Spener urged the Petersens to retain this new conviction as a private opinion. However, in 1699 they publicized their views in the work, *Das ewige Evangelium der allgemeinen Wiederbringung aller Creaturen* (the term "eternal Gospel" became synonymous with universal restoration).

Through the efforts of the Petersens, Heinrich Horche, and others, informal Philadelphian societies were established in many places in Germany during the few years immediately before and after 1700. These societies were viewed as the beginning of a divinely empowered movement which would eventually strip the sects (i.e., the established churches) of all true believers and, in time, their power. It is interesting that the London Philadelphian Society (formally founded in 1694) did not attempt to bring formal organization to the Philadelphians in Germany until 1703, the same year the London society was forced to retire from public view due to lack of interest. One of the documents connected with this organizational effort was a list of influential friends of the Philadelphian movement in Germany. It was compiled by the man appointed as the inspector for Germany, Johann Dittmar. Conspicuous in the list are both leading Pietists and Radical Pietists: Spener, Michaelis, Arnold, the Sprögels, Petersen, Horche, Reitz. However, also noteworthy are the absence of Francke, who was not apparently impressed with Dittmar even during Dittmar's student days at Halle, and Hochmann, who was very much in agreement with Philadelphian ideals.[18]

The attempt to give formal structure to German Philadelphianism proved a failure due to a combination of reasons. (1) Johann Dittmar proved to be a poor choice for inspector (he displayed a gross lack of tact). (2) Radical Pietists were generally averse to anything that appeared as an attempt to form a new sect. (3) Halle Pietists, whom Mrs. Leade especially sought to court, not only had little respect for Dittmar but were also becoming more aware of the differences between the radical party and themselves. (4) The timing of the effort was inopportune; the peak of interest between 1697 and 1703 had already begun to wane.[19] Nevertheless, it is important to note that the Philadelphian ideal of the church continued to be normative for Radical Pietism throughout the history of the movement. Thus they perceived the church as an invisible fellowship of true believers which transcended confessional and national boundaries, which was bound together by brotherly love, and which waited expectantly for the inbreaking of Christ's Spirit.

As intimated above, the years 1697 to 1703 mark a period of unparalleled Radical Pietist activity and can be regarded as the formative stage of the movement. Undergirding this stage were Boehmist themes and movements. Boehme's criticism of the established church combined with chiliastic hopes and the Philadelphian-inspired conviction that the reign of Christ's Spirit was dawning to fuel a frenzied call for separation from Babel. Visions, ecstasies, prophecies, bodily spasms, and uncontrollable laughter and barking[20] served to "confirm" the apocalyptic message of preachers like Heinrich Horche, Samuel König (1670–1750), Johann Heinrich Reitz (1655–1720), Ernst Christoph Hochmann von Hochenau, and the Petersens. The aggressive activity of this period has been given the appropriate label "Babel-storming."

By the turn of the century, Quietism, the third stream of mystical piety which contributed to the complexion of Radical Pietism, began to make its presence felt. Introduced into Radical circles by Peter Poiret (1646–1719) and Gottfried Arnold, Quietism's leavening influence served to calm the enthusiasm that marked the Boehmist-Philadelphian excitement of 1697–1703.

Quietism is a mystical system which found its classic expression in three Roman Catholic mystics of the seventeenth and early eighteenth centuries: Miguel de Molinos (1640–1697), Antoinette Bourignon (1616–1680), and Madame Guyon (1648–1717) (the latter two separated from Roman Catholicism). R. A. Knox posits that Quietism is rooted in "a kind of ultra-supernaturalism" in which human effort is rejected "so as to give God the whole right of spiritual initiative. . . . God alone must do everything; we cannot even co-operate with him, only allow him to operate in us, and forget that he even allows us to allow him."[21] Quietists upheld the "dark way" to spiritual union with God, in which one's will is lost in God's, as superior to the "way of light," in which visions and revelations are received. The highest form of prayer is the "simple intention" of the heart, which makes no use of external aids or mental pictures. The resultant passivity is expressed in such concepts as self-denial and resignation (*Gelassenheit*) and in a "pure" and "disinterested" love in which the individual relinquishes all desire even for personal salvation and happiness.[22]

Numerous German Protestants looked with favor on this new movement as a defense of "inner" religion against externals and as a protest against the expanding institutionalism in Roman Catholicism

which resulted from Jesuit Counter Reformation practices. The fact that Quietists were severely persecuted within the Roman Catholic Church also tended to recommend their beliefs to those Protestants critical of religious establishments in general. In addition, the German mystical tradition's focus on self-denial and *Gelassenheit* helped to pave the way for the acceptance of quietistic views. Even the young Francke, whose translation of Molinos' *Guida spirituale* into Latin in 1687 exposed the learned German audience to quietistic thought, was impressed by the work's emphasis on humility, Christ-centeredness, and trials associated with the religious life.[23]

Within Radical Pietist circles Poiret and Arnold are to be credited with the popularizing of Quietism. Poiret was born into a French Huguenot family at Metz in Alsace. In Frankfurt he became acquainted with a Pietist separatistic circle which at first had attached itself to Spener. However, it was his immersion in the writings of Bourignon and his subsequent attachment to her group in Holland that was decisive for the direction of his later life. Following Bourignon's death, he took Madame Guyon as his spiritual guide; her influence is especially noticeable in his later works. Poiret became the mediator of both Bourignon and Guyon to Germany and elsewhere. His editing of Madame Guyon's voluminous works between 1704 and 1719 paved the way for her wide influence in middle and eastern Europe. Though he himself wrote few mystical works, his chief one, *L'oeconomie divine*, combined the insights from a variety of mystical traditions.[24]

Arnold supplemented Poiret's work in introducing quietistic literature to the German audience. Significantly, his work in preparing prefaces for German translations of the writings of Molinos, Guyon, and Pietro Petrucci was concentrated between 1699 and 1702,[25] the period in which he himself turned from a Babel-storming perspective to an attitude of "holy indifference" toward outward things.

The effect which Quietism had on Arnold is reflective of the impact it had on the larger Radical Pietist movement. It placed a check on the emotionalism and apocalyptic excitement of the Boehmist-inspired Babel-storming period. Indeed, the attitude of outward quietness and stillness fostered by Quietism was inimical to the aggressive spirit characteristic of Boehmism.[26] From about 1704 onward a quietistically informed piety became the controlling spirit in Radical Pietism. It is noteworthy that in 1733 the *Geistliche Fama*, the most influential organ of Radical Pietism, named the era at the beginning of the century the "Poiretischen und Arnoldischen Periodum."[27] These two men exhibited the *Stillen im Lande* ("Quiet Ones in the Land") character which came to dominate the later period of Radical Pietism. The life of the key Radical Pietist figure during this period, Gerhard Tersteegen (1697-1769), exudes such a quietistic piety as do the two great literary accomplishments of eighteenth century Radical Pietism, the *Geistliche Fama*, published by Johann Samuel Carl (1675-1757) and later J. C. Edelmann at Berleburg from 1730 to 1744, and the *Berleburger Bibel*, edited by Johann Friedrich Haug (d. 1753).[28]

As the death dates of the above last great figures in Radical Pietism indicate, the movement as such had run its course by the 1750s and 60s. Nevertheless, Radical Pietism did give birth to two organized fellowships, both of which migrated to America: the German Baptist Brethren, the subject of this work, and the Inspirationists. The latter was a group founded at Marienborn in Wittgenstein in 1714 and led by Johann Friedrich Rock (1687-1749) and Eberhard Ludwig Gruber (1665-1728). The Inspirationists held that the days of direct inspiration from God had not ended. Prophetic utterances were delivered by various "instruments of true inspiration" who often experienced bodily convulsions while prophesying. The society migrated to America in 1842, settling first near Buffalo, New York, and then establishing the Amana community near Iowa City, Iowa, in 1855.

One final observation needs to be made concerning Radical Pietism in general. The Radicals tended to be much more individualistic than the church-related Pietists. Though they kept in contact through correspondence and visits and even worked together at times, each of the Radicals had a distinctive style of ministry and characteristic theological emphases.[29] As noted at the outset of this discussion, the one unifying feature for Radical Pietists was that they had, for the most part, drunk from the same streams of mystical-spiritualistic piety. Individual differences arose when a leader would imbibe more deeply from one stream than the others or when, historically, one stream flowed more heavily than the others. Still, Radicals felt that they were part of a larger, invisible brotherhood of believers which transcended not only ethnic and confessional barriers but individual differences as well.

Gottfried Arnold

INTRODUCTION

Of all the Radical Pietists, Gottfried Arnold and Ernst Christoph Hochmann von Hochenau played the foremost roles in influencing the life and thought of the early Brethren. Hochmann was directly responsible for "awakening" many of those people who would later be prominent in the formation and development of the Brethren fellowship. Though more indirect, Arnold's impact on the Brethren was exerted through his historical writings, especially *Die Erste Liebe Der Gemeinen Jesu Christi, Das ist: Wahre Abbildung Der Ersten Christen* (*The First Love of the Community of Jesus Christ, that is: True Portrayal of the First Christians*) (1696). This work was used by the Brethren as a source book for discerning the practices of the early church. These facts make a more thorough investigation of these men's life and thought important. In the case of Arnold, such an in depth investigation has several added features. First, Arnold's life represents a kind of microcosm of the Radical Pietist movement itself. Not only do his writings reflect his own theological pilgrimage, but they were instrumental in determining the course of Radical Pietism in general. Second, the study of his view of the individual and corporate aspects of the Christian faith and of his understanding of church history in the *Abbildung* reveals elements of thought on these topics which were common to both church-related and Radical Pietists.

The focus of this investigation will be Arnold's *Abbildung* (*Portrayal*), the work directly cited in Brethren primary sources. Written before his radicalism became pronounced, the *Abbildung* does not exhibit the strong spiritualistic and mystical overtones of Arnold's best known historical work, *Unparteyische Kirchen- und Ketzer-historie* (*Impartial History of the Church and the Heretics*) (1699-1700). For the Brethren, who were seeking to follow the early Christians in both inward piety and outward practice, the *Abbildung* proved to be of far greater importance than the *Ketzer-historie*.

THE LIFE OF GOTTFRIED ARNOLD

Arnold was born on September 5, 1666, at Annaberg in Saxony. He studied at Wittenberg, the citadel of Lutheran orthodoxy, but was unimpressed by the orthodox polemicism. Instead, he focused on the thought and practice of the early church. During these studies he came to the conviction that the early church must be the sole pattern or model for all believers. Even though Arnold's life was characterized by some major theological and ecclesiastical shifts, yet this basic conviction that the early church must be the standard for one's faith remained for him as an unshaken guiding principle.

Arnold's adult life can be divided into three distinct periods: (1) his relationship with Spener (1688–1693); (2) his espousal of separatistic Radical Pietism with its Boehmist-inspired, mystical-spiritualistic piety (1694–1700); and (3) his acceptance of service "within" the Lutheran Church (1701–1714).

(1) While studying at Wittenberg, Arnold came under the influence of Spener, who was later able to arrange tutorial positions for Arnold first at Dresden (1689) and then at Quedlinburg (1693). Though their relationship was strained by Arnold's later separatistic activities, they remained friends up to Spener's death in 1705. As was characteristic of him, Spener remained mild in his judgment of Arnold even at the height of Arnold's separatism.[30]

(2) It was at Quedlinburg that Arnold came in touch with a more mystical-spiritualistic piety and quite critical attitudes toward the established church. The Arndtian, Christian Scriver, and the Boehmist, Christian Hohburg, had labored here. A group of separatists was also meeting at Quedlinburg. During his stay here Arnold developed a close friendship with Johann Heinrich Sprögel, the court chaplain. Sprögel was a leading figure among the spiritualists in the town, though he could not be identified with the more radical separatists. By 1697 Arnold had also become acquainted with the English Philadelphians.[31]

Arnold's tutorial responsibilities left him with ample time to devote to writing. In 1696 he published his first major work, the *Abbildung*, in which he viewed the early church as the ideal community of regenerate believers whose lives should be emulated by all Christians. In recognition of Arnold's scholarly ability, Landgraf Ernst Ludwig of Hesse offered Arnold in 1697 the position of professor of secular history at the University of Giessen. He accepted the professorship, only to shock his friends within churchly Pietism by resigning the position a year later. He felt the emphasis on scholarship was hindering his total love and devotion for God.

This decision marks a definite radicalization in his mystical-spiritualism and separatistic attitudes. His *magnum opus*, the *Ketzerhistorie* (1699–1700), was written at the height of his radicalism and served as a vehicle for the expression of some of his most separatistic sentiments. This book was revolutionary and controversial because it opposed the official Lutheran historiography. Its premise was: "Those who make heretics are the heretics proper, and those who are called heretics are the real God-fearing people."[32] In the course of the work, Arnold came to despair that the true church could have visible form. Even the sects and the Reformation churches became

part of the fall through the self-seeking of their teachers and the failure to put away the old Adam with its pride and self-will. Though Arnold is extremely critical of the institutionalization of the church for its debilitating impact on the Spirit-generated, spontaneous community characteristic of the early church, he holds that the ultimate root of the fall is the corruption of the individual. Man's self-love and seeking of honor are the sources for the heresies, divisions, and errors which have spread throughout Christendom.[33]

Arnold's rejection of the visible church and his deep conviction for separation from the world were accompanied by greater emphasis on an inward, mystical relationship with God. Predictably, in 1700 he withdrew from attendance at church and communion.[34] This same year he wrote *Das Geheimnis der göttlichen Sophia*, which is the classical exposition of the Radical Pietist view of "divine Wisdom." In it Arnold reveals indebtedness to the Boehmism of Gichtel (with whom he corresponded between 1699 and 1701) by, among other things, rejecting marriage.

(3) Two events that occurred in 1701 signal a moderating influence at work on Arnold's extreme mystical-spiritualistic perspective. These events were his marriage to Anna Sprögel, the daughter of his close friend at Quedlinburg, and his acceptance of a position within the Lutheran church.

As would be expected, Arnold's marriage shocked his Boehmist friends. They still hoped, however, that Arnold would maintain a "pure" marriage, only to have their hopes shattered with the birth of Arnold's first child. Gichtel, who had considered Arnold his disciple, complained that he had now "even fallen into having children."[35] In *Das eheliche und unverehelichte Leben* (1702), Arnold explains his dramatic change of thought concerning marriage. He had come to see the wisdom of seeking a "blessed middle course" between the inward and outward, the spiritual and the temporal. Purity is not dependent upon total separation from the things of this world; it is primarily a question of one's total inward devotion and commitment to God. A Christian's relationship to the world and to things (including marriage) is to be governed by the God-given principles of moderation and "to the pure all things are pure."[36]

The other indication of a major modification in Arnold's Boehmist-determined radicalism was his acceptance of the position of court preacher in Altstädt at the end of 1701. A number of writings from the years 1699–1701 reveal two important catalysts at work in the reshaping of Arnold's view of the church: (1) the recognition that love for one's neighbor demands that the mature bear willingly the cross of self-denial by remaining within the fallen church in order to lead weak Christians to a firm faith and (2) a turning to a more mystical, inward, passive perception of Christianity which, to a great extent, relativized all outward organization, viewing it as indifferent (for the mature), but necessary (for the weak), means through which God is presently pleased to work for the sake of the weak.[37]

This fundamental reorientation in Arnold's thought should not be looked upon as a rejection of Radical Pietism.[38] Rather, Arnold's change reflects the basic transformation that was beginning to take place in the character of Radical Pietism as Quietism's passive strains began to "quiet" down the aggressiveness of the Babel-storming period. Arnold's considerable interest in Quietism during the period in which his new perspective was evolving is reflected not only in his preparation of the aforementioned prefaces for various quietistic works but also in his poetry from this period which evinces a quietistic spirit.[39]

With this new view of the church derived from Quietism, Arnold felt that he could accept the position of court preacher in Altstädt at the end of 1701 under the patronage of the widowed duchess of Saxe-Eisenach. When Arnold refused to subscribe to the Formula of Concord, however, the reigning duke refused to confirm him in his post. Arnold was accorded a degree of protection in this awkward situation by his installation as royal historiographer by Frederick, the newly-crowned King of Prussia. This action only annoyed the local duke who "begged the King to do 'his historian' a 'favor' by employing him in Prussia."[40] Frederick obliged with his appointment of Arnold in 1705 to the pastorate at Werben which Arnold's father-in-law, Sprögel, had just held. He then served as pastor and superintendent at Perleberg from 1707 until his death on May 30, 1714, at the age of forty-seven.

One other significant contribution made by Arnold during the last period of his life (1701–1714) should be considered: his propagation of "mystical theology." The fullest discussion of this subject appears in his *Historie und Beschreibung der Mystischen Theologie* (1703), though many of his other writings have a strong mystical flavor.

Arnold's use of the term "mystical theology" has reference to the syncretistic system which he builds by combining a variety of mystical traditions. Significant roles in this mixture are played by Tauler, à Kempis, the *German Theology*, Jan van Ruysbroeck, Angelus Silesius, and, in particular, Boehmism and

Quietism. Arnold utilizes the term "theology" in mystical theology to designate the same thing as theosophy, that is, the revealing of the Wisdom of God. The mysteries of God are revealed through the divine Wisdom and are accessible only to the regenerate. God's truth is basically practical; that is, it evidences itself in experience, not mere cognition or reason. Because of this, mystical theology stands in marked contrast to the *Schul-Theologie* (scholastic theology). It does not contend over words or useless questions; it coerces and damns no one for the sake of doctrine; it does not bring income, ease, or positions of honor but, on the contrary, rejection and persecution by "learned men."[41]

The practice of mystical theology in essence means the experience of pure divine love. Such love unites one with the will or understanding of God.[42] Arnold sees the goal of mystical theology as unity, both with God and among all Christians.[43] All mystical teachers agree that God is the eternal, highest good who, as the center of all things, unites all multiplicity and difference in Himself. All great theologians since Adam have shared these basic convictions; any differences among them are not essential. Indeed, Arnold holds that mystical theology is the true message of the prophets and apostles. It was Arnold's hope that by propagating this message he might help to reunite the church.[44]

This concern for the unity and reformation of the church caused Arnold to regret the harsh tone of some of his earlier works, especially the *Ketzerhistorie*.[45] Yet in spite of this change of attitude, he remained true to the seminal thoughts of the major works from his more radical period. Büchsel has noted three major themes which Arnold maintained throughout his life. (1) He continued to uphold a central idea of the *Abbildung* that the character and nature of the corporate church must be a reflection of the new man in Christ, the individual regenerate Christian. Thus the new conception of the responsibilities of the regenerate Christian in Arnold's later life led to a corresponding change in his view of the church. (2) He did not give up the idea of the fall of the church. Though he did tone down his criticism of the church, he did not reject the basic thought of the *Ketzerhistorie*. Indeed, he remained partial to this work his entire life. (3) He approved of and advocated the fundamental ideas of the mystics to an increasing degree throughout his life; this point is demonstrated by the fact that he entitles his last work *Theologia Experimentalis*.[46]

Methodological Considerations

The purpose of the work

The title[47] and dedication (*Zuschrift*) of the *Abbildung* clearly expose the purpose of the work. Though Arnold does present the *Abbildung* as a Church history (*Kirchen-Historie*), his intent transcends the mere recording of historical facts; he desires that the work be edifying (*nützlich*). He therefore portrays the "first Christians" as the purest and truest examples of Christianity. Arnold admonishes the church to return to "the first love" as represented by the early church. In effect, the witness of the first Christians becomes the standard by which all later forms of Christianity are to be measured.[48]

The role of reason, regeneration,
and impartiality

The task of the historian in this endeavor is to set forth the "mere historical account." Arnold's great concern is to be sure that the truth suffers no damage by straying from the historical record.[49] The reader, on the other hand, must approach the *Abbildung* in a quite different manner. He should not be content to acquire mere historical knowledge nor should he approach the *Abbildung* with a judgmental or purely rational attitude. Such approaches focus on only external matters and may lead the reader to reject whatever he does not consider reasonable or as applicable in the contemporary setting.[50] As Büchsel indicates, Arnold does not disdain historical knowledge; he desires only that his readers find a middle-way between a shameful ignorance and a false wisdom and sinful curiosity.[51]

The one characteristic that Arnold considers indispensable if his readers are to be edified by the work is a regenerate life. Only the regenerate man can judge the works of the early writers by the light of the Holy Spirit and determine what is edifying.[52]

The desire of the truly regenerate should be to follow the example of Christ, especially as it is depicted in the life and thought of the Apostles.[53] According to Büchsel, this emphasis on the imitation of Christ and His disciples results in a kind of contemporaneousness (*Gleichzeitigkeit*) that binds together the present with the past and makes possible immediate contact with the first Christians. Thus, regenerate readers and first century believers share a solidarity and unity which is based in a common discipleship to Christ and in the fellowship of Christ's

body.[54] Arnold's history of the first Christians will realize its edifying purpose if it spurs its readers to such active discipleship.

One further characteristic is demanded of both historian and reader for a true understanding of the history of the church—impartiality (*Unparteilichkeit*). Not only does Arnold indicate in his title that his Church history is "impartially set forth" ("unparteyisch entworffen"), but he also addresses his work "to the impartial reader" ("an der Unparteyischen Leser") in his initial foreword. Arnold would appear to have a twofold meaning in mind when he employs the adjective, *unparteyisch*.[55] First, as the historian, Arnold desired to present unbiased, historical, incontrovertible truth by allowing his historical sources to speak for themselves. Nearly every paragraph in the *Abbildung* contains at least one citation of a historical source. His own commentary on these sources is kept to a minimum. Second, as was common in Radical Pietist circles, impartial meant non-confessional, i.e., not belonging to any of the outward forms of the church, whether Catholic, Lutheran, or Reformed, for all these groups were merely "religious parties" and "sects."[56] True impartiality can be realized only by those who reject all the rules and regulations of the external institution and focus on the Lord Jesus as the fundamental content of true Christianity. In reality, only the regenerate are able to be impartial,[57] for only the person who is renewed and enlightened by God is able to free himself from a debilitating party spirit and thereby be receptive to the example on the first Christians.

The sources and contents
of the *Abbildung*

Arnold arranges his source materials thematically, according to his own distinctive outline. The following list of the eight books which comprise the *Abbildung* reveals several important facts about Arnold's view of Christianity and history.

The First Book—Concerning the First Christians' Duty and Relationship toward God.

The Second Book—Concerning the First Christians' General and Special Worship.

The Third Book—Concerning the First Christians' Duties and Relationships toward One Another.

The Fourth Book—Concerning the Duties and Relationships of the First Christians toward Themselves.

The Fifth Book—Concerning the First Christians' Duty and Relationships toward the Godless.

The Sixth Book—Concerning the Private and Domestic Life of the First Christians.

The Seventh Book—Concerning the Special Miracle-Gifts of the First Christians.

The Eighth Book—Concerning the Fall of Christendom, especially under and after Constantine the Great.

One may discern from the titles of the first six books that Arnold viewed church history from the perspective of Christians' duties and relationships to God, other Christians, themselves, the godless, and their households (at this point, of course, Arnold shows his "partiality"). He was not concerned with the development of the institution or of dogma; his focus was *personal*, the life of the regenerate. One could justifiably say that for Arnold church history was to be written by the regenerate historian, read by a regenerate audience, and focus upon the lives of the first regenerate Christians.

To support his portrayal of the first Christians (those of the first three centuries), Arnold cites not only sources from his designated period but also the works of authors who lived centuries later (Gregory the Great and Bernhard of Clairvaux, for instance).[58] He makes no attempt to distinguish or even identify the chronological or historical settings of his sources in the body of his work. This unhistorical (or, more appropriately, ahistorical) use of sources reflects a basic presupposition for Arnold: all Christian truth, as standardized in the early church, is constant. This presupposition leads to the belief on the one hand that the original truth finds expression, more or less clearly, in later centuries, and on the other that any deviation from the original ideal form of Christianity is a distortion of the truth.[59]

In spite of Arnold's desire to be "impartial," his own historical and theological biases creep in with his emphasis on various authors and specific works. Generally speaking, Arnold quotes the great church fathers most often. Oddly, however, citations from the little known Macarius of Egypt appear second only to those of Augustine in frequency in the first book of the *Abbildung*. This occurrence has a dual explanation. First, Arnold edited Macarius' Homilies in a German translation in 1696; and second, Arnold was especially enamored with Macarius' emphasis on inwardness and unity with God. In addition, Arnold shows a tendency to focus on the spiritualism of Augustine (he frequently cites the *Confessions*) and the ethical rigorism of Tertullian.[60] Likewise, Jerome supplies Arnold with criticisms of the development of the church under Constantine toward greater elaborateness and wealth and away from the self-denial of the cross.[61]

Arnold's view of church history

In the first seven books of the *Abbildung*, Arnold develops his picture of the life of the first Christians (for Arnold the "first Christians" included believers up to the fourth century but preeminently designated those of the first century or apostolic period). During this period the church found her purest and truest expression.[62] Yet Arnold not only has a "pictorial" purpose in mind in the *Abbildung*, he also has a historiographic purpose—to present his concept of church history. Arnold gives hints of this historiography in his first seven books but devotes the entire eighth book to its exposition.

Büchsel perceives that Arnold uses the term "fall" (*Verfall*) in three different senses: (1) to refer to the period after 300 A.D., (2) to designate developments in the church prior to this time, and (3) to encompass the general degeneration of the church with no reference to a definite date.[63] Even though his use of the term "fall" is fluid, the various elements of his view of the fall do fit into a consistent and logical pattern. The church remained pure during the time of the apostles, but developments had already begun to appear in the church by 100 A.D. which resulted in the slow erosion of the church's character. Though true Christians remained in the ascendancy until the fourth century, the church was gradually succumbing to practices which tended toward greater outwardness and institutionalization, and away from purity in faith and life. This trend culminated in a complete fall under Constantine when the church became bound to the world. From this time on "neither spiritual nor temporal things became better, but always more wicked and wretched."[64]

For Arnold, a significant change occurs in the church at the time of the fall. Whereas before the fall, the visible church is essentially the community of true Christians, after the fall it comes to represent the distortion of true Christianity, that is anti-Christ.[65] The true church after the fall is the "*invisible* [italics mine] holy community of Jesus Christ."[66] From the time of the fall onward, the histories of the true and false church are intertwined. It becomes the task of the regenerate historian to separate the two strands of the church, using, of course, the ideal of the early church as the plumb line.[67]

Arnold's understanding of the post-fall church is illuminated by considering his view of the heretics.[68] He indicates that the early church considered one a heretic not so much for what he believed but how he lived. More specifically, it would have been considered heresy if one denied God, if he failed to follow the teachings of Christ or live a holy life, or if he so confused nature and grace that he maintained a sinful life by his teaching and example.[69] If error was found in the early church, the offender would be admonished twice (Arnold probably has Titus 3:10 in mind) and, if necessary, the members of the church would separate themselves from him until he repented. By no means would the offender be persecuted, much less killed, for his error.[70]

Arnold opposed defining a heretic as someone whose understanding of Scripture deviated from the generally held sense of Scripture. Such a definition would allow few Christians to escape the designation, heretic, for erroneous views of Scripture continue to be held by many to this day. Arnold did not see Scripture as a resource to be used for deriving theological systems and confessions of faith which then could be turned against those who understood Scripture differently. Rather Scripture, when illuminated by the light of the Holy Spirit, should be perceived as the "true ground of godliness," that is, the aim of Scripture is to show us how to live lives pleasing to God.[71]

Arnold agreed that one could justly be called a heretic if he did not hold to the clear words of Scripture, but placed "new and previously unknown words and forms of speech" over God's Word.[72] It is precisely at this point that Arnold makes his attack upon the *Rechtglaubigen* (Orthodox). He notes that the so-called orthodox were not content with the mere words of Scripture but felt they needed explanation and elaboration. Therefore, the orthodox clergy developed confessions of faith and symbols which they placed over Scripture (thus Arnold could accuse the orthodox of heresy on the basis of his above definition). Adherence to these *Menschen-Satzungen* (human dogmas) was binding upon all Christians; failure to accept these orthodox interpretations earned one the designation "heretic." Fidelity to the opinions of men thus became of greater importance than living a life of godliness based on God's Word. In fact, the clergy, who were so concerned about upholding the external standards of the faith, not only fell into such terrible errors as greed, the seeking of honor, advocacy of persecution for heretics and, ultimately, disdain for the will of God, but they also led their people along these same paths.[73]

As intimated in the preceding discussion, one of Arnold's basic convictions is that a person's devotion to God must arise from an obedience that is uncompelled and free-willing. He is therefore especially critical of four "tools" of the institution used to coerce the consciences of the people: the confessional, the ban, church councils, and confessions of faith.[74] Tragically, those who opposed the clergy and their precepts and sought to live according to the first love of the church were labeled as heretics and even suffered persecution at the hands of the "orthodox." Yet their desire to obey God rather than man demonstrated that their faith was pure and true. Consequently, these people who were proclaimed as "godless" and "hypocrites" were often the most pious.[75]

Because the church of the fall has become "the enemy of the divine truth" by forsaking the true teachings of God and replacing His Word with its own commands, Arnold looks for the representatives of the true church elsewhere. He finds his witnesses of the truth (*Zeugen der Wahrheit*), for the most part, among those who have been labeled as heretics.[76]

Though Arnold's understanding of the fall of the church and his conviction that the true church was often to be found among the heretics were to undergo further elaboration in his *Ketzerhistorie*, these concepts already find clear exposition in the *Abbildung*. Even Arnold's radicalism, which was quite pronounced in the *Ketzerhistorie*, finds occasional expression in the *Abbildung* (for example, the belief that the fall of the church could still be seen in his time).[77]

Regeneration

Arnold views the life of the regenerate individual as a microcosm which ideally contains all that should be characteristic of the larger church. This point is highlighted by a perusal of the contents of book one. Here one finds a consideration of such topics as conversion, illumination, regeneration, active faith, obedience, perfection—all of which deal with Christian faith as it is experienced individually. Arnold does not even consider the corporate life of the early church until books two and three, and here he treats his subject in terms of the foundational principles which he has set forth in book one. On the basis of the organization of this work, soteriology, i.e., salvation applied individually, clearly is the theological locus which, for Arnold, governs the writing of church history and the understanding of the church.[78] Specifically, it is the restoration of the relationship between God and man effected in regeneration which becomes the main theme of book one.

Conversion and illumination

Arnold opens his work with the assertion that, according to both the Lord Jesus Christ and His disciples, true conversion is the genuine foundation of true, active Christianity.[79] Conversion is initially a divine work, for man cannot turn to God on his own. Man is dependent on Christ's work of showing him the way to God and the Holy Spirit's activity in leading him to an awareness of God's will and his own lostness. When a person arrives at this knowledge, he can be moved by the Holy Spirit to evidence the two marks of true repentance: an earnest hate toward sin and a deep love for God.[80] True repentance is possible only through faith. This faith finds Christ in the Word through the light of the Holy Spirit and it finds the Father through Christ. The faith of new Christians finds its entire foundation or assurance in the Spirit's witness to their spirit that they are now God's children. Arnold is careful to point out that all that comes to man in the conversion process—forgiveness of sins, a peaceful heart, justification—is due to God's mercy and love. Whoever has experienced this grace is no longer able to excuse the weakness of the old Adam. True conversion must, therefore, lead to holy living. It is inconceivable that one who is justified should live unholy or one who is raised from the dead should continue to remain dead. Besides, God has not only eradicated past sins, but He also helps man to sin no more.[81]

An integral part of conversion for Arnold is man's illumination or enlightenment (*Erleuchtung*). In illumination the believer is the passive recipient of an outflow of divine love and grace which enables him to contemplate divine things. Arnold does not view illumination purely as an immediate, mystical experience; rather, it is intimately connected with the reception and appropriation of the Word. The process of conveying the Word to man involves God, Christ, the Holy Spirit, and teachers. God Himself must open the heart for illumination to occur. Christ, the mediator of God's Word, must be followed implicitly in discipleship. The Holy Spirit applies the Word to the life of the believer. Teachers convey the letter (or outward Word) which must be vivified by the indwelling Christ. Continued receptivity to the Spirit's gift of wisdom (used synonymously with enlightenment) is conditioned upon a pious life, purity of soul, and Christian godliness. These qualities are attained negatively through the renunciation of the world and of self and positively through the observance of God's commands. Enlightenment is not a once-and-for-all infusing of wisdom into the

believer but involves growth to higher degrees of knowledge concerning Jesus Christ (conditioned of course by a parallel growth in godliness).[82]

Renewal of man in God's image

Arnold perceived one of the essential works of the Holy Spirit as the renewal of the image of God in man. To understand all that Arnold means by renewal, several of his discussions (those regarding regeneration, avoidance of sin, perfection, and restoration of the divine image) need to be considered.

Regeneration or the new birth is the first step toward blessedness (*Seligkeit*) following the forgiveness of sins. The new birth occurs totally apart from man's powers; it must be effected by the supernatural power of the Holy Spirit. The transformation that occurs in the believer is an inward change, affecting the heart (*Gemüth*) and mind (*Sinn*).[83] To help explain this change, Arnold employs an unusual interpretation of the dichotomous and trichotomous views of man's constitution. The unregenerate man consists of body and soul; the regenerate man is composed of body and "two kinds of spirits": the soul and "the image or likeness of God."[84] The first man, Adam, had possessed this image of God. However, Adam and, through him, the human race, lost it through Adam's sin. By means of the saving work of Christ, man may again attain the image of God.[85] Arnold describes the restoration (*Herwiederbringung*) of the lost image of God as the main goal (*Haupt-Zweck*) of the new birth.[86]

The Holy Spirit plays the essential role in effecting the restoration process. The restoration of the divine image (which Arnold seems to equate with man's spirit) occurs as a gift of the Holy Spirit or through the Spirit's power or grace. It is due to the Spirit's indwelling work that man's spirit acts as the vivifying influence upon the body and soul.[87] The Spirit is also responsible for the new valuation of man before God. When men receive the renewing Spirit, they obtain fellowship with God, the rights and status of a son, the pledge of eternal life, and the first fruits of the future goodness.[88]

So wonderful is this intimate fellowship with God through His Spirit that Arnold can say, citing the Fathers' interpretation of 2 Peter 1:4, that man has become a partaker of God. This divinization (*Vergötterung*) does not mean that man takes on God's nature or essence. Rather, the Fathers used this term to indicate a divine illumination of the inner man whereby men come near to God and thus become like God. In this new relationship with God, man acquires a "supernatural" perspective governed by heavenly, eternal goals and values rather than earthly, transient ones. In addition to intimate spiritual fellowship with God, the likeness of God has a second essential meaning for Arnold. It carries a clear ethical demand—to imitate the good works of God.[89]

To explain how man is able to fulfill the ethical demands of the new life, Arnold reverts to his distinctive anthropology. In the unregenerate man, who possesses only body and soul, the soul is under the control of the flesh (body) which will inevitably lead the soul into earthly lusts. In the regenerate man, however, the spirit or image of God is restored by the Holy Spirit. If the spirit truly rules man, the soul will follow the spirit in the desire to please God. Though the flesh comes under the control of the spirit, it still retains its earthly weakness, i.e., original sin. With his new constitution the Christian is able to avoid all intentional (*vorsätzlichen*) sins but continues to experience sins of weakness associated with original sin—evil speech, thoughts, and works. Such sins can be removed to an ever greater degree during the believer's lifetime. Towards this end a constant battle must be waged by the believer through the power of the Spirit against both earthly foes—self and love of the world—and spiritual ones—Satan and evil spirits.[90]

Arnold moves directly from his discussion of the Christian's struggle against sin and Satan to a consideration of Christian perfection. Arnold notes that perfection consists of doing what God desires. In one sense, this perfect fulfillment of God's will remains an unattained goal. Thus daily repentance and renewal are essential if growth into the new life is to take place. In another sense, however, the first Christians could justifiably call themselves perfect, not on the basis of their own imperfect character, but as a result of their new life in Christ. They recognized that they had no other perfection than that one based upon Christ and given them as a gracious gift by the Holy Spirit.[91]

Man's relationship to God

Significantly, Arnold devotes the first book of the *Abbildung* to the discussion of man's relationship to God. It is from this primary relationship that all of the believer's other responsibilities (which Arnold sets forth in books two through six) are derived.

Arnold maintains that the undergirding for man's relationship with God (from the human side) is the person's wholehearted love for God. From this basic attribute of the God-man relationship issue such

other important qualities as fear, trust, hope, humility, praise, thanks, and joy[92] (Arnold treats these qualities in the chapters following his discussion of love). This love for God must be guarded against such usurpers as love for the creature and love for the world. The immediate working of such love demonstrates itself outwardly in the desire to please God by observing His law as it pertains both to God and man.[93]

At the close of his chapter on love for God, Arnold employs the familiar mystical imagery of the love-play between the soul and Jesus. Such love results in a kind of realized eschatology for Arnold. Through this love the Christian already shares in the enjoyment of the eternal blessings, and he awaits only the throwing off of the weakness of the flesh.[94]

Arnold expressly considers the subject of unity with God in the final chapter of book one. He finds basic Biblical support for the believer's unity with God in John 17:20, 21 and bolsters his case with evidence from other New Testament passages and from the Church Fathers. He generally sees Christ or the Holy Spirit as the mediator of unity with God. Again he uses the mystical imagery of the bride (the soul) and the bridegroom (Jesus). Characteristically, Arnold indicates that this inward state of unity with God must be accompanied by outward marks. Thus it is a certain sign of whether or not a person has God and His Spirit within himself if the true fruits of righteousness are found in him.[95]

The life of active faith

As is by now clear, one of Arnold's recurring emphases is that the inner new birth will always be evidenced in outward actions (*Kennzeichen*). This active, visible side of Christian experience comes to the fore in Arnold's thought when he discusses active faith. Even here Arnold is careful to point out that living faith is made possible only through God's superabundant grace in Christ. Though faith must begin with belief and confidence in God from the heart, it *must* proceed to demonstration in deed. It is not that faith needs good works, but works are of its very nature.[96] Thus faith is authenticated or activated by works as well as by love for God and one's neighbor and by overcoming the world.[97]

Because of the importance of demonstrating one's faith, Arnold gives special attention to the theme of obedience to God's will. The truly regenerate man has renounced his own will and surrendered it to God; he desires to live according to God's will and thereby please Him. Obedience to God's will should never be viewed as a difficult or disagreeable task.

Such an attitude indicates an improper understanding of the new birth on several counts. First, God's law commands nothing that is difficult or impossible; rather, His yoke is easy. This is especially true because, second, God has given us His powerful Spirit which is able to overcome the weakness of the flesh. Because of the enabling work of the Holy Spirit, Arnold sees obedience both as a gift and a responsibility: we are expected to obey God because God's gracious gift of the Spirit supplies us with the power. Third, the only type of obedience that pleases God and edifies the believer is obedience that arises from love for God.[98]

The above interplay between God's grace and man's responsibility also arises as Arnold considers the believer's assurance or certainty in the faith. On one side, Arnold cites Philippians 1:6 that God, who has begun a good work in us, will bring it to completion. On the other side, Arnold warns against growing lukewarm in the faith and falling away from the truth. Care, watching, and perseverance are necessary to preserve the treasure of grace.[99] Thus Arnold can define the "elect disciples of Christ" and "children of God" as those who "are reborn and live piously"[100] (combining God's gracious work and man's responsibility).

When a person is obeying God's will, this obedience will manifest itself negatively in the renunciation of self and the world and positively in discipleship. Self-denial is accomplished through the deadening of the old Adam with his lusts and desires, a process which leads, on the one hand, to the weakening of one's own will and, on the other, to peace for the soul and joy in the Holy Spirit.[101] True Christians likewise are called to deny the world with its enticements, riches, and high honors. It is not that the world itself is evil, however, for the world belongs to God; only the worldly evil belongs to Satan. In reality, however, the world and evil are so inseparably intertwined that the Christian is able to separate himself from evil only by removing himself from the world (which has become Babel). Thus the Christian perceives himself as a pilgrim and stranger in this world, longing instead for his heavenly fatherland.[102]

Christians have been given an example of how they are to walk in a holy manner in this world through Christ's words and deeds. Discipleship to Christ is based upon having Christ living within and is expressed in a Christ-like life. The essence of this Christ-like life is love, for positively it is the fulfillment of the law and negatively it destroys evil.[103] Such love is to be the mark of Christians in their relation to each other and to the godless.[104] Imitating the example of Christ's love also means following Christ in the way of the cross—tribulation and suffering. Through the inner battle against evil (see p. 30) and the way of the cross, the believer is purified and perfected. For this reason the early Christians viewed tribulation not as a punishment from God, but as fatherly discipline. Arnold therefore considers suffering as a basic mark for true Christianity.[105]

Though Arnold could advocate renunciation of the world and one's own self, he also counseled the principle of moderation and sobriety in relation to the use of material goods and of the creation in general. However, Arnold does not make a clear distinction between the spheres to which each of these concepts applies (a problem which would surface later in his wrestling with the questions of work and marriage). In counseling moderation Arnold sought a kind of middle way which recognized on the one hand that man could become subjugated by intemperate use of worldly things and on the other that these things had been created by God for our use.[106]

Summary

Regeneration forms the foundation for Arnold's view of the Christian life. This emphasis has implications for several of Arnold's distinctive viewpoints. First, Arnold consistently maintains that regeneration contains both inner and outer aspects, both of which are essential. It is the Holy Spirit's inner work in man which makes every step of regeneration possible. But Arnold also indicates that the Spirit's inner working will always produce outward, visible marks. Inasmuch as regeneration is an inward working of the Spirit, Arnold can describe the Christian life in terms of a realized eschatology: the Christian is illumined, perfect, united with God, enjoying heavenly life (Arnold tends to place more weight on this side of the balance). Inasmuch as regeneration must be outwardly demonstrated, Arnold employs concepts which stress the need for constant growth in grace: the Christian must deny self and the world, obey God's will, fight against sin and Satan, walk as Christ's disciple.

Second, Arnold's emphasis upon regeneration leads to a consequent stress upon Pneumatology as compared with Christology.[107] Christ is viewed as the pattern or model for the Christian life. Just as the fullness of the Godhead dwelt in Christ, so also should God dwell in us. Christ, the new man (as opposed to Adam, the old man), through His conquest of death by the cross and His reconciling ministry, has restored the image of God in man and enabled man to experience new life. The Christian is called upon to follow Christ in the way of the cross—self-denial, tribulation, persecution. Though Christ opened up and marked out the way for men, it remains for the Holy Spirit to actualize the new life. God dwells in us by His Spirit. The regenerate life in all its facets is worked by the Holy Spirit. It is the Spirit's power that gives us victory and a taste of the heavenly sweetness here and now. The Spirit thus becomes the focus of Arnold's attention, for the possibility of regeneration is realized in the Spirit's power.

The Church

The church as the community
of the reborn

Even though Arnold begins the *Abbildung* with a discussion of numerous elements which pertain to the individual's Christian faith, this emphasis should not be interpreted as a depreciation of the corporate aspects of the faith. Arnold demonstrates in two ways that his concern for community, though subordinate to his interest in personal salvation, plays a key role in his understanding of Christianity. First, Arnold holds that it is God's will to establish a "perfect society" among men. To this end God has provided the source and power for this brotherhood in Jesus and the Holy Spirit respectively. Second, Arnold holds that the formation of community is an integral part of regeneration. Just as natural brothers and sisters share a bond of fellowship due to their origin from the same parents, so also spiritual siblings experience a strong sense of community due to their rebirth as God's children. Since each Christian derives his faith from the one true faith in God, a fundamental bond exists which should unite all believers into one fellowship.[108]

Arnold considers the church to be the corporate extension of the regenerate believer.[109] Those characteristics which are constitutive for regeneration— (1) outward marks, (2) the inward working of the Spirit, (3) suffering (see below)—are likewise essential for the true church. From this vantage point, then, the church can never be perceived as an institution; it is fundamentally a fellowship or community of regenerate persons. For Arnold institutionalism, with its authority, coercion, and hierarchy, is inimical to those loving, personal qualities which are basic to a community of faith.[110]

(1) Arnold maintains that the true church can always be discerned by its outward marks. The true church will be visible, demonstrating its faith in a holy, God-pleasing life. Throughout book three Arnold develops a number of visible marks which, he felt, characterized the early church and therefore should be found in all communities of believers— unity, love, humility, mutual support, and admonition. Every believer becomes responsible for maintaining and preserving the church's character by bearing one another's burdens, receiving and giving admonition and discipline, witnessing to the world by his good works, and using his spiritual gifts for the edification of the body.[111]

(2) Inwardness is a second basic mark of both the regenerate believer and the true church. Inwardness is the attitude which perceives the essence of Christian faith as lying in spiritual matters and in a free-willing commitment and obedience to God. Every Christian, by virtue of his priesthood, has the freedom to go to God directly. By no means does the church mediate the relationship between God and man; rather the church itself is constituted by the gathering of the regenerate.[112]

(3) Though he does not explicitly state it, Arnold moves from a visible to an invisible concept of the church at the time of the binding together of church and state under Constantine.[113] This occurrence has ominous results for true believers. Because those who truly desired to follow God felt compelled to oppose the ungodly practices of the fallen church, they were labelled as heretics and became persecuted by the church. Thus these persecuted "heretics" realized Arnold's third mark of the true church—suffering.[114] They became the witnesses of the truth alongside a church which had fallen away from its first love.

True worship

The inner-outer interplay which is so characteristic of Arnold's thought is also found in his understanding of worship. True worship combines commitment of oneself to God as a living sacrifice (Rom. 12:1) together with the practice of good works (James 1:27). Such worship is not confined to open gatherings alone, but should occur everywhere and at all times.[115] This conviction has clear implications for the place and time of worship. Church buildings were not even known during the first two centuries. The early Christians viewed the entire world as God's dwelling place and held that their bodies were God's temple. Originally, Christians met under the open sky or, a bit later, in meeting houses (Arnold calls them "Conventicles") or prayer houses which differed little from private homes.[116] Likewise, worship was not bound to a definite time. The first Christians perceived that Christ inaugurated an unceasing Sabbath which hallowed every day as a time for devotion. This Sabbath begins for the individual at his rebirth.[117]

Though Arnold's definition of worship seems to emphasize the individual's devotion to God, he does not overlook the corporate aspects of worship. Praying, singing, and reading and exposition of the Word were all important aspects of the early church's life. Both praying and singing were considered expressions of the first Christians' unity in mind and spirit while the reading of the Word was important for the instruction and admonition of the body.[118] Yet Arnold cautions that each of these exercises must be accompanied by a corresponding inward quality. Praying is effectual only when it arises from a pure heart and a humble spirit; one must sing not only with the mouth but also from the heart; effective preaching is dependent upon the Holy Spirit's ministration to both speaker and listener.[119] Arnold has only sharp words for those accretions to these practices which placed the emphasis on outward, regulated ceremony rather than freewilling worship. Thus he criticizes the development and use of prayer books and formula prayers; professional singers, instruments, and singing in parts; lectionaries, pulpits, human eloquence, and theological hairsplitting.[120]

Sacraments and church discipline

Arnold opens his discussion of the sacraments by considering the meaning of the word, sacrament. After tracing the development of the meaning of this word, Arnold concludes that one cannot be dogmatic about either the number of the sacraments or the meaning of the word itself.[121] Instead, since "sacrament" does not appear in Scripture, it would be preferable to maintain those practices which have the command and promises of God.[122]

Arnold understands baptism as a sign of an already commenced conversion and rebirth; by virtue of this rite, one is received into the community. For Arnold baptism is integrally tied to the active faith which must follow repentance. Romans 6 and 1 Peter 3:21 indicate that in baptism one pledges to die to the world and sin and live for righteousness. Because baptism effects nothing, it realizes its true meaning only through conversion and a change of character. Thus renewal of the heart and daily repentance are necessary aspects of every Christian's life.[123]

By viewing baptism as a sign of the new birth[124] and a pledge to live a new, holy life, Arnold maintains a close connection between regeneration and baptism without resorting to any kind of baptismal regeneration. However, Arnold holds that the original connection between regeneration and baptism found in the thought of the early church was distorted during the fall of the church by an *opus operatum* interpretation. Thus the outward performance of the rite was thought to convey the grace of God, conversion, and regeneration whether or not repentance and faith in God were present.[125]

Arnold likewise holds that the introduction of infant baptism, for which he sees no historical evidence prior to the third century, tends to distort the connection between baptism and faith. That infants were not originally intended to be baptized is shown by the Lord's command in Matthew 28:19 which indicates that preaching must precede baptism.[126]

Arnold considers baptism and the experiences connected with it—forgiveness of sins, active faith, regeneration—as necessary presuppositions for participation in the Lord's Supper. This repeated act serves not only as a remembrance of Christ's sacrifice but also as a reminder that we are to offer our lives to God as a living, holy, God-pleasing sacrifice in obedience to Him. Arnold develops several other themes that for him are basic to the meaning of the Supper—thanksgiving, sharing, and the unity and fellowship of believers. The themes of sharing and unity were given outward expression in the early church through the practices of the love feast or Agape and the love kiss. Both practices were later discontinued; in the case of the Agape this cessation occurred because of the unfortunate abuse of the rite. Special emphasis is laid on the Lord's Supper as the occasion for the fellowship of *believers*, of the pious, of those who demonstrate their love for God in active faith. It is thus a terrible abuse of the first, pure practice when the church comes to make no differentiation between the pious and the wicked or hypocrites but allows all to attend the Supper.[127] For Arnold the fall of the church becomes quite evident in the observance of the Lord's Supper.[128] As the first love of the church gradually disappeared, people no longer attended the Lord's Supper out of a voluntary spirit. As attendance dropped, various forms of coercion were used to force the people to participate. Such regulations led to hypocrisy, indifference in the observance of the rite, and the introduction of outward show.[129]

Arnold viewed church discipline as a practice which was necessary for the proper observance of the Lord's Supper and for the maintenance of the character of the church. Every believer, when he joins a community, becomes responsible for the holiness of his brothers and sisters. In fact, if one remains silent concerning a brother's sin, he himself becomes guilty and is a hypocrite.[130] Yet Arnold stresses that certain inward qualities must be present before discipline can be exercised in a community. First, holiness in one's own life was essential. Before a person could admonish his brother, he must be free from all blame himself. Second, discipline must be carried out in an attitude of love and humility. Restoration of a fallen brother is possible only when he realizes that discipline occurs out of a loving concern for his welfare. Third, Arnold holds that discipline, when carried out in a loving manner by upright believers, is not an act of force but one of freedom.[131]

According to Matthew 18:15ff., private sins should first be dealt with privately. Open sins must be treated publicly, however. Discipline for open sins is to be carried out by the entire church. Yet, even in this case, love is to be extended to the errant brother.[132]

Arnold may appear to be inconsistent when, on the one hand, he condemns the use of force in the fallen church and, on the other, he maintains the necessity for discipline in the true church. Yet the problem is clarified somewhat when it is analyzed from the perspective of Arnold's inner-outer dialectic. When discipline was motivated by inward principles, when it arose from the community's love and concern for each other, only then could it be practiced in a spiritually edifying manner. When, however, the authority for discipline was wrested from the community and assumed by the hierarchy and institution, discipline became characterized by external force and compulsion.

Teachers, clergy, the state

The teacher (*Lehrer*)[133] plays a key role both in Arnold's conception of the true church and in his discussion of the fall of the church. For him the integrity of the church stands or falls with the integrity of the teacher. To understand the place of the teacher in the early church according to Arnold, his view of church government needs to be considered. Initially, there were no privileged positions in the church; all shared responsibility for the direction of the church. Every member bore the right and responsibility to admonish, test, and discipline his fellow believers. There was even the freedom in the beginning for anyone to preach, teach, or baptize who was so gifted.[134]

Arnold does acknowledge that there were different offices in the church, but the holders of these positions were accountable to the entire community. It is interesting (in the light of recent debates) that Arnold maintains that the leadership must be both "charismatic" and elected. Though office bearers were called to their position by God, this call had to be acknowledged by a "Holy Spirit ruled consensus of the church."[135] Thus there was "in the church no monarchical form of government but an aristocratic or much more democratic" form, "since one did nothing without the judgment of the people."[136] Not only did the community have the right to elect and confirm teachers in their office, but it also was to judge its leaders and could even dismiss them.[137] The officers selected by the early church had distinguished themselves by their holy life and by their knowledge and practice of God's Word.[138]

Arnold posits that the distinctions which the teachers began to recognize among one another and within the church itself were the "first scattered seeds of the Anti-Christ."[139] Originally there was no distinction in the church between the so-called clergy and laity, for they all addressed each other as "brother" or "sister." Later the teachers began to separate themselves from the community by narrowing the application of the word "spiritual" to themselves and by their assumption of the designation κλῆρος or "Erbtheil."[140] The word "clergy" thus becomes a pejorative term for Arnold, to be connected with the institutionalization and fall of the church.

In the early church there were also no distinctions among the teachers themselves. A teacher was not bound to one congregation but was free to go and teach in other churches. It was only later that distinct districts and dioceses came into being, each with its own bishop who held sole responsibility for that area. In time bishops were forbidden to teach authoritatively outside their own diocese. Arnold especially criticizes the bishops for the development of a hierarchical structure in the church. Initially, the bishop was one of the elders who had no more power than the other elders. Though he was considered the first among the elders, his position was one of spiritual service. The placing of a bishop over the other elders was a custom that originated with men. Arnold expressly refutes the view that the bishops were appointed by God alone or received their office through apostolic succession.[141]

Büchsel perceives that the fall of the clergy exhibits itself in three different symptoms according to Arnold: (1) a fall in the Christian life among the clergy, (2) a fall caused by the binding of church and state, (3) a fall deriving from the institutionalization of the church.[142]

(1) Arnold considers at length in book eight the debilitating attitudes and practices (pride, hypocrisy, greed, simony, drunkenness, lust, etc.) which served to undermine the life and witness of the teachers.[143] The enjoyment of outward welfare was especially conducive to the spread of corruption for it enticed the church into increasing outwardness.[144]

(2) Arnold views the binding of the spiritual and temporal realms, which began with Constantine, as the decisive source of the fall. It is an open invitation for the work of anti-Christian forces. Arnold maintains that the church has no right interfering in worldly affairs. The domain of the church involves spiritual, eternal realities and its affairs are handled "through persuasion, admonition, teaching, and discipline."[145] The state rules through outward regulations which always carry with them a form of coercion. The separation of church and state applies equally to both realms: the church and especially the clergy are not to intervene in worldly affairs or seek to pervert the church into a state-church, while the state is not to rule over the church.[146] Arnold acknowledges that the state has an important role to play in the fallen earthly order. It serves as the preserver and protector of society. The Christian is to be obedient to the state in worldly matters but is to be obedient to God alone in matters of faith and conscience.[147]

(3) Nowhere does Arnold's criticism against externalism become more caustic than when he deals with the institutionalizing tendencies that were at work in the church before and after the decisive fall under Constantine. Arnold touches on at least three general areas in which externalism distorted the original purity of the church: Scripture, the ministry of the Spirit, and the practices of the church.

In true Reformation heritage, Arnold maintains that no decree or tradition can stand beside or above Scripture. He sees the violation of this principle at the time of the fall as having corrupting results. He especially criticizes those practices which gradually took the Bible from the hands of the people and burdened it with human precepts—the use of prescribed texts during the year and later the development of lectionaries.[148]

Arnold views the effects of institutionalization as especially debilitating for the ministry of the Spirit. The institution and the Holy Spirit are mutually exclusive principles for Arnold.[149] Whereas the former is characterized by externalism, coercion, regulations, the latter is denoted by inwardness, freedom, sim-

plicity. The effects of institutionalization are clearly seen upon the Spirit's miracle-gifts. These gifts began to disappear as soon as the church started to consign their practice to a particular office.[150] Likewise, the development of an *opus operatum* view of the sacraments had a disastrous influence upon the Christian life. The outward work was emphasized at the expense of the inward, regenerating work of the Holy Spirit.[151]

Arnold further sees externalism at work in the observance of such practices as the sacraments, preaching, singing, prayer, and fasting. From the time of Constantine on, these practices, which had at first been observed out of voluntary obedience, were increasingly encumbered with regulations which made their observance mandatory.[152] Though these regulations may have served a purpose for weak Christians, they were of no help to the reborn.[153]

Summary

Büchsel's contention that Arnold views anthropology (or, more properly, salvation individually applied) as *the* criterion for understanding the church certainly appears to be borne out by the *Abbildung*. Those characteristics which are fundamental for the regenerate individual—a correspondence between inner and outer, suffering, freewilling obedience—are likewise determinative for the church. It does seem, however, that Büchsel's conclusion that ecclesiology lies considerably in the background[154] is not altogether accurate. Though ecclesiology is secondary to anthropology in his thought, one senses Arnold's desire for a true corporate expression of regenerate Christianity. His criticism of the institutional church does not have the despairing overtones of the *Ketzerhistorie*. Rather, his call for the church to test itself by the plumbline of the early church would seem to indicate that Arnold has a deep-seated desire to see the church reformed *corporately* as well as individually.

The same inner-outer dialectic that was crucial for Arnold's view of the regenerate man also plays a key role in his understanding of ecclesiology. Thus Arnold recognizes the place of such worship practices as singing, praying, preaching, reading the Word; but they must not be burdened within external regulations to the point that their internal significance disappears. The sacraments are a central part of the corporate life of the community, but their meaning is perverted by an *opus operatum* view which stresses outward appearances rather than inward realities. Preservation of the character of the church demands discipline, but correction is to be administered only from a sincere love and concern for one's brother, never as a tool of coercion. Church offices are necessary for the proper functioning of the church, but the authorization to exercise one's office is based upon a gift granted by the Spirit and acknowledged by the church. All this can be distilled into one key idea for Arnold: the Holy Spirit, who is central to the very being of the regenerate church, is free to act only in an atmosphere of free-willing, wholehearted commitment to God. It is the inward reality furnished by the Spirit which gives external practices their meaning.

As often happens with reformers and reform movements, excessive amounts of the cure can lead to a situation worse than the initial problem itself. To be sure, some of the implications of Arnold's thought in the *Abbildung* and *Ketzerhistorie* are dangerous: overemphasis on individual regeneration may lead to depreciation of and even despair with corporate Christianity; stress upon the inner witness of the Spirit can create subjective tendencies which, taken to the extreme, may threaten the objective content of the faith; viewing good works as a criterion for true Christianity may cause one to reduce Christianity to an ethical religion; zeal for personal holiness may lead to separation from the world and church and stymie any concern for fellow Christians. Though some of these excesses are to be found in Arnold's own thought and life, it is to his credit that he possessed other principles which tended to rectify his extreme views. Especially important in this regard are his principle of the middle way and his desire for correspondence between inner and outer aspects of the faith. Arnold's life may be viewed as a struggle to find the proper balance between various poles of Christian experience. For the most part, it seems that Arnold was able to moderate the excesses reflected in the *Ketzerhistorie* during the succeeding years. It is therefore much fairer to judge Arnold ultimately by his later life as the pastor, seeking to lead weaker Christians to maturity, than by his earlier life as the author of the *Ketzerhistorie*, advocating separatism because of a corrupt and corrupting church.

Ernst Christoph Hochmann von Hochenau

Probably the most winsome figure among Radical Pietists was Ernst Christoph Hochmann von Hochenau (1670–1721). He was the beloved friend of the awakened among the Reformed, Lutherans, and Anabaptists, the confidant of pietistically-inclined nobility, and the bold proclaimer of the love of God in Christ Jesus to not only the "sects" but also the Jews.[155] His significance lies not in his writings, as in the case of Arnold, but in the people whose lives he touched.[156] The charisma of Hochmann's Christ-centered life gave to his message a forcefulness which left a lasting impress on the many whom he "awakened" in Germany, Switzerland, and the Netherlands. Among his converts were a number of those who were to become the leading figures in the early Brethren fellowship. Because Hochmann's significance is found in the epistle of his life, it is best to weave together the discussions of his life and thought, though a summary of some of his distinctive views will also be presented.

Hochmann was born in Lauenburg on the Elbe. His father, who served as a private secretary to the duke of Saxe-Lauenburg and as a customs official, was raised to a position of nobility with the title "Hochenau" in 1664. Ten years later the family moved to Nürnberg.

Hochmann began to prepare for a law career in 1691, studying successively at the universities of Giessen, Halle (under the celebrated Thomasius), Leipzig, Erfurt, and Jena. While studying at Halle (1693) Hochmann was converted by Francke. However, the direction which Hochmann took in his new-found faith displeased Francke greatly. Hochmann became the leader of a group of spiritualists at Halle whose radical views soon warranted the appointment of an electoral (Brandenburg) commission. In the hearings Hochmann expressed convictions which would remain determinative for him throughout his lifetime. He maintained that the foundation for his new views was his experience of the new birth through the indwelling work of the Holy Spirit. Hochmann considered this experience of decisive importance. In it he received an immediate calling from God to serve as a spiritual priest to God's people. He held that the exercise of this calling was not bound to any outward ecclesiastical office. It is the Holy Spirit alone who grants the power and authority to priests to intercede on behalf of each other for forgiveness of sins and the bestowal of spiritual gifts. The Holy Spirit is even now fashioning a new fellowship of the elect which transcends confessional boundaries. This new *Gemeinde* celebrates through faith the Spirit of Christ's body and blood without the need for the outward elements.[157]

By this time Hochmann had come under Petersen's influence, as is evidenced in his eschatological views. Hochmann was convinced that the outward church, i.e., Babel, must fall and that God's thousand year kingdom would be established on earth. The vanguard of this kingdom was the spiritual priests who were able to recognize the need of the hour through divine inspiration and could therefore lead God's spiritual church. The implications which Hochmann's eschatological views had for his understanding of the state were quite disconcerting to the investigation commission. Though Hochmann acknowledged that the Christian is to obey the state, he maintained a "right of exception" in view of the impending breaking in of God's kingdom. God may, through the inspiration of the Spirit, call upon the spiritual to act contrary to the established laws. The Christian is bound to obey such divine inspiration, for it supersedes any necessity to obey the state.[158]

Faced with such radical views, the commission called for Hochmann's expulsion from Brandenburg. Hochmann reluctantly left Halle at the end of May or the beginning of June in 1693. After a brief stay at Leipzig, he went to Erfurt where he spent the next several years continuing his law studies. Here he stayed with the professor of law at the university, Georg Heinrich Brückner. Brückner was a friend of Petersen and Jane Leade, the English Boehmist and founder of the Philadelphian Society. This friendship, his concurrent correspondence with certain Quedlinburg spiritualists (see p. 24), and his acquaintanceship with Gichtel were significant in shaping the later course of Hochmann's life. Hochmann's association with the Philadelphian Society and Gichtel needs to be explored further.

Oddly, Hochmann's name does not appear of Dittmar's list of German friends of the Philadelphian Society. Yet his acquaintance with the movement is unquestionable as attested by several facts: (1) his association with two men connected with German Philadelphianism, Petersen and Brückner, (2) his knowledge of Leade's works, and (3) the numerous similarities between Hochmann's thought and the emphases of the Philadelphians. Hochmann parallels Philadelphian thought in his eschatological expectations of the fall of Babel and the coming of God's kingdom, his belief in the restoration of all things and the corollary idea of purification after death, and his adoption of the term "priesthood of Melchizedek" (also used by Gichtel) to refer to the fellowship of spiritual priests who were active in a ministry of intercession. For both Hochmann and Leade part of the ritual connected with this priesthood involved the selection of a new name (Hochmann took the name, Aaron). Renkewitz also notes that Hochmann, like Leade, Petersen, and Poiret, was committed to the concept, derived from Coccejus, that a series of steps in the communication of religious knowledge

had occurred in the course of the economy of revelation.[159] Though Hochmann's views on these subjects followed the general outlines suggested by the Philadelphians, the details of his thought reveal some characteristic differences. His view of eschatology gave much more attention to chiliasm; his view of revelation relied more heavily on inner illumination (rather than on extraordinary revelations, voices, visions, and prophecies); he felt the impending fall of Babel obligated him to call the princes to repentance; his view of the community of the Spirit was more spiritualistic than that of the Philadelphians; he refused to engage in the speculations about the Trinity and Christology typical of the English Boehmists.[160]

Hochmann's association with Petersen brought him into contact with not only the Philadelphians but also Gichtel. Hochmann's indebtedness to Gichtel is found primarily in Gichtel's view of the imitation of Christ and the Melchizedekan priesthood. Gichtel held that the life and suffering of Christ is to be repeated in one's own life. This Christlikeness places upon a believer the responsibility for interceding for both the regenerate and the lost. The ministry of intercession is an integral duty of a priest who belongs to the order of Melchizedek. An essential condition of this priesthood involves joining oneself to Christ in uncompromising devotion which, for the Boehmist, Gichtel, necessitated a celibate existence. Likewise, the true priest will rely on God for his needs and not depend on worldly employment. Hochmann was able to fulfill this latter condition through contributions by friends and the interest on his inherited wealth. Unlike Gichtel, however, who did not seek fellowship (even though his home did serve as a way station for Radicals), Hochmann felt a recurring longing for the formation of a new spiritual community.[161]

One other Radical Pietist who played a part in Hochmann's spiritual formation was Gottfried Arnold. The question of whether Hochmann first met Arnold in 1697 or 1699[162] does not bear great significance since Arnold's influence on Hochmann was not through his person but through his writings. Though they were molded by similar forces, each went his own way (as was typical of the Radical Pietists). Hochmann's view of church history (especially the Reformation) was dependent on Arnold's *Abbildung* and *Ketzerhistorie* as evidenced by Hochmann's citation of these works at various times.[163] Hochmann likewise relied on Arnold and Poiret for his understanding of mystical theology and, in his later years, for quietistic terminology and concepts.[164]

The convergence of strong separatistic and chiliastic influences in Hochmann's thought signalled the beginning of a new period in his life in 1699. Hochmann commenced a Babel-storming ministry in which he saw it as his task to witness against the fallen church and assemble believers together who had left "Babel." This task he shared with numerous other Radical Pietists. Thus he itinerated at various times with Dippel, Arnold (only in 1699), Samuel König, Johann Heinrich Reitz, and Carl Anton Püntiner to such places as Solms-Laubach, Frankfurt on the Main, Berleburg, and Lippe-Biesterfeld between 1699 and 1702.

It was at Berleburg in Wittgenstein between October 1699 and April 1700 that the chiliastic and enthusiastic activities of the Radicals reached their high point. Here extraordinary phenomena which were described as "fire of the Spirit"—uncontrollable laughter, violent shaking of the body, visions, ecstasies—seemed to signal a special outpouring of the Spirit prior to the inbreaking of God's millennial kingdom.[165]

As a result of these occurrences, Hochmann felt moved to establish a new community of the Spirit at Berleburg in April 1700—the priesthood after the order of Melchizedek. Renkewitz notes six distinctive features of this spiritual fellowship. (1) The foundation for the new order is the expectation of the soon return of Christ, whom Hebrews pictures as the priest-king in the mold of Melchizedek. Whoever is sealed to this new priesthood will be at Christ's disposal in the establishment of His kingdom. (2) The new order of priests involves the implicit rejection of the priesthood of the established churches. The new priests receive their calling immediately from God as did Christ.[166] (3) The new priests join themselves into a new order. Though in actuality no fixed organization was established, the action of consecrating priests clearly revealed an impulse to form a new community (albeit spiritual). (4) The office of priest demands the exclusive commitment to Christ, the bridegroom; thus one must remain free from all other attachments, whether to parents or spouse. (5) The task of the priests is to seek personal holiness and to offer prayers for others. Personal holiness involves the willingness to follow every impulse of the Spirit and thereby demonstrate one's discipleship to Christ. It was held that intercessory prayer served several functions: it provided the person prayed for with power to overcome temptation and live the Christian life; it aided the coming of the kingdom; it helped to fulfill God's purposes concerning the people of Israel. (6) Hochmann saw it as his special task to warn all the rulers of the states and territories of the impending judgment and to lead them to personal conversion.[167]

Though the Berleburg court was swept away by the enthusiasm, interference from the neighboring court at Lippe-Brake helped to squelch the radicalism in May 1700. Nevertheless, Berleburg and the county of Wittgenstein remained important refuges for the Radicals well into the eighteenth century. The ecstasy which the Radicals experienced at Berleburg gradually subsided, though Hochmann and others continued their aggressive preaching against the princes and the clergy. As a result of his activity, Hochmann was expelled from Wetzlar, Hannover, and Bremen in 1702 and 1703 and suffered imprisonment at Detmold from August to December of 1702.

As a condition for his release from the Detmold castle, Hochmann was called upon to write a confession of faith. The resulting *Glaubensbekenntnis* warrants close consideration because of the clear affinities between the thought of Hochmann found therein and that of the early Brethren.[168] The confession was divided into seven sections with a supplement added on the subject of marriage.[169] Renkewitz speculates that this supplement was demanded by the ruling count due to the stir created by the immoral activities of Eva von Buttlar and her "gang."[170]

(1) Hochmann begins by confessing his faith in God. However, he exhibits the Boehmist aversion, common to Radical Pietism, to conceiving the God-head as three *Persons*, preferring instead to speak of a divine *Wesen* ("essence"; the emphasis is on the unity of God's self-revelation). Thus Hochmann writes of an "ewigen Göttlichen Wesen im Vatter/ Sohn und Geist" ("eternal divine essence in Father/ Son and Spirit").[171] Hochmann concluded the first section by professing belief in the Apostles' Creed "with mouth and *heart*" [italics mine].

(2) Hochmann holds that Christ instituted baptism for adults and not for small children, for there is not an iota of an express command in Scripture for baptizing the latter. (3) The Lord's Supper is instituted only for the chosen disciples of Christ who have renounced all worldly things and follow Christ in deed and truth. God's covenant will be reviled and His anger will be aroused against the entire *Gemeinde* if the godless children of the world are admitted to the love feast as is currently done. (4) Hochmann believes that though he was born and conceived of sinful seed, he can become not only justified through Christ but also perfectly sanctified through Him, so that no more sin remains in him. He acknowledges,

however, that he has not yet attained this state. The great redemptive work of Christ realizes its full purpose only when the soul attains the perfect likeness of God and Christ through Christ's mediatorship. Without holiness no one will see God.

(5) Hochmann stresses that Christ alone, as the Head of the church, can appoint teachers and preachers and give them the necessary ability. Scripture (Eph. 4:10, 11; Acts 20:28) attests that the Holy Ghost and not man makes men to be bishops to feed the *Gemeinde*. (6) Hochmann believes that the state is a divine ordinance in the "kingdom of nature." He acknowledges that he will obey it in civil matters, but he ascribes no power to the state when it conflicts with God's Word, his conscience, or the freedom of Christ. Just because God has ordained magistrates to rule in the realm of nature does not mean that they are *ipso facto* Christian; even the Turk and the Pope are true magistrates. Hochmann will grant the predicate "Christian" only to the magistrate in whom he detects the Spirit of Christ.

(7) At both the beginning and end of this article, Hochmann states that he does not feel the confession to be the right place to consider the restoration of condemned men, for this doctrine demands a detailed deduction and word-of-mouth discussion. Yet he does offer several brief arguments. As in Adam all men fell, so also must all men be restored through the second Adam, Christ Jesus. If this were not so, it would necessarily follow that Christ was not powerful enough to restore the human race which was lost through Adam. Romans 5 indicates how much stronger the restoration through the mediation of Christ is than the fall of sin in Adam. 1 Corinthians 15:22 is also adduced as support. This part of the confession ends with prayers for the count and his household.

The supplement on marriage opens with the customary Boehmist interpretation of the creation and fall. Hochmann thus sees more curse than blessing connected with the married state. He cites Matthew 19:10–12 and 1 Corinthians 7:1 to indicate that celibacy is to be more highly valued than marriage. The remainder of the appendix is devoted essentially to a discussion of the five types of marriage (see p. 254, n. 35) which are introduced with the governing principle, "As men are, so are their marriages."

Following his release from Detmold prison, Hochmann traveled to Hannover and Bremen and then retired to the solitude of Schwarzenau in Wittgenstein in August 1703. During the coming years Hochmann would repeat the pattern of a grueling pace of traveling and preaching followed by a period of inactivity at Schwarzenau. While Hochmann rested at Schwarzenau between 1703 and 1704, he felt the impulse to establish a small community which took up residence in his cottage (which he called the *Laboratorium*). This community sought to live a life of perfect surrender to Jesus Christ. This surrender had eschatological roots: Hochmann saw Revelation as summoning the believer to loose himself from all human bonds, obligations, and duties in order to be free to follow the coming Lamb. As a result of this conviction, Hochmann renounced his rights of citizenship in his native city, Nürnberg. Hochmann continued to believe that the return of Christ was near, and in a certain sense this community was viewed as the vanguard of the coming kingdom of Christ.[172]

After spending only half a year in this community, Hochmann left on another preaching tour. His trip to the Reformed area of the lower Rhine, which included a tour through Holland, was to be the first of three such sorties (1704–1706, 1709–1710, and 1717–1718). This area, already opened for Pietism by Untereyck and Labadie, proved to be the scene of some of the best response to Hochmann's message. His "impartial" spirit was demonstrated by his preaching to and fellowshipping with all the religious groups of the area—the established churches, mystics, Mennonites, Quakers, and Jews.

During Hochmann's first tour, the theme of his preaching was separation from the church. Significantly, however, this demand was not occasioned by eschatological considerations but by the unholy character of the churches.[173] It was in the course of this missionary tour that Alexander Mack, who would become the principal leader among the early Brethren, came under Hochmann's influence.

The most significant occurrence between his first and second trips to the lower Rhineland was a lengthy period of imprisonment at Nürnberg (October 1707–October 1708). This period of confinement gave Hochmann time to reflect on several important subjects. His basic treatment of the demand for freedom of conscience came from this period.

As Hochmann's Detmold confession indicated, one of his special concerns was the freedom to preach Christ's Word without interference from the state. His call for freedom of conscience can be seen as an inevitable result of the banishments and imprisonments that plagued him especially during his Babelstorming period (1699–ca. 1707). It must be stressed that the fundamental base for Hochmann's call did not rest on any humanistic or Enlightenment argument derived from the inherent dignity and rights of man. Rather, freedom of conscience was a principle which found its basis in Hochmann's own experience of conversion: since Christ has given him an immediate calling, no man or government is able to dictate to his conscience. Especially galling to Hochmann was the granting of episcopal privileges to the territorial princes by the imperial law. Through such presumption the state usurped the church's exclusive domain—the inner life—and violated Christian freedom. Hochmann's absolute commitment to Christ likewise made it impossible for him to confess Christ within the framework of one of the three recognized faiths. Limiting worship of God to one of these faiths would make Christ partial and negate the fundamentally impartial character of Christian truth.[174]

To be sure, Hochmann made ready use of other arguments to support his case for freedom of conscience. He utilized historical precedents embedded in the rise and development of Protestantism. The Speyer Protestation (1529) sought nothing other than what he desired; Luther himself held that the state must not exercise compulsion over the conscience; the Peace of Westphalia guaranteed the right of emigration. Hochmann was also quite willing to borrow juristic arguments which were based more on man's natural rights. Grotius, Pusendorf, Thomasius, Conring, and Tulleken provided Hochmann with an imposing arsenal: no prince can ask what the reason opposes; no subject should believe contrary to his feelings and thought; it is contrary to divine and natural rights to punish someone because of his unbelief; the care of the soul is not able to be entrusted to the prince; future blessedness lies outside worldly sovereignty.[175] Yet, all these arguments were aimed at securing a fundamentally religious right: the freedom to travel unmolested between territories, to preach the gospel openly, and to live a life of absolute discipleship to Christ.

An even more important result of his Nürnberg imprisonment was a basic change in Hochmann's relationship to "Babel." From this time on his theme of separation from Babel begins to be replaced by an attitude of indifference toward the church. He sees the crucial battle no longer against the "outward Babel" but against the "inward Babel," with the goal being complete surrender of the heart to the love of Jesus and the fostering of brotherly unity among souls. This change of attitude likewise has ramifications for his eschatological views. No longer does Hochmann seek to aid the coming of God's kingdom by tearing down Babel; rather, he now waits for the kingdom in patient surrender.[176]

Two elements play important roles in this new perspective. The first is the influence of quietistic concepts on Hochmann's thought. With Arnold and Poiret, he speaks of resting in and sinking into the sea of God's unending love. Yet the quiet repose and passivity which came to characterize the later Radical Pietist movement (as typified by Tersteegen) is not to be found in Hochmann. He cherishes (rather than renounces) the overwhelming joy which one feels in being united with Jesus and immersed in the sea of divine love. In addition, in his later life, Hochmann continued to be active in leading men to the experience of God's eternal love.[177]

The second element responsible for Hochmann's new perspective toward the established church was his disappointment with the two groups which were formed in the wake of his work: the Brethren (organized in 1708 while Hochmann was in prison) and the Inspirationists (organized in 1714). In both cases he lamented the narrow sectarianism which demanded that a person subject himself to a requirement (baptism on one hand, recognition of the group's divine inspiration on the other) in order to be accepted into the fellowship of the body. From the time of his Nürnberg imprisonment, he gradually came to see that departure from Babel was not the decisive matter. It was a far too unstable state: some Radicals wandered aimlessly from group to group, some remained "still," others returned to the church, holding only a few points rigidly. Hochmann therefore turned his attention to caring for the communities of the Spirit through his visits and edifying preaching.[178]

Hochmann's new perspective becomes apparent in his second trip to the lower Rhine (1709-1710). In his preaching at Wesel in 1710 he did not demand separation from the church but took an indifferent standpoint.[179] As a result of his work in Wesel, Hochmann also became involved in a sharp literary dispute with the Reformed Consistory of the city. When the generally irenic Hochmann refused to continue the fracas, his old friend Dippel, who was living in Holland at the time, came to Hochmann's defense. Dippel's work, purportedly penned by a Reformed elder, was a bitterly satirical attack on the church authorities. It received a good deal of attention and went through three editions.[180]

Though Hochmann continued to make extended preaching tours up until his last years (to Saxony and Thuringia in 1711, the lower Rhine in 1717-1718, and Ebersdorf and Obergreiz in 1719-1720), he spent more and more time at Schwarzenau. He took up residence in the Valley of Huts near Schwarzenau. Manifesting his desire to live in a place free of quarrels, Hochmann called his dwellings "Friedensburg" after the heavenly City of Peace. He shared his hermitage with one or two "brothers" and maintained only one "rule"—the double command of love of God and neighbor. Hochmann died at Friedensburg in January 1721.

Renkewitz posits that throughout Hochmann's lifetime two thought groups undergirded his faith: a biblical-*heilsgeschichtlich*-eschatological one, which was the force behind the restless, itinerant preacher of God's impending judgment, and a mystical-spiritual one, which was the quieting agent for the restful repose of the solitary mystic. The first thought group derives from Lutheranism and Lutheran Pietism and was most prominent in his thought between 1699 and about 1707. Hochmann held that God had acted in history as the Creator and Reconciler, and, in the near future, would preside as final Judge. He was convinced that Christ's return and the final judgment were near. The signs of the end were already present: wars were breaking out, the princes and the church were being judged, the Jews were being converted. At Christ's return, the pious would reign with Him for one thousand years over the godless. Hochmann showed no desire, however, to work out the details of this eschatological picture beyond this general outline. This eschatological hope became the motivating factor behind Hochmann's call for repentance and conversion (demonstrated by obedience to the commands of Christ) as well as his demand for separation from Babel.

The second thought group was derived from mystical sources. On the basis of this cluster of ideas, Hochmann perceived God's eternal, unchanging essence as unfathomable love. Man had his origin in this divine sea of love and yearns to return to it. Yet sin dissolved the original unity between man and the divine essence and left in its stead disharmony and animosity. Thus, class distinctions, heathen titles, the misuse of power by the state, even the very existence of the state are the result of sin. Man experiences God's anger whenever he turns from God. However, as soon as he is converted and turns toward God by means of the way opened by Christ's reconciliation, God's anger is dissipated. Christ is conceived in this thought group not so much as an example, reconciler (though this idea is present), King, or judge but as the heavenly bridegroom. Spiritual marriage to Christ, the personification of the loving essence of God, is to be valued above earthly marriage. In such a relationship Christ's loving Spirit streams into man, surrounds him, and flows through him into the church and the world. Eschatological motifs persist in this construct, though the coming kingdom is viewed as the perfect kingdom of love devoid of classes, the

state, and the military. Even more important here is the doctrine of the restoration of all things. Since not all men die in a converted state, Hochmann postulated an interim state after death. Eventually all men will come to a recognition and acceptance of God's will. Though both of these thought groups are retained by Hochmann throughout his life, the conception of God as eternal love comes to predominate during the final decade of his life.[181]

The first cluster of concepts is especially significant for this study. It was while these concepts were still regnant in Hochmann's thought that Alexander Mack and other future Brethren leaders came under his influence. During the period of 1699–1707 several themes recur in Hochmann's thought that are of crucial importance for the Brethren. The first theme is that of discipleship to Christ. Renkewitz indicates that this theme played a dominant role in Hochmann's thought during the years 1700 to 1703.[182] At this time in his life Hochmann by no means spiritualized the meaning of discipleship to Christ but sought rather to identify with the outward life of Jesus. As an indication of his resolve, he fasted forty days and nights in 1702.[183] Significantly, as early as 1703 (before Mack had met Hochmann) the question of adult baptism had arisen among Hochmann's followers. Some had expressed a desire for baptism based on a twofold argument derived from Hochmann's own convictions. Not only has Christ given us His example of being baptized in flowing water, but He has also left us a direct command for baptism. Hochmann's reticence toward such a course of action was based on his fear that a sectarian structure would arise which would undermine the community of the Spirit by making an outward form binding.[184] It should be noted that Hochmann did not *ipso facto* reject the observance of the outward practices of the faith. But participation in them was always to be an expression of the essentially inward and spiritual character of Christianity. Their observance must derive from the inward prompting of the Holy Spirit. Thus he participated in a separatist communion service at Gutenstetten, whose purpose was to strengthen fellowship with Jesus, and he gave the Brethren cautious approval of baptism if it was performed on those who had already received the Holy Spirit and become disciples of Christ.[185] Increasingly, in his later life, however, (after his experiences with the Brethren and the Inspirationists), Hochmann came to emphasize following and surrendering to Christ in the inward life rather than in outward precepts.[186]

A second theme found during this period of Hochmann's life was his eschatologically determined desire for community. For Hochmann the church is founded on the Spirit, not on the Word or sacraments. He looked for the approaching millennial kingdom when all believers would share in a visible community of the Spirit. In fact, both his attempts to establish more of a concrete fellowship—the Melchizedekan priesthood at Berleburg in 1700 and his Schwarzenau "Laboratory" in 1703 and 1704—were motivated by a desire to realize the order of the kingdom of Christ prior to His actual return.[187] The success of these two fleeting experiments of outward community was undermined, however, by the competing principle of the invisible community of the Spirit which increasingly dominated Hochmann's later life. He continued to insist that God's truth is impartial, transcending confessional limits, and that, as a result, there can be only one true faith—the true, inward unity of the heart with God and His Son which expresses itself in active love.[188] Yet his increasing indifference toward the outward church allowed him to fellowship with believers whether inside or outside the established church. During his last years he felt free to attend church occasionally, and in the course of his work at Ebersdorf and Obergreiz in 1719 and 1720 he even ministered within the Lutheran church. Renkewitz interprets these actions as indicating that Hochmann continued to experience a conflicting desire for both solitude and fellowship to the end of his life.[189]

In reviewing Hochmann's life, it seems that his most important legacy was intangible—the new religious perspective bequeathed to his "brothers" and "sisters." For this reason it is difficult to measure the impact of his witness. That his impact was considerable is underscored by Ensign.

> He [Hochmann] gathered many a little group of scattered and lonely separatists together for worship, and infused some of the older sects (such as the Mennonites) with his enthusiasm. He had numerous friends all over Germany, and in neighboring countries; of all classes, from the nobility to the lowest. Many were "awakened" by him. Following generations accounted him to have been among the "giants" in those times. Zinzendorf referred to him as "der Selige"; Tersteegen made a pilgrimage to his grave, and composed his *Grabschrift*; Jung-Stilling sketches him with affection and admiration in his novel, *Theobald*, concluding, "er war ein herrlicher Mann."[190]

Concluding Observations
Concerning Radical Pietism

One of the most colorful movements in the history of Christianity is Radical Pietism. Like a mosaic, the overall picture of Radical Pietism is a result of the blending of the distinctive hues represented by the individual lives and thoughts of the Babel-stormers and mystic-spiritualists. How exactly each person contributed to the composition may be difficult to analyze, but the fact that each has provided an essential part to the whole is undeniable. Likewise, the changing tones of the movement as it developed make it necessary to gain a grasp of the entire picture before the relation between individual pieces becomes evident. With this analysis of the larger movement and some of its most important pieces, the evaluation of how it influenced the Brethren will be enhanced.

In the course of this investigation it has been noted that the Babel-storming period of Radical Pietism was extremely unstable. Built as it was on an eschatological foundation, it soon became apparent with the delay of God's intervention that separation from the church could not be viewed as an end in itself. A number of Radicals felt that some form of fellowship was needed to fill the void. Yet a strong bias against any kind of formal organization did not permit easy answers. This bias against outward forms was based on the conviction that (1) no sect could avoid the divisive and controversial spirit that was a manifestation of the fall, (2) the very nature of outward practices is to lead to a formalism which destroys their essential inner meaning, and (3) formal organization must await a direct calling from God through His Spirit (this conviction sometimes had an eschatological basis—formation of a visible fellowship must await the breaking in of the Spirit as the harbinger of the coming kingdom). Basically four options presented themselves during the history of Radical Pietism as solutions to this dilemma. First, some returned to the established church without forsaking the conviction that it had fallen from its initial purity. These people generally viewed outward forms as indifferent and held that ministry to weak Christians was more important than the desire to keep oneself apart from all that is unholy. Arnold is the prototype of this option. Second, some Radicals organized themselves into a body for which the immediate inspiration of the Spirit was the constitutive element. This option, represented by the Inspirationists, tended to spiritualize the outward aspects of the faith. Third, another formal organization of former Radicals, the Brethren, emphasized the Radical tenets of discipleship to Christ and following the pattern of the early church. They held that full obedience to Christ demanded not only inward renewal through God's Spirit but also the observance of the outward rites. Fourth, by far the most common course adopted by Radicals was to await quietly and in stillness for God to work out His plans in His own time and in His own way. Influenced by Quietism, this option emphasized the cultivation of an inward spiritual union with Christ in which one surrenders his will entirely to God. Generally, Radicals who chose this approach maintained an attitude of impartiality and indifference toward outward structures so that they could worship with the various sects when so moved. It is against the background of these various manifestations of the Radical Pietist spirit that the Brethren initially are to be understood.

Chapter 3

ANABAPTISM

Introduction

Anabaptism, especially the Mennonite branch of the movement, came to have great importance for the early Brethren, for it was from Anabaptism that the external structure of the Brethren faith was built. This chapter begins with an overview of the historical development of Anabaptism. More thorough attention will be given to the cultural and religious changes that occurred among seventeenth century Mennonites. The thought and practice of the Anabaptists will then be investigated in some detail. However, two important limitations will be placed on this investigation. First, attention will be focused on the doctrine of the Mennonites, since it is the thought of this branch of Anabaptism with which Alexander Mack was most familiar.[1] Second, as much as possible, source materials will be utilized which will reflect the Mennonite thought with which Alexander Mack would have been familiar. To this end the following primary source materials will be utilized: the works of Menno Simons and Dirk Philips, which formed the doctrinal foundation for Dutch and, increasingly, Swiss Mennonite thought, and *Martyrs Mirror*. This Dutch martyrology was used as a historical source book by Mack. It contains the Dordrecht Confession and two other confessions of faith (all written between 1627 and 1632) and some other important doctrinal material in its preliminary sections. The final part of this chapter will be devoted to a discussion of Radical Pietism's perception of Anabaptism.

Historical Overview of Anabaptism

Anabaptism was born in the same cultural and religious milieu as the Reformed and Lutheran churches. Yet, due to its biblical literalism, its radical obedience to the teachings of Christ, and its emphasis on a disciplined community of believers, Anabaptism

acquired a character quite different from that of the major Reformation churches. Likewise, Anabaptism lacked the degree of unity found in the state churches. A unified movement was obstructed by the Anabaptist policy of congregational government, by the fierce persecution which deprived Anabaptism of its leadership and forced it underground, and by geographical barriers. The simple, unschooled faith of the Anabaptists at times led to aberrations—at St. Gall Anabaptists took literally the Gospel admonition to become as children; certain Anabaptists from Thuringia were so carried away by their apocalypticism that one claimed to be the Son of God; at Münster the attempt to establish the kingdom of God led to violence and oppression.[2] Yet, in the majority of cases, this unlettered and unfettered faith, when guided by responsible leaders, resulted in an unswerving devotion to Christ and His teachings which was willing to face any hardship for His sake.

Anabaptism had its origins in a small group of scholars who had been studying the Bible with the Zürich reformer, Ulrich Zwingli, since 1520. Between 1523 and 1525 major disagreements arose between Zwingli and two of his disciples, Conrad Grebel and Felix Manz, over the role of the Zürich City Council in the progress of the reform. Zwingli was committed to allowing the Council to set the pace of reform. The young radicals felt, however, that reform must progress according to the Spirit's directives derived from Scripture. In question was whether a government, whether Christian or not, has the right to decide matters relating to the church. When on January 18, 1525, the City Council condemned the radicals for their defense of believer baptism, the small circle of disillusioned men was faced with the choice of compliance, exile, or imprisonment. On January 21, about a dozen men met at the home of Manz to seek God's will. After prayer, George Blaurock asked Conrad Grebel to baptize him "with the true Christian baptism upon his faith and knowledge."[3] After Grebel had baptized him, Blaurock proceeded to baptize all the others present. At the same time they commissioned one another to "the ministry of the Gospel" and, in effect, to the establishment of a new church body.[4]

The work of Grebel, Manz, Blaurock, and others in such places as Zollikon, St. Gall, Schaffhausen, Grüningen, Appenzell, Chur, and Basel laid the foundations for the first branch of Anabaptism, the Swiss Brethren. The success of this missionary activity quickly led to suppression by both the state and the established church. From the viewpoint of the ecclesiastical authorities, rebaptism, no doubt, was the most obvious "crime" committed by the Anabaptists, though their concept of the free church was considered destructive to the very nature of a united, territorial church. Likewise, the state felt threatened by the Anabaptist rejection of both the oath and all military service, acts which it deemed treasonous. The decisions of the Zürich Council in 1526 which made rebaptism and attendance at Anabaptist meetings punishable by death[5] were soon followed by other Swiss cities.

The Swiss Brethren were soon deprived of their original leadership. Grebel died of the plague around August 1526, Manz was executed by drowning in the river Limmat (which flows through Zürich) on January 5, 1527, and Blaurock fled from Switzerland in April 1527, only to be martyred in the Austrian Tyrol in September 1529. Nevertheless, other men quickly filled the leadership gaps. A significant meeting of several of these Swiss Brethren leaders together with representatives from the South German Anabaptists occurred in February 1527 at Schleitheim, a village near Schaffhausen. The deliberations of this synod resulted in the Schleitheim Confession of Faith, thought to have been composed by Michael Sattler. The seven articles in the confession give guidelines for the organization and self-discipline of a free church movement. This document clearly distinguished the participating Anabaptist groups, on the one hand, from the main Reformation churches and, on the other, from those groups on the fringes of Anabaptism which tended toward antinomian and spiritualist excesses.[6]

With increased persecution during the 1520s and 30s in Switzerland, the Swiss Brethren sought refuge in the Austrian Tyrol, Moravia, and South Germany. Yet persecution continued to plague them here as well. During the first half of the seventeenth century, native Swiss Brethren congregations were found solely in Bern and around Zürich and Basel. Only the small

community in Bern, which finally received toleration in 1815, has managed to survive to the present. Today it has about two thousand baptized members.

Although there are few Swiss Mennonites (the Swiss Brethren have from the eighteenth century aligned themselves with the Mennonites) left in Switzerland, their descendants are to be found in many places. Swiss Mennonites migrated to the Palatinate and other areas of South Germany during the second half of the seventeenth century and throughout the eighteenth century, to Galicia and Volhynia in Poland in the 1780s and 90s, and to North America in six waves between 1683 and 1880. These American immigrations included Swiss Mennonites and Amish[7] from Bern, the Palatinate, Galicia, and Volhynia.[8]

The second important group of Anabaptists was the South and Central German Anabaptists. The groundwork in these areas of Germany had been laid by Swiss Brethren. Michael Sattler had ministered in Strassburg and Horb prior to his martyrdom in May 1527 and Wilhelm Reublin had worked in Strassburg, Rottenburg, and Esslingen between 1525 and 1528. Augsburg and Strassburg soon surfaced as the main areas of activity while Hans Denck, Hans Hut, and Pilgram Marpeck emerged as the key leaders of the movement. Hans Denck had been baptized by one of the Swiss exiles, Balthasar Hubmaier. Though possessing spiritualistic tendencies, Denck's life manifested a gentle spirit which exuded Christian love and abhorred sectarian divisiveness. Denck labored in Augsburg, Strassburg, the Rhine Valley, Nürnberg, and Ulm prior to his early death, caused by the plague, at Basel in November 1527. It was Denck who baptized one of the most fiery Anabaptist preachers, Hans Hut, in May 1526. It was also Denck whose moderating influence caused Hut to tone down the apocalyptic elements (the early return of Christ and the last judgment) in his missionary preaching.[9] For about one year Hut conducted a profoundly effective preaching tour through Franconia, Bavaria, Austria, and Moravia.[10] He was arrested in Augsburg in August 1527 and died there as a result of a fire in his cell.

The man that gave continuity and stability to the Anabaptist movement in South and Central Germany was Pilgram Marpeck. He led the Anabaptist congregation at Strassburg from 1528 until his expulsion from the city in 1531. During the next twelve years Marpeck visited Anabaptist fellowships in Germany, Switzerland, and Moravia, strengthening them by his presence and correspondence. He turned to Augsburg in 1544 where he ministered to the Anabaptist congregation until his death by natural causes in

1556. Marpeck's special contributions include his concern for unity within the Anabaptist movement and his lengthy literary debate with the spiritualist, Caspar Schwenckfeld.[11]

Anabaptists in South and Central Germany suffered the same rigors as did their Swiss counterparts. Persecution by imperial and Catholic authorities so decimated the movement that by 1600 Anabaptism had almost completely disappeared from the region. The few Anabaptists who were left were absorbed by the Hutterites and primarily by the Swiss Brethren and Mennonites.

The third distinct area of Anabaptist activity was in Austria and Moravia. During the second half of the 1520s, Anabaptism spread rapidly in such Hapsburg territories as Austria (through the work of Hut), Carinthia, and the Tyrol (through the ministry of Blaurock). Increasing opposition from the authorities caused Anabaptists from these lands as well as from South Germany, Bavaria, Württemberg, Hesse, and Switzerland to begin migrating to Moravia in the late 1520s. Here Nicholsburg, the manorial estate of the lords of Liechtenstein, became a popular haven for radicals of various persuasions.[12]

One group of radicals, led by Jacob Wiedemann, was characterized by a strong emphasis on eschatology and by the advocacy of both the principle of community of goods and an extreme form of pacifism which included the refusal to pay taxes. During Hans Hut's brief stay at Nicholsburg in 1527, these characteristics were accentuated to the point that Lord Liechtenstein felt he could no longer give refuge to the radicals. Under the leadership of Wiedemann, about two to three hundred persons moved in 1528 to Austerlitz where they were invited to settle by the tolerant lords of Kaunitz. Due to the special need of caring for many indigent brethren, a community of goods was instituted which gradually extended to both consumption and production.

Between 1529 and 1533 these communitarian Anabaptists were torn by much internal dissension. As a result, several new colonies were formed. It was the nearly two year ministry (1533–1535) of Jacob Hutter that finally helped to solidify the various groups. Hutter had followed Blaurock as the leader of the Tyrolese Anabaptists in 1529. Between 1529 and 1533 he had visited the Moravian communitarians several times not only to oversee the Tyrolese refugees who had come to Moravia but also to mediate the differences dividing the colonies. Though martyred in 1536, his brief period of leadership in Moravia had profound significance for the future of the movement

which bears his name. Williams gives a fitting testimony to Hutter's work:

> [Hutter] released the energies and channeled the skills of his people into the building up of an economically durable and socially cohesive organization with the capacity to colonize and missionize more vigorously and steadfastly than had ever been possible before.[13]

Up until almost the end of the century, the Hutterites flourished (while other communitarian groups languished) due to relative external peace and a series of outstanding leaders including Ulrich Stadler, Hans Amon, Peter Riedemann, and Peter Walpot. In the course of the next two centuries, persecution (during the Counter-Reformation, Turkish wars, and Thirty Years' War) decimated the brotherhood until in 1767 only sixty-seven people remained. During this period the Hutterites sought refuge in Hungary, Transylvania, Rumania, and Russia. In 1874–80 the entire brotherhood migrated to South Dakota. In 1963 the Hutterites had 120 Bruderhofs with about 10,000 members in the Canadian provinces of Manitoba, Alberta, Saskatchewan, and Ontario and nearly 4000 in the Dakotas, Montana, and Washington.[14]

The final major group of Anabaptists originated in the Netherlands. Anabaptism was introduced to the Netherlands and North Germany primarily through the very successful evangelistic work of Melchior Hofmann. Though he agreed with evangelical Anabaptists on many theological points, his views on eschatology and Christ's celestial flesh were to taint the Anabaptist movement in the above areas for many years. Hofmann's speculations concerning the last things convinced him that Strassburg was the New Jerusalem. In 1533 he managed to have himself arrested at Strassburg, for he believed that his imprisonment would set in motion the sequence of events that would culminate in Christ's return. Instead, he died in prison ten years later.

Two parties gradually emerged from the weak foundations laid by Hofmann. The first was a radical revolutionary party which captured the majority of Hofmann's followers. This group was responsible for the misguided attempt to establish the kingdom of God on earth by force at Münster in 1534–35. Though the revolutionaries were ruthlessly overcome, their actions had tragic consequences for the entire Anabaptist movement. The authorities now seemed to have clear evidence that, in spite of the Anabaptist insistence on nonviolence, they harbored revolutionary intentions.

The second group of Melchiorites was firmly nonresistant and possessed a faith that was very similar to that of the Swiss Brethren. The initial leaders of this group, formed in 1534, were Obbe and Dirk Philips. They were joined in 1537 by the converted Roman Catholic priest, Menno Simons, who would give his name to the movement. Dirk Philips and Menno Simons deserve the major credit for the forging of a well organized brotherhood. Their pastoral and evangelistic work helped to spread Anabaptism throughout the Netherlands and North Germany. Likewise, their writings played an important role in defining the Mennonite faith. Philips' *Enchiridion*, a compilation of monographs on various doctrines, was one of the most systematic presentations of Anabaptist theology written during the sixteenth century. Though Menno wrote about twenty-five treatises as well as numerous letters, one of his most important works was *Foundation of Christian Doctrine*. This treatise sought to clear the Anabaptists of any Münster connotations and to state plainly for the brotherhood various doctrinal truths.[15]

The Mennonites experienced much internal discord during their early years. The controversy created by Adam Pastor's denial of the preexistence of Christ was resolved in 1547 only by banning the erring elder.[16] Even more serious was the dissension created by the question of how strictly the ban should be observed. Dirk Philips and the successful evangelist, Leonard Bouwens, took a strict position on the application of the ban. The excommunicated member should be shunned, even to the point of denying the person "bed and board" in the case of married partners. Though Menno finally adopted this position, his loving and pastoral spirit served to mellow the harshness which characterized the position of his two fellow ministers. Disavowal of this rigorous interpretation led to the separation in 1555 of one group of Mennonites. Known as the Waterlanders, a name derived from the region north of Amsterdam in which they lived, this group held a more moderate and open attitude toward discipline and other matters of church practice. A second division over the question of avoidance occurred in 1560 and resulted in the formation of the moderate High German Mennonites who were centered in South Germany and along the Rhine. Though not involving the question of discipline, still another division occurred in the 1660s between Frisian and Flemish Mennonites. Social and cultural differences seem to have played as much a role in this split as did disagreement over church practice.[17] Division continued to plague especially the Flemish up through the 1630s. Though the Frisian-Flemish breach was substantially healed in 1639, a new division occurred in 1664 which led to the

alignment of nearly all Mennonite parties into one of two new camps. The followers of Samuel Apostool, who were known as Zonists, were traditionalists who continued to view the Mennonite Church as the one true church and who insisted on a fixed confession. Galenus Abrahamsz de Haan, the leader of the second faction, the Lamists, had been influenced by his association with the Collegiants. His supporters were more liberal and cautioned against overemphasis on the the idea of the visible church.[18] It was not until 1811 that Dutch Mennonites finally united with the organization of a general conference, the *Algemeene Doopsgezinde Societeit*.[19]

With the granting of toleration in 1579, the Dutch Mennonites began to flourish, reaching a total of 160,000 members and children by 1700. In the following century, however, the *Doopsgezinde* were struck by a crippling internal enemy—rationalism and secularism—which reduced the total population to 27,000 in 1809. A conservative reaction in the present century has revitalized the faith, so that by 1965 the baptized membership had reached about 40,000.

Dutch Anabaptists quickly reached beyond the boundaries of their native land, founding congregations early in the lower Rhine, East Friesland, Hamburg, and Danzig. By 1553 Mennonites had settled in Poland and in 1788 they came to the Ukraine in Russia. During the last one hundred years, persecution in Poland and Russia has caused these Mennonites to emigrate in three major waves to Canada, the United States, Paraguay, Uruguay, and Brazil.

The worldwide population of the Mennonites as of 1966 was about 445,000 members. Of these, 245,000 live in North America, 100,000 are in Europe, and the rest are scattered throughout Central and South America, Africa, and Asia.[20]

The Life and Thought of the Seventeenth Century Mennonites

CHANGES IN THE LIFE STYLE AND FAITH OF THE SEVENTEENTH AND EARLY EIGHTEENTH CENTURY MENNONITES

During the latter part of the sixteenth and throughout the seventeenth and early eighteenth centuries, various influences were at work which substantially changed the character of the Mennonites. Ironically, persecution in the case of the Swiss Brethren and toleration in the case of the Dutch Mennonites brought about new life styles which were open to a more pietistic, inward faith.

With the granting of toleration in the Netherlands in 1579, the Mennonites became an increasingly settled denomination of prosperous middle-class families. Whereas the former, more agrarian setting had fostered a life style which gravitated around the family and church and which permitted the successful maintenance of cultural mores, the new middle-class, commercial environment opened the Mennonites to a wide variety of cultural and religious influences. Gradually, the artificial barriers which the Mennonites had relied upon to maintain their separation from the world broke down. The more liberal Waterlanders were especially susceptible to these influences. They held a broader, more mystical conception of the faith than did the other Mennonite groups. This perspective is typified by their observance of open communion and their relationships with such representatives of mystical, inward piety as Coornhert and the Collegiants.[21]

Tieleman van Braght's famous martyrology, *Martyrs Mirror* (1660), can be seen as an attempt by a conservative Zonist to combat the subtle effects of worldly ease and prosperity by preserving the uncompromising spirit of the forefathers. Yet conservative Mennonites were not free from this new spirit of openness as is evident in a German book, published in Amsterdam in 1664, which was to become quite influential among Mennonites on both sides of the the Atlantic. This work, *Christliches Glaubensbekenntnus der Waffenlosen . . . Christen . . .*, was composed by the Zonist, Tieleman Tielen van Sittert. It contains the first German translation of the Dordrecht Confession of Faith,[22] a collection of prayers, a collection of hymns, and a sketch of Mennonite history. In the preface van Sittert writes:

> As the evening and the morning prayer and the prayer before and after meals of the Reformed Dutch Prayerbook are scriptural and useful for edification, our folk in this country use them often and teach them to our young people. . . . Many of our folk who speak or understand German, or know how to read or sing it, use very much the scriptural hymns by Luther as we do not like to reject or think little of anything we understand to be in accordance with God's Word, it may come from whatever Christian, it makes no difference to us.[23]

Friedmann has suggested that such examples of religious openness are reflective of a basic transformation that was occurring in the Mennonite faith. He maintains that the original genius of Mennonitism can be represented by the German word *Gottesfurcht*, which conveys the idea of "a reverential trust and obedience" which "removes all fear of the 'world' and enables men to become the true salt of the earth." The new perspective, which was becoming more evident among the Mennonites throughout

the seventeenth century, coincided with the rise of Pietism. Attention came to be focused on the experience of the blessedness of salvation by the individual and the cultivation of a godly life by occupying one's mind with devout thoughts and emotions. A new vocabulary, expressed in German in the words *Gottseligkeit* (godliness), *Seligkeit* (blessedness or eternal bliss), and *Erbauung* (edification), gradually came into vogue.[24]

Among the Waterlanders the pietistic spirit made itself evident early. In his popular devotional book, *Wegh na Vredenstadt* (*Way to the City of Peace*), the Waterlander preacher, Pieter Pietersz, utilized a literary type which in the English-speaking world is epitomized by *Pilgrim's Progress*. Written over fifty years before Bunyan's classic (1625 as compared with 1678), the book depicts "in dialogue form the itinerary to the 'heavenly Jerusalem,' where is found 'the unity of spirit under the palms of peace.'"[25] The peaceful, simple spirit, emotional warmth, and high moral character which imbue this and other works by Pietersz are likewise found in *The Wandering Soul* (1635), written by another Waterlander minister, Johann Philip Schabalie. Described as "the first popular Bible history of modern times," this devotional work found its way into Mennonite homes in Holland, Germany, Switzerland, and America.[26]

The eighteenth century would be the period in which Pietism (and, ironically, rationalism) would have its most pronounced influence on Dutch Mennonites. Yet, two developments during the seventeenth century had created a receptive climate among the Mennonites for Pietism: the growth in most groups of an open-minded, "impartial" attitude toward outside religious ideas and the predilection of the Waterlanders and some Lamists for an inward, quietistic piety. The merging of these two qualities prepared many Mennonites for the work of three important representatives of Pietism during the first half of the eighteenth century. On his first trip to the lower Rhine (1704–1706), Hochmann is said to have visited the Dutch Mennonites. He also was well received by the Mennonites in Krefeld who had close ties to the Dutch segment of the church. He first visited the Krefeld Mennonites in 1705, and, on this third trip to the Rhineland (1717–1718), he was permitted to preach in their meetinghouse.[27] The Krefeld Mennonites also opened their meetinghouse in 1751 to the quietistic Pietist, Gerhard Tersteegen. The outstanding representative of Dutch Mennonite piety was Joannes Deknatel (1698–1759), who served the Amsterdam Lamist congregation. His was an impartial, inward Christianity that brought him into contact with Zinzendorf, A. G. Spangenberg, and John Wesley. In his sermons and numerous books, he called for "inner rebirth and revival understood as a quiet piety and inward edification."[28] His piety not only influenced many Dutch Mennonites but, through his writings, it shaped the life of Peter Weber (1731–1781), who became a leading pietistic Mennonite minister in the Palatinate.

Governmental policies in Switzerland forced the Swiss Brethren to adopt a style of life radically different from that of the Dutch Mennonites. Martin Schrag summarizes the effect of continuing persecution on the Swiss Brethren (Mennonites). "In the choice between emphasizing the Great Commission, and thus possibly being exterminated, and living in isolation as the church of the remnant, the Mennonites chose the latter."[29] Two patterns of cultural isolation were adopted by the Swiss Mennonites in coping with this persecution. Those who remained in Switzerland maintained a precarious existence throughout the seventeenth century in secluded valleys and on mountain slopes. Others migrated, especially to the Palatinate, where they received toleration by governments who recognized their agricultural proficiency. In this agrarian setting the Swiss Mennonites generally lived in cultural enclaves which served to insulate them from the surrounding society.[30]

The development of these Mennonite agricultural communities resulted in a distinctive cultural pattern: the focus of life became the family and community; farming was considered a sacred occupation; language was identified with the faith of the fathers; marriage was within the group; cultural forms in matters of dress, food, and social custom were frozen; political life was avoided and higher education rejected; a sharp separation was made from possible worldly influences. Schrag notes that these cultural changes had a definite effect on the faith.

> The missionary surge was replaced by a people becoming *die Stillen im Lande*. The voluntary commitment and believer's baptism became a matter of keeping "Mennonite" children in the fold. Discipleship became a matter of following the accepted cultural patterns of the Mennonite community. The original creative quest for insight was replaced by a strong accent on the faith of the fathers. There was a loss of eschatological expectancy, the remnant status being accepted as more or less permanent.[31]

Robert Friedmann has posited that quietistic Pietism gave the Mennonites a spiritual rationalization for this basic change in life style.[32] Though the Swiss Mennonites, due to their cultural isolation, did not feel the impact of Pietism as soon as their Dutch counterparts, historical and literary evidences of the influence of Pietism become apparent after 1700. Hochmann had close contact with the Swiss Mennonites in the Palatinate in 1706 on his first trip to the area. He stayed with a Mennonite, Hans Bechtold, at Zuzenhausen and frequently visited towns in and around which Mennonites lived: Eppstein, Lambsheim, Guntersblum, and Mutterstadt.[33] The Brethren also seemed to have had ties with the Bernese Mennonites, which might suggest prior Radical Pietist activity among the Mennonites in this area.[34]

The Swiss Mennonite struggle for existence prevented the development of a native literature during the seventeenth century, though four editions of their popular hymnal, the *Ausbund*, did appear. During the first two decades of the eighteenth century two works of Swiss Mennonite origin were published which indicated that "the bitterness of the experiences in Switzerland was still lingering in the soul of the brethren."[35] The latter of these two books, the *Send-Brieff* (1720), was originally written by an unknown Swiss Mennonite in prison at Bern, Switzerland, in 1715. It contains traditional Anabaptist themes: suffering as the inevitable result of faithfulness and obedience to God and the call for perseverance in following the great model of Christ Himself. Of greater importance as a devotional work was *Güldene Aepffel in Silbern Schalen* (*Golden Apples in Silver Bowls*) (1702) which is thought to have been published at Basel. The greater part of this work is composed of the testimonies of five outstanding Anabaptist martyrs of the sixteenth century: Michael Sattler, Thomas von Imbrioch, Susanne von Holtz, Matthias Cervaes, and Konrad Koch. The final part of the book is a reprint of the first two sections of the van Sittert devotional manual of 1664: the German translation of the Dordrecht Confession and the prayer collection. The contents of *Golden Apples in Silver Bowls* are significant because they reflect the changing spiritual temper of the Swiss Mennonites. Though they desired to remain true to the heritage of a suffering church, they were gradually acclimating themselves to the contemporary spiritual climate and adopting more completely the piety and literature of the Dutch Mennonites.[36] This point is underscored by the German translation of Schabalie's *Wandering Soul* sometime between 1700 and 1710. This translation is thought to be the work of Bernhard Benedict Brechbill, an outstanding Swiss Mennonite leader.[37] In addition, in 1739 a prayer book, the *Ernsthafte Christenpflicht*, was printed by Swiss Mennonites in the Palatinate. The appearance of this prayer book indicates a shift away from the traditional *ex-tempore* prayer, a change that had occurred among Dutch Mennonites the previous century.

Even more symbolic of the shift to a more pietistic, inward expression of faith among Swiss and German Mennonites was the non-Mennonite devotional literature that found its way into Mennonite homes during the late seventeenth and first half of the eighteenth centuries. Among these works were Arndt's *Wahres Christentum* and *Paradiesgärtlein*, Arnold's *Ketzerhistorie* and *Abbildung*, Tersteegen's works, Francke's *Glaubensweg*, Johann Heinrich Reitz's *Historia der Wiedergeborenen*, and Madame Guyon's *Heilige Liebe Gottes*.[38] The Radical Pietist flavor of much of this literature should not be overlooked.[39]

The use of this pietistic and quietistic literature merely mirrors the *Stillen im Lande* character of the Swiss Mennonites in Switzerland and Germany. As a means of survival they developed a quiet, inward faith which was expressed within the boundaries of their own community of faith. It needs to be stressed, however, that the Mennonites, especially those in Switzerland, Germany, and, later, America, never lost contact with their heritage but kept it before themselves through the intermittent reprinting of the doctrinal works of Menno Simons and Dirk Philips and of the Anabaptist martyrologies, *Martyrs Mirror* and *Golden Apples in Silver Bowls*.[40]

THE THOUGHT OF THE SIXTEENTH AND SEVENTEENTH CENTURY MENNONITES

Fundamental principles of Mennonite Doctrine

It must be remembered that the Mennonites were as much a product of the Reformation as the Reformed and Lutherans. They would have agreed with both of these churches, and especially with the Reformed, on most of the major points of theology. Where differences did occur, they arose more from emphasis than essence. It is in the areas of soteriology and ecclesiology that departures from Reformed and Lutheran thought are most discernible. This opening section will explore how five sources of authority recognized by the Mennonites—God, Christ, Scripture, the Holy Spirit, and the example of the primitive church—influenced their conception of the church. The theological locus of the church is chosen as the "proving ground" for these sources of authority because the Mennonites have emphasized the work of these authorities in a corporate context (unlike the Radical Pietists who individualized and spiritualized their effects).

The church was ordained and sustained by God from the beginning

According to Mennonite doctrine, one of God's central purposes in the creation is that He might have a people for Himself. Thus Menno, Philips, and van Braght all stress that the origin of the church goes back to the beginning of the world. Philips, in fact, pushes the origin of the church back even farther: "The church of God was originally begun by God in heaven with the angels, . . . to stand before the throne of God praising and serving him, and also that they should minister to and be fellow-servants of the believers (Rev. 21[22]:9."[41]

As can be seen in the above quotation, Philips held that the prerogative for forming the church rests with God. Yet His involvement does not end here, for He is intimately connected with the progress of the church as well. When Adam and Eve fell, God provided for the "restoration of corrupt man, and the renewing in him of the image of God, and the reestablishment of the ruined church of God" through "the promise of the coming seed (Gen. 3:16[15]) of the woman."[42] As represented by Cain and Abel, there exist "two different people, two different congregations and churches, the one of God and from heaven, the other of Satan and from the earth."[43]

Van Braght stresses that in all ages God has ordained teachers in the church so that His will could continue to be proclaimed to the people. Since the time of Christ, there has been a succession of true teachers known by the right teaching of the truth. Significantly, van Braght sees true doctrine including the correct understanding of "holy Baptism."[44] Van Braght's demonstration of this point relies heavily on a work that became extremely important for radical historiography: Jakob Mehrning's S. *Baptismi Historia, Das ist Heilige Tauff-Historia* . . . (1646–1647).[45] Van Braght cites Mehrning's contention that the Waldenses, who are considered the forerunners of the Anabaptists,[46] actually are of ancient origin, being present "even in the time of the apostles." This bold assertion is made on the basis of statements by a certain unnamed Romanist and of the testimony of Matthias Flacius in the *Magdeburg Centuries* that "an ancient papistic book" held that the Waldenses "existed from the time of Sylvester, yea, from the time of the apostles."[47]

God's provision for the true church is also perceived in His nourishing the church in the wilderness for a period of 1260 years (based on Rev. 12:6–11). Van Braght does not specify when this wilderness period actually occurred, noting only that the suggestions of the time of the death of the apostles, the years 300 and 600, and the time of the rise of Mohammed in the east and the pope in the west had been made for the beginning point.[48] Van Braght demonstrates that the Anabaptists are part of the faithful succession by including three confessions (including the Dordrecht Confession) which he holds are in essential agreement with "the most ancient and simple creed," the Apostles' Creed.[49]

Christ is the Head of the church

As the Head of the church, Christ has provided all that is necessary for the life of the church. Philips holds that the church from the beginning has found its existence "in Christ, by whom all things are renewed."[50] As a result of His earthly ministry, Christ has made available both the means and the perfect example for the restoration of the image of God in man and in His body, the church.[51] Thus Christ's death and resurrection provide the power and pattern for the new birth in man.[52] Likewise, during His earthly life, Christ gave believers the commands and the perfect example which are to govern their new life. Representative of the many passages in Mennonite literature which could express the above ideas is the following one:

> ... they [those who accept, in faith, the "proffered means of divine grace, Jesus Christ"] regulate themselves in their weakness to all words, commandments, ordinances, Spirit, rule, example, and measure of Christ, as the Scripture teaches; for they are in Christ and Christ is in them; and therefore they live no longer in the old life of sin after the earthly Adam (weakness excepted), but in the new life of righteousness which comes by faith, after the second and heavenly Adam, Christ . . . [53]

This focus on Christ's role in the salvation and sanctification of believers and the formation of a people of God results in a Christocentric emphasis that permeates Mennonite thought. The new life in Christ and His body is viewed in terms of discipleship to Christ, obedience to His Word, and keeping of His commandments.[54] Christ is thus perceived as the ultimate authority for the church; other important sources of authority—the Word and Spirit—become channels for communicating Christ's authority to the church.

The Word is the outward guide for the church

The Christocentric faith of the Mennonites has important ramifications for their view of Scripture. Menno, for example, insists that it is to Christ that all the Scriptures point and it is through Him that the entire Bible is to be interpreted. "All the Scriptures, both the Old and the New Testaments, on every hand, point us to Christ Jesus that we are to follow Him."[55] Though the Mennonites acknowledged that all of Scripture was written for believers' instruction, admonition, and correction,[56] their Christocentric hermeneutic led them to give priority to the New Testament. It is in the New Testament that God has made His will for man fully known through His Son, who confirmed and sealed this eternal Testament with His blood.[57] The Old Testament period is one of imperfection with its law and ordinances, but it does provide figures and shadows of the perfection that comes in Christ. Likewise, the "glorious promises" of the Old Testament find their fulfillment in Christ.[58] (It should be remembered that the Mennonites see the people of God as *the* element of continuity in the Bible and throughout human history.) Due to the special emphasis on Jesus' words and example in Mennonite thought, the Gospels also tend to be used to interpret the rest of the New Testament.

The Mennonites applied radically the Reformation principle of *sola Scriptura*. They felt that Scripture was plain and clear in its intent[59] and needed no special interpreters other than Christ's indwelling Spirit.[60] Every believer, whether erudite or unlearned, who had through faith been empowered with the Spirit, has the God-given ability and right to interpret Scripture. Yet this privilege and responsibility was not an encouragement for each believer to seek his own personal interpretation. The Mennonites truly sought (with varying degrees of success) to attain a common understanding of the intent of Scripture through the Spirit's leading. This process was to be undertaken in an atmosphere imbued with "the meek, friendly, peaceful, and peace-loving spirit of Christ."[61]

Due to the Biblical literalism of the Mennonites, which sought to follow the plain word of Scripture, the theological categories which developed in Protestant Orthodoxy are completely foreign to Mennonite doctrinal literature. These writings tended to be practical and thematic and show close adherence to Biblical terms and quotations. Though the Mennonites did write confessions of faith, these works lack the systematic and reasoned consistency of the corresponding works of Protestant Scholasticism.

The Holy Spirit teaches and governs the church

For the Mennonites, the Word and Spirit form a dynamic unit which is to govern every aspect of the believer's individual and corporate life. Whereas the Word provides for the church the perfect example and teaching of Christ and His apostles, it is the Spirit's role to apply the Word to the hearts and minds of believers. The Holy Spirit is thus frequently viewed as the Teacher, whose office is "to reveal Christ and to make known his doctrine to man."[62] The Holy Spirit is able to fulfill this function only in the lives of the regenerate. They are enabled by the Spirit's anointing to understand the spiritual intent of the Word.[63] Mention has already been made of the recognition of the Spirit's function in guiding the community of believers to a consensus on questions of Scriptural interpretation. The Mennonite conviction that the Holy Spirit and the Word must work in concert was highlighted in the seventeenth century when the explicit terminology of the "inner and outer Words" came into common usage.

The continuation of the primitive church

One of the great divides between Anabaptism and the established churches was their respective views of ecclesiology. Though some studies have held that the difference arises from Anabaptism's commitment to the restitution of the early church, several recent writers have rightly called this thesis into question.[64] In the writings of Menno, Philips, and van Braght, the explicit theme of restitution is almost nonexistent. Determinate for the Mennonite view of the church are two points already mentioned. (1) "They were concerned that the Bible, and especially the New Testament, be taken as authoritative *in whatever is clearly enjoined*, whether by precept or by example."[65] The admonition to follow the example and teachings of Christ and His apostles is thus a constant refrain in Mennonite literature. (2) The Mennonites felt that they were a part of the true church which could trace its existence back to the apostolic community (and before!). Therefore, they strove for the "*continuation* of the true apostolic church."[66]

Summary

Though the above principles are not explicitly developed in Mennonite literature, a grasp of them is indispensable for understanding Mennonite thought. To a great extent they determine the shape that Mennonite doctrine, especially soteriology and ecclesiology, assumed.

Mennonite Soteriology

The creation and fall of man

Man was created in God's image and likeness, in righteousness and holiness,[67] unto eternal life. Man could have remained in this state if he had not deviated from the command of God. But through the subtle seduction of the serpent and the envy of him, Adam and Eve transgressed the command of God and became disobedient. As a result of this disobedience, "sin has come into the world, and death by sin, which has thus passed upon all men."[68]

The restoration of man through the work of Christ

Man would have been eternally lost had it not been for God's compassion on His creatures and His unchanged will and purpose "to have a man after His own image and likeness."[69] The resultant provision for man's sin through Christ's atonement is viewed in Mennonite literature in terms of satisfaction of God's justice, substitution, and sacrifice. Since the justice of God required that Adam's sin should not go unpunished and since no creature could satisfy God's justice, God promised to send His only Son as a Savior. In Jesus the promises made to the Old Testament patriarchs were fulfilled. By His willing obedience and spotless sacrifice and by His undeserved death, he put away "the guilt and deserved death of Adam."[70] Christ's "obedience undid the disobedience of Adam and all his seed" and therefore made salvation possible for all men.[71] Menno is especially careful to emphasize, however, that Christ's "merits, death, and blood" are the sole means of man's forgiveness and salvation.[72]

The appropriation of salvation

Mennonite doctrinal writings during the sixteenth and seventeenth centuries do not reveal a fixed order of salvation (this would be typical of Protestant theology during the sixteenth century as well). Generally, conversion (or sometimes regeneration) was used as an inclusive term for the initial aspects of the salvation process. Conversion-regeneration was viewed by Mennonites as fundamental to salvation. Typical is Menno:

> We must be born from above, must be changed and renewed in our hearts, and must be transplanted from the unrighteous and evil nature of Adam into the true and good nature of Christ, or we can never in all eternity be saved by any means, be they human or divine.[73]

Menno's treatise, "Foundation of Christian Doctrine," offers a general outline for the Mennonite ordering of the conversion process. The primary features of this order are: (1) divine calling through the Word, (2) repentance, (3) faith, (4) regeneration (inward baptism), (5) and baptism. (1) Menno opens his discussion of Christian doctrine on an evangelical note: the day of grace has arrived in which we are now called to repentance and faith; "let us awake, be sober, and give ear to the inviting voice, and in this accepted time arise from the deep slumber of our loathsome sin, for the Lord is at hand."[74] (2) It is Christ Himself who exhorts men to repentance. Without true repentance "it will not help a fig to be called Christians, [and] boast of the Lord's blood, death, merits, grace, and Gospel."[75] Repentance involves the call "to die unto sin, and all ungodly works, and to live no longer according to the lusts of the flesh . . ."[76] Therefore, in contrast to hypocritical sorrow, it will issue in a change of life and the bearing of "good fruit."[77]

(3) In straightforward terms Menno explains his understanding of faith. That it plays the same pivotal place in Menno's thought that it does in the thought of the Reformers is evident.

> Faith accepts this Gospel [the blessed announcement of the favor and grace of God to us, and of forgiveness of sins through Christ Jesus] through the Holy Ghost, and does not consider former righteousness or unrighteousness, but hopes against hope (Rom 4:18), and with the whole heart casts itself upon the grace, Word and promises of the Lord, since it knows that God is true, and that His promises cannot fail. In this the heart is renewed, converted, justified, becomes pious, peaceable, and joyous, is born a child of God, approaches with full confidence the throne of grace, and so becomes a joint heir of Christ and a possessor of eternal life.[78]

One cautionary note is sounded in the discussion, however. "There is none that can glory in himself touching this faith, for it is the gift of God."[79]

(4) Though Menno considers baptism next in this discussion, it is clear that he holds inward baptism or regeneration as being a necessary precondition for outward baptism: "For only this inward baptism [by which the inner man is washed] . . . is of value in the sight of God, while outward baptism follows as an evidence of obedience which is of faith."[80] Menno defines regeneration as "an inward change which converts a man by the power of God through faith from evil to good, from carnality to spirituality, from unrighteousness to righteousness, out of Adam into Christ."[81] It is received by faith and effected by the Word and Spirit.[82] For Mennonites the radical inward change which characterizes regeneration becomes the presupposition for their call for a life of obedience and discipleship to Christ.

(5) One of the best summaries of the Mennonite view of baptism is to be found in the Dordrecht Confession.

> Concerning baptism we confess that all penitent believers, who, through faith, regeneration, and the renewing of the Holy Ghost, are made one with God, and are written in heaven, must, upon such scriptural confession of faith, and renewing of life, be baptised with water, in the most worthy name of the Father, and of the Son, and of the Holy Ghost, according to the command of Christ, and the teaching, example, and practice of the apostles, to the burying of their sins, and thus be incorporated into the communion of the saints; henceforth to learn to observe all things which the Son of God has taught, left, and commanded His disciples.[83]

As the confession indicates, Mennonites maintained that baptism was only for those who had responded to the Gospel in repentance and faith and experienced the inner workings of God (which were promised to a sincere faith). For Menno and Philips this precondition precluded the practice of infant baptism. Menno's works especially contain detailed responses to both the Lutheran and Reformed arguments for infant baptism. Though Menno utilizes history, logic, and theology to support his position, Scripture remains the authoritative basis for his apologetic.[84]

The Biblical basis for the observance of believer baptism is found in Christ's command and the teaching and practice of the apostles. Yet, from a theological standpoint, baptism also plays an integral part in the conversion process. It is a sign and evidence of the "obedience which is of faith."[85] As such, baptism has a connection with remission of sins, according to Menno. This connection is by no means immediate, for Menno expressly denied that baptism is the means of salvation and the remission of sins.[86] In typical Anabaptist fashion Menno maintains, according to 1 Peter 3:21, that it is inward baptism, i.e., the covenant of a good conscience with God by the resurrection of Jesus Christ, which saves (this interpretation is dependent on Luther's translation and the similar Dutch rendering).[87] In every case Menno mediates the connection between baptism and remission of sins by faith-obedience. Thus, wherever there is an active, obedient faith, the divine promise of remission of sins is realized. Because this faith is signified and betokened in water baptism, it can be said (explaining Acts 2:38) that remission of sins is received *in*, but not *through* (Menno carefully distinguishes the implications of the two prepositions) baptism. The essential factor is therefore not the water but the power of the divine Word received through faith.[88]

The Mennonite ordinance of baptism looks both backward, to the initial working of God in one's life, and forward, to the living out of the new life in Christ. Baptism's retrospective side is found in its being a seal and confession of faith and a testimony to the new birth and a good conscience. Its prospective side is found in its representation of both the burial of one's sinful flesh and the acquisition of new life in Christ, in its incorporation of the believer into the visible church, and in its being a pledge to lead a life of discipleship to Christ.[89] One can sense from this catalogue the great kerygmatic value that the rite of baptism had for the Mennonites.

The living out of one's salvation

The believer's new life in Christ was understood especially in Mennonite circles in terms of discipleship and obedience to Christ. Menno repudiates the idea that they sought "to merit the atonement of their sins and eternal life" by their conformity to the Word and example of Christ. Rather, they saw this new life as an expression of a "bold and submissive spirit of love which is out of a Christian nature, prepared unto all good works and obedience to the holy, divine Word."[90] The dynamic for the life of discipleship was the experience of regeneration through the Spirit's power. This inner renewal caused the Mennonites to have high expectations for regenerate believers:

> . . . all who are born of God, rightly baptized in the Spirit, fire, and water as the Scriptures teach, are heavenly-minded and godly. Their sins they bury. They lead a penitent, pious, virtuous life according to the Word of the Lord. They show the nature and power of Christ which dwells in them by word and work. They bring forth the fruits of the Spirit and suppress the works of the flesh. They are proper members of the body of Christ and labor according to the gift received. In short, they are fruit-bearing twigs of the true vine, and their fruits abide unto eternal life.[91]

With such an optimistic view of the Christian life, it is understandable that the charge of perfectionism would be levelled against the Mennonites. This allegation was directly denied by Menno in a number of writings. Mennonites were keenly aware of the failings caused by the inherited sinful nature which is never entirely destroyed in the Christian; hence the need for discipline. Yet the believer is also to desire to die fully to this inherent depravity so that it will no longer be master over his mortal body.[92]

As the above discussion would indicate, the Mennonites considered a fruitful faith as the sole source of assurance for the believer. It was only to this faith that God's promises of salvation and eternal life were given. Yet the distinguishing feature of this faith, as expressed in the life of the Christian, was its obedi-ence to Christ's Word. In this way emphasis in the Mennonite understanding of assurance tended to shift to the external signs of this faith.[93]

Mennonite Ecclesiology

Overview of the Mennonite view of the church

A description of the church found in Menno's writings reveals some salient features of the Mennonite view of the church.

> . . . the community of God, or the church of Christ, is an assembly of the pious, and a community of the saints, as also the Nicene symbol puts it, which from the beginning firmly trusted and believed in the promised Seed of the woman, which is . . . Christ; the which will accept and believe to the end His Word in sincerity of heart, follow His example, be led by His Spirit, and trust in His promise, as the Scriptures teach.[94]

For Menno, at least four characteristics are fundamental to the nature of the church. (1) The church is a *community*. The Christian faith is not to be lived out in solitude; growth in the faith is possible only within the context of mutual love, support, and admonition. This conviction was basic to the Mennonite and Anabaptist practices of the sharing of goods with needy members and mutual admonition and discipline (elaboration on key Mennonite practices will follow). Likewise, the Mennonite prohibition against marrying outside the church takes its rise from the emphasis on community as the Dordrecht Confession reveals: "the believers of the New Testament have . . . no other liberty than to marry among the chosen generation and spiritual kindred of Christ."[95] *The* time at which the church celebrated its identity as the community of God and church of Christ was during the Lord's Supper.

(2) The church is an assembly of the pious and the saints. The church can be predicated as holy because its individual members have dedicated themselves to a life of discipleship to Christ and have experienced the inner renewing of the Holy Spirit and because the entire body desires to attain the character of its Head, Christ.[96] Since the church is to be composed exclusively of such people, it is a visible church which must be concerned for its character.[97] The preservation of the purity of God's people therefore necessitates the practice of discipline. Discipline must be administered in a loving manner, however, with the restoration of the errant believer as its goal.

The visible character of the church also meant that the church was to be viewed, "at least in part, as the nucleus of God's kingdom on earth or its attempted realization."[98] An element of realized eschatology is thus present in Mennonite thought as can be seen in Philips' affirmation that "the church of the Lord is easily recognizable from its description, namely, 'the holy city, new Jerusalem, coming down from God out of heaven, prepared as a bride adorned for her husband (Rev. 21:2).'"[99] The Mennonite conviction that the believer belongs to God's kingdom had definite implications for their view of the state. They acknowledged that secular authority was ordained of God to punish the evil and protect the good and it therefore should be obeyed by the Christian.[100] Yet one important condition is placed on obedience to the state: "in so far as it [obeying the magistracy] is not contrary to God's Word."[101] Christ's prohibitions of retaliation with the sword and the swearing of oaths therefore take precedence over any conflicting dictate of the state. Given the sharp distinction made by the Mennonites between the church and the world and their uncompromising commitment to what they found explicitly taught in the New Testament, it is understandable that both Menno and Philips would consider (and realize) suffering as a mark of the true church.[102] Undeserved suffering and persecution were the way of Christ, who also predicted that this would be the way of His followers.

(3) The church is composed of the disciples of Christ. Every aspect of the salvation process—repentance, faith, regeneration, baptism—directs the believer to his responsibility to live the Christ-like life. Baptism, though, was regarded as *the* event in which the believer pledged his commitment to God and the church to lead a life of discipleship to Christ. This characteristic of the church was frequently formulated in Mennonite literature in terms of partaking the nature of Christ or becoming like Him. For example, Menno writes:

> For Christ has expressly portrayed Himself in His Word, that is, as to the nature which He would have us understand, grasp and follow and emulate, not according to His divine image, seeing He is the true image of the invisible God . . . , but according to His life and conversation here on earth, shown forth among men in works and deeds as an example set before us to follow so that we thereby might become partakers of His nature in the spirit, to become like unto Him.[103]

The ramifications of this feature as it relates especially to the Mennonite approach to Scripture and their observance of the practices of the early church have already been developed.

(4) The church is led by the Spirit. Notice has already been made of the Spirit's work in enlighten-

ing the heart and transforming the life of individuals and in leading the church through the Word of Christ. The first generation Anabaptists especially sought to pave the way for the Spirit's work through the proclamation of God's Word in missionary outreach. By the end of the sixteenth century, however, the Mennonites had adopted a *Stillen im Lande* attitude which had little place for the missionary zeal of the founders.

The offices of the church

Mennonites recognized the need for church officers, for without them "the church cannot subsist in her growth, nor continue in building."[104] A threefold ministry gradually developed among the Mennonites, as evidenced by statements in the confessions after 1577. The elder (German, *Aeltester* or *Vorsteher*; Dutch, *Oudste* or *Leerar*) was authorized to perform all the functions of the church. The preacher or servant of the Word (German, *Prediger*, *Lehrer*, or *Vermahner*; Dutch, *Dienaar* or *Vermaner*) was ordained to preach only. The deacon was ordained to assist the elders and preachers in their work and to care for the poor. The Dordrecht Confession also mentions the ordination of "aged widows" as deaconesses to care for the poor, sick, and needy.[105]

The practices of the church

The Lord's Supper. The Mennonites held that there were only two ordinances or sacraments (the word "sacraments" was occasionally used by the Mennonites but never in a sacramental sense): baptism (see above) and the Lord's Supper.[106] Like baptism, the Lord's Supper had great kerygmatic value for the Mennonites. It held two essential meanings for them: (1) it was a memorial of Jesus' suffering and death and (2) it constituted a call for the church to *be* the body of Christ. (1) The Dordrecht Confession notes that the bread and cup remind the partaker not only of Jesus' broken body and shed blood but also of the "fruits" of his suffering and death: "redemption and eternal salvation, which He purchased thereby, showing such great love towards us sinful men."[107] (2) The confession also stresses the existential meaning of the rite which calls the body

> to love and forgive one another and our neighbor, as He has done unto us, and to be mindful to maintain and live up to the unity and fellowship which we have with God and one another, which is signified to us by this breaking of bread.[108]

Discipline. Frequently in Mennonite literature the observance of the Lord's Supper and discipline are connected. The Christ-like character which all disciples were called to reflect in the Lord's Supper could be maintained only within a disciplined community. This high regard for the holiness and purity of the visible church was to be accompanied, however, by a special concern for the spiritual growth of each individual believer. Discipline was to be administered with the repentance and restoration of the errant believer as its goal.[109] Menno holds that the exercise of excommunication is ultimately "for reformation and not for destruction"[110] and therefore it is "a work of divine love and not of perverse, unmerciful, heathenish cruelty."[111]

Both Menno and Philips considered church discipline a divine command given through Christ (Matt. 18:15-19 and 16:19—the power of the keys) and Paul (1 Cor. 5 and 2 Thess. 3:6, 14-15).[112] The authority for administering discipline resided in the elder, acting in the name of the congregation. Before he could exercise discipline, however, an approving vote was needed by the congregation.[113]

Disciplinary action was to proceed according to the threefold order of Matthew 18: (1) a private rebuke by the offended party, (2) a private rebuke by representatives of the congregation, and, if necessary, (3) disciplinary action by the entire congregation. Formal disciplinary action by the church took two forms among the Mennonites. The lesser ban involved exclusion from communion while the greater ban involved exclusion from membership accompanied (in the stricter position of Menno, Philips, and Leonard Bouwens) by shunning or avoidance. The strict Mennonites (in contrast to the Waterlanders) held that avoidance should be observed even by the family and spouse ("bed and board").[114] It is noteworthy that Menno understood excommunication as an outward action by Christ's church which confirmed the existing spiritual separation from Christ of the errant brother: "no one is excommunicated or expelled by us from the communion of the brethren but those who have already separated and expelled themselves from Christ's communion either by false doctrine or by improper conduct."[115]

As the above quote indicates, both doctrinal and moral errors were subject to discipline. Open sins, i.e., shameful deeds committed publicly, were to be dealt with directly and openly by the church. However, secret sins, those committed in private against God, did not need to be made public but were "a matter between a man and his God."[116]

Though Menno supported the strict position of Philips and Bouwens on avoidance, his writings reveal a genuine desire to see discipline exercised in a loving, redemptive way. Such a spirit, which expresses its genuine concern for its brother in loving admonition, provides a much needed commentary on both the rigorist position of Menno's contemporaries and the moral and doctrinal laxity of the contemporary church.

Feetwashing. The importance of feetwashing to certain groups of the Mennonites is indicated by Philips' inclusion of the rite as one of the seven basic rules for Christ's church and by its appearance as one of the eighteen articles in the Dordrecht Confession. This latter document offers a concise statement of its import. Christ instituted feetwashing among His disciples who, according to His command and example, "taught believers to observe [it], as a sign of true humility and, especially, to remember by this feet washing, the true washing, whereby we are washed through His precious blood, and made pure after the soul."[117] Feetwashing was generally observed by the Mennonites as a form of hospitality to house guests, especially a visiting preacher or elder. Its practice continued into the seventeenth century especially among the Frisian, Flemish, and High German Mennonites, though during the next century it fell into disuse. Some of the conservative divisions of the above Mennonite groups also observed it in connection with communion.[118]

Concluding observations

One of the most prominent features of Mennonite thought was its existential character. This quality derives from the combined effect of several distinctive Mennonite emphases. The view of Christ as the Example for the new life, the straightforward approach to the Word which emphasized the Gospels rather than the more theological Pauline corpus, a conception of soteriology which saw all the aspects of the conversion experience pointing to the actualization of the new life in Christ, the prominent kerygmatic quality of the ordinances, the mild realized eschatology of the visible church all played a part in making Mennonite doctrine life-oriented.

A second conspicuous trait of Mennonite thought was its simple coherency. The various elements of Mennonite doctrine fit together into a cogent unit which could be readily grasped. Such a system had no use for the contorted arguments of the sophists, but relied for its strength on a simple, literal reading of the Word. These qualities were not devoid of hidden dangers (legalism, factiousness, narrowness), but they also resulted in a Biblical faith that was for the people and of the people.

Finally, the Mennonites appreciated the value which outward practices could have for declaring the faith. Though certainly recognizing the great inner and spiritual significance of baptism and communion, they understood that this meaning could be forcefully portrayed through visible symbols.

The Radical Pietist
Perception of the Mennonites

As was noted earlier, the Mennonites and Radical Pietists developed close ties during the first half of the eighteenth century. They held many emphases in common—a critical view of the established churches, their scholasticism, and their undisciplined bodies; obedience and discipleship to Christ (though the Mennonites extended its application more to outward practices); a strong existential bias regarding the Christian faith; and an optimistic view of realizing the new life in Christ. Likewise, the two groups saw something to admire in each other. The Mennonites were attracted to the devotional warmth and zeal of the Pietists. The Radicals appreciated the degree to which the Mennonites had realized the Christian life exemplified by the apostolic church.

The perception of the Mennonites by Hochmann and Arnold is instructive in discerning the relationship between the two movements. According to Renkewitz, Hochmann found the Mennonite traits of firm discipline, brotherly love, freedom from ties to the state, and the spiritual conception of the sacraments appealing. In 1710 he cited Menno as an ally in his criticism of infant baptism. He also found in the Mennonites support for his argument against state interference in the affairs of the Christian faith. Nevertheless, the "impartial" Hochmann does judge the Mennonites as a sect and places them beside the other sects—Reformed, Lutheran, and Catholic.[119]

Even more illuminating is Arnold's estimate of the Mennonites. Though Friedmann's contention that Arnold was "the true mediator between Anabaptism and Pietism" needs to be qualified somewhat,[120] Arnold does relate to his Pietist audience many Mennonite qualities which he finds commendable. He especially praises their piety, godly lives, brotherly love, simple obedience, steadfastness in persecution, and defenselessness (note that Arnold is evaluating them through Pietistic eyes).[121] Yet he also criticizes them for their following of the letter of Scripture, which resulted in legalism and Pharisaism, and their divisiveness, which Arnold views as a manifestation of self-will, conceit, and Pharisaism.[122] Arnold, of course, ultimately adjudges the Mennonites, along with the other sects, as exhibiting the signs of the fall.

These and other considerations in this chapter help to explain a number of the phenomena peculiar to the Mennonite-Brethren relationship during the eighteenth century: why Mack and the first Brethren, coming as they did from a Radical Pietist background, did not join the Mennonites; why the Brethren had intimate knowledge of, and appreciation for, the Mennonites; why the Brethren had good success proselyting the Mennonites. The subtle changes that had taken place among the Mennonites during the seventeenth century made them quite receptive to a Pietist message, especially one which combined most of the outward features of their own faith.

Chapter 4

JEREMIAS FELBINGER AND THE POLISH BRETHREN

Introduction

The influence of two movements, Radical Pietism and Anabaptism, is sufficient for explaining the derivation of most of the thought of the early Brethren. Yet there is some evidence that a third theological tradition, the Polish Brethren (Socinians), may have made some contribution to the formation of the Brethren mind.

Donald Durnbaugh has pointed out that the possibility of historical contact between the Polish Brethren and the early Brethren is strong. The center of Socinian activity in the early seventeenth century was Rakow, Poland. In the later 1630s the Racovian brethren came under severe attack from the Counter-Reformation and by 1660 the entire movement was expelled from Poland. Among the places they sought shelter were Prussia, Silesia, the Netherlands, and the Palatinate. In the latter place, a settlement existed at Mannheim (near Mack's birthplace) between 1663 and 1666. Eventually, ecclesiastical pressure caused them to remove to Silesia. In the Netherlands the Socinians developed close ties with the Collegiants with whom the Brethren also had direct contact. The description of the Brethren in America by the Baptist historian, Morgan Edwards, is especially intriguing at this point: "They are *General Baptists* in the sense which that phrase bears in Great Britain; but not *Arians* nor *Socinians*, as most of their brethren in Holland are."[1] Unfortunately, Edwards does not give further clues to the identity of "their brethren in Holland." Finally, one of the European members of the Brotherhood, as listed by Alexander Mack, Jr., was a brother Stritzka described as "ein Colischer Edelman." This nobleman may have been from Köln (Cologne), but Brumbaugh simply identifies him as a "Polish nobleman."[2] Further information about this nobleman might be most revealing about a connection between the Polish Brethren and the early

Brethren. Yet this bit of evidence, along with all the rest, still leaves the case for claiming a direct historical relationship between the two groups in the realm of tantalizing conjecture.[3]

Evidence of Brethren literary dependence upon the Polish Brethren is far more definite. In the original edition of his work, *Rights and Ordinances*, Mack notes, "The Greek word for the command *to baptize* actually means to immerse." He then cites his authority as, "It is so translated by most translators."[4] Later editions of Mack's writings attribute this point to Jeremias Felbinger whose *Christian Handbook* (*Christliches Hand-Büchlein*) indeed makes the above point.[5] The binding of Felbinger's work together with the third (1799) and fourth (1822) German editions of Mack's writings is indicative of the importance of this book for the Brethren. These facts suggest that an investigation of Felbinger's *Christian Handbook* would be profitable.

Jeremias Felbinger

HIS LIFE

Felbinger was born in Brieg in Silesia in 1616. Though raised as a Lutheran, he became a Socinian sometime after 1642. He was for a time rector of a school at Köslin in Pomerania (from which territory he was expelled for his views) and later an educator in Helmstadt (from which he was also banished), Bernstadt, Greifswald, and Wratislav in Poland. He also served as co-pastor of a Socinian congregation at Strasswitz near Danzig. He spent the last years of his life at Amsterdam in great poverty (he was still alive here in 1687). His disaffection with the Socinians, partly over their prohibition of holding office and engaging in war, was responsible for his miserable circumstances. They denied him a pension for his variant views, causing him to support himself by teaching and correcting proof. Arnold notes that Felbinger was more inclined to remain true to the views of Arius rather than to identify completely with the Socinians.[6]

Felbinger wrote several noteworthy works besides his *Christian Handbook* (1661). These include a work in Latin on the doctrine of God (1653); a Polish Brethren confession of faith which appeared in German in 1654 and in Latin, French, and Dutch in 1657; a Greek-German lexicon (1657); a German translation of the New Testament from the Greek, providing variant readings derived from the Socinianizing version of the New Testament by Courcelles, a professor at the Remonstrant seminary in Amsterdam (1660); and two writings against the Socinians (1672 and 1681).[7]

FELBINGER'S *CHRISTIAN HANDBOOK*

Basic principles in Felbinger's Thought

The governing principles of Felbinger's thought, as it is represented by his *Christian Handbook*, differ little from the Anabaptist tradition. Fundamental to his understanding of the Christian faith are the teachings of Christ. It is incumbent upon the Christian to follow the Savior in complete obedience. Nothing which He has instituted should be disdained or considered unnecessary.[8]

Felbinger holds that God has given man a clear revelation of all that is necessary for salvation in His Word. Therefore, the Christian does not need to rely upon the sophistry of the scholastic theologians in order to understand Scripture.[9] Like the Mennonites, Felbinger holds that there is clearly progression in the revelation of God's plan of salvation. Thus the promises and prophecies given to Adam (Gen. 3:15), Abraham (Gen. 22:18), and the prophets provide an increasingly clearer picture of the future Christ. All the outward sacrifices, ceremonies, and other regulatory ordinances of the Mosaic law were but shadows representing in a dark form the Priesthood and Kingdom of Christ which were to come in the new covenant. The dark types and ceremonies of the Mosaic dispensation and the prophecies of the prophets find their fulfillment in the life, death, and resurrection of Christ. Felbinger especially encourages his readers to "consider the teaching of the holy Gospels."[10]

A discussion of the Work

Contents

Felbinger's work is divided into seven major sections: (1) the creation of man, his fall, and his restoration; (2) the reception of innocent children into the Lord's visible church; (3) holy baptism; (4) church discipline; (5) holy feetwashing; (6) holy communion; and (7) the prohibition of the swearing of oaths.

The creation, fall, and restoration of man

According to Felbinger, man was created without sin and guiltless; he had no weakness and his soul lacked nothing. Man could have attained a state of righteousness and perfection through a judicious and constant exercise of obedience. In order to test man's obedience, God gave Adam and Eve the freedom to eat of all the trees of the garden with the exception of the tree of the knowledge of good and evil. When Adam obeyed his wife and ate the fruit of the forbidden tree, they lost their innocent state and became sinners.[11]

Felbinger holds that man continued to have the form and likeness of God even after the fall (Gen. 9:6; James 3:9), but this likeness consisted of man's lordship over creation. What man lost through his disobedience was his original innocence. He never did attain righteousness and holiness, for such a state could be realized only through perfect obedience to God. After the fall Adam's children partook of his likeness and form which was now subject to death and possessed a shameful inclination (*Zuneigung*) for sinning.[12]

From his investigation of Scripture, Felbinger deduces six conclusions with respect to the fall. These conclusions clearly have an apologetic aim. (1) The first man and woman freewillingly, without compulsion or unavoidable necessity, succumbed to the temptation of the serpent and disobeyed the command of God. (2) They were not robbed, on account of their disobedience, of some kind of an original righteousness and holiness (which they did not inherently possess). (3) Adam and Eve did not bring on their offspring an original sin which would make all their descendants entirely incapable of good and the sworn enemies of God and all virtue. (4) God condemned neither Adam and Eve nor their descendants to eternal fire on account of the disobedience of the first man and woman. (5) It is incontestable that God drove Adam and Eve from the garden, thereby removing the possibility that they would prolong their misery by eating of the tree of life. (6) God also has not exercised his right to execute His judgment of immediate death on man but has granted man time to repent and many years to better himself.[13]

Felbinger proceeds to note how God, in His mercy, forbearance, and love, has provided a way back to Himself and to the tree of life. This way remained open with the condition that one of Adam's descendants must fulfill all the will and all the commandments of God as well as undergo the suffering of a most horrible death.[14] The first revelation of the way back to God was found in the promised seed of the woman who would overcome the serpent (Gen. 3:15). God has progressively revealed his work of eternal salvation (including resurrection from the dead and eternal life) through Abraham, Moses, and the prophets. The fulfillment of God's promises is found in the earthly ministry, death, and exaltation of Christ. To develop the results of Christ's ministry, Felbinger turns his attention to Romans 5:12–21. Just as sin was introduced into the world by one man, Adam, and death, as the consequence of sin, came upon all men, so also righteousness entered the world by one man, Jesus Christ, whose perfect obedience to the will of God received the gracious reward for righteousness: eternal life (which He is now able to bestow on His followers). All who are begotten of Christ by the Spirit become heirs of eternal life,[15] even though they do not exhibit Christ's perfect obedience due to sins of weakness. Their righteous standing before God is based on Christ's own righteousness and obedience which He carried out for the Father on the cross in order to abolish the sins of the whole world. However, all those who respond with unbelief and disobedience to God's grace are threatened with the terrible punishment of eternal fire.[16]

The Socinian framework of Felbinger's treatment is quite evident. Especially noteworthy are: (1) his denial of original sin and his minimizing of the effects of the fall, (2) his stress on obedience as the condition for acceptance by God, (3) the focus on perfect obedience as the constitutive element in Christ's salvific work, (4) eternal life as the reward for Christ's obedience, and (5) the portrayal of Christ as the Example[17] for our life of faith and obedience.

Felbinger includes one other important discussion in this section. He is emphatic that God does not pronounce death upon innocent children as punishment for Adam's sin. They must die only because they are begotten by a mortal father. Death is thus a natural condition (*Beschaffenheit*) of our temporal existence. Felbinger admits that children exhibit the inclination for evil, but, citing James 1:14–15, he maintains that their misdeeds are not considered sin as long as they are done without knowledge and will. To demonstrate that God holds no one responsible for the sins of another, he cites passages from both Testaments: Ezekiel 18:20; Deuteronomy 24:16; Matthew 16:27; Romans 2:6; Galatians 6:5; 2 Corinthians 5:10.[18]

The reception of children into the church

In the second section of his *Handbook*, Felbinger returns to a discussion of Christ's work of salvation and notes the implications which Christ's ministry has for children. Once again he focuses his argumentation on Romans 5:12–21. Though Adam's disobedience resulted in death for all men, Christ's obedience, which extended itself to the perfect fulfillment of all God's commandments and even death, has overcome the power of Satan and the world. Therefore, no one should say that the disobedience of Adam unto death is more powerful than the obedience of Christ unto life. Felbinger applies these "greater" effects of Christ's obedience to innocent children in two special ways. First, children, before they willfully commit sin, belong to the invisible church because Christ died for them and purchased their salvation with His blood. Felbinger further concludes that since they belong to the invisible church, they must also belong to the visible church. Second, if children do die in their innocent years, parents can be assured that they by no means are condemned to eternal fire but that they will experience the blessed joy of heaven through the power of Christ's death and perfect obedience.[19]

Felbinger acknowledges that the Scriptures prescribe no outward ceremony for the reception of innocent children into the visible church. He suggests, however, that Christ's example of laying hands on young children and praying for them can be followed by pastors. At this ceremony parents should also be reminded of their duties to their children. Felbinger earnestly challenges parents with their responsibility to teach their children about faith in God and Jesus Christ, the need to arrange one's entire life according to the will of God and Christ, and the importance of baptism. He recommends the Apostles' Creed as a good teaching tool for children.[20]

In this section Felbinger also briefly discusses the practice of infant baptism. He sees authorization for the practice neither in Christ's example nor in His express commands. Instead, diligent searching of the books of the new covenant reveals that baptism must be preceded by the hearing of the Word, faith, remorse for former sins, regeneration, and a firm resolve to live according to the will of God (which includes the desire for baptism). An innocent child is able to experience none of these things.[21]

Holy baptism

Just under half of Felbinger's *Handbook* is devoted to a discussion of baptism. Not only does the broader Anabaptist observance of believer baptism call for defense but the distinctive Polish Brethren practice of immersion baptism also demands support.

Felbinger begins his treatment of baptism with the contention: "To baptize and to immerse are one and the same . . ."[22] He defends his thesis by various linguistic, Scriptural, and theological arguments. Noteworthy among his Scriptural arguments is his appeal to John 3:23, where it is stated that John was baptizing at Enon because there was much water there. He concludes that if John had wanted to sprinkle a little water on the forehead he would not have needed to select a site where there was much water. Felbinger's main theological argument is that immersion baptism was commanded by God through Christ. The divine origin of immersion is supported in two ways. First, Jesus Himself testified that John's baptism (by immersion) was from heaven. Second, Jesus, following the way prepared for Him by John, authorized immersion baptism by His own example and teaching.[23]

Felbinger briefly draws two other conclusions concerning baptism: (1) only those who are able to be instructed in all the essential aspects of Christian faith (Matt. 28:18–20) are to be baptized. This condition is not applicable to young children. Instruction concerning obedience to Christ and the maintenance of a godly life and walk is to continue after baptism. (2) The meaning of baptism is summarized by Christ who promised salvation to all those who believe and are baptized (Mark 16:15, 16). (He does not develop further the relation between baptism and salvation.)[24]

All the rest of Felbinger's discussion of baptism is devoted to a historical apologetic supporting the above points. He brings to his defense the testimony of the book of Acts and the early church, the succession of faithful witnesses who maintained the true teaching concerning baptism, and the corroborating witness of various Reformed, Lutheran, and Catholic writers.

Brief notice of several points in Felbinger's historical discussion is called for. He holds that the first changes in the order of baptism instituted by Christ occurred in the third century. It was Cyprian and some others of his opinion that established infant baptism and communion at this time. He appeals, however, to the well-known passage in Tertullian's work, *De baptismo*, and to the delayed baptisms of such men as Constantine, Gregory Nazianzus, Basil the Great, and Augustine to demonstrate that infant baptism was still not considered normative even through the fifth century. After this time infant baptism became more and more accepted.[25]

Felbinger is substantially indebted to Jacob Mehrning's S. *Baptismi Historia* not only for his own lengthy historical discussion but also for his line of faithful witnesses.[26] He utilizes Mehrning's contention that the Waldenses predate the appearance of Peter Waldo in 1160. Indeed, they go back to the time of Pope Sylvester and even to that of the Apostles.[27] This argument greatly simplifies the need to validate the assertion that up until Felbinger's time there had always been Christian churches and especially Christian teachers who had agreed with the baptismal order of Jesus Christ.[28] The Waldenses thus become the direct link between the apostolic church and the Anabaptist movement for the perpetuation of the true teaching concerning baptism.

Church discipline

Felbinger derives his brief treatment of discipline from an anonymous Dutch tract entitled (in German) *Kurze Erklärung über unterschiedene Articul des Christlichen Glaubens*. It was printed at Amsterdam in 1656. On the basis of Felbinger's discussions of discipline and communion, which were also taken from this source, it would appear that the tract might be Anabaptist.

Discipline is considered necessary because the church's character is to be holy and without blemish. Not just the elders but, indeed, every member should be concerned with the life and conduct of the congregation. Discipline is to proceed according to Matthew 18:15–18. If the transgressor is hardened in his sin, he is to be put out of the church. Open misdeeds should be punished openly before the congregation (1 Tim. 5:20). If a grave sin is committed, no member is to have dealings with the transgressor or even eat with him (1 Cor. 5:11). In the case of open sins, it is good for the offender to confess his sin to the congregation and accept its judgment. It is also good to confess secret sins (James 5:16), for this is part of repentance and is helpful in the attainment of forgiveness (at this point Felbinger differs from Menno).[29]

Holy feetwashing

Felbinger's exposition of John 13:1-17 is quite thorough. At the close of his study, he provides the reader with a summary of his major conclusions. (1) The chief founder of feetwashing is God the Father who has given all things, including the institution of this holy ceremony, into the hands of His Son, Jesus Christ. (2) The first servant and inaugurator of this ceremony is Christ Jesus. (3) It is to be observed just before the holy communion. (4) Both the one who washes the feet of another and the one whose feet are washed participate with Christ in eternal salvation and all heavenly blessings (vs. 8, 17). (5) This rite is to be observed by the teachers and overseers of Christians. (6) It is also to be observed by all Christians who have been cleansed of their former sins by baptism. Earlier, Felbinger had noted that Christians inevitably commit unintentional faults due to human weakness which, so to speak, "get one's feet dirty." Rather than being rebaptized, the service of feetwashing is a certain sign of truth (*ein gewisses Wahrzeichen*) that the Christian is purified of these sins.[30]

Holy communion

As noted above, Felbinger's section on communion is borrowed entirely from an anonymous Dutch tract. The discussion is composed of four segments.
(1) Concerning the ceremony of the breaking of bread. The tract confesses that the ceremony of breaking of bread was instituted by Christ, received by the apostles, and transmitted to the church. It is celebrated in remembrance of Christ and for the proclamation of His death. Just as in the Passover ceremony, the lamb was a sign of the Lord's deliverance in Egypt, so also the bread and the cup are reminder-signs (*Gedenkzeichen*) of Christ's body and blood. Yet these signs possess a much more appropriate signification than the lamb in the Passover ceremony because Christ gave His body to death and His blood for shedding.
(2) Concerning the eating of the flesh of Christ and the drinking of His blood. The tract stresses that Christ's body and blood are truly food and drink, for they provide life, i.e., eternal life. Just as physical food and drink must be taken internally, so also must Christ's dead body and shed blood be received inwardly by our souls through faith in His efficacious death.

(3) Concerning the communion of the body and blood of Christ. The belief is stated that the partaking of the bread and cup is a corporate communion of the body and blood of Christ. Thus the many share in the one single bread and in one single body (1 Cor. 10:16-17). The drinking of the cup is a reminder that the bread is partaken as a token, not of Christ's living body, but of His dead body, entirely without blood.
(4) Concerning the dignity of this ceremony. The grave significance of communion is underscored with the warning that those who do not discern Christ's body and blood as being holy, eat and drink judgment upon themselves. Therefore, communion should be partaken only after investigating one's life and walk. Nevertheless, every effort should be made to be present at the celebration of communion.[31]

Prohibition of the swearing of oaths

On the basis of Christ's words in Matthew 5:33-37 and the similar counsel in James 5:12, Felbinger concludes that the swearing of all oaths is forbidden under the new covenant. He then investigates the nature of human oaths themselves. Felbinger observes that when one swears, he is, in effect, acknowledging that he has a part in that by which he swears. It becomes his surety that he is declaring the truth. In the fact of the matter, however, it is presumptuous for man to swear by heaven, earth, Jerusalem, his own head, God, or Christ. Man has no power over the first four items; it is God alone who has created and established them. In the case of the latter two items, there is no guarantee that a man will not swear falsely, declaring thereby that he wishes to have no part with God and Christ. The Christian, however, should speak out firmly his "yes" with a "yes" and his "no" with a "no," knowing that he does so in the presence of God and Christ. Felbinger indicates that the New Testament provides two formulas by which the Christian can declare, both to the church and to the state, the truth and the inner testimony of the heart and conscience. The first is to call on God and Christ as one's witness. The second is to declare the testimony of one's conscience in the presence of God, Christ, and the holy angels. Felbinger admonishes his readers to be ready and willing to testify concerning the truth in every situation.[32]

Concluding Observations

Though the doctrinal point where Socinian thought would be most discernible—the doctrine of God—is not discussed by Felbinger, Socinian theology is evident in Felbinger's treatment of the fall, Christ's work of salvation, and immersion baptism. His discussion of soteriology, especially as it relates to children, is not entirely consistent. He seeks to avoid the intimation that the entrance of sin into the world resulted in the transmission of inherited sin to Adam's offspring, thereby necessitating Christ's atoning death. Yet when he argues for the salvation of children, he indicates that it is not just Christ's obedience but also His death and shed blood which guarantee that children will not suffer eternal condemnation. Considered as a whole, however, Felbinger's handbook presents a view of the church and its rites which conforms with the larger Anabaptist perspective. Only when he insists that baptism means immersion does he add a stricture that is not characteristic of Anabaptist practice. But it is this stricture which made this work a valuable source for the early Brethren.

Chapter 5

ALEXANDER MACK'S LIFE AND THOUGHT

Introduction

The man who was the guiding spirit of the early Brethren was Alexander Mack. It was his association with the Radical Pietist, Ernst Christoph Hochmann von Hochenau, and his sharing with certain unknown Mennonite individuals and congregations which fashioned the theological framework that would characterize the Brethren. It was under his leadership that a group of eight men and women committed themselves to the institution of a "New Testament church" by believers' immersion. It was to a large measure due to Mack's preaching, teaching, and writing skills that the young church expanded to several locations in Germany. Finally, it was as a result of his pastoral leadership that the scattered and, at times, disillusioned flock of Brethren who came to America achieved a new sense of community and mission.

It is true that there were other men from the first generation of Brethren who, with Mack, contributed invaluable effort in laying the foundation of the church. Yet an understanding of Mack's life and writings provides one with a representative overview of that foundation, an overview which includes all the components essential for a basic comprehension of early Brethren life and thought.

The Life of Alexander Mack

The story of Alexander Mack's early life centers in Schriesheim, a small town located in the Rhenish Palatinate, five miles north of Heidelberg. Here Mack was born (he was christened on July 27, 1679), the youngest of John Philip Mack's four sons.[1] John was a well-to-do miller, a trade which had been in the Mack family for four generations. An influential and respected man in the community, he served as a long-time member of the town council as well as a

mayor in 1690 and 1696. He was a devout man and raised his family in the Reformed Church, where he served as an elder.[2]

Alexander's two oldest brothers worked in the mill, while the third became a baker. There is some evidence that Alexander was destined to attend the Heidelberg Neckar School, a college administered by one of his uncles. However, the death of his oldest brother in 1689 changed any such plans. Alexander now began to learn the milling trade. What schooling Alexander did receive probably did not extend beyond the limited offerings of the town.[3]

On January 18, 1701, Alexander married Anna Margaretha Kling. Her father was John Valentine Kling who, like Alexander's father, was a respected Schriesheim townsman, serving as a Reformed elder, town councilor, and at one point, mayor. In November 1701, the first child, John Valentine, was born to Alexander and Anna. He was the first of five children born to the Macks. The others were Johannes, Alexander, Christina, and Anna Maria. The two daughters and their mother died while in Europe; the three sons later accompanied their father to America.

It is not known when Mack first became disaffected with the Reformed Church. It is likely that he had been exposed to radical views prior to his first contact with Hochmann which is thought to have occurred in 1705 in the territory of the religiously tolerant count of Ysenburg-Büdingen.[4] Radical Pietism had appeared in the Palatinate by 1702 when Matthew Baumann openly attacked the established church in his home of Lambsheim. In the spring of the following year, the itinerant preacher, John George Rosenbach, was active in Heidelberg and nearby Mannheim. In an action which reflected more generalized Radical Pietist sentiments, four Lambsheim residents—John Traut, Jacob Bossert, Jacob Berg, and Adam Pfarr—refused to swear an oath required of subjects in April 1706.[5]

Hochmann's initial preaching tour in the Palatinate in the summer of 1706 was occasioned by an invitation from Alexander Mack. Following their arrival in Schriesheim, Hochmann, Christian Erb, and other Radicals boldly proclaimed their message through street preaching and in more private gatherings in homes and Mack's mill. Hochmann's activities met with such success that the Heidelberg Superior bailiwick decided to intervene. On August 22, he attended a meeting at Mack's mill and interrogated those in attendance concerning their activities. When the county clerk threatened to call in a regiment of soldiers to arrest "these dangerous persons," the participants fled. The crackdown on the "Pietist sect" continued with the arrest of Hochmann, Erb, and eight others at Mannheim on September 6. They were sentenced to hard public labor. Hochmann and Erb were released only after being sternly warned against returning to Mannheim and the Palatinate. The Elector Palatine considered this Pietist activity so dangerous that he issued an edict on September 14 that all Pietists found gathering in homes should be seized and placed at hard labor without hearing or trial.[6]

These repressive measures caused Mack to look for a new home where his new found religious convictions could be expressed freely. Therefore, he moved his family to Schwarzenau in the county of Wittgenstein in late 1706. Henry Albert (1658–1723), the count of Sayn-Wittgenstein-Hohenstein, had extended toleration to all refugees who sought the free exercise of their faith within his territory. This policy was made possible by the weak imperial organization of the Holy Roman Empire and was motivated by at least two considerations. First, the county of Wittgenstein was a hilly, ill-favored land which suffered severe depopulation during the Thirty Years' War. To attract settlers, Henry Albert granted newcomers not only religious freedom but also nearly all the rights of subjects in return for a yearly tax. Second, Henry Albert himself inclined toward Pietism. He evidences this inclination in a letter written in 1700 to his brother, August David, in Berlin in which he offered glowing praise of Hochmann. In addition, four of his sisters became Pietists and married commoners in spite of the disapproval of relatives. Though Henry Albert's policy of toleration came under severe attack, he maintained it until his death in 1723.[7]

In 1706 and 1707 Mack sold all of his possessions in Schriesheim. Since he had had extensive holdings in his home town, he was able to acquire a considerable sum of money from their sale. However, during the following years, Mack's wealth was completely expended as he unsparingly used it to pay the fines of those arrested for their beliefs and to aid refugees who had fled to Schwarzenau.

Throughout the spring and summer of 1707, it is thought that Mack and Hochmann traveled together as itinerant preachers to various parts of Germany, including the Palatinate. During this tour they probably visited in Mennonite homes and congregations. Not only is it known that Hochmann had a good relationship with the Mennonites, but Alexander Mack, Jr., also confirms that his father "visited in sincere love, different congregations of Baptists [Mennonites] in Germany"[8] prior to the organization of the Brethren in 1708.

In many facets of their thought, Hochmann and Mack were in complete agreement.[9] However, in the area of church organization and practice they had major differences. Hochmann's spiritualistic separatism undergirded his vision of an invisible church of the Spirit. In it formal religious organization was replaced by the spiritual bonds of love between brothers and sisters committed to Christ, ordained clergy were replaced by priests called immediately by the Spirit, and the outward sacraments were replaced by Spirit baptism and spiritual communion. Nevertheless, Mack and other Radical Pietists were coming to believe that the New Testament supported the institution of an organized church along with the practice of such rites as baptism, the Lord's Supper, and discipline. Both full obedience to Christ and the very ability to fulfill the commandments of the New Testament seemed to involve the need for practicing these rites and the creation of simple organization.[10]

Sometime, perhaps during the late summer of 1707, Mack returned to Schwarzenau, recognizing his obligations to his family and the Christian fellowship there. Mack now had the opportunity to continue his search of the Scriptures with a group of men and women who were also seeking full obedience to Christ and the New Testament. One of the deep concerns among these Radical Pietists was their unbaptized state, for they were convinced that their baptism as infants was unscriptural. In the early summer of 1708, two "foreign brethren" visited the Pietists at Schwarzenau and strongly urged them to be baptized. These unidentified "foreign brethren" were most likely Collegiants or Polish Brethren.[11] These developments spurred Alexander Mack and George Grebe to write to Hochmann, who was imprisoned at Nürnberg at the time (July 1708). They sought his opinion about the administration of water baptism by trine immersion and the observance of the "Lord's love feast." His response was one of cautious encouragement, warning them to "count the cost" of the inevitable trials that would follow and to avoid a purely outward and legalistic observance of these rites which would obscure the essential inward work of Christ.[12]

The little band of Pietists now resolved to proceed with their plans for administering adult immersion. Preparatory to this action, the group chose one of their number by lot to draft a letter to Pietists in the Palatinate inviting them to participate in "this high act of baptism."

Three basic reasons were given for baptism by adult immersion: (1) the example of Christ's baptism in the Jordan River; (2) the commandment of Jesus in Matthew 28 to "make disciples of all peoples, baptizing them in the name of the Father, and of the Son, and of the Holy Spirit"; (3) the example of the early church. It was made quite clear that baptism in and of itself was not essential for salvation.[13]

As the above intimates, the decision to proceed with baptism was derived from their desire to be fully obedient to the example and commands of Christ and His Word. Having "found in trustworthy histories that the early Christians during the first and second centuries"[14] were baptized by trine immersion, eight people covenanted together to follow this example. Sometime in early August,[15] Alexander and Anna Margaretha Mack, Andrew Boni and his new wife, Joanna, John and Joanna Kipping, George Grebe, and Luke Vetter gathered at the Eder River. The portion of Luke 14 about "counting the cost" to which Hochmann had made reference was read. One of the men was then chosen by lot to baptize Mack who then baptized the one who baptized him and the other six.

News of this and subsequent baptisms spread quickly within both political and religious circles. Other rulers in the vicinity of Wittgenstein looked upon these "Anabaptist fanatics" as a severe threat to law and order (the comparison of the Brethren with the Münsterites was explicitly made). In particular, Count Charles Louis of Sayn-Wittgenstein, the brother-in-law of Henry Albert, was incensed by the "blasphemous" and "scornful" attitude taken by the Brethren toward infant baptism. He severely criticized Henry Albert for tolerating such a "fanatic pack" in clear violation of the Treaty of Westphalia.[16]

These baptisms also brought criticism from various Radical Pietists. The Boehmist Gichtel felt the Brethren were "not deeply enough grounded." He criticized them for their sectarianism, their gaining of disciples through the sharing of Mack's means, and their selfish praying.[17] Christoph Seebach, a Lutheran

pastor who had been dismissed from his parish, aired a typical separatist complaint against the Brethren.

" . . . through this fantasy of the necessity of baptism, they fall into a dreadful sectarianism." After Christ's resurrection, there was no longer need for water baptism; those passages in the New Testament referring to baptism have to do with the baptism by the Spirit.[18]

Most painful for the Brethren, however, was Hochmann's increasingly critical attitude. His cautious approval of water baptism when preceded by Spirit baptism had turned to pointed criticism of the Brethren's coarse and subtle sectarianism which was "completely intolerable to a spirit made free by the blood of Christ." In a significant shift, he even counseled that adult baptism was unnecessary if one had experienced infant baptism and was being baptized "each day" by the Holy Spirit.[19]

Not all the publicity was bad. As more people seriously considered the beliefs of this new group, more baptisms occurred. By 1715 the Schwarzenau brotherhood had grown to what Alexander Mack, Jr., could later describe as a "large congregation." By 1720 the members and their families numbered about two hundred. Through the work of Mack, Christian Liebe, John Naas, and others, congregations were also established in Marienborn, Krefeld (to which many of the Marienborn members moved in 1715 due to persecution), and Solingen, near Krefeld. Liebe's presence in Bern may also indicate a Brethren presence there. At the peak of the movement's growth in Europe around 1719 there probably were only several hundred members.

The organization and worship of these congregations were simple. Generally they had at least one lay preacher, who preached, taught, and helped in administering communion, and a bishop (*Vorsteher*), who oversaw the affairs of the whole congregation. Both were chosen by election or consensus while probably only the *Vorsteher* was ordained by the laying on of hands.[20] The similarity to Mennonite organization is obvious. The worship of the congregation would have followed a typical Radical Pietist meeting. In testimony before Heidelberg authorities in 1709, several Radical Pietists, including a future Brethren, Martin Lucas, described such a meeting:

When they come together they sing two or three hymns [usually from John A. Freylinghausen's *Geistreiches Gesangbuch*], as God moves them; then they open the Bible and whatever they find they read and explain it according to the understanding given to them by God, for the edification of their brethren. After they have read, they fall to their knees, raise their hands to God and pray for the authorities, that

God might move them to punish the evil and protect the good; then they praise God that He has created them for this purpose.[21]

Mack's devotion to spreading the Brethren vision of a church conformed to the example of Christ and the early church is evidenced by his work not only as a pastor and evangelist but also as a writer. In 1713, *Basic Questions*, the first publication presenting Brethren principles, appeared. This pamphlet consisted of forty questions submitted by the separatist, Eberhard Louis Gruber, to be answered with "corporate, clear, and candid explanations" of the Brethren's new form of baptism and new church fellowship. Two years later Alexander Mack published the first major theological work of the Brethren, *Brief and Simple Exposition of the Outward but Yet Sacred Rights and Ordinances of the House of God . . .* The format of *Rights and Ordinances* is a supposed conversation between a father and son employed as a literary device to present the unique beliefs of the early Brethren.[22] It considers the "rights" or laws which are to regulate the behavior of believers toward each other and the world and the "ordinances" which the true church of Christ should observe.

Internal and external difficulties caused the Brethren to shift the locus of their movement to America by 1729. The Krefeld congregation was torn by a controversy in 1717 which arose when a young member, John Häcker, married the stepdaughter of a Mennonite minister. Christian Liebe had Häcker placed under the ban for marrying outside the church. This action embittered John Naas, the leading Brethren elder at Krefeld, and led to his withdrawal from the congregation. The dispute may have also been behind the decision by twenty Krefeld families to emigrate to America in 1719, under the leadership of Peter Becker.

In 1720 the pressure of external events caused about two hundred of the Schwarzenau Brethren under Mack's leadership to move to Surhuisterveen in West Friesland in the Netherlands. Continuing official pressure on Henry Albert to restrict his policy of toleration, increasing controversy with the Inspirationists, and ever-present economic problems contributed to this decision. Surhuisterveen was in an area that was religiously congenial to Brethren beliefs and practices. Many Mennonites and Collegiants were to be found here (connections with the Collegiants may have led to their locating at Surhuisterveen). In their new home the Brethren kept to themselves, lived quietly, and worked diligently, probably in the chief occupation of the area, cutting peat.[23]

Even in Surhuisterveen life was difficult for the Brethren. At times the Collegiants provided the Brethren with needed financial support. In addition, their immersion baptisms were still technically illegal.[24] These concerns, together with the glowing reports received from the Brethren in America, were instrumental in the decision to sail for America. In 1729 Mack and a group of about 120 Brethren left Rotterdam for Philadelphia. They arrived on September 15, 1729, and were given a warm reception at nearby Germantown, the center of Brethren activity throughout much of the eighteenth century. Mack, with Peter Becker's full approval, at once assumed the leadership of the Germantown church, a position which he held with great wisdom and skill until his death on January 31, 1735.[25]

Mack's passing was a great loss to the Brethren, for their future in America was still precarious. Yet the testimony of Mack's life and writings continued to guide the Brethren.[26] As a leader, Mack sought to serve his flock with a sensitive, humble spirit. He commanded the respect of those to whom he ministered by his own life of devotion to Christ. He was a diligent student of the Word and believed that Scripture, rather than man's reason, church creeds, or individual inspiration, should be the ultimate guide for one's life. Once he came to a decision based upon study, prayer, sensitivity to the Spirit, and group consensus, he would live by it, no matter what the consequences. However, he tried to antagonize no man but strove for a loving, sharing, caring community of believers who lived in obedience to Christ.

The Thought of Alexander Mack

INTRODUCTION

As one reads and studies Mack's two extant treatises, *Basic Questions* and *Rights and Ordinances*, their background should be borne in mind. These writings were not intended as systematic and complete expressions of faith. From their inception the Brethren avoided creeds and confessions, partly because they felt that they had not yet obtained light on all questions and partly because they were reacting against the scholasticism which was so much a part of Protestant Orthodoxy. In these treatises Mack was presenting the early Brethren position on beliefs and practices which were sources of controversy with the Radical Pietists, Mennonites, and established churches. At the beginning of the discussion between father and son in *Rights and Ordinances*, Mack has the son say: " . . . I am asking you, dear father, that you might better instruct me in accordance with the witness of the Holy Scriptures and the early Christians in all things which are yet so controversial and which cause us such criticism."[27] Durnbaugh adds an additional note of caution:

> The Brethren shared the post-Reformation evangelical beliefs about Christianity, and were definitely influenced by their Calvinist background.[28] It, therefore, does violence to historical accuracy to judge them alone on these two frankly propagandistic tracts, even though they are the only statements readily available.[29]

In spite of this reservation, it is still possible to discern the essential characteristics of Brethren thought from these two propagandistic treatises. What Stoeffler has adjudged a "historically valid principle" applies here: " . . . the ethos of a group can best be preserved if the latter fights vigorously against some real or imagined enemy . . ."[30]

This study of Mack's thought is based upon the translation of his writings made by Durnbaugh in the source book, *European Origins of the Brethren*. Besides *Basic Questions* and *Rights and Ordinances*, reference will also be made to a letter from Mack to Charles August, Count of Ysenburg-Büdingen-Marienborn. This letter was written on behalf of a widow Hoffmann who had been expelled from the count's territory after she had allowed her daughter to be baptized by Mack. It is the only known correspondence from Mack to have been preserved in Germany.[31] As far as is known, Mack published only one other tract. It was written in America to counteract the Sabbatarian views of Conrad Beissel. Unfortunately, there are no copies of this tract known to exist. There are also some fragments from Mack's pen in blank leaves of his personal Bible (a Luther Bible) which is preserved at Bridgewater College in Bridgewater, Virginia.

HERMENEUTICAL CONSIDERATIONS: THE SOURCES OF AUTHORITY USED BY MACK

Before attempting to discuss those theological issues which are the major concern of Mack—soteriology and ecclesiology—it is essential that another consideration be dealt with—the sources of authority recognized by Mack for establishing a church. These sources, in large measure, will determine and give shape to the primary foci of Mack's writings.

The step taken by the initial group of eight brothers and sisters in forming a new church was not a capricious venture—it was undertaken only after they had "counted the cost." Undoubtedly, they had seriously considered the question, "Where does our

authority lie for taking this decisive step?" This very query was put to the Brethren by the Radical Pietist, Eberhard Louis Gruber, several years after the organizing of the brotherhood. He pointedly asked:

> Can any one of you stand up who is willing to state, upon his conscience and responsibility in the hour of his death and on the Day of Judgment, that he had received such a direct calling from God to re-establish the ordinance of baptism which was so long neglected [the Radical Pietists saw infant baptism as a perversion of New Testament baptism, but, like the Quakers, spiritualized away the necessity of adult baptism], and with it to form an entirely new church of Christ here on earth such as has not existed since the time of the apostles and the early Christians?[32]

In answering this question as well as others in the course of his two extant writings, Mack reveals that his vindication of the establishment and perpetuation of the Brethren fraternity rests on six fundamental convictions: (1) the church is called into existence by God; (2) Christ is the Lord of the church; (3) Scripture is the church's objective authority; (4) the Spirit leads the church; (5) the life and doctrine of the early church, i.e., the church of the first and second centuries, provide the normative pattern for the church; (6) the church is responsible for shaping the character of its members.

The church is called into existence by God

The doctrine of God receives very little direct comment in Mack's writings. This was one of the theological loci on which Mack remained faithful to this Reformed upbringing, accepting without question the orthodox understanding of the three persons of the Trinity and their gracious work in the salvation of man. Yet Mack does provide us with one brief glimpse of his view of God the Father in the preface to *Rights and Ordinances*. Here God is represented as a stern Judge and Lawgiver who expects obedience of His children. His transcendence and omnicharacter are emphasized through such adjectives as "almighty," "omnipotent," "all-powerful," and "eternal."[33] Mack has a definite purpose in mind for employing this emphasis upon "the greatness of the Sovereign": to show that the ultimate authority for the Christian and the church is God. He is the "Householder" (*Haus-Vater*), the source of the commandments and the ordinances which are to be kept in His household. The promises for obedience to His statutes and laws are "life eternal, and all of the other gifts of grace of the Holy Spirit which believers possess."[34] Disobedience by His children will be met with wrath and punishment. This view of God as a sovereign Lawgiver and Householder has several possible sources. From Reformed thought could come the stress on God's sovereignty while Mack's precisionism could come from Reformed piety.[35] Both Anabaptism and Radical Pietism used this "household" imagery and could view God as a stern Judge and Lawgiver.[36]

Not only did Mack maintain that God was the source of the "rights and ordinances" governing the church, but he also asserted that God was the ultimate source for the establishment of the church. In answering Gruber's question concerning the authority for "forming an entirely new church" (see p. 69), Mack responds with several assertions which underscore God's role in founding the church.

> No man would dare to appropriate this [establishing a church] for himself, or declare before men that he was sent by God to establish a church, but he would gladly leave the honor to God. Even though God may use some as special instruments for this, they only need to be tested whether they are sent by God, as John says (3:34): "For he whom God has sent utters the words of God."[37]

Mack further insists that God alone could give that direct calling and prompting through His Spirit which were necessary for founding a visible community.[38] No one can follow "the teaching of Christ [which for Mack necessitated a church where the outward ordinances could be properly observed] unless he lets himself be drawn by the Father."[39] Note that Mack's appeal for divine authorization in founding the church rests on both inward and outward evidences. It is the certainty of having been inwardly directed by God confirmed by the outward testimony of following the words of God and teachings of Christ which assures Mack of God's sovereign activity in the formation of the Brethren. This interplay between the inward (a Pietistic keynote) and outward (an Anabaptist emphasis) aspects of the faith will be noted frequently in Mack's writings.

Christ is the Lord of the Church

No other source of authority is emphasized in Mack's writings so strongly as is Christ's authority in establishing and directing the church. Even Mack's appeal to the Father's activity in founding the church results in the accentuation of the objective authority of Jesus Christ.[40] It is Jesus Christ, as the fullest revelation of God's will, who is to be obeyed. In the preface to *Rights and Ordinances* Mack writes:

> . . . it may be readily believed that God most certainly wants everything to be kept which He has made known

and revealed to the whole world in these latter times through His beloved Son. . . . However, none of the teachings and ordinances of our Lord Jesus may be considered insignificant, for they were indeed commanded and ordained by an all-powerful Monarch and King.[41]

What is the believer's proper response to the Lord Jesus? The answer for Mack receives an almost monotonous repetition throughout his writings: wholehearted devotion and *obedience*. One can gain a feeling for this constant refrain in the father's final advice to his son in *Rights and Ordinances*:

> Observe well, that the true believers and lovers of the Lord Jesus have always looked steadfastly and single-mindedly to their Lord and Master in all things. They follow Him gladly in all of His commands, just as He has told them to do, and as He has shown them by His own example. They thus learn in their simplicity to understand well the intention of their Master, even in the simplest matters.[42]

Mack's writings can be understood and appreciated only when this backdrop of obedience is kept in view. It is even more important, however, to understand exactly what Mack meant by obedience. Here again the intersection of the inward and outward aspects of faith is evident. Unlike the Radical Pietists, who tended to spiritualize away the need for obedience in external matters of the faith, Mack felt that all the commandments and ordinances of Christ must be observed. Yet, lest obedience become a pharisaical and legalistic bondage to the minutia of Scripture, Mack tempered his concept of obedience with a recognition of its essentially inward nature. Obedience is a joyous and willing search for the expressed wishes of the Lord in order to manifest one's love and devotion for Him. The only passage which Mack underscored in his *Rights and Ordinances* was:

> SON: I well perceive that man should not only heed that which is commanded, but also the Master Himself, and especially His greatness. Therefore all of the commandments of the great God shall be esteemed great.
>
> FATHER: *Yes, that has always been the true faith and the true love of all saints and believers. They have done what God has commanded them to do, and have bowed all of their reason and will before the will of their God. It can be heard or noticed of no believer that he has ever rebelled against a single commandment of God.*[43]

By stressing the subjective side of faith, the Radical Pietists had subordinated the authority of the historic Jesus to the "direct guidance of the Holy Spirit—or one may say the living Christ."[44] The practices of Jesus and the early church were by no means considered normative in themselves. For Mack and the early Brethren, however, outward obedience to "the Jesus of history" and inward devotion to "the Christ of faith" (borrowing some current phrases) were equally requisite for the Christian faith. Full obedience to Christ therefore necessitated the establishment of a *Gemeinde* in order to practice those ordinances instituted by Christ—baptism, church discipline, the Lord's Supper.[45]

As has been suggested, the very existence of this new *Gemeinde* was an issue that needed defense. Gruber's insistence in *Basic Questions* for some direct calling or "undoubted divinity" validating the divine origin of the Brethren caused Mack to buttress their existence further with a Christological argument. For Mack, the fundamental authority for the church's existence was given by Jesus Christ during his earthly ministry. The Brethren wished only "to remain in simplicity and true faith in the original church which Jesus founded through His blood."[46] The true church can always be known by its obedience to the teachings of Jesus which remain in force until He comes again. Mack affirms that the true church (known by its observance of "the true baptism [believers' immersion] and ordinances") has never ceased to exist (he does not attempt to demonstrate his contention). Even though it had but few members at times and though outward baptism may have been discontinued for a time (because of persecution, not because of unwillingness to perform it), yet there have always been some who "walk in the teaching of Jesus, in baptism and the other ordinances."[47] Note that Mack's case for the divine origin of the Brethren has now utilized both the primary apologetic of the Radical Pietists—the direct calling from the Holy Spirit—and that of the Mennonites-Anabaptists—an unbroken line of teachers who have faithfully maintained the doctrine of Christ, especially baptism.

Mack considered Christ to be *the* authority for the church. Other sources of authority do exist for him—the Word, the Spirit, the example of the early church; but they all become channels for communicating the mind of Christ to the church. This Christological orientation by no means lessens the authority of these other modes of revelation; indeed, since they all bear witness to the One who stands at the center of the faith, they derive their authority directly from Him.

Scripture is the church's objective Authority

Although Mack does not specifically deal with the doctrine of Scripture, it is clear from his writings that he is in full agreement with the great Reformation principle, *sola Scriptura*. Not only does Mack note the divine inspiration and authority of Scripture on several occasions, but he underscores the *final* authority of God's Word again and again through such expressions as "the Scriptures say," "as Scripture has said," and "expressed in Holy Scripture."[48] All other would-be pretenders to this position—whether Christian tradition, human reason, private mystical experiences, theological systems, etc.—must be rejected. This view of Scripture is to be expected, for the three strands of Christianity which influenced Mack—Reformed, Pietist, and Anabaptist—all considered Scripture normative and divine.

A perusal of Mack's usage of Scripture reveals that he considered the whole Bible (Old Testament Apocrypha included) important for discerning Christ's will. In the view of Mack and the early Brethren, the whole Bible "witnesses to one divine event and possesses a wholeness and completeness of meaning for the believer that removes the necessity for a fragmentary quoting of this favorite passage or that."[49] Mack severely criticizes those who take "here a verse of the [New] Testament" and there another verse, and with these verses "make love illicitly."[50] This pick-and-choose theology destroys the order and unity that is inherent in God's Word. For Mack there is a definite continuity between the Old and New Testaments. Time after time, in *Rights and Ordinances* especially, Mack traces the origin and development of various practices (the ban, baptism, examination, marriage) in the Old Testament through to their fulfillment in the life and teachings of Christ. Frequently, these Old Testament practices are said to be prefigurations of their New Covenant counterparts. Martin Schrag is correct when he asserts that Mack's "emphasis in the Old Testament-New Testament relationship is fulfillment and continuity."[51]

Even though Mack sees continuity within God's Word, he also recognizes a hierarchy of authority in Scripture which is Christologically determined. As the revelation of God in Christ Jesus and as the clearest indication of the will of Christ, the New Testament has a higher degree of authority than the Old. Also, within the New Testament itself Mack places more weight on the teachings and commandments of Christ (the Gospels) than on the rest of the New Testament. The following quotations will bear out these emphases. In his answer to Gruber's final question, Mack admonishes, "If we remain in the teaching of the New Testament, we expect this outcome, namely, that the fulfillment of our faith will be eternal life." In his letter to Count Charles August, Mack notes that the true Christian should "seek to carry out everything Jesus has commanded and bequeathed in His testament."[52] Although these emphases on the New Testament and especially the teachings of Christ do exist in Mack, they must not be overemphasized. As Schrag cautions, the focus in Mack's writings "is as much in terms of continuity and fulfillment as of subordination."[53] Though Mack's recognition of the underlying continuity between the Testaments could suggest Reformed influence, the way in which he handles the continuity-discontinuity question has more affinities with Mennonite thought.

Mack and the early Brethren accepted Scripture in simplicity, humility, and all seriousness. As Mack indicated, "If man does them [God's commandments] in true faith and in obedience holds his reason captive, he will gradually become single-minded and childlike. It is just in this single-mindedness that the soul finds rest, peace, and security."[54] Vernard Eller describes the early Brethren approach to Scripture as "uncritical (in a scholarly sense)." As "simple, unlettered believers" Mack and his fellow Brethren merely followed the examples of Christ and His disciples in total obedience.[55] At its best, this uncritical, straightforward method of reading the Bible led to the humble acceptance of the teachings of Christ as a means for expressing one's love to Him. At its worst, this method led the Brethren to a narrow literalism and legalism which seem "to make of Jesus' teachings simply another Mosaic code filled with all the . . . casuistry from which Jesus had joyously delivered his disciples."[56] A tendency toward such casuistry can be found in the following quote from *Rights and Ordinances*:

> . . . it may be readily believed that God most certainly wants everything to be kept which He has made known and revealed to the whole world in these latter times through His beloved Son. That is, all who call themselves Christians should live as children of one household. The good Householder [*Haus-Vater*] has given them rules and laws which they are to keep and respect well and prudently. Along with it, He has promised them eternal life, if they will obey Him in all things—insignificant as well as important ones. However, none of the teachings and ordinances of our Lord Jesus may be considered insignificant, for they were indeed commanded and ordained by an all-powerful Monarch and King.[57]

Durnbaugh notes that the very title, *Rights and Ordinances*, reveals an element of legalism. *Rechte*, the word translated as *rights*, carries the meaning *law, statute, rights*—all legal terms.[58] The dangers implicit in such legalism fortunately tended to be counterbalanced by Mack's emphasis on love for God as the foundation for obedience and the necessity of possessing God's indwelling Spirit as the enabler for an obedient life.

Since Mack was not theologically trained, it is not surprising that in his use of Scripture several characteristics of popular Protestant faith appear. Although Mack generally gives New Testament evidence for asserting that an Old Testament practice is a type or "prefigurement" of a practice in the New Covenant, in other instances he fails to provide this proof. For example, he maintains without Scriptural support that the washing of Aaron and his sons prior to their entrance to the tabernacle (Ex. 30:18–20; 40:12) is the same as the believer's entrance into the Lord's church through baptism and confession of faith; that the eighth day of circumcision prefigures believer baptism; that cleansing by water in the Old Testament is the brotherly discipline in the New Covenant.[59] Judged by today's evangelical standards,[60] such interpretation would probably be termed allegorical. Yet it should be remembered that among the common laymen of Mack's time such Christ-centered allegory was accepted; even a man of the caliber of Luther engaged in it.[61]

Another element of popular Christianity that is evident in Mack's writings is his use of the Old Testament Apocrypha. In his writings Mack quotes from the Old Testament Apocryphal books of Ecclesiasticus, Wisdom of Solomon, and Tobit. Mack appears to make no distinction between these books and the remainder of the Bible, citing these books right along with the canonical Scriptures.[62] Since Mack used a Luther Bible, he had ready access to the Old Testament Apocrypha. Luther himself, however, considered that the Apocrypha were "books not to be esteemed as part of the Holy Scriptures, but nonetheless profitable and good to read"[63] (a statement which appeared prior to the Apocrypha in Luther Bibles).

These items of popular faith in Mack's writings only reinforce the fact that Mack (1) interpreted all of Scripture as a continuing revelation of God's will finding fulfillment in Christ and (2) accepted the entire Biblical record as he had it in a simple, straightforward manner.

The Spirit leads the Church

A second avenue used by Mack for discerning the will of Christ is the guidance of the Holy Spirit—the inner Word. In introducing his discussion of the inner Word, Mack focuses on the place of the law under the two covenants. He points out that, whereas the law was external in the Old Testament, it is internalized by the Holy Spirit in the heart of the believer in the New Covenant.

> The Holy of Holies in the ark of the Covenant, in which the tablets of the law lay, now corresponds in the New Covenant to the heart of each true believer. In it undoubtedly lie the tablets of the law of his God. They are written in each believer's heart, not by the hands of men but rather by the Holy Spirit.[64]

The Holy Spirit who dwells within our hearts is the same Spirit who taught, commanded, and inspired the apostles. Since it is the same Spirit, the Word "inwardly written by the Spirit of God is completely identical with that which is outwardly written in the New Testament."[65]

It is precisely at this point of the relationship between the inner and outer Words that Mack confronts the Radical Pietists. At issue are the content of the inner promptings of the Spirit, the necessity of outward actions, and the criteria for judging the inner and outer Words.[66] Mack leaves no doubt that the inward Word must be limited and tested by its harmony with Scripture (note the emphasis on the final authority of Scripture).

> However, when a person says, out of haughtiness alone, that the laws of his God are written in his heart, while he opposes the orders, statutes, and laws which the Son of God and His apostles have ordained (of which the Scriptures testify outwardly) you may be quite sure that he is still of the world. The law which he claims to have in his heart was written by the spirit of errors and lies.[67]

Mack follows in the tradition of Calvin, Spener, and Menno in his view of the role of the Spirit in the understanding of Scripture.[68] For Mack, the Spirit must be present in order rightly to understand the Word. Mack wrote, "No one may say to a believer that he should and must believe and obey the Scriptures, because no one can be a believer without the Holy Spirit, who must create the belief"[69] (both a Reformed and Pietist emphasis). Again he notes, "A man can indeed read the Scriptures outwardly and talk and write about them, but, if the spirit of faith is not in him, he will not be concerned with the commandments therein, nor be frightened very much by the threats which they contain."[70]

Mack felt that the lack of this spirit of faith in a person's life was the key to understanding Jesus' saying, "He who has ears to hear, let him hear." Such a person had not yet had his "inner ears" opened. To those who did not possess the Spirit, the commandments of God would seem burdensome, and they would not be expected to obey them. But,

> . . . when a believing person whose inner ears are opened reads the Holy Scriptures outwardly, he will hear as the Lord Jesus intends His teaching to be understood. He hears that which the apostles want to express in their writings. He will also be impelled, through his inner hearing, to true obedience which makes him obey even in outward matters. Outwardly, he reads the Scriptures in faith and hears the inner word of life which gives him strength and power to follow Jesus.[71]

Mack thus develops a reciprocal relationship between the inner Word (the witness of the Spirit) and the outer Word. A person must possess the inward testimony of the Spirit if he is to understand Scripture rightly. Yet Scripture itself limits and tests the witness of the inner Word. Although Mack affirms the authority of both the inner and outer Words, the end result of the relationship between the two is to emphasize the outer authority, Scripture.[72]

When this reciprocal relationship between Word and Spirit is functioning properly, the tendency toward legalism and literalism can be checked. A principle that Mack and the early Brethren put into practice was their conviction that the community of believers must always strive for further light. The early Brethren had carried over several Radical Pietist excesses (rejection of the married state and of work) into their newly founded brotherhood. However, through continued discussion of Scripture and openness to the Spirit, these excesses were rectified by the body.[73] In addition, by maintaining that sensitivity to the inner witness of the Spirit was imperative for understanding the Scriptures correctly, a discipleship to Christ could result which was heart-felt and vital.

The Holy Spirit further leads the church through the selection of teachers and elders. Mack reflects Arnold's contention that church leadership is to be charismatic and elected. Thus, the faithful church will choose only those men in whom they discern the Spirit of Christ.[74]

The early church provides the normative pattern for the Church

Mack placed special emphasis upon the example presented by the apostles and the Christians of the first and second centuries. Two sources can be discerned for such an emphasis: (1) the Anabaptists, who emphasized the importance of following the example and pattern of Christ and the apostles and of preserving the unbroken line of true teachers who had remained faithful to the doctrine of Christ (continuity) and (2) Gottfried Arnold, who held that the primitive church was the purest representation of

Biblical Christianity and that witnesses of the truth had perpetuated the true church to the present age. Durnbaugh observes that Alexander Mack, Jr., in discussing the developments leading up to the first baptism,

> ... wrote that the early Brethren "felt powerfully drawn to seek again the footsteps of the first Christians." The group, he goes on, asked their leader, Mack, to baptize them "upon their faith after the example of the first and best Christians"—a clear statement that the primitive church was for them normative.[75]

The elder Mack has the father declare to the son in *Rights and Ordinances*: "You have heard about Christ and His apostles, and many testimonies of the early Christians, that they baptized in flowing waters and wells, and that baptism is nothing else but immersion."[76] As intimated in this quote, Mack and his fellow Brethren were interested not only in obeying the example of the early church but also in recovering the precise practices of the early Christians. This desire led Mack to study several contemporary sources in an attempt to find evidence of the early church's baptismal practices. Alexander Mack, Jr., describes the process whereby the Brethren arrived at the practice of trine immersion:

> They found in trustworthy histories that the early Christians during the first and second centuries were planted into the death by crucifixion of Jesus Christ, according to the commandment of Christ, through trine immersion in the water bath of holy baptism. They therefore diligently searched the New Testament, and found that everything agreed with this perfectly. They therefore had an ardent desire to be furthered through this means, practiced by Christ himself and commanded by Him, for the fulfillment of all righteousness, according to His saving counsel.[77]

This passage is significant, for it throws considerable light on the interpretive approach to the Bible used by Mack and the Brethren. Using historical sources from several different theological traditions,[78] the Brethren found the threefold mode of baptism to be of ancient pedigree; then they examined the New Testament and found this mode to be consistent with Scripture.[79] In commenting on this methodology, Chalmer Faw maintains that the practice of the primitive church as found in the histories was actually used as "a commentary on the simple word of the Scripture."[80] This method is entirely in keeping with Mack's hermeneutics, for though the threefold form was suggested by historians, the final authority for its use depended upon its harmony with New Testament guidelines.

Undoubtedly, the desire of the Brethren to follow the New Testament teachings as exemplified by the early church led to the adoption of a number of distinctive practices: feetwashing, the love feast, the holy kiss, the prayer veil, the anointing service for the sick. The Brethren were quite ready to become a "peculiar people" in their quest to recapture the life and virtue of the primitive church.

The church builds up the character of its Members

Though Mack's view of the church will be analyzed thoroughly in a later section, it should be pointed out that Mack considered the church as a kind of proving ground for the development of Christian character. It is to the church, as God's household, that He has given His rules and laws.[81] It is within the context of the church that His kerygmatic ordinances of baptism and the Lord's Supper are to be observed. It is the church itself which Christ and His apostles have commanded to utilize the ban to maintain the purity of the body of Christ.[82] For Mack, the church is an indispensable agency through which and in which "the good Householder" seeks to realize His will.

Summary

When these six sources of authority are combined, they form a framework by which Mack's views of soteriology and ecclesiology can be readily understood. God is a Sovereign Lawgiver and Householder who has revealed His will fully to man through His Son, Jesus Christ. Jesus has left in His teachings a record of those "rights and ordinances" which the Father desires men to obey. The living record of these teachings is to be found in the example of Jesus, the apostles, and the apostolic church as recorded in the New Testament. People are called to respond to Christ in heartfelt faith and obedience and be led by His ever-present Spirit (the inner Word). This Spirit will never direct believers in ways contrary to the will of God, which the Spirit has caused to be recorded in the New Testament (the outer Word). All believers are directed to the church, the household of God, as the place where God's will is to be realized. These presuppositions reveal a unique interplay of Pietist, Anabaptist, and Reformed elements which will likewise be noted throughout Mack's doctrinal discussions.

DOCTRINAL CONSIDERATIONS

The doctrinal synthesis of Mack and the early Brethren

As noted earlier, the polemical nature of Mack's two extant writings should occasion caution in any attempts to place a facile theological label upon the Brethren. Read at face value, these writings yield a conspicuous Anabaptist ecclesiology. Yet given Mack's cultural context, this element should neither surprise us nor blind us to the existence of other more covert elements in Brethren thought. The immediate group with which Mack was interacting was the Radical Pietists whom he was actively seeking to proselytize. Mack did share much in common with the Radical Pietists (heartfelt devotion and obedience to Christ, the necessity of inner illumination by the Holy Spirit to understand Scripture, antipathy for "Babel" and "the sects"—the established religions). But he sought to bring this group into his fold by emphasizing in his writings the one major difference— the necessity for obeying Jesus' teaching concerning the *outward* practices, not just his teaching relating to inward faith (note the title of Mack's writing: *. . . the Outward Yet Sacred Rights and Ordinances of the House of God*). Any formulation of early Brethren theology must take into account the fact that Mack and many of his fellow Brethren were Pietists "at heart" (several reconstructions of Brethren theology have tried to diminish or have even overlooked this Pietistic influence). It is true that the Brethren rejected the mystical and spiritualistic excesses of the Radical Pietists both in Germany (the Inspirationists) and America (the Beisselites), but the Brethren understanding of the individual Christian life retained many Pietistic elements.

It should be reemphasized that the Brethren accepted the great body of evangelical truths held by the Reformation churches. Though Mack does not speak directly concerning the doctrines of God, Christ, sin, and the atonement, yet the fact that he held orthodox views on these loci finds considerable confirmation in the preceding section of Mack's sources of authority. For him these truths were presuppositions which could be accepted without debate, and of course they were accepted by Anabaptists, Pietists, and Reformed—the three main contributors to Brethren thought.

The orthodoxy of Brethren thought can be inferred from one other form of evidence. On several occasions when Brethren, or people closely associated with the Brethren, were arrested in Germany for their disruptive activities (illegal religious gatherings and baptisms), they revealed in their interrogation that they accepted the greater part of the Heidelberg Catechism because, as one man said, "it is taken from God's Word."[83] Nevertheless, the early Brethren were generally averse to creeds due, in part, to the tendency in established churches to equate faith with doctrinal precision (*assensus*) rather than life-changing commitment to Christ (*fiducia*). As one group of imprisoned Brethren stated, "If the Reformed *conducted* [italics mine] themselves according to the Heidelberg Catechism, and if only the infant baptism, swearing of oaths, and the sixtieth question [on justification by faith] were different, we could soon agree with you."[84]

Soteriology: The doctrine of the individual Christian Life

Man's fall and Christ's atoning work

Mack does not explicitly address the question of man's fall and Christ's redemptive work. Yet the few passages that give a hint of his thought on these subjects suggest that he followed evangelical formulations. Concerning man's creation and fall, he briefly states: "Adam was created in Paradise in the image of God. When he was disobedient to God, he lost his divine stature and had to accept the curse and death."[85] The fullest representation of Mack's view of the atonement is to be found in a poem, generally ascribed to him, which was appended to *Rights and Ordinances*. It presents a substitutionary view of the atonement.

The Sin-Expunging Jesus

A pard'ning Lord I am,
In love I will be found.
The Son of God and man,
To heal the sinful wound.
All is now gained,
My death has bought,
And pardon wrought
That you be spared.

Your sin I cast away,
It shall return no more;
Your debt I had to pay,
And suffered for it some.
My blood I gave,
My life I spent,
Through death I went
For you to save.

This have I done for you;
Be faithful then, and true;
Do not depart from me,
I shall be faithful too.
Then watch and pray,
And love me too,
Who first loved you
And am your stay.[86]

The conversion process

Because of the apologetic nature of his writings, Mack offers no systematic study of the conversion process. Yet by piecing together scattered statements concerning conversion, his *ordo salutis* might be schematized as repentance, faith (obedience), baptism, and rebirth (discipleship).

Repentance. Repentance receives very little direct attention in Mack's writings. From Mack's passing remarks about repentance, it is clear that he considered repentance the first step in the conversion process: " . . . the sinner shall repent and believe in the Lord Jesus and should be baptized in water upon his confession of faith."[87] Mack also gives parenthetic acknowledgment to the activity of God in bringing a person to repentance while discussing the necessity of spiritual food for those souls who "have been awakened by grace to repentance."[88]

Faith and obedience. It is on the subject of faith and its corollary, obedience, that Mack rivets his attention. Occasionally, Mack appears to be a true son of the Reformation fathers. Concerning the doctrine of justification by faith, Mack affirms: "Whoever believes in Him [Christ] is justified." Likewise, he emphasizes that faith is the result of the Spirit's activity: "no one can be a believer without the Holy Spirit, who must create the belief."[89] Yet even these notes of Reformation theology are sandwiched into sections where the overwhelming theme is: saving faith "must produce works of obedience."[90]

For Mack the primary characteristic of faith in Christ is that this response to the Lord "produces obedience and submission to all of His words and commandments."[91] If faith is to be saving faith, it "must be proved by love and obedience."[92] Mack's strongest Scriptural evidence comes from the Johannine writings, where keeping God's commandments is frequently seen as an expression of love for God, and the examples of Abraham offering his son (cf. James 2:21) and of Jesus' willingly humbling and submitting Himself to God's will (cf. Heb. 5:7-9).

Though Mack does maintain that true obedience is outwardly evidenced by keeping all the teachings and commands of Christ (referring most frequently to baptism and the ban), he is careful to temper this emphasis with the idea that obedience must always be an expression of our faith in and love for God (see p. 70). It is against this background that some of Mack's statements which appear to border on works-righteousness need to be interpreted. For example, in *Rights and Ordinances*, Mack writes, "God looks only upon obedience, and believers are bound to

obey the Word. Then they will achieve eternal life by obedience."[93] Mack further seeks to guard himself against what might be perceived as a Catholic view of salvation by noting that this obedience is "not according to the pope's doctrine and command but rather by the command of Jesus the crucified."[94]

The theological tension which some of Mack's statements create is due, to a great extent, to his conception of salvation as a process rather than just a one-time, forensic event. Here his view tends to run counter to the Lutheran emphasis on justification by faith alone. Salvation for Mack begins with justification by faith, but saving faith must continually produce obedience (or works), a view which is expounded in James 2:14-26 (Luther's "right strawy epistle"). Understandably, the former Lutheran pastor, Gruber, queries whether such a view will "not produce a new papacy, and bring about salvation by works."[95] Mack's answer to this question is instructive:

> It has been testified sufficiently above that we do not seek to earn salvation with these simple works, but by faith in Christ alone. If it is to be a saving faith, it must produce works of obedience. Where that faith is not present which produces obedience . . . , then no salvation is promised for a single work done without faith.[96]

Though affirming that salvation must be based on faith in Christ, Mack shared with Pietists in general the conviction that salvation is a state which must be continually evidenced in a believer's life by the fruit of the Holy Spirit (obedience and works).

Baptism. This discussion of the role of obedience in the Christian life forms the basis for Mack's understanding of the next act in the conversion process: baptism. His view of the "obedience of faith" is crucial as he considers some serious points of contention with the Radical Pietists concerning the necessity of baptism and baptism's relation to salvation. (The discussion of the meaning and mode of baptism will be considered under ecclesiology.)

The reason for observing water baptism, according to Mack, is that it has been commanded by both God and Christ.[97] Thus, water baptism is a matter of obedience, and therefore is to be observed. "Since then, Christ . . . considers baptism necessary for believers, obedience to this commandment of baptism is also necessary for salvation."[98] Note that Mack does not make a direct connection between baptism and salvation but always mediates the two by the idea of obedience. He is aware that this view could be construed as baptismal regeneration and therefore points out, "Salvation is not dependent upon the water, but only upon the faith, which must be proved by love and obedience."[99]

Rejection of water baptism has very serious implications. First, it means disobedience to God and Christ.

> Whoever opposes God in one thing—even if it is as insignificant as outward baptism—such a person will be properly punished for this disobedience. However, I do not think that a single commandment of the Lord Jesus dare be considered insignificant, if we consider the power and might of the Sovereign without reluctance.[100]

Second, rejection of outward baptism brings into question the very nature of that person's faith (since obedience is an expression of faith).

> If, however, a man does not desire to be baptized, he is rightly to be judged as unbelieving and disobedient, not because of the baptism, but because of his unbelief and disobedience. Christ has rightly said, "He who believes . . ." [Mark 16:16]. If He had made salvation dependent on the water, men would be much more willing to be baptized, and retain their own will in other things.[101]

In this line of argumentation, Mack is employing themes emphasized by the Radical Pietists—obedience and discipleship to Christ (defined by Radicals, however, in terms of an inward attitude, not in terms of New Testament explicits) and the necessity of faith being evidenced by spiritual fruit—against his former associates. He is pressing his point to its limits in *Basic Questions* in order, no doubt, to gain further support among the separatists. It is this setting which must be kept in mind as Mack unequivocally states his case.

Rebirth. Mack's understanding of regeneration is also colored by his emphasis on obedience: "The spiritual rebirth is nothing else than true and genuine obedience toward God and all of His commandments."[102] Though Mack does not discuss rebirth at length, nearly all his statements deal with the subjective side of regeneration—what should happen in the life of the believer who is reborn? Oddly, he does not link the Holy Spirit to rebirth (especially since inner baptism and rebirth by the Spirit were so important to Radical Pietists). Instead, Mack takes a Mennonite tack, by connecting the experience of regeneration quite closely with baptism. To avoid the position of "baptismal regeneration," however, Mack once again mediates rebirth and baptism by the ideas of obedience or faith. "We can, therefore, answer that the desire for obedience toward water baptism is inseparable from the true rebirth. . . . If . . . true faith is present, and the Word is grasped or accepted in the water bath by faith, then a

considerable rebirth or cleansing occurs in the 'washing of water with the word' (Eph. 5:26)."[103] When questioned further by Gruber, Mack also admits that a person may "have attained a goodly proportion of rebirth before water baptism."[104]

The regenerate life should be a process of growth to greater obedience. It involves the use of the will and mind in following Jesus more closely. (In this sense regeneration and discipleship would be parallel terms for Mack.) Mack certainly would not uphold the idea of "eternal security." Rather, the believer's assurance rests on his continued obedience to Christ. Thus Mack admonishes that a believer "may very easily lose again that which he had previously attained [speaking of progress to fuller regeneration]. The food of the new creation, then, for its sustenance and growth, is true obedience to the Lord Jesus."[105]

Testing (examination)

For Mack, an integral part of the believer's growth process is his being tested by God. "This is the divine intention that man, after he has entered into a relationship with his God, is . . . then tested in the commandments of God."[106] This principle is basic to both Testaments. It is evidenced in God's relationships with Adam, Noah, Abraham, and Israel in the Old Testament and with Jesus and the disciples in the New.

Both Spener-Halle Pietism and Radical Pietism saw testing as an essential part of any Christian's life. Such discipline was the purifying fire by which the believer dissociated himself from selfish pride and worldly entanglements and sought by the power of God's Spirit to lead a holy life. Especially for Radical Pietists, however, accountability was essentially to God and not a body of Christians.[107] Mack began with the Radical Pietist understanding of testing but went one step beyond. To be effective, testing must not be merely a subjective experience between God and man; there must be mutual accountability within a committed community if true growth is to take place.[108] Though discipline will be considered as a corporate responsibility in a later section, it is noteworthy that here again Mack combined a subjective emphasis of the Radical Pietists—testing—with the objective counterpart—discipline.

Summary

At a few points in his view of salvation, Mack deviates from Reformation emphases. He avoids a purely forensic view of justification and instead places the greater weight on faith known by obedience and works. Yet he also recognizes the necessity of God's initiative in making salvation available through Christ's redemptive work and the Spirit's working of faith.

Mack's understanding of conversion has affinities with that of Pietism—salvation as a process, faith as a wholehearted devotion to Christ which must produce fruits, testing. Yet his indebtedness to Anabaptism comes through quite clearly in his understanding of faith and obedience, baptism, regeneration, and discipline. It would appear that Mack was simply taking the Radical Pietist principle of total devotion to Christ through to its logical conclusion: obedience must extend to the *outward practices* of the faith as well. The advocates of this line of reasoning were of course the Anabaptists. It should cause no surprise then that Mack's understanding of the corporate personality of the church is thoroughly Anabaptist.

Ecclesiology: The doctrine of the corporate Christian Life

One of the most evident aspects of Mack's turning from Radical Pietism to Anabaptism is his espousal of the necessity of the corporate Christian life. The Pietists had majored on the importance of personal experience; even the conventicles that were a frequent concomitant of Pietism tended to see themselves as small para-church groups designed for their own mutual edification.[109] Mack, however, without denying the importance of inner experience, maintained that the Christian faith should be lived out in community. Illustrative of this conviction is the following quote from *Rights and Ordinances*. Here Mack chides the separatists for their false, spiritualized love and freedom which they used as a pretext for avoiding any organized church and for emphasizing whatever they pleased in Christ's teachings.

> It is true that this uninhibited illicit love covers all, for it is not a marriage with Christ and His church to walk according to His rules [Mack is turning a common Radical Pietist metaphor—marriage to Christ—against them], in which there is no room for illicit love, but rather a love which hates all that is evil, wicked and sinful, if it is not to be false (Romans 13:9). These lovers may be judged and criticized by those who have entered into the marriage with Christ [i.e., the church] and have committed themselves, who edify one another, work, and admonish.[110]

Mack and the early Brethren concreted the concept of love. They had no desire to remain in the above "pernicious hypocritical love" of the Radical Pietists

but desired to fulfill their love and obedience to Christ by observing baptism, the ban, and the Lord's Supper. All of these practices, however, presupposed the existence of a body of committed disciples. It was this belief that led Mack and seven others to covenant together and form the Brethren fellowship in 1708.

Mack does no abstract, theological writing concerning the concept of the church, but deals only with those practices which are integral to Christian community—baptism, the Lord's Supper, and the ban. It is upon these practices that attention will be focused, together with two other issues which were considered important for the faith and life of the community— marriage and the view of the state.

Baptism

Though Mack places most of his emphasis on the controversial aspects of baptism, he does give cursory treatment to his understanding of the general meaning of baptism. Baptism is a rite which is to be administered to those who have responded in repentance and faith to Jesus Christ. Water baptism has been founded and ordained by the Son as "an efficacious seal and outward symbol of all those who would believe in Him."[111] Though Mack denies that water baptism has any power to save, he does view it as more than a naked symbol, connecting baptism (as a seal of faith or obedience) closely to salvation and regeneration. Baptism likewise symbolizes the burial of a person's sins and, according to Romans 6:2-4, his burial into death and his arising to newness of life in Christ Jesus. Finally, citing 1 Corinthians 12:13, Mack notes that baptism represents the believer's incorporation into the church.[112] Perhaps reacting against the Pietistic emphasis on the baptism of the Spirit, Mack almost totally omits any reference to the inward working of the Spirit and how this inner baptism relates to water baptism (with the exception of citing 1 Cor. 12:13).[113]

There are issues which are causing more serious difficulties for Mack and the Brethren than the theological meaning of baptism, however. Mack is in fact waging a three-pronged attack in his discussions of baptism. At issue with the Radical Pietists is the question of the necessity of outward baptism (see pp. 76-77); at issue with the Mennonites is the question of the proper mode of baptism; and at issue with the established churches is the question of believer baptism. It is no wonder that of the forty questions in *Basic Questions*, twenty-three deal with baptism, while of the fifty-nine questions in *Rights and Ordinances*, twenty-nine involve baptism.

Mack disposes of the question of infant baptism more rapidly than he does the other two.[114] He rejects the practice of infant baptism because "there is not a single example" of it "in the New Testament" and because infants are not capable of repentance, faith, or instruction. "The apostles baptized only those who confessed their faith in Jesus through true repentance. Jesus, their Master, commanded them only that those were to be baptized who could be taught before and after baptism [Matt. 28:19-20]."[115]

Mack next considers the arguments raised by Paedo-baptists in favor of infant baptism. He tersely dismisses Matthew 19:14 (Jesus' blessing of the children) by noting "it says nothing of baptism." He then offers a curt response to the argument that households were baptized among which there must have been children: "Only reason says that children must have been among them. The Holy Scriptures do not say a single word about it."[116]

Citing Gottfried Arnold, Mack gives a rather vague summary (the fault clearly is not Arnold's) of the introduction of infant baptism.

> We find in Gottfried Arnold's *Portrayal of the First Christians* that infant baptism began to be practiced only at the end of the second century after Christ's birth. At first, they did it only upon request for those who desired it. Later, baptism was only at Easter. Finally, a certain pope issued an order that no child should die without being baptized. Thus it has prevailed through long-continued custom until everyone now thinks that infant baptism was commanded by Christ.[117]

With his rejection of infant baptism, Mack feels constrained to discuss the issue of the state of children who die without baptism. Mack stresses that "children are in a state of grace because of the merit of Jesus Christ, and they will be saved out of grace"[118] (the usual Mennonite formulation of the problem). To bolster this view Mack relies on an elaborate argument. Mack sees a positive relationship between circumcision and baptism. Circumcision was required by God in the same way that He now requires baptism of Christians. Just as there was no penalty if a child died before the eighth day before he could be circumcised, the same holds true of baptism. In the case of baptism, the "eighth day" refers to the "day on which it could have repented and believed in the Lord Jesus, and could have been baptized upon this, its faith."[119] The promise of salvation still applied to children who died before the eighth day of circumcision or baptism. The source for this

unusual argument with its reinterpretation of the "eighth day" is, no doubt, Anabaptist. Dirk Philips, in fact, employs this very apologetic in his discussion of infant baptism.[120]

Mack now focuses on the question of immersion. He has already, at the opening of *Rights and Ordinances*, shown how water baptism was prefigured in the Old Testament. Although he does not specifically mention immersion in this initial discussion, it is clear from the evidence which he marshals that he has immersion baptism in mind. For example, his evidence from Old Testament prefigurations includes the Noahic flood, in which the wicked were drowned, the lifting of Moses from the water by Pharaoh's daughter, the passage of Israel through the Red Sea, the washing by the priests before entering the tabernacle, and the washings by lepers and women.[121] This opening section concludes with various New Testament arguments. He underscores Jesus' submission to John's baptism, noting also that John was baptizing at Enon near Salim, because there was much water there.[122]

It is at this point that Mack picks up his argument that immersion is the proper mode of baptism. He reiterates the example of Jesus' baptism by John and the fact that baptism took place where there was much water. Mack then has the father address the son: "You should be able to see sufficiently from these two testimonies that if the commandment of baptism could have been fulfilled on dry land, John would not have gone where there was so much water."[123]

Mack reinforces his position with linguistic and historical evidence. He notes, "The Greek word for the command *to baptize* actually means to immerse. It is so translated by most translators."[124] With citations from *Martyrs Mirror*, Jeremias Felbinger's *Christian Handbook*, the New Testament Apocryphal book, the Gospel of Nicodemus (see p. 85), the Mennonite work, *Golden Apples in Silver Bowls*, and possibly Gottfried Arnold's *Abbildung*, Mack adds historical evidence that the early church baptized by immersion.[125]

As Mack did with the Radical Pietists, he again uses one of the presuppositions accepted by his antagonists (the Mennonites): the authoritative nature of Jesus' teachings. Jesus, in the Great Commission, has commanded His disciples to baptize, i.e., to immerse, all new followers of Jesus. Immersion is therefore a directive from the Lord himself.

The conclusion to the case for immersion is an argument derived from the meaning of baptism.

Mack makes the valid proposition that for any symbol to be meaningful the outward symbol should be as similar as possible to the inward essence. Noting that baptism symbolizes the burial of sins, he stresses that the most meaningful representation of burial in terms of water baptism would be immersion, not sprinkling or pouring.[126]

The Lord's Supper

In *Rights and Ordinances* Mack deals with the Lord's Supper immediately after his discussion of baptism (the Lord's Supper is not discussed in *Basic Questions*). As in the case of baptism, Mack decries the incongruity between the way the ordinance was practiced in the early church and the current custom. He provides a detailed exposition of his understanding of the primitive church's observance of the Lord's Supper.

> When . . . the believers gathered in united love and fellowship and had a supper, observing thereby the commandments of the Lord Jesus that they wash one another's feet after the example and order of the Master (John 13:14, 15), yes, when they broke the bread of communion, drank the chalice (the cup) of communion, proclaimed the death and suffering of Jesus, praised and glorified His great love for them, and exhorted one another to bear the cross and endure suffering, to follow after their Lord and Master, to remain true to all of His commandments, to resist earnestly all sins, to love one another truly, and to live together in peace and unity—that alone could be called the Lord's Supper.[127]

Note that, for Mack, the Lord's Supper consists of three parts: feetwashing, the *Agape* or love feast, and the Eucharist. Mack's view of the Lord's Supper is tinged throughout with Anabaptist practices and themes—the observance of feetwashing,[128] the commitment to bearing the cross and suffering, discipleship to Christ, the Supper as the living portrayal of their desire to be a regenerate community. Throughout the history of the Brethren, the Lord's Supper has been *the* occasion when the church proclaimed in existential fashion its beliefs concerning the meaning of the church.

Mack challenges some specific facets of the ordinance, as it was currently practiced, which he felt were contrary to the original pattern. First, attendance at the Supper is to be limited to the regenerate, those who have "separated from the body of Satan, the world, yes, from all unrighteousness, and from all false sects and religions." Second, the rite is to be an *evening* meal, a supper, and not a meal in the morning or at noon. Third, it was to be a *meal*. The

meal should be big enough that people would not need to go away hungry. Fourth, examination should take place before the Lord's Supper; obvious sinners are not to be permitted to partake of the Supper.[129] In typical Anabaptist fashion, the discussion of exclusion from the Supper leads directly to a consideration of discipline and the ban.

The ban

The authority to administer baptism was not the Brethren's sole catalyst for the conviction that some type of formal organization was needed to observe Christ's commands. They also understood that the Biblical teaching regarding brotherly admonition and discipline necessitated the existence of a body of disciples committed to Christ and each other.[130] Thus, it is to be expected that discipline should be second only to baptism in importance in Mack's writings.

Mack broaches the topic of discipline by noting that God's intent for separation between dissimilar elements has antecedents in the Old Testament. He finds the principle of separation present in creation— God separated the intermingled light and darkness into day and night; in the fall—God had to remove man from His presence after man's disobedience; and in the rite of circumcision—those who bore the sign of circumcision were separated unto God and could therefore enter the temple. The principle of separation must apply likewise in the New Covenant. Because in the New Testament the church has become God's holy temple, it is to be "separated from the world, from sin, from all error, yes, from the entire old house of Adam."[131]

It is true, nevertheless, that the church still walks "in a state of humiliation in this wicked world," being tested by Satan through divine permission. This testing is a necessary and positive process, for not only does it test believers' faith and love but it also reveals to the church whether a person truly accepts or rejects discipleship to Christ.[132] Sin can occur in the church if one does not remain in constant prayer and watching.

In the case that sin does enter the church, one of two methods of discipline is to be administered, depending on the seriousness of the sin. If a brother sins "against one of his fellow members or even against the ways and statutes of the Lord," he is to be disciplined according to Jesus' teaching in Matthew 18. No separation need take place unless he "rejects the counsel of the Spirit of God" through his hardness of heart and arrogant pride. If a member commits a gross sin (those listed in Gal. 5:19), however, he is to "be expelled from the church according to 1 Corinthians 5:13."[133] Reminiscent of Dirk Philips and Menno Simons, Mack maintained that expulsion should be accompanied by avoidance in spiritual and physical relationships (at home this meant "bed and board" if the spouse was a member).[134] The purpose of such an extreme measure is twofold: (1) so that the errant brother may be cleansed of his sin "by true penitence and repentance" and (2) so that "the entire body or church is not contaminated by it [the sin]."[135] Ultimately, Mack sees avoidance as an expression of divine love. He laments that, in the case of close friends and family, observance of the ban is difficult because "often natural love is much stronger than divine love."[136]

Mack places special emphasis upon the attitude of believers toward discipline. True believers do not sin intentionally, but if they do unwittingly commit sins they "are truly sorry for it in their hearts.... When they are corrected by their fellow members, they listen very willingly, and allow themselves to be told where they have fallen short."[137] Others, however, who respond "in arrogance and selfishness" to the "discipline of love" in effect exclude themselves from the body by their attitude. Though their sin can be readily forgiven if they repent, they hold themselves outside the community by despising the counsel of the church. Thus it can be that "two men can commit the same sin: one may be lost and the other may attain mercy" simply by their attitudes toward the church's counsel.[138]

The *church* is responsible for ejecting "sinful, offensive, self-seeking spirits" from its fellowship. "Whatever these believers bind on earth, that will be certainly also bound in heaven; what they loose on earth, that will also be loosed in heaven." True believers can exclude and avoid offending members "because they have in themselves already rejected and banned such a mind and spirit."[139]

Mack considers one other issue that is related to the idea of discipline: whether or not the church should examine people carefully before baptizing them. The Brethren had been criticized for accepting persons through baptism, who, in a short time, had to be excommunicated. Mack answers that throughout both Testaments God has to accept people on faith, some of whom later rebelled against Him. The church likewise should accept all on the basis of their outward profession. Only after a man has entered into a relationship with God and His church is that man tested in the commandments of God.[140]

The view of the state

The transition in *Rights and Ordinances* from the subject of the ban to that of the relation between the church and civil government is made with a query (probably hypothetical) by the son: "If then a church conducts a ban and separation for itself, would the civil authorities permit this?" Mack formulates his response along traditional Anabaptist lines:

> Mark well, that this good ordinance is not opposed to the authorities, but, on the contrary, is conducive to the station of civil government. The faithful are taught by Paul (Romans 13:1–7) that they should be subject to the human regulations made by the authorities for the sake of the Lord, who instituted them. They should give the government taxes, imposts, honor, and respect, for all authorities are ordained of God to punish the evil, and to help to protect the good, provided that they desire to carry out their offices in accordance with the will of God.[141]

With regard to the swearing of oaths, Mack simply counsels, "If the true believers affirm with 'Yes' what is 'Yes' and deny with 'No' what is 'No' in accordance with the teaching of Christ, that is much better than many oaths which are mostly sworn and not kept."[142]

When faced with a practical situation in which the dictates of the state violated what he felt to be God's will, Mack demonstrates that he felt obligated to obey God rather than the authorities. In September 1711 Mack was expelled from Marienborn for his baptismal activities there and told not to return. However, he reappeared in Marienborn on two other occasions, once in October 1711! Though Mack's justification for his return is not available, he no doubt shared the sentiments of one of the people whom he baptized: one "must obey God more than the authorities."[143]

Marriage

One of the Radical Pietist excesses on which the Brethren obtained "further light" was the belief that celibacy was a higher form of spirituality and therefore should be observed by all true believers.[144] That marriage was an issue which Mack felt needed continuing clarification among the Brethren as well as defense vis-à-vis the Radical Pietists is reflected in the son's question to the father in *Rights and Ordinances*: "May believers marry, or how should marriage be practiced?" Mack cites several Old Testament passages to show that God has placed His blessing and sanction upon marriage. Mack notes, nevertheless, that God has declared that "the state of marriage must be conducted in purity and in continence, and not in the plague of lust as do the heathen who do not know God."[145]

Though Mack rejected the Radical Pietist belief that true believers should not marry, he did hold a high view of celibacy. He cites Paul's counsel that it would be good for unmarried persons to remain as he, Paul, was (1 Cor. 7:8). "If the unmarried state is conducted in purity of the Spirit and of the flesh in true faith in Jesus, and is kept in true humility, it is better and higher. It is also closer to the image of Christ to remain unmarried.[146]

Mack viewed marriage as a rite which had an intimate connection with the life of the entire faith community. Marriage can be approved only when "it occurs in the Lord Jesus, and is performed in the true belief in Jesus Christ."[147] For Mack, this meant that marriage was to be allowed only within the Brethren fellowship. Confirmation for this belief was found in numerous Old Testament passages which called for the purity of the Israelites in their marriage relationships.

Mack concludes his discourse on marriage with a consideration of two special cases. First, he treats the situation where one spouse is converted and the other is not. Mack advises that in most cases the believing spouse should continue living with the unbeliever. If, however, the unbeliever should commit shameful and adulterous acts, the believer would be justified in leaving "such a vicious person."[148] The second special case is that of adultery. Mack is unequivocal on this point. An adulterer must be banned or else "the entire church would be defiled." The innocent partner would be expected to observe the ban as well. If the person does repent before the church, "he or she could continue to live with the innocent partner. However, it would be unclean to have relationships with each other again, according to the pure mind of God."[149]

Mack's discussion of marriage is instructive, for it provides valuable background for several important facets of early Brethren history. The part that marriage played in dividing the Krefeld congregation has already been noted. The high view of celibacy and the strictures placed upon sexual relationships also help to explain the captivating effect which Conrad Beissel's celibate community of Ephrata had upon many of the early Brethren.

Summary

The conclusion is inescapable that the Brethren view of the church is thoroughly Anabaptist. William Willoughby is entirely justified in claiming that the "Anabaptist pattern of the 'New Testament' Church was taken over by the Brethren almost *in toto*."[150]

The indebtedness is obvious in such aspects as strict discipline, the use of the ban, the concept and practice of adult baptism and communion, the respect for marriage, and the view of the state. Nevertheless, it should be noted that many of these practices had their spiritual counterparts in Radical Pietism and that all of them had been discussed by Gottfried Arnold as being ingredients of the ideal: the primitive church. These spiritualized and idealized Radical Pietist elements were either fulfilled or, in the case of celibacy, toned down by outward "rights and ordinances" of a clear Anabaptist flavor.

Eschatology: *The doctrine of the future Life*

In discussing the doctrine of the last things, Mack's attention is focused on matters of personal eschatology: the reward of believers, the punishment of unbelievers, and the doctrine of universal restoration. (His only mention of Christ's return is in his citation of Revelation 1:7.) Mack vividly contrasts the states of believers and unbelievers. The heavenly existence of believers "is a life of joy which is no longer subject to death and remains everlasting. For eternity there is no illness, pain, fear, want, discomfort, war or disputes; neither weeping nor mourning will be heard." Unbelievers, however, must

> ponder all of these things—how they spent their lives in sin, how they did not love God as the highest good, and lost through folly all this great blessedness. Then they will experience torment, grief, and misery which no tongue can express, for they are banished from the presence of God and all the saints.[151]

It is clear that Mack also believed in the Philadelphian and Radical Pietist doctrine of universal restoration. He writes: "According to the testimony of the Holy Scriptures, 'the smoke of their torment goes up for ever and ever' (Revelation 14:11). However, that it should last for eternity is not supported by Holy Scripture."[152] Nevertheless, Mack stresses that those who are restored will never attain the special status accorded those who chose to follow Christ in this world. He also counsels that this belief "should not be preached as a gospel to the godless." This is because

> Many who have heard about universal restoration commit the great folly not to deny themselves completely but rather hope for the restoration. This hope will most certainly come to naught when they enter the torment, and can see no end in it.[153]

Concluding Observations

It cannot be claimed that Alexander Mack was a religious innovator; he accepted simply and uncritically the sources which were available to him—Scripture, histories, and discussions with Mennonites and Radical Pietists. It cannot be said that he was a skilled theologian and systematician; he was too much of a pastor for that, focusing his attention on the special problems that faced his small flock. What can be stated about Mack is that he was a devoted disciple of Jesus Christ who sought to obey Him and follow Him in every facet of his life. By this plumb line Mack judged the theological terrain (Reformed, Anabaptist, Pietist) on which he was to build the Brethren fellowship.

The theological structure which was erected by Mack and his fellow Brethren must be termed eclectic. Certainly the visible exterior is Anabaptist; but to judge the entire structure by the outside and conclude that the Brethren are primarily Anabaptist (as Durnbaugh tended to do[154]) is too facile. One must also explore the interior of the edifice. Here Radical Pietism is seen to be a significant theme. Yet it should be remembered that the contribution of a third building material—Reformed thought (with which Radical Pietism and Spener-Halle Pietism had affinities)—lies imbedded in the foundation where it is difficult to detect.

The clearest indication that all three of these religious influences played a part in the formation of the Brethren is not to be found by investigating ecclesiology (which is obviously Anabaptist) or soteriology (which contains both Pietist and Anabaptist thought). Instead, one must consider the theological presuppositions Mack brought to these two loci with which the greater part of Mack's writings deal. Though Mack does not explicitly treat the doctrines of God, man, and sin, the sources of authority Mack cites in formulating his views of salvation and the church indicate that these undeveloped subjects are necessary foundations for all that follows. It is in these sources of authority—the sovereignty of God in forming the church, Christ as the Lord of the church, Scripture as the church's objective authority, the Spirit as the Director of the church, and the early church as the normative pattern for the church—that Mack's indebtedness to Reformed thought as well as to Anabaptism and Pietism becomes evident.

It is clear, however, that the actual expression of Brethren faith and practice is primarily Anabaptist and Pietist. Though on this point Brethren scholars are agreed, there was much discussion in the 1950s and 60s as to the way in which the early Brethren mixed these two ingredients. The various formulations were as follows: David Ensign stressed Radical Pietism and minimized Anabaptism, William Willoughby claimed equal influence, Donald Durnbaugh stressed Anabaptism and minimized Radical Pietism, and Vernard Eller proposed a dialectical tension between the two elements.[155] Since the mid-60s a consensus has been reached which Durnbaugh has depicted as a creative tension between Radical Pietism and Anabaptism, balanced on a fulcrum of Protestant faith.[156] This study of Alexander Mack's life and writings would seem to confirm this consensus. The historical and literary sources for the European Brethren reveal that the early Brethren maintained a balance between inward piety and outward obedience, between subjectivity and objectivity. Mack recognized that a vital faith must contain *both* these elements. Eller has located a passage in Mack's writings which clearly reflects this balance.

> That which the Holy Spirit ordained for the faithful was written outwardly. All believers are united in it, for the Holy Spirit teaches them inwardly just as the Scriptures teach them outwardly.... Therefore, when a believing person whose inner ears are opened reads the Holy Scriptures outwardly, he will hear as the Lord Jesus intends his teaching to be understood. He hears that which the apostles want to express in their writings. He will also be impelled, through his inner hearing, to true obedience which makes him obey even in outward matters. Outwardly, he reads the Scriptures in faith and hears the inner word of life which gives him strength and power to follow Jesus.[157]

In the course of this study, it has been seen how the tension between inward and outward expressions of faith was maintained in several important areas: the Holy Spirit (the inner Word) and the Scriptures (the outer Word), inward faith and outward obedience (fruit bearing), the indwelling "Christ of faith" and the exemplar, the "Jesus of history," personal piety and corporate responsibility, subjective testing and corporate discipline. Eller indicates the beauty of this dialectic when it is operating properly.

> The two emphases check and balance each other. When the Radical Pietist tendency would slide off into subjectivism, private inspiration, mysticism, enthusiasm, or vaporous spiritualism, it is pulled up short by the demand for concrete, outward obedience to an objective Scriptural norm. Conversely, when the Anabaptist tendency would slide off into formalism, legalism, biblical literalism, or works-righteousness, it is checked by the reminder that faith is essentially a work of God within the heart of the individual believer, an intensely personal relationship rather than a legal one. Thus, within Brethrenism, Anabaptist

influences *discipline* Pietism at the same time that Pietist influences *inspire* Anabaptism.[158]

Though Mack may be criticized for not maintaining this balance at all times in his own writings (he does tend towards legalism and literalism at points), he has bequeathed to his spiritual descendants a conception of the faith that captures the best elements of Anabaptism and Pietism and places them in a creative and viable tension.

There can be no doubt that Mack avoided many of the extreme ideas and practices of the Radical Pietists. All traces of Boehmism are missing except for the perception of the established church as Babel; Brethren piety is expressed more in terms of discipleship to Christ and ethical preciseness than mystical-spiritualism; celibacy and the refusal to work are rejected as normative states. Yet, as has been noted, Mack by no means rejected all Radical Pietist distinctives; some are integral to his apologetic arsenal. Mack thus begins with the separatist emphasis on total devotion and discipleship to Christ (defined in terms of personal piety) and concludes that obedience should include the outward practices of the faith as well.[159] Even more importantly, Mack borrowed the thought form of an inner-outer dialectic utilized by Hochmann and Arnold to conceptualize many aspects of the Christian life.[160] Though Hochmann's dialectic placed the greater weight on the side of the inner and spiritual, Arnold's dialectic, as developed in the *Abbildung*, showed more balance. Thus he maintained that the inner, spiritual essence of the faith will always express itself in outward, visible ways. However, outward qualities must never supersede the inner meaning; rather they should serve to enhance it. It would appear that Mack not only borrowed this thought form but expanded its use (see p. 83).[161] Unlike either Hochmann or Arnold, however, Mack laid special stress on the objective, corporate side of the faith, feeling, no doubt, that the Radical Pietists in general had consistently overweighed the balance on the side of the Spirit and inwardness.[162]

Radical Pietism thus equipped Mack with some foundational principles which he merely carried to their logical conclusions in Anabaptism. This observation may explain why Mack's practice of using Pietistic principles to his own advantage in his attempts to proselyte the separatists was apparently quite cogent.[163] For Mack, Anabaptism was the logical extension and fulfillment of the principles he had learned as a Radical Pietist. To express this point in a different way, Radical Pietism seems to supply Mack with the presuppositions of his faith; Anabaptism with his ecclesiology.

There are other theological principles in Mack's writings which deserve continuing attention. Mack worked with the concept that contemporary expressions of the faith need to be assessed continually for their faithfulness to the Word of God. No theological tradition—Anabaptist, Radical Pietist, or Reformed—was above scrutiny by Scripture. He therefore criticized the deterioration in life and doctrine of the Mennonites,[164] the private inspiration and asceticism of the Radical Pietists, and the scholasticism and rigid orthodoxy of the Reformed. Yet he firmly upheld the Anabaptist distinctives of obedience, discipleship, believer baptism, and discipline, the Radical Pietist stress on a pious, regenerate, Spirit-directed life, and the Reformed penchant for sound doctrine and "preciseness" in the faith.

The eclecticism of Mack and the early Brethren not only led them to evaluate traditional expressions of Christianity, but it also caused them to remain open to new insights that might be garnered from Scripture through the Holy Spirit's illumination. The fact that the first Brethren were willing to organize themselves into a new fraternity by believer baptism, knowing that such an act would open them to persecution; the fact that they rejected the Radical Pietist excesses with regard to marriage and work; the fact that they did not write binding creeds all suggest that the Brethren lived with the expectancy that God would lead them into new and deeper understandings of the faith. Such a process for discerning truth places a great deal of responsibility upon the entire body—for knowing the content of the faith, for critiquing current forms of Christianity, for individually and corporately being open to the Spirit's direction. Yet it also tends to build Christians who have a mature and strong faith. One of the signs of a gifted leader is the ability to pass on to his people the tools whereby they can carry on the mission. This Mack did, not only by helping to lay out the foundation and the basic form of the church but also by demonstrating in his life various principles which, if followed by later generations, would provide guidelines for the church's future struggle for meaning and relevance.

In many ways Mack was like a trusting parent who, having fulfilled his responsibility in instilling his children with godly virtues and beliefs, must entrust the future of his grown progeny to the care of God.

When asked by Gruber to speculate about the future of the fledgling Brethren movement, Mack replied:

> If we remain in the teaching of the New Testament, we expect this outcome, namely, that the fulfillment of our faith will be eternal life. In return for insignificant shame and suffering, we will obtain immeasurably momentous glory. We cannot testify for our descendants—as their faith is, so shall be their outcome.[165]

Though the divisions and dissensions which have marred the outcome of the Brethren would rend Mack's heart, it is a tribute to him that all Brethren groups continue to look upon him and the early Brethren as their spiritual fathers.

Addendum
The Literary Sources
Utilized by Alexander Mack

The study of the literary sources used by Mack in his two extant writings, *Basic Questions* and *Rights and Ordinances*, is a profitable endeavor for at least two reasons. First, it reveals some of the major influences which shaped Mack's thought, and, second, it reflects upon Mack's abilities as a critical (or uncritical as the case may be) researcher. Basically, Mack's sources fall in three categories: Gottfried Arnold's writings, Mennonite works, and Jeremias Felbinger's *Christian Handbook*.

No doubt, Gottfried Arnold deserves much of the credit for the historical sources cited by Mack as well as some of his theological and ethical insights.[166] In Mack's effort to explain and defend the Brethren mode of baptism, he borrowed some of his key historical sources from Arnold's *Abbildung*. Not only does he twice cite this work by name in *Rights and Ordinances*,[167] but other citations on baptism used by Mack appear in Arnold's work—from Cyprian, the council of Ilibris, Gregory, and Justin.[168]

Mack borrowed heavily from Mennonite sources. His known indebtedness to Mennonite literature includes three works: *Martyrs Mirror* (*Bloedig Tooneel*[169] in Dutch), the Gospel of Nicodemus (or the Acts of Pilate), and *Golden Apples in Silver Bowls*. *Martyrs Mirror* is specifically mentioned by Mack in *Rights and Ordinances*. He cites it three times in one paragraph, giving exact page references, to bolster his case that the ancient church administered baptism by immersion. It is also possible that Mack's reference to the testimony of Justin and Gregory concerning baptism derives from *Martyrs Mirror*.[170]

In the original edition of *Rights and Ordinances*, Mack, while offering historical evidence for immersion as the ancient mode of baptism, includes two paragraphs of evidence purportedly deriving from the New Testament figure, Nicodemus.[171] This material comes from the New Testament Apocryphal book of the Gospel of Nicodemus (or the Acts of Pilate).[172] This work was probably occasioned both by suggestions and statements made by Justin and Tertullian and by the spurious Acts of Pilate officially published under Maximus Daza in 311 or 312 for use against the Christians.[173] Written no later than the fourth century, the Gospel of Nicodemus contains a supposedly official report by Pilate concerning Jesus and reflects a tendency to use the procurator as a witness to the history of Christ's death and resurrection. The influence of the Gospel of Nicodemus was especially strong in the Middle Ages and continued into the Reformation period when the work was translated into German by Philip Ulhart of Augsburg in 1525. It became a part of Mennonite literature through the debates of Marpeck, Schwenckfeld, and Bucer over Christ's descent into hell, one of the sections of the book. William Klassen notes that the Gospel of Nicodemus gained popularity among the Mennonites as a source of Sunday afternoon reading entertainment.[174] One may infer from the manner in which Mack begins his citation from the Gospel of Nicodemus that not only he but his readers were familiar with this work: "Yes, Nicodemus testifies in his description of the crucifixion of the Lord Jesus . . ."[175] The intimate association of the early Brethren with the Mennonites would account for Brethren familiarity with this work.

Mack did not regard this New Testament Apocryphal book as having Scriptural authority, for he placed it in a list of historical sources for immersion. But he was uncritical of the historical veracity of the account. The uncritical, straightforward attitude which Mack evidences in his use of Scripture is likewise true of his use of historical sources. It is interesting that later editions of Mack's *Rights and Ordinances* have left out this reference to the Gospel of Nicodemus (the second edition appeared in 1774).

A second instance of Mack's uncritical acceptance of source materials is also found in *Rights and Ordinances*. In referring to early testimonies on the mode of baptism, Mack attributes the following statement to Tertullian: " . . . they are immersed three times and baptized. This custom was maintained until 801, and the time when Ludovicus was made emperor in 815."[176] Durnbaugh traces this obviously incorrect quotation (Tertullian died around 223 A.D.) to the Mennonite work, *Golden Apples in Silver*

Bowls (1702). The larger passage in this work from which Mack probably lifted his citation is:

> ... thus says Tertullian (in his book *On the Chaplet*): "Those who are to be baptized profess there, and also some time previously in the church before the bishop that they renounce the devil, his pomp and angels; after this they are immersed three times and baptized." Renan notes at this passage that the old custom was that the adults were baptized and washed with the bath of rebirth, [and that] this custom was maintained until the time of Charles the Great, Ludovici the emperor, in the year 801; Ludovicus became emperor in the year 815 after Christ's birth.[177]

Durnbaugh certainly seems correct in concluding that "the similarity between the passage in the Imbrioch writing and the incorrect quotation by Mack is so striking that there can be little doubt that Mack condensed his quotation from the earlier Anabaptist publication" and, in the process, incorrectly attributed to Tertullian the note of Rhenanus.[178] Incidentally, the only two statements in Mack's writings which testify that early baptism was by trine immersion come from Mennonite sources: the Gospel of Nicodemus and *Golden Apples in Silver Bowls*. Also of note is that all three Mennonite sources were reprinted in America at the Ephrata Cloister: *Golden Apples in Silver Bowls* in 1745, *Martyrs Mirror* in 1748–51, and the Gospel of Nicodemus in 1748 and 1764.[179]

A third major source used by Mack was Jeremias Felbinger's *Christian Handbook*. Mention has already been made (see p. 58) of Mack's probable use of Felbinger to demonstrate that baptism means immersion. Equally substantial evidence for Mack's indebtedness to Felbinger results from a comparison of the historical sources cited by both men in their argument for the historical priority of immersion over other modes. Both men include statements by Bede, Wallfried Strabo, and Honorius Augustodunensis (among others). Felbinger's and Mack's wording of each of the three quotations is almost identical in the German and the order of the three is identical with the three following one upon the other in Felbinger's work and the first two quotations being separated from the Honorius Augustodunensis quote in *Rights and Ordi-*

nances only by the quotation from the Gospel of Nicodemus. Such a coincidence would seem to indicate that Mack borrowed these quotations from Felbinger.

On the basis of the literary sources used by Mack, it is clear that influences from both Anabaptism and Radical Pietism (Arnold's works) were strong. These two movements alone are sufficient for explaining the derivation of most of Mack's thought. Nevertheless, citations from the works of Jeremias Felbinger suggest contributions from another theological tradition: the Polish Brethren. The analysis of Mack's thought in this chapter reveals no Socinian influence on Mack's view of anthropology and soteriology, but he clearly can find support for the Brethren view of baptism, communion, discipline, and oath-taking in Felbinger's work. As Durnbaugh concludes, though proof of direct ties to the Polish Brethren "would hardly change the interpretation which emphasizes the predominance of Radical Pietist and Anabaptist strands in the Brethren fabric, it could provide a striking accent."[180]

This brief study provides further evidence that Mack was a foreigner to the domain of the academic world. The same uncritical (in a scholastic sense) attitude which Mack brought to Scripture is seen in his selection and citation of historical sources. He relied upon the testimony of others more qualified than himself to guide him in his pursuit of knowledge concerning Scriptures. Even though he did reveal a lack of theological and historical expertise at points, this shortcoming does not detract from the principle which motivated his search of the historical sources: Mack sought to come to a deeper understanding of the meaning of Scripture by learning how the early Christians expressed and practiced their faith. These historical works became a valuable commentary on the Scriptures, not as authorities alongside of the Word, but as aids to illuminate the Word's intent. Appreciation of this point again underscores Mack's high regard for Scripture and his desire to apply the Scriptures in order to follow more closely the footsteps of Christ.

Chapter 6

THE CRYSTALLIZATION OF THOUGHT AND PRACTICE IN AMERICA

Historical Developments in America

Between 1719 and 1735 most of the adherents of the fledgling Brethren movement in Germany emigrated to America. Though there are some references to Brethren in Europe as late as the 1770s, most of the remaining members of the brotherhood either merged with the Pietistic circle surrounding Terstee-gen or joined similar groups such as the Mennonites.[1]

The initial group of Brethren emigrants from Krefeld arrived in the Quaker-directed colony of Pennsylvania in 1719. Some families settled in the vicinity of Germantown, while others moved farther inland, into the "back country," in search of cheap land. Oddly, the Brethren held no worship services until 1722 when Peter Becker (1687–1758) and two others visited the scattered Brethren and told them of their intention to hold services in the fall of 1722 at Germantown. Though the lingering memories of the dissension at Krefeld may have contributed to this delay in organization, other significant factors were, no doubt, the difficulties posed by getting established in the new land and by the dispersion resulting from the search for land. The meetings, discontinued during the winter because of difficult traveling conditions, resulted in a revival of spiritual fervor in 1723. As a result of this revival, six individuals asked to join the group by baptism. This request presented a problem for the Germantown Brethren, for, without an ordained minister, they did not consider themselves a fully organized congregation. However, after due deliberation, they chose Becker as their first minister. The baptisms and an accompanying love feast were held on December 25, 1723, the date which is recognized as marking the reactivation of the Brethren movement in America.[2]

In the fall of 1724 the entire male population (numbering fourteen) of the Germantown congregation conducted an evangelistic tour into the wilds of "Penn's Woods." This effort led to the organization of two new congregations, Coventry and Conestoga. The bright prospects for continued expansion were dimmed for a time by a division within the young brotherhood. One of the converts at Conestoga was Conrad Beissel (1690–1768), a charismatic speaker and leader. Due to his native abilities, he was elected as the leader of the Conestoga congregation, and all went well for a while. Soon, however, Beissel began to preach his own distinctive form of Christianity which combined Boehmist and Radical Pietist tendencies such as celibacy and direct revelation (as superior to Scripture) together with Sabbatarianism and monasticism.[3] The introduction of these practices led to a split in the Conestoga congregation in 1728. Repeated efforts by the Germantown Brethren and Alexander Mack, after his arrival in 1729, were unable to effect a reconciliation.

In 1732 Beissel and his followers moved farther into the wilderness and established the monastic community of Ephrata in present-day Lancaster County. The monastic and cultural achievements of Ephrata (singing, printing, the illuminating of manuscripts) became renowned on both sides of the Atlantic.[4] Ephrata reached its zenith in the middle decades of the eighteenth century but was in decline by the end of the century due to Beissel's death, the inroads of civilization, and the spread of epidemic diseases caused when the community turned the institution into a hospital following the Battle of Brandywine in 1777. Its last members died in the nineteenth century.

Especially during its peak years, Ephrata had great appeal for those Brethren who yearned for closer personal communion with God. By the mid-1730s much of the initial zeal of the Brethren movement had died down.[5] In 1735 a pietistic revival, centering around Stephen Koch (1695–1763) and Alexander Mack, Jr. (1712–1803), occurred in the Germantown congregation. A number of leading figures in the congregation who were touched by this revival spirit, including Koch, Valentine and Alexander Mack, Jr., Ludwig Höcker, John Hildebrand, and John Henry Kalcklöser, a minister, ultimately went to Ephrata in 1739. Similar defections from other German religious groups (notably the gifted Reformed minister, John Peter Miller) testify to the mystical appeal of Ephrata and its visionary leader.

Even though the Ephrata movement and the Brethren eventually developed a relationship in which they agreed to disagree with each other, the haughty attitude of the Cloister toward the Brethren is reflective of the general Radical Pietist critique of the Brethren. Note the illuminating distinction between the groups made by the *Chronicon Ephratense*:

> Those who know how the affairs stood between the two congregations know also that a close union between them was impossible; for they were born of diverse causes, since the one [the Brethren] had the letter as its foundation, and the other [Ephrata] the spirit; and while both had the same Father, they had different mothers.[7]

To both the Ephrata Brethren and the Radical Pietists, who shared a common mystical-spiritualistic piety, the Brethren emphasis on outward obedience to the "letter," i.e., Scripture, could lead only to legalism and sectarianism.[8]

In spite of the Beissel schism, the Brethren continued their outreach into the colonies. The focus of their evangelistic activity was the German settlers of Mennonite, Reformed, and Lutheran background.[9] By 1770 there were at least fifteen churches in Pennsylvania, one in New Jersey, and seventeen others scattered in the colonies of Maryland, Virginia, North Carolina, and South Carolina. Morgan Edwards, who collected materials for a history of Baptists in America and from whose research the preceding statistics are derived, compiled in 1770 a list of over fifteen hundred baptized members and forty-two ministers.[10]

A significant part of the literary and political life of the Brethren was wrapped up in the careers of the Christopher Sauers I, II, and III. Sauer I (1695–1758) established a printing concern in Germantown which made available newspapers, almanacs, and Bibles to the German-speaking colonists. Though he never joined the Brethren, remaining a confirmed Radical Pietist all his life, Sauer I did much of the printing for the Brethren and guided the political course of the Brethren and other peace groups during the Indian Wars of the 1750s. His son, Sauer II (1721–1784), did unite with the Brethren and became a prominent minister in the Germantown congregation. Sauer II continued the printing establishment and became one of the wealthiest men in Pennsylvania at the time of the Revolutionary War.

During the Revolution the Brethren, together with the Mennonites and Quakers, experienced various degrees of persecution and harassment for their refusal to bear arms for and swear allegiance to the revolutionary government. Sauer II had all of his property confiscated and suffered physical abuse. (Unlike Sauer II, who tried to give no offense to either side, his son, Sauer III [1754–1799], became an active Loyalist though he did not bear arms.) Other Brethren were fined heavily for refusing to bear arms, and some even refused to pay the fines voluntarily, insisting that they be taken from them by force. The Brethren position was based upon their firm belief in nonresistance (which had brought about the massacre of dozens of Brethren settlers during the Indian Wars) and in forsaking all oaths. The Brethren refusal to take the oath of loyalty to the new government naturally resulted in the charge that they were Tories. In actuality, the Brethren did feel a debt of appreciation toward the British because of the religious freedom and the opportunity for material prosperity realized under the Crown's rule. In addition, either they or their fathers had affirmed their loyalty to the Crown when they entered the colonies (the Brethren made a distinction between swearing and affirming). In response to the shifting political and military scene, the Brethren formulated the following policy in 1779 (borrowing Durnbaugh's summarization): "Where a government did not have clear *de facto* power, it was obvious that God had not definitely spoken. Therefore, the prior allegiance should be maintained."[11] Church discipline was brought upon those who allowed themselves to be forced into mustering or into taking the oath of loyalty to the revolutionary government. Though some Brethren historians have overemphasized the effects of the Revolutionary War experience on the Brethren, it did tend to increase their withdrawal from worldly affairs and gave added impetus to their migration to new territories.

The Individual and Corporate Lives of the Colonial Brethren

THE PERSONAL DEVOTIONAL LIFE

That a strong pietistic undercurrent continued to flow in the lives of the eighteenth century Brethren in America can be discerned from a number of vantage points: individual testimonies, pietistic revivals among the Brethren, Brethren devotional literature, pietistic themes in Brethren thought, and an appreciation of certain mystical traditions.[12]

The personal testimonies of Stephen Koch, Alexander Mack, Jr. (related by Koch), and George Adam Martin reveal spiritual struggles reminiscent of those of Francke and Wesley. Koch's experience is especially noteworthy. Reflection upon the death of a close brother in the faith caused Koch to be overwhelmed by the conviction that he himself had not yet attained a true relationship with God. His "breakthrough" came during a vision on May 3, 1735.

> While I lamented thus to God it seemed to me as though suddenly a flame of God's voice struck me, which entirely illumined me inside, and I heard a voice say to me: "Yet one thing thou lackest." I asked, "What is it then?" The answer was, "You do not know God, and never have really known him." I said, "Yes, that is so; but how shall I attain to it?" Then it seemed as though I were beside myself. But when I came to myself again, I felt an inexpressibly pleasing love to God in my heart; and on the other hand all anxiety, with all the temptations of the unclean spirits, had vanished. Yea, it seemed as if all my transgressions were pardoned and sealed, and day and night there was nothing else in my heart but joy, love, and praise to God.[13]

Peter Becker's opposition to the pietistic revival occasioned by Koch's experience indicates that a more sober form of religious expression was settling in among the Brethren. Yet the steady growth in the number of Brethren congregations and members during the eighteenth century manifests a continuing concern for evangelism.

During the colonial period, the Brethren composed a remarkable amount of devotional material including hymns and edifying works. One recent anthology of American poems written in the German language includes the works of no fewer than eleven Brethren.[14] Prominent themes in this devotional literature include the cultivation of loving communion with God, the denial of self and the world, perseverance in the Christian life, faithful discipleship to Christ, eternal salvation and judgment, and frequent reference to Christ's life and work—Jesus is our preeminent example; Christ is our Redeemer, Reconciler, Mediator, and the Restorer of the divine image; and the blood of Christ was shed for our forgiveness and redemption (a substitutionary and sacrificial view of Christ's death is found in several places).[15] There are also several examples of Christ-mysticism in this literature, using the common Radical Pietist imagery of the soul as the bride of Christ (though one does not find the sensual language that accompanies this imagery in much Radical Pietist devotional literature).[16]

Radical Pietist concepts and phrases continue to appear in Brethren literature of the colonial period, though by no means as frequently as in the literature of Ephrata. The confessional churches continue to be labeled as "Babel," the Philadelphian schema of church history and eschatology is retained, enlightenment of one's understanding is still needed for true spiritual sight.[17] A Radical Pietist phrase which Hochmann at times used is especially common in Brethren correspondence during this time. Frequently, Brethren begin or close their letters with the greeting: "I kiss you in the spirit."[18] This expression of warm brotherly love, derived no doubt from the practice of the holy kiss, is suggestive of the invisible, spiritual brotherhood which Hochmann sought to foster.

A most intriguing passage from the hand of Alexander Mack, Jr., who returned to the Germantown congregation by 1748, reveals a number of concepts common to Radical Pietists. The passage, the opening paragraph of his preface to his father's reprinted works (1774), sounds strikingly similar to Arnold's counsel to his readers in the forewords of his *Abbildung*:

> Kind and dear reader, whoever thou art, into whose hand this little book may come:
> Just as it may contribute much to apprehend usefully the true sense of a treatise, when a person is considering the testimonies contained therein with *an impartial mind* and with *a sincere love for the truth*, to *compare them* prayerfully (invoking divine mercy) *with the testimonies of the apostles and prophets* that he may examine them in an humble spirit;—so it is on the other hand very hurtful, when *one prepossesses with prejudice*, permits himself to be carried away inconsiderately by *a prematurely judging spirit*; as by so doing the truly noble spirit of investigation is in a manner locked up, and *real wisdom remains hid*, and then nothing but darkness and confusion are revealed from the fountain of human selfishness, and these cause such a state of moral night, that he who walketh in it, stumbleth and Christ himself and *the testimony of his everlasting truth* become to such a man a stone of stumbling and a rock of offense.[19] (Italics mine.)

One other indication of a continuing pietistic legacy is the Brethren attitude of ambivalence toward mystical experience. This attitude has already been seen in relation to Ephrata, and it is also evident in the celebrated Catherine Hummer affair. Catherine, the daughter of a minister in the White Oak church, experienced visions for a period of several years. The markedly divided opinion about her visions caused the Brotherhood to adopt a mediating position at the 1763 Yearly Meeting:

Although we have no consensus about the occurrence in question, those who believe in it are not to judge those who do not. Likewise, we shall not look down on those who derive some lesson and benefit from it. In general, we admonish you, beloved brethren, to receive one another as Christ received us, and to forgive one another as Christ has forgiven us also.[20]

Though the Brethren were opposed to mystical experiences or writings which claimed an extra-Biblical authority, they seemed to have accepted mystical literature if it was of an edificatory nature (as above). Works by such men as Arndt, Tauler, and à Kempis, with their emphasis on fellowship with and devotion to Christ, the importance of self-denial and humility, and the Christian's responsibility to God and his fellowman, were popular among the Brethren.[21] Mystical and pietistic devotional literature was readily available for the German-speaking colonists, for both the Sauer and Ephrata presses majored in such works.[22] This literature included works from a variety of pietistic and mystical traditions—Lutheran, Mennonite, English Puritan, Boehmist, Philadelphian, Radical Pietist, Quietist, medieval mystical—as well as several New Testament Apocryphal writings—the Gospel of Nicodemus and the Apostolic History of Abdias.[23] All of the above pietistic influences created for the individual member a devotional, semi-mystical religious atmosphere in which he was constantly reminded of his relationship and duties to his Creator and his fellow man.[24]

THE CORPORATE LIFE

Just as important as the cultivation of inward piety for the colonial Brethren was their relationship to the covenanted community. This emphasis is reflected in the criticism by a former member of the Ephrata Community, Henry Sangmeister (1723-1785?): "these blinded people [the Brethren] say, man cannot live without community."[25] Expressions of brotherly love and admonition for the members of the body to love and serve one another, to care for each other's temporal and spiritual needs, and to forbear and prefer one another in love are replete in the literature.[26]

Due to the greater availability of sources, the picture of the formal organization of a Brethren congregation during this period is more complete than that of the European phase. The early Brethren observed congregational government. A typical congregation would have had deacons and "ancient widows" as deaconesses. The ministry was composed of the exhorter and the ordained elder (or bishop). The deacons and elders were elected on trial and

had to prove themselves worthy during a period of probation (usually several years) before being ordained with the laying on of hands (the other officers may also have been installed with the imposition of hands).[27]

Initially, the Brethren met in private homes for their worship services, consciously following the pattern of the primitive Christians according to Morgan Edwards.[28] Though the first plain meetinghouse appeared in 1770 at Germantown (Quaker and Mennonite influence is to be noted here), such worship centers were not generally accepted until the 1830s and 1840s. A rare glimpse of Brethren worship practices is offered in a book entitled, *The Alert Traveller through Europe and America*. Written by an anonymous Radical Pietist in 1761, it presents a critical, but informative, caricature of a typical service as well as some remarks on the character and ordinances of the Brethren. The writer observes that the Brethren meetinghouse in Philadelphia

struck the eye because of its beautiful paint. Above the door was a lamp which had been overturned, with this inscription:

We sing and preach with great outcry;
If only the Spirit could be thereby.

These people seem rather peaceful and modest in their conduct. Their clothing is middle-class [*bürgerlich*]. Most of the men wear beards. They do not tolerate infant baptism. When they become adults, and wish to be baptized, they go where there is water and are immersed three times. They hold communion or love feast often. Their meetings are zealous and their preaching and praying often take place with great clamor, as if their God were hard of hearing. One hymn chases another as if they lack [inner] silence. They teach their cherished truths after the letter.[29]

Screening out the critical tone of the portrayal (the Radical Pietist complaint is clear: the Brethren, with their emphasis on external practices and Scripture, have lost the Spirit), one may conclude that the Brethren had zealous and enthusiastic preaching and praying in their meetings, enjoyed singing,[30] and used Scripture to defend their basic tenets.

The Brethren generally discouraged baptism until the later teens or after marriage in order to be sure the applicant was fully aware that baptism involved both faith in Christ and the surrender of one's life in complete obedience to Him. A typical baptismal service began with the reading of Matthew 18:10-22 (with the focus on the covenantal responsibility of giving and receiving exhortation and discipline in verses 15-20)[31] and the singing of a hymn. The applicant then kneeled in the water (one account suggests that the questioning was done while the applicant was standing) and was asked: (1) if he believed Jesus Christ was the Son of God; (2) if he rejected totally the devil, the world, sin, and all hypocritical worship; and (3) if he would remain faithful to Jesus' teaching to his death. He was then immersed forward three times. The laying on of hands and prayer were performed while the person was still in the water. When he arose, he was given the kiss of peace.[32]

The love feast or communion was held at irregular times, with the interval between observances being sometimes well over a year.[33] During the colonial period some major changes occurred in the order of the three parts of the communion service. The order as originally practiced in Germany and until at least 1736 in America[34] was love feast, eucharist, and feetwashing. It was then changed to love feast, feetwashing, eucharist no later than 1755[35] and sometime around 1770 it became feetwashing, love feast, eucharist. Mack, Jr., explains that this latter change occurred "after Reitz had published his New Testament [translation], and a brother joined us who knew Greek and properly explained to us that Jesus washed the feet before supper."[36] This willingness to alter the practice of the ordinances whenever new light became available is one of the remarkable traits of the colonial Brethren.

The maintenance of the character of the church through discipline continued to be an important aspect of the community's life. In assessing the application of discipline by the Brethren during this period, Durnbaugh concludes:

> The impression is given of firm but brotherly action designed to correct errors, while conserving the unity of the Brotherhood. Great respect for individual personality was paired with keen criticism of dubious action and improper attitude.[37]

Controversy did arise, however, over the use of the ban. George Adam Martin reveals that the question of the ban was continually a source of contention at the Annual Meeting. Abraham Dubois (1679–1748) and Michael Frantz (1687–1748) advocated a strict application of the ban with avoidance, while Martin sought a more moderate form of discipline. Martin's disagreement with the Brethren on this and other points resulted in his being placed under the ban along with about sixty others who would not observe avoidance in relationship to him. Ultimately, he aligned himself with the Ephrata Brethren.[38] Given the mixed composition of the early Brethren—Mennonite, Reformed, Radical Pietist, Lutheran—such disagreements would seem inevitable. Yet, to the credit of the Brethren, a warm, loving fellowship was evolving throughout this period which was learning to forbear one another in love until a consensus of thought could be reached on controversial issues.

Relationships with other Religious Bodies

The German culture and "plain" life style of the Brethren inclined them to having recurrent interaction with three other religious bodies: the Moravians, Quakers, and Mennonites. This interaction led the Brethren on one hand to the adoption of several features characteristic of these groups and on the other to closer definition of their own faith.

Brethren practice was influenced by both the Quakers and Moravians during the colonial period. Indebtedness to the Quakers is to be found in the plain style of dress, meetinghouse architecture, and some of the terminology connected with the yearly meetings (for example, the terms "query," i.e., an item of business brought before the meeting, and "Annual Meeting"). The initial impetus, however, for the holding of yearly meetings seems to have been a direct response to the ecumenical councils sponsored by Count Ludwig von Zinzendorf and the Moravians in 1742.[39] These conferences, to which representatives from the various German religious groups in Pennsylvania were invited, were designed to effect greater unity among the German sectarians and ultimately form them into "the Congregation of God in the Spirit." Each of the groups in time withdrew for varying reasons.[40] George Adam Martin explains how Zinzendorf's synods served as a catalyst for the Brethren yearly meeting.

> We consulted with each other what to do [after sensing Zinzendorf's ulterior motives], and agreed to get ahead of the danger, as some Brethren had already been smitten with this vain doctrine, and to hold a yearly conference, or, as we called it, a great meeting, and fixed at once the time and place. This is the beginning and foundation of the great meetings of the Brethren.[41]

The Pietistic zeal of the Brethren was especially appealing to the quieter Mennonites. The great similarity in faith and ordinances between the two groups made the transfer relatively easy. Even the one major difference in practice between the two groups, the mode of baptism (Mennonites baptized by pouring), could serve the Brethren as a means for proselyting Mennonites. Morgan Edwards reports many Mennonites "desired a restoration of *immersion* and have gone off to the Tunkers for want of it."[42]

The tension and strife between the Mennonites and Brethren that are evidenced quite frequently in Brethren sources from the eighteenth and nineteenth centuries are no doubt due to the similarities shared by the two exclusivistic groups[43] and their propensity for settling in the same areas—beginning in Germantown and Lancaster County and continuing in the migration of both groups to Virginia, Ohio, and Indiana. It is instructive to note the conclusion concerning the Brethren rendered by Zinzendorf's General Synod:

> The Dunker Church [*Täuffer Kirche*] failed to prove its origin and by this very fact demonstrated sufficiently that they have nothing to do with the Anabaptists who were condemned by the Augsburg Confession. It is a congregation of God-fearing folk, who act after their conscience but without illumination, who are earnest and therefore appealing people. We would consider it only natural if they united with the Mennonites and came to an agreement about the method of baptism. That would make one sect less in the country.[44]

Apparently, the difference in the mode of baptism was the only significant barrier between the two groups from the Synod's perspective.

Doctrinal Developments

Brethren doctrine underwent further refinement during the colonial period. The refinement process occurred as the Brethren continued to test their thought and practice against the new light gained from Scripture and contemporary literature and as they interacted, sometimes heatedly, with other groups. This discussion will therefore focus on areas of thought where the Brethren developed more fully the basic structure laid out by Mack, Sr., and on the literary debates engaged in by the Brethren.

SCRIPTURE

The Brethren continued to show a strong commitment to Scripture, so much so that their Radical Pietist and Quaker contemporaries criticized them for following a "dead letter." Typical of the Brethren regard for the outward Word is the view expressed by the anonymous writer of *A Humble Gleam*. The treatise was written in response to a booklet penned by the Quaker, Benjamin Holmes, and dealt with three key issues: Scripture, conversion, and baptism. The opening statement in the discussion of Scripture is: "The Holy Scriptures is [sic] a letter of God which He has written to the human race through the operation of His Eternal Spirit."[45] Priority is given to

the New Testament because it has been confirmed and sealed through Christ's death (a Mennonite concept). Scripture must be read with a prayerful, contrite heart. "This is so that the entire New Testament is written into the heart of the reader by the finger of God in which one can read all of the commandments of Jesus Christ (2 Corinthians 3:3)."[46] The writer also insists that Scripture be understood contextually. He notes that the tract to which he is responding contains "many beautiful and glorious scriptural passages . . . , especially if the reader took enough trouble to look these up in the Holy Scriptures, where they are all in their proper context, so that every well-disposed, sincere soul can easily find the correct meaning from what precedes and follows."[47]

A treatise by Mack, Jr., on feetwashing which was appended to the 1774 edition of his father's writings is a second source for the Brethren understanding of Scripture. Of greatest importance are the principles of Scriptural interpretation demonstrated in this work. True to the Pietist heritage, Mack, Jr., insists that spiritual enlightenment of one's "eyes, mind, and understanding" is required for the true discernment of Scripture.[48] A Pietist theme is also present in his desire to remain open to new truth. Speaking for the Brethren, he held that they wanted to avoid the temptation of conforming their interpretation of Scripture to their received tradition: "we do not intend to rest upon old practice but the word of the Lord alone is to be our rule and guideline."[49] Durnbaugh observes that Mack, Jr., placed two strictures upon the openness to "new revelations of God's truth": "such revelation would of necessity be in harmony with the Scripture" and "the agreement of the Brotherhood would be brought into play in establishing new understandings."[50]

The principle of being open to new truth based on Scripture bears upon several other traits characteristic of the Brethren. They accepted differences of opinion on questions of *adiaphora* as long as the unity of the body was not disturbed. In a letter to John Preisz, dated October 23, 1798, Mack, Jr., stated:

> Although I have diligently read your letter several times in the fear of the Lord, I still cannot say that all of the Scriptural texts which you quote make the same impression on me as I understand they made on you. What am I to say? The flowers in the garden are quiet and peaceful even though one is embellished in blue, another in red and still another in white. They peacefully praise their creator and laud in complete harmony the manifold wisdom of the being of all beings. One praises thee, God, in the quiet of Zion.[51]

This freedom of expression allotted to the individual, a trait which probably derived from the Pietist antipathy for "coercion of conscience," existed in dynamic tension with a strong desire among the Brethren for corporate responsibility and unity. The working out of the tension between these two characteristics is exemplified in the Brethren method of resolving conflicts. When differences of opinion arose on questions of practice and there was no consensus of thought leading to a resolution of the problem, the Brethren generally counseled the various sides to "bear with" one another until an acceptable solution was found (see pp. 89-90). Evidently, there was a high regard for brotherhood, peace, and love which superseded any desire for quick solutions to pressing problems. Mack, Jr., gives eloquent testimony to this principle in discussing the logistics of changing the order in which the various parts of the Brethren communion service were observed.

> Yet I say this, that if I came to a brotherhood which wished to have breaking of bread and the elders of that brotherhood did not acknowledge other than that the feetwashing should be after the supper, I would participate quite simply in love and peace and would nevertheless explain it to them according to the Scriptures. I would wait in love and have patience with them until they too gained this insight . . . [52]

The Brethren exhibited one other Pietist trait in relation to their understanding of Scripture: antipathy for autonomous reason.[53] Mack, Jr., following the sentiments of his father, maintained that the greatest honor for reason is when it is "in the bonds and shackles of the heavenly wisdom"; outside this captivity, reason is an "outlawed harlot" which seeks to control Scripture.[54]

CHRISTOLOGY

A doctrine which caused some controversy among the colonial Brethren was belief in Christ's celestial flesh, derived, no doubt, from the Mennonites. George Adam Martin relates that he was involved in a dispute over this question with Abraham Dubois and, in particular, Michael Frantz. Frantz reportedly maintained that Jesus "had not received more from the Virgin than a wanderer who passes through a town receives from the town; or than a ball which passes through a gun, or the water which runs through a pipe."[55] Martin, at Martin Urner's urging, openly challenged Frantz. He notes that it was "two days before this Mohammedan Goliath was slain." Martin's account strongly suggests that Mack, Sr., also held the celestial flesh idea.[56] Frantz's advocacy

of this belief is corroborated by two stanzas of poetry in a collection of doctrinal writings, in both prose and poetry, which was published posthumously.

163. His body has no sinful error
Nor anything corruptible, says Scripture,
Decay has not touched Him
He ascended to heaven together with his body.

165. Thus will I not also believe
Then only as Scripture states quite clearly
That when Jesus came from heaven
He possessed nothing from human seed.[57]

As the first stanza intimates, Frantz's espousal of this doctrine was an attempt to remove any possibility of Christ having a part in sinful flesh. This, of course, was Menno Simons' concern as well.

A few brief observations should be made about the colonial Brethren view of the atonement. Numerous passages in the literature from the period exhibit a substitutionary and sacrificial view of the atonement with special emphasis on the blood of Christ as the price of our salvation.[58] This theme indicates that the Brethren followed an evangelical and pietistic view of the atonement rather than a Boehmist or Socinian scheme. Occasionally, the more Pietist and Radical Pietist focus on Christ as the restorer of the image of God in man also appears.[59] Interestingly, these concepts appear frequently in the testament written by William Knepper (d. 1755) on his deathbed to his children. He had joined the Brethren in Germany (Solingen). Other Pietist and Radical Pietist themes are prominent in the work: Christ as the Bridegroom of the soul, the Philadelphian schema of history and eschatology, fellowship with God. As the first and second generation Brethren pass away, the Radical Pietist themes especially become less prominent and by the 1820s and 30s they have generally dropped into disuse.

SALVATION

The literature from the colonial period indicates that the Brethren discerned a basic interplay between God's work in initiating salvation and man's responsibility in responding to this work. The Brethren understood that salvation accrues initially only through God's sovereign and gracious work of redemption in Christ. As a result of Christ's atoning death, all men are placed in a salvable state.[60] Yet, as the anonymous writer of *A Humble Gleam* stresses, the application of this salvation also awaits God's initiative: "No beginning of true conversion occurs without the finger of God appearing and breaking the stubborn selfishness of man so that the words of God may penetrate the heart."[61] In the above treatise, God's work of creating a new being in man and man's responsibility for responding to God in repentance and faith basically follow a Pietist pattern.

> . . . the complete and perfect conversion consists mainly in this—that all the works of the devil in us are destroyed (1 John 3:8). Secondly, that we are completely cleansed by the blood of Jesus Christ from all sins and vices (1 John 1:19 [9]), and made holy (Romans 1:4); and therefore reconciled with God (2 Corinthians 5:20). And thirdly, that we turn away from the world and from ourselves through repentance (Acts 20:21), and that through faith we come to God in Christ and become new creatures through the rebirth (John 3:3), as those who were created in Christ Jesus for good works (Ephesians 2:10).[62]

As this quote indicates, the Brethren considered the new relationship to God as an essential part of the conversion process. The best discussion of this point in colonial literature is that by Michael Frantz in his previously mentioned work, *Simple Doctrinal Considerations (Einfältige Lehr-Betrachtungen)*. In a section of prose, Frantz develops the twin ideas of inward and outward communion with God. He views the communion of love between God and the believer in a cyclical and trinitarian fashion. God has given believers everything, i.e., the heavenly inheritance and possessions, through Jesus Christ. Believers then return the spiritual fruits of an obedient life to God through the Holy Spirit. "That is communion with the Father and with His Son Jesus Christ, because the Father gave them the divine nature and the entire holy life of virtue of Jesus Christ, and because He gave them everything, they in turn give Him everything out of love, yes, their whole heart."[63] Frantz gives a Brethren twist to this Pietist and Radical Pietist theme by insisting that divine communion is to be shared with the community of believers. "They admonish, edify and stimulate one another to cling to the Lord and to follow after Him to love Him from their whole hearts."[64] Frantz maintained that "if the inward communion with God has been truly realized, it will issue in outward communion."[65] Outward communion is evidenced by bringing forth all kinds of virtues of love and by loving one's neighbor as one's self.

The new life which results from communion with God is understood by the Brethren in Pietistic terms: it involves the denial of self and the world, the willing desire to do all that God has commanded, the acceptance of testing as a necessary means of growth to a better life through God's grace.[66]

Due to the tendency of Pietists to measure the temperature of their spiritual lives by feeling states, they were continually plagued by the related problems of assurance of salvation and of certainty of continuing fellowship with God.[67] The Brethren were no exception to these problems (as indicated by the previous testimony of Stephen Koch). Typically, those who faced these problems struggled with two options: (1) a quietistic approach which took the tack: "You must hold still and patiently surrender yourself to your God and be content, however He may be dealing with you now or later"[68] and (2) a more active option of fighting against one's flaws and weaknesses. In counseling people with such problems, Mack, Jr., took a moderating position. He did not deny the importance of finding a resolution to inner spiritual struggles, but he stressed that God would act in one's life in His own time. He then shifted his emphasis to the believer's responsibilities toward God: we are to deny ourselves and pray to "the Lord to keep us from sin and to guide us into the pleasure of His will, so that our will, our desire and all our pleasure may become a daily burnt offering to the pure love of God."[69] Mack's counsel of total surrender to God's will thus retains an active, outwardly directed element (His will is evidenced by self-denial and obedience) which is lacking in the stillness of the Radical Pietist.

BAPTISM

The meaning and mode of baptism continued to be a major issue of contention between the Brethren and their religious neighbors. The major part of the aforementioned *A Humble Gleam* was devoted to the topic of baptism. It answered eight objections to water baptism raised by the Quaker, Benjamin Holmes, and concluded with the admonition that "no professor of Christ has a right to omit water baptism and to separate it from the work of conversion." Water baptism is not to be neglected, because the Spirit of God commanded it and because He does not disdain it—He hovered above the face of the waters at the work of the first creation (Gen. 1:2) and descended to the water of the Jordan to bless the baptism of Christ at the work of the second creation (Matt. 3:16). Yet, Spirit baptism is not to be minimized, for "where Spirit and water are together the water cannot bless the Spirit but the Spirit must bless the water."[70]

Alexander Mack, Jr., the most prolific writer of this period, produced the most important discussion of baptism in the colonial period. He became involved in a pamphlet war, primarily concerning baptism, with a Lutheran clergyman, John Christopher Kuntze (1744–1807). In his *Apologia or Scriptural Vindication* (1788), Mack responded to Kuntze's *The Refuted Anabaptist* by reprinting it with his own comments interwoven under the pseudonym "Theophilus." Kuntze quickly replied with *The Conquered Anabaptist* (1788) to which Mack responded with his *Appendix to the Conquered Anabaptist* (1788). He followed his father in using historical, linguistic, and Biblical arguments to uphold his contentions. Mack's basic position in these involved disputations can be summarized with a statement taken from his last mentioned work.

> For almost sixteen hundred years, the dear Messrs. Infant-baptizers have now been seeking in the Bible a well-founded proof for infant baptism and have not yet found it. Therefore the Baptist-minded still insist on this one point and say: "Show us one single commandment or example for infant baptism in the Holy Scriptures and we shall be in harmony with you!" But as long as this does not happen, you must not take it amiss that we believe the history of baptism which reports that infant baptism was instituted by the popes and that it was a commandment of the Roman Catholic emperors.[71]

In these two discussions several points, not developed in the writings of Mack, Sr., need to be highlighted. Two Anabaptist motifs are used by the writer of *A Humble Gleam* to defend water baptism. First, he appeals to the concept of the threefold baptism with water, Spirit, and blood experienced by Jesus and His disciples. The writer argues that this threefold baptism is one just as spirit, soul, and body make only one man. Though many early Christians experienced the baptism of blood by their martyrdom, others may share in this baptism "through an inward martyrdom by the crucifixion of their desires (Galatians 5:24)." Second, citing 1 Peter 3:20–21, he holds that "the covenant of a good conscience with God saves us, and that only in the resurrection of Jesus Christ." It is held that this covenant is made in the water, for, according to Paul in Romans 6:4, we are resurrected with Christ to walk in a new life in baptism.[72]

Especially important in these works is a more thorough development of the relationship between the divine elements of the forgiveness of sins and the gift of the Holy Spirit and the human elements of faith—obedience and baptism. Mack, Jr., rejects the idea in his debate with the Lutheran, Kuntze, that

either the Holy Spirit or the forgiveness of sins is dependent on baptism. Citing Acts 8:16–17 and 10:44, Mack notes that the reception of the Holy Spirit may precede or follow baptism. Likewise, he refers to Ephesians 5:26 and John 15:3 and concludes that "the powerful cleansing agent is and remains the Word and not the water."[73] In the case of both the gift of the Holy Spirit (Gal. 3:2) and the forgiveness of sins (above), the hearing of God's Word with faith is the determinative factor (though the entire salvation process is dependent initially on "the blood of Christ").[74]

What relation does baptism have to these elements then? Mack maintains that water baptism actually makes its beginning inwardly, through the attitude of an obedient faith. Those who have put on Christ inwardly through faith also put on "the entire counsel of God" and on the basis of this obedient faith will desire outward baptism. Thus Mack attributes the reception of both the inward and outward elements of conversion to saving faith. Typical of the Brethren, he sees these elements working "most generally inwardly and outwardly at the same time," though, as has been noted, he is not dogmatic on this point.[75]

A final point, related to the question of baptism, comes out in Mack's discussion. He insists that children are innocent before God and are part of the covenant of grace (the Brethren utilized Coccejus' covenantal terminology). However, Mack does not build his case upon a rejection of original sin, but upon the efficacy of Christ's death (as did the Mennonites).[76] The pivotal verse for Mack's argument is Romans 5:18. "Just as this text proves that condemnation included even all children because they too are human, it also proves on the other hand that the justification of life will also include children because they too are human."[77] Mack is careful to point out that all innocence given to children "is of God and for God" and that children who die "are made righteous through the blood of Christ."[78]

ESCHATOLOGY

Brethren interest in eschatology was wrapped up in personal eschatology primarily. They looked forward to sharing eternity with "God's worthy host divine" in the "Holy City." Here they would share intimate fellowship and joy with their Lord and receive the reward for their faithfulness to Him during their earthly walk.[79]

Occasionally, the expectation of the soon return of Christ is expressed, especially at the time of the Revolutionary War.[80] Eschatological hopes also continue to be cast in a Philadelphian mold. Beissel held that the world was in "the evening of the sixth time-period, that is, . . . the holy Ante-Sabbath" while William Knepper observed that the Laodicean church was spreading throughout all Europe and even America.[81] Both Beissel and Knepper are indicating by these statements that they believed the Lord's return was near, for Philadelphians held that the seventh period, the Laodicean, would be only a short period of temptation prior to the return of Christ.

One of the most detailed eschatological discussions from this period is found in Michael Frantz's *Simple Doctrinal Considerations*. He devotes four pages of poetry to the exposition of his understanding of the last things. Like Beissel, he feels that it is the evening of the Sabbath rest or millennium. This event will be preceded by Christ's return, the binding of Satan, and the first resurrection, i.e., the resurrection of the just to rule with Christ one thousand years. It is noteworthy that little emphasis is placed on Christ's return itself; the major interest is in the glories of the thousand year Sabbath rest. At the end of the millennium, Satan will be loosed and he will lead Gog and Magog into battle. However, he will be defeated by God and thrown into the pit of fire for eternity. Then occurs the final judgment unto eternal life in heaven or eternal death in the fiery pit.[82] After all Christ's enemies are put at His feet, the end will come when Christ will deliver up the kingdom to God the Father. From the foregoing, it can be seen that Frantz presents a remarkably thorough development of a classical premillennial view.

Universal restoration continued to be held by many Brethren during the colonial period. One of the most significant works on this doctrine to appear in colonial America was *The Everlasting Gospel, Commanded to be Preached by Jesus Christ, Judge of the Living and the Dead Unto All Creatures.* It was written by a German pastor, George Klein-Nicolai, who used the pseudonym "Paul Siegvolck," and was translated into English by the Brethren minister and poet, John S. Price. This book was instrumental in converting Elhanan Winchester to "the everlasting gospel" of restorationism.[83] The undergirding argument of the work appears early:

> As the whole Divine Being is pure Love, so are likewise all the Attributes of God, as for Instance, his Wisdom, Omnipotence, Holiness, Mercy, Truth, &c. at the Bottom nothing else but Love.[84]

Since God is "unchangeable Love," punishment must not be "never-ceasing and endless" but it must "aim

at and be designed for their [all creatures'] final Preservation, Melioration, and Restoration."[85]

Of additional note is the work bound with *The Everlasting Gospel: The Fatal Consequences of the Unscriptural Doctrine Of Predestination and Reprobation; With a Caution against It.* This work follows in the same vein as its companion volume, attacking the "doctrine of *Calvin, Beza* and *Piscator*" more for its view of God than for its understanding of redemption. Thus God "has no need to create and ordain some Creatures to an infinite, everlasting, Damnation, like a tyrannical Monarch."[86] Any affliction He sends on the wicked is to the end

> that he may have Compassion on them, as on the prodigal Son, and deliver them out of all Troubles, or Torments, in Time and Eternity, so as he loves to do. Isa. 24:21, 22, Hosea 13:14. Yea, *God will disannul their Covenant with Death, and their Agreement with Hell shall not stand,* Isa. 28:17, 18, 19, and he will swallow up Death in Victory, Isa. 25:7, 8, *and make* every Thing new. Rev. 21:5.[87]

In spite of these publications, the Brethren generally did not make their belief in universal restoration a matter of public record. The Baptist historian, David Benedict, mentions this fact in 1820: "It is said, however, that they [the Brethren] hold the doctrine of universal salvation, and hence they are often called Universalists; but this sentiment they are not forward to advance, nor strenuous to defend."[88]

FRANTZ'S *SIMPLE DOCTRINAL CONSIDERATIONS*

The initial section (thirty-three pages) of Frantz's *Simple Doctrinal-Considerations* contains 507 stanzas of poetry of four lines each. Divided into 23 parts, this poetry forms the most systematic presentation of Brethren thought available during the colonial period. The various parts include: self-examination, the foundation and covenant of faith, the church, baptism, feetwashing, the breaking of bread, the office of spiritual shepherd, Christ's incarnation, spiritual marriage, outward marriage, discipline, heavenly citizenship, earthly citizenship, the state, revenge and resistance, worldly warfare, spiritual warfare, the swearing of oaths, the eating of blood, Sunday, the Sabbath, the inner sabbath, and the resurrection of the dead. Nearly all of these subjects have already been discussed, but brief consideration should be given to two subjects which are directed at the Ephrata community: the discussions of marriage and the Sabbath. Frantz acknowledges, like Mack, Sr., that celibacy is a special spiritual state which allows greater devotion to God.[89] Unlike Mack, however, he pointedly undermines the belief that supports the

Boehmist bias for celibacy—marriage was instituted after the fall.

> 187. The married state instituted by God
>   Still before the Fall was entirely inviolate:
>   At that time Adam was not tempted
>   As Paul himself clearly says.[90]

The Sabbatarian emphasis of Beissel not only caused Mack, Sr., to pen a tract (not extant) against the practice but also impelled Frantz to devote fifty stanzas in his work to the topic. Frantz bases his argument against observance of the Sabbath on the relationship between the Old Testament law of Moses and the New Testament grace in Christ. He sees the law as a figure and the Sabbath as a shadow of Christ. Both find their fulfillment in Christ. The only law applying to Christians is the duty of love, the inward spiritual law. Frantz sees the Old Testament law of the Sabbath fulfilled in Christ, the Lord of the Sabbath. Not only does Jesus' breaking the Sabbath indicate that it is not to be observed any longer, but there is also no command in the New Testament for its observance. Moreover, since every day is now the Lord's, Sunday, the day John refers to in his Revelation as the Lord's Day, may be observed as the Sabbath.[91] It is interesting that Brethren writers must again address this issue during the latter half of the next century when the Sabbatarian influence of the Seventh-Day Adventists becomes pronounced.

CONCLUDING OBSERVATIONS

One of the prominent features of the thought of the colonial Brethren was their application of the Pietist and Radical Pietist principle of seeking a balance or middle-way between inner and outer expressions of the faith. Following the lead of Mack, Sr., in whom this principle was more implicit, the colonial Brethren explicitly extended the use of the principle to many facets of their faith. Michael Frantz, in whom this dialectic is most visible, has even composed a stanza of poetry explicating the inner-outer dialectic.

> 126. The outward proceeds from the inward
>   Otherwise it is the letter which only kills,
>   The outward has merely shown,
>   That man submits himself afterwards.

Below is a listing of some of the middle-ways explicitly or implicitly found in colonial Brethren theology and practice.

Inward, individual	*Outward, corporate*
The leading of the Spirit	The authority of Scripture
Inward communion with God—love for Him and His people	Outward communion with God—love for one's neighbor
Inner spiritual baptism	Outward water baptism
Spiritual feetwashing	Outward visible feetwashing
Individual freedom of expression	Corporate unity and peace
Openness to new truth	Corporate consensus based on Scripture
Concern for an individual's spiritual growth	Concern for corporate purity
Spiritual marriage	Outward marriage
Inner Sabbath	Outward Sabbath day

Though in each of these pairs the Brethren recognized the validity and necessity of each, their interaction with Radical Pietists, Quakers, and the Ephrata community caused them to place additional emphasis on the outward, corporate aspects of the faith.

During the colonial period the Brethren continue to exhibit a dynamic, creative spirit in their poetry, literature, and practice. They are willing to change their practice when new light from Scripture is received, though the voices for "tradition" are present. Their evangelistic outreach continues to attract converts throughout the middle and southern colonies. They manifest a deep love and concern for the spiritual growth of the community and a willingness to defer individual opinions for the sake of corporate unity. The Brethren excel at hymn writing and the apologetic writings of Mack and Frantz reveal further elaboration and development of Brethren thought.

Changes are noticeable, nevertheless, in the thought and piety of the Brethren. Radical Pietist themes, though present in the older Brethren, are less noticeable toward the end of the century. Brethren worship services reveal less of the pietistic zeal and fervor of the earliest period. A more sober mode of worship is settling in among the Brethren. Yet, any noticeable inroads by outside influences are blocked during this period by the exclusive, closely disciplined community which holds tenaciously to its German sub-culture.

Chapter 7

HISTORICAL, PRACTICAL, AND DOCTRINAL DEVELOPMENTS

Historical Developments

It has been traditional to view the period from the end of the Revolution to 1850 as the "wilderness period" of Brethren history. The term "wilderness" was used to depict not only the location of many Brethren congregations but also the cultural isolation of the Brotherhood. More recently, however, a new appreciation for the important advances during this era has been developing.[1] It was during these years that the geographical spread that is found today among the Brethren occurred, and during the same period Brethren doctrine and polity underwent further development and refinement in response to the changing needs of the growing Brotherhood.

One of the most significant aspects of Brethren life following the Revolution was the migration to new territories. This expansion was due to rising land values in the East, the bitter experience during the War, and the glowing reports concerning the frontier which were circulated among the Brethren. During and immediately following the War, numerous Brethren moved into the Shenandoah Valley and across the Alleghenies into western Pennsylvania. Brethren from Virginia and North Carolina had crossed the Cumberland Gap into Kentucky and Tennessee by 1800.[2] The first Brethren settlers had moved into Missouri in the 1790s, Ohio in 1793, Indiana in 1809, and Illinois in 1812. As these dates indicate, the Brethren often were part of the first waves of migration to enter a new territory, following closely on the heels of the explorers and trappers. By 1850 Brethren were to be found in Wisconsin, Michigan, Iowa, Minnesota, and Oregon. From 1850 on, Brethren settlers moved into the territories between the Mississippi River and the Pacific Ocean: Kansas, Nebraska, Colorado, California, the Dakotas, Texas, Louisiana, Idaho, and Washington. During this process, the Brethren grew steadily, from about fifteen hundred members in 1770 to an estimated twenty thousand in 1865.[3] By 1880 this latter figure had nearly tripled to fifty-eight thousand members.

There are several noteworthy characteristics of this expansion process. First, Brethren and Mennonites frequently settled in the same areas in these migrations, especially in the Midwest. This fact led to occasional friction between these "religious cousins." Second, during the initial stages of Brethren expansion, migration was primarily undertaken by individual families; only later, during the settlement of the prairie states especially, did migration in large groups occur. This practice was in contrast to that of the Mennonites who, for the most part, moved in large groups or colonies. This difference may indicate a stronger sense of individualism among the Brethren. Third, the Brethren, like the Mennonites and Baptists, possessed a pattern of church life which was well adapted for meeting the challenges of westward expansion. Their free church or believers' church pattern included the "free ministry" (unpaid, self-supporting ministers), worship in homes, and lack of formal liturgy.[4] Ministers were elected by the congregation so a church seldom lacked an elder for any more than a brief period of time. Fourth, the congregations that came to be established on the frontier were generally made up of people who had been traditionally Brethren. The Brethren pioneers were joined by other Brethren settlers until a nucleus of a congregation could be formed. The evangelistic spirit, which had faded to a great extent by the end of the eighteenth century, was not quickened again until the 1860s and 70s when the Brethren came under the influence of revivalism.

Brethren peace principles were again tested during the Civil War. As much as the Brethren would have liked to distance themselves from all the issues attending this conflict, they could not for three important reasons: (1) their opposition to military service, (2) their opposition to slavery, and (3) their proximity to the battle zones.[5]

(1) The Brethren as a whole remained firmly committed to their nonresistant principles during the Civil War. To secure legal recognition of their nonresistant position, Brethren in the North and especially the South labored to secure exemption from military service. John Kline, a leading Brethren elder from Virginia, and a pamphlet written by William C. Thurman, who had recently left the Baptists for the Brethren, played significant roles in acquiring Brethren exemption in the South. On both sides of the Mason-Dixon line the Brethren received exemption generally upon the payment of fines which ranged from two hundred to five hundred dollars or which were levied on one's property. In several cases the option of securing a substitute was offered, but the Brethren counseled against this alternative.[6]

(2) From 1782 on, the Brethren had taken an uncompromising stand against slavery. The prohibition on buying, keeping, selling, or even hiring slaves was adhered to strictly even south of the Mason-Dixon line and was enforced by church discipline. The Brethren position against slavery was, needless to say, unpopular in the South. Many Southern Brethren therefore decided to avoid the problems associated with their principles by migrating to free states.[7] Those who remained sought to balance a desire not to offend public feeling with their own Christian convictions. Many sensed the inevitable outcome of the slavery issue. In 1847 John Kline rather prophetically stated concerning slavery:

> . . . I do believe that the time is not far distant when the sun will rise and set upon our land cleansed of this foul stain, though it may be cleansed with blood. I would rejoice to think that my eyes might see that bright morning; but I can have no hope of that.[8]

Little did Kline know that he would lose his own life as a result of the conflict which secured the freedom of the slaves (see p. 106).

(3) The Brethren who suffered the most hardship during the Civil War were those living in the Shenandoah Valley. Many of these Brethren lost their homes, barns, livestock, and produce to Sheridan's scorched earth policy. Yet, at the 1865 Annual Meeting, the Brethren, demonstrating their commitment to mutual aid, set up a fund to aid their needy brothers and sisters in Virginia and Tennessee. Unlike the Baptists, Methodists, and Presbyterians, the Brethren were solidified by the events of the Civil War. This unity can be traced to their common stand on slavery and nonresistance, their aversion to political

involvement, and their loving response to needy members of the body.

Brethren Practice and Polity

Brethren worship practices show a trend toward greater form and order during the nineteenth century. Because the area served by most congregations was quite large, preaching points were usually established in several places. Thus services might be held in a given location only once a month. Though smaller gatherings continued to meet in homes or barns, more and more congregations built plain meetinghouses from about the 1820s onward. In a typical meetinghouse the men and women would sit on opposite sides of the room on backless benches while the minister(s) (Brethren congregations frequently had several ministers) faced the congregation from behind a table. The table was never on a raised platform but was on the same level as the people to signify the equality of each member of the congregation. A typical Sunday worship service opened with an unaccompanied hymn which was "lined" by a minister or deacon.[9] Prayer was offered followed by the selection of the "preacher of the day" who would choose the Scripture text to be addressed.[10] The passage was read by one of the ministers or a deacon and then the preacher of the day and possibly several other ministers would develop the meaning of the text. After the sermon(s) a younger minister or deacon "bore testimony" by briefly exhorting the congregation to actualize the message of the day's preaching. The service was closed with a final hymn and prayer (not a formal benediction, however). Brethren preaching tended to be devotional, emphasizing such typically Brethren themes as self-denial, nonconformity, discipleship to Christ, obedience to the precepts of Scripture, love to God and one's neighbor; somewhat apologetic, defending the Brethren views of baptism and the love feast especially; evangelical, based on one Biblical text which the speaker developed by using Biblical and non-Biblical illustrative material; and, at times, evangelistic, giving a low-key invitation to believe in Christ.[11]

The observance of baptism and communion (commonly referred to as the love feast) was a special occasion for the Brethren. Baptism was especially important for young adults, for it represented the confirmation of a person's desire to join the church, to turn from the ways of the world, and to lead a life of Christian discipline and discipleship. In 1848, Annual Meeting formalized the order of baptism, recommending the following practice in order to remove differences which existed in its observance.

> First, the applicant to be examined by two or more brethren; then, the case to be brought before the church council, before whom the applicant is to declare his agreement with us, in regard to the principles of being defenseless, non-swearing, and not conforming to the world; then, in meeting, or at the water, to read from Matt. 18, verses 10 to 22, in public, the candidates being asked if they will be governed by those gospel rules; then, prayer at the water, and in the water, the following questions to be asked:
>
> Question: Dost thou believe that Jesus Christ is the Son of God, and that he has brought from heaven a saving gospel? Answer: Yea.
>
> Question: Dost thou willingly renounce Satan, with all his pernicious ways, and all the sinful pleasures of this world? Answer: Yea.
>
> Question: Dost thou covenant with God, in Christ Jesus, to be faithful until death? Answer: Yea.
>
> Upon this thy confession of faith, which thou hast made before God and these witnesses, thou shalt, for the remission of sins, be baptized in the name of the Father, and of the Son, and of the Holy Ghost. After baptism, while in the water, the administrator to lay his hands on the head of the candidate, and offer up a prayer to God in his behalf, and then the member is to be received, by hand and kiss, into church-fellowship.[12]

What is truly remarkable about this recommended order is that there are no substantial differences between it and a record of a Brethren baptism which occurred 114 years earlier (see pp. 90–91 and n. 32). Though examination of the applicant is provided for, the questioning deals primarily with the applicant's willingness to live according to the principles of the Brethren.

The Brethren love feast was the social and religious high point of the year. It was preceded by the deacons' "annual visit" to each home to examine the members in preparation for the love feast. Each member was asked the following questions: "Are you still in the faith of the Gospel, as you declared when you were baptized? Are you, as far as you know, in peace and union with the church? Will you still labor with the Brethren for an increase of holiness, both in yourself and others?"[13] If discord was found in the membership, the love feast would be postponed until the problem was resolved. The love feast was a two-day affair commencing Saturday before noon with a worship service. A noon meal was followed by a solemn service of spiritual preparation and examination. The love feast proper occurred Saturday evening with feetwashing, the Lord's Supper (a common meal), and the bread and cup. The event was concluded on Sunday with a regular worship service. Because the love feast attracted Brethren from many miles around, visitors were housed either in private homes or, if the meetinghouse was so equipped, in the sleeping quarters above the assembly room. For the Brethren, the love feast was the visible demonstration of the love, unity, and brotherhood which they felt were the heart of the Christian life and Gospel.

The attendance of non-members at the Lord's Supper came to be more closely regulated during this period. In 1832 Annual Meeting decided that non-members could partake of the supper if there was room and the churches so desired. In 1841 it was deemed permissible for friends to be admitted to the supper if they did not partake of the bread and the cup. By 1849 the counsel was more negative: "Considered, to be a divine and sacred ordinance, as all the Lord's ordinances are, and should be eaten by the members only."[14]

During this period definite guidelines for the practice of discipline were spelled out by Annual Meeting (in 1794, 1805, 1822, 1837, 1840, 1842, 1843, 1844, 1848, 1849, and 1850). The decisions rendered show a general uniformity of thought. A distinction was made between Matthew 18 and 1 Corinthians 5. Matthew 18 was held to refer to sins and offenses which a member commits against a fellow-member. The member who refused to acknowledge his fault should be "put back" or disowned from the church council, communion, and the holy kiss. It was considered that 1 Corinthians 5 referred to vices and crimes committed against God and the truth. Members who fell into these gross sins should be dealt with by avoidance, i.e., withdrawal of fellowship, including not eating in his company.[15] The Brethren also dealt with the difficult problem faced by the Mennonites concerning the relationship between a person put in avoidance and his family. Though it was held that the full effect of avoidance would be felt if the spouse and children withdrew fellowship, those who felt they could not observe avoidance were still to be regarded as members but were not to partake of communion.[16]

The study of Brethren church polity during the nineteenth century can be a perplexing endeavor because (1) Brethren polity has never fit neatly into any of the three classical forms of church government (congregational, presbyterial, episcopal) and (2) Brethren polity was undergoing rapid development in this century to meet the needs of a body growing numerically and territorially. These characteristics can be appreciated in a consideration of the organization of the local church and of those structures which transcended the life and, in given circumstances, the authority of the local church.

The most basic unit of polity among the German Baptist Brethren was the local congregation. This fact provided a strong congregational cast to Brethren polity. The governing body of the local church was the council meeting, made up of all the members of the congregation. Its decisions on moral, spiritual, and practical questions relating to the life of the church and her members were binding. Not to "hear the church" led to the admonishment of the brother and, if he did not repent, to his being "put back" or avoided.

The officers of the congregation included deacons and ministers.[17] Both were elected for life by the congregation (though the congregation could remove them from office) either to meet the needs of a growing congregation or to replace those who had left the area or died. Deacons or visiting brethren were responsible for (1) caring for the poor, (2) conducting the annual visit of all the members prior to the love feast to ascertain their spiritual state, (3) investigating problems in the church either along with the ministers or by themselves, (4) assisting in the meeting (worship service) when asked by the minister by reading Scripture, leading singing, praying, and exhorting the members to faithfulness, and (5) taking charge of the preparations for the love feast.

The Brethren gradually developed a three degree ministry which was first mentioned in the Annual Meeting minutes in 1858 (Art. 19) and was given final form at the 1874 Annual Meeting.[18] On occasion the church would call a promising young man to the ministry of the first degree. His responsibilities included (1) preaching when given "liberty" by the older ministers, (2) conducting a meeting if none of the elders were available, and (3) preaching at funerals. If he showed himself faithful during this trial period, he was advanced to the second degree. Besides his former duties, he now could (1) make his own "appointments," i.e., arrange to preach at a certain preaching point on a given date, (2) administer baptism, (3) take the counsel of the church concerning the admission of an applicant for baptism if the elder was absent, (4) serve communion in the absence or at the request of an elder, and (5) perform marriage. Upon the faithful execution of these responsibilities, he could then be advanced by the congregation to the third degree or full ministry (only those advanced to this level were ordained with the laying on of hands). The so-called elder or bishop could not only perform all his former preroga-

tives but also (1) preside at any council meeting whether in his home congregation or in another, (2) give the charge to ministers and deacons in order to install them, (3) serve on the Standing Committee of Yearly Meeting, (4) ordain other elders, and (5) share equal status with all other elders, except where appropriate to defer to elders with seniority.[19]

A significant concomitant of the rapid expansion of the Brotherhood was the desire to maintain unity in doctrine and practice and to foster fellowship among the scattered congregations of the Brethren. Two forms of polity served to bind local congregations more closely together. The first of these was the adjoining elder system which was the Brethren form of the "circuit rider" phenomenon. Philip Boyle explained this practice in a description of the Brethren published in 1848. In defining church leadership he stated:

> It is the duty of the bishops to travel from one congregation to another, not only to preach, but to set in order the things that may be wanting; to be present at their love-feasts and communions, and, when teachers and deacons are elected or chosen, or when a bishop is to be ordained, or when any member who holds an office in the church is to be excommunicated.[20]

These traveling brethren served as a vital communication link among the scattered membership, providing physical, social, and spiritual support.

The adjoining elder system also served an important role in helping to resolve conflicts in a local congregation. When a congregation could not settle a matter itself, a committee of elders from adjoining churches would be called in to help resolve the issue. The counsel of this committee was generally accepted by the local church as a kind of "binding arbitration." It is noteworthy that the first instance in which the Annual Meeting of the Brethren sent a committee apparently without formal request from the local congregation occurred in 1849.[21] In the following years the Annual Meeting assumed this prerogative to a greater degree.

The second form of polity that served to unite the Brotherhood was the Annual or Yearly Meeting. Significant changes occurred in the functioning and authority of this body during the nineteenth century (the first minutes from an Annual Meeting come from 1778 though the minutes continue to be incomplete until the 1820s). Held at Pentecost, Annual Meeting rotated between the eastern and western parts of the Brotherhood. The dividing line between east and west moved steadily westward, reflecting the westward expansion of the Brethren (it shifted from the Susquehanna River to the Allegheny Mountains, and in 1864 to the Ohio River). The Annual Meeting was a special time of fellowship for ministers and private members (those not holding office) from throughout the Brotherhood. The sense of spiritual unity was enhanced by well attended preaching services, common meals, and a love feast (discontinued in 1851).

The conduct of business occupied an increasingly important place on the Annual Meeting docket. Business during the Annual Meetings of the late eighteenth century and early nineteenth century was conducted in an informal and simple manner, much as an ordinary council meeting. Having sought the guidance of the Spirit, the assembled elders would consider any questions raised. Some queries received a verbal response; the more important cases were answered by letter either to the congregation submitting the question or, if the case was of general interest, to each of the congregations in the Brotherhood. As the number of questions presented increased, it was decided that the host church should select five or more of the oldest ministers who would then retire to a private place to prepare responses to the queries addressed to Annual Meeting. In this way the entire slate of business did not have to be aired before the whole assembly and before strangers. As was done previously, some queries received verbal response; others were disposed of by sending a written response to the congregation presenting the question. Only matters of general interest were reserved for public discussion and consideration. This latter practice continued until 1830 or 1831 according to Henry Kurtz, who was writing in 1867.[22]

Until 1847 any member of the Brotherhood could attend Annual Meeting and participate in the decision making process on items of general interest. Unanimity was sought on all questions brought before the general assembly, and, if a consensus was not achieved, disposition of the query was deferred until the next year. The 1847 Annual Meeting made several important changes in this system, forming a delegate body and placing responsibility for considering queries into the hands of this body. The relevant minutes state:

> The council to consist of delegates, not more than two to be sent from each church, with a written certificate, containing also the queries to be presented (by the church whom they represent) to the yearly meeting. The delegates to constitute a committee of the whole to receive and examine all matters communicated to the Y. M. [Yearly Meeting], and to arrange all the queries and questions for public discussion, and after they are publicly discussed, and the general

sentiment heard, then the delegates are to decide, and if two-thirds or more of the delegates agree, let the decision thus made be final. But if the nature of the case be such that two-thirds do not give their consent, then let it be delayed (postponed) until it receives the voice of at least two-thirds of the legal representatives. The yearly meeting to be attended by as many teachers and members as may think proper to do so, and the privilege in discussion to be free and open to all who may desire to participate in the same as heretofore.[23]

In an effort to facilitate further the conduct of business, the 1848 Annual Meeting decided to continue the general committee of five to seven elders (this committee came to be known as the Standing Committee) and to establish as many special committees as were necessary to dispatch the business. The general committee and special committees were to act in concert to prepare the queries for discussion.

The increasing number of queries caused the 1856 Annual Meeting to approve the establishment of districts of five or more adjoining churches to answer any local questions.[24] The relationship between Annual Meeting and the district meetings was further refined in 1866. Any business items brought to the district meeting had to be passed by a local church and brought by that church. The district meeting was to refer to Annual Meeting any question of general concern or any matter which could not be settled. Any member had the right to appeal a decision made by a district meeting to the Standing Committee at Annual Meeting. The 1866 Annual Meeting also gave specific instructions for the composition and officers of the Standing Committee and dispensed with the special committees. This action, along with the decision in 1863 which gave the Standing Committee authority to open and examine all questions brought to Annual Meeting in order to expedite their discussion, placed considerable power in the hands of this select group. Furthermore, a significant statement was contained at the conclusion of this organizational resolution of 1866:

> The proceedings of the Annual Meetings shall be published, and it is earnestly recommended that all the overseers of churches, whether ordained or not, have them faithfully read and observed in their respective charges. And if it be represented to the Annual Meeting, that this recommendation is disregarded, it shall be the duty of the standing committee to appoint faithful brethren, whose duty it shall be to visit said churches, and see that the Minutes are properly read and observed, and to set in order things that are lacking.[25]

In 1868, Annual Meeting agreed that the Standing Committee should be of representatives elected by the respective districts of the church, rather than being selected by the elders of the church hosting the Annual Meeting as before. The organization of the Annual Meeting of the German Baptist Brethren was now complete.

A perusal of the minutes of Annual Meeting between 1800 and 1870 reveals several important characteristics which are important for understanding the nineteenth century Brethren. The most conspicuous characteristic of these minutes was the movement toward greater order, structure, and uniformity. Dale Brown applies the term "legalism" to this movement, but he cautions that the usage of this word does not imply that the Brethren of this period were guilty of a loveless application of religious mores or of a form of works-righteousness.[26] Rather, this tendency toward less flexibility and greater detail and definiteness was motivated by the desire to maintain the Brethren principle of nonconformity in the face of an enveloping society, to maintain the principles of order and unity in response to the rapidly increasing geographical and numerical size of the Brotherhood, and to maintain the principle of respect for the decisions of the "old Brethren" against those who agitated for "innovations." During this period Annual Meeting formulated casuistic rulings against the use of tobacco, life insurance, lightning rods, likenesses (photographs), musical instruments, salaried ministers, membership in secret societies, attendance at shows and fairs, flowered wallpaper, carpets, and bells.[27] At first these decisions were all based on Scripture or "Gospel principles,"[28] but increasingly past minutes alone came to be invoked.[29] Gradually, the concept of a "Brethren's order" emerged—a kind of unwritten creed composed of the rulings made by Annual Meeting and of usages adopted by common consent which governed the faith and practice of the Brethren. The first explicit reference in Annual Meeting minutes to the "order" of the church appeared in 1821 with regard to baptism and spoke of those who "acknowledge the Brethren's order as right." Again in 1849 a query asked that a group of Brethren "experienced and sound in the faith . . . [be sent] with the decisions of the Annual Meeting . . . [to] visit all the congregations in the United States, and establish them all in the same order, according to example (Acts XV)."[30] In time the order of the church assumed a position of authority beside that of Scripture. In 1858 Annual Meeting was asked: "Is the gospel itself sufficient to preserve a union of practice throughout the brotherhood?" Its response was: "Considered, that the gospel, with the practice or order consistent with the gospel, will preserve the union of the brotherhood."[31] After this the twin powers of the gospel and order of the church commonly appear side by side in the minutes.[32]

Paralleling this emergence of church order was the development of the power of Annual Meeting itself. It became the final court of appeal for decisions at the local and district levels, and local churches were expected to observe the order established by the united counsel of the Brethren at Annual Meeting (see p. 103). Nevertheless, there was a certain amount of ambiguity attached to Annual Meeting decisions. For instance, in 1860 Annual Meeting was asked if it was not contrary to the Brethren profession that the New Testament was their only rule of faith and practice "to make a strict observance of the minutes of the Annual Council a test of fellowship." The answer was, "The decisions of the Annual Meeting are obligatory until such decisions shall be repealed by the same authority."[33] Yet in 1865, responding to the query, "Does the Annual Council make laws, or give advice only, in cases where it has no direct gospel on the subjects?," Annual Meeting counseled, "It gives advice only."[34] Dale Brown reflects on a discussion by Henry Kurtz regarding this ambiguity found in the minutes of Annual Meeting.

> He [Kurtz] opposes one view in the church by emphasizing that they are not binding laws or rules legislated for the governing of others. We find the perfect law only in Christ and his teachings. Neither will he accept the antithesis of the above view by regarding the decisions as mere vain traditions of men. The traditions of our Christian Elders tend to help our obedience to the law of Christ and protect us from the vain traditions of men. If the minutes constitute neither laws, nor vain traditions, what are they? Kurtz appropriates the analogies of the court process with the jury and [of] parties making treaties of peace to point to the necessity of periodically coming to collective judgments in order to be reconciled and to renew the covenant which each one has made at the time of baptism.[35]

As long as a middle way was steered between these two poles, the ambiguous nature of Annual Meeting's authority caused no problems. But as Brown indicates, a polarization of the attitudes toward the decisions of Annual Meeting had already begun by the 1860s. This polarization "was pronounced enough to nourish the seeds which were to erupt in the major schisms of the last half of the nineteenth century."[36]

That segment of the Brethren which sought to give greater authority to the growing body of Annual Meeting rulings seems to have departed from the view which early Annual Meetings took toward their own deliberations. This point becomes evident by observing the way in which the early councils administered their decisions. Queries were answered either verbally or by letter if the concerned parties were not present. The only decisions which received general distribution were those of interest to the church at large. Apparently, little effort was made to collect or preserve past decisions, which would explain why records from many early Annual Meetings are missing (of the fifty-three Annual Meetings between 1778 and 1830, the year when continuous records begin, minutes of only thirty-four councils are extant). Even as late as 1858, Annual Meeting denied a request to have all the extant minutes of past councils printed, though a similar request was approved in 1861. One might conclude that the early yearly councils considered their decisions applicable for only their own particular situation and time. They did not wish their counsel to be binding upon later generations of the Brethren who should come to their own understanding of the truth based on Scripture and the leading of God's Spirit.[37] It is quite clear that tradition played a part in these decisions. The opinion of the "old Brethren," the contemporary elder statesmen, was held in high regard. But by the mid-nineteenth century "old Brethren" had also come to refer to the Brethren forefathers whose counsel in the extant minutes was raised to a level of authority beyond the original intent of the "old Brethren" of yore.

To give a true picture of how the decisions of Annual Meeting were actually received by the church at large, one more important characteristic of the Brethren needs to be added. The principle of individual freedom and openness was by no means lost during this period; in fact it helped to temper the rise in the authority of Annual Meeting up through the 1850s. While on certain issues the Brethren remained solidly united in their opposition—freemasonry, gambling, lotteries, nonresistance—on others the Brethren showed a willingness to change. For example, in 1827 and 1828 Annual Meeting ruled that Brethren should not have carpets in their houses, since such would lead to elevation and pride. However, the issue was raised again and again until, by 1878, Annual Meeting conceded the possession of plain carpets. In commenting on Annual Meeting's decisions on carpets, Henry Kurtz reveals the Brethren attitude toward the "things of the world":

> While such improvements were yet new, and only found in homes of the great and rich in the world, it was proper for brethren to advise as above (1827 and 1828 decisions); but after such improvements had become a common thing, and it was a convenience generally known, there was no further objection to their introduction. Thus it was almost in all cases.[38]

Similarly, the original opposition of Annual Meeting to such issues as Sunday Schools, revival meetings, the taking of interest, and the use of beef at love feasts changed to an attitude of cautious acceptance through the process of continued queries from the grass roots. This fact indicates that Annual Meeting was not intransigent on issues which it deemed adiaphorous but was willing to change and adapt albeit in a slow, cautious manner. Likewise, it shows that there was not universal adherence to the counsels of Annual Meeting and that there was an openness on the part of the majority to struggle anew with the validity of previous actions.[39]

This discussion of polity was begun with the observation that Brethren church government defies classification into any of the traditional forms of church government. Only a hybrid form of polity could express those political principles which were dear to the Brethren—individual freedom of conscience, the desire to attain unity in the faith based on consensus, respect for the counsel of the elders, recognition of the equality of believers (the priesthood of all believers). One of the best attempts at characterizing Brethren polity was made by a Church of the Brethren elder, I. D. Parker. Written in 1908, this statement is reflective of Brethren polity of the last half of the nineteenth century as well.

> What then is the New Testament Church Polity? . . . It may be called an Ecclesiastical Democracy, a government of the people, by the people, and for the people. It comprises a combination of forms:
>
> 1. It is Democratic in the sense that the highest authority is vested in the membership.
>
> 2. It is Republican in the sense that the church chooses representatives to execute her will.
>
> 3. It is Congregational in local matters, but general on all questions of doctrine and matters of a general character.[40]

Biographical Sketches

Several of the literary and administrative leaders in the mid-nineteenth century came from outside the Brethren tradition.[41] Henry Kurtz (1790–1874) was born in Binnigheim, Germany, but left his family and native land to come to America in 1817. He became a Lutheran pastor in 1819, serving churches in Northampton County and Pittsburgh, Pennsylvania. Serious disputes in his second pastorate which arose over Kurtz's efforts to institute church discipline and Christian communitarianism caused him to leave the Lutheran Church. He moved to Stark County, Ohio, in 1826 or 1827 where he became acquainted with the Brethren and finally joined the church in 1828. Kurtz played significant roles in the church as the editor of the first church paper, the *Gospel Visitor*, and as the clerk of Annual Meeting every year from 1837 to 1862, with the exception of only 1839.[42]

James Quinter (1816-1888) came from a non-religious background in eastern Pennsylvania. He joined the Brethren in 1833 and distinguished himself as a preacher and evangelist. He served as either writing clerk or assistant writing clerk of Annual Meeting from 1855 to 1885. From 1856 until his death, Quinter was involved in church-related publication work, and he was also a prime mover in making higher education available to Brethren youth.

There were also several outstanding Brethren leaders of the nineteenth century who came from families with Brethren ties. John Kline (1797-1864), an elder from the Shenandoah Valley, was an influential figure at Annual Meeting, serving many years on the Standing Committee and from 1861 to 1864 as the Moderator of Annual Meeting. He logged over 100,000 miles (estimated from his diary) as a traveling preacher for the church. He was murdered in 1864 by Confederate guerrillas possibly due to his anti-slavery sentiments or because his travels between enemy lines on church business were interpreted as disloyal or treasonous actions. Peter Keyser (1766-1849) was the leader of the Germantown congregation for forty-seven years and was known for his keen knowledge of Scripture and able preaching. George Wolfe, Jr. (1780-1865), served as the leading figure among the "Far Western Brethren" (Illinois), a group of Brethren isolated from the main body of the church by distance (and later by some differences in practice) for over forty years. He helped to effect the final merging of the two groups in 1859.

The Devotional Lives of the Brethren

The pietistic, semi-mystical faith that characterized the religious life of the eighteenth century Brethren carried over into the first part of the nineteenth century.[43] This is evidenced by the continued composition of hymns and devotional works and the regular appearance of new editions of the Brethren hymnbooks every few years. Yet, clear signs that a religious era was ending for the Brethren are also present by the end of the eighteenth century. The two principal hymn writers around 1800 are Alexander Mack, Jr., who died in 1803, and Jacob Stoll, who was seventy-five years old in 1806 when a volume of his poetry and devotional writings was published at Ephrata. The poetry of both these men continued to reflect that sweet, pleasurable experience of intimate communion with Christ which typi-

fied the more mystical Pietistic circles. Yet, these men, in reality, represent a previous era. Not only does the genre of Christ-mysticism slowly pass from currency but of even greater significance is the fact that few new hymn writers of note appear to carry on the rich tradition of Brethren poetry.[44]

The same phenomenon can be seen in Brethren devotional literature. Several noteworthy works appear during this period: John Valentine Mack's (1701-1755) *Ein Gespräch zwischen einem Pilger und Bürger, auf ihrer Reise nach und in der Ewigkeit* (published posthumously in 1777; reprinted 1792, 1817, 1862); the aforementioned publication by Jacob Stoll, *Geistliches Gewürz-Gärtlein Heilsuchender Seelen . . .* (1806); David Landes' *O lieben Freunde! dies ist der sicherste Himmels-Weg, wenn man sich selber richten thut, und andern neu sagen und offenbaren. . . . Das Güldene A B C Für Jedermann, der gern mit Ehren wollt bestahn* (1825). The themes and/or titles of all these works reveal indebtedness to pietistic works of the seventeenth and eighteenth centuries. Mack's work utilizes the literary tool of a conversation between two people (some such works employ more characters) on an imaginary journey to eternity. This motif, which has medieval roots, has already been noted in the work of the Dutch Mennonite, Pietersz, and in Bunyan's *Pilgrim's Progress*. The theme of a spiritual flower or, in this case, spice garden which provides enjoyment or "seasoning" to the soul as it passes through also has medieval antecedents. Yet the proliferation of this theme occurs in pietistic literature. Examples of it can be found in works by Arndt, Schabalie, Tersteegen, and an anonymous Lutheran writer.[45] Landes' spiritual primer (the "Golden ABCs" likewise have medieval and pietistic roots) contains esoteric and mystical views of the Christian faith drawn from the Berleburg Bible and Gottfried Arnold.[46]

These works indicate that a quiet, devotional, somewhat mystical spirit continued among the Brethren at least into the third decade of the nineteenth century. This spirit was fostered by public worship and even more by family devotions, which included the reading of Scripture and devotional works, singing, and prayer.[47] Yet, the very fact that the above works use borrowed themes and imagery suggest that this pietistic spirit is losing its vitality and certainly its originality. The further fact that these works are the last clear representatives of the devotional spirit that was so strong during the previous century has ominous significance for the perpetuation of the spirit. Tied as it was to the German sectarian sub-culture, this spirit was, to a great extent, dependent on the continued availability of appropriate literature in the German language. Furthermore, as the Brotherhood shifted from a German-speaking to an English-speaking body between the 1830s and 1850s, the Brethren became linguistically severed from the traditional piety.

An important transition figure between the old piety and a new spirit of openness to the religious ways of the larger American setting is Henry Kurtz. The communitarian emphasis which had led to his departure from his Pittsburgh congregation was motivated not only by contact with George Rapp and Robert Owen but also by concepts derived from Boehme and Arnold. He felt the three major problems of the contemporary church were

> the hierarchical structure, creedalism, and the confusion of Christianity with philosophy. The threefold answer to these problems could be found by improving one's heart, organizing Christian communities, and introducing strict discipline in the church. Complete decay of Christianity could be staved off only by returning to the "first love" or simplicity of the early Christians, the simplicity of the Gospel, and the simplicity of nature.[48]

After joining the Brethren, Kurtz continued to show attributes of the old piety. He published a German translation of a portion of Menno Simons' complete works for the sake not only of the Mennonites but also of every "truth-loving reader." Noting that Menno was a "witness of the truth," Kurtz was assured such readers could find and treasure the "kernel" in the "hard shell" by applying the apostolic rule: "Test everything, and hold to the good" (1 Thess. 5:21).[49] Likewise, he held the belief that the Brethren were part of an unbroken line of persecuted dissenters which could be traced back to the apostolic church. Kurtz developed this thesis in the first volume of his *Gospel Visitor* in an article with the revealing title: "The Church in the Wilderness: Testimonies on the Existence of an Apostolical Church from the Beginning of the Gospel up to our Time." Utilizing the "Waldensian connection" which has been noted in the works of Mehrning, van Braght, and Felbinger, Kurtz contends:

> . . . when their [the Waldenses'] most inveterate adversaries themselves admit, that the age of the Waldensian churches reaches up to the apostolic time, then it is a pleasing confirmation of the truth, that at all times, even in the most corrupt centuries of the (Roman) church, there existed always a true church of the Lord . . .[50]

Following the Waldenses in this chain were the Bohemian Brethren and the Anabaptists and Mennonites, the intermediaries for the early Brethren.

One other indication that Kurtz retains a form of piety and faith whose antecedents are in the Radical Pietist spirit of the previous century is his reaction to the use of the word "sacrament" by a member of the church. He was livid, exclaiming that the word originated not from the Bible but "in New-Babylon, the city built on seven hills, and here also was invented or rather misapplied the word sacrament to the same number of Seven. A remarkable coincidence."[51]

Though manifesting these characteristics of the former Radical Pietist-Anabaptist faith and piety, Kurtz played a part in opening the Brethren as a body to the broader vistas of American society and religion. Kurtz desired his *Gospel Visitor* to be a means of edifying and unifying the brotherhood. Yet his inclusion of selections from other religious and secular periodicals, his dialogue with other denominations on doctrinal questions, and his occasional notice of news items of religious significance (e.g., Jewish plans to return to Palestine) helped to nudge his readers out of their cultural and religious isolation. With the coming of the more progressive James Quinter as his assistant in 1856, Kurtz was persuaded to advocate more forcefully through the *Gospel Visitor* such "innovations" as educational institutions for Brethren youth (which he had initially opposed) and, later in the decade, the introduction of Sunday Schools. Though Kurtz himself remained conservative to the end of his life, his own life and work portray the changes that were occurring in the Brotherhood especially after 1850.

Doctrinal Developments

Doctrinal writings during the period between the Revolutionary and Civil Wars show little new or creative work. Rather, the central concern of the Brethren was closer definition of their faith and practice in order to be certain the Brotherhood shared the same, united faith and, even more importantly, to defend their faith against the encroachments of the outside world and of other denominations. Symbolic of this concern is Peter Nead's utilization of the imagery, common to religious dissenters (see pp. 259–260, n. 48), of the well enclosed garden (Song of Songs 4:12):

> The Church is a *garden* which should be well enclosed. There should be no gaps or openings left for the enemy to enter. And a *strong guard* should be stationed all around the enclosure, so that no "tares" (false doctrine) be sown in the garden, by the enemy.[52]

The following discussion will focus on several important facets of Brethren thought: areas in which change is to be noted, doctrines which undergo further definition, and interaction with the doctrine of other denominations or movements.

THE SOURCES OF AUTHORITY USED BY THE BRETHREN

The Brethren during this period remain true to the sources of authority recognized by the early Brethren: God, Christ, Scripture, the Holy Spirit, and the pattern of the primitive church. However, as was noted earlier, several additional sources of authority for the church gain prominence during this period: Annual Meeting and the order of the Brethren. The growth of the power of each of these two elements actually is linked together, for Annual Meeting increasingly becomes recognized as the conservator of the order of the Brethren while the past minutes of Annual Meeting are, to a great extent, considered the embodiment of the "ancient order." In addition, certain "gospel principles" were discerned by the Brethren as being fundamental to the character and nature of the church: simplicity, liberty, order, subordination of reason to the Word of God, due regard for the decisions of former Yearly Meetings, sincere love of the Brethren, and a constant aim for union.[53] All of the sentiments expressed in these principles are generally consistent with the values emphasized by the early Brethren. Even the regard for past decisions of Annual Meeting and the order of the Brethren can be seen arising from the respect accorded the decisions of the elders gathered at Annual Meeting. The important new features are the high esteem given *former* decisions and the prominent place given the "ancient order" in the deliberations of Annual Meeting.

THE DOCTRINE OF SALVATION

Refinements and changes in the Brethren order of Salvation

The Brethren formulation of the order of salvation during this period reveals the influence of and interaction with other religious groups. The writers at the beginning of the nineteenth century continue to reflect a Pietist and Radical Pietist understanding of the conversion process. Christian Longenecker (1731–1808) holds that the process includes: (1) Repentance. A penitent heart is dependent on the inner workings of God's grace, which leads consecutively to the fear of God, the reading of His Word, a recognition of one's sinful state, the tug of the Father and one's own

conscience, and, finally, complete surrender "into the hand of God for grace or disfavor"[54] (a clear quietistic note!). (2) Faith. This belief in things not seen is induced by the tug of the Father directing the person to the Son and requires the prostrating of one's self in spiritual powerlessness and humility. To a person in such a state, God will give the gift of the Holy Spirit. The person will then learn to know Jesus Christ who will forgive his sins, cleanse his flesh and spirit of defilement, and give him a new leader, the Holy Spirit. The Son then gives the believer inner joy and the assurance of forgiveness for previous sins. (3) A love for God known by obedience. In his new relationship to Christ, not only is the believer ready to kiss Him (note the Christ-mysticism), but he will also obey Him in all things—including baptism. (4) The Christian life. The soul must still be saved from the clingingness of sin and all unrighteousness. This comes to pass through the power of Jesus and His Spirit and the free will of man, who must separate himself from all uncleanness. Longenecker considers celibacy to be an aid in this cleansing process.[55]

Peter Bowman (fl. 1800) also begins his discussion of conversion with the initial working of God. Man must become enlightened by the light of God's mercy in order to be convinced of his sinful nature and the guilt of sin. When a man recognizes his true state, a change will be wrought in his soul involving (1) the resolution to sin no more due to the fear of the consequences of sin and (2) the conviction that he needs to obtain grace and the forgiveness of sins from God. He thus becomes a seeking soul who will find in the Scriptures God's promise to save sinners "through the sacrifice of his [Christ's] life and blood on the cross." By Christ's sacrifice, He "has procured for us . . . the remission of sins, and has promised unto us the gift of the Holy Ghost." Through baptism, as "the answer of a good conscience toward God," one is promised the remission of sins and the gift of the Holy Ghost (Acts 2:38).[56]

The noteworthy features of these formulations of conversion are the highly subjective or "psychological" analysis of the process, especially as it involves the working of God through His Word and Spirit in the soul of the believer. This characteristic of Pietism, along with the Radical Pietist and Quietist overtones of Longenecker's discussion, indicate a continuation of the older piety into the second decade of the nineteenth century. However, a noticeable change comes over the discussion of the conversion process by the Brethren by the 1820s and 30s. Formulations of the *ordo salutis* during this period generally follow the earlier pattern of enlightenment or self-knowledge, repentance, faith, and baptism, to which are promised the remission of sins and the gift of the Holy Spirit. Yet the strongly subjective quality of the treatments by Longenecker and Bowman are replaced by a far more objective analysis which is preoccupied with the proper ordering of the elements of salvation. The source of this change is reflected in the minutes of the 1815 Annual Meeting.

> And inasmuch now, at this time, among the many religious parties and denominations there are such whose doctrines on repentance, on baptism, and on forgiveness of sins through the atoning sacrifice of Jesus, and on the sanctification through the Holy Spirit, seem to differ not much from those of the old brethren, only that they, according to our views, as the Word teaches us, do not put every thing in the right place.[57]

Interaction with revivalist groups like the Methodists and River Brethren, who called for "a lively experience of the forgiveness of sins" or even "complete sanctification" prior to baptism,[58] forced the Brethren to focus attention on the defense of their order of salvation. Typical of Brethren pronouncements during the 1830s concerning the conversion process is Peter Nead's declaration:

> The terms of the Gospel in order to salvation, are Repentance, Faith and Baptism, and the promise is, the remission of sins, and the reception of the Holy Ghost. . . . Now these prerequisites [to salvation] are connected,—and what God hath joined together, let not man put asunder.[59]

Rather unconsciously perhaps, the Brethren were doing exactly what Walter Scott, the outstanding Disciple of Christ evangelist, sought to do for the Campbellites: develop "an *objective* plan of salvation, in contrast to the subjective plan preached by the revivalistic groups."[60]

The objectifying of the salvation process can be seen in two other developments during the nineteenth century. (1) By the 1840s discussions had arisen over whether the proper order of repentance and faith was repentance-faith or faith-repentance. One might speculate that some Brethren maintained that a degree of faith must precede repentance in order for a change of heart to take place while others insisted that there could be no true, saving faith without repentance. (Could the firm Campbellite order have been behind this discussion?) The traditional, informal order of self-knowledge, repentance, faith left the question open. In 1845, Annual Meeting was asked to resolve the issue. Its answer was:

> Out of this faith [one which recognizes the righteousness of God (Rom. 1:17) and which causes a person to believe in

God's existence and to seek Him diligently (Heb. 11:6)], when it is quickened, repentance will come; and when the repentant sinner hears and receives the blessed gospel, an evangelical and saving faith will issue therefrom, which worketh by love, and maketh itself known by keeping the commandments.[61]

In effect, then, the Brethren developed a faith as *assensus* (knowledge of God and His demands)-repentance-faith as *fiducia* model. Though some writers during the second half of this century do follow this model in their discussions of conversion, most tend to simplify the entire matter by dealing with the various facets of faith in a single treatment. In the latter case, both the repentance-faith and faith-repentance schemas continued to appear without causing much stir.[62]

(2) The second development during the nineteenth century demonstrating an objectifying of the view of conversion is found in the manner in which the Brethren connected baptism with salvation and regeneration. Both Alexander Mack, Sr., and Jr., had carefully mediated the relationship between baptism and regeneration with the concept of faith acting in obedience. Some Brethren writers, emphasizing that the saving element in baptism is not the water but the "spirit of obedience" or "the answer of a good conscience toward God" demonstrated in the act, continued to uphold this traditional view.[63] Yet this view of baptism, which balanced the importance of its inward and outward elements, tended to be superseded by a more formal, objective formulation of baptism's connection with salvation and regeneration. Without doubt, the predominant argument for the observance of baptism during this century is that it is connected with repentance and faith as a unit to which God has promised remission of sins and the gift of the Holy Spirit. Thus God has ordained baptism as one of the means for the attainment of salvation. Not only is baptism commanded by God but it is also essential to salvation.[64] When questioned about teaching a form of baptismal regeneration, one Brethren writer welcomed the implication, claiming baptismal regeneration was Biblical,[65] though other writers resolutely denied the charge by maintaining that the Brethren, unlike the proponents of baptismal regeneration, hold that baptism would do no good unless preceded by repentance and faith.[66] In several other cases, it was held that those who raised such questions were disputing "the subject with God." Why should one "complain about the grace of God merely . . . because he has appointed means to bring you into Christ?"[67]

Accompanying this new emphasis was also a new phrase which is reflective of the more objective view of baptism: means of grace. This phrase came into general usage during the nineteenth and early twentieth centuries and was applied not only to baptism but to all the Brethren worship practices. It appears as early as 1817, in reference to the outward practices in general, in a document from the Philadelphia congregation, though Peter Bowman, in the same year, refers to baptism as a "means of salvation, to try our obedience."[68] James Quinter succinctly explains the import of the phrase for the Brethren.

> By the phrase, "means of grace," we understand those means which if properly used, or those conditions which if properly complied with, will put us in possession of the grace of God. As this grace is the gift or production of God, it is given by him as all his blessings to man are given.[69]

The classical expression of the Brethren understanding of means of grace is to be found in C. F. Yoder's book, *God's Means of Grace* (1908). All the ordinances, church worship practices, and distinctive teachings of the church (nonconformity, nonresistance) are placed under the rubric of means of grace.[70]

It would seem that the source of this new formulation of the necessity for baptism was both the objectifying reaction to revivalistic groups and, even more, the Biblicism of the Brethren as they dealt with such passages as Mark 1:4 (the Brethren, like Calvin, generally viewed John's baptism as essentially the same as Christian baptism), John 3:5; Acts 2:38–39; Ephesians 5:25–26; and Titus 3:5. The Lutheran roots of Nead, Kurtz, and other Brethren also should not be overlooked. This argumentation is, however, a significant departure from the emphasis of the early Brethren. For them, baptism was the outward sign and expression of an inward faith and obedience. It was the answer or testimony of a good conscience toward God. Emphasis was placed on the inward elements of the salvation process as fundamental and antecedent to the outward practice. Though the early Brethren did assert that the forgiveness of sins was promised to the obedient reception of baptism, the Brethren of the nineteenth century reversed the prior emphasis by focusing on the inward grace that *followed* the rite: baptism was for the remission of sins. It is noteworthy that this shift to a more outward, objective view of the salvation process has ramifications for the baptismal practice of the Brethren: the correct *form* becomes increasingly important. In 1821, Annual Meeting allowed people "content with their baptism" by single immersion to join the

church without rebaptism, provided they acknowledged the correctness of the Brethren order. In 1828 it was counseled that it would be better if they were rebaptized. In 1833 trine immersion alone was recognized as valid.[71] This latter conviction remained ascendant in all Brethren groups for well over a century.

Interaction with other Denominations

The process of defining more rigidly the church's position on the doctrine of salvation was fostered, to a great extent, by interaction with other denominations. Brethren literature of the period between 1785 and 1865 reveals that the Brethren were reacting to at least three groups on soteriological questions: the Mennonites, Reformed, and revivalist groups.

The main topic of contention with the Mennonites during this period was the proper mode of baptism.[72] Between 1804 and 1858 no fewer than six Mennonite and five Brethren works (written by Christian Longenecker, Peter Bowman, Peter Nead, and John Kline) appeared which continued the rivalry between these geographic and theological neighbors.

Like Alexander Mack, Sr., and Jr., the above Brethren writers employed a variety of arguments in defense of trine immersion: linguistic, Biblical, theological, and historical. In some of these arguments a rather elaborate (and somewhat problematic) exegetical method is employed.[73] It is noteworthy that the earlier writers, Longenecker and Bowman, relied on authorities that were familiar to a Radical Pietist and Mennonite audience: Felbinger, Reitz, the Berleburg Bible, Luther, Menno, *Martyrs Mirror*, and the Froschauer Bible (used especially by Swiss Mennonites). Nead paves a new direction in Brethren apologetics, however, by turning more completely to English and American authorities of Anglican, Methodist, Presbyterian, and Baptist persuasion.

Occasionally during the period under consideration, the Brethren reacted to various Calvinistic doctrines. Nead warns his readers against those who teach "that God works by irresistible means" and that one "cannot fall from grace."[74] Likewise, he cautions against those who "declare that man is only free to choose evil, and not free to choose good; that his situation is such, that he cannot give consent, or subject his will to the will of God."[75] These criticisms derive basically from the conviction that God has given man free will to accept or reject the right. Further, "it is only that service and worship that flows from a free and willing mind, that is acceptable with, and glorifies the name of God."[76]

With these basic convictions, it is understandable that the Brethren would react strongly against the Calvinist doctrine of predestination. It was felt that this doctrine placed God's own justice in question and, in effect, made Him responsible for sin.[77] The Brethren did not, however, strike predestination and election from their vocabulary, but held that election was based on foreknowledge of men's fitness.

> God foresaw that man would fall; and to remedy the loss and restore man to the divine image again, Christ was, as a Lamb, slain before the foundation of the world. In the Divine estimation Christ was slain before the foundation of the world; but to us, visibly, not until four thousand years afterward. In the divine foreknowledge the church was established before the world was made, and God *fore-ordained* who should compose it, basing this foreordination, not on one in preference to another on any personal ground, but on the ground of fitness as to quality.... The penitent, believing, loving and obeying, humble, self-denying soul is *foreordained* to be one of God's ELECT, now, henceforth and forever.[78]

Though the Brethren generally did not fit into any theological mold (nor did they seek to), they would have been more Arminian in their understanding of election, the efficacy of the atonement, the free will of man, and perseverance.[79]

The movement which posed probably the greatest threat to the Brethren during this period was revivalism. This point is underscored by the reaction against revivalist theology in the Annual Meetings of 1815 (Art. 1), 1820 (Arts. 1, 2), 1855 (Art. 9), 1857 (Art. 25), and 1859 (Art. 3) and against revivalist practices like protracted meetings and mourner's benches in 1842 (Art. 2) and offering invitations and singing an additional hymn to induce "mourners to come forward" in 1855 (Art. 21). Though the Pietist and Anabaptist heritage of the Brethren caused them to view conversion as indispensable for the Christian life, they were critical of the revivalist theology of groups like the Methodists and River Brethren and the "new measures" of men like Charles Finney. Especially disturbing to the Brethren was the teaching that forgiveness of sins, the new birth, reception of the Holy Spirit, and even complete sanctification should precede baptism. The emotionalism of revival services also bothered the Brethren, for by this time a more quiet, formal mode of worship had developed.

Reflecting these concerns, Brethren criticism came from several different vantage points. First, such requirements prior to baptism are nowhere found in Scripture.[80] Rather, Scripture links remission of sins, the gift of the Holy Ghost, and regeneration with baptism (John 3:5; Acts 2:38; Eph. 5:26; and Tit. 3:5).

Second, the "new converting means" have not been appointed by Jesus Christ or the apostles; they are man's appointment alone.[81] Singled out for special criticism were the anxious bench, protracted meetings, emotional preaching, the telling of thrilling anecdotes, the use of singing to rouse the emotions, the production of "animal magnetism" (hypnotism), and "praying characters" offering their services to pray for sinners.[82] Third, it was held that the aim of these new measures was to stir the emotions "to such a degree as to get the individual to believe that his sins are pardoned, and that he is born of God."[83] This use of emotions is not able to bring about the genuine change in man required by Christ. Indeed, it is perilous to "rely on the feelings of our hearts alone, as testimony that we have passed from death unto life; for our hearts are deceitful above all things and desperately wicked, and Satan, that vile deceiver, is ever on the alert to draw our precious immortal souls into ruin."[84] Fourth, much revival preaching "appeals to the feelings, but does not inform the mind." People "are told to believe, . . . but what their faith is to lay hold of, and what the Lord requires them to do that they may serve him acceptably, is not made clear to their minds."[85] The crucial criticism here is that revivalism too often fails to educate the believer concerning the costly life of discipleship to which Christ calls his followers. John Kline protests against the sentiment found in the revival song:

> "Nothing, either great or small;
>   Nothing have I now to do:
> Jesus died and paid it all,
>   Long time ago."

> This would surely be getting salvation at a cheap rate. There is in this no "trial of faith, more precious than gold," no "cleansing of the flesh and spirit, perfecting holiness in the fear of the Lord." This means receiving the crown without bearing the cross.[86]

The Brethren were not against so-called "experimental religion" but maintained that a true change of heart must issue in a life of humble obedience and crossbearing discipleship to Christ.

THE CHRISTIAN LIFE

Not until the 1860s and afterward does the term "sanctification" come into common usage among the Brethren (through interaction with holiness groups) to describe the Christian life in general. Instead, the Brethren retained traditional Anabaptist and Pietist conceptions of the new life in Christ. The goal of the Christian life was the formation of a Christ-like character in the believer. In the conversion experience the believer receives both the motivation and enabling power for the new life. The desire to live a life pleasing to God must derive from the relationship of love between God and the believer. The ability to live the Christian life is dependent upon "the Lord's power in us through his Holy Spirit."[87] The Brethren would agree with Kline's assertion that God gives the believer "the strength and will" to live the new life, but "man has his work to do. He must be a coworker with God."[88]

The visible character of the new life is delimited by two key principles: negatively, by denial of self and the world and, positively, by obedience to God and discipleship to Christ. During this period self-denial, humility, and nonconformity to the world are Christian virtues which are stressed over and over again in the devotional and periodical literature. These virtues are especially emphasized as the Brethren are forced to come to terms with the surrounding culture in the course of the nineteenth century. Obedience, recognized by God-pleasing works, continues to receive special notice from the Brethren, so much so that they are at times criticized for preaching the doctrine of salvation by works. Kline responds to this charge by stressing that the entire Christian experience is based on faith:

> . . . We as Brethren believe and teach that "faith without works is dead." All good works are done in faith. And no man can believe in the Lord Jesus Christ with his heart, without loving him; because faith is a loving acceptance of all the truth revealed by the Lord to man. Our heartfelt reception of that truth leads to obedience, and obedience is good works.[89]

The only significant difference between this conception of the Christian life and that of the previous century is one of emphasis. The mystical theme of love for and union with God becomes less pronounced during the period while the outward expression of the principles of self-denial, nonconformity, and obedience are more clearly delineated through the developing order of the Brethren and the decisions of Annual Meeting.

ESCHATOLOGY

Some changes were taking place in the Brethren view of eschatology during this period. With regard to personal eschatology, the Brotherhood was slowly moving away from universal restoration, possibly due to the influence of revivalism and evangelicalism. In the Annual Meetings of 1794, 1798, and 1800 the Brethren demonstrated that they would not tolerate universalistic beliefs that were contrary to Scripture.[90] Though belief in universal restoration continued throughout the nineteenth century, it was to be held as a private opinion and not openly preached.[91] In 1858 James Quinter noted that belief in the doctrine was "by no means universal among us."[92] About the same time articles begin appearing in the *Gospel Visitor* which are quite critical of the teaching.[93]

The Brethren continued to hold a premillennial view of Christ's return, though this belief is expressed through several different constructs. At the beginning of the nineteenth century, Peter Bowman used a Philadelphian schema. The church was passing from the Philadelphian church phase to the Laodicean. In a short time the antichrist would appear and the time of great tribulation would commence.[94] Peter Nead utilizes one of the models common to the Adventists (and the early church): just as the seventh day of creation was a day of rest so also the seven thousandth year will usher in the rest of the millennium.[95] In general, however, the Brethren ordered the end events as: the apostasy, the tribulation under the antichrist, the gathering of the elect at Christ's return, the Millennium, the general resurrection and judgment.[96]

Several observations should be made about the Brethren approach to eschatology during this period. First, though the Brethren generally expected the soon return of Christ, they were not caught up in detailed speculations about the time He would return. Benjamin Bowman's skeptical view of Adventist attempts to date Christ's return would probably typify the Brethren.[97] Second, Brethren literature during the period of 1785 to 1864 contains very little discussion of eschatology. It was definitely part of the Brotherhood's Christian hope,[98] but the primary concern of the Brethren related to the demonstration of the Christ-like life. Like the Anabaptists, the Brethren possessed a realized eschatology derived from the conviction that the body of Christ was already realizing, by God's power, the life of the future kingdom. Thus John Kline could state:

> . . . the church, in its purest form and highest sense, is heaven begun on earth. . . .
>
> Since the church is the outward, visible form of God's kingdom on earth, it is of the utmost importance that the church give expression to and be a representative of the soul and spirit of the kingdom.[99]

Concluding Observations

This period is of decisive importance for the history and thought of the Brethren for several reasons. First, the geographical spread which characterizes the Brethren today was, to a great extent, attained by the end of the period. Second, the Brotherhood made the shift from a predominantly German-speaking group to a predominantly English-speaking one. Third, the Brethren begin to interact to an ever greater degree with their surrounding cultural and religious neighbors. Fourth, during the course of this period, Brethren thought and practice assumed definite form. In reality, all four of these phenomena are interrelated. Brethren faith, practice, and piety were able to maintain their distinctive features through the early decades of the nineteenth century primarily because of the artificial barriers created by their migration to the edge of the frontier, their German sub-culture, and their German devotional literature. With the opening of the last new territories, the shift to English, and the utilization of English religious literature, the Brethren were forced to come to terms with the outside world. During the 1830s and 40s, several changes indicate that the impact of American culture is being felt by the Brethren: the old piety, dependent on their German Pietistic litera-ture, gradually disappears; church practice becomes more rigid and formal in an effort to unify the scattered congregations and "fence the church in"; a more objective view of salvation develops in response to the subjective formulations of revivalism; power increasingly is centralized in Annual Meeting as the conservator of the old order. Nevertheless, by the 1850s it is also becoming apparent that some of the Brethren are willing to accept "innovations" (Sun-day Schools, education) from American society and religion which are considered advantageous for the church's future course.

Brethren thought and practice undergoes several important changes during this period as the church seeks to come to terms with the outside world. Because Scripture is used increasingly to defend the "received tradition" of the Brethren, little of the open-ness to new ideas or practices found in the previous century is evidenced. Emphasis comes to be placed on the outward expression of the faith. Discussions on Brethren doctrine frequently were reduced to the ordinances of baptism and the love feast; a closely regulated outward community came to be looked upon as the place where the Christian life was to be lived out with the result that the inward piety and fervency of the earlier period were dimmed; one's Christianity came to be judged by outward marks—nonconformity to the world, nonresistance, faithful-ness to the order of the church. What J. C. Wenger has said of the Mennonites in America during this same period is likewise true of the Brethren:

> These formulations [the theology developed by nineteenth century leaders] tended to cluster about nonresistance, nonconformity, and the ordinances: but nonresistance was thought of too exclusively in terms of a rejection of military service in time of war and little effort was made to develop a broad social ethic in terms of New Testament Chris-tianity; nonconformity was often misunderstood as involv-ing merely the maintenance of a cultural *status quo* rather than a dynamic spiritual tension with a Christ-rejecting world; and there developed an enumeration of "ordinances" [or among the Brethren, "means of grace"] which was utterly foreign to the Anabaptist tradition, as well as an undue emphasis on outward forms.[100]

The concept of an inner-outer dialectic, which had become an explicit principle of Brethren thought and practice during the colonial period, is far less visible during the following era. With the focus on defend-ing Brethren practice and maintaining the order, the balance had clearly shifted in the direction of out-wardness. Yet, counterbalancing forces can be seen in the life and work of Quinter and Kurtz. It is unfortunate that the attempt to regain equilibrium resulted in the shattering of the Brotherhood in the 1880s.

Chapter 8

PETER NEAD'S LIFE AND THOUGHT

Introduction

Without doubt the most thorough and detailed exposition of Brethren thought during the nineteenth century comes from the pen of Peter Nead (1796–1877). In his two major works, *Theological Writings* and *Wisdom and Power of God*, Nead covers the major themes of systematic theology and considers at length the distinctive practices of the Brethren. His works received wide circulation among the Brethren and undoubtedly served to effect greater unity of thought throughout the Brotherhood. Albert Ronk pays tribute to Nead and his theological writing by observing that his "theology was so pungent and convincing, the minds of the people were so thoroughly settled as to the sacramental rites, that, in the disagreements which later caused three divisions among the Brethren, none of them arose over the Sacraments."[1] For an in-depth understanding of the thought of the nineteenth century Brethren mind, the investigation of the thought of Peter Nead becomes mandatory.

The Life of Peter Nead

It is traditionally held that Nead's forebears came from Germany to America prior to the Revolutionary War. Peter's father, Daniel, settled in Hagerstown, Maryland, where he made a living as a tanner. The Daniel Nead family consisted of four sons: Matthias, Daniel, John, and Peter. Though the family was staunchly Lutheran, the sons were religiously independent. Only Matthias remained Lutheran while Daniel and John joined the Brethren and became ministers in Tennessee.[2]

Peter was born at Hagerstown on January 7, 1796. Apparently, he was an apt student, for a grandfather offered to subsidize his education to prepare him for the Lutheran ministry. For some reason the offer did not appeal to him. As a youth, he worked as a clerk in a local store. When the family moved to Frederick County, Virginia, Nead became apprenticed to a tanner and also taught school during the winters.

During his early twenties Nead joined the Methodist Episcopal Church. His leadership abilities were quickly noticed and he was installed as a class leader. However, he became disenchanted with the Methodists and began a brief career as an itinerant preacher. During 1823 and 1824 he traveled up and down the Shenandoah Valley, preaching wherever anyone would listen to him. This was a period of great uncertainty for Nead as he searched for a religious body whose tenets he felt were in accord with the teachings of the New Testament. In the course of his search, he became acquainted with the German Baptist Brethren through a booklet written in 1823 by Elder Benjamin Bowman of Rockingham County, Virginia. Nead visited the Brethren during his travels and was impressed that they observed the ordinances "according to the Scriptures."[3] He decided to unite with the Brethren and on June 14, 1824, was baptized by Elder Daniel Arnold in the Potomac River.

On December 20, 1825, he married Elizabeth Yount, a daughter of a Brethren member. They settled on the Yount homestead in Rockingham County, Virginia. For a living Nead carried on a tanning business and taught school. In 1827 he was called to the ministry at the same council meeting that elected John Kline as a deacon.

Nead applied himself to his ministerial responsibilities with great devotion. Because he joined the Brethren at the time they were making the transition from German to English, the bilingual Nead was able to meet the special need for preaching in English. His speaking ability, already polished during his earlier religious experiences, was frequently called upon, and he became affectionately known as "the English Preacher."

Nead's systematic frame of mind is revealed in his daily regimen. It is said that he arose at three o'clock, ate a bit of dry bread, walked about the room a few minutes, and then devoted himself to reading, writing, and memorizing Scripture until six o'clock.[4] This schedule not only prepared him for his ministerial duties but gave him time for writing as well. His first book, *Primitive Christianity, Or a Vindication of the Word of God*, was completed in 1833 and published the following year in Staunton, Virginia. In it, Nead gave an overview of the doctrine of redemption and detailed discussions of the distinctive Brethren practices. This work became a means of outreach for the church. A neighbor commented that it was "the cause of persons coming to the church that never heard Brother Peter preach."[5] A German translation of the work appeared in Pennsylvania in 1836.

That same year Nead completed another theological work, *An Exhortation of Certain Evangelical Truths*, a second edition of which appeared in 1845. A larger pamphlet was also released in 1845. Its title reveals the basic content of the writing: *Baptism for the Remission of Sins; The Faith Alone and Prayerless Doctrine Considered; Observations on the Present State of the World; Corrupted Christendom and the True Church of Christ*. This work's lengthy section on baptism presented numerous historical and theological citations which were utilized in many of the later debates and books on the subject.[6] Appended to the writing was a treatise on the Lord's Supper by John Kline.

Following his resettlement near Dayton, Ohio, in 1848, Nead revised his three previous writings, added some new material, and published his best known book, *Theological Writings on Various Subjects* (1850). This book, totaling 472 pages, was in such demand that a second large printing occurred in 1866. Its impact on the Brotherhood was considerable. It became recognized as a standard work for the Brethren and did much to stabilize and unify the membership in all parts of the Brotherhood.[7] It served as an evangelistic tool, for many people came into the church after acquainting themselves with the doctrines of the Brethren as presented in Nead's book. Significantly, Roger Sappington observes that Nead's *Theological Writings* "had more influence on the development of the ideas of the Church of the Brethren from 1850 to 1900 than any other single volume, except the Holy Bible."[8]

Nead wrote one more major work, *The Wisdom and Power of God* (1866). This work follows a traditional outline of theology, treating the doctrines of God, creation, sin, redemption, the church, and consummation. In addition, he was instrumental in starting the Old Order monthly publication, *The Vindicator*. Begun in 1870 by Samuel Kinsey, his son-in-law, this periodical featured a steady stream of articles from his pen.

For twenty-seven years up until his death, Nead served the Lower Stillwater congregation near Dayton. He frequently served in district conferences, and twelve times he was chosen as a member of the Standing Committee of Annual Meeting. His last years were troubled by the tensions created by the introduction of such innovations as Sunday schools, academies, revival meetings, and foreign missions. Though he was at the forefront of the Old Order movement, which opposed these practices, his counsel was, as always, motivated by a deep love for and commitment to the church as he knew it at his baptism. He "was not able to accept any change, however slight or far-reaching, which to his mind would move" away from this standard. "This rigidity was both his strength and his tragedy."[9]

The Thought of Peter Nead

INTRODUCTION

Peter Nead was the first writer among the Brethren to present a systematic and expanded discussion of Brethren doctrine. Nead's writings can be trusted as a reliable reflection of Brethren doctrine during the mid-nineteenth century for a number of reasons. First, Nead was totally committed to the church of his choice: the German Baptist Brethren. He was willing to conform his thought and practice to the order of the church because of his deep love for the Brotherhood.[10] Second, as J. H. Moore suggests, Nead probably read all the Brethren literature he could find.[11] His writings reveal a thorough acquaintance with every facet of Brethren life and thought. Third, Nead's *Theological Writings* became recognized as almost an unofficial creed of the church. Its acceptance by the Brotherhood indicates that Nead had captured the life and spirit of Brethren thought.

Nead's writings are not theological in the technical sense of the word. The cogency of his argumentation does not rest on carefully reasoned propositions, but on the combined testimony of appropriate Bible passages. He does not generally use the technical terms found in the standard systematic works, but utilized instead Biblical terminology. Though at times he does exhibit these characteristics of a more systematic approach to theology (especially in *Wisdom and Power*), his overall approach is more in keeping with the Biblical theology of the Pietists and Anabaptists.

Nead does, nevertheless, introduce a significant new source for the defense of Brethren doctrine—the supportive testimony of works from a variety of theological traditions. In his two major works Nead cites over fifty sources, including commentaries, theological works, patristics, theological dictionaries, and religious encyclopedias. Though his purposes were thoroughly apologetic, he actually helped to heighten Brethren awareness of the larger theological world.

The published works of Peter Nead include a fragment of his diary, two volumes of doctrine, a few articles in the *Gospel Visitor*, a total of seventy-seven serial articles in the first eight volumes of the *Vindicator*, and several miscellaneous articles and answers to queries in the latter periodical. This study will utilize nearly all these sources.

THE SOURCES OF AUTHORITY USED BY NEAD

The sources of authority recognized by Nead for determining the life and thought of the people of God are quite similar to those utilized by the early Brethren. Yet at several significant points Nead supplements or modifies the emphasis of the original hermeneutical synthesis. These changes are critical for understanding the varied Brethren response to American secular and religious culture during the nineteenth century.

God provides for and preserves His People

Nead sees God's hand at work both in the "wonderful construction" of the first man, Adam, and in His loving provision for Adam's sin in the promised Redeemer of Genesis 3:15.[12] Furthermore, in every dispensation God has preserved a remnant. Nead views the primary character of this remnant as its observance of the ordinances according to God's will. On one occasion he also singles out the continuation of "the true administration and intention of baptism" from the time of the apostles (like the Mennonites and Mack) as a special attribute of the true church.[13] Nead does not attempt to trace any line of continuity. Yet he does casually mention the Waldenses in a section where he argues that the true church has always practiced the commands of the Lord.[14] It would seem that Nead assumes that his readers know the "direct" connection which the Waldenses have to both the early church and the early Brethren.

Christ is the Head of the Church

For Nead, the Christian life, in its individual and corporate aspects, is to be patterned after Christ, "our exampler [sic]."[15] The special authority ascribed to Christ derives from His unique relationship to the Father. Nead testifies in the preface to *Theological Writings*:

> . . . the only motive which has induced me to write this book, was to bear testimony to the truth as it is in Jesus; and also impress upon the minds of the children of men, the great necessity of obeying God, our Heavenly Father, in all His precepts, as they have been revealed by Jesus Christ, and are now upon record in that well know Book called the New Testament.[16]

Because Christ has fully revealed the will of the Father, He can be rightly called the "Author" of the Christian religion, "the only law giver in the church," and the head of the church.[17] The household imagery, which plays an important part in Mack's conceptualization of the Christian faith, is almost nonexistent in Nead's thought.

The Christian's responsibility with regard to the precepts delivered by Christ is unqualified obedience. The Brethren tendency of viewing the new life in Christ in legalistic terms is especially strong in Nead. Not one commandment of the Lord Jesus Christ is to be taken lightly or overlooked. Indeed "the highest learned and the greatest scholars in the School of Christ" are those who are "the meekest, humblest and the most unassuming and yet the most scrupulously particular in the observance of all the points or precepts and institutions in the doctrine of Christ."[18] Even the underlying motive for the believer's life of obedience—love for God and free-willing subjection to His will—is cast in such a way to reinforce the necessity of obedience.

> If our knowledge of the word of God has the right tendency, say, to love God and man, our knowledge is true; because no man can, in the true sense, have this affection for God and man and not *obey* all the precepts and institutions of the New Testament of our Lord and Savior Jesus Christ. See John XIV. 21-24.[19]

Nevertheless, for Nead and his contemporaries the new life of obedience and discipleship to Christ was not burdensome; rather, they willingly submitted themselves to their Lord and Master, knowing that all His commandments were for the spiritual welfare of His people.[20]

*Scripture is the perfect standard
for the Church*

Nead felt that Scripture contained all the truth necessary to accomplish the divine will for man: salvation and sanctification.[21] Since the Word of God perfectly reveals His will for His people through the precepts and example of Christ and the apostles, it is the sole "standard, the only infallible rule to judge by, and to know how matters stand betwixt us and our Creator."[22] Nead again discloses a legalistic bias when he refers to Scripture as the "one law book" for the church.[23] With such a view of Scripture, it is understandable how he can insist, for example, that the true church "believes that not only the mode [of baptism], but all that is connected with the institution is strictly essential, and that a willful omission in any one part of the institution would be an infringement upon the holy name of Jesus."[24]

Nead affirms the divine inspiration of Scripture on several occasions in his writings. He notes that the Old Testament prophets were "filled with the spirit of inspiration,"[25] and that the apostles

> . . . were under the influence of one spirit—being divinely inspired by the Holy Ghost in all their instructions and proceedings in holding forth Christ and Him crucified; for the reconciliation of man to God,—the salvation and redemption of a lost and ruined world. (2nd Cor. 5:18, 21.) Hence, their understanding, preaching and practice of the gospel or doctrine of Christ, was a unit. Now this concord or harmony, which characterized the ministry of the apostles, must be attributed, as already intimated, to that one Holy Spirit by which they were called and baptized into one body. 1st Cor. 12:13.[26]

Nead believed that the inherent unity found in the New Testament was likewise an attribute of all Scripture. "The book of God is not a book of confusion, but of harmony. It reveals but one order . . ."[27] Nevertheless, not all Scripture possesses the same degree of light. The New Testament, as the clearer revelation of the will of God through Christ, has primacy over the Old Testament, while the words and example of Christ, as the revelation of God Himself, occupy a central position in Scripture. Note, for example, the following affirmation by Nead.

> It is in the New Testament that life and immortality are brought to light. Therefore when we exhort our fellow man to work out his soul's salvation, we have no reference to the law that we should labor with those tools which Moses gave to the Jews—but to the Gospel, that we should perform the commandments of our Lord Jesus Christ.[28]

Even though Nead does see degrees of authority in Scripture, he nevertheless upholds the perfection of the entire Word of God[29] and the need to acquaint oneself with all of Scripture, including the Old Testament. A knowledge of the Old Testament is indispensable for all Christians, for it contains the basic patterns and figures developed and fulfilled in the New Testament (Nead at times resorts to an allegorical interpretation of these prefigurations).[30] This knowledge, therefore, "has a great tendency to fortify the mind against those objections which are made in opposition to the institutions of the New Testament."[31] In addition, Nead allows for an element of continuity between the Testaments which must be Christologically determined. Though he does not detail the nature of this continuity, he holds that Christ, the "founder of the Christian religion," determines what is abrogated and what is retained in proceeding from the dispensation of law to that of grace.[32]

Nead encourages his readers to "unite, harmonize, and obey the whole will of God."[33] Systematizing God's Word has its place, but only when it is done according to the true sense of the Word of God and with the humble desire to obey the whole will of God. A stern warning is levied against quoting or preaching "the word of God in a disconnected way in order to prove a false idea of the doctrine of Christ or the plan of salvation."[34] Such a prejudicial approach to the Word is entirely incompatible with the humble, respectful attitude of a true follower of Christ. Nead believed that "a meek and lowly mind will never rebel against any part of the doctrine of Jesus Christ."[35]

For Nead, the Bible is an "open book." It is so clear in its intent that even the uneducated could understand its message. "You probably have heard it said that common people have not the learning to understand the will of God; but don't you believe in such sayings, for it is a very plain Will, written in common style and adapted to the meanest capacity."[36] Each member of the Brotherhood should seek to develop a basic knowledge of Scripture. He must not rely solely upon his preacher for expounding its meaning, for preachers are not infallible.[37]

Nead's view of Scripture results in some commendable emphases—Scripture is the sole authority for the church; it is to be read in its connective sense; every believer should arrive at a basic knowledge of Scripture on his own. Yet his legalistic and literalistic approach to the Word tends to emphasize the external features of the faith, especially the ordinances, at the expense of the inner spirit and faith which vivify the obedience of faith.

*The Holy Spirit is the inner guide
for Believers*

All of God's elect, i.e., those who have conformed
their will to God's, "entered into the church of
Christ, and are living up to their christian privileges,"
have received the anointing of the Holy Spirit. The
effect of this anointing is to teach the elect "not only
a part, but the whole will of God, and the observance
of it."[38] Because the indwelling Spirit is thus indispensable for a complete understanding of Scripture,
Nead holds:

> The testament, separated from the Holy Spirit in the
> church, is not *all*-sufficient for the illumination and con-
> version of the sinner. If that were the fact, there would
> have been no necessity for Christ to appoint a ministry
> under the Christian dispensation. Neither would he have
> said that the spirit will "reprove the world of sin, and of
> righteousness," &c.; and, also guide the believer into all
> truth. (See John 14:26; 16:8, 15.)[39]

Nead is optimistic that if Christians are "operated
upon by his Spirit; and if led by that Spirit, they
need apprehend no danger of swerving from the
truth or imbibing error." This is the case because "it
is the Spirit's office to guide the believer into all
truth."[40] Yet, believers must beware, for there are
false spirits active in the world. Therefore, it is
necessary to try or prove the spirit

> . . . .by the word of God. For example—If that spirit from
> whose operations we act and move, and if those actions
> and movements do not in every respect agree with the
> Gospel of Jesus Christ, we may take it for granted, that it is
> a spirit of error, and not the spirit of truth, that operates
> upon us.[41]

Thus, Nead is true to the Brethren-Anabaptist heritage in seeing an inherent coincidence between the
Word and the Spirit. The Spirit is needed to guide
the believer into the truth while the Word becomes
the plumb line for judging supposed manifestations
of the Spirit.

*The primitive church provides the norm
for the contemporary Church*

Occasionally, in his two main theological works,
Nead sets forth the primitive church as the standard
for all contemporary expressions of the church. For
example, he admonishes those people seeking a
church home to make their selection with the "full
persuasion that your choice resembles Primitive Christianity, when under the control of Jesus Christ and
the twelve apostles."[42] The cloak of authority that
surrounds the apostolic church has a Christological

base: the apostles were inspired in "their understanding, preaching and practice of the gospel or doctrine
of Christ."[43]

It has already been noted (p. 116) that Nead's
earliest writings view the Brethren movement as a
continuation of the true apostolic church. However,
in the *Vindicator* Nead casts the relation between the
apostolic and Brethren churches in terms of *restoration* (suggesting that the establishment of the true
church does not depend upon a discernible line of
continuity). Thus Nead's longest running serial in the
Vindicator was entitled "The Restoration of Primitive
Christianity." This subtle change could be explained
on the basis of two factors. First, restorationism had
a strong apologetic appeal as shown by its effective
utilization by the Disciples movement. During the
turbulent 1870s, Nead used the term to call the
church back to the purity of the apostolic church.
His fear was that the church was progressing into the
same path as "a blind and corrupted christendom."[44]
Second, the Brethren were coming to doubt the
viability of arguing for the authenticity of the church
on the basis of an "apostolic line of succession." The
problem faced by those who made the claim of
apostolic succession was that "they cannot well get
around the church of Rome, and everybody knows,
or, at least, ought to know, that to trace religious
practice there, and then, call it a protestant religious
practice, is rather humiliating."[45] Whether Nead came
to share this same skepticism is not certain (his
continued use of the idea of a remnant would
suggest he retained the concept of continuity), though
even in his earliest works the theme of continuity is
used sparingly.

*The early Brethren were divinely inspired
in their interpretation of Scripture*

Though not appearing in his two major works, the
conviction that the early Brethren were guided by
the Spirit in the organization of the church is frequently expressed in the *Vindicator*.

> Upon the whole, we say, that our first brethren through and
> by whom God reorganized the church in America, were
> finally endued with the Holy Ghost to understand and
> practice the ordinances according to the will of the Master;
> and the observance of those institutions had the desired
> effect.[46]

Whereas Scripture provides the basic outlines and
patterns for Christian practice, the founders of the
German Baptist Church were endued with authority
to establish the specific details of Brethren practice.

Where the Testament is silent on the order or mode of observance, the brethren, by whom God organized the church, were clothed with authority to say in what way the commandments or institutions of his house are to be practiced.[47]

Obedience to "the ancient order, and self denying principles of the church, as taught by the Savior and held forth by the early fathers of our Fraternity"[48] created for Nead a tightly knit and unified institution which served as a sturdy defense against the encroachments of a corrupted Christendom and devious Satan. At times Nead appears to leave some freedom in his system through what he calls the "tendency" or "spirit of the gospel." He encourages every member of the body of Christ to have a knowledge of the tendency of the gospel, that is, an understanding of Scripture which is deep enough to discern whether a given practice is of God or of the flesh and Satan.[49] Yet even at this point, Nead generally limits the extent of this freedom by interpreting the tendency of the gospel in the light of traditional Brethren practice.[50]

From the above, it can be seen that Nead recognizes the freedom of the early Brethren to interpret Scripture under the guidance of the Holy Spirit. Yet he is not willing to extend this freedom to later generations of the Brotherhood. Nead thus limits the contemporary working of the Spirit by freezing the outward expression of the church in her dress, institutions, and ordinances. The order of the old Brethren to which Nead committed himself when he joined the church became a fixed standard for Nead that would allow no additions or subtractions.[51]

The church is the conservator of the ancient Order

Nead felt that the church, and especially Annual Meeting, should function as the guardian and enforcer of the faith of the church as handed down from Christ and the apostles and understood by the early Brethren. Thus Nead maintains: "The true church is clothed with authority from on high to enforce the admonitions of the apostles strictly, and all who will not hear the church should be separated or excommunicated."[52] Annual Meeting's special role in conserving the established order is likewise underscored by Nead:

Here let me again say that our yearly meetings, as they are termed, *have no right to make laws*, or change any of the administrations of the ordinances of the established church or house of God, but to enforce upon all the churches the observance of the whole doctrine of Christ

and his holy apostles, as understood by those brethren through whom God organized his church.[53]

What Nead and the Old Order Brethren sought was a church in which unity was expressed in terms of *uniformity* of faith and practice. The church, in its local and national structure, was to be the conservator of this order and enforce its observance, if need be, through discipline. Here again, Nead limits the contemporary activity of the Spirit by his rigidity. The original view of Annual Meeting as a gathering of believers who should arrive at a Spirit-directed consensus on issues facing the church is completely lacking.

Summary

Nead's sources of authority, taken as a unit, form a tightly knit structure with firm and easily defined boundaries. God has worked throughout history to preserve a remnant who have faithfully observed His ordinances and will. The full revelation of the Father's will was made in Jesus Christ who presented all that the Father wishes to be observed in His precepts and example. The apostles were inspired by the Holy Spirit to record perfectly in Scripture and in practice the doctrine of Christ. The Holy Spirit has now been given to all believers to guide them in their life of obedience to these patterns. The early Brethren were endued by the Spirit to fill in the details of the divine pattern and the church and Annual Meeting now become the conservators of the old order. In a day when many Brethren felt their faith was being threatened by a worldly and corrupted Christendom, this authority structure provided an objective standard by which they could easily critique departures from the faith.

THE DOCTRINE OF GOD

Nead deals specifically with the doctrine of God in *Wisdom and Power*, his last major work, which follows the outline and utilizes a few of the traditional categories of systematic theology. Nead recognizes that there are few new ideas that can be advanced on the subject of God's existence. Yet, he feels it necessary to "advocate the existence and character of the *one true and living God*, for the enlightening of the world and the strengthening of their [those who believe in divine revelation] faith, and thus prevent the rise and spread of infidelity."[54]

Nead begins his apologetic by affirming that there is but *one* God. If there were more than one, it would be reasonable to expect rivalry and war among the gods, more than one revelation (or Bible), and conflicting manifestations of glory and power. Yet no such manifestations have ever been witnessed.[55]

The existence of God can be known be His effects: His works and word. Thus God's existence is demonstrated by an orderly universe, the judgments against the wicked in the Old Testament, fulfilled prophecy, and the very existence of matter, for which there must be a first cause. Further evidence is found in the exhibitions of God's glory to Moses and to Peter, James, and John (at the transfiguration of Jesus). Nead concludes his discussion of God's existence with an admonition to accept the evidence of Scripture by faith: "Take the Bible for the man of your faith—be governed by its counsel, and a crown of eternal life will be your reward."[56]

Nead next considers the divine nature of God. He maintains an orthodox conception of the Trinity, i.e., that there is a "unity of three persons in the Godhead": Father, Son, and Holy Ghost.[57] In support of the doctrine of the Trinity, he cites both Old and New Testament passages. He notes the plurality of the statements found in Genesis 1:20 and 3:22—"Let us make man" and "man is become like one of us." He even sees evidence for the Trinity in the threefold name by which God revealed Himself to Moses: "I am the God of Abraham, the God of Isaac, and the God of Jacob" (Ex. 3:15). For New Testament support of the Trinity, Nead cites Matthew 3:16–17, Matthew 28:19, 2 Corinthians 13:14, and the disputed passage of 1 John 5:7–8. Nead recognizes the textual problem with these latter verses, but he maintains that the passage does not conflict with other passages of Scripture and that, if it is dropped, the connection between verses seven and eight is broken.[58]

Nead specifically states that he has no objections to the use of the word "person" when applied to the Father, Son, and Holy Ghost.[59] He interprets "person" somewhat anthropomorphically, however, holding that man's creation in the image and likeness of God refers to the body as well as the soul.[60] In another passage Nead states:

> We read in the Scriptures of the eyes, ears, face, mouth, arm, hand, finger and feet of the Lord. See 1 Kings XV, 5–11; Gen. VI, 8; Psa. XXXII, 15, 16; Isa. LII, 10; Deut. XXXIII, 3; Exo. VIII, 9; Lam. III, 8. That those members when applied to the Lord may be understood spiritually— that is, denote his protection, judgments, etc., we readily admit. But this would be no proof that God *has* no eyes, ears, face, etc.[61]

Typical of the Brethren, Nead does not stray far from the clear declarations of Scripture. He refuses to speculate about the subsistence of the Godhead and, as a result, says little about the attributes of God. (Mention is made that God is a spirit and therefore is invisible to mortal eyes.) Likewise, he refuses to delve further into the mystery of the Trinity or incarnation (to be examined later).

THE PROBLEM OF EVIL

Nead feels constrained to deal with the question of the origin of evil (in relation to the fallen angels) because it reflects on God's own character. God certainly cannot be the author of sin, for Scripture reveals that "God is love" (1 John 4:8) and that "He cannot tempt anyone to do evil" (Jas. 1:13). Therefore, Nead feels that he must posit another source.

In resolving the question of theodicy, Nead refers to Jude 6 and 2 Peter 2:4. All of God's creation was good and all of His creatures were originally holy, but not infallible.

> The angels like men were created for the glory of God. Hence they were created free agents, with liberty and intelligence; as it is only a voluntary service that can glorify the name of God.[62]

However, Satan, who was of the highest order among the angels, abused his position and power by becoming filled with pride and ambition. He was *self-tempted*, misusing the volition inherent in the freedom of his will.[63]

Ever since that initial rebellious act of desiring the praise and honor that was alone due to God, Satan has been the enemy of God and His creation. Not only did Satan involve other angels in his rebellion against God, but he also seeks to turn man away from God, having "for his object the destruction of all mankind."[64]

Nead maintains that the present home of Satan and the fallen angels is hell, or earth,[65] where they were banished by God for their rebellion. Here they are bound with everlasting chains. However, though their power is limited, their chains are long enough to reach every man. He can tempt but not force or compel individuals to rebel against the government of God.[66]

DOCTRINES OF MAN AND SIN

Nead refers to man as "the *master piece* of the creation."[67] He was created after the image and likeness of God, which, Nead maintains, refers to both body and soul. The first man, Adam, was created in righteousness and holiness and had a perfect knowledge of his Creator and of the entire creation.[68]

"At this time, man was in a state of innocency, pure and harmless, resembling his Creator, and for the continuation of man in a state of purity, the Lord God planted a garden eastward in Eden, and there He put the man whom He had formed."[69] At this juncture Nead develops two postulates that are basic to his understanding of man and sin. First, he notes that man was created a free moral agent, "endowed with understanding and will, and of course free and capable of obeying."[70] This conception of man is derived from Nead's understanding of the relationship between man and his Creator. Reflecting ideas common to both Pietists and Anabaptists, Nead argues:

> Dear reader, it is plain to me, that that faculty of the mind called will, is free in all men, to accept or reject, choose or refuse. And this freedom of acceptation and rejection was not conferred upon man for his destruction, but for the better qualification of the enjoyment of that God, who made man for his glory . . . It is only that service and worship that flows from a free and willing mind, that is acceptable with, and glorifies the name of God; whereas, if man had not the power over his will, he could not obey and worship God from a right of choice, but his conduct would be unavoidable, and of a compulsory nature.[71]

Nead's second postulate is that, in order to demonstrate his true righteousness and holiness, man's obedience had to be tried.

> God, for wise purposes, put Adam under restrictions, and thereby gave him to know, that notwithstanding his noble extraction and extensive dominion, he was not as yet at the summit of happiness, but in a progressive state or condition, and that in order to his preservation and advancement in glory and happiness, obedience to his will would be indispensably necessary. The law given to Adam, was a fair trial of his love and obedience.[72]

The trial of Adam's obedience came through the agency of Satan (Nead is careful not to lay the responsibility for the actual temptation on God). If Adam had not sinned, his descendants could have derived from him an "undepraved nature" and, like him, they could have been justified by the law.[73] However, both Adam and Eve failed the test of their obedience by breaking the law of God. Nead sees a number of results stemming from man's disobedient act of eating from the forbidden tree. The union that existed between God and man was dissolved and Adam and Eve died a spiritual death that very day.[74] They were stripped of their innocency, became mortal, and lost the image of God which had been impressed on their soul.[75] The loss of God's image

affected every aspect of man's being: "the whole man is depraved—all the faculties of the soul, even the mind, sight, will, judgment and understanding, are affected by reason of this spiritual malady."[76]

Adam's sin also had tragic consequences for his descendants. "Adam being the head and representative of his progeny, or human family, acted not only for himself, but also for his posterity."[77] Consequently, all of mankind partake of Adam's corrupt nature because they were in Adam's "loins, or blood."[78] Nead considers the salient feature of this corrupt nature as a "fleshly and corrupted mind" which is continually prone to wickedness. Left entirely to himself, man could never have recovered from his deplorable condition. God's merciful interposition on man's behalf first comes to light in Genesis 3:15 in "the glorious gospel communicated in the promise of a Redeemer."[79]

CHRISTOLOGY AND THE ATONEMENT

Nead holds that Christ is equal with the Father and has existed from eternity.[80] His assumption of human flesh, which commences the fulfillment of the Old Testament prophecies of a coming Messiah, has as its object the salvation of man and the destruction of the works of the devil. Christ came to do what depraved man could not do: make an atonement for the sin of the world.[81]

Statements made by Nead indicate that the theory of the celestial flesh of Christ, derived from the Mennonites, still was being discussed among the Brethren in the 1830s. He states: "whether he [Christ] derived his body, that is, took flesh and blood, from the Virgin Mary is a disputed point by some."[82] Though Nead holds that Scripture does not say whether Christ derived His body from Mary, he does stress that the body of Christ was conceived in Mary's womb, that He took on flesh and blood, and that Christ proceeded from Mary. He is willing to "let this knowledge suffice."[83]

In narrating Jesus' life Nead emphasizes several characteristics which he feels are basic to all followers of Christ. First, he dwells at length upon the self-denial and humiliation that Jesus accepted by forsaking His place in glory and identifying Himself with humanity. His birth, His circumcision, His subjection to His parents, and His baptism by John all demonstrate His willingness to humble and deny Himself.[84] Second, Nead stresses that Jesus was obedient both to the law and to His Father's will. Quoting from John 4:34, John 6:38, and Philippians 2:9, Nead affirms that Jesus was obedient to His Father in His life and His death.[85] Yet, He also fulfilled the law in every point. This obedience involved the preceptive part of the covenant between God and man as well as the penal part of the covenant. He who was holy, pure, and undefiled became cursed to atone for the sins of guilty man.[86] Finally, Christ is also our exemplar. It is incumbent on every believer to follow in His footsteps and to pattern his life after Christ's. No better example of living can be found than the One who is the way, the truth, and the life.[87]

In order to understand more fully Nead's conception of the atonement, it is necessary to consider briefly his view of law. Nead notes that God gave the law to His chosen people, Israel, for two purposes: first, to show the character of God—holy and righteous—and, second, to show the character of man—weak, helpless, and unrighteous. The law was of two types—moral and ceremonial. The moral law revealed to man his impotency and his inability to obtain righteousness. The ceremonial law revealed the necessity for the atonement of sins and the means of expiating sin: through the sacrificial death of animals. Yet, in reality, all the animals slain and all the blood that was shed were unable to take away man's sin.[88] The ceremonial law merely prefigured or was the type of Christ's own death.

> All those victims that were slain . . . had for their substance, the holy and patient Jesus, bearing our sins away, by suffering a painful and a shameful death, "the just for the unjust, that he might bring us to God." 1 Pet 3:18.[89]

Thus the perfect One, who kept the law in its totality, took on the curse of the law as the only being who could make a complete atonement for sin. Nead maintains that the real agony which Jesus suffered on the cross was not the physical pain. "The real cause of the Saviour's agony was that full view which he had of the demerit of sin, and which he, as the substitute of the sinner, would have to endure in his own body on the cross."[90]

Nead emphasizes the great price of our redemption—the blood of Christ, which indeed was his very life.[91] He also notes that the efficacy of the atonement is dependent on the person and character of Jesus Himself. "He was the Son of God, the second person of the trinity, hence no other being either in heaven, on earth, or under the earth could have made satisfaction to divine justice for man's delinquency."[92] From the above, it can be seen that Nead views the atonement in terms of substitution, penal satisfaction, and sacrifice.

There are several important results that Christ's atonement produced. First, it canceled Adam's transgression so that Adam's sin is no longer imputed to his descendants. However, the atonement does not eradicate the depraved nature inherited from Adam.[93] Second, the effects of Christ's atoning death are universal. Though the way is now cleared for all men to be saved, there is one important proviso for the realization of salvation: the atonement must be received and applied according to God's prescription.[94]

THE APPROPRIATION OF SALVATION

Introductory observations about Nead's order of Salvation

Several noteworthy characteristics concerning Nead's *ordo salutis* can be gleaned from his discussion of salvation. First, Nead at times states in unequivocal terms what he considers the proper order of the initial aspects of salvation: repentance, faith, and baptism to which elements are promised the forgiveness of sins and the gift of the Holy Spirit. On one occasion he adds: "you will find there is no other way for the sinner to be saved, than by a conformity to that order which God has so plainly revealed in the New Testament."[95] Examination of the context of such dogmatic declarations reveals that Nead is reacting against revivalism.[96] Of all the movements against which Nead reacts in his major writings, revivalism comes in for the harshest and most frequent criticism. This point needs to be remembered for it has definite ramifications for the way in which Nead formulates his *ordo salutis*. Second, when not placed in a polemical setting, Nead's understanding of the order of salvation tends to be less rigid and objective. This is especially true of his discussion of salvation in the less polemical and more theological *Wisdom and Power*. Here he treats many facets of salvation almost untouched in his *Theological Writings*: justification, adoption, regeneration, sanctification. Third, Nead's consideration of salvation reflects the religious controversies and discussions that were occurring both within and without the Brotherhood. His shifts on the order of repentance-faith have already been noted (see p. 272, n. 62). Nead's fuller development of the topics of regeneration and sanctification in *Wisdom and Power* are probably dependent upon interaction with revivalism and the holiness movement respectively. In this respect, Nead reflects the ever-increasing dialogue that the Brethren are having with American religious trends in the course of the nineteenth century.

Nead's order of Salvation

Enlightenment

Nead holds that enlightenment precedes the conversion process proper. The Word and Spirit work in concert to make the sinner aware of his lost condition. Thus the seed of the new birth is sown in a general invitation given to sinners through the Word while the Spirit "strives with sinners, not willing to give them over to a hard heart and reprobate mind."[97] When the sinner is enlightened concerning his lost state, he becomes an inquiring soul, seeking release from the weight of sin and the sense of guilt created by the knowledge of God's law.

Repentance

When the mind has been enlightened, the sinner is prepared for repentance. Nead notes that there are several essential aspects to "evangelical repentance": (1) a heartfelt sorrow for and bitter hatred of sins committed against the Author of our existence, (2) confession to God, and (3) the amendment or reformation of life. He especially emphasizes the last aspect, reformation of life, as "the main property of repentance."[98] Thus, a man can know if he has perfectly repented "if he is willing to forsake and renounce all the works of the flesh, and to submit or be subject to the word and will of God." If, however, a man is unwilling to surrender totally to Christ, "it proves that there still remains some darling lust which he is not willing to part with."[99]

Faith

Though Nead does not make the point in *Theological Writings*, he observes in *Wisdom and Power* that a certain degree of faith precedes repentance. This faith must believe in the existence and character of God and must be *active*, leading on to repentance; otherwise it remains a dead faith. Nead sharply criticizes the view that the mind is passive in believing (he probably has Calvinists and Lutherans in view). If such is the case,

> I cannot see *why* man should be commended for believing, or blamed for not believing . . . If the objection to the voluntary exercise of the mind in believing or disbelieving be *true*, the *whole tenor of the Old and New Testament is a false representation of the preceptive will of God—a mere sham or contradiction* of truth and justice.[100]

Nead describes faith as the reception of that testimony which God has given us in His word concerning the Father, Son, and Holy Ghost. It is confidence or trust in God and also in Jesus Christ, our Redeemer, and the gospel.[101] Faith is obtained by hearing and reading the Word, though the Holy Spirit also "works and co-operates with the gospel, that the testimony of God might be received."[102] Nead stresses the indispensable relationship between faith and works by noting that the strength of one's faith is known by his "*subjection* and *obedience* to the word and will of our Heavenly Father."[103]

Baptism

Repentance and faith qualify the penitent for baptism. That baptism is just as necessary for salvation as repentance and faith is emphasized again and again by Nead. For him it is the pivotal act in the entire conversion process.

> Faith and repentance do not convert, but prepare us for conversion to God. The word conversion, signifies a turning to God, we, therefore, argue that the unbaptized cannot in the Gospel sense of the word be said to be converted to God. They are no where from the 2d chapter of Acts to the end of the Testament said to be so. Baptism we repeat is the converting act. In the days of the Apostles whenever a person was baptized, he was said to be converted, and not before, See Acts xv.[104]

As noted earlier (pp. 108–110), an objectifying process was taking place in the Brethren ordering of salvation during the nineteenth century as the Brethren interacted with revivalist groups. Nead plays a key role in formulating and popularizing this more objective view in which baptism played such an important role. Nead stressed the essential character of baptism by maintaining that it, together with repentance and faith, formed a unit to which was promised the forgiveness of sins and the gift of the Holy Ghost.[105] "God has seen fit to adapt means to certain ends, and it is only by observing the means, in the spirit of the gospel, that the promised blessings can be obtained."[106] Though baptism alone cannot save, yet, as one of God's appointed means, it is essential to God's promise of salvation. Nead defends his view of "baptism for the remission of sins" by appealing to such Scripture as Acts 2:38; 22:16; Ephesians 5:26; Titus 3:4–7; Hebrews 10:22; 1 Peter 3:21.[107] He also cites for support various Methodist, Episcopalian, Lutheran, Baptist, and Calvinist[108] writers and confessions as well as numerous early church fathers.[109]

Though Nead devotes considerable attention to his contention that baptism is for the remission of sins, he also recognizes that the rite has several other significant meanings. Baptism is the admission rite whereby a believer is "recognized as a fellow-citizen of the saints and of the household of God." In baptism the believer renounces his former realm of allegiance—"the sinful practices of the world, the lusts of the flesh, and the devil"—and vows his "allegiance to King Jesus, to obey him in all things."[110] In baptism the believer enters into a covenant with God, he is ingrafted into Christ, and he becomes a child of God.[111] Finally, baptism is intimately connected with the divine workings of justification, regeneration, and adoption (see below).

Nead's conception of baptism is significant primarily because his understanding of the rite remained dominant among all Brethren groups well into the twentieth century. Especially important in this regard is his emphasis on baptism as the means of the remission of sins and as the initiatory rite into the church. The impact that Nead's conception of baptism had upon the traditional view of baptism was twofold. First, the older view that based its argument for the observance of baptism on an inward-outward dialectic—the outward rite of baptism is to be observed because it is an expression of the obedience of faith and the answer of a good conscience and it is therefore *in* such an act that one receives God's promised forgiveness—is replaced by a far more objective, outward argument—baptism is essential to salvation because it is a means of grace appointed by God. Though not denying the essentiality of repentance and faith, Nead raises baptism to a level of equal importance to these inward qualities. The second change is closely related to the first. Whereas the older view placed the emphasis on the *antecedent* inner qualities leading to baptism, Nead's view reversed the emphasis by basing the apologetic on the spiritual qualities which *followed* the observance of this means of grace. Thus the outward is no longer viewed as the expression of the inward, but it becomes the means for receiving the inward. These observations become very important in understanding developments in the Brethren Church (Progressives) in the next century.

Justification, adoption, regeneration

Because Nead views baptism as the converting act and the final condition of the salvation process, he deals with the divine workings of regeneration, justification, and adoption after his discussion of baptism. He does not seem to place these aspects of the conversion process in any definite relationship, though his discussions of justification and adoption sometimes precede that of regeneration.

As expected, Nead is emphatic that justification before God, i.e., the pardon of our sins, is dependent upon obedience to God's order of salvation. It is just as dependent on the renunciation of sin and the entrance into covenant with God (baptism) as it is on faith. Averring that Paul "does not say that we are justified by faith only," Nead insists:

> we find upon an examination of the Gospel that justification by faith always has a reference to baptismal justification[!]; when, by baptism we enter into covenant with God, and into a justified state, through the redemption that is in Jesus Christ.[112]

Compliance with the word united with the consequent promise of God based upon that compliance form "the *first* and most *important* evidence" for justification.[113]

Nead likewise ties adoption to the observance of baptism. It is in baptism that we are made the children of God, for according to John 3:5 we are not "born of the spirit until we are born of the water."[114] The believer can know that he has become a child of God by both internal and external evidence. Not only does he have the word of promise "if he has proceeded agreeably to the word" but he also has the internal witness of the Spirit assuring him that he is a child of God (Rom. 8:16–17).[115]

It is noteworthy that each of Nead's three writings where he treats the doctrine of salvation (the 1834 and 1845 works in his *Theological Writings* and his *Wisdom and Power*) gives an increasing amount of attention to the doctrine of regeneration. This characteristic, typical of Brethren writings of the period, is a response to the emphasis given to the doctrine of regeneration in revivalistic theology and represents a desire to give the doctrine firmer rootage in Brethren thought.

Nead's basic conception of regeneration remains fairly consistent between the 1830s and 1860s. He utilizes the imagery of conception (begetting), quickening, and birth to conceptualize the meaning of regeneration. A person is begotten of God in enlightenment when the Word of God is implanted in the sinner as the seed of the new birth. The change of heart and mind that occurs in repentance and faith represents the quickening of the sinner by the Spirit. These two elements must necessarily precede the new birth.[116] Regeneration is a change of state produced by the Word and Spirit. While faith is the "instrumental cause" (note the theological language in *Wisdom and Power*) of this change, baptism is the "act of regeneration." Thus, according to the Gospel, being born of the water precedes being born of the spirit.[117] Regeneration produces several significant spiritual effects. In regeneration the believer becomes "a *partaker* of the divine nature, and hence is spiritually-minded." He loves God and man and delights in the law of God. He experiences the hope of eternal life, divine reconciliation, and peace with God. True regeneration can be known by both internal and external evidences. Internally, one has the witness of the Spirit that he has passed from death to life, while, externally, regeneration is expressed in the love of God's commandments.[118]

Nead's objectifying tendency is quite noticeable as he deals with justification, adoption, and regeneration. All three of these spiritual workings are tied to the act of baptism in such a way that makes the outward act indispensable for the realization of the spiritual component. Here again Nead appears to limit the working of the Spirit.

The Christian life

Though not foreign to his vocabulary, the word "sanctification" is not generally used by Nead to refer to the overall goal of the Christian life. As with other Brethren writers of the period, Nead portrays the new life of the believer in Anabaptist and Pietist categories.

The experience of regeneration is crucial to the new life. Not only are those who are born of the Word and Spirit now operated on by the Spirit, but the new relationship of love between God and the believer becomes the catalyst for subjecting oneself to the will of God and keeping the commands of Christ.[119]

Nead constantly reiterates the point that the truly converted person will always express his change of state outwardly. Characteristic of the Brethren is Nead's conviction that this new outward conduct is exhibited positively in humility, love for God and man, and obedience and discipleship to Christ and negatively in self-denial and nonconformity to the world.

Throughout Nead's writings the principles of self-denial and nonconformity appear as a constant litany in response to the dangers of a corrupt society. He felt that the "Church, which is the body of Christ, will be found in a state of self-denial, walking in all the ordinances and commandments of the Lord, blameless."[120] In his later life Nead again and again admonished his fellow Brethren to beware the subtle temptations posed by a corrupted Christendom and an even more corrupt world. He called upon them to return to the self-denial and humility that characterized the early church and the early Brethren.

> No person can be a true subject of the Kingdom of heaven—an acceptable member of the family of Jesus, who is unwilling or ashamed to profess and observe the self-denying principles of the gospel of Christ as understood by our ancient brethren and by them required of all the members of the church.[121]

Just as important to the character of the people of God is nonconformity. "The people of God are a distinct and separate people from the world—that is they are of another character and party, engaged in a calling which is opposed to the sinful maxims, customs and practices of the world . . ."[122] Although the body of Christ is not to conform to the world, Nead contended that "the people of God should be united, and be as uniform in their customs and habits as possible, that there be no difference of character among them."[123] One gains the impression in reading Nead's articles in the *Vindicator* that he

> . . . wanted to capture and hold fast the spirit of nonconformity to the world that was common to many early Brethren. He wanted to perpetuate a spiritual principle by institutionalizing the forms in which that spirit had manifest itself in the past.[124]

Nead sees the goal of the Christian life as perfection or sanctification, though his conception of perfection is thoroughly Pietistic. It is therefore "the bounden duty" of the believer "to go on to perfection—from one degree of grace to another, unto a full state of sanctification."[125] Nead recognizes that sinless perfection is not possible in this life (in the same discussion he opposes the belief that one cannot fall from grace) due to sins of weakness. Yet, he does affirm that "as long as they [the children of God] preserve that love and affection for God and his word which they received at the first they cannot sin—that is, willfully . . ."[126] Both testing (a Pietistic theme) and the baptism of suffering or fire, i.e., the crucifixion of the old Adam (an Anabaptist theme), are important features in the sanctification process.[127]

Summary

The most significant difference between Nead's conception of the conversion process and that of the early Brethren is Nead's strong objectifying tendency in response to the subjective salvation system of the revivalist. Consequently, he emphasizes a particular order of salvation; he views God and the Spirit working through outward means to provide the promised spiritual blessings; he ties remission of sins, the gift of the Holy Spirit, regeneration, justification, and adoption to baptism. There are other indications as well that Nead is moving away from a subjective, inward view of the faith. He tones down the earlier tendency to discuss the conversion process in strong "psychological" terms, that is, the emotions of the soul as it is worked upon by the Spirit and Word. Likewise, Nead's discussion of the relationship of love between the believer and God is entirely devoid of the mystical themes found in earlier Brethren works. Of special note is that Nead begins to use theological categories and terminology in his *Wisdom and Power*, a characteristic that is becoming more noticeable in Brethren writings of the 1850s and 60s.

THE CORPORATE CHRISTIAN LIFE

The character of the Church

From the beginning of the Brethren fellowship, a strong filial bond had pervaded Brethren life. It was felt that "it is in, and not out of the church that the believer can live the life of the son of God."[128] This fundamental belief meant that those qualities which typified the true child of God—love, obedience to Christ and His Word, humility, holiness, self-denial, nonconformity—were likewise to characterize the whole people of God. These "gospel principles" were so important for the expression of the corporate existence of the Brethren that Nead maintains: "the church of God is a congregation of believers in Christ Jesus; and how may she be known? Answer; by her profession and general character."[129] Nead holds that the profession of the true church involves the acknowledgment of Christ as the one head and the New Testament as the "one law book" of the church. This one law book governs the entire life of the family of God, not only calling all brothers and sisters to love, humility, unity, nonconformity, and mutual aid but also prescribing the polity of the church. The character of the church as it is known in the world is delimited by the above gospel principles— complete truthfulness, nonresistance, nonlitigation, care for the needy.[130] The true church can therefore be discerned by the practical expression of the Gospel of Christ.

Church Officers

Nead contends that ministers, who have been entrusted with the preaching of the Word, derive their authority from Jesus Christ. Yet, this authority is never self-assumed, for the Lord uses the church to choose His ministers. In the business affairs of the congregation, the minister is to lay the matter before the church, but he has no more power in deciding the issue than the private members. Nor is he to proceed in "affairs of the kingdom of grace" without taking counsel of the church. Ministers should remember that they are servants and not masters of the church. They are to be examples to the flock, being sure that their life corresponds with their doctrine. Finally, they are not to seek pay for their services, though the church should be ready to help her poor ministers and those who incur expenses in traveling for the sake of the church.[131]

The ordinances of the Church

Nead mirrors the Brethren trait of viewing the ordinances as visible declarations of the church's fundamental beliefs. Yet, he also contends that their very observance fosters spiritual growth. "Now when these institutions are well studied in the school of Christ and observed by the believer in the literal and spiritual sense, they will promote love to God and love to man."[132]

Baptism

Baptism had special significance for Nead's understanding of the church. The Brethren of the nineteenth century normally waited for a person to apply to the church for membership. After being visited by two or more ministers who heard the applicant's profession of repentance and faith, the applicant appeared before the church council. If the church was satisfied with his profession of conformity to the church's faith and practice and accordingly voted to receive him, he would then be baptized. For Nead and the Brethren baptism thus was viewed as the admission rite into Christ's body and into the blessings and promises of God's kingdom.[133]

No other subject receives as much attention in Nead's writings as baptism.[134] This preoccupation with baptism is directly due to the controversial nature of the Brethren form of baptism, trine immersion.[135] Nead leaves no doubt about his commitment to this mode, for he dogmatically affirms: "the Church of Christ . . . believes that not only the mode, but all that is connected with the institution is strictly essential . . ."[136] Nead's certitude about the Brethren mode of baptism derives from his conviction that every aspect of the rite can find authorization in the words and example of Christ and His apostles.

Nead's fullest defense of trine immersion is found in the work that forms the first part of his *Theological*

Writings. Nead feels that the proper formula to be used in the baptismal rite is that given by Jesus in Matthew 28:19. There is no reason to adopt, as some have, those baptismal formulas found in Acts, namely, "In the name of the Lord Jesus" (Acts 8:16) and, "In the name of the Lord" (Acts 10:48). Nead presents three reasons for this conclusion: (1) We cannot infer from the expressions, "in the name of the Lord Jesus," and, "in the name of the Lord," that the form recorded by Matthew was not used; (2) the name of the Lord generally signifies, "according to the Lord's direction"; and (3) no good reason can be found to explain why the apostles would not have used the formula given them by their Lord and Master.[137]

Nead's apologetic for the Brethren mode of baptism followed a fourfold line of argumentation: (1) baptism is in water; (2) it is by immersion; (3) immersion is threefold; (4) the action in immersion is forward. (1) Although Nead does note that some of the baptismal narratives in Acts are indefinite as to where the baptisms were performed, he argues on the basis of John's baptism of Jesus and the detailed narrative of Acts 8:38–39 that baptism is to be performed in water. The Greek prepositions associated with baptism, ἀπό, ἐπί, and εἰς, support this same conclusion.[138]

(2) Nead next contends, "That immersion, or an overwhelming in the water, is the ancient mode of Baptism, is very obvious from the meaning of the word itself."[139] He cites Luther, Calvin, Owen, Beza, and Joseph Mede to corroborate this contention. Likewise, the "representations and figures" in baptism found in the New Testament are further evidence that immersion is the Scriptural mode of baptism. In this connection, Nead cites the comparison of baptism to burial and resurrection (Rom. 6:3–5 and Col. 2:12), the baptism of the Israelites in the cloud (1 Cor. 10:1–2), and (a bit more problematical) Noah's salvation in the ark (1 Pet. 3:20–21) and Jesus' baptism of suffering (Luke 12:50).[140]

(3) Nead turns to Matthew 28:19 to substantiate his argument for trine immersion. "To baptize in the names of the Father Son and Holy Ghost [sic] implies but one immersion—whereas, to baptize in the name of the Father, and of the Son, and of the Holy Ghost, implies a trine immersion."[141] Some of his strongest evidence for trine immersion comes from the practice of the early church. He cites Ambrose, Jerome, Tertullian, and Basil and notes the practice of the Greek Orthodox Church to show that trine immersion was the uniform mode in the early church.[142] He also relies on the theological argument that, since each member of the Trinity performs a particular office in the salvation of sinners, each person of the Godhead should be honored in baptism.[143]

(4) Nead looks upon baptism as a form of worship of God, and, from this understanding, he develops his argument for the forward motion in baptism. He notes that "in all those various examples for the worshipping of the true God, in the Holy Scriptures, not one is to be found in which the posture of falling upon the back was observed"; rather one finds that "the posture of kneeling and falling upon the face, was observed by the old Fathers, Jesus Christ, and the apostles, in divine worship."[144]

Though Nead's dogmatic approach to every detail of the observance of baptism appears excessively legalistic by today's norms, it must be remembered that he wrote in a day when doctrinal discussions and debates were taken very seriously (the phenomena of interdenominational public debates between the 1850s and 1880s is an evidence of this spirit). Nead's view of Scripture and the "order of the Brethren" likewise mandated a great concern for every detail of Christian life and thought.

Threefold communion

Nead is consistent with Brethren tradition in maintaining that "in the same night in which he [Christ] was betrayed into the hands of sinners, he did establish three . . . institutions, to be all observed in order, at one meeting—namely, Feet Washing, the Supper, and the Communion."[145]

Feetwashing. Nead considers that Jesus' words in John 13:12–17 give unequivocal authorization for the practice of feetwashing. He places the observance of feetwashing prior to the meal, appealing both to Hebraic custom and to the comments of Adam Clarke and Bishop Pearce. Feetwashing holds several significant spiritual meanings for Nead. First, it represents "that brotherly chastisement, which the children of God are sometimes called upon to exercise one towards another." He sees feetwashing as a symbol of the application of Matthew 18:15–17: "You observe, that in order to wash a brother's feet, you must bend or stoop yourself; and, secondly, your brother gives his feet into your hands, and then you can wash them." Second, "Feet Washing represents that state of purification through which the believer must pass, so as to be received at the coming of Christ."[146] In another discussion of this rite, the kerygmatic quality of feetwashing is stated even more forcefully:

> This institution tends to humility and the love of the brotherhood, and in it we also have a revelation of the necessity of a present salvation and the method of its

preservation, in order to admission to the marriage supper of the Lamb . . . The church militant is in a preparative state, for an introduction into the heavenly or triumphant state.[147]

The Lord's Supper. Nead is careful to distinguish the difference between the Brethren observance of the Lord's Supper and that of other denominations. He observes that the term, Lord's Supper, is taken from 1 Corinthians 11:20 and refers not to the bread and wine but to the meal which Jesus ate with His disciples on the night in which He was betrayed. The Supper is observed because it is appointed by Christ. It is to be a full, common meal, partaken at night. Its purpose is not only to refresh the body but to invigorate the inner man as well.

> The bodies of the members are not only strengthened by this institution, but the mind and soul of the believer is built up and encouraged, to perfect holiness in the fear of God, in anticipation of the heavenly supper which the Saints of the Most High will enjoy in the evening of this world.[148]

The eschatological motif is prominent in Nead's interpretation of the rite, for in another passage he holds that the meal reminds the believer of the coming of the bridegroom and of the heavenly state as well as of the marriage supper of the Lamb.[149] Also of note is that Nead expressly denies the assertion that the Brethren were eating the Jewish Passover in observing the Supper. Brethren defense of this point takes on significant proportions during the last half of the nineteenth century.[150]

Communion (Eucharist). Nead's discussion of the eucharist generally reflects an Anabaptist perspective. He views the bread and wine as being emblematical of the broken body and shed blood of Christ. He therefore opposes the doctrine of transubstantiation, insisting that the Scriptures which deal with the elements should be interpreted in a spiritual and not in a literal sense. He adopts the Zwinglian-Anabaptist view that the elements are a memorial of Christ's death and are to be shared "until he shall come."[151] Typically Anabaptist is the imagery he connects with the bread and cup.

> Flour is manufactured out of many grains of wheat. Bread represents the body of Christ and the body of Christ's church. Wine is made out of grapes, the grapes are bruised and pressed; the juice thereof is wine. Wine represents the blood of Christ, which was profusely shed for the sins of the world.[152]

Nead admonishes his readers to examine their life and conduct closely; if someone senses that he is unworthy, especially as a result of an unreconciled relationship, he should exempt himself from communion and seek reconciliation.[153]

The holy kiss

Nead considers the holy kiss a command of Scripture (Rom. 16:16; 1 Cor. 16:20; 1 Pet. 5:14). It was laid aside by "a degenerated christendom" but has always been observed by the true church. It should be observed often, especially when members meet for divine worship, when a newly baptized member comes out of the water, immediately after feetwashing, and just before communion. The holy kiss is a demonstration of spiritual affection and "is intended to promote mutual love among the fraternity."[154]

Anointing

The Scriptural support for anointing comes from James 5:14–15, but Nead also notes Mark 4:13. He considers it a great pity that this practice has almost become "extinct," especially since great promises are attached to it. Anointing is the privilege of every brother and sister, but it is up to the individual to decide if he wants to receive it. If he does, he should "be perfectly reconciled unto the will of God" with regard to the outcome of the affliction. The order of the service follows that described by James.[155]

Discipline

Nead holds that discipline is a necessary part of the church's government because of human frailty— members are "liable to commit trespasses against each other and against the church." The church is to be concerned about its character and purge itself of disobedient members. Yet discipline must always be administered with the design that it save and not destroy the erring member.[156]

In cases where a brother sins against a brother, the guidelines prescribed in Matthew 18:15–18 are to be followed. If, after the third step, the offender refuses even to hear the church, he is to be disciplined with the lesser excommunication or withdrawal, i.e., exclusion from the holy kiss, church council, and communion.

Since public transgressions bring a stigma against "the whole mystical church," such grave sins are to be dealt with according to 1 Timothy 5:20 and Titus 3:10. Those committing sins like those in 1 Corinthians 5:11 are to be expelled from the church and avoided or shunned. The object of avoidance in this greater excommunication is always "to save the soul."

The church should always seek to induce excommunicated members to repent, reform, and return to the church. All who "return by a *sincere repentance and reformation of life*" are to be warmly welcomed and received (without rebaptism).[157]

The state and civil Responsibilities

Nead sees the establishment of civil government as a necessary effect of the fall. Because of the fallen nature of man, the state has been ordained to punish the lawless and disobedient and protect the righteous.[158]

In all of Nead's discussions of the believer's relationship to the state, there exists an underlying principle. The Christian is fundamentally a citizen of God's kingdom and it is to this kingdom that he owes his primary allegiance. Nevertheless, the Christian is to obey the state in all things not contrary to Gospel precepts. This principle is the guideline which Nead uses as he discusses going to law, paying taxes, swearing, and bearing arms. Nead argues against going to law in order to settle differences with one's fellow man. The children of God are not to take vengeance on any man (he cites 1 Tim. 1:9–10). If, however, a believer violates the law, he is no longer under the Gospel but becomes liable to the law and its punishment.

Nead views the payment of taxes as authorized by both Christ and Paul. The Brethren are even to pay those fines imposed for their refusal to bear arms. Nead also uses the standard of Christ's word to advocate nonresistance and nonswearing (here James as well). In both cases Christ has given plain commandments and, in the case of nonresistance, believers have the promise of Christ and the Apostle Paul that they would be rewarded for their perseverance in suffering (Matt. 5:11–12) and that no power could separate them from the love of God and Christ (Rom. 8:35–39).[159]

ESCHATOLOGY

Personal Eschatology

Nead soberly reminds his readers that death is a certainty for everyone, though no one can know when it may come. Yet, he quickly holds forth the gospel message: "the grave is not the end of man. No. They that have done good shall come forth unto eternal life; but they that have done evil, shall come forth unto everlasting destruction."[160] Nead utilizes this eschatological truth to reinforce the call for responsible living now. During our stay on earth we should spend our days "with an eye to the glory of God, and the salvation and sanctification of our souls."[161] Likewise, because our souls will one day be reunited with our bodies, we should keep our bodies pure and free from fornication. "We should take care of them and present them a living sacrifice, dedicated to God and his service."[162]

Nead holds that the proof of believers' resurrection is founded upon Christ's own resurrection. It was the real physical body of Christ that was raised, though it was in a glorified form. In like manner, the natural body of believers will undergo a change and become a spiritual body at the time of the resurrection.[163]

Corporate Eschatology

In both of his major works Nead describes those events that will take place in the last days. He focuses his attention on the apocalyptic passages of Matthew 24, Mark 13, and Luke 17. He asserts that these passages mix together prophecies relating to both the destruction of Jerusalem and Christ's second personal appearance.

Nead discounts the possibility that the exact time of Christ's return can be known. Yet believers have been given signs by which they can have a "knowledge of his near approach." Most of the signs found in the above Synoptic apocalypses have already occurred, but it is not said how often they will recur before Christ comes. This very fact should cause all believers to live in a state of readiness for His coming.

Nead seems to be opposing postmillennial views when he challenges the "general opinion" that religion will be in a prosperous state before Christ's return. He holds that things will grow progressively worse for the true church prior to Christ's coming, though human society will become more advanced and prosperous. The true church, consisting of only a small number of true disciples, will pass through affliction in the last days. An especially clear sign of the nearness of Christ's second coming will be the return of the Jews to their homeland (written in 1833!). At His return Jesus will be seen by all the inhabitants of the earth, both saint and sinner. Nevertheless, His coming will be sudden and unexpected; watching and perseverance are needed by the children of God.[164]

Nead believes that Christ's return has special significance for both the church and Israel. At His advent, Christ will gather the believers to Himself in the air, first those who have died and then those who are alive. This is the first resurrection. Christ's millennial reign of peace and well-being will be followed by the second or general resurrection and the Day of Judgment. Nead opens his discussion of the sequence of events centering on the Jews[165] by observing that a great army will come against the restored House of Israel in order to destroy it. The Lord will then save Israel in its great peril and will be recognized by Israel as the Messiah. Immediately after the conversion of the Jews, the beast and the kings of the earth (Rev. 19:19-21) will wage war against Christ. Yet the Lamb will overcome them and Satan will then be found and thrown into the bottomless pit for a thousand years (the Millennium). At the end of this period, Satan will be loosed and will again seduce a host to oppose Christ. This time his defeat by Christ will result in his eternal punishment in the lake of fire. The general resurrection and final judgment follow these events.[166]

The judgments wrought on the Day of Judgment will be final and sure. Nead perceives three classes of men at this time:

> ... first, the saints—those which were Christ's at his coming;—secondly, the righteous, or the blessed of the Father—these are justified persons, and in consequence of their justification will stand on the right hand of the judge,—and thirdly, the unrighteous, or disobedient—such as would not have the man Christ Jesus to reign over them—in consequence of which they shall be placed on the left hand of the judge ...[167]

The saints will not be subject to the judgments handed out on this day. The righteous will be welcomed into the kingdom of heaven while the unrighteous will be cast into the lake of fire, which is the conflagration of the earth spoken of by Peter (2 Pet. 3:10).[168] Nead believed that there would be degrees in both the punishment of the wicked and the happiness of the righteous.[169]

It appears that Nead, like many other Brethren, held the doctrine of universal restoration as a private opinion not to be published before the unconverted. Though hints of the doctrine are to be found in his *Theological Writings*,[170] he does not explicitly discuss the belief. The main evidence for his espousal of restorationism comes from the report that "he with others published *Winchester's Lectures on the Prophecies*" a little before 1866.[171]

Several general observations should be made about Nead's eschatological views. First, he follows the basic outlines of eschatology found in earlier Brethren works. In *Wisdom and Power* he even utilizes the Philadelphian schema in his observation that the Laodicean church is considered "a type of the state of the church when the Savior shall come."[172] Yet, he also reflects current (Adventist) modes of schematizing eschatological events when he considers reasonable "the belief of some" that the seven thousandth year of the world will begin the Millennium. The seventh day on which God rested "may also represent the Millennium Dispensation."[173] Second, Nead believed Christ's return was near. This conviction was based on the universal apostasy and decay which he saw in Christendom.[174] Yet, Nead refused to speculate when Christ would return. Though his discussion of eschatology is one of the most complete up to his time in Brethren literature, it is far less detailed than the eschatological treatments of Brethren writers in the late nineteenth and twentieth centuries. Third, Nead used the eschatological motif to reinforce his emphasis for obedience to the Word. Every believer should prepare himself for Christ's near return by obeying all the commandments and ordinances of the New Testament.[175]

Peter Nead's Role
in the Division of the Brethren

Though Nead did not live to experience the anguishing divisions of 1881-1883, his spirit lived on in the Old Order Brethren. His articles in the *Vindicator* to a great extent guided these conservators of the old "landmarks" (cf. Prov. 22:28) up until his death in 1877. In his writing Nead utilized powerful sectarian imagery and compelling eschatological motifs which set the stage for the withdrawal of the Old Order Brethren from the Brotherhood. As early as 1833 Nead had written:

> The wilderness is the place for the children of God; and they are safe as long as they remain there; but whenever they come up out of the wilderness—that is, unite themselves with the world in it vanities, and live according to the customs of the times, they are no longer the true children of God; they may have the name, but are not his children indeed.[176]

Nead returned to this wilderness imagery in 1871 when he was distressed by the continuing openness of the Brotherhood to various elements of "popular religion." After citing Revelation 12:14, Nead raised the poignant plea:

> The spiritual wilderness is the place which God has appointed for His church. But, lamentable to say, many of God's people have become dissatisfied with the place that God has appointed for the church and are leaving and preparing to leave the wilderness and resorting to the world and the popular religion of the times as fast as they can.

O, brethren, pause for a moment! What will this world and this popular religion profit you in the spirit land! It may serve you very well for the present, but it will not do for the future. *We tell you* that the popular religion of the day, *cannot* qualify you for heaven and eternal glory. I beseech you therefore: STAY IN THE WILDERNESS, which is THE PLACE and THE ONLY PLACE of safety.[177]

When Nead perceived that his pleas were having little effect upon the inroads of popular Christianity, he began to call in 1872 for the use of strong disciplinary action in order to purge the church of "those inroads or innovations which are made either by adding to or subtracting from the ancient order and practice of the precepts and institutions of the gospel."[178] He desired to "dispose of" that element in the church that was copying "mystery Babylon," i.e., "the popular and fashionable religion of our day."[179]

By 1874 Nead was becoming disappointed with Annual Meeting's failure to take firm action against innovations and those agitating for them.[180] Nead gave fateful counsel to his readers the following year in his call for the "remnant" to remain faithful. Referring to Revelation 18:4, he advised:

Conference must be reformed; and if this can not be effected, then the only remedy or alternative, in order to save the churches, will be for those who believe in and practice the ancient order of the church to withdraw from all who contend for and practice an order of things which conflicts with the older established order and principles of the church.[181]

Nead placed the drift of the church into "corrupted Christendom" within an eschatological framework. He believed that what was happening to the Brethren was part of the apostasy and union of the sects which would lead to the persecution of the true church and in a short time to Christ's return.[182] Eschatological impetus was therefore given to the desire to remain true to the old order. There can be no doubt that such compelling use of sectarian and eschatological themes helped to set the stage for the events of the 1880s.

Concluding Observations

Peter Nead's impact upon the thought and practice of the German Baptist Brethren during the last two-thirds of the nineteenth century is profound. Yet it is ironic that this impact has both conservative and forward-looking aspects; it combines both traditional and novel elements.

The heart of Nead's conservatism is seen in his desire to enclose the church like a fenced-in garden. He sought to preserve and defend the order of the Brethren which he accepted at his baptism. To this end Nead thoroughly immersed himself in the thought and practice of the Brethren, completing the work which formed the major part of his *Theological Writings* just nine years after he joined the Brotherhood. In his writings he aggressively defended Brethren doctrine against "popular religion," especially revivalism. For Nead the Brethren faith, as formulated by the old Brethren, more nearly conformed to the ideal of primitive Christianity than any other with which he was associated. This conviction was fundamental to his rigid rejection, later in life, of any additions to or subtractions from the "ancient order" of the Brethren.

It was Nead's very zeal in defending Brethren doctrine, however, that placed the Brethren in touch with new ideas. Nead's role in helping to convert the Brethren to an English-speaking group through his preaching and writing created the possibility for more rapid acculturation of the Brethren. His broad reading, his citation of corroborative testimony from a wide variety of theological traditions, and his introduction of theological terminology, though done in order to support Brethren views, actually paved the way for a more educated Brotherhood. J. H. Moore has noted the irony attached to Nead's diligent study and research:

. . . as far as blazing the way for the Brethren to become a reading and thinking people, well rooted and grounded in their accepted church principles, he was certainly a real pathfinder. While not an advocate of high schools and colleges among us, . . . he nevertheless, by the seed his book planted . . . [opened] up the way, unintentionally, for every Brethren educational institution west of the Alleghenies.[183]

Finally, Nead's objectifying reaction to revivalistic theology gave a new emphasis to the Brethren understanding of baptism and the outward ordinances. The outward was no longer the sign, seal, or answer of the inward but the means to the inward. This subtle theological change is basic to the formalism and externalism which characterized Brethren practice during the nineteenth and early twentieth centuries.

Peter Nead's life and writings epitomize the "multiple personalities" which were developing among the Brethren as they were forced to adapt to the American religious and cultural scene. Though Nead was the unassailable defender of the old landmarks, his tactics for defending the old order utilized progressive means. In truth, a part of Nead's legacy can be seen in each of the three groups that emerged from the turbulent 1880s. His allegiance was with the Old Order; his spirit (in using the new to preserve the old) was like that of the Conservatives; his methodology was like that of the Progressives.

Chapter 9

ISSUES CONTRIBUTING TO THE SCHISM

Introduction

The year 1851 has traditionally been recognized as a pivotal point in Brethren history, for in April of this year Henry Kurtz began his monthly paper, the *Gospel Visitor*, at Poland, Ohio.[1] Yet, church periodicals represented only one of a number of issues (including education, a paid and educated ministry, Sunday Schools, evangelism, prescribed dress, mode of feetwashing) that would lead to a polarization of the progressive and ultraconservative forces in the church and ultimately to schism between 1881 and 1883. This chapter will investigate how each of these issues served to undermine the unity of the Brotherhood during the course of the 1860s and 70s.

Periodicals

Kurtz had tried to establish a religious periodical twice during the 1830s but discontinued both ventures due to lack of support. In 1850 he queried Annual Meeting about the propriety of starting a paper. When the query was deferred until the following year, Kurtz decided to begin publication of his paper in order to give the Brethren something specific to discuss. The 1851 Annual Meeting placed the paper on a one year trial period during which the Brotherhood was to examine the paper impartially and report any objections to the next Annual Meeting. In 1852, noting the mixed response to the journal, Annual Meeting permitted its continuation and urged opponents of the paper to exercise forbearance. The next year the *Gospel Visitor* was recognized as a "private undertaking" which should meet no further church interference. The acceptance of the periodical by Annual Meeting was in great measure due to Kurtz's special ability to work within the Brethren system—balancing his individual freedom in pursuing

the enterprise with respect for the wishes of the Brotherhood.[2]

Kurtz felt that the *Gospel Visitor* could help to preserve the unity of the widely scattered Brotherhood and solve doctrinal and practical problems by providing a sounding board for insights and conclusions. He also saw the paper as a means to promote those values and ideals distinctive to the Brethren.[3] The *Gospel Visitor's* contents, with the exception of letters from readers and doctrinal queries, were almost entirely devotional and written in a refined and dignified style. Kurtz also published a German edition, the *Evangelische Besuch*, which retained the same high standards of style as the English edition.

Opposition to Kurtz's publishing venture came from those who felt that the paper created disharmony by publishing articles of a critical nature and that it represented an attempt to "merchandize" the gospel.[4] Notwithstanding, a journal with denominational orientation was an undertaking whose time had come among the Brethren.

Though the paper faced financial pressures for the first several years, it continued to grow, requiring the hiring of James Quinter as assistant editor in 1856. Albert Ronk sees Quinter's coming as significant: "To him more than to Elder Kurtz is credit due for forward thinking relative to the pressing questions of the day."[5] The same year a second significant addition to the staff occurred with the hiring of Henry R. Holsinger (1833–1905) for a one year apprenticeship. Though Holsinger remained only the one year (he was disappointed that Kurtz did not follow his suggestion to change the *Gospel Visitor* into a weekly), the printing training he received was of great importance to the later course of his life and that of the church.

Holsinger was born in Morrison's Cove, Pennsylvania and was a direct descendant of Alexander

Mack. He joined the church in 1855 and was called to the ministry in 1866. Following his stint with the *Gospel Visitor*, Holsinger returned to his home in Pennsylvania where he engaged in farming and teaching school. In 1863 and 1864 Holsinger returned to the printing trade, publishing a local newspaper at Tyrone, Pennsylvania in support of the newly formed Republican Party. Yet his real desire lay in establishing a weekly paper serving the interests of the Brethren. Thus, in January, 1865, Holsinger began the *Christian Family Companion* and disposed of the secular paper shortly afterwards. It had a column devoted to "worldly matters" (Civil War news and farm market reports) and possessed a more casual and less devotional format (it had extensive advertising) than the *Visitor*. More importantly, it was designed as an "open forum" to provide a medium for opinions to be expressed openly on a whole range of controversial topics with little editorial comment.

There was just as great a difference between Holsinger and Kurtz as there was between their respective papers. Holsinger showed little of Kurtz's tact in dealing with the church leadership and was quite impatient with the slowness of the traditional channels for change in the Brotherhood. Characteristically, he pushed on an issue of reform so forcefully that opposition from the conservative forces was almost inevitable. Only when the reactionary movement had commenced would he back off. Holsinger's abrasive overstatement of an issue (behind which there was usually an element of truth) is reflected as he (later in life) stresses one of the primary purposes for establishing the *Christian Family Companion*.

> The first work undertaken was to remove certain hindrances to the prosperity of the church. As in the case of the young prophet Josiah, it appeared that the book of the law had been lost in the rubbish of tradition. It was imperative that this dead weight be removed before the light of intelligence could shine upon the sacred page with such brilliance as to reflect into the heart of mankind.[6]

The controversial and critical nature of Holsinger's paper led to increasing opposition from Annual Meeting. The constant pressure caused Holsinger to "seek relief"; indeed he even felt that perhaps he had been going "too fast."[7] He therefore decided to sell the paper in 1873 to James Quinter who combined it with the *Gospel Visitor*. In 1876 Quinter renamed the paper *The Primitive Christian* and, after he bought *The Pilgrim* the same year, he changed the name to *The Primitive Christian and Pilgrim*. In 1883 this paper merged with *The Brethren at Work* and be-

came *The Gospel Messenger*, the official organ of the Church of the Brethren. Today this monthly periodical is simply called the *Messenger*. Following his acquisition of Holsinger's paper, Quinter continued a progressive stance, advocating the introduction of such measures, especially education, which would serve to fulfill better the mission of the church.[8]

For several years following 1873, Holsinger retired from an active role in denominational affairs, thereby hoping to quiet complaints about his progressivism and promote "the peace and prosperity of God's people."[9] He was encouraged by the slow advances being made in education, an educated ministry, Sunday Schools, and missions. Yet he felt the progressive movement needed even a stronger voice, so in 1878 he returned to the publishing field with another weekly, *The Progressive Christian*. From this point on Holsinger became the catalyst for the Progressive wing of the church while *The Progressive Christian* became its mouthpiece. In 1883 this paper was renamed *The Brethren's Evangelist* and in 1885 its name was changed to *The Brethren Evangelist*. In 1892 it became the official publication of The Brethren Church and has continued as such up to the present.

Amid this chorus of progressive voices, the ultra-conservative wing of the church, the Old Orders, decided to publish their own journal, *The Vindicator* in 1870. This journal, which continues to be the official publication of the Old German Baptist Brethren Church, was begun at Dayton, Ohio, by Samuel Kinsey with the support of his father-in-law, Peter Nead. The purpose of this paper was well expressed in the first issue.

> . . . we feel willing to apply our little might and influence, as well as we can, in wielding the sword ingeniously and powerfully, yet *friendly* and *kindly*, against the popular inventions, as well as modern improvements, continually attempted to be made upon the simple doctrine taught by the Saviour. Our object is to labor against all such innovations.
>
> To contend for the order of the brethren as it has been established.[10]

Unlike Holsinger, the Old Order wing sought to keep controversial material out of their journal and tended to rely more on the exertion of pressure on Annual Meeting and the Standing Committee during the conflict.

It is true that the contents of the church papers were only one of the major issues that plagued the Brethren. Yet the periodicals played a central role in keeping attention focused on all the controversial questions and in popularizing the disputes concerning these questions.

Education

Traditionally, the Brethren considered that a "common school" education, the basic elementary education provided by most states, supplied the children of Brethren parents with all necessary skills. As stated by the Annual Meetings of 1831, 1852, 1853, and 1857, all higher education—high school and college—was to be avoided because it was a worldly endeavor which tended to lead youth astray from the faith and which inculcated a spirit of pride. Kurtz took this position in the first article to appear in the *Gospel Visitor* on the subject in 1854 (he had purposefully avoided the topic until 1854 because of its controversial nature). By the end of the year, however, he was beginning to change his mind on the subject when he realized that an increasing number of Brethren children were attending academies and colleges.

The leading proponent of the establishment of Brethren-related schools was Quinter. In March, 1856, he wrote the *Visitor*, advocating that a Brethren school be established where Brethren young people could train for teaching in the public schools. Since many of the older Brethren school teachers could no longer meet the stricter requirements for school teachers, these younger Brethren could take their places, ensuring that moral and religious training would continue to be a part of children's education. Kurtz concurred with Quinter's proposal and further argued in June, 1856, that Brethren children should receive training to pass the requisite examinations in order to be able to help children from German-speaking homes make the transition to the English classroom as well as to instill Christian values into the public classroom.

A key opponent of the growing sentiment for education and schools was a pseudonymous writer, "Rufus." He voiced his opposition in the *Visitor* in January, 1855, and again in September, 1856. In the latter article, Rufus contended that establishment of a Brethren school could lead that institution to a worldly concern for fame and renown. Even more serious was the very real danger that the founding of a Brethren school might lead to pressure for an educated ministry.[11] A present day historian for the Old Order Brethren, Marcus Miller, indicates that the greatest concern that the Old Order wing of the German Baptists had concerning such a Brethren

school was its effect on the traditional form of Brethren ministry.

> It was the feeling of many of the Brethren that the proposed Brethren academies would cultivate or create the desire for an educated ministry which would preach, not under the influence of the Spirit, but, for hire. They then envisaged not only a salaried ministry but also a solitary ministry (as opposed to the plural). They believed these to be contrary to Holy Scripture . . . [12]

Quinter responded to Rufus' objections in the same September, 1856, issue of the *Visitor*. His arguments were: (1) If Annual Meeting continues to be against anything more than a common school education, this opposition would either lead Brethren parents to disobey Annual Meeting or, if parents enforced the ruling, cause their children to go their own way when free from parental authority. (2) If Brethren children do go to institutions of higher learning, these schools are often devoid of the pure Christian influence desired by parents. (3) The church may lose many promising youth if it is not sympathetic to their desire for education. Quinter then calls it a duty owed to God, the church, and the rising generation to encourage and build such institutions. Quinter did not respond, however, to the objection that such schools might also train ministers.[13]

That the arguments of Quinter and Kurtz were swaying church sentiment is shown by an investigation of the minutes of Annual Meeting from 1857 and 1858. As was noted earlier, the 1857 Annual Meeting continued its customary opposition to the worldly pursuit of education, but in 1858 Annual Meeting made a significant change: "Concerning the proposed school in the Gospel Visitor, we think we have no right to interfere with an individual enterprise, so long as there is no departure from gospel principles."[14] The principle of individual freedom which ensured the continuation of Kurtz's *Visitor* now was extended to permit the establishment of Brethren-related schools.

Efforts to establish a Brethren high school had actually begun prior to Annual Meeting's provisional acceptance of the idea in 1858. In 1852 Jacob Miller began a high school at Buffalo Mills in Bedford County, Pennsylvania. Miller's death in 1853 ended the venture, however. Two other short lived attempts at establishing high school level academies occurred in the early 1860s. In 1861 Kishacoquillas Seminary was opened by S. Z. Sharp, a leading figure in Brethren educational circles, but remained in Brethren hands for only four years. Quinter and Kurtz opened the New Vienna Seminary in Clinton County,

Ohio, in 1862, but due to financial problems related to the war, the school closed in 1864.

During the first half of the 1870s, the Brethren attempted to establish their first colleges, but all these schools were short lived.[15] The first college (and indeed the first Brethren educational institution) that withstood the test of time was Juniata College (1876) which opened as Huntingdon Normal School and Collegiate Institute. This venture was followed by two other successful institutions—Ashland College (1878), which was established in Ashland, Ohio, and came into the hands of the Progressives at the time of the split, and Mount Morris Seminary and Collegiate Institute (1879), which was organized at Mount Morris, Illinois, and merged with Manchester College in North Manchester, Indiana, in 1932.

A second front of the battle over education was opened by Henry Holsinger and the Progressives when they began to advocate openly an educated ministry. The fears of the Old Order Brethren that agitation for greater freedom concerning education would lead to the desire for an educated ministry were well founded. Holsinger indicates that the Progressives were especially disconcerted by the incompetence of many of the elders and bishops. This incompetence was a direct result of their lack of education. Holsinger felt that the German Baptist Brethren were stagnating numerically and spiritually because their leadership lacked the education necessary to participate in the modern world.

> ... the church was in great need of reformation. ... I can even now close my eyes and name a dozen churches with whose elders I was personally acquainted who could not read intelligently a chapter from the Bible or a hymn from a hymnbook, nor write an intelligent notice or announcement of a communion meeting for a paper. Some of them could deliver a pretty fair discourse in an extemporaneous way, more or less satisfactory to the people of the community in which they lived, but the more discreet of them could not attempt to preach at a strange place or in a town.[16]

Holsinger continued by pointing out that since such men controlled the church, a young "aspirant with short hair or store-bought garments and a worldly education with a godly life and holy conversation" stood little chance of advancement in the ministry.[17] This desire among the Progressives to provide special training for Brethren ministers was not fully realized until 1888 when Ashland College received a new charter. This charter provided that "the training of Christian ministers" would always be "regarded as one of Ashland College's major functions."[18]

Paid Ministry

From the beginning of the denomination, Brethren ministers had labored for the church without remuneration, supporting themselves through their secular professions (usually farming).[19] It was not until the 1850s that the practice of the free ministry began to be challenged. In 1856 Annual Meeting was asked about receiving public collection "for our laboring Brethren." The counsel of Annual Meeting was that such a practice was "not agreeable to the gospel."[20]

The first mention of support for ministers in a positive light in the Annual Meeting minutes occurred in 1860 in a report of a committee commissioned the previous year to devise plans for fulfilling the Great Commission. This report proposed that district treasuries be established to help defray the expenses of traveling evangelists. Yet it was also suggested that any ministers undertaking evangelistic work should "labor as they have been accustomed to do, without money and without price, as far as their circumstances will permit . . ."[21] This report was not adopted by the 1860 Annual Meeting due to the meager attendance resulting from the location of the gathering (Tennessee was removed from the centers of Brethren strength). It was eventually accepted in 1868.

Annual Meeting made some concessions on the issue in 1861, permitting support in cases of necessity or hardship.[22] As reflected in the previous paragraph, the real stimulus for a paid ministry was the growing conviction that the church needed to take the Great Commission seriously, both at home and abroad. This issue became hotter during the 1870s and 1880s when traveling evangelists became more common and their support was necessitated by their lack of full-time employment.

The Old Order Brethren were solidly opposed to the concept of the paid ministry because they felt a paid minister would be more likely to preach what his congregation wanted to hear. Though Henry Kurtz would probably be considered a Conservative (he died before the split), he does reflect, in a sermon presented at Annual Meeting in 1845, the sentiments of the Old Orders:

> ... God never meant for the Gospel to be used as a means for getting water to the preacher's mill, or grain into his garner. When the Gospel is converted into merchandise, the preacher becomes a merchant, and like all other merchants it becomes his interest to handle his goods in a way that will please his customers, and put them in such shape and procure for them such kinds, whether good, bad or indifferent, as will suit their fancies and please their tastes.

"The love of money is a root of all evil," no less in the ministry than anywhere else.[23]

The issue of a paid ministry received regular attention in Holsinger's *Christian Family Companion* during the last half of the 1860s especially. The Progressives felt that it placed an excessive burden upon a minister to expect him to fulfill all his ministerial obligations as well as to provide for his family in secular employment. In 1866 J. W. Beer wrote an article in the *Christian Family Companion* reflecting this Progressive stance.

> When I say that ministers of the gospel should be supported by the church, I mean they should receive their temporal substance—their food and raiment, for their services. I mean to say, that, when a congregation sets apart a brother to attend to the sacred duty of preaching the gospel, it is the duty of that congregation, while the brother thus set apart labors in his holy calling among them, to see to it, that he, and his dependent family, . . . have suitable clothing and proper food. . . . Paul taught that the Lord had ordained that they who preach the Gospel should have their temporal subsistence for their services.[24]

It is important to note that the Progressives drew a distinction between a paid ministry and a salaried ministry during this controversy. Writers like J. W. Beer were not promoting a salary arrangement between a church and its elder; rather, they were advocating that ministers be given support to cover the essential needs of their families. The salaried ministry gradually grew out of the paid ministry during the years following the split.

Evangelism

Up until about 1860, the Brethren made little effort to evangelize their non-Brethren neighbors. The passing of the evangelistic zeal characteristic of the early Brethren can be attributed to several factors. First, the German sub-culture of the Brethren severely limited their opportunities for outreach. Second, a "passive evangelism" developed which was content to wait for people to apply to the church for membership. The Brethren relied on their distinctive life style and literary publications to speak for them. Third, the strong corporate consciousness of the Brethren, their defensive theological posture, and the conviction that they represented a remnant of the true church in a hostile world all tended to foster an attitude of withdrawal which had many similarities to the *Stillen im Lande* posture that reigned in Mennonite circles from the seventeenth to the nineteenth centuries.

Attention has already been given to the strenuous resistance of the Brethren to revivalistic methods and theology. Yet indications appear by the late 1850s that many Brethren were ready to utilize certain revivalistic practices if given Brethren moorings. Noteworthy in this regard is the counsel concerning protracted meetings (a series of meetings with preaching designed to lead to conversion and baptism). In 1842 Annual Meeting was asked about the use of such "new measures" as protracted meetings and mourning benches. Annual Meeting cautioned against the introduction of such innovations and counseled that one should follow the doctrine and example of the apostles in the matter. In 1848 Annual Meeting held that it was not profitable for members to attend camp meetings and protracted meetings held by other denominations. By 1858, however, Annual Meeting had softened its position. It was now held that a series of meetings was "not contrary to the gospel, if the believer is proceeded with according to the gospel, and the order of the brethren . . ."[25] At the same Annual Meeting the principle of holding a series of meetings was upheld but the Brethren concluded concerning the term, protracted meetings, "we know nothing of it in the gospel."[26] Yet by 1874 the term itself could be used in a query and accepted without questioning its lack of Biblical precedent (though qualifications continued to be placed on how these meetings were to be conducted).[27]

As was noted in the discussion of the paid ministry, Brethren interest in evangelism increased greatly from 1860 onward. Instrumental in the agitation for more concerted evangelistic outreach was John Kline. His selfless dedication in bringing the message of salvation to countless numbers of people throughout the Shenandoah Valley and the hill country of present day West Virginia between 1835 and 1864 was the inspiration for many other ministers to take up his standard. Kline played a key role in the request from Virginia in 1856 that Annual Meeting devise a plan of evangelism. When action on this and other requests was taken in 1859 by the appointment of a committee to devise such a plan, Kline was included. He also signed the final report (along with D. P. Sayler, John Metzger, and James Quinter) in 1860. The report called for the establishment of districts with district treasuries which were to be used to defray the expenses of evangelists. Special requests for evangelists were to be sent to Annual Meeting though individual ministers were encouraged to continue their evangelistic endeavors.[28]

This plan was eventually adopted in 1868 but it was felt by some that Annual Meeting was dragging its feet in implementing the plan.[29] Therefore, several evangelistic efforts were begun during the late 1870s without initial Annual Meeting sanction. Early in 1876 Christian Hope, a native of Denmark, was authorized by the northern Illinois district to return to Denmark and begin mission work for the Brethren there. The Danish mission, the first foreign missionary endeavor for the Brethren, gained Annual Meeting approval in 1876. Continued agitation for a more thoroughly organized approach to home missions resulted in the convocation of a missionary convention at Meyersdale, Pennsylvania, in December, 1877. Proponents of the resulting Brethren's Church Extension Union sought to win Annual Meeting sanction for their organization and plans in 1878. When Annual Meeting rebuffed this attempt, ostensibly because the plan did not come up through a district, the mission enthusiasts sought to make the plan more acceptable, a desire that was reflected in the selection of a new name for the organization: "The Work of Evangelism." A new effort to gain Annual Meeting approval resulted in the deferral of the matter in 1879 but finally bore fruit in 1880 with the establishment of a Domestic and Foreign Mission Board.[30]

The chief exponent of the use of some of the new evangelistic techniques was Stephen H. Bashor. This charismatic speaker is said to have added over ten thousand members to the church between 1875 and 1882. He was but twenty-two when he was elected to the ministry and began his evangelistic work. Bashor presents his own view of the role of an evangelist and the special opportunities which were open to the Brethren if they would avail themselves of evangelism:

> It is a fact that cold, logical, learned and intellectual discourses [though the Brethren were not generally known for these, Bashor wants to underscore the lack of zeal exhibited by many preachers] do not as a rule arouse enthusiasm and win men to practical acceptance of the truth preached or the cause accepted. It is one thing to reach and control the judgment, and quite another to enlist the life in service to that which the judgment accepts. The work of the pastor is to instruct and convince; that of the evangelist is to arouse the instructed to allegiance. . . . I saw open then, one distinctive and effective line of labor. That was as an exhorter. Appeal to the affections, the fears and the conscience of those yet out of Christ, in the families of the Brethren and their friends. It seemed to me that the church had been planting and cultivating in a prolific soil for over a century, and had neglected to lay down the plow for the sickle. The harvest was ripe—dead ripe—and the reaper should gather in the ripened grain.[31]

Bashor especially criticized the failure of Brethren parents to encourage their children in the faith. Many of these children were lost to the church either because they were never confronted with the gospel or because they could not accept the strict order of their parents' church.[32]

The Old Order response to the growing acceptance of revivalistic practices was stout resistance. In a petition sent to Annual Meeting in 1869, a group of southern Ohio elders who would form the core of the Old Order movement insisted that protracted meetings be conducted in "strict accordance with the gospel."[33] During the 1870s the Old Order Brethren regularly registered their opposition in the *Vindicator* to the way protracted meetings were generally conducted. Criticism was especially levelled at the use of various means to excite the emotions—the singing of revival hymns, giving invitations to rise or come forward, preoccupation with hell, calamities, and death-bed scenes—and the tendency for sinners in an emotional state to be so hurried that they failed to count the cost.[34] Such elements were held to be not in harmony with the old order of the church. It was also feared that evangelistic and missionary work would encourage support for a paid ministry.[35]

Sunday Schools

The same slow modification of Brethren attitudes which occurred with regard to protracted meetings can also be seen in connection with Sunday Schools. Initially opposed by Annual Meeting in 1838, they were sanctioned by Annual Meeting in 1857 "if conducted in gospel order."[36] Sunday Schools (or, as they were generally called at this time, Sabbath Schools) had begun appearing in some progressively-minded congregations during the 1850s and found increasing acceptance by Conservatives and Progressives alike in the following decades.

In the years immediately following Annual Meeting's approbation of Sunday Schools, James Quinter wrote several articles in the *Gospel Visitor* advocating that "such Sabbath Schools as are not contrary to the gospel, and such as the brethren will approve of, [be] established among us where it can be done in union"[37] (note the traditional Brethren concern that change should not occur at the expense of unity). He stressed that Sabbath School should never be viewed as a substitute for parental instruction and teaching by the ministry; yet it can serve "as a very efficient auxiliary to the Christian ministry, in helping it perform its work of teaching the knowledge of the Lord."[38] Reflecting a progressive stance on the authorization for Sabbath Schools, Quinter argues:

The authority of Scripture then for Sabbath Schools, is seen not so much in any positive commandment, as it is seen in the general precepts of the gospel, and in the spirit of Christianity, which lays hold of every agency which may be rendered subservient to the promotion of the welfare of mankind, and puts it under contribution, in accomplishing its holy purpose in spreading the knowledge of the truth of Jesus.[39]

Quinter sees several special benefits accruing from the introduction of Sabbath Schools: they will help children to "advance in Scriptural knowledge," they may prevent children from forming evil habits, and they will offer children from non-Christian families the opportunity to obtain religious instruction.[40]

The Old Order Brethren considered Sabbath Schools as another popular innovation of man, lacking Gospel principle and authority, and out of harmony with the apostolic order of the church.[41] They maintained that the command to bring up children in the nurture and admonition of the Lord was directed to *parents* and not Sunday School teachers. They especially feared that the Sunday School would reduce the hold the parents had over the Christian education of their children and increase the "danger of imbibing the principles and faith of a false Christendom" (especially if children attended union Sunday Schools).[42] The Old Order Brethren were given additional ammunition for their cause when Progressive attempts to find historical precedent for Sunday Schools backfired. Progressives cited Ludwig Höcker's Sunday afternoon youth meetings begun in 1748 as a Brethren forerunner of Robert Raikes' Sunday School. When, however, it became common knowledge that Höcker belonged to the Ephrata group, the ties of the Sunday School to the Ephrata schismatics was not overlooked.[43]

One other Sunday School practice heartily adopted by the Progressives and rejected by both the Old Order and Conservatives was Sunday School Conventions. These district-wide gatherings at which lectures and workshops were offered on various theoretical and practical aspects of the Sunday School had made their appearance among the Brethren by 1876. These conventions were opposed outright by the Old Orders, and, although many Conservatives played an active role in the early gatherings, Annual Meeting ruled in 1882 that "Sunday-school Conventions . . . follow the course of popular Christianity and are contrary to the principles of the Gospel and contrary to the Scriptures. See Rom. 12:2."[44]

Dress

The distinctive plain dress of the Brethren, whose basic features derived largely from the uniform of the Quakers during the eighteenth century, was another source of conflict between the various factions. The authority for this plain dress rested in the "gospel principles" of simplicity and nonconformity. The specific features of the Brethren uniform continued to evolve during the first half of the the nineteenth century through common consent with Annual Meeting providing little specific counsel. From 1850 to 1880, however, numerous detailed rulings were offered by Annual Meeting on queries regarding the style and cut of a man's hair and beard, the wearing of jewelry, and the specific style of men's and women's clothing.[45] Adherence to this prescribed form of dress was viewed with increasing gravity by the main body of the church, the Conservatives, between 1850 and 1880 so that by the 1880s conformity to the prescribed dress was beginning to be made a test of fellowship.

No doubt, this move toward uniformity in dress came as a result of Brethren interaction with the fashion-crazy modern world. The Brethren considered conformity to the fashions of the world as an evidence of a sinful spirit of pride. They therefore sought to hedge the church against the incursion of this spirit by defining strict limits between acceptable and unacceptable dress. It should be noted that all groups of the Brethren were agreed that the gospel requires plainness and modesty in dress; disagreement arose over the questions of whether the features of the Brethren dress should be strictly itemized, who should be ultimately responsible for determining the application of gospel principles with regard to dress, and whether a specific uniform should be made a test of fellowship. The perspective of the three groups on the above questions reveals a great deal about the underlying issues which divided the parties. The Old Order Brethren felt that a distinctive dress was an essential characteristic of the true church. Uniformity is an indispensable feature of dress for it not only identifies the Brethren in their relationship to the world as Christians of a special character—nonresistant, inoffensive, mild, humble— but it also helps to inform the heart with a moral and holy character (note the stress on the outer as the indicator and even the shaper of the inner). Since every part of one's dress, as an aspect of the whole, has a bearing upon the heart, close attention should be given to every item of dress. It is the church, as the body of Christ, which has been authorized to establish "the things for which there is no written letter," and its decisions are to be the rule or practice. Those who do not hear the church on matters of dress are to be dealt with according to Matthew 18:17.[46]

In sharp contrast, the Progressives believed that individual conscience should rule in adiaphorous issues. Though nonconformity must remain the controlling principle on this issue, mandatory uniformity destroys that vital spirit of inner obedience which is at the heart of the Christian life. The following editorial statement by Holsinger and Bashor in the *Progressive Christian* is a good summarization of the Progressive position:

> We have yet it seems to learn the lesson, that Christian life does not consist in the "outward adornment," of the body, but in the heart and life.—I Peter 3:2. When we learn this as a church, we will cease to preach uniformity in dress, as the central figure of the Christian life. When we make uniformity in dress a test of Christian fellowship, we do make "outward adornment" the adorning of the Christian life, and thus stand in direct opposition to the teachings of the apostle, when he says our adornment should not be outward but inward; or of the heart.[47]

The Conservatives sought to follow a middle course between these two extremes. Harshey's two articles cited above (from 1877 and 1878) were written in response to the Conservative tendency to avoid the itemization and detailing of the order of dress. Though defending nonconformity in dress in general terms, the Conservatives were not willing to itemize every detail of Brethren dress.[48] In the previous decade James Quinter had reflected the Conservative viewpoint when he observed:

> . . . the Brethren have never, we believe, laid down any particular form of a garment either for the male or female members of the church, though as a body, they have adopted a plain garment. In this they have showed their wisdom and prudence. Where we have no Scripture in the minute details of Christian duty, we should claim none.[49]

The Conservatives were attempting to retain a balance between respect for the traditions of the elders and openness, within the contemporary context, to the guidance of the Spirit of truth.

With the appearance of the *Progressive Christian* in 1879, however, the Conservatives were forced to shift their emphasis to a defense of the received tradition and of the authority of Annual Meeting in determining adiaphorous questions. R. H. Miller, a leading spokesman of the "right wing" of the Conservatives, maintained that "the Brotherhood has ever held . . . the position that the counsels of the church, in all things where there is no positive thus saith the Lord, is the only safe and Gospel plan of church government and Christian conduct."[50] Besides maintaining the mandatory nature of the counsels of Annual Meeting in their polemic against the Pro-

gressives, the Conservatives also upheld the *doctrine* of uniformity in dress: "it is natural and reasonable that they [God's children] should have the same oneness and harmony in the external appearance as the internal."[51] As can be seen, the Conservatives were being forced to slant their arguments in entirely opposite directions depending on their particular antagonist.

Feetwashing

An issue that created a great deal of dissension in the Brotherhood and was especially disquieting to the Old Order Brethren was the lack of uniformity in the practice of feetwashing.[52] During the course of Brethren history, two forms of feetwashing had come into use. In the single mode of feetwashing, each person both washed and wiped the feet of another. In the double mode, one washed consecutively the feet of several while another followed and wiped them. The single mode seems to have been used at the Germantown church from the beginning while the double mode was practiced at two of the daughter churches of the Germantown congregation—Conestoga and Coventry. These two churches were the great feeders of westward expansion so that the double mode came to be practiced in the main body of the church. Besides the Germantown and Philadelphia congregations, one other group of the Brethren, the Far Western Brethren (see p. 106), practiced the single mode.[53] In the unification proceedings during the 1850s, it was agreed that the two groups should practice forbearance toward one another on the question of feetwashing. When the Western Brethren communed with Eastern churches, the double mode should be observed, while the single mode should be practiced when Eastern Brethren communed with Western churches. In this way two modes came to be practiced in the church, though the double mode continued to be recognized as the "general order of the brethren."[54]

The uneasy truce that existed between the practitioners of the different modes was first disturbed by a work by William C. Thurman, the vocal advocate of Adventist convictions in the Brotherhood. In *The Ordinance of Feet Washing, As Instituted by Christ, Defended and Restored to its Original Purity*, Thurman offered Biblical support for the single mode and then charged that the double mode is "*an ordinance of your own invention.*" He held that it originated in the Indian Creek church in 1800 and therefore "cannot be the institution of Christ." He further observed that the Germantown church has "never yet been prevailed upon to adopt your new method" and he relates Mack, Jr.'s charge from his death bed "not to leave 'the old order of the brethren'" regarding feetwashing.[55]

Though some discussion concerning which was the original mode occurred in the *Gospel Visitor* and *Christian Family Companion* in 1865 and 1866, the next important development took place in 1868 when Annual Meeting sent committees to the Philadelphia, Germantown, and former Far Western Brethren congregations with the hope that a more complete union could be effected. The 1869 Annual Meeting minutes reveal that none of these churches were willing to discontinue the single mode, maintaining that it was the original practice of their bodies. Annual Meeting agreed to bear with these churches but advised that all new churches should observe the double mode.[56]

The appointment of the Annual Meeting committees in 1868 was probably behind the resumption of the debate concerning the original mode in the *Christian Family Companion* in 1868 and 1869. The principal figures in this exchange were Samuel Kinsey and A. H. Cassel, who was recognized as the premier Brethren antiquarian. In the course of the discussion, Cassel provided supportive evidence for his contention that the single mode was the earlier form of feetwashing. Interestingly, Kinsey resorts to a progressive argument when he contends that, even if the single mode was older, the Brethren may have obtained further light on feetwashing and, as a result, changed to the double mode. So heated did the debate on feetwashing become, that editor Holsinger decided to stop the discussion in April, 1869![57]

The 1869 decision did not put to rest the controversy and in 1871 a committee was appointed to ascertain "which was the first mode practiced by our brethren in America."[58] The actual investigation was conducted by D. P. Sayler whose research was felt by some to have been quite inadequate (Sayler was a staunch supporter of the double mode).[59] A. H. Cassel in particular was critical of Sayler's "loose and unsatisfactory" investigation and Annual Meeting's continued attempts to suppress the growing sentiment for the single mode.[60]

Deliberations concerning the committee's findings were held privately among the elders assembled for the 1872 Annual Meeting. The official decision of the Annual Meeting was: "Make no change whatever in the mode and practice of feet-washing, and stop the further agitation of the subject."[61] The Old Order Brethren, firm advocates of the double mode, were pleased with this decisive statement on the issue, but the ruling did little to end the agitation concerning the proper mode. The problem came before Annual Meeting again in 1876, but ruling on the queries was deferred until 1877. In 1877 Annual Meeting gave the following counsel to a query requesting approval, for those Brethren who so desired, to practice the single mode of feetwashing:

> Inasmuch as the so-called double mode of feet-washing is the order of the general brotherhood, this Annual Meeting cannot sanction the practice of different modes; but those churches which wish to observe the single mode we will bear with, when it can be done unanimously and without giving any trouble or offence in the church.[62]

The Old Order Brethren felt that this decision was contradictory to the 1872 decision and that, rather than assuaging the controversy, it opened the door for even greater agitation. Eventually, both the Conservative and Progressive groups would adopt the single mode of feetwashing while the Old Order Brethren retained the double mode.

Observations

This overview of the issues that contributed to the divisions of the 1880s yields some noteworthy observations. Major changes occurred between 1857 and 1860 with the acceptance of Sunday Schools, series of evangelistic meetings, and Brethren-related educational enterprises. These progressive steps were received with a noticeable lack of severe conflict. This relatively peaceful progression is to be credited to James Quinter's keen insight into the mechanics of Brethren thought and polity. He, like Kurtz, waited until the time was ripe for change so that he needed to exert only a moderate amount of pressure to open the door for new practices. After a lull from 1860 to 1865, probably due to the disruptive character of the Civil War, Holsinger entered the picture with his *Christian Family Companion*. Lacking the discernment of a Kurtz and Quinter, he felt that he could force the progressive movement ahead by constant and, at times, vigorous pressure. It must be questioned whether Holsinger's tactics were not actually counter-productive to progressivism. It comes as no surprise that Marcus Miller denotes the decade of 1865 to 1875 as the period of the growth and solidification of Old Order sentiment.[63] These years match almost exactly the period during which Holsinger was publishing the *Christian Family Companion*. Likewise, one can only speculate along with a host of others since the time of the split whether there would have been a Progressive-Conservative division if Holsinger had been less impatient and less critical.

Yet, in fairness to Holsinger and the Progressives, it should be reiterated that theirs was not an emphasis which was selfishly motivated. They possessed a great vision for what the church could become if it would loose itself from the formalism and cultural baggage that were hindering the church's mission.

The Platforms of the Parties

Though the issues already cited were the most visible sources of conflict among the Old Orders, the Conservatives, and the Progressives, there was another set of differences which was, in reality, the fundamental cause of tension. These differences consisted of the crucial questions of polity, the authorities used for determining faith and practice, and the attitude toward adaptation to the world.

As has already been shown, the Conservative leadership of the church had sought more efficient and effective methods of organization to handle the ever-increasing number of issues the church was facing in its struggle to come to terms with the modern world. Towards this end specific guidelines were laid down regarding the composition of Annual Meeting, the selection of the Standing Committee of Annual Meeting, and so forth. This organizational development was paralleled by an increase in the authority of Annual Meeting.

Both the Old Orders and the Progressives were disenchanted by this growing institutionalization in the church. In a petition submitted to Annual Meeting in 1869, the Old Order Brethren cried for greater simplicity in the organization of Annual Meeting. They singled out for criticism the selection of a certain portion of the Standing Committee from each state (as opposed to selecting the committee from all the elders present), the appointment of a "human moderator" (rather than allowing the Holy Spirit to be the guide or moderator for the committee's discussions), and the practice of listing all the members of the Standing Committee in the minutes. The Old Orders felt that, besides creating a barrier to the movement of the Holy Spirit, these practices tended both to "elevate and exalt the mind" and to concentrate "too much [power] in the hands of a few." Also criticized was the power recently assumed by Annual Meeting of sending committees to various churches where difficulties were present. The Old Orders preferred the older practice of settling such difficulties—the local church should call in elders from the adjoining districts to help resolve the problem. Only when a local issue remained unsettled or in cases where the ordinances or doc-

trines of the church were involved should the ruling of Annual Meeting be sought.[64] Annual Meeting decisions on the ordinances and doctrine should be uniformly observed in all local churches.[65] After the Old Orders reorganized following their withdrawal from the Conservatives, they also repudiated district organizations and meetings.[66]

The Progressives, like the Old Orders, objected to the prerogative assumed by Annual Meeting of sending committees to local congregations. The Progressives, the most congregational of any of the groups, felt such a practice was a violation of the rights of the individual congregation. Though they maintained that in matters of doctrine "the church of Christ should universally harmonize," they upheld the right of local congregations to decide questions of "government and custom."[67] All decisions of Annual Meeting for which there was no Gospel precept should be considered advisory only. The Progressives maintained that they were following the traditional Brethren understanding of these decisions and cited for additional support the testimony of such a departed statesman as John Kline.[68] The importance of District and Annual Conferences was recognized but it was felt that they should be held primarily "for social advantages, and for consultation upon general methods of church work, and to beget a unity and concert of action in all important matters."[69] The Progressives were also critical of the increasing authority of the Standing Committee because it "made bishops separate and superior to the body and authority of the church, whereas the gospel declares them servants of the church."[70]

Though there was some disagreement among the Conservatives concerning what authority the decisions of Annual Meeting should have, the view that these decisions should be mandatory had gained the ascendancy by 1882. This year it was decided that all queries should be decided according to Scripture

> where there is anything direct . . . applying to the questions. And all questions to which there is no direct expressed Scripture applying, it shall be be decided according to the spirit and meaning of the Scripture. And that decision shall be mandatory to all churches having such cases as the decision covers. And all who shall not so heed and observe it shall be held as not hearing the church, and shall be dealt with accordingly.[71]

Such was the protest against this minute that it was modified the next year by the statement that this "decision shall not be so construed as to prevent the Annual Meeting from giving advice when it deems it proper to do so, and that given advice, shall be so entered upon the minutes."[72] These developments clearly indicate that the Conservatives felt that the unity in faith and practice of the total community must have precedence over the liberty of the individual member or church. R. H. Miller gives expression to this concept.

> Uniformity is but one of many peculiarities that separates God's people from the world. One by one they may all be taken out of the way and every form that manifests the Christian spirit of humility and strict obedience, be supplanted by forms that manifest the flesh. This is one thing that congregationalism has never failed to do. . . . When a single congregation assumes the right to decide,—it assumes the right to change, and it changes to suit itself without regard to the judgment of the Brotherhood, or the feelings of adjoining congregations . . . [73]

The second fundamental difference among the three factions concerned the question of what authorities should be used for determining Brethren faith and practice. The position of the Old Order Brethren on this question is succinctly stated by the standard which Samuel Kinsey adopted for the *Vindicator* and which appeared on the title page of every issue: they sought obedience to "the ancient order, and self-denying principles of the church, as taught by the Savior and held forth by the early fathers of our Fraternity." The Old Order Brethren followed Peter Nead in holding that

> Where the testament is silent on the order or mode of observance [of the ordinances], the brethren, by whom God organized the church, were clothed with authority to say in what way the commandments or institutions of his house are to be practiced.[74]

Between the gospel and the ancient order of the Brethren, the Old Orders had a tightly knit and unified framework which they felt constrained to preserve in the face of a worldly culture and corrupted Christianity. They therefore felt that Annual Meeting should serve primarily as a conservator of the established order. Along these lines Samuel Kinsey writes:

> It never was the object of the Annual Meeting—neither has she a right—to sanction new rules and orders, and to instill new principles, but rather to see that the established rules and old principles be *preserved*; that all preach the same and practice the same; and, that thus offences, a variety of practices and divisions, be warded off, and the sweet harmony, peace, love and *purity* of the church be maintained.[75]

The Progressives were in agreement that Gospel explicits must be observed but differed with both Old Orders and Conservatives about practices on which Scripture is silent. Holsinger addresses this issue.

> We are in perfect accord with the practice of the church in its administration of the ordinances of the Gospel. So far as we have plain instructions in God's word as to how we should proceed, we believe it is well that we should have uniformity; but when the Scriptures are not definite, no such regularity is required. The Scriptures must be the basis of our uniformity. Our methods of bringing about a uniformity differs [sic] from some of our brethren in this wise: They have adopted an order or custom which obtained by accident or otherwise among their predecessors, we by teaching the gospel, inculcating scriptural sentiments upon all points, and the aggregation of effects thus brought about is our uniformity.[76]

The Progressives charged that, by stressing the "order of the Brethren," the Conservatives and the Old Orders especially were majoring on "externals" and neglecting "the weightier matters of the law of God." The Progressives held that the ancient customs of the church should be respected,[77] and they even maintained at the time of the split that they were "the only true conservators and perpetuators of the brotherhood and its original doctrines and principles."[78] Yet they felt that no tradition, including their own, could be elevated to a position in which it could not be scrutinized by the touchstone of the gospel.

The Conservatives sought a middle way between these two positions. Though emphasizing that the Bible must be the only rule of faith and practice, the Conservatives placed a great deal of respect in the "councils of the ancient Brethren." Note how J. H. Moore deals with the issue.

> There are two extremes in . . . [this] matter, each one equally dangerous. The one consists in ignoring and positively rejecting everything done, and recognized by those of former years, and the other is to claim that those who lived just before our time were, in some way, so influenced by the Holy Spirit, that what they did was right, and therefore, we dare not set aside or alter their decisions on any point. The actions of our ancient Brethren were not inspired in any divine sense, but were simply the result of their best judgment and careful reading, and should be respected by us only as they harmonize with the "thus saith the Lord" and the general tenor of the Gospel.[79]

The Conservatives thus combined belief in the priority of Scripture with a high regard for, yet a willingness to change, the received order.[80]

A third basic point of contention was their respective attitudes toward the acceptance of new practices. A number of factors actually come into play on this point—both of the preceding differences (polity and sources of authority) and also the factor of acculturation, that is, whether and how fast the church should become a part of the outside religious and cultural world. The Old Orders showed rigid opposition to any kind of acculturation (though they have softened somewhat on this point), rejecting higher education, Sunday schools, revival meetings, etc. as "innovations" and seeking to conserve the order of the church as they knew it. The Progressives were the most open to the outside secular and religious world, earning themselves the label, "the fast element." They accepted new practices if they were not contrary to the gospel and contributed to the mission of the church. Holsinger clearly expresses the Progressive position:

> . . . The Progressive Christian will advocate an onward movement by the use of all lawful and expedient means. We hold it our duty to keep pace with the times. And we mean what we say, an onward movement, and not a backward movement. . . .
>
> By keeping pace with the times, we have more direct reference to the using of such improvements as the advancements of science and art may introduce, for the promulgation of the religion of Christ. . . .
>
> . . . And we would keep up, fully up, and not a year or twenty-five years behind the times, as the Brethren have been all along in most things, such as newspapers, colleges, Sunday Schools, and the like.
>
> And again; we believe in keeping pace with the times in matters outside of religion.[81]

Practically, this was the essence of progressivism to the Progressives. Yet the term "progressive" also had a spiritual meaning which was accepted by both Progressives and Conservatives. To be progressive in a spiritual sense meant advancement, development, or progression in Christian maturity and truth. The Conservatives, however, were much more careful to distinguish between a Christian and non-Christian form of progression.

> A "Progressive Christian" is one who is approaching still nearer to the Bible—one who is moving toward the Bible and away from the world. . . . Progression is all right . . . if it makes people more humble, more honest, more consistent and more obedient to every part of God's Word . . . ; but if it makes them high-minded, self-willed, proud, boastful, and disobedient to the Bible and the church, it follows that there may be considerable progression, but very little Christianity.

The Conservatives tried to steer a middle course between the Old Orders and Progressives on this issue of *adiaphora* as they did on others. They were willing to see change, but it had to be gradual. During the process of change on an issue, the Conservatives consistently pled for forbearance on the part of the Orderites and the Progressives. The unity of the main part of the church was more important than "keeping pace with the times" or "maintaining the ancient order of the Brethren."

Chapter 10

THE DIVISION AND AN ANALYSIS

The Withdrawal of the Old Order Brethren

The first stirrings of the faction that came to be known as the Old Order Brethren occurred on October 13, 1868, when a group of about twenty Ohio Brethren, purportedly called together by Peter Nead and Henry Kurtz,[1] met to share their concern about "the present digression of the church, in many localities, from her ancient order and practices." Further consultation was called for on November 13, 1868, which resulted in the drafting of a petition to be presented to Annual Meeting in 1869. The immediate concern of the group was "that in the future our Annual Conference Meetings be conducted more in *simplicity* and after the manner of the first brethren."[2] The seriousness which attended the framing of this petition is reflected in the final paragraph:

> ... if this Conference Meeting shall hear and grant this petition well; but in case it shall refuse to do so, it is very probable that many churches will not be represented at our next Annual Conference, and hence the result will be a reorganization of our Conference Meetings by said churches in accordance with this petition.[3]

Feeling that the petition should address their broader concerns rather than just the conduct of Annual Meeting, these Brethren met again on March 29, 1869, at the Bear Creek Church in the Miami Valley in southwestern Ohio. A supplement was added to the petition wherein they registered their opposition to protracted meetings, Sabbath schools, prayer meetings, social meetings, and Bible classes. The petitioners were hoping that Annual Meeting would exert its authority to effect greater uniformity of thought and practice.

The Annual Meeting of 1869 gave careful consideration to the petition and supplement as the opening paragraph of its reply indicates:

> ... Annual Meeting desires to maintain all the practices and ordinances of Christianity in their simplicity and purity,

and to promote the "unity of the spirit in the bonds of peace;" therefore, though it cannot grant the changes and objects desired by the petitioners to the full extent petitioned for, it will make the following changes in the manner of holding Annual Meeting, and endeavor to guard, with increased vigilance, against the abuse of the practices referred to in the supplement ...[4]

The limited concessions that Annual Meeting made on the specified issues produced the desired effect for several years, holding in check the progressive forces in the church. Yet the progressive mood of the church could not be restrained for long, and agitation for recognition of the new practices, especially the single mode of feetwashing (the Old Orders considered it an innovation), returned with added impetus in the second half of the 1870s.

The Old Orders reacted to this new wave of progressive sentiment by sending a petition to the Annual Meeting of 1879 that requested "that she [Annual Meeting] do away with those changes and new movements which were more and more introduced, and that she cease giving encouragement and latitude to the things that were evidently destroying the union of the brotherhood."[5] However, the Standing Committee did not allow the petition to come before the Annual Meeting and returned it to the senders "with a sort of threat."[6] Though the Old Orders acquiesced to the rebuff at the time, it was decided to appoint five Brethren to correspond with leading elders of various states in order to discern what course of action should be taken next. As a consequence of these efforts, the Old Order Brethren in the Miami Valley, who were being urged by their compatriots in other parts of the Brotherhood to lead the decisive stand, met in November, "perhaps on the twenty-fifth day," of 1879 at the Salem Church in the Miami Valley. The tangible result of this conference was a petition, known as the Miami Valley

145

Petition, that was to be sent to the 1880 Annual Meeting.

There are a number of prominent features in this document. (1) The overriding concern of the Old Orders, which resounds throughout the petition, was for union and peace in the church. They felt the church was drifting away from the ancient and apostolic order upon which it was founded. The diversity of practice and disunion in spirit were visible signs of the grave state of the church. (2) The best way to heal the divided state of the church was to remove the "fast element." (3) Basing their arguments upon Scripture, the ancient order of the church, and the authority of Annual Meeting, the Old Orders again called for firm action against various innovations which they considered were the sources of the disharmony: high schools, Sabbath-schools, protracted or revival meetings, a salaried or paid ministry, the single mode of feetwashing. (4) The Old Orders desired firm action, not the Conservative ethic of forbearance. For, "Forbearance, we think, is the door by which these things [the innovations] came into church one after another, and now it seems there is no door to be found by which to get them out again."[7] (5) The Old Order Brethren candidly stated in the petition that they were very concerned about their authority within the Brotherhood: "Our plain decisions have been disrespected and overruled, and if this state of things shall continue to exist, we will lose all our power in the controlling of the church."[8]

The District Meeting of Southern Ohio passed the petition on to Annual Meeting without giving it its unanimous approval. At the 1880 Annual Meeting the petition was read to the meeting but a substitute paper, "formed by the Standing Committee," was presented by R. H. Miller. This paper was received by the meeting in place of the Miami Valley Petition. The wording of one of the resolutions in this substitute document is significant in revealing the position of the Conservative leadership of the church:

> RESOLVED, . . . that while we declare ourselves conservative, in maintaining unchanged what may be considered the principles and peculiarities of our fraternity, we also believe in the propriety and necessity of so adapting our labor and our principles to the religious wants of the world as will render our labor and principles most efficient in promoting the reformation of the world, the edification of the church, and the glory of God. Hence, *while we are conservative we are also progressive* [italics mine].[9]

The paper proceeded to urge "considered restraint"[10] with respect to the five practices mentioned in the Miami Valley Petition.

Though the action of Annual Meeting and the wording of the above introductory section irritated the Old Orders, they were incensed by Annual Meeting's counsel concerning the feetwashing question: "The best way to stop the agitation of this question is to allow the same liberty of conscience for our brethren that we ask for ourselves."[11] The Old Order Brethren retorted that such counsel

> . . . was only kindling the fire for further disunion and contention—every one do as their conscience may choose to dictate! Conscience the guide! One of the most dangerous doctrines ever preached, and it came from the brethren's Annual Conference Meeting. The tendency, if the "conscience" may be a guide in one of the Lord's ordinances, it may be the same in another, and where, in such an order of things, can exist the Lord's people who are to be of "one mind" and "speak the same thing?"[12]

A sense of despair was felt by many Old Orders following this further setback. "Many now declared as entirely useless and fruitless to go to Annual Meeting any more."[13] In a meeting of Old Order elders on November 9, 1880, it was decided to convoke a general council of the Old Order Brethren in order to determine what course of action to take next. To this end an announcement appeared in the *Vindicator* calling for the general consultation to be held on December 8, 1880, at the Wolf Creek Church in Montgomery County, Ohio. The announcement extended an invitation to "all our faithful and steadfast brethren . . . who are in favor of the *ancient and apostolic order of the church, as set forth in said petition.*"[14]

The council meeting was well attended, with Old Order Brethren from a number of states and even some members of the Conservative leadership of Annual Meeting—D. P. Sayler, James Quinter, and R. H. Miller—being present. The decision of the consultation was to resubmit the Miami Valley Petition, with some minor changes and additions (in the form of resolutions), to Annual Meeting. It was concluded, "with the agreement and advice of the Annual Meeting leaders," to send the petition directly to Annual Meeting without going through the district. It was felt that "this special conference was really of higher authority than any district meeting."[15] Though one wonders what the Old Orders hoped to achieve by resubmitting the petition, it could be that, as Lauderdale posits, with the action or inaction of Annual Meeting "upon these specifics, the Old Orders could take whatever action they thought necessary with considerable more justification."[16]

The substance of the Miami Valley Petition never was discussed during the Annual Meeting of 1881.

After it was read along with the minutes of the Miami Council, Jesse Calvert questioned the legality of its presentation since it had not come to Annual Meeting through District Meeting. Though R. H. Miller argued forcefully for its legality (as it seems he was obliged to), the conference voted overwhelmingly to remove the paper because of the technicality.

This action by the 1881 Annual Meeting was decisive for the future course of the Old Orders as an Old Order historian, John Kimmel, indicates:

> The Annual Meeting's second and ultimate rejection of the Miami Valley Petition was the leading immediate cause of the Old Order Brethren's movement of separation from the general brotherhood of the German Baptist Brethren church.[17]

Understandably, the Old Order Brethren were deeply embittered at having been betrayed by the Annual Meeting leaders who had given favorable counsel to the plan of action taken. The disillusioned leaders of the Old Orders called for a meeting of their Old Order compatriots to be held at the Ludlow and Pointer Creek Church, near Arcanum, Darke County, Ohio, on August 24, 1881. The purpose of the meeting was to "consult with regard to the necessary provisions for the preservation of a unanimity of sentiment in faith and practice."[18]

The result of this meeting was a document called the *Resolutions*. Principal features of the *Resolutions* included: (1) the conviction that the Old Orders were faithful both to "primitive Christianity as taught by Christ and his apostles" and to the ancient order of the church; (2) the charge that the main body of the church had allowed innovations and deviations from the apostolic order of the church to creep in thereby destroying the peace and union of the Brotherhood; and (3) the call for separation based on numerous New Testament passages which warned against those who preach a false gospel or who depart from the tradition handed down.[19]

The approval of the *Resolutions* by this meeting was regarded by the Old Order Brethren as an act sealing their withdrawal from the German Baptist Brethren and the authority of Annual Meeting.[20] Old Order Brethren in other parts of the country, especially in Iowa and Indiana, followed the Miami Valley Brethren in separating from the Brotherhood (Old Order Brethren in Maryland had already separated from the church in 1880).

Some of the immediate consequences of the Old Order withdrawal were hasty excommunication proceedings by the Conservatives against the Old Orders and conflicts between the factions regarding the ownership and occupancy of the meetinghouses. In several cases the Conservatives even brought law suits against the Old Orders (nonlitigation was one of the traditional principles of the Brethren).

The Old Order Brethren took the step of formal reorganization on November 25, 1881, at the Salem Church in Montgomery County, Ohio. They assumed the designation *Old* German Baptist Brethren, thereby "setting forth their position and desires for the old church worship, and to designate them from the *new*, or those who introduced and admitted new measures into their body."[21] Likewise, the use of the world "old" was consistent with the fact that they had been called for many years the "old brethren" or the "old order brethren." At this meeting arrangements were made for the Old Orders' first "Yearly Meeting," to be held at Brookville, Ohio, on Pentecost, 1882. Delegations were also sent out to assist various groups of Old Order Brethren to form themselves into congregations.

Though the Old Order Brethren were fully organized by the time the German Baptist Brethren held their Annual Meeting in 1882, the Old Orders did take a special interest in a query brought to Annual Meeting by the Southern Ohio District. This query requested that Annual Meeting "indorse the action [excommunication] of the churches in southern Ohio and elsewhere in regard to those who have gone with the resolutions, and also to enter the same upon the minutes." The counsel of the Standing Committee was passed without discussion: "This Annual Meeting does endorse the action of the churches which expelled the members who accepted the resolution referred to above."[22] This proceeding, coupled with the acceptance of the mandatory clause (see p. 142), had a special sting for the Old Order Brethren:

> . . . it is just to state that this Annual Meeting did pass a decision in the early part of its deliberations, making its decisions mandatory . . . , and then they ratify this expelling and house-locking without bringing before that body what was done, and how those who were expelled were treated. This shows advantage-taking and unfairness, and it *binds*, according to the mandatory clause, those who did not have a full knowledge of what was done, having no chance to know, because the question was not explained before it was passed.[23]

These actions by the Conservatives only confirmed the Old Order Brethren in the rightness of their cause and gave them added resolve to maintain the purity and unity of the ancient order of the Brethren.

The Expulsion of the Progressive Brethren

The course of the progressive movement in the German Baptist Brethren Church from 1865 to 1881, though influenced by a number of men from the Conservative as well as the Progressive wings, seemed inevitably to gravitate around the life of one man— Henry Ritz Holsinger. Albert Ronk explains the reasons for Holsinger's prominence.

> It might not be entirely true that Elder Henry Holsinger was the leader of progressive thought, but it is true that he was credited with, or blamed for, the progressive movement as it gained momentum. He was in the center of it for at least three reasons: (1) because of his aggressive, outspoken, impatient personality; (2) because his papers, *The Christian Family Companion* and *The Progressive Christian*, were published as open forums that discussed both sides of leading questions; and (3) because he had a keen prophetic sense. . . .
>
> It was this prophetic sense that caused Holsinger to look ahead fifty or more years and see what would come to pass among the German Baptist Brethren.[24]

As Lauderdale quips, "Holsinger not only saw ahead, but did all he could to make it come true in his time."[25]

As previously noted, Holsinger was at the forefront of the agitation for many of the practices which embodied the platform of the progressive movement. In his editorial positions Holsinger wielded considerable influence upon the course of the progressive movement, and it was especially in this capacity that Holsinger ran into difficulties with the leadership of the church. Sharp opposition had caused Holsinger to sell the *Christian Family Companion* to Quinter in 1873, and similar reaction was not long in coming after the inception of the *Progressive Christian* in 1878 by Holsinger and Joseph W. Beer. This paper was founded "with the avowed purpose of advocating progressive measures and reforms."[26] So critical and aggressive were the editorials in the *Progressive Christian* that five districts sent queries to Annual Meeting in 1879 (just six months after the publication began) protesting the paper's radically progressive and schismatic tone. The action of Annual Meeting and the charges leveled against the editors were as follows:

> . . . it is required that the editors of the *Progressive Christian* make an humble acknowledgement to the Annual Meeting for publishing erroneous statements in regard to church members; charging a part of the church with idolatry [Holsinger had criticized some features of the church's stand on dress in an article entitled "Idolatrous Clothes Religion"]; stigmatizing some of its members with terms of reproach, ridiculing some of the peculiar practices of the

church, and admitting into the paper inflammatory and schismatic articles some even from expelled members.[27]

In accordance with Annual Meeting's decision, Holsinger and Beer made acknowledgement before the conference and accepted the above statement.

Following Annual Meeting Holsinger and Beer disagreed over the future course of the paper. Holsinger wanted to maintain a radically progressive stance while Beer favored a more moderate course. Holsinger decided to allow Beer to test his policy on his own and sold his interests to Beer. Beer's experiment with the new policy was a financial failure and the paper was discontinued on December 12, 1879. Not until April 30, 1880, was the *Progressive Christian* resurrected with Howard Miller publishing it in his and Holsinger's name. Soon afterwards Holsinger took over again as editor, publisher, and proprietor.

Holsinger continued his radically progressive policy in the periodical and predictably met with increasing hostility from Old Orders and Conservatives alike. Holsinger's comments about the opposition from these two factions of the church are illuminating.

> While in many things I was in sympathy with the old-order brethren because of their consistency, as a matter of fact they were the indirect source of all my trouble and persecutions. They furnished the ammunition, while the conservatives fired the guns, not intending to injure anybody. I grant them the credit of having been sincere in their motives, but sadly mistaken as to the matter itself.[28]

Interestingly, Holsinger's compliment of the Old Orders for their consistency was reciprocated by the Old Orders toward their Progressive foes.[29] Implicit in this mutual sympathy, however, is the charge that the Conservatives were inconsistent. This charge was almost inevitable, for the middle ground which the Conservatives sought to maintain was often vaguely defined and was by no means stable. The Conservative position fluctuated depending upon the particular adversary. Likewise, the "Conservative element consisted of all degrees of position from progressive to old order. They did not want to depart too far from the historic, but desired some new avenues of approach to growing needs. Many were progressive but wanted to move slowly."[30] The mixed composition of the Conservatives explains why opposition to Holsinger continued to mount even after the Old Orders had commenced their withdrawal from the Brotherhood in 1880.

At the Annual Meeting of 1881, four more districts presented grievances against Holsinger and his paper.

The report of the committee appointed by the Standing Committee to consider the grievances stated:

> ...H. R. Holsinger is publishing a paper in which many articles have appeared criticising the work of Annual Meeting, and against the order of our church government, as also against our order of observing the Gospel principle of non-conformity to the world in wearing-apparel after having been again and again admonished by our Annual Meeting to be more guarded in his publication, and promised to do so, which promise he has not performed, but has continued his former course with increased effort. We therefore recommend that this meeting appoint a committee to wait on him in his church and deal with him according to his transgressions.[31]

Annual Meeting's acceptance of this report did not please Holsinger on two counts. First, the phrase "according to his transgressions" seemed to prejudge his case. Second, he felt that the charges were general and contained no evidence which he could dispute before Annual Meeting. With the appointment of the five man "Berlin Committee," Holsinger had one further complaint—only one of the members of the committee had even a casual knowledge of Holsinger's paper.[32]

The committee sent by Annual Meeting to Holsinger's home church in Berlin, Pennsylvania, was to begin its investigation of the charges against Holsinger on August 9, 1881; however, the proceedings never went beyond a discussion of the ground rules for the hearing. Serious difficulties arose between the committee on one hand and Holsinger and his home church on the other[33] regarding two issues: whether a stenographer should be employed and whether the hearings should be held in private (church members only). Holsinger insisted that, since he had been charged publicly at Annual Meeting, he had a right to a public trial. Therefore, he proposed that a stenographer be hired to record the trial and that the public be allowed to witness the investigation, though only church members should vote during the proceedings. However, the committee contended that, according to established usage, the hearings should be held in private without any record being taken.

Holsinger claimed that the traditional usages of the church should not apply in his case since no one had ever been charged with offenses similar to those brought against himself. Furthermore, his church had requested that a recorder be present and that the hearings be open, and Holsinger felt the church's desires should be honored.[34]

The hearings were now at an impasse. The committee refused to continue as long as an agreement could not be reached on the ground rules for the proceedings, and neither side was willing to compromise its position. When no further progress was made on the second day, the committee decided to withdraw in order to prepare its report. The report concluded:

> In view of the above considerations, especially in view of the fact that Brother H. R. Holsinger refused to have his case investigated by the committee in harmony with the gospel as interpreted by our Annual Meeting, and the consent of our general brotherhood, and inasmuch as brother H. R. Holsinger and the Berlin church assumed all responsibility in the case, therefore we decided: That H. R. Holsinger cannot be held in fellowship in the brotherhood, and all who depart with him shall be held responsible to the action of the next Annual Meeting.[35]

The committee's report received the signature of only one member (Elder John P. Cober, M.D.) of the Berlin congregation.

After the departure of the committee, the Berlin church continued its meeting and unanimously passed the following resolution:

> Inasmuch as Elder H. R. Holsinger had not violated any gospel order of the general brotherhood, and not having a trial of the charges brought against him at the annual meeting of 1881, therefore the Berlin congregation, including the Meyersdale branch, will continue to work together with Bishop Holsinger as our bishop, and we invite all who are willing to take the gospel of Christ as the man of their counsel, into church fellowship with us.[36]

During the period from the meeting of the Berlin Committee in August, 1881, to the Annual Meeting in May and June, 1882, tension was mounting in the Brotherhood as reflected by the numerous articles which appeared in the church papers discussing Holsinger's case and the issues which divided the Progressives and Conservatives. Two significant Progressive statements concerning the proceedings came out during this period. Bashor's widely distributed pamphlet, "Where Is Holsinger?," questioned the significance of the committee's decision since no formal trial was held. Howard Miller's article in the *Progressive Christian* of September 16, 1881, sized up the problem as follows:

> Divested of all its verbiage, the trouble with Henry is that he is now, and always has been, too far ahead of his day and generation. The other side of the house would put this to the credit of his being wickedly fast. . . .
> . . . I think it may be laid down as a broad principle that no one should ever be put aside except for doctrinal and moral defections. Holsinger's morals or faith were not questioned. He was shelved because he presumed to question the wisdom of his fellows.[37]

All parties concerned were awaiting the 1882 Annual Meeting, for it would be here that the question of Holsinger's expulsion would be resolved with the acceptance or rejection of the committee's report. The Annual Meeting of 1882 quickly addressed itself to the committee's report as the second item of business on the first day. The report was read and a motion was made and seconded that it be accepted. The ensuing discussion concerning the report and related matters lasted nearly the entire day.

D. C. Moomaw first introduced a motion to delay action on the matter until the next day in order to explore more fully the serious ramifications of acceptance of the report: not only Holsinger but also all those sympathizing with him would be under the ban. Moomaw offered a compromise proposal which had been written by Holsinger himself (Holsinger had lost his voice and was "obliged to appear in proxy"). In this "olive-branch of peace," Holsinger made some remarkable concessions. He asked forgiveness for all past offences and promised to remain in harmony with church practice and not to speak or write anything antagonistic to the general order of the church or Annual Meeting.[38] Holsinger's compromise was offered as a substitute for the committee report and therefore required the rejection of this report. The lengthy discussion which followed centered on two issues: whether action on the entire matter should be deferred until the next day and whether Holsinger's confession could still be presented if the Berlin Committee report was passed. However, Holsinger stated that he would withdraw his concessions if the report was passed. As he writes later, he could not conscientiously allow his paper to be presented after passage of the committee report, for to do so would be to "acknowledge the justice of the action of the committee."[39]

As discussion over these issues continued into the afternoon with seemingly increased confusion, Holsinger urged Moomaw to withdraw the motion to delay consideration of the committee report. This being done, Holsinger, having sufficiently recovered his voice, delivered a final emotional appeal which concluded with the statement that his primary concern had always been the union and prosperity of the Brotherhood. The moderator then put the motion for adoption of the committee report before the Annual Meeting. It was passed and Holsinger was expelled.

The same evening a number of Progressives met at a nearby schoolhouse to determine what response should be made to the action of Annual Meeting. With Elder P. J. Brown acting as chairman, the group declared in a resolution that Holsinger had been expelled illegally since he had violated no explicit gospel or moral principle. On the following day the Progressives accepted a memorial which was addressed to the Standing Committee and called for "a joint committee, say of twelve brethren, half to be selected by the progressive brethren and the other half by your body, and they prepare a plan for a general reconciliation . . ."[40] The Standing Committee rejected this memorial on the basis of the same technicality by which the Miami Valley Petition of 1881 had been ruled out—it had not come through a district meeting! Just as in the case of the Old Orders, the Conservatives had already committed themselves to a division in spite of a final peace overture.

At this point the Progressives felt that all avenues toward reconciliation had been exhausted. In the final meeting at the schoolhouse on June 1, the Progressives adopted a set of resolutions whose primary features were: (1) the conviction that the Word of God must be the only rule of faith and practice for the church; (2) the assertion that the Conservatives had departed from the standard of Scripture through the enactment of mandatory legislation on issues which the gospel granted liberty; (3) the belief that continual reform is needed to maintain the primitive purity of the church; and (4) resolutions to continue fellowship with like-minded Brethren, to restore the church to its historic roots, and to hold a convention to carry out the needed reforms. It was decided that the convention should be held at Ashland, Ohio, on June 29, 1882. At this final meeting the Progressives also adopted the motto: "The Bible, the whole Bible, and nothing but the Bible."[41]

The fruits of this Ashland Convention included: (1) the establishment of preliminary plans for a new denomination (in the event that further efforts at reconciliation failed); (2) the initiation of efforts to effect a union with other groups that had separated from the Brethren, such as the Congregational and Leedy Brethren; and (3) the adoption of the "Declaration of Principles." This document, written by S. H. Bashor and clearly modeled after the Declaration of Independence, exhibits many of the same themes which were prominent in the resolutions passed by the Progressives on June 1 (see above). Noteworthy in the "Declaration" is the conviction that in doctrinal matters there should be universal harmony while on questions of government and customs the church is to observe congregational polity. It was also emphasized that the Conservatives were the ones who had departed from the historic principles of the church. In a separate resolution the Progressives asserted that

... we are the true Conservators of the doctrines of the Brethren church, and have never strayed from the church founded by our fathers, that nothing done in this meeting shall be construed as secession or departure from the original church organized in Germany, in 1708, or from the principles of the gospel as interpreted by our fathers ... [42]

Though the Progressives were moving ahead with the work of reorganization, they did not formally organize until after the Conservatives held their 1883 Annual Meeting. It was hoped that the Conservatives might offer some sign (particularly the repeal of the mandatory clause) which would point the way to reconciliation. As Holsinger related in the *Progressive Christian*:

It is the desire of the Progressive portion of the Church to prevent a split in the body, if possible. All our convention work and church business has been so shaped as not to encourage or recognize a schism, and we "shall fight it out on that line" until after the Bismarck conference, next May.[43]

The Progressives received an unmistakable sign from Annual Meeting that the division was a reality. Not only was the mandatory rule not repealed (though it was modified), but Annual Meeting authorized the rebaptism of all those baptized by the Progressives and Old Orders, disavowed Sunday School conventions, sustained the work of the expelling committees, and "virtually endorsed" the locking of meeting-houses.[44] The Progressives now proceeded with the formal organization of The Brethren Church at a convention held at Dayton, Ohio, on June 6, 1883. "After the Dayton convention the Brethren Church was regarded as a fixed institution, and charters were obtained in all states where congregations existed."[45] The three-way division of the German Baptist Brethren was completed. Of the approximately fifty-eight thousand members of the entire denomination prior to the splits, about four thousand went with the Old Order Brethren and about six thousand joined the Progressive Brethren.

Analysis of the Division

During the years since the three-way division of the German Baptist Brethren, there have been numerous attempts to explain and interpret the intricate interplay of issues contributing to the schism. A brief summary and analysis of several of the more important interpretations will be helpful in making our own analysis.

One of the first major attempts to interpret the split is to be found in John L. Gillin's doctoral dissertation. Gillin (1871–1958) pastored the Brethren churches at Waterloo and Enon, Iowa, until 1901 when he began graduate studies at Union Theological Seminary and Columbia University. He received his doctorate in sociology from the latter institution in 1906 and was thus one of the first Brethren ever to earn such a degree. He served as president of Ashland College from 1906 to 1911. The last several years of his tenure were spent in a nonresident capacity, having joined the faculty of Iowa State University. In 1912 he became a professor of sociology at the University of Wisconsin, a position he held until his retirement. He continued to exert much influence on the church until about 1920 through his writing for the *Brethren Evangelist* and his active participation in General Conference. A conservative and funda-mentalist backlash to his liberal leanings in the 1910s caused him gradually to withdraw from an active role in the Brethren Church after 1920.

Gillin based his study of the Brethren upon a sociological theory developed by one of his Columbia University professors, F. H. Giddings. This "modified 'instinct' theory" is based on the assumption that

the mental activity that produces society is the response of sensitive matter to a stimulus. In the like response of people to the same given stimulus we find the origin of all concerted activity [homogeneity], and in the unlike and unequal response is the origin of the processes of differentia-tion [heterogeneity], which in their relations to the con-certed activity give rise to the complex phenomena of organized society.[46]

The stimuli which make possible that interaction of homogeneous and heterogeneous groups which leads to a more highly organized society are of two kinds: environmental and cultural. "The character of the physical environment determines whether the population of a country shall be homogeneous or not, while the character of the population determines its type of mind, character and disposition, its ideals, its ability to unite in concerted action and its social organization."[47] It can be seen that this social theory is built upon a kind of Hegelian dialectic. Various segments of society react to a given stimulus, result-ing either in greater heterogeneity or increased homo-geneity. In either case a more complex societal structure is created. This structure is then acted upon by a new stimulus, leading either to further "differen-tiation" or to greater "consciousness of kind." This theory is viewed as being especially appropriate to both the American and Dunker experience. The stimulus of the "physical nature" of America was determinative for the future course of the wide variety of people who were attracted to the continent. In spite of the heterogeneity, these diverse elements possessed potential for homogeneity. "This fact determined that American society should be progressive." Thus the original heterogeneity gave way to greater "consciousness of kind" as the various segments of society began to respond to each other by opening up "means of communication and association." This socialization process, resulting in greater consciousness of kind, is the distinctive feature of the American development.[48]

Gillin also explains the origin and development of the Dunkers on the basis of this theory. With specific reference to the causes of the schism, Gillin sees two opposing stimuli at work in the church: the desire for uniformity in one segment of the church and for liberalization in another. The push for uniformity in the church began about 1835 when it was realized that variations of Dunker thought and life had developed. This push was evidenced in the ceaseless effort to unify "her organic structures, her practices and her beliefs." The culmination of this unification process was the passage of the mandatory clause in 1882 together with the withdrawal of the Old Orders in 1880 and the expulsion of the Progressives in 1882. The liberalizing influences in the church commenced about 1850 when certain progressive individuals in the church began to coax the church into the larger American society by advocating such advancements as periodicals, education, and evangelistic outreach. The Progressive Brethren were the most liberal of all the groups, though the Conservatives have become increasingly more progressive since 1882.[49] Gillin's vision for the Dunker church is significant.

> The liberalization of the Dunker church, however, is not yet complete. As the process began before the division in 1882, so the policy of coercion [arising from the drive for uniformity] did not cease altogether at that date.... While, on the whole, liberal policies, and rational sentiments dominate the Dunker church today, all the respect for tradition and all coercion upon the individual has not ceased. But the Dunker church has achieved a social organization that maintains essential unity and is stronger than it ever was, while, at the same time, it allows a greater measure of individual and social liberty than ever before. Those are the marks of a progressive and liberal society.
>
> ... The Dunker church has not reached the stage of social development represented by American society as a whole, but under the influence both of the environing society and also of causes operating within itself, it is rapidly evolving toward such a stage.[50]

Gillin's interpretation of the causes of the split has several positive features. First, it recognizes that the split must be understood on the basis of (1) factors lying within the matrix of Brethren thought and practice and (2) differing responses to the surrounding American social and religious spheres. Second, it isolates one of the fundamental causes of the split—the conflict between the drive for uniformity and the desire to become a part of the larger American society ("liberalization"). However, Gillin's interpretation of the split also contains some serious weaknesses which are carried over into his application of Giddings' "modified 'instinct' theory." Since this theory seems to fit in quite naturally with the evolutionary and liberal mood of the period, it offers Gillin an appropriate framework for presenting not only his thesis that the Progressive movement among the Brethren was a part of the larger liberal tide in American society but also his vision that the Brethren should be a significant part of the socializing forces remaking American society. This perspective causes Gillin to depreciate tradition, former standards of faith, and corporate responsibility for an individual's actions; in a corresponding fashion he elevates individual freedom and experience, rationalism, and social advancement as the means to improve society.[51]

That this interpretation of the Progressive movement has a serious flaw is dramatically evidenced by the strong conservative reaction by the majority in the Brethren Church against Gillin and several other liberal-minded ministers during the teens. The source of the flaw in Gillin's analysis can be summarized in two interrelated points: (1) Gillin equated progressivism and liberalism (see the above quote) and (2) he failed to realize that the founders of the Brethren Church were progressive yet conservative. (1) The dual definition of progressivism (see p. 144) is important to keep in mind at this point. It is true that the Progressives desired to make use of modern advancements to facilitate their outreach; yet they realized that progression must be delimited by Scripture. When, in the early twentieth century, many members of the Brethren Church came to fear that liberalism was progressing beyond Scripture, the brakes were set. (2) The Progressives by no means jettisoned their tradition at the time of the split (though there was a tendency to depreciate aspects of it). Both in theory and practice they showed continued commitment to the conservation of that part of their Brethren heritage which was firmly grounded in Scripture. They saw progressivism as a reform movement, calling the church to purge herself of those human traditions which were encumbering her original God-given mission.

A second interpretation of the division has been offered by Floyd E. Mallott, a former professor of

Church History at Bethany Theological Seminary (Church of the Brethren). He views the schism as a three-way response to industrialism. The Old Orders emphatically rejected all "new techniques, modes, and manners of the era, insofar as the Church and the direct service of God were concerned." The Progressives took the opposite extreme—"enthusiastic adoption of the new techniques and the cry for change and progress."

> The majority party came to be called "conservatives," although one wonders whether "moderates" or "middle of the roaders" would not have been a more accurate designation. . . . it had the weakness of a poorly defined position. Many had not thought on the issue at all, and merely stayed with the majority party. The moderate always has a certain advantage in having elements of truth from all views of the subject.[52]

Donald F. Durnbaugh, in a similar vein, designates "acculturation" as the primary problem faced by the Brethren during the last half of the nineteenth century.[53] These interpretations are helpful in calling attention to the cultural impact of American society upon the Brethren as a fundamental issue of the schism. Yet they fail to explain why the various groups responded as they did to the surrounding culture.

Albert T. Ronk has offered a third interpretation for the division. He frequently refers to "Brethrenism" as the ideal or standard by which all of Brethren history should be judged. Though Ronk's usage of this concept is rather vague, he does venture one broad definition: "The measure of brethrenism in The Brethren Church is limited to the degree that its adherents live up to the principles taught by the Master."[54] Brethrenism thus encompasses all divine truth as revealed in Jesus Christ; as such every embodiment of the true Church throughout history has possessed the characteristic of Brethrenism. "Brethrenism means Brotherhood—brotherhood in Christ."[55] Ronk feels that the "Mind of the Brethren" (he uses this term frequently to refer to the core truths of Brethren faith and practice) was distorted at the time of the split by the "Germanic trait of needing a regulatory set of rules." This predilection toward legalism was most pronounced in the passage of the mandatory clause which transformed the minute book into a "law book."[56] Opposed to this legalistic tendency were the progressives who were to be found in both the Progressive and Conservative wings of the church. The platform of the Progressives is simply that the Christian must continually grow "in knowledge and spiritual magnitude." Ronk

maintains that progressivism is inherent in the thought of the "Brethren from Mack on until the disturbing days of the 1870's and 80's."[57] On the basis of these statements, one may infer that Ronk viewed the course taken by the Old Orders and many Conservatives as a departure from true Brethrenism and that the Progressive wing was actually a reform movement which was calling the church back to her historic Biblical faith. With justification Ronk places special weight on the inner workings of the Brethren mind. Yet the vagueness and generalities with which Ronk describes Brethrenism causes one to wonder whether Ronk had a clear understanding of the "mind of the Brethren." He is able to sense when a statement rings true to the spirit of historic "brethrenism," but he fails to identify those features which qualify it as genuinely "Brethren."[58]

One of the most intriguing interpretations of the division is that offered by Kerby Lauderdale in an independent study at Bethany Theological Seminary. Lauderdale applies the thesis formulated by Vernard Eller that the essence of the Brethren heritage is to be found in a creative tension between the Anabaptist emphasis on corporate discipleship and the Radical Pietist stress on individual piety (see pp. 83–84). The division occurred when these two elements became polarized with the Old Orders emphasizing the Anabaptist perspective to the exclusion of the Radical Pietist and the Progressives stressing the Radical Pietist perspective to the exclusion of the Anabaptist. The Conservatives sought to maintain the creative tension between individualism and community.[59] The strength of this interpretation is found in its identification of those factors within the Brethren tradition which fostered the schism—a polarizing conflict between the principles of uniformity and congregationalism/individualism.

This analysis of the split does contain some weaknesses, however. First, Lauderdale tends to absolutize the differences between the Old Orders and Progressives. For example, he writes:

> The Old Orders fought for absolute community, the Progressives fought for absolute congregationalism, and the Conservatives fought for them both [?]. . . . The Old Orders fought for absolute separation of church and world, for no additions to the Gospel but the traditions of the Elders, and for absolute uniformity. The Progressives fought for separation of church from world in faith alone and avid mission activity, for no additions to the Gospel at all, and for uniformity only in faith. The Conservatives fought for definite separation but definite mission activity, for the sense of the church in matters where the Gospel is silent, and for uniformity in faith and practice.[60]

The exclusive terms which Lauderdale employs to describe both the Old Order and Progressive positions misrepresent each position. This point becomes evident especially after the clouds of controversy had dissipated and calm reason returned. The Old Order emphasis upon community did not lead to absolute uniformity or absolute separation from the world. Likewise, the Progressive battle cry for congregationalism and individual liberty did not lead to absolute congregationalism, a disregard for community, or disunity in practice.[61] It would be a truer representation of the positions of each of the three groups to place them on a continuum with community/uniformity/separation at the extreme right and congregationalism/individuality/adaptation at the extreme left. At the midpoint of the continuum would be the Conservatives, though the composition of this group would include both progressive and ultraconservative members. The Old Orders would occupy a position between the midpoint and the extreme right and would be a rather homogeneous group. The Progressives would occupy a place between the midpoint and the extreme left and would also be fairly homogeneous (see the diagram below). The differences between the three factions thus should be perceived more as differences of *emphasis* rather than of *essence*.

Martin is correct in criticising the use of the terms "Radical Pietist" and "Anabaptist" as if these two movements continued to influence the Brethren in their pure forms (though it would seem justified to speak of an Anabaptist or Radical Pietist tendency or spirit). From their very start, the Brethren represented a *tertium quid* between Radical Pietism and Anabaptism. Though the Brethren clearly adopted elements from each group, these elements were given a new character when the Radical Pietist emphases on Spirit, individuality, and openness were placed in dialectical tension with the Anabaptist stress on outward form, community, and order. Later generations of Brethren no longer manifested a conscious indebtedness to the Radical Pietists or Anabaptists, but the creative tension between the inner and outer, though not always formulated in the same way, remained as a significant feature of Brethren life and thought.

Martin appears to overstate his case, however, when he claims that the Progressives and later the Conservatives gradually abandoned historic Brethrenism and capitulated to the modern world.[63] Though both groups have made major compromises in their historic faith to the modern world, the Progressives on the side of outward expression (nonconformity to

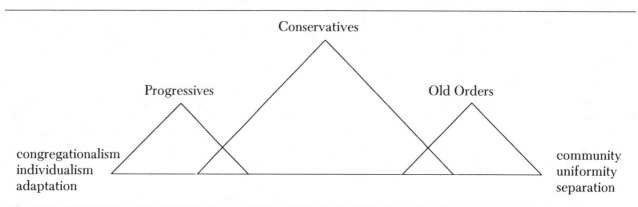

A second criticism of Lauderdale's analysis comes from an independent study written by Dennis Martin at Wheaton College (Martin has roots in the Grace Brethren, one of the branches of the Progressive group). Martin writes:

> . . . it is incorrect to place the emphasis on radical Pietism and Anabaptism as major factors. The Brethren left their European origins behind in the early eighteenth century and became an American sect. The enticement to the Progressives in the 1870s . . . was Pietistic only insofar as the entire American revival movement was Pietistically influenced.[62]

the world and loving service to society) and the Conservatives on the side of inner piety (the stress upon personal conversion and close fellowship with God), it is still premature to sound the death knell of historic Brethrenism in either group. Martin's pessimistic evaluation seems to make too close of a connection between historic Brethrenism and the "religious and ethnic subculture" of the nineteenth century Brethren. To institutionalize the expression of Brethren life in one given period is to distort the true core of the Brethren faith. This faith is founded upon an individual conversion experience and the continuous cultivation of personal fellowship with God. This personal faith will make itself manifest in commitment to a community of faith, in a life of corporate discipleship, and in a willingness to actualize such gospel principles as simplicity, liberty, order, love, unity, and respectful subordination to other Christians, especially one's elders. Though certain outward forms which are built upon gospel authority (the ordinances and various gospel explicits—nonresistance, nonlitigation) would remain unchanged, other externalities which are adiaphorous (modern inventions, dress, personal appearance) may change (though there would be debate on how much change should be permitted and who should set the limits on the change). Much of the distinctive Brethren subculture of the last century did rest upon adiaphorous practices, so that the abandonment of these forms did not impair the core of the Brethren faith. This is not to deny, however, that serious concessions have been made by the Progressives and Conservatives in particular during the last hundred years.

The insights and evaluation of the above interpretations provide a useful foundation for our own view of the division. The thesis of Lauderdale forms the best starting point for understanding the events of the 1880s. The Brethren faith can be best understood as a dynamic tension between inward spiritual qualities and outward, corporate forms. In the writings of Alexander Mack and early Brethren, this tension was maintained by several important principles. (1) Scripture was allowed to reign as the supreme authority in the church. Traditional forms and usages were not permitted to acquire such a position that they impeded the Spirit's ability to speak through Scripture and lead to new truths and forms. (2) The principles of unity and love for the Brotherhood were so ingrained into the minds of the Brethren that they not only were willing to set aside personal rights for the sake of the Brotherhood but also were able to bear with differences until the Spirit brought all to a oneness of mind.

During the middle of the nineteenth century two polarizing trends began to appear within the Brotherhood. The first trend, which started to become evident around the 1840s, was a gradual move toward greater rigidity, order, and legalism as manifested in the minutes of Annual Meeting. No doubt, this reaction was fueled by the increasing interaction of the Brethren with the surrounding culture. An opposite trend began in the 1850s with the desire to make use of modern developments which would aid the church in her mission.

Clearly, the immediate cause of both trends was the question of acculturation. It acted as a catalyst which accelerated and heightened the differences between the "orderites" and the progressives. By the end of the 1860s the two bonds which had maintained the tension between the inner and outer expressions of the faith began to come unglued. The Old Orders, feeling that the Brethren faith as they knew it was in danger of being lost, appealed to Annual Meeting to bring about greater uniformity in relation to the traditional forms. The Progressives, sensing that the Spirit's call to meet the spiritual needs of the modern world was being hampered by increasing traditionalism and the mandates of Annual Meeting, fought for greater freedom on adiaphorous matters. Likewise, the Old Orders came to feel that they could no longer bear with this progression toward apostasy and placed purity of the church above unity of the Brotherhood. The Progressives, headed by Holsinger, became impatient with the drag placed upon their efforts by Annual Meeting and attacked the Conservative leadership's movement toward mandatory legislation and the suppression of individual liberties.

By the 1880s the Conservatives had grown weary of maintaining the balance between the two factions. They relied upon a technicality to dismiss the final Old Order attempt to restore the church to her former character and a non-trial and a technicality (the same one used against the Old Orders) to effect the excommunication of the Progressives. It is most interesting that the Conservatives used the dialectic to their own purposes during the schism. In the Annual Meeting substitute for the Miami Valley Petition in 1880, Annual Meeting scandalized the Old Orders by emphasizing its progressive side in two statements: "while we are conservative we are also progressive" and "we advise more forbearance and liberty" of conscience. After the Old Orders had withdrawn, the 1882 Annual Meeting emphasized the opposite side of a the dialectic by maintaining its commitment to uniformity with the passage of the mandatory clause. This was the final slap in the face to the Progressives who had thought that reconciliation with the Conservatives might be possible. The 1883 Annual Meeting, which gave no hope to the Progressives, also moderated the mandatory clause by acknowledging that some of its decisions were only advisory.

Because the questions involved in this division were of a dialectical nature, it would appear that each of the three groups was correct in part of its position but in error at other points. The Old Order Brethren properly maintained the importance of the principles of community, nonconformity to the world, and a simple and self-denying life style. Yet the danger in their position is found in legalizing the specific forms in which these principles are to be cast, thereby creating a rigid, closed system. The mission of the church became self-preservation rather than outreach to a needy world.

The Progressives were correct in "criticizing the Conservatives for their near idolatry of the past"[64] which the Progressives felt was hampering the church's freedom to develop new means for meeting the spiritual needs of society. The very real danger in the Progressive position was that the strong emphasis on individual freedom and adaptation to the modern world could lead to a loss of corporate unity and the exposure to every new wind of doctrine which would blow across the American religious scene. Holsinger and the Progressives can also be criticized for their lack of sensitivity to the unity of the Brotherhood and their impatient and radical reform methods.

The error of the Conservatives was to be found in their abuse of their position of power at Annual Meeting and their use of the dialectic for their own purposes. Though it may have been difficult to prevent the withdrawal of the Old Orders, leaders from both the Progressive and Conservative groups expressed their belief following the split that the division could have been avoided if greater forbearance and forgiveness had been exercised. It is true that the Conservative position was often vaguely defined with the result that the main body was censured by both extremes for deliberate inconsistency in playing both ends against the middle.[65] Yet in fairness to the Conservatives, this ambiguity was frequently the result of trying to maintain a creative balance between the Old Order and Progressive positions. At one extreme were the Old Order Brethren who tended to formalize the expression of the inner spirit, thereby making it dependent upon a specific "order." At the other extreme were the Progressives who, in their revolt against externalism and formalism, lost sight of the principle of mutual submission for the sake of unity and brotherhood. That some of the leaders of the Conservative faction realized the importance of upholding the truths contained in both positions is demonstrated by the following quotes.

> Holiness is the result of regeneration. The quickening, lifegiving power of God's Word, applied to our hearts, produces holiness of life. Then having holiness of life—new life, it seeks manifestations, and communication, through the various avenues of the body . . .
>
> Holiness in *principle* is invisible. Holiness in *form* is visible—is principle lived out by physical action. Hence the essential part of holiness is in the principle. Its form is simply the outgrowth of the principle. Holiness is the link that connects *form* with *principle*; otherwise form would be mere dead works. . . .
>
> In writing this article we have not designed to refer to our order of dress in disparaging terms. We are satisfied with the order, if complied with from proper motives. But we hear so much about the order; *the order*; THE ORDER, and very little about the *principle*, that must underlie, and support all order . . . [66]

> All finite organic existences are based on the counterprising conditions of conservatism and expansion, always as a unit and never in antagonism of *life* and *end*. . . . A nonprogressive church is a suicidal church. A non-conservative church ditto. And so of individuals. . . . But some want a conservatism that makes a mummy of the church; while others fight for progression that converts the Bible of the Lamb into the mother of harlots, committing fornication with every new suitor of fashion and worldliness that presents himself. Some cling to a hobby that stunts life, binds the church hands and feet, chills her very blood, and makes her haggard and ghastly and inactive as a corpse, while others not content with breaking away from the trammels of obsolete tradition and conventionalism, break away from the cross itself, and put Christ to an open shame. . . .
>
> Progress and conservatism in equipoise—This is the Divine idea, the incontrovertible fact of his economy.[67]

Had the wisdom expressed in these excerpts prevailed, the decade of the 1880s might have held a far different meaning for the German Baptist Brethren.

Chapter 11

DOCTRINAL DEVELOPMENT AND INTERACTION

Introduction

The period from 1865 to 1883 was one of doctrinal and practical ferment among the German Baptist Brethren. As more Brethren received high school and college training and as a larger number of Brethren were coming into contact with urban culture, the Brotherhood was gradually gaining an awareness of the larger social, economic, and political issues of the day.

America itself was undergoing great change during this period. The industrial revolution had come to the United States along with the accompanying phenomena of social and economic upheaval. Revolutionary forms of modern thought, most notably historical criticism of the Bible and Darwinian evolutionary theory, were challenging traditional Christian thought. American evangelicals were turning their attention to temperance and foreign missions and were following with great interest the results of the Moody-Sankey revivals. All of these concerns of the American scene left their impression upon Brethren thought and practice.

The Developing
Theological Mind in the Brotherhood

One of the indications that the Brethren are moving into the wider stream of American church life is their utilization of terminology and apologetic methods characteristic of systematic theology. This trait has already been noted in Peter Nead's *Wisdom and Power.* In 1858 a correspondent to the *Gospel Visitor* remarked:

> Nevertheless, I have observed ever since I am in the church, an insatiable desire among the brethren to gain information wherever they can. And I observe of late, that many of our brethren try to explain scripture passages by grammatical constructions or explanations, or explanations

made by some learned man, they themselves not understanding grammar more than I do, which fits them like the armor of King Saul on little David.[1]

The writer then uses this observation to advocate education for Brethren youth (the armor will then fit better).

A phenomenon of this period which no doubt forced leading Brethren to become conversant with theological, philosophical, and linguistic modes of thought and argumentation was interdenominational debating. Leading defenders of the Brethren faith like James Quinter, R. H. Miller, and J. W. Stein continue to employ a strong Biblical apologetic but also utilize the newer means of defense. Especially in these debates the Brethren reveal their willingness to make use of all available resources to buttress their apologetic for the distinctive Brethren practices (especially baptism, feetwashing, and the Lord's Supper).

Indicative of the changing theological mind of the Brethren are the following items. (1) In 1876 J. T. Meyers, one of the younger, well-educated elders in the church (he had attended the Lutheran Theological Seminary in Philadelphia) called for a systematic approach to the study of the Bible. Noting that theology is a science involving Biblical facts and that the mind is a "speculative organ" that desires order, he challenged the Brethren to engage in the task of systematic theology, not just biblical theology. He observes that "systematic theology consists in the collecting of these facts [of the Bible] together into a systematic order, determining their relation to each other, with many other cogent truths, as well as a vindication of their harmony and consistency."[2]

(2) Noah Longanecker and C. H. Balsbaugh became involved in a brief exchange on the philosophical and systematic theological question of whether God suffered on the cross. In response to

Longanecker's contention that the divine forsook the human on the cross, Balsbaugh asserted, "But 'God in Christ,' in the Manger, on the Cross, and on the Throne, is the imperative requisition of Divine Law and human apostasy."[3] (3) James Quinter, after distinguishing between the objective and subjective aspects of salvation, commented: "This distinction is frequently met with in theological writings, and is useful in expressing the different relations in which salvation stands to us."[4] Quinter's attitude toward systematic theology would have been representative of the more progressive-minded members of the fraternity. They were willing to borrow insights from non-Biblical sources when they illuminated the meaning of the Word. Though it is true that this utilization of methods and materials more characteristic of systematic theology is still an isolated phenomenon, it does indicate the trend of the times toward a better-educated, theologically aware membership.

Theological Issues in the Church

INTRODUCTION

The Brethren periodicals during the years preceding the split provide a detailed picture of the issues which were troubling the mind of the fraternity. Though one of the controversial questions—the proper mode of feetwashing—had roots solely within the church, sources outside the church were responsible for nearly all the other major doctrinal discussions. Some of these discussions related to Brethren doctrines and practices which were not generally recognized by other Christian groups—the love feast and whether it was originally celebrated as the Jewish passover, closed communion, baptism for the remission of sins, the prayer covering, plain dress, and avoidance. Some were occasioned by the influence of other denominations and religious groups on the Brethren—soul sleeping, annihilation of the souls of sinners, Sabbatarianism, adventism (all convictions of the Seventh-Day Adventist), regeneration (revivalism), sanctification (holiness groups) and whether miracles continued beyond the apostolic period (Spiritualism). Some reflected methods and movements which had gained prominence in other evangelical denominations—church-related educational institutions, protracted meetings, Sunday Schools, foreign mission, women preachers, and a paid ministry. Finally, some issues derived from a desire to take advantage of modern techniques—church periodicals and literature and a full stenographic report of Annual Meeting proceedings. Though some of these

controversial questions have been discussed already and others are of minor significance, a more thorough investigation of several of these issues is important for understanding the forces molding Brethren thought of the period.

SOTERIOLOGY

The Brethren perception of the proper order of salvation remained fairly consistent during this period. Nevertheless, revivalism and the holiness movement caused the Brethren to give more attention to several facets of salvation. One of the subtle ways in which revivalism influenced the Brethren was to fill the void left by the gradual disappearance of the old piety. A quite significant difference exists, however, between the former piety, based on Classical Pietism and Radical Pietism, and the new piety, which possessed predominantly American roots. The pietistic spirit of the eighteenth century Brethren centered in an affective relationship of love between the believer and God and Christ, often with mystical overtones, which was founded in the new birth and was cultivated through personal prayer, the reading of the Bible and devotional literature, and meditation. This personal experience with God resulted in a deep concern for other people, because love of and communion with God impelled the believer to love the community of faith and one's neighbor. The revivalistic piety also emphasized personal experience with God and individual appropriation of salvation. However, it was cultivated in corporate "prayer and social meetings" and especially in seasonal (usually the fall and winter months) revival services with gospel hymns and preaching which personalized and individualized Jesus' death and salvific work.

At least three differences can be noted between the two forms of piety. (1) Revivalistic piety tended to subserve the interests of the corporate community to those of the individual. Corporate worship was organized in such a way as to lead the sinner to Christ or revive the faith of the believer. As a result, the strong corporate commitment of the earlier piety, which moved from the individual to the community, was severely weakened. (2) Closely connected with the above observation is a change in the perception of the Christian life. The older piety viewed Christian growth as gradual and progressive while revivalism perceived the Christian life as "a struggle across dull plateaus between peaks of spiritual refreshing."[5] This characteristic of revivalism was conducive to the concept that there may be several "works of grace" in an individual's life. Though the Brethren polemic against the form of revivalism found in the holiness movement militated against any significant influence from holiness or, later, pentecostal groups, the Brethren adoption of the more Reformed style of revivalism[6] found especially among the Baptists would open them up at the end of the century to Keswick teaching. (3) It has been demonstrated that revivalism during the mid-nineteenth century had a sensitive social consciousness and even paved the way for the social gospel.[7] Yet by the early twentieth century the conservative piety of revivalism was beginning to react against the clamorous proclaimers of social Christianity.[8] The bifurcation between social and individual salvation that resulted was foreign to the earlier piety which maintained an integral relation between one's individual experience with God and one's responsibility to his neighbor.

Revivalism's preoccupation with the new birth and regeneration was the catalyst which caused the Brethren to discuss regeneration increasingly in a technical, rather than informal, sense. The lack of attention given to the new birth by the Brethren is reflected in a statement by Benjamin F. Moomaw, an elder from Virginia:

> . . . there is no subject in Theology so imperfectly understood; and in fact it is rarely ever discussed before a congregation. Since I have occasionally lectured upon it, I have met with many persons, young, middle aged, and those three score years and over, who have never heard it discussed.[9]

Though there is still a good deal of diversity in the understanding of the new birth among Brethren writers, the most frequent schematization of the doctrine is to compare it with natural birth (as did Nead).[10] It thus includes generation, quickening, and birth. Writers prior to the 1860s tended to use regeneration in an inclusive sense for all three aspects or shift its primary focus to the new birth (Nead and Zelotes). Writers during the period under discussion tend to use the word, new birth, as the inclusive term for the process and limit regeneration to the initial step in the process (though new birth and regeneration are sometimes used synonymously).

Moomaw's work can be considered representative of Brethren views regarding the new birth in the 1860s and 70s. He holds that the new birth "does not mean simply external reformation, but it is obvious that it includes an entire change of heart; the renewal of the soul in the likeness of the divine image"[11] (note he is defining the term by using traditional Brethren concepts). The new birth, like natural birth, includes three aspects. (1) Regeneration, correspond-

ing to generation, "means to beget anew, reproduce, and is the work of the Spirit of God through the word, while the creature is passive." (2) "Conversion is the turning from one state or condition to another, in which the creature is active, and answers to quickening in the process of the natural birth." (3) "Being born again means to be introduced into the family of God." Herein we enter into covenant relations with Him, receive the Spirit of adoption, become children of God and recipients of the "benefits and immunities of the kingdom of God."[12]

Moomaw then discusses the interrelationship of regeneration with other aspects of the salvation process. He considers the Holy Spirit as the "efficient means" of regeneration and the word of God as the "instrumental means"[13] (note the theological terminology). He criticizes a view of the new birth which is too dependent on either (1) "the action of the creature, in the performance of ordinances" or (2) "spiritual influences, independent of secondary instrumentalities, and the co-operation of the creature."[14] He therefore dismisses the idea of baptismal regeneration on the one hand and the claim that baptism is merely a sign of regeneration on the other. Just as man is a unit composed of soul and body so also the new birth should be seen as a unit affecting both parts of man. "Hence the Spirit must renew our spirits, and the body must be baptized in water to signify that as Christ's redeemed property it is now given unto him visibly."[15] Moomaw concludes by maintaining that regeneration must have both internal evidence (assurance of forgiveness and the feeling associated with the certainty that we are God's children) and "external evidence [obedience] corroborating the internal operation." Either alone "is not reliable—the feelings without corresponding obedience, nor a cold formal obedience without the corresponding emotions of the soul."[16]

Moomaw's discussion of regeneration contains two especially noteworthy elements. First, the traditional inner-outer dialectic is quite explicit throughout the treatment. Second, Moomaw attaches to the doctrine of the new birth a thoroughly Brethren signification.

In addition to regeneration, discussions of the doctrine of sanctification become much more common during this period. The increasing currency of the term is no doubt due to the proliferation of the holiness movement. As early as 1856 John Kline noted that he occasionally heard of some people "professing sanctification" and observes that thereby they were claiming to have attained sinless perfection. Though he is nonjudgmental on such claimants, he does deny earlier in his diary the possibility of sinless perfection in this life.[17] The Brethren characteristically rejected the possibility of realizing "perfect sanctification" or "entire sanctification," though, true to their Pietist heritage, they held that one could be perfect in his desires and intentions.[18] Brethren writers also criticized the notion, implied by revivalism, that the Christian life is composed of emotional peaks and valleys. Thus James Quinter rebukes those "who suppose that religion is a fitful sort of life; an alternation of excitement and insensibility."[19]

Brethren treatments of sanctification and holiness reveal a strict fidelity to traditional conceptions of the Christian life. Representative of the Brethren definition of sanctification are comments by Samuel Kinsey:

> Sanctification is not instantaneous; it is gradual. We are to "purify our souls *in obeying the truth*" [italics mine]. As is the purifying process, so is the sanctifying process. We are to "grow in grace and in the knowledge of the truth." As our growth in grace and spiritual manhood advances, so does sanctification advance. We may enjoy *degrees* of sanctification just in proportion to the perfect state of our heart.
>
> . . . To be as perfect in our walk, talk, thoughts, and actions as God is perfect, can not be expected while we are in the flesh. But our *desires* can be holy, pure, and perfect.[20]

ECCLESIOLOGY

Though some of the ecclesiological subjects that generated discussion in the Brethren periodicals reflected interdenominational tensions—the observance of the holy kiss, love feast, and feetwashing *as church ordinances*—others reflected developing differences within the church—avoidance and questions of dress (whether women could wear plain hats in place of the prayer cap; the necessity of men, especially ministers, wearing full beards). Developments with regard to avoidance are particularly revealing for they suggest a weakening of the sectarian nature of the church. During the eighteenth and early nineteenth centuries, when a strong sectarian and exclusivistic conception of the church prevailed, avoidance remained a vital part of the church's disciplinary activity. With the weakening of the conviction that the church was the sole "ark of salvation" and the broadening social and religious horizons in the church, avoidance gradually slipped into disuse (though it remained on the minutes). In 1865 Holsinger could testify that he never saw it practiced or applied, while Grabill Myers, an elder from Pennsylvania, commented the same year: "I am aware that avoidance was practiced by the church in former years, and by some to this day, yet I have

known more or less about the church for fifty years, and I never saw it practiced, but heard of it all this time."[21]

Another indication that the former exclusivism of the church is weakening is the new perspective taken toward the question of apostolic succession (this question was a live issue at this time due to the Baptist Landmark movement). Though many still claimed a historical connection to the apostolic church through the Waldenses,[22] other men were coming to realize the problematical character of the entire issue (see p. 118). The new apologetic for the existence of the church was based upon the faithful observance of the doctrine of Christ and the presence of the Spirit, irrespective of the continuous practice of this doctrine. Note B. F. Moomaw's discussion of the issue.

> We are well aware that we cannot in the pages of history, discover an unbroken line of apostolical succession, in the history of any professed Christian organization. Nor do I think it necessary that we should do this to prove the presence of the church. If we can find a church that preaches and practices the doctrines preached and practiced by Christ and the Apostles, it should be satisfactory as to the presence of the Spirit. "If they speak God's Word," i.e., "declare the whole counsel of God," it is evidence "that God has sent them," and the promise is sure that the Savior will be with them, by his Spirit . . . John 14:17.[23]

The Progressives, after reorganizing themselves into The Brethren Church, used several ideas suggested in the above passage as an apologetic for their uniqueness among Christian groups: their preaching of the whole gospel, their commitment to the New Testament as their only creed, their practice of all of the ordinances.

ESCHATOLOGY

The man who shaped Brethren attitudes toward eschatological questions more than anyone else during the latter nineteenth century (and even into the next century) was the former Baptist minister, William C. Thurman (d. 1906). Though he was a member of the Brotherhood for only a few years (see pp. 140–141 and n. 55), his repeated unsuccessful attempts to establish the date of Christ's return caused his name to be used as a by-word in the church for misguided date setting.

The few personal references Thurman makes in his works as well as his approach to Scripture reveal several striking similarities to William Miller, the founder of the Adventist movement. Thurman, like Miller, had been an avowed deist. Yet following his conversion he became convinced not only of the utter truthfulness of God's Word but also the remarkable exactness of all revealed chronology. In fact, for Thurman the "unerring records of God's celestial calendar" provided "a new internal evidence of the divine inspiration of our Bible."[24]

Thurman's interest in prophecy began during the 1840s through reading the Adventist periodical, *Midnight Cry*. Through intensive study of Biblical chronology, he became convinced that the great Millennial Sabbath rest would begin in 1875 and that in 1868 the dead in Christ would rise and, together with the living believers, meet the Lord in the air (this is the first time that a pre-tribulation rapture [he does not use the word "rapture"] is found in Brethren literature). His conclusions were published in his *Sealed Book of Daniel Opened*. The detailed study of prophecy, astronomy, and Biblical chronology in this 304 page book testifies to his seven year investigation of Scripture to pry "into the chronological order of the holy oracles of God." The certainty that Thurman attached to his calculations, which, he felt, opened up the hidden truths of Daniel, is revealed in the preface of his work:

> Having . . . thus discovered the truth as to the correct chronology of our Bible, which removes the seal and opens the book of Daniel, my object in this work is to "Write the vision and make it plain upon tables" (Hab. ii. 2); to disclose that portion of the "sure word of prophecy" (2 Pet. i. 19) which was "shut up and sealed till the time of the end" (Dan. xii. 4, 9) . . . [25]

Thurman's calculations involved a reworking of the earlier Adventist proofs for Christ's return. However, they met with the same disappointing fate as Miller's reckonings. He set and reset the time of Christ's return for at least five different dates— September 27 and October 26, 1868; October 17, 1869; April 19, 1875; and April 7, 1876.[26] In announcing the last date he finally began to show some uncertainty about his conclusions: "But if Jesus does not come this year, I shall honestly admit that my arrangement of these prophetic dates is incorrect, for after much mature deliberation, and the closest investigation, I can extend them no farther."[27]

Thurman continued to have a small impact on the German Baptist Brethren even after his second disfellowshipping in 1867. Among his Adventist supporters in Virginia were a number of former Brethren. Some of these former members slowly filtered back into the church following the repeated disappointments. Others joined other churches while, in two individual cases, one man reportedly lost his faith

and another his mind.[28] A group of Thurman's followers whom he had baptized and who would have had to be rebaptized to join the German Baptist church refused to submit to rebaptism and later joined the Progressives following the split.

Thurman's activities remained a subject of interest in the Brethren periodicals. In 1876 and 1877 he was publishing a monthly paper, *The Word of God*, in Charlestown, Massachusetts, and in the latter year he debated with an Adventist, Miles Grant, on the topic of trine immersion.[29] In 1886 Holsinger met Thurman in Virginia and heard him preach.[30] Thurman apparently remained a restless prophet, trying to discern the signs of the times, for in 1882 it was reported that he was "having more visions."[31]

Interestingly, the initial Brethren response to Thurman's calculations was one of openness, though there were some critical voices. The *Gospel Visitor* actually promoted the sale of *The Sealed Book of Daniel Opened*. After his falling out with the church over feetwashing, the Brethren were more cautious, although some members still accepted his chronology.[32] After 1868, however, the general mood of the church was decidedly against detailed chronological speculations and date setting. Samuel Kinsey's comments are illustrative of the general Brethren attitude toward definite dates and the responsibility of believers relative to Christ's return:

> From reading the Testament I would not judge that God ever intended that man should be able by calculations which he might make, to determine the time of Christ's coming.
>
> But because the "Son of Man" will come at an hour when we "think not," it is necessary that we are ever watching and continually holding ourselves to readiness to depart at the shortest notice.[33]

Brethren discussions of eschatology during the 1860s and 70s show great diversity of thought. Though treatments of eschatology are, almost without exception, premillennial, Brethren writers reflect the great contemporary ferment of thought on this subject occurring in the larger American evangelical community. The traditional post-tribulation view of Christ's return continues to be prevalent but both pre- and mid-tribulation views are present. Though no dispensational schemas are yet discernible, questions are being discussed which show that the ground is being prepared: whether Christians will have to go through the tribulation, what to do with Daniel's seventieth week, whether the "kingdom of God" and the "kingdom of heaven" are synonymous (the Brethren almost always indicate they are during this period).[34] It is also interesting to note the ebb and flow of eschatological interest. Discussions of the last things predictably proliferate in the *Gospel Visitor* and *Christian Family Companion* between 1865 and 1868 but diminish by the end of the decade. Articles on eschatology appear in Quinter's publications only infrequently during the 1870s but the greatest interest in the events of the end during this decade is to be found in the *Vindicator* where the troubles in the church are regularly linked to the apostasy that is to precede Christ's return (see p. 131). One gathers the impression from this data that the Brethren were agreed on several eschatological points—the fact of Christ's personal return prior to the millennium, the inadvisability of setting dates—but allowed great latitude to individuals to understand the details of the end times within these parameters.

Thurman's Adventist message was not the sole instance of Adventist influence on the Brethren. Brethren periodicals reflect the impact of other beliefs of the Seventh-Day Adventists on the church. Numerous articles are thus addressed to the issues of Sabbatarianism, soul-sleep after death for believers, and the annihilation of the soul of sinners after death. The latter two beliefs were reproved by Annual Meeting in 1858 while M. M. Eshelman and R. H. Miller addressed themselves to the Sabbath question in widely circulated treatises.[35] Intermittent discussions of these issues throughout this period (and the rest of the century in the Brethren Church) indicate the continuing unsettling impact of Seventh-Day Adventism.

The Brethren
Response to Contemporary Scientific,
Social, and Religious Movements and Issues

Articles written for the Brethren periodicals indicate that the membership was gaining a greater consciousness of the major issues facing America. James Quinter kept his readers abreast of significant national and international news especially if it possessed special religious importance. Some writers were also expressing their viewpoints on such contemporary issues as evolution, labor problems, and temperance. An overview of Brethren perspectives on some of these problems provides and excellent gauge of changing attitudes in the church toward American society.

SCIENCE

As was true of the wider American church scene, the impact of evolution was not evident among the

Brethren until the 1870s. Prior to this date, Brethren writers express the conviction that there is a basic harmony between science and Christianity and that a knowledge of science can fortify Christian faith.

> . . . the Bible is the great moulding power which is to fit the mind to embrace christianity, but this does not prevent the sciences from having the same effect, . . . for the mind that simply deals in matters of common daily concern cannot possess such noble thoughts of the Creator as he who is seeking the design in the different departments of nature . . . [36]

The religious controversy over evolution reached its most critical stage in the late 1870s in America, for not only had the American scientific community generally accepted the new theory but several leading theologians had expressed their support for Darwinianism, notably President James McCosh of Princeton University and President Paul A. Chadbourne of Williams College.[37] It is at this time that intermittent discussions of evolution appear in the Brethren periodicals. Several writers stated their belief that the conflict between religion and science on this issue would disappear if theologians and scientists would remain in their own proper spheres of interest. "The mistake of both theologians and 'scientists' is in the attempt of either to furnish a standard by which to judge of the other's conclusions."[38] Yet a crucial presuppositional difference is to be noted in two men making this point. S. H. Sprogle perceives an "inherent conflict between science and religion" while Howard Miller expresses the belief that "no real difference exists between genuine knowledge classified and called science and pure faith in God called religion."[39]

Articles appearing later in 1877, however, reveal great alarm over the philosophical underpinnings of evolution, especially materialism and rationalism. Lewis Hummer, for example, challenges the materialism of "Darwin, Huxley, Tyndall, Spencer, Underwood":

> If Materialists extend the province of "matter" over the province of spirit [he has previously cited a statement by Huxley intimating this], and call the combination "matter," then of course matter would have the inherent power that Materialists claim it has got: Put God to matter [i.e., limit the means of God's activity to material forms] then evolution is simply a new name for creation."[40]

Alex Reese attacked what he perceived as the supplanting of revelation by the "established facts" of science and reason.

> Revelation is set aside as unworthy of reason, and because it (revelation) conflicts (?) with the "facts" of "science." . . .

... And now the spirit of the modern philosophy is to deify Reason—to ignore Revelation and to set God and his claims aside. It is skepticism and infidelity masked in their disguise of scientific research.[41]

Brethren opinion seems to have been solidly against the theory of evolution in the late 1870s and early 1880s. Several writers between 1880 and 1883 even felt that the tide was turning against evolution through the literary efforts of several men whom God had "raised up." Notable in this latter regard was Wilford Hall of New York who was reported to have sent a copy of his work, *Problem of Human Life, Here and Hereafter*, to leading evolutionists throughout the world.[42]

Though exhibiting general consensus on the question of evolution, the Brethren were debating other related issues, especially the age of the earth. The problem of reconciling the Genesis account of creation with the fossil record had led to the proposal of the gap theory (an indefinite span of time exists between Genesis 1:1 and 1:2) as early as 1867 and the day-age theory (each day of creation represents an unspecific period of time) by the 1870s. Proponents of six literal solar days of creation were quite vocal, nevertheless.[43] In these discussions the dogmatic literalism of the advocates of the latter view was in marked contrast to the rather condescending tone of those in the "scientific know." Note J. Keim's response to an article which had approached the above question "according to the Bible."

> Now, my dear friend, if you are not acquainted with the Nebular theory, astronomy and geology, you cannot understand this scripture [the Genesis account of creation] by the light of these sciences, but you must be content to read the plain simple words of Moses and take it just as it reads. This will answer your purpose best . . . do not cry down the sciences simply because you do not understand them.[44]

This quotation is eloquent testimony to the tensions being created in the church as more men received higher education. Those who retained the traditional literal approach to Scripture felt their faith threatened by the new learning which seemed to subordinate God's Word to the word of science. Those Brethren who had received college and university training maintained that they were fully committed to the truth of Scripture but believed that this truth could be more fully illuminated by a thorough knowledge of scientific data. They harbored great optimism in believing that an intelligent and systematic study of God's creation could supplement the revealed Word in extending the realms of man's knowledge.

SOCIAL ISSUES

The social problems which accompanied the industrial revolution in America attracted some Brethren attention during the 1870s and early 1880s. J. B. Brumbaugh, an associate editor of the *Primitive Christian and Pilgrim*, took special editorial note of the rise of a "communistic element" in the United States that utilized anarchistic tactics to attempt to gain reform. Though deploring their "lawless and brutish course of action," he placed a great deal of blame upon the "capitalists" for the problem. Rather than making more jobs available and paying working men sufficient wages to live, they were "using the money of our country to subserve their own selfish purposes."[45]

The spiritual needs of America's towns and cities were a concern to the Progressives in particular. They called upon the church to realize its responsibility for fulfilling the Great Commission in the urban centers. They felt the fact that Brethren were to be found in only two cities in 1883—St. Louis and Philadelphia—showed a callous neglect which "some of us will have to account for."[46]

The Brethren felt strong sympathy for the temperance movement that was gaining momentum during the 1870s. Annual Meeting had taken strong and repeated stands (beginning in 1781) against the manufacture, sale, and use of intoxicating beverages. Yet Annual Meeting characteristically felt that the proper place for advocating this and other principles was within the church and therefore advised against joining temperance societies.[47] Reflective of these convictions was the frequent claim that the German Baptist Brethren represented the oldest temperance society in the United States. So strong was Brethren sentiment for temperance that many parted with tradition and advocated participation in elections in which the sale of intoxicating liquor was an issue.[48] Historically, the Brethren groups as a whole have maintained their fidelity more to this principle than any other with the possible exception of nonresistance.

CONTEMPORARY RELIGIOUS MOVEMENTS

Many of the "innovations" which were so disruptive to the church's welfare during this period had roots in American evangelicalism—revivalism, church-related schools, Sunday Schools, foreign missions. In this chapter it was seen that several other features of Brethren thought—eschatological interest and temperance—gained added prominence due to contemporary religious developments. Other data, such as the occasional reports in the Brethren periodicals of the work of Moody and Sankey and information about the 1878 Prophetic Conference at New York in both the *Vindicator* and *Primitive Christian and Pilgrim*, likewise reveal that the Brethren are both aware of and interested in current evangelical occurrences. For better or for worse the Conservative and Progressive Brethren were accepting the necessity of moving into the main stream of American life.

Concluding Observations

As much change occurred among the German Baptists in the quarter century between 1857 and 1882 as in any other twenty-five year period in Brethren history. Up until the former year the Brethren, through Annual Meeting, had vigorously resisted nearly every attempt to introduce nontraditional practices into the church. Significantly, however, in 1857 and 1858, series of meetings, Sunday Schools, and Brethren-related schools received conditional acceptance by Annual Meeting. A new era of what might be termed "controlled openness"[49] was inaugurated. The Brethren showed a willingness to accept new practices if they were expressed *within* the context of the church and her stated principles. James Quinter expresses succinctly the attitude that dominated this period of Brethren history.

> We think that every principle and every institution should be impartially examined in the light of gospel truth and its own practical tendency, and be dealt with according to its merits. And if it is worthy of our regard, it should have it [our regard], though it may have been rejected by some, and abused by others, and be found associated in systems with things that are wrong.[50]

Chapter 12

DENOMINATIONAL REORGANIZATION AND CULTURAL INTERACTION (1883-1915)

Introduction

The years immediately following the division of 1882-1883 were precarious ones for the Brethren Church. Though the Progressives were generally united in their fundamental sentiments, their unity was based more in their *opposition* to the policies and authority of the Conservative leadership of Annual Meeting than in any constructive alternative (this point is underscored by the contents of the "Declaration of Principles"). Whereas the Conservatives had the considerable advantage of retaining essential control over the local, district, and denominational organization of the church and whereas the Old Order Brethren had the psychological and practical advantage of being fully committed to the idea of withdrawal for the sake of preserving the old order, the Progressives faced the trauma of being unwillingly excluded from the main body. The harsh reality of this fact was only slowly realized[1] and the reorganization of the church was a slow and painful process. Not until about 1900 had the emotional scars healed sufficiently for the church as a whole to develop a positive, new self-consciousness of its mission in society. During the first two decades of the new century, remarkable progress was made in home and foreign missions, the definition of polity, and the growth of the existing institutions and auxiliaries of the church. The Brethren became actively involved in the larger life of the American church and took advantage of the many interdenominational movements which distinguished the period. Yet in the teens the forward movement of the Brotherhood was temporarily stymied as the church became embroiled in a liberal-fundamentalist controversy which can be viewed as a direct result of the spirit of openness which pervaded the denomination especially up to 1900.

The Process of Reorganization

The reorganization of the Brethren Church, begun at the 1883 Convention, was not formally completed until 1887.[2] The work of the 1883 Convention at Dayton, Ohio, reveals that the Brethren were by no means ready to face the difficult task of defining their understanding of church government. The duties and qualifications of ministers were defined in five simple statements derived from 2 Timothy 1:15, 4:2; Matthew 28:19-20; 1 Timothy 3:1-11; Acts 6:4; and 1 Corinthians 9:1-14. A brief five point report by the Committee on Church Government was sent back to committee because of fear that its adoption would be tantamount to establishing a creed. For its resubmitted report, the committee presented a copy of the New Testament as the creed of the church and the report was adopted with the singing of the doxology! The Convention also reiterated the church's support for a paid ministry, Sunday Schools and Sunday School Conventions, and higher education (through Ashland College). The "literary tone" of the *Progressive Christian*, which was renamed *The Brethren's Evangelist* beginning July 18, 1883, was now to be "under the control of the general Brotherhood," a move that was welcomed by the German Baptists' *Gospel Messenger.*[3]

At the close of the 1883 Convention, a National Executive Committee of five was appointed "to arrange for a future convention whenever occasion may demand."[4] Though there may have been an informal agreement to wait at least five years before another convention was called,[5] the feeling that the denomination still lacked proper organization was expressed both at the beginning and end of 1884. Yet fears that a new centralized hierarchy would destroy congregational church government effectively offset the growing clamor for another convention. Sentiment for the second convention finally caused the

Executive Committee to call for the convention to be held at Ashland, Ohio, on September 21–23, 1887. There seem to have been two factors in particular which were instrumental in the decision to call the convention: the need to coordinate evangelistic efforts and the desire to foster greater unity, fellowship, and brotherly love.[6]

At the 1887 Convention the church clearly indicated that the Progressive understanding of congregationalism did not imply belief in absolute congregationalism. Thus it was decided:

> it is the sense of this Convention that the apostolic idea of congregational church government relates alone to the incidental affairs of the local congregation, and not to doctrinal practices and tenets which must be general or universal—the same in all congregations, the doctrinal conditions of membership in one congregation shall be the doctrinal conditions in every other.[7]

Beyond this simple declaration, the Brethren were not prepared to go. Other important features of the Convention were (1) the appointment of a General Mission Board and the call for state conventions to establish State Mission Boards to coordinate mission work; (2) the adoption of regulations for the convening and governing of future conventions; (3) the organization of a women's society; and (4) detailed discussions regarding the status and finances of Ashland College and the Publishing House.

It was decided at the 1887 Ashland Convention that future conventions would be held once every five years. Accordingly, the next convention (this gathering was renamed "Brethren General Conference" in 1892) was held at Warsaw, Indiana, in 1892. Such was the press of business and the need for continued attention to the educational, missionary, and publishing interests of the church that a conference was called for 1893. These same concerns resulted in the authorization of a conference for 1894. By 1894 so much progress was being made in all the major departments of the church as a result of the three consecutive yearly conferences that a consensus developed that conferences should be held annually[8] (annual gatherings were formally authorized in 1898). Thus over a period of ten years the fear that annual conferences would lead to a diminishing of congregational rights gradually was overcome by the realization that "failure in every important church enterprise, and in that general display of denominational energy and unity which always impresses the world, is a dear price to pay for the absence of them."[9]

The void left by denominational inactivity between 1883 and 1892 was filled to a great measure by the

district organization. Sunday School Conventions were held annually in a number of states. The 1887 Convention called for the establishment of state organizations to facilitate evangelistic work and by the late 1880s and early 1890s many of these districts were holding annual conferences in conjunction with the Sunday School Conventions. Until the 1980s the districts had generally been given preference over the national organization of the Brethren Church in questions relative to church polity and authority (provision for the ordination of elders, disciplining of ministers, organization and recognition of new congregations, resolution of difficulties in a local church).

The Establishment and Growth of Auxiliary Organizations and Institutions

A significant part of the life of the Brethren Church during this period was wrapped up in its various auxiliaries, many of which were organized between 1887 and 1900. The National Ministerial Association, proposed in 1887, was organized in 1892. It provided ministers with fellowship and training (through a recommended reading list) and the families of deceased ministers with financial assistance.

At the 1887 Convention a Sister's Society of Christian Endeavor (SSCE) was established. Though this women's organization grew slowly, it could boast about two thousand members in 1897. This society was extremely active during this period, providing support for evangelistic work, funding a Theological Chair at Ashland College, assuming the support of needy ministers (through the Superannuated Ministers' Fund) until 1912, and underwriting the college tuition of young men preparing for the ministry. The SSCE also sponsored a girls' organization, the Sisterhood of Mary and Martha, which was formally organized in 1913. The name of the SSCE was changed to The Woman's Missionary Society in 1919.[10]

In 1890 the first chapter of a youth organization, the King's Children Society, was formed, though concern for the church's youth had been evidenced throughout the 1880s through regular columns for children and youth in the *Brethren Evangelist*. In 1893 a national King's Children Society was organized with a Board of Directors and a youth paper. The organization grew rapidly, from 250 members in 1893 to 2000 in 1894 and 4500 in 1895.[11] A growing desire to work more closely with the burgeoning interdenominational Christian Endeavor movement (begun in 1881) caused the organization to be renamed the Young People's Society of Christian Endeavor of the Brethren Church in 1901.

Sunday Schools, whether Brethren or union (held in conjunction with other denominations), continued to be an important part of the work of the church.[12] Annual Sunday School Conventions provided state-wide fellowship and instruction for Sunday School personnel. Though the Brethren used a variety of Sunday School literature during the 1880s and early 90s (International Lessons and literature from D. C. Cook, the American Baptists, and United Brethren), by 1893 Brethren Sunday School literature was available. Two Sunday School papers were also published, *Cheering Words*, containing edifying material, and *Words of Wisdom*, a temperance paper.

The Progressives were fully aware of the importance of church literature; they had made full use of the periodicals to foster and mold Progressive sentiment among the German Baptists prior to the split. Articles of incorporation for a Brethren Publishing House were therefore procured by a committee appointed by the 1883 Convention and both the 1883 and 1887 Conventions recommended the purchase of the *Evangelist* and the existing (privately owned) Publishing House. Yet these later recommendations were not realized until 1892 due to the financial burden of the young denomination. The 1892 Convention also authorized the production of a complete series of Brethren Sunday School literature and tracts[13] which were published separately by A. D. Gnagey in Meyersdale, Pennsylvania, until 1894. In this year the printing of the *Evangelist* (which was being published at Waterloo, Iowa, at the time), the Sunday School literature, and tracts was placed under the business management of a single Board and the Meyersdale and Waterloo interests were moved to Ashland where they have remained to the present.

Ashland College maintained a precarious existence until the end of the century due to persistent indebtedness. In 1888, with the debt amounting to about $41,000 (between 1884 and 1886 Holsinger had worked feverishly to retire the debt), the college was placed in receivership. The institution was sold in a private sale at which the Conservative trustees paid $4,000 for some nonessential land and five Progressive trustees paid $18,500 for the main campus. The trustees made up the deficit from their private resources. This arrangement had been made by the two parties and thereby Ashland College passed into the hands of the Brethren Church.[14] In August, 1888, a new charter was secured which, for the first time, made the training of ministers a prominent feature of

its purpose. Nevertheless, continuing indebtedness resulted in the closure of the college between 1896 and 1898 until the arrival of the new president, J. Allen Miller, who served in this capacity from 1898 until 1906. Under him and his successor, J. L. Gillin (1906–1911), the debts against the college were finally liquidated. Between 1900 and 1919 the enrollment consistently remained around one hundred.

In 1906 J. Allen Miller resigned to head the new Bible department, which, for the first time, was designated as a seminary. A second professor, J. A. Garber, was added to this department in 1915 during the presidency of W. D. Furry (1911–1919). The seminary department granted a Bachelor of Arts Degree in Divinity to those completing the classical divinity program while a modified English divinity program led to a diploma but no degree.

Evangelistic activity, which had been a large part of the Progressive program prior to the split, continued to have a high priority in the Brethren Church.[15] During the 1880s and early 90s, however, much of the evangelistic work was necessarily focused on the organization of churches where members of the German Baptists had either left the church or were expelled. The 1883 Dayton Convention authorized two evangelists, J. H. Swihart and P. J. Brown, to attend specifically to the work of "reconstruction and organization of churches."[16] At the urging of the 1887 Ashland Convention, district organizations were established in order to facilitate evangelistic activity. These districts formed Home Mission Boards and also selected a state evangelist whose function was to effect new organizations. Though a General Mission Board was created in 1887, its primary function was to oversee the district work. A permanent National Mission Board was therefore established in 1892 to "promote the missionary work of the Brethren church."[17]

By the mid-1890s support began to mount for more concerted evangelistic activity in new fields— urban America and foreign missions. Though there was opposition initially to these new efforts, it had generally subsided by the second decade of the new century.[18] By 1910 city missions had been initiated in Washington, Pittsburgh, Philadelphia, Columbus, Canton, Chicago, St. Joseph, and Montreal. In 1914 it was reported that the church had 144 rural congregations, 48 in towns, and 21 in cities.[19] The Brethren were awakening to the fact that America was becoming increasingly urban and that the future of the Brethren Church was, to a great extent, dependent upon reflecting this trend.

Sentiment for foreign mission activity began to grow in earnest in 1896, especially as a result of J. C. Cassel's zealous advocacy. It was fostered through the holding of missionary conventions in local congregations in the Brotherhood during 1897 and 1898, regular articles on the subject in the *Evangelist* (Cassel is a frequent proponent), and by focusing attention on the mission activity of the larger evangelical community.[20] Advocates of the cause were determined to do something tangible at the 1900 General Conference. Cassel's proposal to organize a foreign mission agency within the structure of Conference was given a cool reception. As a result the famed organizational meeting of the Foreign Missionary Society of the Brethren Church (FMS) occurred "out under the trees." The FMS was an entity separate from the authority of Conference and the control of its Board of Trustees was left in the hands of its contributors.[21] During the years 1909-1912 attempts were made to unify the work of the National Missionary Board and FMS. Though unification was not realized, in 1912 it was decided that the two organizations should hold joint meetings to coordinate their work. In time, the National Missionary Board's province came to be recognized as home missions (the term "Home Mission" Board first appears in 1920) while that of the FMS was considered foreign works.

The initial attempts to field a missionary were not illustrious. J. C. Mackey's endorsement by the 1897 Conference for service in India went no further. The attempt to establish a mission in Persia in 1902 by supporting a national, Yonan Auraham, failed due to lack of careful planning and opposition by such men as Gillin and B. C. Moomaw. Learning from these lessons, detailed preparations were laid between 1907 and 1909 for the opening of work in Argentina by C. F. Yoder (1873-1955), his wife, and sister. This planning resulted in a fruitful field of work for the Brethren which has continued up to the present. A second successful mission field was opened in Africa, primarily through the individual work of James Gribble. A member of the Philadelphia First Brethren Church, Gribble had gone to Africa in 1909 under the auspices of the African Inland Mission. So glowing were his reports of missionary opportunity in Africa that Conference authorized the opening of this field in 1914. After a period of deputation work back in the States, Gribble returned to Africa with four others in 1918 under the oversight of the FMS.

L. S. Bauman (1875-1950) deserves much of the credit for stirring interest in foreign missions among the Brethren. Louis was the son of W. J. H. Bauman

(1837-1922), one of the important leaders of the Progressives at the time of the division. Louis was born in Iowa but grew up in Morrill, Kansas. He was ordained in 1894 and served pastorates at Morrill (1894-1895), Auburn and Cornell, Illinois (1895-1897), Mexico and Roann, Indiana (1897-1900), and the Philadelphia First Brethren Church (1900-1908). Between 1908 and 1912 he not only traveled as the field secretary for the FMS but he also engaged in much evangelistic work. Bauman suffered two personal losses during the first decade of the twentieth century—his son, Glenn, died of diphtheria in 1907 and his wife succumbed to tuberculosis in 1909 (he remarried in 1912).

In 1912, after a most successful prophetic conference/revival meeting in Long Beach, California, Bauman decided to stay "for a year or two" as the pastor of the newly founded Long Beach congregation. His stay as pastor stretched until 1946 when Charles Mayes succeeded him in this role. Bauman pastored the First Brethren Church in Washington, D.C., from 1948 until his death in 1950. Long Beach became the FMS headquarters under Bauman's influential position as the secretary/treasurer of the organization (he remained in this capacity until his death). Not only was the FMS organ, the *Brethren Missionary*, published here but the Long Beach church also assumed a large portion of the financial support of the Society. In addition, Bauman's church vied with the Philadelphia First Brethren Church for the honor of furnishing the most missionaries.[22] Significantly, Philadelphia and Long Beach become the centers of fundamentalist sentiment in the Brethren Church.

As this review of the church's auxiliaries and institutions indicates, the Brethren Church made significant progress between 1883 and 1915. From a disorganized group of Progressives whose main unity was found in their dissent to the authority of Annual Meeting, the reorganized Brethren Church gained a new sense of mission and showed a ready spirit to face the challenges of the twentieth century.

The Growth and Distribution of the Brethren Church

Though statistical reports are scarce until 1915, irregular records give a general outline of growth patterns in the church. In the chart below an attempt is made to provide statistics at five year intervals. These figures are not entirely accurate for usually they are based only upon churches which reported that year. Nevertheless, it can be seen that steady denominational growth occurred during the period.

Year	Churches	Membership
1889	144	7,513[23]
1895	138	10,031
1900	173	12,727
1905	157	14,117
1909	219	18,607
1915	210	23,044
1920	171	21,848[24]

The statistical reports reveal several additional noteworthy facts. A report of Brethren congregations in 1889 indicates that the Brethren were concentrated in Pennsylvania, Ohio, and Indiana with lesser representation in Maryland, Virginia, West Virginia, Michigan, Illinois, Iowa, the Dakotas, Oregon, California, Colorado, Missouri, Nebraska, and Kansas. An addendum to a report for 1895 manifests one of the pressing problems in the church: the shortage of ministers. 79 pastors were serving 117 congregations; there were 123 places reported where mission work could be undertaken; there were 77 inactive ministers![25] No doubt many congregations languished and died in the late nineteenth and early twentieth centuries because of the lack of active ministers. As confirmation of this, Albert Ronk, who began active ministry in 1907, testified in 1966 that he found many congregations that were unknown to him before he began his research into the *Evangelists* covering the years 1883 to 1900.[26] One would suspect that these harsh facts contributed to the recurring calls for better coordination between pastorless churches and ministers seeking charges.[27]

The Development of Church Practice and Polity

Though the Brethren Church remained firmly committed to the major aspects of traditional Brethren practice, minor charges did occur. With regard to baptism, the Progressives insisted that the questions asked of penitents at the time of baptism (see pp. 100-101) were contrary to apostolic practice (Acts 8:36-38) and that Scripture gave no authority for the laying on of hands while the candidate was in the water.[28] Rather, the practice of the Brethren Church has been to question the penitent person concerning his faith in Christ, commitment to Scripture, and surrender to the Lord's service at the time of public confession (in accordance with the revival practice)

and to separate the laying on of hands from baptism by observing it at the next regular worship service (usually within one week).

In its observance of communion the Brethren Church adopted the single mode of feetwashing, placed the supper on the table prior to feetwashing (the Conservative practice had been to have it off the table at feetwashing), limited the love kiss to the time of feetwashing (see p. 128), extended freedom to local churches to decide what should be served at the common meal, and opened its communion to those groups which practiced trine immersion (some churches were more liberal on this point). In addition, unlike the Conservatives, who insisted that the sisters receive the bread and cup individually from the elder, the Brethren Church allowed sisters to break bread and pass the cup among themselves.[29]

By making the individual conscience and corporate persuasion rather than the decisions of Annual Meeting the arbiter of nonessentials, the Brethren Church also moved away from other traditional practices. Women substituted plain hats for the prayer cap (eventually women came to wear no head covering) and men began to wear modern, yet unpretentious, clothing. Ministers quickly switched to nontraditional hair styles, including the moustache alone (traditionally associated with the military). There also appears to be a relaxing of the prohibition against joining secret societies, though moral persuasion continued to be brought against the practice.[30] The manner of discipline also changed. The ban generally fell into disuse and informal methods—reproving, rebuking, thorough teaching, simple and practical preaching, leading exemplary lives—were recommended to mold members' behavior and thought.[31]

The catalysts for these changes appear to be varied. In some cases the Brethren Church sought an order which was felt to be closer to Scripture (in baptism and communion especially). The single mode of feetwashing was considered the original mode observed by the early Brethren. Adaptation to religious practices in the wider evangelical community also played a part (when confession of faith should occur, a limited form of open communion, changing patterns of dress). In addition, the memories of the sometimes harsh dispensing of discipline among the German Baptists led to a less regulated church body. As a result, practices like the joining of lodges and, later, military service gradually became more common.

Changes relative to the officers of the local congregation are also to be seen. The office of deaconess was reinstituted by the end of the century[32] though she was usually a deacon's wife rather than the "ancient widow" of early Brethren practice. The ordination of deacons (and later deaconesses) was also reestablished (during the first half of the nineteenth century ordination of deacons was gradually replaced by installation with "the hand and kiss," i.e., handshake and holy kiss).[33]

The second degree of the ministry was quickly discontinued in the Brethren Church. Though there was some discussion about a two degree ministry—probationers or licentiates and ordained elders,[34] no such arrangement ever came into practice. Rather, a single degree ministry (ordained elder), with no formal probationary period, remained the standard until 1934 when licensure was adopted by the Ministerial Association. Further standardization of the procedures for calling, licensure, and ordination has occurred in the 1970s and 80s.[35] The paid ministry gradually evolved into a professional ministry and the plurality of elders of German Baptist practice necessarily gave way to the "solitary" elder due to the shortage of pastors. While ministers were still called to their office by their home church, they rarely remained there. During this period changes in pastorates were frequent, occurring in many cases after less than two years in one congregation.[36]

A significant departure from nineteenth century Brethren practice was the encouragement of women to preach and even be ordained.[37] A number of districts in the late 1880s and early 1890s welcomed "sisters to enter the ministerial field when possessing the necessary qualifications."[38] Likewise, the 1892 National Conference extended "to the sisters all privileges which the brethren claim for themselves."[39] This development derived from the conviction in the Brethren Church that women should have "equal rights and privileges with men"[40] and it should be set in the broader context of the women's movement in America.[41] A. L. Garber (1853–1942), a progressive among the Progressives, seems to have been instrumental in overcoming initial resistance to the idea,[42] while Laura E. N. Hedrick (nee Grossnickle, 1858–1934), who was ordained in 1891, lobbied strenuously for women to take an active role in ministry.[43] In addition to Laura Grossnickle, twenty-one other women entered the Brethren ministry in the 1890s and 1900s.

One of the most important issues of the organizational period of 1883–1915 was the question of church government. The 1887 Convention had set forth a limited form of congregationalism as the apostolic ideal (see p. 166). Yet fears of the loss of congregational authority continued to undermine efforts to

define more clearly the nature of this limited congregationalism. In 1892 B. C. Moomaw, an elder from Virginia, presented a detailed proposal for the delimitation of local, district, and national church government entitled, "A Manual of Church Organization and Administration." Action on this paper and on one presented by A. D. Gnagey entitled, "Call, Preparation and Qualification of Ministers," was "postponed indefinitely."[44] In 1895 J. C. Mackey renewed the effort to provide "a better system of government for the Brethren church."[45] His paper on the "Appointment of Pastoral Charges" was instrumental in the appointment of a Commission of Ten (five ministers and five laymen) which was to "make a study of government and discipline, and report a system of expediency for the Brethren church which shall be in agreement with, and subordinate to the Word of God."[46]

During the two year period which the commission took to finalize its study, comments in the *Evangelist* reveal the concerns which were foremost in the minds of the opponents and proponents of greater centralization. G. W. Rench, who was a firm advocate of the simplest form of congregationalism, was quite straightforward.

> I wish it could be understood once, that what is called our "National Conference" is no law-making body. It has no right over any other body other than itself. . . .
> I repeat it, Conference has never been commissioned by the divine word as a body of authority over the congregations.[47]

Other men like B. C. Moomaw desired a well formulated and structured form of polity and saw extreme congregationalism as an overreaction to the past experience of the Progressives.

> . . . the intense feeling against Annual Meetingism naturally impelled the organizers of the Brethren church to rush to the opposite extreme of incoherent congregationalism, the logical result of which is weakness, confusion and final disintegration.[48]

Besides harboring a deep concern about inefficiency, many desired a governmental means to oversee the actions of ministers (there were a number of congregations irreparably damaged by designing or unprincipled ministers during the 1880s and 90s). For example, W. H. Miller, the younger brother of J. Allen Miller, observed:

> As a means to an end I care not what you may call the desired instrument, a confession, rules of faith, church manual or discipline. Some plan along this line seems to me is one thing we need to give us greater unity and vitality as a church. It will devise a way to take care of weak

congregations, and adjust local misunderstandings. It will to a great extent put a stop to the use of the church organ as an advertising medium for "ministerial tramps" who wend their way to us, create lots of trouble and then fly to other folds.[49]

In 1897 the Committee of Ten presented a "Manual of Expediency" which detailed the organization, officers, and duties of the local, district, and national structures.[50] It resembled the paper read to the 1892 Conference by B. C. Moomaw. Yet a mysterious shroud covers the Conference's deliberations. Not only are no minutes for the 1897 Conference printed in the Brethren Annual but there is no article dealing with the Manual in the *Evangelist* until six months later. This article, which is actually a paper read by G. W. Rench at the 1897 Conference, lists three points of opposition to the Manual: (1) it is not necessary for the world's salvation, (2) through it Conference would seek to regulate the affairs of the districts, and (3) it would commit himself and every member of the church "to the defense of some things which I would not want to defend nor wish to see defended." He does suggest, however, that Conference adopt the part which pertained to the regulation of General Conference.[51] Significantly, the 1898 Conference took Rench's latter recommendation and established permanent conference rules. Ronk's conjecture that the Manual was tabled in 1897 and that the discussion may have been rather unpleasant is quite plausible given the counsel of several men prior to the 1898 Conference that rancor, scheming, and hobby riding be given no place.[52]

The passage of conference rules in 1898 quieted the question of polity for several years. Nevertheless, there seems to have been general discontent with the adopted conference rules, for in 1901 a committee of three was appointed "to formulate a body of rules and order of business for General Conference, such rules and order of business to supersede all preceding ones."[53] At the same Conference the Executive Committee assigned C. F. Yoder with the task of preparing a paper on "The Apostolic Church: Its Organization and the Limit of its Authority."[54]

The three-man committee apparently decided to make a thorough, unhurried investigation of its assignment, for it did not bring its report until 1906. Ronk speculates that J. Allen Miller, who probably had as much insight into the Brethren character as any man, may have deliberately delayed the report until he knew the time was opportune. If this was the case, the plan worked, for Conference passed the proposed rules for its own governance in 1906. The

major difference between these rules and those passed in 1898 is the enumeration and description of the Standing and Special Committees of Conference. There is another possible explanation for the delay. Between 1901 and 1906 Yoder was apparently giving detailed thought to Brethren polity as occasional articles in the *Evangelist* during the period suggest. In late 1906 (probably after the 1906 Conference)[55] his eighty-three page treatise on *Gospel Church Government* appeared. Could Miller and his committee have been biding their time in the hopes that Yoder's research would help to shape sentiment for greater organization? Curiously, however, Yoder's work is little known in Brethren circles; Ronk does not even mention it.

During the first decade of the twentieth century intermittent discussions in the *Evangelist* reveal continued dissatisfaction with the ill defined and inefficient organization of the Brotherhood. Thus articles appeared calling for (1) a clarification of the relationship between the local, district, and national organization, (2) a more unified method of fund raising (every agency was doing its own), and (3) greater cooperation among all levels and agencies of government. Frequent appeals in these regards came from J. L. Gillin and J. Allen Miller. A statement by the latter illustrates the frustration with the status quo.

> . . . The difficulties in my opinion, into which we fall can be laid directly to the door of the inefficient organization of our work, both district and general. . . . I believe increasingly in organization, not in multiplying organizations, and creating diverse and often antagonistic interests thereby, but *in organization.* . . .
>
> Organization, such as I here plead for, should mean the unification of our whole church life and work. . . . *Organization would mean the unification, correlation and exploitation of every legitimate interest committed to the church.* Every word in the last sentence is measured. . . . Two facts establish it beyond controversy; namely, the experiences of other bodies who are meeting with success and our own experience of twenty years with but indifferent success and constantly clashing interests.[56]

These and other concerns resulted in minor revisions of the conference rules in 1910 and eventually to the appointment of a Committee of Twenty-five in 1912 "to endeavor to arrange and better organize the work of the church in all departments."[57] Though the committee's report was given in 1914, action was deferred on it until 1915 in order to give the Brotherhood time to consider it carefully. After an unhurried and deliberate presentation of each article at the 1915 Conference, the "Manual of Procedure" was passed with almost a unanimous vote.

The Manual bears strong resemblance to the Manual presented to the 1897 Conference and thus to B. C. Moomaw's 1892 paper. The greatest difference between the 1897 and 1915 Manuals was the detailed definition of the purpose, authority, membership, and organization of General Conference, which details had been, to a large measure, worked out between 1901 and 1910. The "Manual of Procedure" carefully defined the organization, officers, authority, and duties of the local, district, and national structures and left to each of these structures the responsibility for the adoption of the sections appropriate to its own functioning. District conferences and their officials were given preference to General Conference in all areas where oversight of local matters was deemed necessary—examination of candidates for ordination, the providing of counsel for pastors and local churches, the reception of a "certificate of standing" for pastors assuming a charge within the district, and provision for the transferral of church property to a district Board of Trustees in the event a congregation disbanded. The General Conference, like district conferences, was to be a self-organizing and self-perpetuating body. It had the right to control all cooperating organizations of its own creation. But it "had no power to interfere with the work of any local church nor with the work of the several District Conferences."[58]

After thirty-five years the reorganization of polity in the Brethren Church was complete. As testimony to the excellence of the committee's work, this Manual has remained in force to the present with but minor revisions (the most significant changes have been the recent shifting of the some of the district powers to national organizations). It would seem that the *process* which led to the adoption of the Manual was just as important as the final product. An analysis of the process is illuminating for it reveals how various factors can serve either to hinder or enhance the development of a consensus on controversial issues. Probably the greatest hindrance to progress on the subject of church polity was the nagging memories of the authoritarian character of Annual Meeting and its expelling committees. The fear created by these experiences caused many Brethren (notably S. H. Bashor) to guard jealously the rights of the local congregation. In addition, behind the scenes lobbying and scheming seemed to have played a part in the 1897 problems.

The Brethren were forced to relearn by painful experience many of the lessons that the early Brethren had discovered in their own search for unity in faith and practice. It was slowly realized that strictly individual or congregational interpretation of gospel principles led only to disunity and inefficient organization.[59] On the other hand, J. Allen Miller and other advocates of greater organization had learned some valuable wisdom.

> Another essential to a good Conference is the full, open and free discussion of all questions. After a discussion practical agreement ought to be easily attained. My observation has been that a Conference action forced against a large minority or without due consideration is worthless to the church as a whole. A long and quite active participation in the affairs of the Conference has taught the writer that it is better to go as fast as the most of the folks are willing to go. If you cannot succeed with the work as you think do the best that can be done and WAIT. . . . It took us five years to get the report of the Committee of Twenty-five perfected and adopted. But we do now have what we might have had and ought to have had thirty-five years ago. But we had to wait. It goes without controversy that any steps taken for the furtherance of the work of the church must be quite unanimously agreed upon to be of any real value.[60]

The Brethren were rediscovering the wisdom of forbearing one another in love for the sake of unity and that the best possible results are to be gained, not by forcing a solution through, but by waiting for a consensus to develop based on open and free discussion.

The Spirit of the Times: Openness and Distinctiveness

Having been cut off from the German Baptist Brethren and thus the restraints of Annual Meeting, the Progressives experienced a sensation of freedom which they had not known before. The sentiment of many ministers in the Brethren Church was that the German Baptists had been too exclusive and that the Brethren Church should cooperate more fully with kindred organizations. W. J. H. Bauman, in reflecting these convictions, also indicates the extent of cooperation: fidelity to Scripture.

> We may consistently co-operate in all that is good. Follow after and work with men as far as they walk and work in the gospel. In preaching Christ as the only Savior, in opposition to moral or any other evil, we not only *may* but emphatically *should* co-operate. . . .
> The Brethren cannot consistently co-operate with any sect in anything unscriptural . . . We should cry against error wherever found; but give men due credit for all the good they have and do. . . . The Brethren may therefore co-operate in all that elevates for the better, and in all that is worthy of merit at the hands of God. People who are too exclusive and who are ready at wholesale denunciation of those who happen to differ with them, must necessarily be proud, bigoted and ignorant, or terribly dishonest.[61]

This attitude differs from that held by the German Baptist (see p. 163). While the German Baptists were willing to take advantage of modern trends and movements only if they could be incorporated into the structure of the church, the Brethren Church was willing to cooperate with organizations outside the church if they were consistent with the gospel. Notable is the different stand taken toward temperance societies like the Women's Christian Temperance Union. Annual Meeting had advised against joining temperance societies because the church itself was a consistent advocate of temperance. However, members of the Brethren Church, even before the split, took active parts in WCTU functions.[62] Beginning with the 1887 Convention a steady flow of resolutions issued from both district and national conferences condemning the "traffic in intoxicating liquors" and commending the work of the WCTU. Beer also started a "Band of Hope" for the children in the church in 1885. To join one had to promise not to drink any intoxicating liquor, chew or smoke tobacco, or use profane words.[63]

This openness to causes and movements outside the church resulted in a readiness to take an active part in many of the interdenominational movements which characterized the period: Christian Endeavor, YMCA, YWCA, the Student Volunteer Movement, and the Laymen's Missionary Movement. The change of the name of the youth organization in the church from King's Children to Young People's Society of Christian Endeavor and the adoption of a new constitution in 1901 are indicative of the desire for closer cooperation with the interdenominational organization. J. C. Cassel and particularly C. F. Yoder were instrumental in arousing support for the changes.[64] Starting in 1896 Brethren leaders began attending the international Christian Endeavor Conventions and in 1903 the Brethren held their first denominational rally at such a convention in Denver.[65] Undoubtedly, such interdenominational contact was broadening the vision of the Brethren. For example, C. F. Yoder praised the ecumenical impact that Christian Endeavor was having on the American church. He noted that "while editors and others are discussing Christian union the Sunday schools and C. E. societies are practically accomplishing it."[66] Significantly, Yoder himself had become rather prominent in Christian Endeavor circles, for in 1903 he attended the Denver convention "at the special request of several men who have International reputations and stand at the head of the world's C. E. movement."[67]

C. F. Yoder (1873-1955) is of special importance for he reflected the emphases that came to the fore in the Brethren Church during his lifetime. His father, Eli L. Yoder (1842-1913), played an active role in the reorganization process of the Brethren Church. Charles was born near Ashland, Ohio, but raised in Falls City, Nebraska, and Morrill, Kansas (he was acquainted with L. S. Bauman at Morrill). Mirroring the Brethren priority on education, he attended Taylor University (1892-1893), Manchester College (1893-1894), and the University of Chicago (1896-1899). He received his B.A., B.D., and Ph.D. from the latter institution. His Ph.D. was granted in recognition of his research done in writing *God's Means of Grace*. Though he was influenced for a period by liberal higher criticism, his roots were too firm in the Brethren tradition to doubt seriously the inspiration of Scripture.[68]

Yoder pastored the Warsaw (Indiana) Brethren Church from 1894 to 1902. Between 1903 and 1907 Yoder served as the editor of the *Evangelist* and taught hermeneutics and practical theology at Ashland College. The rest of Yoder's life was devoted to missionary work. He pioneered the Brethren missionary effort in Argentina in 1909, and served there until his "retirement" in 1937. When the Argentine mission field came under the control of the Grace Brethren in the 1939 split, Yoder returned to Argentina in 1940 to establish a new work. After his second retirement in 1945, he remained in Argentina, devoting his time to writing.

Nowhere was the spirit of cooperation with these Christian agencies as pronounced as at Ashland College. As one student indicated in 1902, "Ashland College is affiliating herself with every movement that looks toward the deepening of Christian character and activity."[69] Thus a Christian Endeavor Society was begun by 1901, a YMCA chapter was organized in 1901, a YWCA chapter in 1902, and an organization of the Young Women's Christian Temperance Union in 1909. All of these groups were quite active, with both professors and students enrolled.[70] Programming in these organizations included emphases on the study of Scripture, development of Christian character, and opportunities for evangelistic and missionary work. Regular statewide and national conventions opened the way for select individuals to gather with delegates from other colleges.

One of the most enthusiastically received movements of the period, the Student Volunteer Movement, left its impact on the Brethren both at the college and in the church. Begun in 1888 by John R. Mott, the SVM challenged youth at international conventions held every four years with the call to foreign missions. Its famous motto was, "The evangelization of the world in this generation." In 1900 a

Student's Volunteer Band was organized at Ashland College. W. D. Furry, who was the Professor of Philosophy at the time, seems to have played an active role in its inception and programming.[71] The Brethren were well represented at the Quadrennial conventions. Six Brethren attended the 1902 Convention in Toronto, seven were present at the 1906 gathering in Nashville, and ten went to the Rochester Convention in 1910. Besides creating interest in missionary work among leading Brethren, the movement also fostered interdenominational intercourse.

Another mission organization of the period, given impetus by the student movement, was the Laymen's Missionary Movement (LMM). Begun in 1906, the movement sought to arouse interest in foreign missions among laymen and stimulate generous giving to the missions cause. W. D. Furry, during his presidency at Ashland College, was actively involved in planning conferences for the movement as the coordinator for the Northern Ohio LMM. In this capacity he was in touch with Mott and J. Campbell White, the general secretary of the movement. In 1912 and 1915 Ashland College hosted LMM Conferences at which White spoke.[72]

The above evidence should not be construed to mean that the Brethren were ready to forsake their traditional distinctives. It needs to be remembered that C. F. Yoder, one of the most cosmopolitan of the Brethren, was the author of *God's Means of Grace*, a defense of traditional Brethren ordinances and beliefs. However, it is also true that there is noticeable concern expressed in the *Evangelist* in the late 1890s about an indifference to the Brethren distinctives. Likewise, the developing sentiment for a better organized polity structure derives in part from a perceived lack of supervision over local matters (see p. 171). It is thus possible to view the years of 1883 to about 1900 as a period of "transparency" to the external religious environment with the final years of the century ushering in a new concern to "tighten the borders."

Reflective of the growing sentiments to preserve the Brethren identity was a conscious shift (beginning about 1895) in the apologetic used for upholding the distinctive doctrines of the church. Desiring to develop an apologetic that was amenable to the new ecumenical atmosphere, the church no longer argued that it was the true church because it possessed direct historical links to the apostolic church and practiced the ordinances in their original purity.[73] Rather, the Brethren turned to a variation of the more recent argument (p. 160) that the church of Christ was to be found wherever the doctrines and

teachings of Christ were faithfully observed.[74] This concept formed the foundation for the "Gospel alone" plea of the Progressives in their controversy with the Conservatives and, in a modified way, the "whole Gospel" slogan which the Brethren fully exploited particularly between the later 1890s and 1930s to highlight their distinctiveness from other Christian bodies. Though recognizing the work that other denominations and organizations were doing in the cause of Christ, the Brethren began once again to maintain their uniqueness. Statements by A. D. Gnagey, the editor of the *Evangelist* (1894-1902, 1908-1915), exemplify the new apologetic.

> There are certain doctrines and practices which make the Brethren Church a *distinctive* organization—a *peculiar* organization, we might almost say *unique*, there being none other like it. These doctrines and practices we hold as ordained of God and commanded by Christ, and therefore essential to the highest spiritual welfare of mankind [the Brethren of this era were very careful not to say that the distinctives were essential to salvation[75]]. Can we enjoy the fruits of these doctrines in any other outside of our communion? If not, then the reason for our existence becomes apparent. If we hold these doctrines as fundamental, then it becomes us to form an organization in which we may practice them and enjoy the fruits which come from a perfect obedience to the whole law of the Gospel.[76]

A central place continued to be accorded the ordinances in the discussion of doctrine. In a day when ecumenical and liberal influences were resulting in an attitude of indifference toward the sacraments, the Brethren felt that they had to defend their ordinances more forcefully. Thus, Gnagey, noticing the adverse effect that ecumenical efforts were having on sound doctrine, publicized the "doctrinal session" at the 1898 Conference during which "the spiritual significance of the ordinances" was to be discussed.[77]

Gnagey's comment is significant for another reason as well. By the turn of the century, those men who had received college and university training, notably Gillin and Yoder, were advocating that a new justification for the observance of the ordinances be adopted. The best known statement of the "new philosophy" of the ordinances was found in the preface of Yoder's *God's Means of Grace*.[78]

> The symbols or ordinances are helps to character and means of teaching, and because they are truly "God's means of grace" they have an intrinsic value which makes them worth contending for. The old apologetic made much of technical arguments and formal obedience. Such arguments now fail to appeal to thinking people so much as arguments based on utility [!]. And, although the point has been much ignored in the past, here is the greatest reason for faithfulness to God's institutions. They are given for

man's good by Him who best of all knew man's needs and how to supply them.[79]

The new apologetic for the observance of the ordinances, as formulated by Gillin and Yoder, therefore placed the major emphasis on the purpose which they served. In one article Gillin held that the ordinances acted as "parables intended to teach great fundamental principles of the Christian life"[80] while in another he stated:

This purpose [which the ordinances serve] was and is, that through them we may learn more of God's will and more of how to minister to the needs of men. The burden of God's efforts with humanity has been to bring it to a higher, a more *god like* life.... Hence it is reasonable to conclude that the things he commanded were not the result of tyrannical caprice, but of beneficent love.[81]

Not only did this philosophy serve to contemporize the Brethren apologetic for the observance of the ordinances but it also began to have a subtle influence on the traditional nineteenth century view of the rites. Though it is true that the emphasis continues to be placed on the beneficial results of observing the ordinances, the increased attention to the inner meaning and intent of the ordinances served to soften the strong objective bias that permeated the older view of the ordinances. Gillin indicates that the new view was gaining support among the church leaders (most of whom had college training).[82] Nevertheless, there were many others who retained the traditional Brethren apologetic (symbolized by a strong appeal to "baptism for the remission of sins") up through the 1930s. These defenders of "Brethrenism" were to add to the tensions of that decade.

Doctrinal Development and Interaction

Those doctrines which traditionally had been the focus of Brethren attention—the *ordo salutis* of repentance, faith, baptism, remission of sins, the gift of the Holy Spirit and the ordinances of trine immersion, threefold communion, and anointing—remained quite stable throughout this period (though the justification for the observance of the ordinances did change). Nevertheless, subtle changes and sometimes unsettling conflicts arising from interaction with other movements during the period are to be noticed. It should not be overlooked that most of this interaction occurred between 1883 and 1900, the period when the church in both attitude and polity was most susceptible to outside influence.

Revivalism had a continuing influence on the Brethren. Notice has already been made of the impact revivalism had on Brethren piety (see pp. 158-159) and at least one aspect of Brethren practice—confession of faith (see p. 169). One other significant practical effect of revivalism was the lowering of the age of baptism. Holsinger intimates that after 1855 "child membership" (he cites examples of youth aged nine to sixteen being baptized) became more common.[83] Significantly, H. L. Goughnour, one of the young ministers in the Brethren Church (b. 1893), advocated child conversion because of the basic Christian qualities children bear.[84] Child conversion could become a common practice in the church only when special prominence was placed on profession of faith in Christ while the meaning of baptism as total commitment and surrender to Christ in discipleship was lessened (the reason why the Brethren normally discouraged the baptism of youth was that they desired them to "count the cost" of the step). That this is in fact what was happening is borne out by the influence that another movement was having on the Brethren Church—Keswick teaching.[85]

Keswick concepts appear in the *Evangelist* by 1895 with the use of pithy fillers by F. B. Meyer. In 1895 Editor Gnagey also discoursed on a topic that has strong Keswick overtones: "The two words most suggestive of victory in the Kingdom of God, are: *Consecration* and *concentration*."[86] Similar sentiments from a number of other writers during the late 1890s suggest a developing acquaintanceship with Keswick ideas.

Two men in particular popularized Keswick teaching in the church: J. C. Cassel and C. F. Yoder. Cassel began to advocate greater personal spirituality in 1895 and continued his crusade until 1899. He maintained that Scripture spoke of two separate baptisms—water baptism at justification and the baptism of the Holy Spirit at sanctification. He also distinguished "the baptism of the Holy Ghost" from the indwelling of the Spirit and from spiritual birth. For Cassel this "definite second blessing, or experience" was not essential to salvation, but it was "absolutely necessary to accomplish a mighty work for God."[87] Included in this "mighty work" were both prophecy and the healing of diseases.[88] The baptism of the Holy Spirit involved the awareness of one's carnal life and the active seeking of victory. Cassel held that there were several important steps to the "obtainment" of Holy Ghost baptism: "First, we must be convinced that it is a definite blessing apart from justification. Next, we determine we want it, next, ask for it, and accept it, and behold it is ours, if our consecration has been true and complete . . ."[89] In 1898 Cassel intimated that the sources of his concern for greater spirituality were the Christian and Missionary Alliance and C. I. Scofield.[90]

As one might expect, Cassel's articles called forth a flurry of response. J. B. Wampler in particular championed what was the general Brethren viewpoint.[91] He took strong exception to Cassel's claim that the baptism of the Holy Spirit was for the present age (no doubt Wampler and others saw overtones of the holiness movement in Cassel's position). He maintained that Holy Ghost baptism, i.e., the Pentecostal outpouring of the Holy Spirit, was limited to the apostolic period and had nothing to do with the effects that Cassel claimed for the experience. This baptism served to inspire and qualify the apostles for their mission and for the transmission of the written Word to the church.[92] J. Allen Miller developed the same idea a bit further.

> I believe the baptism of the Holy Spirit took place on the day of Pentecost. I believe that was the *only* baptism of the Spirit. He is now as he has been since then in the Church. He fills men's hearts even now and fills them often. You may call that a baptism of the Spirit. To me it is only the inevitable result of the Indwelling Spirit being given full control of the man. The Holy Spirit dwells in the whole body of Christ. So he also dwells in each individual believer.[93]

About a decade later Yoder, during his term as editor of the *Evangelist*, occasionally discussed the topic of sanctification and always gave it a Keswick twist. But his discussion of the subject brought forth no response primarily because he used terms for the experience which were acceptable to the Brethren: entire consecration, total surrender. He felt that "the testimonies of such men as B. F. [sic] Meyer, Dr. Chapman, A. J. Gordon, Francis Ridley Havergal, Andrew Murray and others" were not to be taken lightly.[94] He held that the goal of sanctification was complete surrender which could be either instantaneous or a process. Complete surrender does not mean that sin is eradicated, only that one is now able to gain victory over sin through the Spirit's enabling power.[95] Those who have attained this experience testify that there are "several stages of growth": the new birth, assurance, surrendered will, abiding, Spirit filled, victory over sin, the life of surrender involves fellowship with God.[96]

Though Yoder may have become acquainted with Keswick teaching through Christian Endeavor activities, a more probable source is his regular attendance at the Winona Bible Conferences.[97] Begun in 1895 at Winona Lake, Indiana, as a "religious chautauqua,"

the Conference annually attracted speakers with "mild-Calvinist," Fundamentalist backgrounds: representatives from the Bible institutes and key figures in premillennial/dispensational circles. Among these speakers were several with Keswick sympathies, notably J. Wilbur Chapman, the most prominent figure in the early Conferences, and R. A. Torrey. G. Campbell Morgan was frequently present in the teens and 20s. Yoder had a very high regard for the Conferences and encouraged Brethren pastors and lay people to attend.[98] These Conferences no doubt had some influence upon Brethren thought, for Brethren National Conference was held at Winona Lake usually immediately following the interdenominational Bible Conference every year between 1896 and 1939 with but five exceptions.

The Keswick view of sanctification espoused by Cassel, Yoder, and Bowman remained a minority view in the church into the 1930s.[99] The majority of members retained traditional Brethren conceptions and terminology. Thus, the experience of sanctification was held to begin with the indwelling of the Holy Spirit at conversion when one receives the spiritual power necessary to do God's will. It deepens through continued surrender and obedience to God's will. Nevertheless, that many Brethren leaders were concerned about a noticeable lack of spirituality in the Brotherhood is a definite part of the record as well.[100] The priority given to simple profession of faith in Jesus Christ at conversion,[101] (a by-product of revivalism) had created a situation which was conducive to the development of a nominal church membership. This development was paralleled by a diminishing concern about two concepts which were quite prominent in the German Baptist baptismal vows—the unconditional surrender of one's life to Christ and the acceptance of the responsibility to give and receive admonition. Had these traditional emphases not been weakened, the perceived spiritual laxity and the impact of the Keswick concept of a complete surrender subsequent to conversion might not have been as pronounced.

Espousal of Keswick teaching is symptomatic of one other change that had occurred in the Brethren view of the Christian life. Whereas traditional Brethren thought had given a large place to the concepts of negation—self-denial and separation from the world and its values—and of trials as necessary and on-going aspects of the growth process, the religious atmosphere which fostered Keswick thought placed far more emphasis on the positive experience of victory in overcoming sin. Several subtle differences exist between the two approaches. (1) The Brethren-Pietistic view was based on the conviction that there is a basic dichotomy between the worldly and spiritual realms. In Keswick and (Baptistic) revival thought (both of which possessed a definite Reformed slant) this sharp distinction is considerably levelled. The hostile world of the Anabaptist-Pietist perspective is giving way to a more affirmative world view in the Brethren Church. (2) Although the early Brethren and Pietists accepted spiritual trials willingly as a requisite part of the "baptism of fire" all Christians must pass through, Keswick and revival thought (and that in the Brethren Church) gave far less attention to this side of Christian experience. (By focusing on "mountain-top experiences" these two movements tend to imply that the "valleys" of inner spiritual struggles are not a normal or necessary part of the Christian life.) In reality, both of these differences can be associated with the radical transformation that occurred when the Progressives left a body which could still be viewed as an exclusivistic sect and formed a denomination which sought respectability in the midst of other American church bodies.

Though the Brethren showed a willingness to bear with a Keswick understanding of sanctification which allowed for the traditional Brethren position, they firmly opposed holiness teaching. Nevertheless, the denomination was not impervious to the influence of the holiness movement (especially because of their loose polity). Thus Holsinger in 1894 notes that most of the Brethren located in Los Angeles were "carried away with the holiness delusion" while G. W. Rench mentioned that two ministers (Bicknell and McGreggor), who had given undue emphasis to the Holy Ghost, had left the church, apparently after creating some disturbance.[102]

A movement which had stirred forceful reaction from the German Baptists prior to the division—Seventh-Day Adventism—continued to unsettle the Brethren Church in the years following 1883. The influence of Seventh-Day Adventism can be seen in occasional discussions of the immortality of the soul, soul-sleeping, and Sabbatarianism. The *Evangelist* carried two lengthy discussions of the immortality of the soul in the 1880s. In 1885 a debate was touched off by an anonymous writer "A." He contended:

> The fact is, there is nothing immortal about the soul. It is perishable to the same extent that any other fabric or earthly object is, under the command of divine Omnipotence. He is able to destroy both soul and body in Gehenna, and under the exercise of that power, the destruction of the one would be just as complete as the other.[103]

In one of the more consistent and logical presentations in the debate, Edward Mason offered what was probably the majority opinion. After citing Matthew 10:28; 25:19–31; and Luke 16:19–31, Mason remarked:

> We are to fear him who is able to destroy, not kill, both soul and body in Gehenna. The meaning of destroy is not necessarily to put an end to existence. . . .
> . . . The future punishment and happiness of the soul after death, are taught everywhere. If a soul lives in distress and punishment in eternity and continues to live, that implies immortality.[104]

This phase of the discussion was closed in September 1885 by the editor (E. L. Yoder).

The second debate was sparked in 1889 when J. H. Swihart published a tract[105] in which he argued against the idea of an immortal soul, holding that Scripture taught soul sleep for the righteous and the annihilation of the souls for sinners at their respective deaths. The publication of his work resulted in a flurry of response in the *Evangelist*. The debate was sharpened when the editor, A. L. Garber, sent out to Brethren pastors a questionnaire which was obviously slanted against belief in the immortality of the soul (Garber shared Swihart's view). Though the bias of the questionnaire makes generalizations difficult, it does appear that Swihart's position continued to have some support, at least as a private opinion. Even those holding the opposite view generally agreed that there should be forbearance on the issue.[106] It is noteworthy that Editor Gnagey one decade later could challenge the Adventist teaching against the immortality of the soul without receiving any adverse response to his position.[107]

Sabbatarianism became a special issue in California where a Brethren elder, Zed H. Copp, was advocating that Saturday was the Christian Sabbath. Copp, who had been hired in 1893 as the district evangelist, continued teaching his views in spite of warnings from several California elders. Ronk, a native of Northern California, reports that Copp's persistence eventually ruined the Vernalis, California congregation.[108]

In 1894 the California Conference disfellowshipped Copp, but officially reported only that "under existing circumstances we can not hold Bro. Z. H. Copp as a minister in the Brethren Church."[109] The next year Copp's brother, George A. Copp, a Brethren elder in Virginia, sought to clarify the ambiguous California statement. He observed that "'under existing circumstances' is to be construed only to mean that he holds Saturday as the Christian Sabbath."[110] The limited congregational polity of the Brethren Church permitted Zed Copp to find pastorates in Hagerstown,

Maryland and Ashland and Dayton, Ohio, between 1896 and 1900. The first two of these pastorates were cut short by internal difficulties, the nature of which is not explicitly revealed. However, the Dayton troubles were created by his "arbitrary rulings" in "suspending members from fellowship without trial or hearing."[111] As a result Copp was disfellowshipped by the Ohio District in 1900. Though his case was discussed before the 1900 National Conference, Copp's pastoral career was now ended. He turned to Washington, D.C., where his work as a probation officer won the praise of President Theodore Roosevelt.[112]

Even after the Copp case was ended, the Sabbath question continued to create occasional disturbances. The zealous proselyting activity of the Adventists in Brethren communities in both America and Argentina evoked apologetic responses against Sabbatarianism as late as the 1930s.

Two movements that had their genesis in the late nineteenth century had a special impact upon certain segments of the Brethren: Dowieism and the Christian and Missionary Alliance. Brethren interest in the healing ministry of John Alexander Dowie began in 1894.[113] S. J. Harrison, the editor of the *Evangelist* at the time (1892–1894), had gone to Chicago to seek medical treatment for his young son's abdominal tumor. While waiting in Chicago in April, 1894, Harrison attended and was favorably impressed by the services at Dowie's International Divine Healing Association. By mid-month he reported that he was staying in the Dowie home. Though his son died around May first, Harrison placed no blame on Dowie. Instead, he continued to praise the work done by Dowie through the editorial columns of the *Evangelist*.[114]

Harrison's plaudits caused others to investigate for themselves. A steady stream of first hand accounts appeared in the *Evangelist*. The reports by several were quite favorable—Z. T. Livengood, S. M. Minnich, J. O. Talley. The only critical article was written by Dr. A. Pearson. The church had become so caught up in the discussion about Dowie that it was decided to set aside one entire issue of the *Evangelist* for the airing of the various opinions.[115] After this issue, all discussion was ended. As a result of the entire affair, Harrison was replaced as editor by A. D. Gnagey. Harrison then returned to Chicago and began publishing Dowie's weekly paper, *Leaves of Healing*. This arrangement lasted until the end of the year when Harrison severed his ties with Dowie purportedly because of disagreements over business

principles.[116] He eventually helped to organize the Brethren congregation in Sunnyside, Washington.

Other Brethren ministers and leaders stayed with Dowie much longer—J. R. Keller, W. H. Piper, and Dr. Speicher.[117] Keller eventually returned to the Brethren in 1906 only after the self-proclaimed "Elijah" and "First Apostle" had left his utopian Zion in financial shambles through misappropriation of funds.

There is one other fascinating piece to this rather unfortunate saga. During Harrison's stay with Dowie in 1894, he convinced Dowie that trine immersion was the correct and apostolic mode of baptism. Dowie asked Harrison to baptize him by this mode and declared that he would observe no other form of baptism. Reportedly, Dowie practiced only trine immersion after this.[118]

The movement which probably had more impact than any other in shaping the future course of the Brethren Church and especially its fundamentalist wing during the twentieth century was the Christian and Missionary Alliance. The Alliance was organized in 1881 by A. B. Simpson, a former Presbyterian. Simpson's ministry was built around his "four-fold gospel": Christ our Savior, Christ our Sanctifier, Christ our Healer, and Christ our Coming Lord.[119] The first Brethren notice of the movement in the *Evangelist* was in 1894 when S. B. Furry was invited to a Christian and Missionary Alliance convention in Altoona, Pennsylvania. He reported that missions and healing were principal features of their teaching.[120]

Alliance influence was mediated to the Brethren Church through the considerable impact that the movement had on the Philadelphia church and especially J. C. Cassel. Cassel's first mention of the movement was in 1895. He had visited New York City and there toured several of the rescue missions in the company of Dr. Samuel E. Furry, a former German Baptist who was currently associated with Simpson's Christian and Missionary Alliance (one would guess he was related to S. B. Furry). It is most significant that in 1895 Cassel introduced distinctively Keswick teachings to the church and the following year he began his great push for missions![121] In addition, Cassel remained a staunch supporter of the concept of "divine healing" even after Dowie had brought disgrace upon his own movement[122] and was among the first (along with I. D. Bowman, the pastor of the Philadelphia church) to advocate a dispensational view of premillennialism in the church.[123]

Associations between the Philadelphia church and the Alliance movement were apparently quite cordial. In 1898 Cassel reported that an Alliance pastor had spoken at the Philadelphia church and L. S. Bauman disclosed that he had gained a concern for missions and been won to the "blessed hope" of premillennialism when Cassel convinced him to attend an Alliance convention near Lancaster, Pennsylvania.[124] Cassel further stated:

> I am however happy to know that the Alliance does in the main teach what I believe to be true on these points [premillennialism] [so I] consequently feel drawn towards that people. On other important points they lack rich truth that are [sic] prominent among us as a church. We want to hold all the good we have, and learn as much more as we can from others.[125]

Response from other quarters of the church was highly critical of the Alliance, however. Reports of mismanagement of funds and of insufficient training and support for Alliance missionaries elicited warnings about the movement from several ministers.[126] It is also noteworthy that, during the liberal controversy of the 1910s, the liberals occasionally sought to discredit the dogmatic premillennial position of Bauman and Cassel by noting its source in "Christian Allianceism."[127] Nevertheless, these verbal assaults did not curb the subtle yet consequential influence which the Alliance had had and would continue to have (via the Philadelphia church) on the Brethren.

Concluding Observations

During the three decades which followed the organization of the Brethren Church in 1883, the denomination made remarkable progress. From scattered clusters of Progressives struggling to rebuild their church psychologically, spiritually, and physically, the Brethren Church had progressed to a self-respecting denomination. It had quadrupled in size and boasted successful home and foreign mission programs, active auxiliaries, financially stable institutions, and a polity structure consistent with its ideal of limited congregational government. Yet the road to these ends had not been easy. Between 1883 and about 1900 the fears instilled by painful memories of the past blinded many to the dangers of an extreme congregationalism. During the same period an attitude of openness to the beliefs and practices of other movements began to be modified by a more discerning perspective only after irreparable damage had been done to the lives of several congregations. By the turn of the century polity structures[128] and a new spirit of mutual concern and brotherhood were forming which were conducive to more stable growth both physically and spiritually. It is unfortunate, however, that this growth was stymied by severe dissension in the 1910s and again in the 1930s. In both cases the roots of the problem can be traced to emphases acquired during the period of almost unrestrained openness (1883–1900).

Chapter 13

THE LIBERAL CONTROVERSY (1913-1921)

Introduction

The conflict which shook the Brethren Church during the teens was actually a microcosm of a phenomenon that was disturbing the entire American church scene—the liberal-fundamentalist controversy. Though the interaction among the various parties in the dispute and the resolution of the conflict were primarily a product of the Brethren milieu, the forces which created the divergent perspectives were essentially external to the church's environment. In this chapter attention will be focused on the roots of the liberal-fundamentalist controversy in the American culture, the principal figures and issues in the Brethren rendition of the conflict, and how the dispute was resolved.

The Background to the Liberal-Fundamentalist Controversy

American liberalism between 1860 and 1930 was given its essential character by several philosophical presuppositions. First, liberalism was humanistic; it viewed man as a being possessing infinite value and dignity and, as a consequence, inherent rights and needs. Likewise, human reason and experience were recognized as autonomous authorities. Second, liberalism was naturalistic; it tended to conceive of God working through natural means rather than supernatural. Third, it was positivistic; it placed high regard in the inductive, scientific method. Fourth, liberalism was optimistic; it believed the unbridled use of man's moral and rational powers could create a new world order. It was these basic philosophical foundations which, when applied to the pressing scientific and religious issues of the day, resulted in the hallmarks of classical liberalism: theistic evolution, comparative religion, higher criticism. Likewise, the social gospel, though early claiming some more

conservative proponents, was essentially based upon the above presuppositions.

Two different strains of American liberalism can be identified. Evangelical liberalism was denoted by a desire to maintain fidelity to the historic doctrinal and ecclesiastical traditions of Christianity except insofar as modern circumstances required adjustment or change. Such liberals were thoroughly Christo-centric, viewing Christ as God's supreme revelation of moral and religious truth. This revelation was regarded, however, as standing in direct continuity with human reason and experience. The Bible then was not to be appealed to arbitrarily as a source of authoritative doctrine, but, as a witness to the act of God in Christ, its religious truth validated itself "in experience by virtue of its own inherent reasonableness and practical value."[1] Major theologians who fall into this category are William Newton Clarke, William Adams Brown, Harry Emerson Fosdick, and Walter Rauschenbusch.

Modernistic liberalism was more concerned about maintaining a twentieth-century outlook than continuing in the heritage of the historic faith. The representatives of this perspective took the "scientific method, scholarly discipline, empirical fact, and prevailing forms of contemporary philosophy as their point of departure." They therefore "approached religion as a human phenomenon, the Bible as one great religious document among others, and the Christian faith as one major religio-ethical tradition among other."[2] Such a modernistic viewpoint flourished at the University of Chicago among men like Shailer Mathews, Shirley Jackson Case, E. S. Ames, and Henry Nelson Wieman.

FUNDAMENTALISM

Fundamentalism resulted from the convergence of several nineteenth century movements. One facet of the picture is formed by the Bible and Prophecy Conference movement. Emerging from the Niagara Conferences begun in 1868, the International Prophetic Conferences of 1878 and 1886 brought together a number of men who not only were millenarians but also formed the early leadership of Fundamentalism: James H. Brookes, William G. Moorehead, Adoniram Judson Gordon, A. T. Pierson, Nathaniel West, and W. J. Erdman. The great concern of the conference was the reaffirmation of what was considered a neglected doctrine of God's Word: "the precious doctrine of Christ's second personal appearing."[3] Though interdenominational in character, the conferences had a heavy Presbyterian representation within which were several men closely linked to Presbyterian seminaries.[4]

A second facet of Fundamentalism revolved around the person and work of Dwight L. Moody (1837–1899). Moody, the outstanding urban revivalist of the last quarter of the nineteenth century, made three special contributions to the Fundamentalist movement. First, his Northfield conferences (begun in 1880) became an important means of disseminating both premillennial and Keswick teaching (Moody had become a millenarian by 1877). Second, the Student Volunteer Movement, which evolved from a Bible study conference at Northfield in 1886, had premillennial overtones, though it was never dominated or controlled by millenarians (the founder, John R. Mott, was a non-millenarian). Third, Moody played an important part in shaping the character of the millenarian movement through the founding of Bible institutes, notably the academies at Northfield and Moody Bible Institute.[5] R. A. Torrey, who headed Moody Bible Institute from 1889 to 1912, became dean of the Bible Institute of Los Angeles (founded in 1907) in 1912.

In the publishing of *The Fundamentals* (1910–1915) the various facets of the picture come together. The twelve volume statement of conservative theology was financed by two wealthy Los Angeles laymen, Lyman and Milton Stewart. A total of three million booklets were mailed to ministers, professors, theological students, and lay leaders. The sixty-four writers represent a practical alliance between two otherwise distinct groups: the Bible institute, premillennial/dispensational group and a denominational (Presbyterian and Baptist), seminary-oriented group[6] (the English Keswick Convention was also well represented). What linked the writers together was a common belief in an inerrant Scripture and a mutual concern about the advances of liberalism and the social gospel. Though the 1920s would usher in a

period of "clangor and strife" that "turned Fundamentalism into a term of reproach,"[7] the movement had demonstrated in *The Fundamentals* that it could state its case in a dignified, rhetorically moderate style, and with considerable intellectual power.

By 1910 a noticeable change had occurred in the ranks of premillennialists. Almost the entire leadership of the Bible and Prophecy movement had died by 1915 and a new breed of men, typified by Cyrus I. Scofield and Arno C. Gaebelein, came to the forefront. This fact, combined with an earlier occurrence, had momentous importance for premillennialism. During the 1890s much of the old leadership (Erdman, West, Moorehead, Gordon), following the lead of Robert Cameron, had come to reject the Darbyite teaching of the any-moment rapture. However, Cameron's criticism of the concept caused others, particularly Gaebelein, to propagate the concept and its corollary, the pre-tribulation rapture, all the more. For the older leaders "our blessed hope" had referred to premillennialism in general. With their passing, and the increasing influence of Gaebelein between 1900 and 1920, "our blessed hope" gradually became associated with the pre-tribulation view. This position was given added strength and coherency with the completion of the *Scofield Reference Bible* in 1909.[8] Scofield, who received the full backing of Gaebelein for the project, incorporated into the reference material the theology of Darbyite dispensationalism which included the pre-tribulation rapture and the concept of the postponement of the kingdom.[9] The 1914 Bible and Prophecy Conference at Moody Bible Institute is quite significant because of the decisive dominance of the dispensational camp. Noteworthy as the leadership of the conference were four dispensationalists: James M. Gray, William Bell Riley, Scofield, and Gaebelein.[10]

Though all the phenomena discussed to this point may be seen as aspects of a Fundamentalist movement, Fundamentalism did not become a self-conscious network until 1919 and 1920.[11] Symbolic of this transition is the 1919 World's Conference of Christian Fundamentals held at Philadelphia. Prominent in this conference were the dispensationalists and leaders of the Bible institutes. Though the conference shared with the *Fundamentals* a concern for the fundamental doctrines of the faith, its special identity was gained by its aggressive opposition to liberalism and modernism. The militancy of this Fundamentalism not only distinguishes it from the earlier manifestation of the movement but it also caused the gradual disassociation from the militants of both the more moderate Fundamentalists, particularly the seminary-oriented Presbyterians and Baptists, and English Keswick figures.[12]

The Principal Brethren Figures

In order to understand how both liberalism and fundamentalism made their way into the Brethren Church, a consideration of a number of key personalities and the factors which molded their thinking is necessary. Basically, the central figures in the liberal controversy of the teens can be divided into three groups: liberals, men who had been trained in liberal circles but later rejected or modified their liberal perspective, and fundamentalists.

The primary proponents of liberalism in the Brethren Church were John L. Gillin,[13] Herbert L. Goughnour, and Charles E. Weidner. Goughnour was born at Johnstown, Pennsylvania, in 1893. He attended Ashland College from 1901 until 1905, and received his B.A. degree from Temple University in 1910 and his M.A. from Columbia in 1916. He held pastorates at Philadelphia (1908-1910), Meyersdale, Pennsylvania (1910-1916, 1921-1926), and Waterloo, Iowa (1917-1920). Goughnour left the denomination apparently in 1926, for this is the last year that he is listed on the ministerial roll.

Charles E. Weidner was born in 1879 at Topeka, Kansas. He attended Ashland College between 1899 (he began in the preparatory course in the academy at the college) and 1905. He pastored Brethren churches at Nappanee, Indiana (1906-1908), Carleton, Nebraska (1908-1914), Johnstown, Pennsylvania (1914-1916), and Hudson, Iowa (1916-1919). He is last listed on the ministerial roll in 1918.

The initial contact that both of these men had with liberal ideas was apparently at Ashland College. By the turn of the century evolutionary concepts had won the support of academicians in many American colleges and universities. Ashland College was no different. The science professor at the college from 1899 until 1904 was C. Orville Witter, the brother of a Brethren minister, M. A. Witter. Witter was a firm advocate of theistic evolution. He presented his beliefs in an article which was part of a symposium for the first issue of the *Evangelist* in the twentieth century. Editor Gnagey had invited men and women representing different segments of the church's life to share their outlook for the new century. Witter wrote:

> Men are coming to see that the Bible can not from the nature of things be an authority on questions of science and at the same time they see that in order to make a law that

would evolve a human being from a protoplasmic cell [note he is working from this assumption], there must be a Being whose omnipotence and omni-science can not be questioned. The scientist and theologian of this century will clasp hands and confess that the mind which formulated the book of nature and inspired the Word of God was one mind.[14]

Evolution perfectly fit the intellectual temper of the times; its premise of an orderly and progressive universe applied equally well to science, economics, sociology, and religion. Writing for the *Evangelist* at the end of the decade, Witter refers to evolution as a "doctrine." For him, God was the "one who in the beginning created that first living cell of protoplasm with powers within it whereby it should grow and develop through unnumbered ages until it should reach its present dignity and power as a cell in the brain of a man." [15]

A modified form of evolution was also apparently accepted in the religion department of the college. Goughnour shares his initial and later convictions about the teaching:

> Evolution as the process of God's operation in nature is so firmly established that Christians simply must take account of it. The writer clearly remembers how he rebelled against the idea when he first met it. Dr. J. A. Miller, patient and kind as he is, had to send him out of class room one day because of his pugnacious, Pennsylvania dutch hyperorthodoxy. Today I could not surrender my belief in evolution as a process used by God if I should try.[16]

By the turn of the century, theological liberalism was being taught at Ashland College by W. D. Furry (see below) and possibly C. F. Yoder (by 1902). It was J. L. Gillin in particular, however, who introduced more critical forms of liberalism by 1906. Albert Ronk autobiographically underscores the difference in the approaches of J. Allen Miller and Gillin:

> The first year at Ashland [1906-1907] developed nothing that disturbed my conservative theology of Brethrenism. The Bible teaching under Dean Miller was true to the historic form. . . .
> However, during my second year a new teacher [Gillin] with liberal theological leanings taught in the seminary department. We were gradually introduced to higher criticism, especially of the destructive sort. . . . Books were suggested that rationalized much of Scripture.[17]

Gillin's acceptance of a position at Iowa State University around 1908 removed a major source of theological liberalism from direct contact with the college and church.

There were other men who had been trained in liberal circles but completely rejected or modified their earlier liberal views. Significant in this regard were W. D. Furry and George Ronk. Furry (1874–1959) was born in Maryland. He completed bachelor and master degrees at Notre Dame University and in 1902 was taking advanced work at the University of Chicago. He received his doctorate from Johns Hopkins University in 1907. He served the South Bend Brethren Church (1895–1900) and the Philadelphia First Brethren Church (1910–1911). His long-time association with Ashland College included service as professor of Philosophy (1900–1904, 1943–1957) and president (1911–1919). During the 1920s and 30s he served as professor of Philosophy and Psychology and eventually president of Shorter College.

Liberal sentiments are quite noticeable in Furry's thought during the first decade of the twentieth century. In 1901 he advanced the belief that both Testaments contain an evolutionary world view. The ultimate goal is attaining the fullness of the stature of Jesus. "It must thus be seen that Jesus Christ is the typical man and that the end of creation is the making of a world of men like him."[18] For Furry, the validity of Scripture was not to be found in any claim of inerrancy but in the fact that the experiences recorded therein are reduplicated in our own lives.

> We have not placed sufficient stress upon the element of human experience in the interpretation of the bible.... Since it is human to err we need not be surprised if we should find some errors in the bible.[19]

> It [the Bible] proves itself our book not because of any pretentious name or claim but because in the experiences of the men that wrote the book we find our own life—our own longings and desires expressed and satisfied. Eliminate the element of experience from the Bible and it will at once lose it's [sic] hold upon men.[20]

Furry further mirrors liberal ideas in his conception of Jesus and the nature of His relationship with God.

> The unique distinction of Jesus is his consciousness of one-ness with God.... The God-consciousness of Jesus remains the most indubitable argument of his divinity.... But Jesus always expressed his one-ness with God in terms purely ethical. Never has the Immanence of God been more vividly experienced and more emphatically expressed than in the person of Jesus.[21]

During the second decade of the twentieth century, Furry's thought takes a more conservative bent. He is still remarkably in touch with the critical scholarship of his day, but he stresses more forcefully the historic emphases of the faith. Thus in 1911 (the year he became president of the college) he calls upon the church to "lay hold of the eternal deity of Jesus." He appeals for "whole-hearted and whole-minded devotion to the Word of God" and observes that "theology

has today gone wrong because it no longer finds its basis and authority in the Word of God."[22] In stark contrast to his earlier position is a statement appearing in 1911.

> The antinomy that has today been established between doctrine and experience is without foundation and can be met only by a return to the historical Christ. *Religious experience however* profound can never supply the content of belief.[23]

The concern for balance manifested in this quote (between history [or doctrine] on the one hand and experience on the other) also led Furry to warn against overemphasis on the social aspect of the Gospel in the teens. Furry unfortunately gives us no clues to the catalyst for his modified perspective though strong Brethren ties and his associations with the Student Volunteer Movement and the Laymen's Missionary Movement may have played important roles.[24] Nevertheless, his continued citation of liberal writers and his developmental and non-millenarian view of God's kingdom would suggest that he should be classed among evangelical liberals.

George Ronk (1881–1964), an older brother of Albert, was born in Albia, Iowa. The Ronk family moved to Turlock, California, in 1887. He attended Ashland College intermittently between 1908 and 1911. From 1909 until 1911 he pastored the North Manchester, Indiana, church and attended Manchester College (Church of the Brethren). He devoted his attention to denominational evangelistic work before returning to the pastorate at Leon (1913–1921) and Des Moines, Iowa (1921–1924). In the mid-20s he began a successful business career, though he remained very active in church work, serving on the Board of Trustees of Ashland College from 1924 until 1963 (for a number of years he served as president of the Board).

Ronk's struggle with liberalism began on the West coast. He obliquely notes that he was surrounded by an atmosphere of agnosticism and skepticism "under the shadow of the great university" in California.[25] A passing remark by a supporter of a more liberal stance in the church, J. B. Lambert, reveals that this university was Stanford and that its president, David Starr Jordon, had an early influence on Ronk.[26] It was only by coming to Ashland, Ronk reports, that he loosed himself from this skeptical perspective, though his struggle with liberalism was not over. In 1915 Ronk wrote: "Two years ago we would have agreed with our learned brother [Gillin had denied the infallibility of Scripture], but we have slept on that question day and night ever since and see not only its fallacy but its suicidal implications for Tunkerism."[27] This latter statement is significant, for Ronk felt the very foundation of the Brethren faith demanded commitment to an infallible Word.

The third group of participants in the liberal controversy were the Fundamentalist Brethren: J. C. Cassel, L. S. Bauman (see p. 168), and Alva J. McClain. Jacob C. Cassel (1849-1919) was born in Philadelphia and became a member of the German Baptist Brethren in 1876. He played a major role in organizing a Progressive Brethren congregation in Philadelphia in 1887.[28] Though Cassel did not enter the ministry until he was forty-seven, he was extremely active in local, district, and national church affairs. His role in fostering sentiment for foreign missions and in organizing the Foreign Missionary Society has already been discussed. Besides serving as the treasurer of the FMS from its inception until 1918, he was also a member and officer of the other major boards of the church: the General Mission Board, the Publication Board, and the Board of Trustees of the College. He pastored the mission work in Montreal, Canada, between 1909 and 1912.

Though Cassel had only twenty months of school training, he was, like his uncle, Abraham Cassel, an avid learner. He was a very cosmopolitan figure, participating in a wide range of religious activities outside the Brethren Church (note his attendance at interdenominational missionary conferences, Christian and Missionary Alliance conferences, and even a convention of tongue-speaking Triune Immersionist Adventists![29]). Nevertheless, he was firmly committed to a conservative, fundamental view of the faith and forcefully advocated this position against any opponent.

The roots of Fundamentalism in the Brethren Church are to be found in the Philadelphia First Brethren Church and in the person of J. C. Cassel particularly. The fact that Christian and Missionary Alliance teaching inspired the four main emphases in Cassel's thought between 1895 and 1900—faith healing, foreign missions, a Keswick view of the Christian life, and premillennialism/dispensationalism—has been documented earlier (see pp. 178-179). Significantly, several of these emphases came to be held by the two main pastors at the Philadelphia church in the 1890s and 1900s, I. D. Bowman (1862-1953) and L. S. Bauman. I. D. Bowman, the pastor of the Philadelphia church between 1892 and 1901, shared Cassel's views of sanctification, foreign missions, and eschatology, though Bowman notes they were studying the subject of the Holy Spirit independently at

first.[30] Bowman also had a high regard for the Christian and Missionary Alliance.[31]

Cassel indirectly and directly mediated to L. S. Bauman the two themes about which Bauman's later life and ministry gravitated: foreign missions and prophecy. It was the General Conference address by Dean Peck, the Methodist Seminary dean invited by Cassel (see p. 282, n. 20), and a tract by J. Hudson Taylor which first challenged Bauman with the importance of missions. His interest in missions and premillennialism was further bolstered by his attendance (at the urging of Cassel) of a Christian and Missionary Alliance convention near Lancaster. Bauman reports the impact of this conference:

> I saw that according to the plain, unmistakable language of the Word of God, that my Savior's return was personal and premillenial [sic], and that the time was drawing nigh. I was led further to see that the fulfilment [sic] of "the blessed hope" was vitally connected with the evangelization of the world.[32]

Bauman testifies that the incident which, for him, confirmed the importance of prophecy occurred following the death of his son, Glenn, in 1907. Reflecting on this incident some thirty years later, Bauman related how he was assailed with doubts concerning God's promises of the resurrection.

> I opened the Book itself. I fell on my knees. I begged of the living God assurance—absolute evidence! And there in the old Book were the words: "Produce your cause, saith Jehovah; bring forth your strong reasons, saith the King of Jacob.... Declare the things that are to come hereafter, that we may know that ye are gods" (Isa. 41:21, 23, R.V.).[33]

From this point on prophetic study and lecturing occupied a central part of Bauman's ministry.[34]

Bauman's first contact with men who were staunch premillennialists/dispensationalists and who would become key figures in the Fundamentalist movement occurred in Philadelphia. Here he became acquainted with R. A. Torrey, Arno C. Gaebelein, Henry G. Western (president of Crozier Seminary), William G. Moorehead, and A. T. Pierson.[35] It was Bauman's church at Long Beach, however, that became the center of dispensational and fundamentalist convictions in the Brethren Church.[36]

Under Bauman's direction the Long Beach congregation experienced remarkable growth—from 140 members in 1913 to 450 in 1920, 640 in 1927, 1119 in 1934, and 1555 in 1941. There were several keys to this steady growth. Bauman was a dynamic and persuasive speaker who used revivalistic and prophetic messages to stir the hearts of his audience. For Bauman, prophecy was a practical doctrine with great evangelistic potential. In 1913 he testified that the doctrine of premillennialism, more than any other, "has endeared the Brethren church to the hearts of the people of Long Beach, and is drawing scores toward our ranks whose hearts ache to hear more of the blessed, imminent hope of His [Christ's] return."[37] By the 1920s the church was also supporting an assistant pastor and by the 1930s a "Committee of Seventy" was doing most of the calling for the church.

Because the pastoral duties did not rest solely on Bauman, he was freed to do a great deal of evangelistic work not only in Southern California but also in the church at large (the Long Beach church, in fact, sought a pastoral assistant in 1921 for the express purpose of allowing Bauman to do as much as six months' revival work). The Long Beach church itself established new works in Long Beach, Glendale, Compton, and San Diego, among others, in cooperation with the Southern California District Mission Board.[38] In addition, Bauman was active on the Bible Conference circuit and regularly submitted articles, especially on prophetic themes, to the *Evangelist*, the *Sunday School Times* (a Keswick-oriented periodical), and the *King's Business* (published by the Bible Institute of Los Angeles [BIOLA]).

The Long Beach church regularly welcomed non-Brethren Fundamentalist-dispensational-Keswick speakers to its pulpit, especially for the annual Bible Conference of Southern California Brethren Churches (begun in 1912). The list of outside speakers between 1914 and 1938 reads like a Who's Who of the above movements: R. A. Torrey, W. E. Blackstone, A. C. Gaebelein, Thomas C. Horton (who organized BIOLA), L. W. Munhall, Arthur W. Pink, Cortland Myers (a Fundamentalist Baptist pastor), Robert C. McQuilkin (a noted Victorious Life speaker), T. T. Shields, J. H. Webster (professor of New Testament and Exegesis at Xenia Theological Seminary), P. B. Fitzwater (dean of Moody Bible Institute and a former member of the Church of the Brethren), Lewis Sperry Chafer, Louis Talbot, Charles E. Fuller, Charles O. Trumbull (editor of the *Sunday School Times*), William L. Pettingill (a founder of the Philadelphia School of the Bible), William G. Scroggie, W. H. Houghton (president of Moody), Paul W. Rood (president of BIOLA), and Oswald J. Smith. The Long Beach church also regularly hosted prominent missionaries and Christian Jews.

Another facet of Bauman's ministry at Long Beach was his challenge to young men and women to consider pastoral and missionary work. A steady stream of able men issued from Long Beach. Bauman

urged these men to seek special theological training at BIOLA and Xenia Theological Seminary.[39] Through these men the influence of the Long Beach church spread throughout the denomination.

One of the outstanding figures among "Bauman's boys" was Alva J. McClain (1888–1968). His father, W. S. McClain, had married a sister of A. D. Gnagey and had been ordained to the Brethren ministry in 1890. The McClain family lived successively in Aurelia, Iowa; Glendale, Arizona; Los Angeles, California; and Sunnyside, Washington. Alva was converted in 1911 during the revival service held by Bauman at Sunnyside. He attended the University of Washington, BIOLA (1911–1915), Antioch College, Xenia (1915–1918, Th.M. 1925), and Occidental College (B.A. 1925). The theological perspective at Xenia was Presbyterian Calvinism, though premillennialism was the dominant view of eschatology due to the influence of three successive millenarian presidents: William G. Moorehead (1899–1912), Joseph Kyle (1912–1922), and Melvin G. Kyle (1922–1930).[40] While serving the Philadelphia First Brethren Church (1918–1923), McClain began his long educational career as a professor at the Philadelphia School of the Bible (1919–1923). He taught at Ashland Seminary (1930–1937, dean 1934–1937) and served as professor and president at Grace Theological Seminary (1937–1962). He authored one major theological work, *The Greatness of the Kingdom*, as well as a number of briefer works and scholarly treatises. He was also a member of the revision committee for the *New Scofield Bible*.

McClain and Bauman shared a deep friendship until Bauman's death. Though Bauman may have been McClain's spiritual father, McClain was Bauman's theological tutor. Bauman relished the opportunities to acquire greater theological discernment from the far more systematic and scholarly mind of McClain. Gradually, Bauman's loose Biblical theology that typified the traditional Brethren approach to Scripture was transformed into a logically consistent, systematic theology under McClain's guidance.[41] This new theological perspective included emphasis on salvation by grace through faith, a corresponding view of salvation as punctiliar rather than as a process, the conception of baptism as a sign and seal of an inward grace rather than as a condition of salvation, stress on God's sovereignty, and eternal security for the believer (though Bauman did not accept this latter doctrine until the 1930s). Thus, while Bauman remained the charismatic leader of the Fundamentalist wing of the Brethren, McClain supplied the theological structure which undergirded the movement.

Early Skirmishes Between
Liberals and Conservatives/Fundamentalists

One of the earliest symptoms that two mutually exclusive world views were developing in the church is evidenced in the first issue of the *Evangelist* in the twentieth century. The editor had solicited various denominational leaders to share with *Evangelist* readers their visions for the new century. The contrasts are vivid. C. Orville Witter (see p. 182) and the pseudonymous contributor, Quiet Observer, provided the optimistic note:

> It is painful to note the gloomy outlook that many good people are taking at the dawn of the twentieth century, a century which I think has been ushered in with the most flattering prospects that ever attended the advent of any similar epoch. I do not understand how the pessimist brings himself to his sad beliefs. . . .
>
> After all, the world is growing better. Life is richer, fuller and sweeter than it was in the "good old times" to which the pessimists love to refer.[42]

J. C. Cassel's tone was entirely different.

> Humanly speaking I do not look for as great a proportionate advancement during the twentieth century over the nineteenth as there was during the nineteenth over the eighteenth. My reasons for this are twofold; first, because of physical limitations, and secondly I believe that the dispensation will close and the Lord will come again before the century closes, and thus cut short purely human genius and enterprise.[43]

The message of the optimists was undergirded by evolutionary concepts: "evolution unmistakably teaches that Creation is a continuous process and points forward toward a far off golden age."[44] The Progressives had also been predisposed toward such optimism by their simple and unqualified confidence in education. Note J. H. Worst's sentiments in appealing for support of Ashland College at the 1882 Ashland Convention:

> We are progressives, every one of us, by virtue of intelligence, and we owe this progressive movement to the schools of our country. Education, light and knowledge is the great factor of progression . . .
>
> . . . [There is a] vital difference between reaching the true stand of Christian character by growth, development, or education if you please, in the Gospel and attempting to reach it by the heresy of prohibitory law . . .[45]

The gloomy vision of the pessimists, on the other hand, was eschatologically determined. Feeling that Christ's return was near, they looked for "the seduction, the deceptions, the heresies, the anti-Christ that the Word of God warns us with."[46]

These two radically different perspectives predictably led to occasional debates in the *Evangelist* prior to the heated exchanges which began around 1913. The first important discussion between representatives of these two viewpoints concerned the question of the millennium. Cassel and Editor Gnagey had exchanged views on the subject of chiliasm in 1898. Gnagey rejected chiliasm in favor of what Cassel termed "evolutionary salvation": the gospel will finally triumph in a general salvation, preparatory to the Lord's return (Gnagey cited John 12:32; 16:8–9). Cassel, on the other hand, presented a pre-tribulation, premillennial view of Christ's return.[47]

Between 1900 and 1902 the advocates of premillennialism were becoming more forceful in their argumentation. In 1900 I. D. Bowman attacked postmillennialism as "anti-scriptural" while in 1902 L. S. Bauman, in his characteristic style, blazed away at several ideas connected with postmillennialism: the "church-kingdom theory" (the kingdom of God is evolving through the church's leavening action in society) and the "heart-kingdom theory" (the kingdom is within, changing the hearts of men through social and educational processes).[48] Significantly, in 1902 the first articles reflecting a distinctively dispensationalist approach to premillennialism appear. Both Cassel and Bauman maintain that "the kingdom of God is *not* the Gentile church [this is emphasized in view of postmillennialism's identification of the kingdom and the church]. When the kingdom of God is restored to earth it will be restored to literal Israel . . ."[49] Other writers, like B. C. Moomaw and C. F. Yoder, however, cautioned against a dogmatic approach to the question and sought the freedom to hold postmillennial and evolutionary, optimistic views of the kingdom.[50] Though both of these views continued to be propounded in the *Evangelist* (especially premillennialism), the next direct clash between the two positions did not occur until 1915.

A second subject of contention between the dispensationalists and those with a more moderate or liberal perspective centered on the question of whether certain Scripture passages should be interpreted in a literal or symbolic/spiritual manner. This question arose in discussions over several different topics. In 1902 B. C. Moomaw began an exchange on the Genesis creation account by condescendingly quipping:

> . . . literalists used to believe that the world was created in six days of twenty four hours each, which according to Bible chronology could not have been quite six thousand years ago. Science has shattered all this mistaken conception, and proven beyond cavil, not that the Bible account is

wrong, but that our understanding of that narrative, our literal construction of it, is wrong.[51]

Answers from P. J. Brown and L. S. Bauman were not long in coming. Bauman faced the issue squarely: "Nothing is done more to subvert the truth, the authority, and the power of God's Word today, than is the spiritualizing, idealizing, and allegorizing of Scriptures in which there is nowhere any intimation that they mean anything but exactly what they say."[52]

B. C. Moomaw again begged the question in 1904 when he charged that literalists were "destitute of imagination" and claimed (rather injudiciously for a Brethren) that John 13:14 was a hyperbole and Jesus' teachings were an assemblage of ideals, not laws.[53] In response to Moomaw, Cassel and Yoder contended that John 13:14 was a literal command and Cassel and D. C. Moomaw maintained that there was more literalism and law in Jesus' teachings than B. C. Moomaw allowed.[54] Significantly, this exchange prompted Yoder to begin a lengthy series of articles during 1905 on "Bible Interpretation."

The issue was raised again in 1909 when Cassel leveled a blast against those who, in his opinion, relativized the literal meaning of prophetic passages by calling them apocalypses.[55] J. Allen Miller, in a response to this article, revealed that Cassel had him in mind. The typically irenic Miller was concerned that the truth on the matter be clearly set forth in a balanced fashion. He therefore stated his own position in two carefully weighed, italicized statements:

> Let it not be forgotten that all visional symbols, parables, metaphors, similes, and every other form and species of figurative and symbolical language are the vehicles of thought and may and do as truly convey the thought of God as a bare literal statement. . . . To spiritualize literal historical narrative and to literalize any form of figurative language are both equally vicious and contrary to well understood and fundamental rules of interpretation.[56]

Questions which were inevitably drawn into these discussions concerned the nature of Scripture and higher criticism. Both Gillin and the earlier Furry advanced views of Scripture which were similar to those held by modernistic liberals. The Bible is to be analyzed by "the same tests as are applied to other writings." Because it is a "reasonable book," we "should not make any foolish claims for it [inerrancy, no doubt, is implied] which God never intended should be made." Nor should it be used as a textbook on science for God intended it to be a textbook only for religion.[57]

Both Cassel and Bauman were categorically opposed to the work of the higher critics. For Bauman the integrity of Scripture was at stake. He held that "there was no possibility of error" in the writings of Scripture. "Furthermore, the original scriptures were verbally inspired,—stenographically or phonographically, just as you please."[58] In addition, Cassel viewed critical scholarship as a "fad" which sought "to harmonize the Scriptures to twentieth century thought."[59]

Yoder and J. Allen Miller sought to mediate these two positions. Yoder softened Furry's radical statements by carefully setting forth the purpose and aims of biblical criticism and the differences between higher and lower criticism. He further observed that "the extreme views of a few radicals [among the higher critics] have been taken by many as the conclusions of all."[60] Miller responded to Cassel's attack with his characteristic desire for middle ground. He cautioned: "To be fair Brother Cassel must distinguish between Christians who are critics and always constructive and those who may be destructive and unbelieving critics." Miller himself could not agree with all the "sure result of . . . Biblical criticism," but he did wish to obtain "all the light the arduous and life-long study of the Bible can give up upon its meaning."[61]

These discussions rarely lasted for more than a month or two, but they are reflective of two radically different thought constructs and world views. In 1914 J. C. Cassel astutely listed several of the watershed issues between the "old religion" and the new one built on evolutionary and scientific foundations. These issues included supernaturalism vs. immanence, divine salvation vs. culture and education, Christ as Savior vs. Christ as Exemplar, a spiritual kingdom vs. an earthly one.[62] Though moderates like Yoder and Miller sought to reconcile the opposing positions whenever possible, they had no taste for controversy. When the two extremes found co-existence impossible in 1913, Yoder could view events only from distant Argentina while Miller understood the blinding and counterproductive nature of unrestrained conflict.

The Liberal Controversy

The immediate catalyst which touched off the theological controversy which lasted from 1913 to 1921 was the subject of the social gospel. Discussions relating to the social gospel had begun in earnest in 1911 in both pulpit and press. Indicative of the ferment this year are articles in the *Evangelist* which evaluated the social emphasis. Charles A. Bame and

Cassel were ranged on the negative side of the issues while Goughnour and Weidner stood on the positive. Representative of the vision which the young liberals had for the church are remarks presented by Weidner to the National Ministerial Association at General Conference in 1911.

> I believe the Gospel of tomorrow will be a different Gospel from that of today. The great fundamentals as proclaimed by Jesus will be its fundamentals, but because of changed conditions and needs, it will be necessary to change the appeal so as to meet the needs if it is to be effectively proclaimed. Judging from the voice of the prophets of today, the Gospel of tomorrow will be a social gospel.[63]

In the latter part of 1912 the proponents of the social gospel, especially Goughnour, Gillin, and L. L. Garber, began a literary campaign in the *Evangelist* apparently to mold sentiment in favor of greater social involvement. This campaign met with success in the 1913 General Conference when a Social Service Commission was approved. Appointed to the commission were Gillin, Goughnour, Weidner, L. L. Garber, and R. R. Teeter.

During this entire process notes of caution were being raised by Editor Gnagey. He spoke for the majority of ministers in the church in calling for a balanced, Biblical approach to the issue.

> Primarily, it is not the duty of the church to solve these so-called sociological problems. It is the duty of the Christian church to make known Jesus Christ, to carry the blessed Gospel of salvation to the uttermost parts of the earth, to urge men and women to accept Christ as their Savior and build up for herself a membership strong in her most holy faith, sure and undefiled, and unspotted from the world. Having done this the problems of society will be solved, even if unconsciously solved. It is the only way Christ ever attempted to solve such problems.[64]

More reactionary was a memorial passed by the 1914 Southern California District Conference.

> Resolved. That we deplore the publishing of certain articles that have appeared from time to time in the columns of the *Brethren Evangelist* in which something less than the whole gospel of our Lord and Savior Jesus Christ, has been set forth as the fundamental appeal of the Brethren Church, and that we consider all such articles as most serious blows at the very foundation of our beloved church.
> Resolved. That this annual conference of Brethren churches for the Southern California district hereby requests the next National Conference of Brethren churches in the United States, to likewise reaffirm the original position of the Brethren church as stated above; and to declare that no minister, publication, nor institution, is to be considered thoroughly loyal to the purpose of the Brethren church that sets forth in any way anything less than the whole gospel of

> Christ as set forth in the New Testament alone, as the true doctrine and polity of the Brethren church.[65]

General Conference acted upon the memorial by passing the following resolution:

> Resolved, that this General Conference of Brethren churches re-affirm our position that the Word of God, revealed in the Bible, is our only rule of faith and that we continue to reject all man-made creeds, and all declarations of faith aside from the whole gospel of Jesus Christ.[66]

The spirit manifest in the Southern California memorial touched a sensitive spot in liberals like Gillin and Goughnour. Both struck back with thinly veiled attacks against Bauman and his "theological dogmatism." Gillin responded first by calling the church to free itself from all legalism and dogmatism and by turning the Southern California charge against its authors.

> Is the analogy far-fetched that we Brethren have found in the doctrines and teachings of certain dogmatists substitutes for the pure gospel of Jesus? Have not Dowieism, Christian Allianceism, the dogmatism of the Moody Institute, and allied theological doctrines, proved to be Canaanitish gods to the Brethren church?[67]

Goughnour followed in Gillin's wake.

> There is no doubt that all the ministers of the Brethren church, with, perhaps, a few exceptions who have been led astray by placing certain theological dogmas above the plain teachings of Jesus, believe that social service forms an indispensable part of a true Christian life.[68]

The respondent to these articles (and Gillin's especially) was not the expected Bauman or Cassel but a relatively unknown theological student, Alva J. McClain.[69] He put the matter quite frankly:

> In an address, reported recently in the Evangelist we noticed an extremely confusing (to us) use of the words "dogma," "theology," "theological," and the phrase "theological dogma." It is apparently left to the ordinary reader to choose between two conclusions, either that the words were used carelessly and in a thoughtless manner or that the speaker was condemning "theological dogma" in a general way and wondering why it should be made a test of fellowship in the Brethren church. Are we to take his words seriously when he declares that "Theological dogmas spell the death of Christian freedom"?[70]

McClain proceeded to argue that both theology, as the true knowledge of God, and dogma, as authority deriving from God, are true to the Christian faith.

The controversy broke wide open in 1915 when George T. Ronk and J. L. Gillin exchanged a series of bitterly critical and sarcastic articles. Ronk felt that the time had come to face squarely the dangers posed by liberalism.

> The question involves the whole field of Biblical scholarship—theological training, interpretation, inspiration, eschatology, ministerial activities, church objectives. We do not hesitate to say the very foundation of Brethren faith is in the balance.[71]

In his five articles on "The Present Issue," Ronk attacked head-on liberal emphases which he felt were in clear contradiction to Biblical and Brethren standards. In the first article, Ronk upheld the right of each person to interpret Scripture for himself. Nevertheless, he maintained that this does not imply that the church has no right to enforce correct teaching. Rather, the church has a "scriptural duty to interpret and state the truth for the immature, to safeguard the interpretation which generations of righteous and like-minded men have apprehended as truth and given their hearts' blood for."[72]

In his second article Ronk challenged the liberal view of the kingdom. He charged that the belief that the kingdom would come through spiritual and moral evolution was based on the authority of experience rather than the authority of Scripture and Jesus. In this article and the next two, he set forth a basically dispensational view of the kingdom. He distinguished the church from the kingdom (which was rejected by the Jews and awaits a future restoration with Israel) and maintained that the age would be consummated in apocalyptic fashion with great tribulation.[73]

In his final article Ronk confronted Gillin on a subject raised in several articles by the latter. Ronk observed that for the first time in the pages of the *Evangelist*, a church leader (Gillin) had proposed "to shelve the Bible as the inspired product of the Holy Ghost and substitute therefore [sic] experience, denying the primary authority of the Bible, asserting the infallibility of experience alone." Ronk called upon liberalism to come down from its "high horse" of intellectual superiority. He set forth his own view of Scripture: "the Bible is the Word of God, infallible in all matters of doctrine, directly inspired by the Holy Spirit, each writer using his own vocabulary and background."[74]

Following Ronk's third article, Gillin began his response. He charged Ronk with "mediaevalism" and the denial of fundamental principles of the church when Ronk suggested that those who differ with the majority on issues which were open to different interpretations "are bound in honor to separate themselves from the society of the majority."

Gillin averred that "the Brethren have ever stood for freedom of thought and for purity of life. In her fold the only test of fellowship is piety of life."[75]

Gillin continued his assault in a speech at the 1915 General Conference by claiming that

> the Brethren church is not a theological church. It originated in protest against the barrenness of the formal dogmatism of protestant theology. In its essence and nature it is pietistic, having to do with life rather than doctrine, using the term in the theological sense. The church was not concerned with such theological questions as predestination, virgin birth, relation of the three persons of the trinity, definition of the exact relation of man to God, or any of the other historic theological doctrines and controversies.[76]

Such was the negative reaction to Gillin's sentiments that, when asked to give his impressions of the recent Conference for the *Evangelist*, Gillin resorted to biting satire. He presented eleven resolutions which he felt might have been offered by the Conference. The last one states in part: "FINALLY BE IT RESOLVED, that our preachers be admonished to make their preaching as unreasonable as possible, for the more unreasonable their message the more marvelous their success if they attract people to it."[77]

After Conference Gillin opened up a second front of controversy (following the social gospel fracas) with a three part series touching on the inspiration of Scripture. Gillin contended in this first article that there are only four bases on which one could build his faith: an infallible church, an infallible creed, an infallible book, and an infallible experience. Gillin dismissed the first three as valid bases (the absolute inerrancy of Scripture cannot be upheld because of "inconsistencies" and "some ordinary mistakes") and held that "every man who is a Christian has a fundamental fact in his life to which these [other aspects] are mere supports, namely, his own experience with Jesus Christ."[78]

In his second article Gillin posited that Jesus' source of "confidence in God" was the "fact that he knew God." Derivatively then, the foundation of faith is to be found "in the experience which the gospel of Jesus generates in the souls of sinful men."[79] In his final article Gillin considered the value of Scripture. He contended that "inspiration does not depend upon some magical grace which flows through a man and guarantees the divinity of his utterances. Inspiration is no such superficial and wooden thing as that." Hence the inspiration of Scripture does not depend upon its inerrancy but whether it inspires us or not.[80]

Gillin's articles elicited a spate of responses upholding the infallibility of Scripture not only from the more vocal conservatives/fundamentalists like Ronk (his fifth article above), Cassel, Bauman, and McClain but even from the "silent majority-moderates" like Charles A. Bame and W. S. Bell. McClain's article is illuminating for it reflects the orthodox Presbyterian/Fundamentalist training he was receiving at Xenia. He maintained that the delimiting term "verbal" needed to be added to "inspiration" because of the ambiguity of the latter term. For McClain verbal inspiration meant that the words of Scripture were "absolutely correct," though he carefully noted that such inspiration adhered only to "the original words of the record." For support of his position, McClain listed a number of scholars who had endorsed verbal inspiration. This list includes: Hodge, Gaussen, Canon Westcott, Dean Burgon, Torrey, Gray, Moorehead, Pierson, Munhall, West, and Warfield (note the prominence of Reformed/Princeton theologians and leaders of premillennialism/dispensationalism and the Bible institutes). He upheld both verbal inspiration and literal interpretation as crucial foundations for the Brethren view of the ordinances, the permanent unity of the church, and missionary endeavor.[81]

A third area of controversy, relative to premillennialism, was opened up in late 1915 and 1916. In reality, this topic was directly linked to the previous question as W. S. Bell indicates: "A man must to my mind deny verbal inspiration, and the literal interpretation of the Bible in order to defend his position in rejecting the personal return of Christ to earth."[82] It is interesting that in this debate, which pitted a premillennial/dispensational view of the kingdom versus an evolutionary/developmental view, the proponents of each side claimed support from Brethren heritage. E. M. Cobb testified that in his long association with the Brethren he had heard numerous premillennial sermons by the Millers, Brumbaughs, Holsingers, Florys, Studebakers, Earlys, and Wolfes. He also cited the witness of an eighty-two year old, long time member: "I have never heard a postmillennial sermon preached until very recently."[83] George A. Copp, however, contended that, from the time of the reorganization of the Brethren Church in Virginia (mid-1880s), he had never heard or himself preached a sermon on premillennialism. Significantly, however, he notes the negative impact that Thurman's activities had on the doctrine.[84]

The next act in the drama occurred at the 1916 General Conference. L. S. Bauman presented a resolution to the Conference that stated:

> Resolved, that it is the faith of the Brethren church that the holy scriptures as originally written were altogether a

record from God, inspired of the Holy Ghost, who so moved the writers thereof as to keep a record absolutely free from error. Therefore, the Bible as we now possess it, when made free from any error or mistake that translators, copyists, or printers possibly may have made, is the infallible Word of the living God, the one, and only authoritative message of God to men.[85]

When no final action on this and substitute resolutions was realized in the sharp discussions which ensued, a committee of eleven, having equal representation of the differing opinions, was chosen to draft a statement. Their product, unanimously adopted, is significant. The relevant section stated:

> Resolved, That this conference of Brethren churches, without attempting to establish a creed, desires to bear testimony to the belief that God's supreme revelation has been made through Jesus Christ, a complete and authentic record of which revelation is the New Testament; and to the belief that the Holy Scriptures of the Old and New Testaments, as originally given of God, are the infallible record of the perfect, final and authoritative revelation of God's will, altogether sufficient in themselves as a rule of faith and practice.[86]

Several crucial differences exist between Bauman's resolution and that finally adopted. (1) The resolution adopted carefully stipulated that it was not to be considered a creed. (2) The wording of Bauman's resolution reveals indebtedness to Fundamentalism and the Princeton theology of the Hodges and B. B. Warfield while the compromise resolution is more in keeping with traditional Brethren emphases. These emphases include viewing Christ as the fullest revelation of God and the New Testament as the complete record of this revelation. (3) Bauman's resolution argues for the authority of Scripture primarily on the basis of a divinely inspired, inerrant *autographa*. The Conference resolution, however, shifts the emphasis to a Christological base of authority for the New Testament and replaces the essentially negative concept of "free from error" with the positive wording "perfect, final, and authoritative." (4) The compromise resolution defines more fully the purpose and aim of Scripture: a sufficient rule of faith and practice.

The passage of this resolution together with the launching of a denominational "Four Year Program" at the 1916 Conference had an almost immediate calming effect on the controversy. The Four Year Program, proposed by the Moderator, William Beachler, was a bold venture which set goals at the local, district, and national levels for the various departments of the church. Albert Ronk conjectures (and he is probably right) that Beachler made his proposal as a diversionary tactic. "There was a double result, of course—circumventing the controversy and accrual of values from concentrated organized effort."[87] Though poorly organized the first year (the doctrinal discussions provided little time for concrete planning), the program was given renewed vitality with the appointment of Charles A. Bame as the director in 1917. In evaluating the results of the program, Ronk observed that some noteworthy numerical gains were achieved but he questioned whether there was much "spiritual deepening and fervor."[88]

About the time this campaign was drawing to a close, the coals of controversy, which had laid dormant for several years, were fanned to flame by the Interchurch World Movement (IWM).[89] This movement was distinctly a product of the period. By the second decade of the twentieth century the liberal view of the kingdom of God had undergone a dramatic change of emphasis. The ascendant view at the turn of the century—an evolutionary conception which was essentially impersonal, materialistic, and deterministic—had gradually been replaced by a developmental view which held that man plays a key role in bringing in the kingdom. Whether the kingdom ideal was sociological, as in the social gospel perspective, or more evangelical, as in Mott's hope for a world transformed by American missions (see p. 286, n. 24), the result was an idealistic drive to hasten or bring in the kingdom through large-scale, concerted activity. This idealism was not shattered by World War I but, ironically, enhanced. The nation as a whole had united behind the war effort and expectantly awaited the return of its victorious doughboys who had "made the world safe for democracy." Optimism that a new era of world peace was on the threshold ran high.

The Protestant Church had actively backed the war effort with key leaders such as Mott, Robert E. Speer, and William Adams Brown heading various interdenominational war time programs (and learning valuable organizational skills in the process). With the close of the war, it was the feeling that American Christianity was now being tested to see whether it could lead the way in ushering in this new era of peace and Christian brotherhood. The IWM was designed by such men as Mott and Speer to meet this challenge.[90] A grand program, uniting every phase of Protestant church work, domestic and foreign, and an extravagant budget (eventually set at a billion dollars) to fund the manifold projects were formulated in 1919. It was the plan that each denomination should be responsible for drawing up its own budget and for administering its own part of the program.

Initially, Brethren response to the movement was enthusiastic. J. A. Garber, a professor at the Ashland Seminary, Editor George S. Baer, and E. E. Jacobs, the recently elected president of Ashland College (1919-1935) were excited about the venture. In November, 1919, Baer, who gave the IWM strong editorial backing, remarked:

> Nothing more promising has arisen in many years than the Interchurch World Movement. It is promising not only because it purposes to bring about a united front on the part of the Christian forces of the world, but because it would bring the wonderful influence of a united church to bear upon every phase of life which the church seeks to save.[91]

On January 1, 1920, representatives of the various Boards and of the General Conference of the Brethren Church met in Ashland to determine a denominational policy. It was resolved that it was the sense of the meeting (though not unanimous) that those boards which desired to participate in the campaign could do so, "so far as is consistent with our denominational genius and identify."[92] Both ministers and laymen from the church subsequently attended regional conferences leading up to the united financial drive (April 25 through May 2). The Ashland College Trustees decided on behalf of the College to cooperate with the campaign. William Kolb, Jr., a layman from Philadelphia and president of both the College Trustees and Brethren Publishing Company, suggested a denominational budget of $200,000.

Opposition to the IWM was first registered in the *Evangelist* by Louis S. Bauman. In February, 1920, he made a veiled attack against the movement by fitting it into the dispensational prophetic schema. He observed that the hour "seems even to be upon us" when the great religious federation, i.e., the beast of Revelation 17, "will enter into a gigantic and unholy alliance, with the ostensible purpose of conquering the world for Christ and establishing the Kingdom of God on earth."[93] Bauman aimed a direct broadside against the IWM a month later. He challenged the doctrinal silence of the movement on such questions as the deity of Christ, the doctrine of salvation, the inspiration of Scripture, the resurrection of Christ and of the saints, and the personality of the Holy Ghost. He charged that the program of the IWM was that "of post-millenialism [sic] and of Modernism with its 'social gospel' program. . . . This world will be won for Christ, but it will be done according to God's program, and not man's."[94]

The *Evangelist* devoted its April 28, 1920, issue, which appeared during the week of the IWM financial campaign, to articles for and against the project. Interestingly, almost no mention is made about the movement in the *Evangelist* after this date. Without doubt, the disappointing results of the national campaign disillusioned its proponents among the Brethren and heartened its opponents.

The final act in the liberal controversy occurred in 1921. The previous year the National Ministerial Association had appointed a Committee of Twenty-five to formulate a statement of faith which would be agreeable to the ministry of the entire church. The committee was composed of men representing the theological spectrum of liberal to fundamental. It was hoped that a greater measure of unity and understanding would accrue from the committee's work.

Prior to the gathering of the ministers at General Conference in 1921, several articles appeared in the *Evangelist* which reveal that there was much unrest about *how* the statement should be viewed. G. W. Rench maintained that the historic plea of the church—"The Bible, the whole Bible, and nothing but the Bible"—was sufficient in itself. Official creeds or "pronouncements" have "but one purpose, and that is to stir up strife and bitterness among us."[95] B. T. Burnworth was disturbed by what he saw as a developing trend to make "sonship, membership, fellowship in the church" dependent on subscription to a creed. He argued that one's experience with Christ was "bigger than any creed." The historic appeal to the New Testament as the Brethren creed should be sufficient; within these bounds one should have the personal liberty to interpret this creed for himself.[96]

Taking the opposite viewpoint were E. D. Burnworth (a brother of B. T.) and McClain. Burnworth held that the church has a right to clarify what it means by its Whole Bible plea. What makes the church distinctive is its own particular interpretation of the Whole Bible. "Now to permit each one to interpret this general statement of faith in their [sic] own way makes absolutely impossible a Brethren church."[97] McClain is more dogmatic in his insistence on standards of faith.

> . . . the Christian must be "intolerant" in order to be a true Christian! But there are two qualifications. First, we are to be intolerant only of *false teaching* which strikes at the Fundamentals of the Faith, and of sin. Second, we must exercise our "intolerance" in love, and never let it find expression in physical violence. Within these limits INTOLERANCE is a righteous attitude—the mark of every true child of God.[98]

The committee's finished product, "The Message of the Brethren Ministry," was actually the work of McClain, J. Allen Miller, and a third member of the committee.[99] Because of its importance to later developments, it is reproduced here in full.

> The message which Brethren Ministers accept as a Divine Entrustment to be heralded to a lost world, finds its sole source and authority in the Bible. This message is one of Hope for a lost world and speaks with finality and authority. Fidelity to the apostolic injunction to preach the Word demands our utmost endeavor of mind and heart. We, the members of the National Ministerial Association of the Brethren church, hold that the essential and constituent elements of our message shall continue to be the following declarations:
>
> 1. Our Motto: The Bible, the whole Bible and nothing but the Bible.
>
> 2. The Authority and Integrity of the Holy Scriptures. The Ministry of the Brethren church, desires to bear testimony to the belief that God's supreme revelation has been made through Jesus Christ, a complete and authentic record of which revelation is the New Testament; and, to the belief that the Holy Scriptures of the Old and New Testaments, as originally given, are the infallible record of the perfect, final and authoritative revelations of God's will, altogether sufficient in themselves as a rule of faith and practice.
>
> 3. We understand the Basic Content of our Doctrinal Preaching and teaching to be:
>
> (1) The Pre-existence, Deity, and Incarnation by Virgin Birth of Jesus Christ, the Son of God;
>
> (2) The Fall of Man, his consequent spiritual death and utter sinfulness, and the necessity of his New Birth;
>
> (3) The Vicarious Atonement of the Lord Jesus Christ through the shedding of His own blood;
>
> (4) The resurrection of the Lord Jesus Christ in the body in which He suffered and died and His subsequent glorification at the right hand of God;
>
> (5) The justification by personal faith in the Lord Jesus Christ, of which obedience to the will of God and works of righteousness are the evidence and result; the resurrection of the dead, the judgment of the world, and the life everlasting of the just;
>
> (6) The personality and Deity of the Holy Spirit who indwells the Christian and is his Comforter and Guide;
>
> (7) The personal and visible return of our Lord Jesus Christ from heaven as King of Kings and Lord of Lords; the glorious goal for which we are taught to watch, wait, and pray;
>
> (8) The Christian should "be not conformed to this world, but be transformed by the renewing of the mind," should not engage in carnal strife and should "swear not at all;"

(9) The Christian should observe, as his duty and privilege, the ordinances of our Lord Jesus Christ, among which are (a) baptism of believers by Triune Immersion; (b) confirmation; (c) the Lord's Supper; (d) the Communion of the Bread and Wine; (e) the washing of the saints' feet; and (f) the anointing of the sick with oil.[100]

The stamp of both Miller and McClain is quite visible in this document. Miller's mark is seen in the Christocentric apologetic for the authority of Scripture and the triad of words describing the nature of this revelation: perfect, final, and authoritative.[101] McClain's thought is evidenced in the Reformed view of salvation (justification by faith) and the characteristic emphases of Fundamentalism: the virgin birth, the utter sinfulness of man, the vicarious atonement, the resurrection of Christ, and the personality of the Holy Spirit. Noticeably missing is the traditional Brethren formulation of salvation: enlightenment, repentance, faith, baptism, remission of sins, and the gift of the Holy Spirit.

Shortly after the adoption of the "Message" by the Ministerial Association in 1921, Gillin reflected what was probably the general response of the liberals in the church to the document:

> I cannot but wonder what some of the old Brethren who in the early eighties fought their hard battle against man-made rules and definitions, and who decided that the New Testament is a "sufficient rule of faith and practice" on the ground that anything more is too much, anything less is too little and anything "just the same" is superfluous, would think of this new endeavor to bind the consciences of the Brethren ministry....
>
> ... It is much more difficult today than it was twenty years ago for a man to think for himself and interpret his "only creed, the Bible" in the way Paul interpreted his, viz., in the light of knowledge and experience and by the guidance of the Holy Spirit.[102]

Though the statement was adopted with the stipulation that it was to be viewed "as the message of the Brethren Ministry, and not as a creed for the denomination,"[103] Ronk asserts that it was the cause for "practically all" of the young liberals to leave the denomination during the next five years. Many of these men joined the Presbyterian Church.[104] Gillin himself retired from General Conference activities though he continued to contribute occasional articles. He also retained his membership in the Brethren church at Waterloo and the Ministerial Association. It is noteworthy that he reversed his theological stance during the 1940s, not only upholding the authority of the Bible in a Conference lecture in 1945 but also publicly asking forgiveness from Conference for his former position.[105]

Concluding Observations

The investigation of the liberal controversy in the Brethren Church provides valuable insights regarding (1) the nature of Brethren thought and (2) the factors that would issue in the division of 1939. (1) Classical liberalism and the social gospel had a special appeal to those men in the Brethren Church who sought advanced training. The Progressives' clamor for a reasonable faith and the individual's right to interpret scripture for himself under the Spirit's direction were likewise championed by liberalism. The traditional non-credal conviction of the Brethren which was intensified by the revolt against the trend to make Annual Meeting minutes mandatory was paralleled by German liberalism's antipathy for "dogma." The readiness of Brethren to aid not only their brothers in the faith but also their neighbors in the world predisposed them to viewing social service as an integral part of the Gospel.

Each of these traditional emphases, however, was in danger of being distorted by liberalism. Making reason or experience autonomous and subjecting Scripture to the authority of either undermined the foundation upon which the Brethren built their faith (George Ronk and C. F. Yoder sensed this truth). The fact that the Brethren never developed creeds was based on the desire not to limit the Spirit's ability to interpret the Word anew in the contemporary setting. It did not give every individual the right to interpret Scripture for himself *irrespective* of the faith of the community (note E. D. Burnworth's comments, p. 192). Likewise, freedom of thought regarding the Christian faith extended no further than the limits of revealed Scripture. Finally, the Brethren traditionally held that the primary problem of man is spiritual. Though the ultimate design of God is the consummation of His eternal kingdom, this goal is realized now primarily through the Holy Spirit's work of renewing individuals into the image of God through conversion and sanctification. Nevertheless, the community of the redeemed is commissioned to reflect the divine image to the world and this task involves material and social responsibilities as well as spiritual.

(2) Opposition to liberalism came from a wide theological spectrum in the church. There were staunch Fundamentalists like Bauman, McClain, and Cassel; there were men trained in liberal settings who either modified their liberalism (Furry) or took a more conservative Brethren position (George Ronk); there were the traditional Brethren who tended to deplore controversy but would speak out when they

felt the foundation of their faith was being challenged (A. D. Gnagey, G. W. Rench, R. R. Teeter, Charles A. Bame, W. S. Bell).

The spirit and tactics used by each of these groups in challenging liberalism were quite different, however. The Fundamentalist Brethren were militant in their resistance to liberalism and the social gospel, viewing them as categorically opposed to the Word of God. Their means of defending the fundamentals of the faith was direct confrontation and the development of statements of faith to be used as tests of orthodoxy.[106] Though very much within the traditional Brethren camp, Ronk shared the aggressive spirit of Fundamentalism, possibly because he realized the dangers posed to the Brethren faith by liberalism. Finally, those men whose faith was nurtured primarily within Brethren circles tended to be more irenic and emphasize the Brethren distinctives (the ordinances, peace principles) rather than closely reasoned theological formulations. It is true, however, that most Brethren leaders did receive *The Fundamentals*[107] and that there is an inherent conservative bias built into the Brethren faith due to its emphasis on "the whole Gospel." Yet, even though the traditional Brethren leadership was willing to adopt statements of faith to clarify the Brethren position on controversial issues, this group refused to view these statements as creeds and use them as tests of fellowship. The college and university trained Brethren in particular desired to remain open to new light on God's Word wherever it might be found— whether among evangelical liberals or Fundamentalists.[108] These differences between the various groups which had united in their stand against liberalism (especially modernistic liberalism) and the social gospel are crucial for understanding the division of 1939 between the Fundamentalist Brethren and the "Brethrenists."

A word needs to be said about the laity of the church during the controversy. For the most part, the laity was detached from the theological battles and desired peace to be restored. Many thought the entire issue was theological hair-splitting by certain ministers. More important issues faced the church, notably evangelism, the cultivation of the spiritual life, and the propagation of the Brethren distinctives, especially the ordinances.[109]

Chapter 14

THE LIFE AND THOUGHT OF J. ALLEN MILLER

Introduction

If any man epitomized Brethren ideals in the Brethren Church in the years following the 1883 division, that man would, without doubt, be J. Allen Miller. It is true that Miller was shaped by the characteristics of his time. He grappled with the challenges to faith posed by science, history, and philosophy and demanded of himself and his students the cultivation of an intelligent, reasonable faith. Yet the factors which were determinative for his life and thought were wholly religious: his Lord was Christ, his Book was the Bible, and his faith was that of the Brethren. During his over forty years of service to the church and especially Ashland College and Seminary, Miller modelled a winsome Christocentric faith which touched the lives of countless students, professors, church leaders, and laity. Miller's scholarship, leadership at the College and in the church, and devotional fervor made him a dominating figure in the church during the first third of this century.

The Life of J. Allen Miller

John Allen Miller was born near Rossville, Indiana, on August 20, 1866. His parents, Mr. and Mrs. William Miller, were both of Pennsylvania Dutch descent and had come to Indiana from Pennsylvania. His mother was a daughter of a German Baptist minister. His father was a schoolteacher.

J. Allen "was blessed with an inquiring mind, anxious to explore the fields of learning, and in this desire he was given every possible encouragement by his father."[1] At the age of seventeen Miller began teaching school and continued until 1887 when he entered Ashland College. He received his B.A. from Ashland College in 1890. He pursued advanced studies at Hillsdale College and Hiram College, earning B.D. and M.A. degrees from the latter insti-

tution. He also did graduate work at the University of Chicago and in 1904 he received the honorary D.D. from Ashland College.

His relation with the Brethren Church began at the age of eighteen when he united with the church at Edna Mills, Indiana, under the ministry of J. H. Swihart. From the first he was encouraged by the congregation to enter the ministry, a suggestion to which he was not at all averse. Thus, just a few months after his baptism, he was called to the ministry by his congregation, and within a week he had preached his first sermon. Miller served pastorates at Glenford, Ohio (1890–1892), and Elkhart, Indiana (1892–1894), and for many years was pastor of the Ashland church in connection with his work at the college.[2]

Miller's long service to Ashland College began in 1894 when he filled in as president of the institution (1894–1896) after the newly elected head, S. S. Garst, died a month after assuming office. After the precarious financial status of the college had forced the closure of the school for several years, he and his new bride, Clara Worst Miller, were prevailed upon to reopen the college in 1898. Between 1898 and 1906 he again served as president of the college. In the latter year he relinquished the presidency to J. L. Gillin in order to devote himself fully to the Bible department which for the first time was designated as a Seminary. From the beginning of the Seminary, Miller continued as its Dean until 1933 when he asked to be relieved and was made Dean Emeritus. Nevertheless, he continued teaching until two weeks before his death even though he was severely weakened by cancer. He died March 27, 1935.

Miller was a dominant figure in the denomination throughout his lifetime. He served on every significant committee from 1895 on: the Commission of Ten on church polity (1895), the Committee of Three on General Conference rules (1901), the

Committee of Twenty-five on church polity (1912), the Committee of Eleven to consider L. S. Bauman's 1916 Conference resolution, and the Committee of Twenty-five which formulated the "Message of the Brethren Ministry" (1920). He twice served as Moderator of General Conference (1907 and 1924) and many times as Moderator of the Ohio District Conference. Miller possessed the rare ability to discern solutions to controversial questions which satisfied all parties involved. As W. D. Furry testified: "Again and again on the floor of the General Conference when profound and controversial issues had reached a dead-lock, he was first to reach a certain unhesitating assurance of conviction which seldom failed to carry conviction and endorsement."[3] For Miller the search for truth was not to be done at the expense of the peace and unity of the Brotherhood.

Miller was a charter member of the Foreign Missionary Society. He served on the Executive Committee (renamed the Board of Trustees in 1915) of the Society from its inception and as president of the Executive Committee from 1903 until his death. He was frequently elected to the Publication Board and was the first president (1901–1934) of the Board of Directors of the Brethren's Home (a retirement home for both ministers and laity).

Not only the church was the beneficiary of Miller's service but also the city of Ashland. He was a member of the commission which framed the charter under which Ashland is governed and also a member of the Civil Service Commission. He was respected and loved by the people of Ashland and known as widely as any man.[4]

Miller epitomized the classical, liberal-arts student/scholar that was the goal of the college and university training of the period. He was an exceptional linguist, being proficient in Latin, Greek, Hebrew, and Aramaic. His technical skill in the Biblical languages and his unqualified commitment to the authority of God's revelation through Christ in the Word made Miller a highly respected exegete. He also had a strong philosophical bent which lent to his thought a distinctively broad and inclusive quality. L. L. Garber, the English professor at the college, further described his scholarship:

> As a student Dr. Miller had characteristics worthy of modern emulation. He was delightfully thorough, painstaking, and efficient in his daily work. His efforts were nearly always some shades superior to the best of others and he was early ranked as a superior student. His passion for accuracy, for correctness and fullness of detail laid the foundation for that solid and enduring scholarship, which won him wide renown and made his name almost a household word as a leader in the church in which he labored.[5]

As a teacher Miller was always considerate to the views of his students. Charles A. Bame's testimony that "one will search in vain, I believe, to find dogmatism in his writings"[6] would apply equally well to his teaching methods. He never belittled his students and never gave the impression that he had complete possession of all truth. He refused to become entangled in speculative theories but placed the emphasis instead on the practical and vital. His goal for himself and for his students was the development of a mature faith through an open and honest evaluation of all data. In 1928 Miller wrote:

> We must hold a faith that is reasonable, intelligent and compelling. We ought never as ministers and teachers of the Word of God have to beg the question when asked for the grounds upon which our faith rests by replying evasively or charging our questioners with unbelief.... I plead for an informed and intelligent ministry. I covet a ministry for the Brethren church that knows the grounds upon which faith can be rested,—grounds that can not be shaken by any discovery of history, science or philosophy.[7]

What made Miller a respected figure in the church above all else was his own Christian life. It was his humble, patient, loving spirit that "gave weight, and power, and point to this teaching."[8] Miller, probably more than any other person of his time, sensed that the true genius of Christianity and "Brethrenism" was the daily desire to be transformed into the spirit of Christ. It was this inner Christ-like quality that earned Miller the respect and praise of both "Ashland" and "Grace" Brethren leaders.

The Thought of J. Allen Miller

INTRODUCTION

It is unfortunate that Miller never published any major theological works. The only work that provides the reader with any detailed conception of Miller's thought was the posthumous publication of his class lectures and some selected sermons. Yet this very fact may be reflective of Miller as a Brethren theologian. He was convinced that the Brethren had a perfect, unchanging credal standard in the New Testament, but he also realized that the "eternal spiritual and social principles [of the New Testament] await interpretation in every age in the terms of the life and experience of that day."[9] Miller himself continually sought to translate the Brethren creed into the contemporary setting. Yet he may have felt that a full written presentation of his own understanding of Scripture might hinder later generations from wrestling with the necessary task of applying the principles of the unchanging Word to their own culture.

This study of Miller's thought will utilize three separate systematic discussions of theology prepared by Miller: his class lectures on theology published posthumously in the volume, *Christian Doctrine— Lectures and Sermons*, a series of doctrinal articles published in the *Evangelist* between June, 1910, and January, 1911, and a pamphlet, *Doctrinal Statements*, composed of brief doctrinal essays prepared for Sunday School lessons in 1922. Even though each of these treatments derives from a different decade of his life, his seminal thoughts remain quite consistent. Use will also be made of some of the articles which Miller at times submitted to the *Evangelist*. The outline and discussion of doctrinal loci in this study follows, for the most part, those in *Christian Doctrine*.

THE SOURCES OF AUTHORITY USED BY MILLER

Miller shares all the sources of authority utilized by the early Brethren, though the relative emphasis given to these sources does undergo some change in his thought. The only significant difference is the role given reason in Miller's authority structure.

God, the Creator, is Personal

In a number of his writings and published sermons, Miller begins the discussion of his particular topic with the assertion that a fundamental postulate of the Christian faith is the assumption of a *personal* God. With this "given," he argues that the created universe must be purposeful, meaningful, and end-realizing.[10] It takes on the character of its Creator.

God's purpose is revealed and worked out through Christ

Miller's faith is thoroughly Christocentric. He repeatedly affirms that God's eternal purpose is centered in Jesus Christ. God's eternal plan, as conceived in Christ, "embraced in its sweep not alone the un-created world, but man and his salvation."[11] As regards man, "the purpose of God in Christ was the perfection of individual character, redemption from sin, the recreation of man in the image and likeness of Him."[12]

It is in Christ that the revelation of God the Father and of His will is perfectly manifested. Not only has Christ effected man's redemption by his atoning death, but He also set forth the supreme ideal of life for man in His earthly ministry.[13] In Christ "man first begins to see his own matchless character and infinite possibilities."[14]

It is also in Christ that God will sum up all things in the fullness of the times. "Christ is to bring to a head, to bring to a point, to make everything gather around a common center."[15] Given such a Lord, Miller confessed that his premier loyalty was "to Jesus Christ and His Word. With me He is an authoritative teacher, and His word for me is final . . ."[16]

Scripture is God's supreme revelation to man through Christ

Miller remained true to the Brethren and Reformation insistence that Scripture must be "the sole and sufficient authority . . . in every and all matters of religion."[17] A characteristic stamp of Miller's view of Scripture is the following development:

> Jesus Christ came into our world as God's Son, incarnate in perfect Man;
> Jesus Christ spoke for God to men; he revealed the will of God to Men;
> Jesus Christ commanded men to hear his message, believe it and obey it.
> This Message which he revealed personally and through chosen men is the New Testament; as such record it is God's Revelation given through Inspiration.[18]

A second distinctive trademark of Miller's view of Scripture is his use of a triad of adjectives to describe the nature of the revelation made by Christ and contained in the New Testament. (1) It is a *perfect* revelation. The revelation given by the Son of God is, by virtue of His very nature, faultless and perfect. (2) It is a *complete* revelation. There is "no part or element of God's will concerning man and his salvation wanting." (3) This revelation is *final*. "We shall need to look for no other from God. It is God's final word on man's relation to Himself."[19]

As is evident from the foregoing, Miller stresses the fact that there is progress in Biblical revelation. Since the New Testament contains God's perfect, complete, and final revelation, it is the fulfillment of the Old Testament revelation. Jesus has "preserved in the New Testament System all that was of value and of permanent religious validity in the Old."[20] Though the Old Testament System is thus abrogated, it does retain value for the Christian. It serves as a tutor that brings us to Christ (Gal. 3:24). It flashes forth divine glory, even though it is a passing glory (2 Cor. 3:10ff.). It helps the Christian to understand the historical fulfillment of the Old Testament system in the New Testament.[21]

Miller upholds the divine inspiration of *all* Scripture (in responding to German higher critics). He defines inspiration as

> that God-inbreathed influence or power which qualifies chosen men to receive and communicate the Revelation of God; or the supernatural influence of the Holy Ghost upon the powers of man through which he is enabled to apprehend clearly and to communicate what God has manifested to him.[22]

Reflecting the contemporary controversy over the doctrine of inspiration, Miller devotes considerable attention to validating his claim that all Scripture is inspired. As testimony for the inspiration of the Old Testament, Miller cites God's direct communication with Adam, the patriarchs, Moses, and the prophets; the prophetic formula, "Thus saith the Lord God of hosts"; and the testimony of Jesus and the Apostles. As a general deduction for the inspiration of the New Testament, Miller asserts (on the basis of the priority of the New Testament revelation in Christ): "Whatever characteristics of infallible truth the Old Testament possesses to recommend itself to us, the New possesses with an equal degree."[23] He does argue, however, that the inspiration of the New Testament can be specifically demonstrated by (1) Jesus' claim to possess all power (Matt. 28:18), (2) the commissioning of the apostles by "such a superior authority," (3) Jesus' promise to guide the apostles into all truth by the Spirit, and (4) the apostles' conviction that they were under the guidance of the Spirit.[24] In addition, Miller upholds that three other "unimpeachable witnesses"—history, miracle, and prophecy—should be sufficient to establish the veracity and consequently the inspiration of Scripture for any "fair critic."[25]

The doctrine of plenary or verbal inspiration calls for Miller's special attention. He seeks to arrive at a mediating position between an undue stress on the divine disclosure of the exact words of Scripture (emphasized by fundamentalists) and the opposite emphasis on the distinctive mode of expression used by each writer (highlighted by liberals). He therefore held that in some cases God did make known the very words to be used by the writers of Scripture. In other instances, however, the choice of words and manner of expression were distinctively those of the writer. Yet even in such cases, the Holy Spirit guided the writer in his selection of the material to be recorded and influenced him to use "just such language as was adequate to express the truth intended." Thus, plenary inspiration is not dependent upon God's making known the very words of Scripture.[26]

Though Miller considered the above questions concerning the nature of Scripture quite important, he cautioned that the fundamental purpose of Scripture was realized only in the search *to know the will of God*. This search demands that Christians approach Scripture in "the true spirit of Bible study." Such a spirit includes: (1) the deep conviction of the truth of the Bible, (2) "the *thorough conviction* that we have personally to do with the contents of the Bible," (3) a childlike faith, and (4) a spirit of prayer.[27]

Miller's respected exegetical ability derived, no doubt, from his commitment to some basic hermeneutical rules. He worked from three major premises: (1) "Every passage has but one true meaning." (2) "There is, therefore, a unity of Biblical truth." (3) "The meaning of each passage is capable of being investigated."[28] Miller advocated the use of any light which historical and literary criticism could shed upon the text. In addition, he insisted that one's interpretation must be contextual and take into account the general teaching of Scripture.[29] Characteristic of Miller's approach to Scripture is his insistence that we "take our stand on the New Testament as the Word of God" and not squander our time on idle speculations or quibbles about things of doubtful value.[30]

The Holy Spirit guides believers in the understanding of the Word

It is noteworthy that Miller gives far more attention to the inspiration of and interpretive tools for Scripture than do preceding Brethren writers while he devotes far less attention to the Spirit's relationship to the proper understanding of the Word than his predecessors. This shift is to be expected, however, given the controversy regarding the inspiration of Scripture in his day.

What Miller does say about the relation between the Word and the Spirit is entirely consistent with the Reformed-Anabaptist-Pietist heritage of the Brethren. Miller holds that "until the darkened understanding of the mind has been illuminated by the Holy Spirit the individual is unfit to explain the word of God to others."[31] Hence, it is through the Holy Spirit's influence that the Word becomes the guide for believers. Miller likewise insists that the test of the genuineness of the Spirit's witness must be found in the Word of God. "The witness of the Holy Spirit and that of our own spirit dare not contravene the spoken word."[32]

The early church provides testimony for the practices of the apostolic Church

The argument that played such a key role in Mack's and, to a lesser extent, Nead's authority structure—the example of the early church provides a normative pattern for later expressions of the church—is nearly nonexistent in Miller's writings. Miller does appeal to this apologetic a few times when he marshals evidence for the Brethren practices of trine immersion and threefold communion. For example, he affirms that "the universal testimony of all antiquity is that *Trine Immersion* was the practice of the Apostolic Church."[33] Yet such phrases as "the example of Christ and the Apostles" and "the example of the first Christians" are extremely sparse in Miller's writings. It would seem that the traditional appeal to the example of the early church was weakened somewhat by the demise of the claim of a direct link to the apostolic church through the Waldenses and by the emphasis in the Brethren Church on progression.

The church guides the growth of its Members

Like Mack and Nead, Miller holds that the church has been entrusted with several special powers. The church derives its authority from Christ and the Spirit. Christ himself is the builder of the church while the Holy Spirit vivifies the entire divine corporation. The body of Christ "has interpretative and executive powers under the direction of her Lord and the enlightenment of the indwelling Holy Spirit."[34] These powers (and responsibilities) include arbitrating difficulties between Christian brothers, preaching and teaching the Word as a means of perfecting God's people, and upholding the body of belief and the worship practices entrusted to the church.[35]

The role of Reason

Miller harbors none of the antipathy toward reason found among the early Brethren. Rather, he is far more typical of his age in mirroring a fairly optimistic view of the powers of reason. Reflective of such a view of reason are Miller's apologetic arguments for the existence of God, the reasonableness of revelation, and the veracity of Scripture[36] as well as his strong philosophic bent. For Miller, it was not a question of whether or not to use one's reasoning powers but whether or not one will seek to be logically consistent within the limits set by Scripture. Miller asserts:

> . . . the New Testament is and must remain our ultimate source of information and the final word of authority. One must of necessity hold some philosophic world-view. But there must be consistency in one's thinking and one's conclusions ought not contradict this philosophy and dare not be contrary to the Teachings of Christ and the New Testament Revelation.[37]

Miller thus differs from liberalism in that he rejects the power of autonomous reason to deal with the problems of human existence. He is quite clear on this point.

> Apart from Revelation, Reason is the ultimatum of man's capacity, and Conscience of his power. But neither reason nor conscience can solve the great problems of human life. Reason itself is by far too narrow in its range to be an unerring guide through life. Reason illumined, and Conscience quickened by a Divine Revelation will be adequate.[38]

Reason and man's sense of right are both aspects of man's God-likeness but they realize their potential only when renewed by the power of God's indwelling Spirit.

Summary

By combining the salient ideas in each of the above discussions, it is possible to discern the perspective from which Miller approached the theological task. Miller begins with the assumption of a personal God to whose creative works purpose and meaning necessarily inhere. The focus of God's purpose in history is to be found in Jesus Christ who has given to man a perfect, complete, and final revelation of God which has been recorded in the New Testament. It is God's ultimate purpose to sum up all things in Christ while His purpose for man is his recreation in the image of Christ. This divine purpose is effected through man's commitment to Christ's Word, the indwelling of the Holy Spirit, and the molding influence of the church. When renewed by the indwelling Spirit and guided by the Word, reason and conscience become significant means by which to realize God's purposes for one's life.

OVERVIEW OF MILLER'S THEOLOGICAL METHOD

A few brief comments concerning Miller's theological method will help to introduce the discussion of his theology proper. Miller's treatment of doctrine is well outlined and follows the traditional order found in Protestant theological works. In these characteristics as well as in his more philosophical/theological approach to doctrine, Miller differs from traditional Brethren methodology. Yet elements of a Biblical theological approach, in contrast to a purely systematic approach, are still to be found in Miller's method. His citation of corroborating Scripture is profuse; he avoids involved discussions of controversial topics, preferring instead simply to set forth the Biblical data; he does not make much use of the technical theological terms associated with systematic theology. In addition, Miller's discussions are almost devoid of explicit interaction with other theological positions and he cites the thought of very few scholars. (He refers to only one writer in the Brethren tradition—D. L. Miller of the Church of the Brethren.) His approach is to discern the meaning of Scripture passages relevant to his discussion with the exegetical tools at his disposal.

THE DOCTRINE OF GOD

Miller opens his discussion of the doctrine of God in *Christian Doctrine* with the observation that the Bible everywhere assumes the existence of God. Belief in the God revealed in Scripture and through Christ is fundamental to the Christian faith. Miller outlines the basic Christian conception of God by utilizing a quote from William Newton Clarke's *Outline of Christian Theology*: "God is the personal spirit, perfectly good, who in holy love, creates, sustains, and orders all."[39] (1) The nature of God is defined as Personal Spirit. The term "spirit" connotes "a living and active, a thinking, feeling and willing being who has personality." Hence God may be conceived to be self-conscious and self-directing; He possesses every essential of personality in its perfection. (2) The character of God is perfectly good. (3) The relation of God to all other existence is expressed in the words creation, providence, and government. (4) The motive of God in His relation to all other existence is that manifested in Jesus Christ: holy love.[40]

Miller posits that certain characteristics underlie all of God's activity: personality, life (independent existence), unity, eternity, incorruptibility, and immortality. Special emphasis is given to the characteristic of personality which Miller considers as basic to the supreme conception of God. Not only is such a conception of God necessary to distinguish Christianity from Monism and Pantheism, but the very facts of an intelligible universe and of the personal constitution of man (who bears God's image) cause one to postulate an intelligent Personality as Creator.[41]

God also bears certain unique attributes related to His *modes of activity*—omnipresence, omniscience, and omnipotence—and others related to His *moral qualities*—holiness, love, and immanence/transcendence. Miller develops further these latter attributes. "Holiness in God describes that standard of being and conduct which is the norm for Himself and for His children."[42] It includes such aspects as righteousness, faithfulness, purity, justice, goodness, and wisdom. Miller describes love as the divine attitude of grace toward His children. The supreme manifestation of divine love is in the sacrificial death of Jesus Christ which demonstrates that God's love is as just as it is merciful. Miller insists that immanence and transcendence must never be used exclusively; to do so distorts the nature of God. "Immanence without transcendence is pantheism and results in the denial of the personality of God. Transcendence without immanence is deism and leads to the denial of the providence of God."[43]

Miller observes that the Christian doctrine of the Trinity is a mystery which is simply set forth in Scripture. He makes no effort to develop the significance of the term "Trinity" by the use of an analogy but merely summarizes the relevant teaching of Scripture. (1) The unity or oneness of God is taught everywhere in the Scriptures. (2) This unity is one of essence. Scripture teaches that God, who is one in essence, subsists in three Persons truly and really distinct from each other. (3) The Trinity is a Revelation. The reality of the Trinity is a historical doctrine that is gradually revealed in the course of Scripture. Thus, there is a threefold self-revelation of God in Father, Son, and Holy Spirit. Each of the members of the Trinity is revealed as personal, divine, and co-equal.[44]

THE DOCTRINE OF CREATION—THE WORLD AND MAN

Miller's philosophical frame of mind is evident as he considers the meaning of God's creative works. Miller stresses that God is the sole and efficient cause of creation and that, as the Sustainer and Moral Governor of the world, He is vitally connected with the course of His creation. It is a fundamental conviction of Miller that God is guiding the world "toward the realization of an eternal and supreme purpose."[45] Miller posits that God's interests in His creation center in man. In spite of the fact that sin has entered the world contrary to the will of God,[46] human history is still tending toward the realization of God's ultimate goal—His Kingdom.[47] Meaning in this world is to be found in Christ. "We must hold that Jesus Christ is central in the plan of Creation, Providence and Redemption." Because of this fact, the whole world is meaningful and purposive; nothing can thwart the ultimate purpose of God in creation.[48]

Miller upholds man as God's "crowning work" of creation. As a creature man shares in the material order and is subject to it; as God's special child, man "rises in his self-conscious reason and freedom above all nature and shares likeness with God his maker." This divine image affords a standard by which man's entire conduct can be judged and "gives a supreme significance to and presages a supreme destiny for every man."[49] When he comes to the question of man's origin, Miller again adheres to the Biblical facts without trying to reconcile his position with scientific theory. Thus, Miller insists that man has a common origin. This point, together with man's spiritual capacity, divinely appointed destiny, and kinship with God, fixes a great chasm between man and animal. With regard to the origin of the individual soul, Miller is satisfied with the assertion that it results from a creative act of God.[50]

Miller maintains that, because man is made in God's image, he must share some of God's qualities of personality. Man therefore (1) is a free and personal Spirit, (2) possesses self-conscious reason, (3) is moral (recognizes right and wrong), and (4) is religious and worships. Miller focuses his attention on the first of these propositions. He upholds both God's sovereignty and man's freedom without feeling constrained to apologize for either. He does indicate, however, that God's sovereignty "does not make fatalism the doom of man" and that man "can never escape the sense of personal guilt for sin." Somewhat reminiscent of Luther's famous dictum on freedom and bondage (though approaching the idea from the pole of man's freedom), Miller holds: "The best Christians realize their truest freedom when they surrender in fullest measure to the will of the Heavenly Father."[51]

In his physical constitution man is wholly God's creation. While his body is part of the physical order and therefore subject to physical laws, man's spirit is immaterial, though the body is the medium of the spirit's expression in the earth-life.[52]

Miller perceives the Christian view of man as embracing a splendid destiny for this crown of God's creation—eternal life. This life is one of special quality and is epitomized in the life and character exhibited by Jesus Christ. It is thus marked by holiness of character, power (the absence of limitations of personal attainment and achievement), and blessedness beyond the power and fear of death.[53]

THE DOCTRINE OF SIN

In discussing the doctrine of sin in *Christian Doctrine*, Miller does not utilize the traditional Brethren/ Mennonite Biblical theological approach with its thorough discussion of the account of the fall in Genesis 3.[54] Rather, he avoids the somewhat controversial question of the origin of sin and deals instead with the nature and consequences of sin as taught in the New Testament. Miller holds that sin is the transgression of God's law and therefore is an offense against God Himself. The motives at the root of sin are self-will and self-interest. The New Testament does not teach that the flesh is inherently evil, but it does hold that sin has its seat in the flesh. Miller views sin as a debt involving both guilt and liability. According to Paul such guilt carries with it the penalty of death—not only physical death but also spiritual death. This latter death is the eternal loss of communion with God.[55]

Miller observes that the "common facts of human experience prove" that sin is universal (again Miller uses self-evident facts to build his case). Death, as the penalty of sin, has "reigned over all since the creation of man[56] and Adam's fall." According to Paul sin has entered the world through one man and has passed unto all men since all have sinned.[57]

In his discussion of the imputation of sin, Miller takes a somewhat liberal slant and bypasses the traditional Brethren/Anabaptist resolution of the problem. He acknowledges that "the unity and solidarity of the race and the power of heredity in the moral sphere of life must be taken into account." But he rejects the idea that Paul teaches "that newly born children are guilty sinners before God and therefore objects of His wrath. Guilt is not inherited nor transmitted." What is inherited is "a tendency to sin. We begin with a predisposition toward sin. A bias toward sin is propagated. There is entailed upon each life a moral inheritance from all the past."[58] Nevertheless, Miller distances himself from any liberal notion of the perfectibility of mankind through moral and social development by averring: "The one phase of human inability which we can assert with positive certainty is that man can not save himself. Jesus is the only Savior."[59]

THE DOCTRINE OF REDEMPTION

Introduction

Unlike Mack and Nead, who stressed the distinctive Brethren practices of baptism, the Lord's Supper, and the ban, Miller focuses his attention on the doctrines of redemption and salvation in all his doctrinal writings. Miller sets the stage for his discussion of Christ's person and redemptive work in *Christian Doctrine* by presenting four propositions which summarize man's need and God's provision for salvation. (1) The fact of sin makes redemption imperative. (2) Self-redemption is not possible.[60] (3) There is no redemption save that centering in Jesus Christ. (4) The redemption provided is of God.[61]

For Miller the person and work of Christ are inseparable, for "the main object of the incarnation is . . . found in the accomplishment of the purpose of Christ."[62] He therefore opens his consideration of redemption with a discussion of the person of Christ. This discussion follows a conservative Protestant outline of the topic.

The person of the Redeemer

His Messiahship

Miller first devotes his attention to a demonstration of the contention that Jesus is the Messiah of the Old Testament promises. He develops his case through the cumulative force of five basic points: (1) The Redeemer is the Messiah of the Old Testament. Jesus claimed to be this Messiah. (2) Jesus is demonstrated to be this Messiah by the fulfillment of Old Testament prophecy. (3) Jesus is shown to be the promised Messiah by the types and symbols employed in the Old Testament and the worship of God's people and house. Significant here is the typical quality of the offices of Melchizedek and Moses and of the ritual connected with the great Day of Atonement. That Jesus was the Messiah is also shown (4) by what He was in His person and (5) by the Messianic works wrought by Him.[63]

The doctrine of the incarnation

Miller observes that the doctrine that God in Christ Jesus has manifested Himself in the flesh possesses several important implications. (1) Kinship between God and Man. There is implied in this doctrine a kinship between God and man (often designated in Scripture as the image and likeness of God) which inheres especially in the spiritual constitution of man.

This spiritual kinship or likeness means that God can communicate with and make Himself known to man. The supreme expression of this communication is the condescension of deity, in assuming human form, in order to reveal the will of God. (2) The Kenosis. The phrase "emptied himself" in Philippians 2:7 does not mean the Son divested himself of any essential qualities or attributes of divine personality. Rather (note the conservative view expressed), it means "the voluntary renunciation of his rightful position of equality with the Father and the laying aside of the glory that belonged to him by virtue of his eternal Sonship."[64] (3) Our Lord's Preexistence. Miller cites John 1:1ff.; Philippians 2:5-11; and Hebrews 1:1ff. in affirming that the unique relation that subsisted between God and Jesus had existed from eternity. (4) The Miraculous Conception. Both Matthew and Luke testify that the birth of Jesus was occasioned without a human father and that the moving cause of the conception was the Holy Spirit.[65]

Miller's conservative, Biblical approach to the above issues is also reflected as he considers Christ's divine and human natures. Miller holds that the humanity assumed by Deity in the incarnation was a perfect, true, and real humanity. Likewise, Christ's deity was absolute and perfect. Though Jesus was tried during His earthly existence, He lived a life that was sinless, thereby distinguishing Him from all other men.[66]

Our Lord's exaltation

Miller takes a conservative Protestant approach to the subject of Christ's exaltation. He summarizes the teaching as follows:

> His [Christ's] humiliation ended in his death. Thereupon follows the resurrection as not only proof of his Messianic calling but also the sign and seal of God upon his gracious Mediatorial work. Next in order is the Ascension which follows as a necessary condition to his administration of His Mediatorial office in God's redemptive scheme. Glorification, or the re-investing of the eternal Son with the glory which he had with the Father before the world was, is the fitting climax in our Lord's supreme exaltation.[67]

Curiously, Miller does not add Christ's second coming (which he affirmed) as a fourth stage of Christ's exaltation. Rather, he subsumes this event under glorification. (He may be reacting to the preoccupation with this doctrine in Fundamentalist circles.)

The work of the Redeemer

Miller indicates that the doctrine of redemption properly includes not only the salvation of men but also "the ground upon which that salvation rests and the source whence it proceeds as a divinely bestowed gift upon man." He disavows any desire to formulate a theory of the atonement, preferring instead to "state the facts relating to the doctrine."[68]

Miller holds that God's provision for man's salvation arises from a twofold motive: grace (or love) and righteousness. Thus, salvation issues from God's freely bestowed favor and love but it also demonstrates God's absolute conflict with sin. Grace and wrath (the divine disapproval of sin) are viewed as integral aspects of the Holy Love of God (which Miller sees as God's basic character in relation to His creatures).

Jesus Christ is the divinely appointed agent of God's redemptive work. There is a perfect unity of purpose between the Father and Son in this work, for Scripture teaches both that God sent His Son as the world's Savior and that Jesus gave Himself willingly as an offering for sin. Jesus' obedience to the call and will of the Father in this world mission is an act of His own choosing.[69]

The atoning efficacy of Jesus Christ's life and Death

Introduction

Miller underscores the point that Jesus' entire life must be seen as part of His redemptive work. "The death [of Christ] cannot be separated from the whole life that went before nor from the completing acts of the redemptive process and purpose of God that followed after."[70] Likewise, Jesus' death was no unforeseen accident but an essential part of the original and eternal purpose of God. Throughout the New Testament Jesus' death is intimately connected with God's plan to save man from his sin.[71]

Atonement for sin

Miller summarizes the teaching of the New Testament concerning the meaning of Christ's death under five statements drawn from Scripture. (1) Christ died for us. Miller feels constrained to address the question of the vicarious aspect of Jesus' death at length. For him, Christ's death for us bears no technical or legal overtones; it was done in our behalf. Miller affirms that there is a profound vicarious element in Jesus' death. But he rejects the views that man's guilt was transferred to Jesus and that He was punished on the basis of this transferred guilt. He insists that guilt attaches only to sin committed and to him who commits it; in no way can it be transferred. Philo-

sophical considerations were also behind Miller's position.

> In the judgment of the writer, to transfer, were that possible, the guilt and penalty of one to another who knew no sin and was utterly innocent and thus attempting to make him the object of God's wrath, not only violates these moral distinctions but it contradicts God's justice.[72]

Miller argues that Christ is our substitute in that He, the sinless and guiltless One, took our place and paid the penalty deserved by our guilt by suffering its punishment. Christ's bodily dying thus delivers us from spiritual, but not physical, death. His death is therefore "symbolic of the death from which he saves us"; it is not strictly and literally the same. By His death Jesus has met the ends of our sin and penalty "and on the ground thereof he pardons our sins and remits our punishment." Thus, "instead of dealing with a sinner on the basis of retributive justice he [God] deals with him on the basis of a gracious accomplishment of the ends of his moral government."[73]

Miller considers more briefly other New Testament statements concerning Christ's death which further illuminate his position. (2) Christ died for all. The merit of Christ's atoning death avails for all. (3) Christ died the righteous for the unrighteous. Through all the circumstances connected with his death, Christ remained the righteous One. (4) He was made sin for us. Christ was treated as (not made) a sinner; He was a sinner not in a personal but in a representative manner. (5) Christ became a curse for us. Jesus was cursed not in the sense that He became the object of God's wrath but as a result of the shame of being hung on the cross.[74]

The death of Jesus Christ viewed as a covenant

Miller cites both the eucharistic passages in the Gospels and Paul's writings and the relevant passages in Hebrews in affirming that the shedding of Christ's blood forms the basis of a new, eternal covenant between God and man.[75]

Special aspects of the atonement

Miller gives particular attention to three terms used in the New Testament which accentuate different phases of Christ's atoning work: propitiation, redemption, and reconciliation. He integrates the Scriptural teaching on these terms into the following summary statement:

In the voluntary offering of Jesus Christ as a ransom for the sins of the many we have an everlasting redemption brought in, and upon which offering as a ransom redemption is effected. Further we may add that faith upon man's part brings him into a relation of gracious acceptance with God and adoption into sonship.[76]

Our Lord's mediatorial Ministry

Miller develops one further aspect of Christ's redemptive work: His mediatorial ministry. He notes that the mediatorial ministry of Christ may be seen as beginning with His incarnation, for He came as the mediator of the divine gift of salvation. In a stricter sense, however, Christ's mediatorial ministry began after His passion for it was by His death that a new covenant was established.

Essentially, this new covenant involves God's gracious undertaking to save sinful men upon the conditions of the salvation which He provides. His provision involves a universal atonement whose efficacy is conditional. Thus, God's offer of the pardon of sin is unlimited but human responsibility, involving the will to choose, enters in as a condition. Though it is God's good pleasure that all men be saved, He does not decree that the man who rejects Christ shall be saved. Miller further notes that the Holy Spirit, who makes compliance with the conditions of salvation possible, can be yielded to or resisted by man according to the New Testament.[77]

Christ's intercessory work, begun on earth and now continued in heaven, means that we have a mediator who is constantly working in behalf of our salvation. Miller notes that the mediatorial offices traditionally attributed to Christ—Prophet, Priest, and King—provide a useful depiction of Christ's mediatorial work. As Prophet, Christ reveals the will and word of God to man. He continues to exercise this prophetic function through the divinely appointed ministry of the church. As our High Priest, Christ "represents man before God in worship offering sacrifice in his behalf and offering prayer for him." As King, Christ is the exalted Lord with all authority in heaven and on earth.[78]

Miller briefly considers the nature of Christ's kingdom. He notes that Christ's authority is universal and that the church has been entrusted with the affairs of the kingdom in this age. Thus the church, through the ministry of the Holy Spirit, is the medium through which Christ works in this age. Miller further indicates that Christ's kingdom is a spiritual one. "The laws, blessings, and penalties of the kingdom are spiritual."[79]

Observations

As is evident from this overview of Miller's discussion of redemption, he was not dependent upon any one theological position. He borrowed insights from liberal and conservative theology. He sought to weave these insights into a unit that was Biblically based and philosophically consistent.

THE DOCTRINE OF SALVATION

Introduction

While Miller has paved new ground for the Brethren in his detailed discussion of Christology and the atonement, he follows more closely the traditional Brethren development of the doctrine of salvation. Miller begins his discussion by making it quite clear that Christ's death is the ground of man's salvation. His death has removed all the barriers between God and sinful man and, on man's part, salvation now becomes a matter of compliance with the conditions laid down by God.

The conditions of Salvation

Enlightenment

Miller, like Nead, indicates that enlightenment of a man's understanding by the preaching and teaching of the Word of God is necessarily the first step in salvation. Since the sinful mind is darkened in its understanding and alienated from God, the knowledge of the Word of God must be interpreted to the soul by the Holy Spirit. Miller insists, however, that one must maintain balance on this point, recognizing on the one hand that sinful man has "will and the power of choice" and on the other that no man can ascribe salvation to his own effort.[80]

Faith

Miller notes that faith is the first requisite on man's part since enlightenment is a condition "assured the soul by God's gracious and saving love." For Miller, faith consists of two essential aspects: belief and trust. Initially, faith involves belief in the facts of the Gospel; they must be assented to as true. Yet this "historical faith" is not sufficient to meet the required condition. One must also yield loyal and willing assent to and place unfaltering trust in Christ. Such commitment to Christ will result in obedience to Him and the demands of the Gospel as well as a mystical and spiritual union with Him. Such a view of faith necessarily comprehends "a course of life, a conduct, a fidelity to a norm of righteousness and right living."[81]

Miller affirms that one may speak of faith as a special gift of God and of the Holy Spirit. It grows out of testimony borne to the facts of the Gospel and therefore is dependent on the hearing of the Gospel. The personal object of faith is the Lord Jesus Christ, though Scripture also speaks of believing in the Gospel and God Himself. The benefits and results of the exercise of faith include (1) obedience to the will of God, (2) purification of the heart, (3) the remission of sins (note the significant break from the nineteenth century emphasis), and (4) the blessing of a vital and personal relation with Christ.[82]

Repentance

Miller considers the point that came in for a good deal of discussion during the previous century in Brethren circles: the relation between faith and repentance. He views these as the positive and negative sides of conversion. Thus, faith in Jesus as Messiah can be seen as the converse of turning from evil and toward God. Each is impossible without the other.[83]

Miller identifies a number of "moving causes" leading to repentance: (1) godly sorrow (as an emotion, sorrow cannot be equated with spiritual change), (2) the goodness of God, (3) the long-suffering of God, (4) chastening and reproof, (5) the appeal of heaven, and (6) the coming judgment. Whereas these causes may or may not be present for repentance to occur, there are certain elements which are essential antecedents to repentance. These include faith in the person and work of Jesus Christ, consciousness of the burden and penalties of sin, and a genuine desire for a new life. Thus, some knowledge of the Gospel is necessary for repentance to take place.

Repentance itself is depicted in Scripture as a change that affects the whole of man. It involves a change of mind, will, thought, and heart, i.e., a complete surrender of one's self to the will of God. It likewise involves a change of life and conduct which must be evidenced in a new life. Consequently, there must be in repentance a repudiation of sin and open confession of Christ as well as a turning to God and the desire to lead a life conformable to the requirements of divine sonship. Connected with repentance (and other conditions) is the divine promise of remission of sins.[84]

Obedience

True to the historic Brethren emphasis, Miller insists: "Where there has been a genuine faith and repentance, obedience follows without quibble or hesitancy."[85] Miller holds that a willing obedience to the whole will of God is necessary from the very threshold of the new life if the blessings of salvation are to be received. Three obligations in particular are present at the genesis of the Christian experience.

Confession. While faith and repentance pertain to the heart and inner life, confession is the first outward expression of one's desire to break from the old life. Confession is the open declaration before men that one is convinced of the facts relating to the person and work of Christ and that one is ready to fulfill the obligations thereby assumed.[86]

Baptism. Miller sees baptism as the second command (he emphasizes that it is a command) imposed by the New Testament at the beginning of the Christian life. Miller reveals a significant shift from the view of baptism which dominated Brethren thought during the previous century. He admits that baptism may not be "an additional condition of salvation viewed in its relation to faith and repentance"; it may be "only the expression and completion of a penitent faith."[87] He instead takes a position similar to that of Mack: a penitent faith followed by a full and complete obedience is to be viewed as a single condition upon which ensues salvation. Yet, in what may be seen as a mediating position between those of Mack and Nead, Miller stresses: "when we speak of the separate acts of obedience required as a condition to salvation, baptism stands in the most vital relation to the believer's initiation into the body of Christ."[88] Miller's uncharacteristic vagueness on this point is significant, for it reflects the continued weakening of the former position which emphatically upheld baptism as a condition of salvation. The combination of Miller's less dogmatic position in his class lectures at the seminary, the "new apologetic" of Yoder and Gillin (emphasizing the inner meaning of the ordinances—see pp. 174–175), and the increasing impact of revival theology (salvation is tied to confession of faith in Christ) served to undermine the view which dominated nineteenth century Brethren thought. It is noteworthy that this development was paralleled by the general disuse of the term "means of grace" in a technical, overly objective manner. In fact, by the 1920s and 30s the term is almost nonexistent in Brethren literature.[89]

Miller maintains that subjects for baptism must have a knowledge of the Lord, faith in Him as the Savior, and a sincere repentance. Miller stresses the symbolic nature of baptism (another indication of a switch in emphasis *from* the inward graces which are conditioned upon the reception of baptism *to* the inner spiritual realities to which baptism testifies). Hence "baptism is the outward sign which signifies the inward work of grace wrought in the heart of a believer." It is a symbol of the forgiveness of sins, the new birth, and the death and burial of the old man and the resurrection to newness of life. Miller does continue the strong emphasis upon baptism as the initiatory rite into the church and therefore advocates the rebaptism of believers baptized by a mode other than trine immersion. In rebaptism the motive for the rite becomes "obedience to the divine command."[90]

Confirmation. Miller maintains that confirmation or the laying on of hands is the final act of obedience required of believers at the threshold of the new life (he cites Heb. 6:1-2). It is the outward sign which signifies that the baptized believer has received the gift of the Holy Spirit. Concerning this gift Miller states: "whatever of the Spirit's leading one may have to be brought to repentance, whatever of the Spirit's empowering to have faith and of the Spirit's grace in baptism—such an one is yet to receive the anointing and sealing of the Holy Spirit." It is this anointing and sealing (2 Cor. 1:21-22; Eph. 1:13-14; 3:16; 4:30; 1 John 2:27) to which confirmation testifies.[91]

Concluding remarks

Miller ends his discussion of the conditions of salvation with the caution: "we must not lose the truth that God's gracious work accompanies every step in this process representing the human side of the beginning of the new life."[92]

The nature of Salvation

For Miller, salvation was a process which encompassed "deliverance from the present evil world and its sin and the enjoyment of all the blessings of children of God."[93] In this section Miller thus considers the spiritual transformation and new life enjoyed by the believer.

The beginning of the new life

In commencing his discussion of the initial aspects of the new life, Miller underscores the point that the order of the several phases of the new life are not fixed in Scripture. Indeed, these phases may be said to be contemporaneous. However much theology would desire to provide a definite arrangement, "it seems out of the question in the soul's experience to indicate the priority of one or the other."[94]

Regeneration

Miller defines regeneration as the act of God, wrought by the Holy Spirit, "by which the new life after the likeness of the life of Christ is begun in a man."[95] Though acknowledging that "the work of God is preliminary to that of man" in regeneration, Miller unequivocally affirms that there is both a divine and human side in such spiritual processes. "Indeed his [God's] purpose and activity attain their end only in-so-far as human activity responds to the divine call."[96] Thus, Scripture often sets side by side the divine acts of calling, electing, and foreordaining men and the human acts of believing, repenting, and obeying. Scripture by no means disregards the will of man in setting forth the doctrines of divine election and foreordination.

Miller holds that the divine work of the new birth is necessitated by the unregenerate man's moral inability to free himself from the bondage of sin and death and to perform the will of God. All men have incurred guilt and are under the condemnation of sin due to their own personal choice of evil.[97] In regeneration this moral inability is overcome not by the addition of any "new or additional faculties or powers." Rather, this marvelous change is effected by the Holy Spirit through the moral powers present even from birth.[98]

Scripture presents a variety of figures and descriptive terms to depict this change. These include illumination, a knowing of God, passing from death unto life, union and fellowship with Christ, a partaking of the divine nature, i.e., godliness, putting on of the new man, a change into the divine image, a renewal, a resurrection, and a new birth. What these figures depict is a "mystical and spiritual, yet real and vital change that takes place in the life of every person born again."[99]

Justification

Whereas Brethren writers during the eighteenth and nineteenth centuries gave only brief attention to the doctrine of justification, Miller gives it detailed consideration. He begins by noting God's purpose in giving the law: to make it clear to man that he needed a salvation beyond all that he could do. Had man been able to maintain perfect obedience to the law, he would have merited eternal life. Yet man is without the strength to obey and is condemned by the law for failure to exhibit the perfect and complete obedience required. The law therefore represents a preparation for the Gospel. For the Christian, who has received the Gospel, the law is abolished not in part but as a whole.[100]

In Paul's usage, "to justify" means to declare or pronounce just and therefore to be acceptable to God. It does not mean to make just for that would be a mere fiction, nor does it mean to acquit in the ordinary sense, for that would be a declaration that man had done no wrong. Rather,

> righteousness is the act of God in which a man is declared acceptable to Him. Righteousness is the state of acceptance upon which a man enters upon being divinely approved. The righteousness of Christ is reckoned to him by faith. God's free grace is the source of our justification. The sacrifice of Christ is the "meritorious ground" upon which God proceeds. It is apart from the works of the law that a man is justified and yet it is by "good works" that he is perfected. Jas. 2:14–16.[101]

Adoption

Miller observes that we receive the adoption of sons by faith in Christ Jesus. By adoption we are brought into the family of God, invested with the privileges of sonship, and assured of an inheritance with God's children.[102]

The benefits salvation Confers

Miller holds that salvation, as technically used in the New Testament, means "negatively, to save from the penalties of Messianic judgment; and positively, to bestow the blessings of God through the Messiah."[103] This definition provides Miller with an outline for his discussion of the benefits of salvation.

Negative aspects

(1) The most striking term with reference to salvation viewed negatively is the forgiveness of sins. When a sinner turns to God in repentance and faith, divine forgiveness is assured. Forgiveness is depicted in Scripture as the removal of the consequences of sin, escape from the power of sin, the putting to death of sin in the believer's life, the removal of enmity between man and God, and personal reconciliation with God through Jesus Christ. Negatively, salvation is also characterized as a (2) deliverance from this present evil world and (3) deliverance from the wrath to come.[104]

Positive aspects

The New Testament variously describes the positive aspects of the benefits bestowed by God's salvific work. The main positive features include (1) cleansing and purification of the soul, (2) membership in the kingdom of God, (3) sonship (which includes first the idea of individual salvation but, consequently, definite social implications), (4) union with Christ, (5) the impartation of the gift of the Spirit (which becomes a "certain proof of divine acceptance"), and (6) the impartation of eternal life.[105]

The development of the new life in Christ

Miller considers the new life in Christ from the perspective of several New Testament themes which tend to overlap but which emphasize different aspects of the Christian life: (1) the Christian life viewed in terms of growth and renovation, (2) sanctification, and (3) communion with God.

Characteristics of the Christian life

Miller is fully in keeping with the traditional Brethren view of salvation as not just an event at the outset of the Christian life but also a process whose goal is the ideal exemplified by Christ when he affirms:

> The saving work of grace conceived of as beginning in the new life in Christ Jesus is not regarded as fully accomplished in these [above] initial acts. These are indispensable and primary conditions to salvation. . . . We find that the New Testament holds before the believer an ideal of life and character, of behavior and accomplishment, to be attained in Jesus Christ. This attainment is a gradual and prolonged process.[106]

Miller relates several truths, with regard to this growth process, which are noteworthy. First, he observes that progress in the new life in Christ varies from person to person. While for some it may be like a "leap into superb dimensions of spiritual experience," for others it is like "the tedious climbing of the altar stairs." Second, whatever progress we may make, we must feel, like Paul, the vast gap that lies "between the ideal in Christ and the actual attainment of any moment" in our lives on earth.[107] Third, the goal of renovation cannot be reached by a single act. Throughout the Christian's whole life he is acquiring in character the perfection and righteousness with which he is accounted in justification. Finally, there is both a human and a divine side to the renovation process. The human side involves not only the negative aspects of self-denial and abstinence from sin (Miller depicts this aspect as cleansing) but also the positive "effort to attain by divine grace and approval by a course of conduct such as is defined by the will of God unto a righteousness" like that exemplified in

Christ (Miller describes this aspect as renewal).[108] Miller is emphatic, however, that all such endeavor must be coupled with divine help. Note should be taken of Miller's use of traditional Brethren themes in this discussion—self-denial, viewing the ideal of the new life as Christ, maintaining a balance between the human and divine aspects of the new life.

Sanctification

Miller observes that the dominant idea in the New Testament words relating to sanctification is that of separation unto, consecration to, or setting apart for the service of God. Sanctification is a divine work wrought by God for and in behalf of the believer. As such, it is closely related to, though distinct from, the act of justification. The believer must ever seek to attain, by the Spirit's power, that righteous character which was counted to him by faith. Miller views sanctification as embracing the whole man. Thus, one's whole life, with the thinking, feeling, and willing self, is to be not only cleansed from unrighteousness but also wholly consecrated to God for His purpose and work. The ideal to be attained in sanctification is the perfection of personal character. Progress toward this ideal is attained gradually and is made possible only by the work of the Holy Spirit. Miller employs several different modes for describing further the nature of sanctification: it involves the restoration of the divine image in the soul; it is the attainment of holiness; it secures for the believer a character corresponding to his high calling in Christ Jesus.

From the divine side, sanctification is preparation for the Master's service and must proceed from God. In the highest New Testament sense God both prepares a man for service by cleansing him and consecrates him for His work. Sanctification, whether viewed negatively as cleansing from sin and guilt and as breaking of sin's power or positively as setting apart for God's service, will be complete only at the revelation of the Lord. Miller concludes his discussion of sanctification by cautioning that the danger of apostasy is ever present. The state of perfect divine acceptance is attained, maintained, and perfected by faith. Interestingly, Miller does not want to develop a dogmatic position on entire or complete sanctification, though he considers this point within the context of his warning against apostasy.[109]

Communion with God

Miller devotes a good deal of attention to a motif that was strong among the early Brethren but had been overshadowed by the definite objective and external bias (derived from preoccupation with the ordinances and marks of the separated life) of the German Baptists and of many in the Brethren Church. Miller holds that communion with God is made possible because of "the likeness that obtains between God and his Spirit-filled child."[110] This spiritual kinship with God rests on the adoption attained on the basis of faith in Jesus Christ. Miller further describes the nature of communion with God by noting the spiritual qualities that are integral to it. Communion with God involves (1) the sharing of the divine ideals in union with God, (2) unfaltering trust in Him, (3) a life of prayer, (4) genuine worship of God, and (5) the internal witness of the Spirit (which should be tested, however, with the Word).[111]

Notable characteristics of the life in Christ

Miller concludes his consideration of the doctrine of salvation by describing the preeminent qualities of the Christ-like life. (1) Love. God's children are to reflect His character of love, visibly demonstrated in Christ, to both their brethren in the Lord and their neighbors in the world, including their enemies. (2) Righteousness. Believers are likewise to mirror in their life and conduct the righteous character of God. (3) Humility. Humility is denoted by a spirit of submission to God's will and of subordination of one's own interests for the sake of others. The Christian life is further characterized by (4) a variety of virtues and graces which add beauty, power, and worth to our earthly lives and (5) the fruit of the Spirit which, if present, provides visible evidence of the Spirit's inner domination and control.[112]

Observations

It is noteworthy that, in his discussion of salvation, Miller interweaves traditional Brethren motifs with developments of themes frequently slighted by previous Brethren writers. For example, Miller devotes considerable attention to justification and sanctification, terms which found sparse discussion during the previous century. Yet he evidences complete fidelity to traditional Brethren emphases such as the ordering of the initial aspects of salvation (enlightenment, faith, repentance, obedience to the command of baptism), viewing salvation as both an event and a process, holding the inner and outer aspects of the faith in dialectical tension, upholding Christlikeness as the goal of the Christian life, and maintaining communion with God as an integral part of the salvation experience. Miller can also be credited with aiding the trend to correct the objective, external emphasis of the previous century. In his view of the ordinances as essentially symbols expressing an inner faith and his emphasis on communion with God, Miller not only helped to provide a better balance between the inward/spiritual and outward/practical but he can also be seen as recovering insights that were important to the faith of the early Brethren.

THE DOCTRINE OF THE CHURCH

Introduction

As with all other prior major Brethren writers, Miller perceives the church playing an indispensable role in the new life set forth in the New Testament. He maintains that it was Jesus' intention early in His public ministry to "form a society into which he would gather his faithful disciples." This intention is exemplified in his choice of the twelve and His announcement of the founding of the church in Matthew 16:18. Hence, the faith founded by Jesus is to be conceived preeminently as a life to which there is a social-side—the Christian church.[113]

The church, its meaning and Usages

Miller indicates that the word ἐκκλησία means simply an assembly or congregation. As used in the New Testament, it refers to both the local and general manifestations of God's people.

The composition, purpose, and organization of the Church

Miller defines the church as "a body of believers in Christ who have been called out of the world, who have been born again of the Holy Spirit and are, therefore, alive in Christ, and who, under the authority of Christ, are accomplishing the will of God on earth and among men."[114] God has commissioned His people with the task of making known His wisdom, the Gospel. In consequence of this commission, the church bears the responsibility of not only evangelizing the world with the message of Christ but also overseeing the spiritual upbuilding and nurture of its members. Both of these tasks necessitate the church's fidelity to the deposit of truth entrusted to it.[115]

It is without question that the New Testament church had an organization, for it had officials, rules for its governance, and clearly defined purposes. Miller further emphasizes that the New Testament

considers attachment to this organization as normative: "The picture of the Church as the body of Christ precludes the possibility of any Christian living apart from the church."[116]

The offices of the Church

Miller adduces two principles from the New Testament which establish the importance of the ministry. First, there is a church of "divine appointment founded by Christ, beloved of God, called and commissioned to do a special work in the world." Second, "the ministerial office exists in the church by divine appointment and represents officially and authoritatively the continuance in the church of the permanent elements of her prophetic and pastoral, her teaching and evangelistic functions."[117] Miller holds that these functions have been entrusted to the bishop/elder.[118] The only other permanent offices of the church are those of deacon and deaconess. All officers are to remember that they are not the rulers but the servants of the church. Miller makes one other statement of interest relative to the ministry (in light of the fact that the Brethren Church has made significant changes in the procedure for ordaining ministers following the split in the 1880s): the organization of the ministry with its grades, training required, distribution, and limitations is not spelled out in the New Testament but is "left to the historical development and the exigencies and needs of the times."[119]

Discipline of the Church

Reflecting the trend in the Brethren Church toward less disciplined congregations, Miller devotes only brief attention to the matter of discipline. His discussion follows traditional Brethren thought, however. The church is entrusted with the matters of discipline affecting her members. Personal differences are to be settled according to the principles of Matthew 18:15–17.

Grievous moral offences require severe discipline according to 1 Corinthians 5:7–11 and 2 Corinthians 2:5–7. The penitent are to be restored. Characteristic of Miller's irenic spirit is his insistence that those matters causing divisions and dissension in the church are to be turned away from.[120]

Ordinances of the Church

Unlike Brethren writers of the previous two centuries, Miller gives only minimal attention to the distinctive Brethren practices of trine immersion and threefold communion. Yet his discussion of both is thoroughly consistent with traditional Brethren formulations.

Baptism

Miller is emphatic that trine immersion was the all but universal practice of the church for the first four centuries.[121] In an *Evangelist* article in 1896 he provided abundant evidence for the contention that the original mode of baptism was immersion. He cites the "sum and spirit of Scriptural teachings," the practice of the Apostolic age, the use of the word βαπτίζω in contemporaneous literature, and the opinions of numerous leading scholars.[122] For support of the threefold action, Miller cites the witness of Tertullian and Augustine as well as the elliptical construction of the Great Commission.[123]

Communion

For the most part, Miller follows the "received tradition" with regard to communion. He conflates the Gospel accounts and that of Paul and argues that the order of the three parts should be feetwashing, love feast, and eucharist.[124] He sees the authority for threefold communion resting in "both the command and the example of our Lord Jesus Christ or of the Inspired Apostles." John 13 provides such support for the practice of feetwashing. This church ordinance is a fitting symbol of service (Miller nowhere notes the other meaning traditionally given to the rite by the Brethren—cleansing).[125]

Miller breaks with Brethren tradition when he argues that the term Lord's Supper refers to the entire communion service, not just the love feast. He does uphold the Brethren conviction, however, that the Last Supper was not the Jewish Passover. Miller argues that the love feast is to be considered a church ordinance for both Scriptural (Jude 12; 2 Pet. 2:13) and historical reasons (he cites the testimony of Tertullian, Origen, the Didache, and church histories). The meaning of the love feast is threefold. (1) "It symbolizes a pledge of Brotherhood founded upon Love." (2) "It is a symbol of Fellowship among the members of the Body of Christ." (3) "It is the type of the Marriage Supper of the Lamb."[126]

The authority for the observance of the eucharist is to be found in the words of institution by the Lord Himself, the practice of the apostolic church, and the almost unanimous witness of the Christian church. Miller delimits the "spiritual significance" of the bread and cup in four statements. (1) The eucharist service is a symbol of remembrance of Jesus Christ.

(2) The bread is a symbol of the body of Christ. As such, it presents Jesus as the living bread of which all true believers partake in the Communion and it also symbolizes the body of Christ as a sacrificial offering. (3) The cup is a symbol of the blood of Christ. The shed blood of Christ has two central meanings in the New Testament: it is connected with the inauguration of a new Covenant and it gives a sacrificial character to Jesus' death (He shed His blood for many for the remission of sins).[127]

Other ordinances

Miller briefly notes other New Testament ordinances practiced by the Brethren: the laying on of hands (see p. 206), the anointing of the sick, and the kiss of peace. With regard to the anointing service, Miller observes that "the Brethren church believes that the healing function of the church is perpetuated."[128]

Public Worship

Miller underscores the importance of public worship by noting that "both the precept and the example of Christ and the apostles encourage this necessary practice."[129] This means of grace offers every believer a great opportunity for spiritual uplift and encouragement.[130]

Marriage

The same high view of marriage which had obtained in every preceding period of Brethren history is to be found in Miller's discussions of the family. Marriage is a sacred, inviolable, divine institution (it is not merely a civil contract) which cannot be broken except for the sole ground of infidelity. "It is a mystical union between a man and a woman so close and intimate, so divinely effected and so spiritual in significance that Jesus declares that the two become one flesh."[131] The family and home that issue from this union are the very foundation of our civil, social, and moral life. Love is to be the great governing principle in all family life. Mutual respect and affection should be integral to every relationship in the family.

The State

In Miller's thought there is none of the sharp dichotomy between the church and state evidenced in Mack's thought and to a lesser degree in that of Nead. He notes that both Paul and Peter recognize the divine institution of government among men as well as the authority of its representatives. Further-more, in the American setting every citizen is an integral part of the state by its very constitution. The Christian thus bears an obligation to exercise the right to vote and to practice the right and just in relationship to all other men.

Miller does, nevertheless, uphold the necessity of a radical break with the spirit, values, and purposes of the present evil world order. This principle of non-conformity will express itself in several distinct ways. Christians should not bear arms in carnal warfare for natural aggrandizement.[132] They should swear no oaths in order to conform to the spirit of Jesus Christ. They should separate themselves from a world-spirit which manifests itself in the greed for gain, the sinful pleasures of life, and the improper clothing of one's person.[133]

ESCHATOLOGY

Introduction

Miller's independence from any one theological viewpoint is most clearly manifested in his discussion of eschatology. He is critical of emphases in both liberal and fundamentalist views of eschatology in his desire to remain faithful to what he considers the Biblical teaching on the subject.

Personal Eschatology

Miller holds that the separation of the wicked from the saints occurs at death. Though death is viewed in the New Testament as an enemy which all men must face, Christ's conquest over death means that those who are in Christ are able to share in His victory over death. Thus, for the Christian, death brings heavenly rest, the experience of the personal presence of Christ in glory, the crown of endless life, the joy of eternal service, and the blessedness of spiritual perfection.[134] Miller departed from the traditional Brethren/premillennial conception of the resurrec-tion in his belief that Christians would receive a resurrection body at death. This conviction was based primarily on 2 Corinthians 5:1–8 in which Miller sees Paul arguing that the souls of believers will not be left disembodied at death (he sees other Pauline texts harmonizing with this view: 1 Cor. 15:35–38; Phil. 1:21–24; 1 Thess. 3:13, 4:14).[135] "In this body, which God shall give, the saints shall realize the creative purpose of God, their highest perfection in Jesus Christ."[136]

Miller perceived the fate awaiting unbelievers at death as quite different. The New Testament depicts utter and hopeless ruin for the wicked beyond the grave. Miller notes that the New Testament is surpris-ingly silent about the resurrection of the wicked, but he infers it from John 5:29; Acts 24:15; and Revelation 20:12–13 and from the teaching of a general judg-ment.[137] The Judgment at Christ's Second Coming would be according to works. The doom of the wicked is certain and final: it is described as utter perishing from the face of the Lord; it involves the loss of everything that gives distinctive value and content to human life.[138]

Miller feels that the ultimate destiny of the wicked is a mystery not entirely revealed in Scripture. He sees three possible solutions to this problem: (1) uni-versalism, which does not satisfy the necessity of ridding the universe of sin's work, (2) conditional immortality and annihilation, which involves the in-conceivable notion of how the image of an undying and eternal God can be dissolved into nothingness, and (3) an eternal hell for the devils, angels, and unreconciled humanity, which involves the problem of reconciling the idea of an endless dualism in God's world with God's nature and purpose. Miller admits his own inability to come to a resolution of such issues and is content to allow the answers to unfold in God's own time.[139]

Corporate Eschatology

Miller's view of eschatology is, to a great extent, determined by four principles, most of which have been encountered earlier. These are: (1) a strict and consistent regard for the language used; (2) a compre-hensive New Testament view of any subject in hand; (3) distinction between what is certain and permanent and what is local or incidental; and (4) distinction between that which is essential to the life of Christ and that which is mere opinion or belief about Christ or His teachings.[140]

Miller sees the theme of the kingdom of God as the golden thread running through both Testaments. In contrast to liberalism, he carefully distinguishes the kingdom and the church. The church is the means or agency by which God is working out His plan in the present age. The kingdom, as the goal toward which God's plans for this age point, lies in the future.[141] Yet Miller also rejects "the fanciful divisions of time" advocated by many (he is thinking of dispensationalists no doubt). He sees only two divisions of time indicated in the New Testament: the present age, consummated in the kingdom of

Heaven, and the Age to Come. The last days in which we now live therefore began with the birth of Jesus. Jesus' earthly ministry began the process which will culminate with His second coming. Thus we are already, as a result of Christ's first coming, able to taste somewhat of the powers of the age to come.[142]

Miller deduces from the parables of the Ten Virgins and the Talents three conclusions relative to Christ's Second Coming: (1) they contemplate a long process of time between Christ's departure and return; (2) the Master may return at any moment; and (3) the hearers are admonished to be on guard to do their best. He also sees the return of Christ linked to the preaching of the Gospel in all the world, the salvation of the Jews, and (he admits as plausible) a great apostasy headed up by some anti-Christ.[143]

In his eschatological discussions, Miller either explicitly or implicitly rejects certain key tenets of dispensationalism. He challenges anyone to find the idea of a secret rapture prior to the tribulation anywhere in Scripture. He notes the words referring to Christ's second coming, παρουσία and φανέρωσις, denote personal presence and manifestation respectively and are used of His first coming as well. He holds that the great tribulation mentioned in the apocalyptic writings referred to the overthrow of Jerusalem and the persecution of the Jews. For Miller, the church is anything but a parenthesis. The process looking toward the consummation of God's kingdom began in the days of the apostles and involves the church as the means by which God is working out His plans in this age. He also tends to be critical of the concept of a millennium since it is not found in the didactic or narrative portions of Scripture.[144]

Miller holds that Christ's personal return will precipitate the final crisis which will usher in the Age to Come. At Christ's return the resurrection of the dead (presumably the wicked) and the judgment will occur. The present evil order of things will be overthrown; the re-creation of the material order will result in a new heaven and a new earth (Miller rejected the idea that the present earth would be completely destroyed); and the eternal kingdom of God will be established.[145]

Miller sees these eschatological considerations having practical value (though they do not affect conduct as essentially as other aspects of practical theology). First, they keep before us the facts that the present order will pass away and that we are presently strangers in it. Second, we are reminded that we must be connected with the plan of God and not fight against it. Third, they stress the fact of personal responsibility to Jesus Christ.[146]

Concluding Observations

From this discussion of J. Allen Miller's thought, several characteristics which gave a unique stamp to his work become quite evident. Miller sought to gain a comprehensive, unified picture of divine truth from which perspective he could better distinguish between what was of universal, permanent value and what was merely incidental and of secondary import. He therefore kept central in his thought the great purpose which God had determined for His world and creatures. For example, while exploring the question of how the problem of evil would be resolved (see p. 211), he stated:

> We shall, I think, steer clear of great difficulties if we rightly interpret the purpose of God, remember that there is no limit upon His grace or His goodness and that He was wise enough to plan a world that will ultimately meet His character and strong enough to accomplish that purpose.[147]

This concern led Miller to avoid controversial questions which he considered of secondary importance (the nature of man's creation, the origin of sin, the formulation of an exact theory of the atonement). He felt, no doubt, that those who became preoccupied with these issues were "losing the forest for the trees."

Miller's development of Christian doctrine combined the themes common to Protestant theology together with those which were distinctively Brethren. Miller therefore gave far more attention to the doctrines of God, Christ, the atonement, justification, and sanctification than did Mack and Nead. The result was a far more balanced presentation of Christian truth than is to be found in earlier Brethren works. It is true, however, that the traditional understanding of these themes of Protestant theology, taken for granted by the Brethren and most other Protestant groups through much of the nineteenth century, came under increasing attack during the late nineteenth and early twentieth centuries. This development made teaching on these themes all the more necessary. In spite of Miller's attention to themes not emphasized by Brethren in the past, he demonstrated great fidelity to the truths which had traditionally typified the Brethren, as can be seen in his discussions of salvation and the church. He even brought to the fore several emphases that had been obscured during the nineteenth century: a better balance between the inward and outward aspects of the ordinances and a recognition of the truth that the Christian life must contain a mystical, spiritual relationship with God denoted by the desire to have the character of Christ informed in one's own life.

Finally, Miller sought to gain light concerning God's Word from whatever source he could. Thus, citations from both liberal scholars (William Newton Clarke, William Adams Brown, George Barker Stevens) and conservative scholars (G. Campbell Morgan, A. T. Pierson, James Orr) appear in his works. Yet he remained free from both liberal and fundamentalist systems. He was bound only by his unwavering commitment to Scripture and the philosophical/theological world view developed by a reason enlightened by the Word and the Spirit. Though we may question some of Miller's theological conclusions, our dispute is with a belief gained by thorough study of the Word rather than by inheritance of a prevailing wind of doctrine.

Though no theological label can be attached to Miller, W. D. Furry probably comes as close as is possible to describing and depicting his theological position:

> By inheritance, as he often and with a high degree of satisfaction expressed it in private conversation and public address, by temperament and engrained character of mind, he could be best labeled neither conservative nor liberal alone in all moral and religious matters but rather a liberal conservative . . . This characteristic was . . . evident in his doctrinal positions and churchmanship. Always on both these points he was conservative. Yet again in these sermons and addresses [in *Christian Doctrine*] as well as in discussions on the floor of district and general Conferences he would express himself with views of surprising breadth. Once discussing doctrinal and denominational trends and shifting emphases touching the distinctive and historic beliefs and practices of the Church, Dr. Miller said . . . : "After all, whether conservative or liberal, the best way is to seek to do the right thing by remaining loyal to our original deposit of faith."[148]

Miller's Conception of Brethrenism

During the teens the term "Brethrenism" first came into vogue in the Brethren vocabulary to designate that which distinguished the church from other denominations. In his writings for the *Evangelist*, Miller, as much as any other person during his lifetime, seems to have been able to articulate those elements which constituted "Brethrenism."

Miller understood that the foundation for the church must always be the Word of God. This standard "must ever stand first in all Brethren theology, in all Brethren teaching and preaching. The teachings of that Word must determine the convictions that control life and conduct."[149] Yet Miller understood equally well that this credal standard needed to be reinterpreted for each new age. He challenged the church

to take the Gospel of Jesus Christ and interpret it anew to the men of our times in the terms of the life of our day. Here we have made mistakes in the past and are still making them. Such mistakes continued will be all but fatal to any marked degree of success in the days to come. Now it is not with the Gospel that we have to find fault. It is with our handling of the gospel that we must break. . . . What I am insisting upon now is that we should be less held by man's apprehension of the Gospel and his interpretation thereof than by the Gospel itself. We must take the Gospel as it comes from Jesus and give it to men as we find them today.[150]

These emphases give to Brethren thought both a conservative and a progressive quality. Yet, as Miller makes clear, it is a conservatism based on God's Word not man's traditional interpretation of it, while it is a progressivism that is guided by the Holy Spirit not by the spirit of the times.[151]

A second characteristic which Miller felt should typify the message of the church (it certainly is evident in his thought) is expressed during the liberal controversy in the church.

> . . . two things stand out in great boldness and prominence which mark a Brethren preacher. The first is this,—THE GREAT UNANIMITY WITH WHICH WE ACCEPT THE GENERALLY ACCEPTED TRUTHS OF PROTESTANTISM. But these do not make us BRETHREN any more than they make us Methodists or Baptists or Lutherans. . . . The second is this,—THE GREAT CONVICTION WITH WHICH WE HOLD TO AND PREACH AS ESSENTIAL PARTS OF THE GOSPEL WHAT OTHER PROTESTANT BODIES DISREGARD, NEGLECT OR REJECT. . . . To state our contention in other words it takes the WHOLE GOSPEL as the content of one's faith to make one truly Brethren,—shall I not say CHRISTIAN?[152]

This twofold mark gives to Brethren thought both a conforming and an exclusivistic quality. Yet both aspects are wholly determined by fidelity to God's Word.

In the same article as above, Miller stresses that commitment to the whole Gospel

> makes us dogmatic. It makes us doctrinal preachers. Mark the words and their order—*belief, conviction* then *character*. Also these words in their order, *the truths of the Gospel, their unequivocal acceptance* then *their fearless proclamation to men*. This means that character cannot be divorced from conviction and conviction grows out of one's beliefs. Therefore it does make all the difference possible what a man believes.[153]

Yet this statement emphasizing belief must be balanced with another stressing the resulting life and character.

> In seeking to characterize what I like to call the spirit and genius of Brethrenism I always find myself at a loss for

words. In the first place this is true because it is a LIFE that I am trying to depict. And what makes this all the more difficult at least for me is the fact that it is not the life of a particular man or woman but the life of a community that I am trying to describe. . . .

. . . My deepest conviction is that Brethren doctrine and practice, the Brethren spirit and genius, sincerely and truly lived makes a type of character the most nearly Christ-like possible to attain. I am pronouncing no judgment on others but I know what Brethren ideals will do for character and life, for the life that now is and the hope of the life to come.[154]

This characteristic of unswerving commitment to correct belief from which must issue a Christ-like life gives to Brethren thought both a dogmatic and a dynamic quality. For Miller, overemphasis on either side of the balance or an attitude of indifference toward either doctrine or life leads to a distortion of the original deposit of faith.

In these attempts by Miller to distill from Brethren thought and life the essential ingredients of Brethrenism, he reveals a concern for balance which is reminiscent of the early Brethren and later discerning leaders such as Kurtz and Quinter. He holds in dialectical tension the Word and Spirit, doctrine and life, conservatism and progressivism, conformity and exclusivism. Though Miller confessed his own inability to articulate the essence of Brethrenism, his own life and thought were an eloquent demonstration of the qualities which have typified the Brethren spirit.

Chapter 15

THE BACKGROUND AND COURSE OF THE BRETHRENIST-FUNDAMENTALIST CONTROVERSY (1920-1939)

Introduction

With the gradual departure of the liberals from the Brethren Church during the 1920s, the conservative and fundamentalist Brethren enjoyed a period of harmony and united action which had been unknown for nearly a decade. Progress was registered in many departments of the church, especially in the foreign and home mission programs. Yet by the early 1930s many leaders in the church were conscious of the fact that two different theological viewpoints were developing in the church. Beginning in 1934 a series of disputes occurred which gradually polarized the Brethrenist and Fundamentalist groups in the church.[1] Though the controversy surrounding Ashland College, which was brought to a head in 1937, commenced the division process, the final break occurred in 1939 at General Conference. This chapter will explore the sources of the developing tensions, the actual process of the split, and the major theological issues involved in the controversy and will conclude with an analysis of the division.

Developments in the Church

The church auxiliaries, most of which were organized between 1887 and 1900 (see pp. 166-168), remained active during the 1920s and 30s. Several new organizations, however, made their appearance between 1920 and 1939. The initial impetus for a laymen's organization began in 1919 when a Laymen's Conference met, apparently at the suggestion of J. A. Garber, during General Conference. These conferences continued until 1923 when the National Laymen's Organization was formally organized through the adoption of a permanent Constitution and By-Laws.[2]

New features were added to the denominational youth work. At the 1933 General Conference a

National Boys' and Young Men's Brotherhood was established as a counterpart to the Sisterhood of Mary and Martha.[3] Summer youth camps, pioneered at Camp Shipshewana, Indiana, in 1927,[4] gradually became a significant means of ministering to youth. About this same time Vacation Bible Schools were also introduced into many local churches as means of reaching out to the youth of the community.[5]

Sizeable gifts donated in Ohio (1901) and Indiana (1921) for the express purpose of providing a home for retired ministers and laity made possible the construction of the Brethren's Home at Flora, Indiana, in 1923.[6] Such concern for the elderly members of the church can be seen as a manifestation of the brotherly love that has typified the Brethren.

Evangelism retained its prominent place in the agenda of the church during the 1920s and 30s. Not only had the Four Year Program (1916-1920) given special attention to evangelism in its goals, but evangelism was also a key feature in the two programs which followed: The Bicentenary Movement (1920-1923, marking the two hundredth anniversary of the organization of the German Baptist Brethren church in America)[7] and a less pretentious two year program (1923-1925).[8] The latter program lacked the organization, zeal, and promotion (and, consequently, results) of the former two.

During the 1920s a major part of the evangelistic work of the church was conducted by the Evangelistic and Bible Study League. Though it was organized in 1919 by the Southern California District Conference,[9] the merging of the National Evangelistic Association (formed in 1918) with the League in 1919 gave it denominational representation and backing.[10] The League put several men[11] in the field each year to conduct Bible Conferences and revival campaigns. It functioned vigorously until the early 1930s when financial hardships during the Depression caused its discontinuation. Nevertheless, the void was ably filled during the 1930s by R. Paul Miller, the field secretary of the Home Mission Board (his success may have played a part in the decline of the League).

Interest in home missions had gradually increased during the 1920s under George C. Carpenter, the president of the Home Mission Board from 1914. With the hiring of R. Paul Miller in 1929 as the first full-time field secretary, the Board's program was greatly expanded. Miller, who had succeeded McClain at the Philadelphia First Brethren Church and, like McClain, had taught at the Philadelphia School of the Bible, had already earned a reputation as a capable evangelist. In his new position Miller became responsible for overseeing the home mission churches, holding evangelistic services, and fund raising. Analysis of the statistics for the 1920s and 30s reveals a marked increase in the accessions to the church by baptism during the first part of Miller's tenure, though the developing controversy in the church reversed this trend by 1935.[12] The church as a whole registered steady growth between 1920 and 1939.[13] Under Miller's leadership the Board also focused its attention on beginning mission works in urban centers (e.g., Compton, Glendale, and Tracy, California; Roanoke, Virginia; Cleveland, Ohio; Spokane, Washington; and Fort Wayne, Indiana). Gradually, the church was taking on more of an urban character.[14]

The foreign mission program grew rapidly during the 1920s and 30s. At the time of the division in 1939, thirty-two missionaries were serving in the two Brethren mission fields: Argentina and French Equatorial Africa. Interest in missions, as registered in the yearly offerings to the FMS, grew apace.[15]

Support for traditional Brethren beliefs during this period was mixed. The Brethren Church was firmly united on the temperance question. In 1919 Editor Baer had hailed the Eighteenth Amendment as "the greatest victory since the Civil War."[16] Throughout the 1920s the *Evangelist* regularly contained articles on prohibition. Readers were kept informed of each shift in the congressional lineup of "wets" and "drys" and counterarguments were aired against the charges that prohibition was not working.[17] The Brethren were admonished to get out and vote in the Presidential elections in 1928 and 1932 because of the prominent place in the party platforms given to the issue of prohibition.[18] Following the repeal of the Eighteenth Amendment in 1933, Editor Baer lamented the "fruits" which it quickly bore—auto accidents, violence, lax morals, etc. [19] A steady chorus of resolutions from district and National Conferences also recorded Brethren opposition to the liquor trade.

The Brethren peace position suffered during World War I especially from liberalism's view of America as God's chosen people who bore the responsibility to preserve the world for democracy and for the advance of God's kingdom.[20] Many ministers advocated the justness of the war and some even counseled Brethren men to enlist.[21] Apparently, many Brethren young men did volunteer. Seven members of the Ashland College class of 1918 enlisted (out of a class of sixteen of both sexes) and a Students' Army Training Corps was organized at the college in 1918 apparently with W. D. Furry's full support.[22] Charles A. Bame was one of the few who upheld the Brethren peace position without apology. With the close of the war, Brethren sentiment, as evidence in the *Evangelist*, returned to a more traditional stance. Various Brethren registered opposition to universal military training and support for disarmament.[23] The Kellogg-Briand pact, which renounced war as a means of settling international disputes, received strong Brethren endorsement[24] and Brethren conferences regularly passed resolutions affirming their "unalterable" opposition to war. Though representatives from both factions upheld the historic peace position of the church, it was generally the older men who did so (Charles Bame, George Baer, L. S. Bauman, and Charles Ashman).

The principle of nonconformity and simplicity in life suffered the most during this period. Editor Baer, knowing he was treading on sensitive ground, queried in 1924: "Where has Brethren simplicity gone? Does any one find any left in his congregation? Should we be concerned about the lack of it? Or is the world not in need of that quality in its life today?"[25] He solicited responses to his questions but, significantly, he received only one answer. The reply was quite discerning, however.

> But in leaving the non-essentials that we [the Progressives at the time of the split in the 1880s] were taught, in our endeavor to swing back to the primitive Christian teaching, we have swung to the opposite extreme. We are giving too much time to the frivolities . . . [26]

What, then, were the primary concerns of the church during the 20s and 30s? Prior to the years of controversy (1934-1939), the temper of the church, as evidence in the Moderators' addresses at General Conference, may be described as one of urgency. The church recognized its responsibility at home and abroad to carry the Gospel to the unsaved. It also was conscious of the need for sound Biblical teaching at home in the face of the dangers posed by liberalism and modernism. Regular calls for the teaching of the Brethren distinctives, especially the ordinances, were raised as were concerns about the need for greater spiritual growth. The church possessed a whole gospel plea that it felt the world ought to hear.

The Dilemma of Ashland College

Under the presidency of Edwin E. Jacobs (1919–1935), Ashland College made great strides forward, but progress was not easily achieved. Jacobs (1877–1953) came from firm Brethren roots. His father, H. S. Jacobs, had attended the 1883 Dayton convention and pastored several Ohio congregations. E. E. Jacobs received his education at Wooster (B.A. 1901), Mt. Union, the University of Chicago, Harvard, and Clark (Ph.D. 1917). He had joined the faculty at Ashland in 1904 as the science professor and, except for time spent elsewhere for study, had remained on the staff from this time. Jacobs' two major goals as president were the securing of an adequate endowment and the gaining of accreditation by the North Central Association of Colleges and Secondary Schools as well as by various state agencies (these goals were, in reality, linked). The first of these goals was realized through two denominational canvasses: the 1919–1921 campaign by William H. Beachler and the 1926–1933 campaign by William S. Bell. Total endowment (both permanent and "living") stood at $600,000 in 1930 (the city of Ashland had also made contributions toward the endowment).[27]

Jacobs had initiated the campaign to achieve accreditation by the North Central Association in 1926. The motivation was twofold. First, the State of Ohio Department of Public Instruction in 1927 required accreditation of all four year institutions of higher education by September, 1929. Though this decision forced the closure of thirty-six Ohio colleges due to the inability to meet accreditation standards, Jacobs was determined to meet the challenge.[28] The college lacked only the required endowment. Second, accreditation was entirely consistent with Jacobs' vision for the school. For him, a Christian liberal arts college of the first order demanded solid commitment to not only Christian ideals but also high academic standards. Like J. Allen Miller, Jacobs felt that the way to build a solid faith was to explore intelligently all facets of a given question. For example, in discussing the problems posed by organic evolution, Jacobs stated: "With a clear understanding of the facts coupled with a sound knowledge of the Bible, they [every school boy] would be better fortified against the errors which this problem involves."[29] The acquisition of accreditation would

establish Ashland College in the eyes of northcentral Ohio communities as an institution upholding academic excellence and would thereby be a great bonus in recruiting students. In seeking accreditation Jacobs' vision extended beyond the limited financial and human (students and faculty) resources of the denomination. He doubtlessly perceived that the future of the college demanded such a course. The goal of accreditation in the North Central Association was achieved in 1930.

Enrollment at the college grew rapidly during the early 1920s (from 129 students the first semester of 1921 to 279 in 1925). However, enrollment remained around this figure into the early 1930s.[30] In 1927 more than fifty percent of the student body came from the Ashland area. In 1933 Brethren students accounted for only about fifteen percent of the total enrollment, though the percentage may have been slightly higher before accreditation[31] (which was a drawing card for recruiting students from northcentral Ohio). In spite of the small Brethren representation, Ashland College still was deemed as *the* school for Brethren interested in college and seminary training.[32]

Undercurrents of criticism against Ashland College are first to be noticed in the teens. In 1915 H. L. Goughnour noted that the leaders of the college were being looked upon with suspicion because they "would not become advocates of this interloping doctrine of 'the blessed hope.'" He claimed students and money were consequently being turned away from the college.[33] In 1919 J. L. Gillin revealed that the college and its teachers were being

> threatened unless they stultify themselves and deny themselves liberty of thought and teaching . . . and teach only one interpretation of certain Biblical statements, and a science which has been exploded for fifty years.[34]

This same year Bauman called upon the college to adopt a statement of faith. Similarly, he demanded that "our schools," i.e., Ashland College,

> tell us exactly what the teaching is that we are being called upon to support with the Lord's money. They must tell us exactly what they are going to teach our children when we send them off to college. WE HAVE AN ABSOLUTE RIGHT TO KNOW, AND TO KNOW EXACTLY.[35]

For the Fundamentalist Brethren (as Bauman's comments intimate), Beachler's endowment campaign made it all the more necessary to settle the whole question of the college's orthodoxy. The Southern California District's method of forcing the issue was to propose to send in their money with a condition attached (apparently regarding the issues of teaching postmillennialism, evolution, and views of baptism other than the Brethren mode[36]). President Jacobs let it be known in personal correspondence with Southern California leaders in mid-1922 that he would accept no such gifts; that the future policy of the College must be left to the Board of Trustees; that the only theological statement he would accept was that adopted in 1919 (which was printed in the Ashland College Catalog); and that this statement should apply only to the Seminary, not the College.[37]

By 1923 the tactics of the Southern California District had become known in the Brotherhood. J. L. Gillin, without making direct reference to the situation, warned that acceptance of conditional gifts restricted a college's freedom and would lead eventually to the "decay of intellectual life." E. G. Mason criticized the factionalism in the denomination, especially the attempt by one group to force its views on the college. He further held that the laity of the church viewed the question of pre- vs. postmillennialism as nonessential and that the materialistic form of evolution was not being taught at the college. In response to these articles, George T. Ronk (who would champion the cause of the college in the next decade) maintained that the supporters of the college did have a say in its affairs and L. S. Bauman averred that the pre- vs. postmillennial question was of importance to his laity and he attacked the haughty manner in which "education" advocated evolution.[38] This dispute over conditional gifts is merely symptomatic of the fact that by the early 1920s two vastly different philosophies of truth and education (we might classify them as a liberal arts view in contrast to a fundamentalist view) were already present in the church (for further discussion of this point see below). The grave seriousness with which Fundamentalism viewed the questions of evolution and premillennialism had already led to rumors of heresy at Ashland College among Fundamentalist Brethren by the mid-1920s.[39]

During Alva J. McClain's first term of service at Ashland College (in the Seminary department) between 1925 and 1927, there were no overt signs of conflict between him and the college administration. He assured President Jacobs at his departure in June, 1927, and *Evangelist* readers somewhat later that his removal to California was wholly for health reasons. He also praised Jacobs and the college faculty for their commitment to Christian education.[40] Statements made by McClain twenty-five years later reveal, however, that he harbored dissatisfaction with the existing situation. He noted the college's lack of interest in a graduate seminary program, the resulting tendency among students interested in graduate theological studies to take regular B.A. degree work rather than a Bible major (to meet entrance requirements), and "liberal" tendencies in the life and faith of the campus.[41]

By this time McClain had already set forth his ideals for a Christian education. In a 1925 General Conference address, McClain outlined three distinguishing features of a "Christian education": it must "yield to Jesus Christ complete lordship over the educative process," "teach Christian truth as well as Christian ethics,"[42] and "be carried on by Christian men and women." McClain further put his finger on the issue that was the dilemma of Ashland College.

> In order to build any kind of a college he [the Christian college president] must have three things: money, teachers and students. If the church supplied all these, his task would be much easier. But the church seldom does this. As a result, the administration turns to the general public. And the moment this is done, certain dangers are incurred. The general public like to patronize educational institutions which maintain a fair degree of moral and ethical respectability, but it is not greatly interested in education that is definitely Christian. Therefore, there is constant pressure brought to bear upon the management to soften the Christian emphasis, and to strengthen the emphasis upon the interests of the non-Christian public. I have no sympathy with his tendency. I would rather fail than compromise.[43]

Note both the either-or nature of McClain's position and its basic incompatibility with the course of action pursued by Jacobs relative to the North Central Association (see p. 217).

McClain's style of teaching likewise differed markedly from that of Miller. Miller used an "open" method of teaching and gave the impression to his students that his search for God's truth was an ongoing task.[44] He was eclectic and Biblical, committed to no one theological system. His desire for his students was that they develop a mature faith based upon the full consideration of all facets of a given issue, using whatever interpretative (linguistic, exegetical) tools were available.

McClain was a skilled systematician and utilized a propositional approach to theology (Delbert Flora has termed Miller's approach "behavioral," i.e., dealing with life). In his teaching he was more dogmatic than Miller and projected a far more confident, self-assured aura with respect to his theological conclusions than his colleague. He was far less committed to traditional Brethren thought than Miller. The basic ingredients of McClain's system were Calvinism, dispensationalism, and Fundamentalism, though within these parameters he demonstrated much creativity.

He accepted Calvinism's emphasis on the sovereignty of God, salvation by grace alone, and the security of the believer but did not hold the view of a limited atonement. With Fundamentalism he shared an uncompromising commitment to the fundamentals of the faith: verbal inspiration, the virgin birth, the substitutionary atonement, the bodily resurrection of Christ and believers. He also affirmed the importance of a dispensational approach to eschatology as well as dispensationalism's sharp distinction between law and grace. Yet he modified dispensationalism's radical time divisions with their disparate forms of divine intercourse with man by means of his distinction between the universal Kingdom of God, which has always existed under God's providential guidance, and the Mediatorial Kingdom. This latter kingdom, understood as God's rule through a divinely appointed, human mediator, is a historical kingdom having its roots in the Old Testament in the nation of Israel (though it was presaged in earlier periods of human history). This kingdom, together with its King, was rejected by the Jewish nation, is presently in abeyance during the interregnum period of the Church Age, and will be fully realized when the Mediator, Christ, returns to establish the millennial kingdom. The mediatorial and universal kingdoms will then coincide in the final triumph of Christ following the millennial kingdom.[45] Such a formulation may be seen as an attempt to counterbalance dispensationalism's emphasis on the discontinuity of God's dealings with man by adding elements of continuity consistent with a more Reformed conception of God's oversight of human history.[46]

It should be emphasized that both McClain and Miller were respected by their students, whether eventually of "Ashland" or "Grace" persuasion.[47] As colleagues, McClain and Miller had great professional respect for each other. However, Miller would not have gone along with McClain's uncompromising fundamentalist spirit whose concern for the truth tended to be divisive.[48] Miller, though concerned about the problems at the college, did not consider a "battle" (McClain's terminology) as the proper means for their rectification (this is true of other "Ashland Brethren" as well).[49]

During his three year stay in Southern California, McClain first taught at BIOLA (1927–1929) and then served as the minister of education in Bauman's Long Beach First Brethren Church (1929–1930). The renewed contact with Bauman further stimulated McClain's vision for a graduate level theological seminary in the church. He envisioned a "school where the competent scholarship of a seminary might function within the warm spiritual and practical atmosphere of a Bible institute."[50] Definite plans were made toward the realization of this dream in the facilities at the Long Beach church.

When news of the proposed venture reached the administration at Ashland College, fears were expressed that a school at Long Beach not only would draw off significant support from Ashland College but eventually might lead to the loss of the college. Bauman and McClain were therefore encouraged to meet with the Board of Trustees in 1930 to arrive at a mutually acceptable agreement. McClain was persuaded to locate the graduate seminary at Ashland but only after he had won some significant concessions from the Board. These included (among others): (1) a minimum of four professors would compose the faculty staff;[51] (2) "the dean of the seminary should have complete jurisdiction in all seminary matters similar to the jurisdiction of the president in the arts college"; (3) "the continuance of the seminary on the college grounds should be regarded as an experiment" only; and (4) a plan was to be devised to insure the financial autonomy of the seminary. In addition, it was decided that Miller was to remain as the titular dean of the new seminary but McClain, with Miller's consent, was to assume "complete responsibility and authority in the reorganization and direction of the seminary."[52]

In the same issue of the *Evangelist* which related the establishment of the new graduate seminary, George Ronk also announced a forward-looking Ten-Year program for the college.[53] In spite of the latent tensions, both the college and seminary embarked on the 1930s with a measure of optimism.

The initial public attack against Ashland College came from the pen of H. C. Marlin, the pastor (from about 1925) of the Pleasant Hill, Ohio, congregation. He was a firm supporter of George Drushal's Brethren mission and educational work in Lost Creek, Kentucky.[54] The large percentage of the Home Mission Board's funding (46% in 1927[55]) that was taken up by the Lost Creek work became a source of contention with the Board especially after R. Paul Miller became the field secretary. He advocated the limitation of the work to evangelism only in order to be able to provide more funds for his zealous church extension program. The conflict between Miller and Drushal led to the appointment of a fifteen member investigating committee. Its recommendation to the 1931 General Conference to close the Riverside Institute was accepted. The independent-minded Drushal reopened his school, however, on a limited basis a short distance away. The dispute lingered on as

Drushal initiated court proceedings which he eventually lost in 1933.

Marlin came to the aid of Drushal's work in his fortnightly paper, *The Postscript* (begun in 1931). Though his primary reason for publishing the paper was to support the Riverside program,[56] Marlin used the *Postscript* as a medium for attacking Ashland College, the Home Mission Board, and the General Conference leadership (undoubtedly to put the church on the defensive). In vilifying language, he denounced the denominational leadership as "the narrow minded bigots that had control of things," the "machine that ruthlessly crushed any man who became conscience stricken and protested," the "self-extolling individuals at the helm" of the denomination. He charged the faculty of the college with teaching sexual license, evolution, and behaviorism.[57] These accusations were aired before an interdenominational, Fundamentalist readership of about one thousand.

No small stir was created throughout the denomination by the *Postscript*. At the 1932 General Conference Marlin was summoned to appear before the National Ministerial Association to produce evidence of his charges. He admitted that he had received his information from a student and that he could not verify its veracity. He was called upon to make full apology for the injury he had done to the school and denomination and to publish his apology in the *Postscript*. Having received his apology, the Ministerial Association extended him full forgiveness. However, he did not desist from his campaign against the denomination as is evident from later *Postscripts*.[58] It is true that Bauman, McClain, R. Paul Miller, Charles Ashman, and other Fundamentalist Brethren were just as incensed at Marlin's unsubstantiated accusations as such Brethrenist leaders as W. S. Bell, Charles A. Bame, Claud Studebaker, and C. C. Grisso. Yet, Ronk's conclusion about the affair is likewise valid: "Suspicions were aroused, not only by the published charges in 'The Postscript' but by the whispering gallery as 'The Postscript' revealed."[59]

Ronk's contention is borne out by the fact that President Jacobs felt compelled in February 1933 to answer "reports" that were "current" regarding the teaching of evolution at Ashland College. Jacobs, who taught biology at the college, insisted that a basic problem was the lack of definition in the usage of the term, "evolution." After identifying several distinct meanings of "evolution," Jacobs focused on the real issues: the general evolution of advanced species from lower forms and the evolution of man from primates. He stated directly:

> First, let me say, that so far as the various species of plants and animals having arisen in nature from preceding ones, the evidence is imperfect, partial and speculative. I myself have never so taught.
>
> And secondly, so far as man having arisen from some early order of Primates, this has never been taught in this college, at least not since I have been president. But I want to warn my readers against one thing and that is, that there is a world of difference between TEACHING evolution and TEACHING ABOUT evolution.[60]

As Martin observes, however, "all that mattered to many opponents of Ashland College was that textbooks propounding the theory of evolution had been used and all Jacobs' distinctions between teaching about evolution and teaching evolution had little effect."[61]

McClain, who had been questioning students about the content of teaching in the college since his return in 1930,[62] decided to force the issue at the meeting of the Board of Trustees in 1933. He demanded that the college faculty sign a fundamentalistic statement of faith similar to the one signed by seminary professors in order to insure that the arts faculty would not damage the "life purpose" of pre-seminary students.[63] Though the college administration fought the move to impose the statement (prepared by McClain) on the faculty, it finally acceded when the board added the provision that it would not require each teacher to sign it. The seminary quickly adopted the new statement but the faculty, "in an atmosphere of restrained hostility," adopted the statement as a group by voice vote with the majority not even voting. McClain felt that this was an empty victory, however, for the administration did not enforce the standards with the stringency he desired.[64]

By this point it was evident that grave differences existed between the college and seminary[65] (a matter which is said to have caused J. Allen Miller great distress).[66] Events in 1934 only heightened the tensions. The depression was taking its toll on both enrollment and financial backing of the college.[67] There was increasing friction between the college and seminary. Most severely felt, however, was the loss of accreditation in the North Central Association due to revised requirements for accreditation. It was a combination of these problems, no doubt, that led to Jacobs' resignation (under some pressure) as president in 1935.

The appointment of Charles L. Anspach as the new president in 1935 was greeted with great optimism by McClain and Bauman.[68] Anspach had graduated from Ashland College in 1912 and had earned his Ph.D. from the University of Michigan in 1927.

He served as the dean of the arts college and the head of the department of education at Ashland from 1923 until 1930 at which time he became the head of the education department at the State Teachers' College at Ypsilanti, Michigan. In a letter to McClain, Anspach reportedly stated that he planned to "reorganize with the Wheaton [College] viewpoint" and "contact conservative men in all denominations" as professors.[69] In a similar vein, he told *Evangelist* readers that it would be the policy of his administration to take a conservative viewpoint, to emphasize pure and righteous living, and to furnish liberal arts and theological training in a distinctly Christian atmosphere.[70]

It was soon apparent, however, that Anspach's view of a conservative, Christian, liberal arts education was far different from McClain's more fundamentalist, separatistic conception.[71] Disagreement began at once. Thus, Anspach criticized the seminary teachers for their protest against the inclusion of certain "modernist" speakers (local clergymen) at his inaugural program. This protest, together with developments at the 1936 Board of Trustees meeting (below), caused McClain to feel betrayed. In McClain's later analysis of the split, he laid a great deal of the blame on Anspach for his "almost cynical violation of his promises."[72]

McClain's seminary-oriented perspective of the issues provides little light on the problems inherited by Anspach when he came to the college. Two issues demanded his immediate attention: the regaining of accreditation and the dim financial picture. These realities forced the college to develop policies which greatly distressed the Fundamentalist Brethren. Already in 1934 non-Brethren professors with Ph.D.s were being hired to meet the new accreditation standards. But it was developments at the 1936 Board of Trustees meeting which precipitated a storm of controversy. The first development was a proposal to amend the Ashland College constitution. The proposed change, which awaited final action at the 1937 Board meeting, would alter the composition of and method of election to the Board of Trustees. (It was undoubtedly occasioned by the lack of sufficient financial support from the denomination and the resulting appeal to the Ashland community for greater financial backing.) The amendment would enlarge the Board from 36 to 42 members with the 6 new positions divided among the Ashland community (3), the alumni (1), and members-at-large appointed by the Board (2).[73] Just as significant, the procedure for the election of all trustees was to be modified. Until 1927 the district conferences of the church

nominated members to the Board and the Board itself selected from the nominees the number of members allotted to the particular district. In 1927 the constitution was amended to permit direct election by the districts. It was found that this new method was contrary to the constitution which governed the college and that a return to the pre-1927 procedure was necessitated. It was therefore proposed that each district nominate twice its allotted number of trustees and that the Board should select thirty-three trustees from the nominees. This procedure, of course, would make the board, to a great extent, self-perpetuating and thereby reduce the church's direct influence on the college.[74]

Two other events took place at the same Board meeting which raised the ire of the Fundamentalist Brethren. In his report to the Board, Anspach attacked a group of pre-seminary students for distributing tracts on the college campus. He also proposed a so-called "double standard" for the student body—a "restricted" standard for those preparing for pastoral and missionary work and a less strict standard for those training for secular service (Anspach felt that it was not feasible to require a completely separate life for the high percentage of local students who lived at home[75]). The Board's passage of this latter proposal occasioned the resignation of L. S. Bauman and Charles H. Ashman from the Board.

As a result of these occurrences, the controversy took on denominational proportions. The Southern California District Ministerial Examining Board sent a letter to Anspach demanding a response to nine specific protests: (1) the alleged use of a "gag rule" on the minority members of the Board; (2) the "dominant place" on the Board given to "wealthy men of Ashland" who "are not in sympathy either with Brethren doctrines or standards of life"; (3) what was deemed as a transfer of control of the college and seminary to men who are not only non-Brethren but not even "numbered among the *Fundamentalist* [italics mine] forces outside our Church"; (4) the "double standard" passed by the Board; (5) Anspach's alleged personal favor for the lower standard (he maintained his family's right to attend movies); (6) his attack on tract passing; (7) the very existence of conflict between the college and seminary; (8) the reduction of the seminary staff from four to three (the position left vacant by Monroe's resignation in 1935 was not filled); (9) the alleged effort "to wrest the College from the control of the Church" and turn it over "to a group of Ashland people."[76]

The letter, dated June 16, evidently demanded a response by June 27. Anspach, who had been absent from Ashland on church-related work, replied to Paul R. Bauman (L. S. Bauman's son) by cable on June 25 and letter June 26. In his letter Anspach suggested that the matter by handled prior to National Conference in joint consultations between a committee from Southern California and a group from the college Board and faculty.[77] The Southern California leaders felt that this offer was a ploy for time and thought the contents of the letter should be broadcast to the denomination. Therefore, the "Open Letter" was distributed throughout the church on July 31.

Understandably, the 1936 General Conference was greatly agitated by the problem at Ashland College. The conference appointed a committee to investigate the situation, disapproved the proposed amendment to the college constitution which would increase the Board's membership to forty-two, and tabled a vote of confidence in Anspach.[78]

These actions served only to heighten the tension at the college. Early in 1937 a faculty meeting was held to consider a proposed code of rules and regulations for the faculty. When the grounds for dismissal came under consideration, McClain moved that one further ground be added: "teaching anything contrary to the college Statement of Faith." When a roll call vote on the matter was demanded, only five affirmative votes were recorded, three of them from the seminary professors.[79] Without doubt, McClain's attempt to turn the statement of faith into a binding creed grated the administration.

The 1937 Board of Trustees meeting brought the crisis to a head. The new constitution with the controversial amendment was adopted. The two trustees from Southern California who had resigned from the Board in 1936 presented themselves as the elected members of the district. The Board, however, apparently considered the two positions vacant and proceeded to nominate and elect two other men to the "vacancies." Further, an investigation committee appointed by the president of the Board made several momentous recommendations. It not only favored the rejection of McClain's proposal to separate the seminary from the college, but called for the resignation or dismissal of McClain and Herman A. Hoyt (who had assumed the position left vacant by Miller's death) "because of a continued lack of harmony and cooperation between the arts college and seminary." This report was accepted.[80] When McClain and Hoyt refused to resign, they were dismissed. The seminary was then reorganized with the following personnel: Willis E. Ronk (dean), Melvin A. Stuckey, and Leslie E. Lindower.[81]

The ousted professors quickly gathered with other sympathizers and formed the Brethren Biblical Seminary Association. This group laid plans for a new seminary, Grace Theological Seminary.[82] It opened its doors in the Akron (Ellet), Ohio, Brethren church in the fall of 1937 and in 1939 moved to its present location, Winona Lake, Indiana. The faculty included McClain, Hoyt, and Homer A. Kent and the student body was composed of all but two of the current Ashland Seminary students.

Almost overshadowed by these developments in June, 1937, was the investigation of the college by the seven man committee appointed at the 1936 General Conference. The committee was informed that its investigation had to await the invitation of the Board of Trustees, so the committee did not function actively until the Board meeting on June 1, 1937. The actual investigation, however, was conducted by only one man due to the resignation of two members, the ineligibility of another who served on the Board of Trustees, and the nonparticipation of three others. The finished report was highly critical of Ashland College for (1) the adoption of the new constitution with the controversial amendment, (2) the antagonism between the college and seminary, (3) unorthodox teaching at the college, (4) the printing of highly objectionable matter in the college paper, and (5) the friction between the administration of the college and the faculty of the seminary.[83] It was roundly criticized, however, by Ashland partisans as being grossly biased. A 1938 college report faulted the investigator for his (1) failure to interview any professors or administrators, though this courtesy was extended by the Board, (2) prejudiced selection of student witnesses without corroborating their testimony or examining their character, and (3) blanket indictment of professors without giving any opportunity for defense.[84] The report was rejected at the 1937 General Conference[85] but it did reveal one undeniable fact: the church was dividing into two distinct camps.

This overview of the difficulties at Ashland College reveals that the underlying source of the problem must be viewed as philosophical/theological, a point that Martin has rightly emphasized:

> The basic tension was a philosophical/theological one between Ashland College, its faculty, administration, and students on the one hand, and Ashland Seminary, its faculty, student and backers—philosophical/theological differences which grew out of differing educational experiences and the resulting differing philosophies of education. In the process of criticism, denials, hopes, and disillusionment, personal antagonisms developed. College professors

viewed the seminary leaders as meddlers and troublemakers and seminary professors felt betrayed and deceived by some college administrators and frustrated by the open opposition of others. Personal antagonisms, as they developed, heightened the tensions but they did not create them.[86]

From Fundamentalism, McClain inherited a crusading spirit against anything which had the appearance of liberalism and its "outgrowth," modernism. His sincere attempts to rid the college of what he perceived as liberal tendencies by gaining the enforcement of a fundamentalist statement of faith caused the administration and Board, which were committed to a more open, liberal arts education, to react in ways which would preserve and ensure such an education. These developments were read by McClain and the Fundamentalist Brethren as an attempt to protect liberal sentiments. The record indicates, however, that continuing pressure from the Fundamentalist Brethren forced the college to do exactly what the Fundamentalists feared—seek greater support from non-Brethren sources due to decreasing financial backing from the church.

Polarization and Schism

Though by 1936 the Ashland College controversy had taken on denominational proportions, the split in the Brethren Church did not ultimately derive from this source. Rather, it acted only as a catalyst, drawing attention to far deeper philosophical, theological and methodological differences between the two factions.[87]

Though there were some denominational leaders who had sensed a growing divergence of thought in the 1920s and early 1930s, the first painful realization that differences existed in the church occurred at the 1934 General Conference. At this time a number of controversial topics were discussed: the doctrine of eternal security; a Fraternal Relations Committee report favorable to reunification with the Church of the Brethren, which was tabled indefinitely; a report by the Church Administration and Government Committee which would have given District Mission Boards "spiritual and governmental oversight of the churches . . . within the limits of our cooperate congregational government"[88]; and a proposed change of personnel at the Publishing Company. Nevertheless, none of these issues (with the exception of the last one) was of a strictly partisan nature.

The first intimation of factionalism in the church itself occurred in relation to the Publishing Company.

Because of the poor financial status of the *Evangelist* during the depression years of 1930–1932, it was proposed to merge the four Brethren publications— the *Evangelist*, the *Brethren Witness* (home missions), the *Brethren Missionary*, and the *Woman's Outlook* (Woman's Missionary Society). The 1935 General Conference approved the merger and a new Publication Board was created. Each of the former independent publications was to have one issue of the *Evangelist* per month to present its special concerns and its respective editor was given considerable freedom as to content. It was originally announced that the merger was to be effected May 1, 1934, and that the editor, George S. Baer, and business manager, R. R. Teeter, would terminate April 30, 1934.[89] However, these changes did not take place until January, 1935, when J. C. Beal replaced Teeter (the new *Evangelist* format appeared at this time) and January, 1936, when Charles W. Mayes replaced Baer. This delay was apparently occasioned by a mixture of theological/personal tensions in the Publication Board similar to those brewing at the college.[90] The personnel changes indicate that the Fundamentalist faction in the new Board eventually prevailed over the Brethrenist group.

During the last year of Baer's tenure, the fact that severe theological differences existed in the church became abundantly clear in the *Evangelist*. Such subjects as eternal security, the relation of baptism and works to salvation, and legalism were thoroughly aired. After Mayes assumed the editorship, however, a fairly tight editorial clamp was put on the *Evangelist* between 1936 and August, 1938. A brief flare-up did occur in 1937 following the 1937 College Board of Trustees meeting, and some propaganda made its appearance in news items and the special numbers (missionary, home missions, WMS).[91] Under Mayes the content of the *Evangelist* underwent a decided change. As Martin indicates, the balance of articles shifted from 62% by future Ashland supporters versus 23% by later Grace loyalists in 1930 to 21% and 74% respectively in the first half of 1936. News from Ashland College, frequent in the first part of the decade, is almost entirely absent after 1936. Articles dealing with prophecy and home missions become quite frequent.[92]

By January, 1939, when the controversy had reached a critical stage, both sides began to take full advantage of the editorial freedom in the special numbers. In addition, a feature called "Our Public Forum" was added in 1939 which was devoted entirely to controversial articles. Editor Mayes even admitted in March 1939 that he made "no claim to be present controversy."[93] The chief organ of the church thus became filled with charges, countercharges, rebuttals, and, at times, quite vindictive propaganda.

One other significant development contributed to the polarization of the two camps. At the Home Mission Board meeting during the 1937 General Conference, R. Paul Miller was relieved of his office. When the Conference, by a majority vote, requested the Board to reinstate Miller, it did so. However, in 1938 he was again dismissed. Another attempt was made to reinstate Miller by attaching the appropriate request as a rider to a resolution which would have established a peace committee composed of representatives from the two factions. The resolution failed to gain the requested two-thirds approval. Though the Board initially refused to reveal the reasons for his dismissal, it eventually came out that Miller was released because of a questionable (but unintentional) real estate dealing. Martin is undoubtedly correct, however, in attributing the dismissal also to personality conflicts and theological/methodological differences between himself and the Board.[94] Especially galling to the Board was Miller's placement of Grace-oriented pastors in the mission churches in spite of the fact that two-thirds of the Board represented the Ashland faction.

Not long after Miller's ouster from the Home Mission Board, the Grace partisans created a rival board, the National Home Mission Council. The two boards then proceeded to vie for the Thanksgiving offering which traditionally went for Home Missions. This new development was viewed by the Ashland group as a further sign that the Grace group was indeed a separatist movement while the other side held that they were merely giving the denomination the choice of another organization to support or not.[95]

The Ashland College loyalists moved to unite their supporters more thoroughly by mid-1938. The Brethren Loyalty Association was therefore organized with such stated purposes as: "to preserve and propagate Brethrenism" and "to foster and promote Christian Education" at Ashland College and Seminary.[96] Thus, by the end of 1938 both groups were organizing for the inevitable showdown. Each had developed a powerful apologetic and was using it to its full potential. The Ashland group was the preserver of historic Brethrenism while the Grace group was the defender of the fundamentals of the faith against all tendencies toward liberalism and modernism.

In the midst of this dissension there were some voices calling for peace. At the 1938 General Conference L. S. Bauman had proposed the selection of a committee of twenty elders and twenty laymen to meet and "give full consideration to all the difficulties that now confront the Church."[97] However, Bauman added to his resolution the provision that R. Paul Miller be reinstated for another year. This rider was quite distasteful to the Ashland group which called for a two-thirds vote on the resolution, insuring its defeat (though the majority favored it). However, a similar resolution by W. S. Bell minus the objectionable provision also failed. The Grace group saw such a resolution as a *de facto* approval of Miller's dismissal.[98]

The Grace partisans again pushed the idea of a peace conference in early 1939 but the Ashland group rebuffed the effort. The latter faction pointed out their own attempts to settle the disputes in 1936 (Anspach's offer to meet with Southern California leaders) and 1938 (Bell's Conference resolution). In addition, they held that they had no authority to appoint such a committee apart from General Conference approval. Martin's analysis of these peace initiatives is unquestionably accurate:

> Though the Grace leaders continually expressed their willingness to "settle" the dispute, as long as neither side expressed the slightest willingness to compromise, (since for the one side "truth" was at stake, for the other, the "faith of our fathers") a peace committee would seem to have been doomed from the start.[99]

The actual process of division in the church may be considered to have begun with the founding of Grace Seminary. Yet, it was the establishment of the Home Mission Council which precipitated a steady stream of resolutions, printed in the *Evangelist*, announcing various churches' withdrawal of support from the Home Mission Board (and, in some cases, Ashland College) and backing of the new Board. These resolutions played significant roles in the events that would culminate in the schism.

At both the Indiana District Conference and the General Conference in 1939 the credential committees were dominated by the Ashland group. In both cases, the committee rejected certain credentials on the basis of whether the delegate or his church had severed relationships with any Conference Board or district organization.[100] In spite of the objections by Grace partisans that this action was a violation of congregational rights, the maneuver realized its goal—the control of the Conference organization.

Following this General Conference action, the Grace group quickly organized itself into the National Brethren Bible Conference which, the following year, assumed the designation, National Fellowship of Brethren Churches (in 1976 the official name was changed to the National Fellowship of Grace Brethren Churches). This organization has continued to hold its annual conferences at Winona Lake, Indiana, while the Ashland group has located its General Conferences at Ashland, Ohio, since 1940.

Both groups immediately moved toward reorganization. Charles Mayes and J. C. Beal were dismissed by the Publication Board in September, 1939, but, when they challenged their removal, appropriate court action was taken to secure control of the Publishing Company assets. A settlement was finally reached with Mayes and Beal who received $7,000 worth of the graded Sunday School materials. An emergency staff composed of Willis E. Ronk, A. L. DeLozier, E. G. Mason, and Claud Studebaker oversaw the publication of the *Evangelist* beginning in October while C. F. Yoder and Dyoll Belote assumed the responsibilities of contributing editor and office editor respectively in December, 1939. All controversial material was to be kept out of the *Evangelist* and emphasis was to be placed on church news (including Ashland College again) and the promotion of Brethren distinctives.[101]

The present organ for the Grace Brethren, the *Brethren Missionary Herald*, appeared in January 1940. It was an outgrowth of the *Brethren Herald*, a paper begun early in 1939 by R. Paul Miller to promote the interests of the Home Missions Council. Charles Mayes assumed the editorship of the *Brethren Missionary Herald* while J. C. Beal became the secretary of publications. The Foreign Missionary Society aligned itself with the Grace group, with the Ashland group relinquishing all rights to the Society in 1940. In all but the Southern California and Northwest districts, where the Grace Brethren retained complete control, new district structures had to be established.

The process of reorganization was most painful in the local churches. In four cases litigation was brought by the Ashland side (the courts ruled in favor of the Ashland group twice and the Grace group twice).[102] In the realignment of churches, the Southern California and Northwest districts went entirely with the Grace Brethren, while Indiana, Illiokota, Midwest and Northern California districts stayed predominantly with the Ashland Brethren. Pennsylvania, Southeast, and Ohio districts were nearly evenly divided. The approximately thirty thousand members were nearly equally divided between the two groups while 99 churches went with the Ashland Brethren and 74 with the Grace Brethren.

The Theological Basis for the Division

It has been intimated throughout this chapter that theological/philosophical differences formed the basis for the later power plays and acrimony which eventually splintered the church. The philosophical differences have been spelled out quite thoroughly already in the discussion of the Ashland College turmoil. This section will focus on a number of theological issues which distinguished the two groups.

THE DOCTRINE OF GOD

Fundamental to many of the issues which divided the Ashland and Grace groups was a crucial difference in their respective views of the divine-human relationship. The Fundamentalist Brethren, in their reaction to modernism, sought to guard the gospel against any ethical or social conception of salvation. This they did by stressing the sovereignty of God and the supernatural character of salvation. Charles Mayes gives an excellent depiction of these concerns in his Moderator's address at the 1931 Southern California District Conference:

> We must guard against the secondary emphasis upon the Grace of God in bringing our salvation. Our Gospel is a message of Grace, with salvation as the first thing to be presented to men. We dare not forget this truth. Some are confusing this, preaching a Gospel of morality, and a message of social ethics. . . . If we maintain the Gospel of the Grace of God and his supernatural salvation, we will be protected from the subtle attacks of modernism.[103]

It is obvious that such a view of God and His work of salvation would revolt against the traditional Brethren emphasis on salvation as not just a supernatural event but also a process which includes a human response to God's gracious offer of redemption—repentance, faith, and obedience.[104]

The Brethrenist leaders, without denying the essentiality of God's sovereign interposition on man's behalf, felt that the Grace group was upholding only one side of the Biblical teaching regarding "particular salvation." Claud Studebaker thus observed:

> It would be far from my thought to infringe on the sovereignty of God in omniscience and omnipotence and his infinite mercy and grace, but to me God has spoken plainly in his word, that man has something to do to be saved in particular salvation, both in receiving it and retaining it. Man in the image of God must choose the salvation that God has freely offered to every man.[105]

The significant difference in emphasis between these two conceptions of God's provision for and man's appropriation of salvation is basic to some of the controversy's most heatedly discussed theological issues.

THE VIEW OF SALVATION

The issue on which the Ashland and Grace Brethren clashed most sharply was the doctrine of salvation. The standard for the Grace group with respect to salvation was: salvation by *grace* through faith (hence the derivation of the name of their seminary). McClain and the Grace Brethren viewed Paul's discussion of salvation in Romans and Galatians as determinative. In 1934 McClain stated: "Paul's greatest battle was not against those who denied the whole principle of Grace, but against those professed Christians who accepted Grace and then sought to add some small modicum of works."[106] Even more revealing are the following statements, penned a number of years following the division:

> If even the smallest item of the law should be added to the gospel and made binding upon believers, so that the requirement now becomes "believe" plus something else in order to be saved, the soul which accepts this "plus something else" automatically becomes "a debtor to the whole law" ([Galatians] 5:3). For such a one, the apostle warns, "Christ shall profit you nothing" (5:2).
> And so the problem becomes very simple: Either Christ will save you by *grace through faith plus nothing* [italics mine], or He will not save you at all![107]

The problem that the Brethrenists had with McClain's dogmatic position was not the matter of grace; they too recognized God's salvific work through Jesus Christ as indispensable for redemption.[108] The irritant was McClain's exclusion of all but faith as a condition of salvation and, further, the tendency to limit faith to confession of faith in Christ. Note, for example, I. D. Bowman's labeling of the position that one is saved by faith alone as "deceptive." Likewise, he contends that it is "heartfaith, which includes ready acceptance of the commandments as well as every other part of the whole gospel . . . that sums up the whole plan of salvation."[109] The problem thus boiled down to two mutually exclusive views of salvation: one which was punctiliar and the other which involved a process.[110] This difference gave rise to all the other distinctions to be noted between the two groups with regard to salvation: (1) baptism, (2) obedience (or works), (3) legalism vs. antinomianism. (1) Such Brethrenists as Claud Studebaker, I. D. Bowman, and Martin Shively held firmly to the Biblicist position of the previous century that baptism is essential to or a

condition of salvation. They pointed to the traditional passages of Mark 16:16; Matthew 28:19–20; John 3:5; Acts 2:37; 22:16; and 1 Peter 3:21.[111] The Grace Brethren labeled such a view as baptismal regeneration. For them

> Christian baptism is the outward sign and seal of the righteousness that is appropriated by faith. We are not baptized to *be* saved; but we are baptized because we *are* saved. The man who is saved will not reject God's appointed sign of his entrance by faith into the finished work of Christ . . . To so reject would be evidence, not of saving faith, but of unbelief.[112]

(2) Both Studebaker and Bowman also upheld the traditional Brethren emphasis that obedience and works are of the essential nature of faith. Bowman, seeking to offset what he considered a preoccupation with faith alone, stated: "*That some kind of works is essential to salvation is certain.* Those who teach that we are saved alone by faith have no use for James."[113] Studebaker, whose theme song was obedience, stressed:

> When folk hear the gospel, believe it, are convicted of their sin and are ready to confess the Savior presented in the gospel, they are told, what they must do to be saved. The instruction is quite plain in various portions of the scripture. God always fulfils his promises and gives the assurance to all them that obey him. . . . The Brethren church came into existence to emphasize OBEDIENCE to every command of our Lord, as the only true evidence of faith.[114]

The Grace Brethren position on this question was that obedience and works issue from an already experienced salvation. Note Bauman's statements:

> . . . when a man is saved,—"born again"—he gives THE EVIDENCE OF HIS SALVATION in a life that is obedient to the will of God as expressed in the commandments of his Lord and Savior Jesus Christ. . . . Grace bringeth salvation, and salvation bringeth obedience and "good works."[115]

(3) It was apparent to each side that there was an inherent danger posed by the emphasis of the other. As the controversy intensified full exploitation was made of the opponent's position. By 1935 the Fundamentalist Brethren were charging the Brethrenists with legalism (Bowman and others were even charged with being "legalists, modernists, and pagans" for their position that works play a part—i.e., they were lumped together with "social gospelers").[116] Studebaker provides a definition of the term as used in the current conflict: "That group of believers who interpret the scriptures to teach that, *man must do something* to be saved and to keep saved, are called legalists."[117] From the Brethrenist side, however,

came the charge, especially from George Ronk, that the Fundamentalists were antinomian. He felt that the Calvinistic Fundamentalism as found in the Grace group possessed a form of "Antinomianism that places salvation squarely as a fiat of God, beyond the free will of man, and disjunct from the moral law and human conduct."[118] Though both these terms represent an extreme view of the opposing position, they do reflect a basic difference between the Grace and Ashland groups: the Ashland side sought a balanced view of the divine and human in the *appropriation* of salvation while the Grace group sought to uphold God's sovereign work in *all* phases of salvation.

THE DOCTRINE OF ETERNAL SECURITY

This same difference in emphasis is to be noted in the position of the two groups on eternal security. In 1939 McClain set forth the doctrine as he himself taught it at Grace Seminary:

> . . . *positively, the doctrine of Eternal Security does mean that God secures the final salvation of all true believers, and by means of this very security He keeps us from that practice of sin or apostasy which would lead surely to perdition . . .*
> . . . *Like many other Biblical truths there are two distinct sides of the truth of Eternal Security:* First, on God's side, He *preserves* the believer. Second, on our side, we must *persevere.* . . . *But we must never forget that our perseverance is the result of God's preservation.*[119]

For the Ashland group, the strong emphasis on God's sovereign power of preservation as found in McClain's statements and those of other Grace leaders militated against Scriptural passages that upheld man's responsibility and free will. Also, it was felt that the more popular form of eternal security, that one could remain in good *standing* with God, although out of *fellowship* with Him, would weaken the traditional Brethren emphasis on obedience and an ethical Christian life.[120] The Ashland group, however, did not deny that the Bible teaches security. A "conditional security" or a "security of the faithful believer" was to be found in Scripture. "There is no possible failure for the faithful. I know of no promise for the unfaithful anywhere in the book."[121]

ESCHATOLOGY

When one compares the eschatological thought of the Ashland and Grace groups, it becomes apparent that the major difference is one of emphasis rather than essence. Both groups believed in the premil-lennial return of Christ,[122] both groups took a dispensational approach to eschatology,[123] both made wide use of the Scofield Bible,[124] both had some prominent exponents of prophecy (L. S. Bauman, R. I. Humberd, and Charles Ashman on the Grace side; I. D. Bowman, W. S. Bell, and J. Ray Klingensmith on the Ashland side). Yet, several characteristic emphases tended to differentiate the two groups. The Grace group gave far more attention to prophecy than did the Ashland group.[125] The Grace group was much more prone to speculate about the identity of prophetic imagery.[126] In 1939 Studebaker chided those who had spent so much time in the effort to "set the exact date [the Grace Brethren avoided this danger] or the approximate time when our Lord could return."[127] Though the extent to which dispensationalism was applied varied within the Grace group,[128] the exponents of a sharper distinction between dispensations tended to be found in Grace rather than Ashland circles. For example, note Bauman's views concerning the Sermon on the Mount.

> It is the law of the highest order, absolutely holy and absolutely perfect. It is the Constitution—*the fundamental law*—of the Kingdom of Heaven. There are some ministers, who do not believe it contains *the gospel of the grace of God.* We might safely challenge you to point out a single sentence in it that bears the "good news" of the grace of God to the sinner who is under condemnation.[129]

Though the Grace Brethren rejected the hyper-dispensationalism of Bullinger,[130] the Ashland group held that even Bauman's dispensationalism was an unwarranted narrowing of the definition of the Gospel and a neutralizing of the ethical teaching of Jesus.[131]

A SEPARATED LIFE

There probably was not a great deal of difference between the two groups in their practical expression of the Christian life. However, the motives and ideal for such a life were quite different. The ethic of the Ashland Brethren was still built especially on the teaching of Christ in the Gospels. George Ronk could thus characterize the Brethren ethic as "piety, renunciation, brotherly love, non-violence, meekness and humility."[132] The ethic of the Grace Brethren reflected, to a great extent, the "marks" of the Christian life peculiar to Fundamentalism. Thus, the by-laws of the constitution of the Second Brethren Church of Los Angeles stated:

In order to maintain a Christian standard of ethics, and to lead exemplary lives, as those professing godliness, this church desires to sight her membership to Rom. 12:2 . . . We therefore admonish those who compose the body of Christ to abstain from dancing, gambling, playing with gambler's cards, theaters, motion picture shows, Sunday desecration, prize fighting, the use of tobacco, intoxicating liquor, narcotics and opiates, or any other intemperate [sic] or pernicious thing that tends to ruin the body, soul, and spirit; also, *we call attention to the facts* [italics mine] that for 200 years the Brethren have been opposed to secret societies, taking of the oath, and going to war.[133]

THE VIEW OF CREEDS

For the Grace Brethren the surest way to guard against liberalism was the adoption of statements of faith. Bauman had set forth the basic utility of creeds in 1923: the fundamentalist demands "loyalty to a creed as the source of all real character," the liberal belittles or throws creeds "to the wind as altogether unnecessary for the production of character."[134] For Fundamentalism one's attitude toward standards of faith determined one's theological position; there was no middle ground. Thus, McClain interpreted the college administration's refusal to adopt standards of faith as "the protection of 'liberalism'"[135] and he apparently had similar designs at the 1938 General Conference when he attempted to have the General Conference adopt the "Message of the Brethren Ministry" as its creed.[136] The Brethrenist position on creeds was that "the moment we begin to write out what we believe and practice and require of our communicants, that moment we step off our Bible-alone foundation and throw ourselves liable to the almost certain danger of adding to or taking from the whole Gospel of Christ."[137] God's truth is larger than any man-made creed and is necessarily limited when the attempt is made to form a binding statement of its content.

CONGREGATIONALISM

It is noteworthy that, as the split became imminent, the two groups tended to polarize the traditional view of Progressive Brethren polity: cooperative congregationalism. The Grace Brethren, who would gain most in the case of future litigation by emphasizing congregationalism, could declare: "It is historic Brethrenism to recognize the supreme authority of the local congregation."[138] On the other hand, the Ashland group tended to emphasize the limitations which cooperation entail:

> The very effort at unity under a corporate name, the evident intent of autonomous churches to unite under the

corporate shield [i.e., the articles of incorporation of the church], and the record that this was done, taken together, *bespeak a voluntary self-limitation*, by the free will of the various autonomous congregations.[139]

This difference between the two groups, together with the preceding, though not causing the division, provided the apologetic for driving the wedge.

Analysis of the Division

In order to provide background for this analysis, notice will be taken of other important interpretations of the division. These interpretations will include both those that were offered at the time of the division and those which have been made subsequent to the split.

During the course of the division a number of writers sought to explain the reasons for the dissension; in fact, the attempt to find an explanation became a source of controversy in itself! Some perceived the difficulties merely as a conflict of personalities or as a power struggle.[140] Others recognized that far deeper theological and methodological differences were the source of the tensions.

The Ashland group generally perceived the controversy as arising from theological innovations introduced into the church through a Calvinistic Fundamentalism. W. S. Bell could trace the "seed of controversy" back "to the beginning of the blending into the theological training of our men of the teachings of the school of Calvin and the Bible Institutes."[141] Robert F. Porte, who received his Th.D. from Drew University in 1933, set the problem in a larger historical-theological framework. He perceived the origins of the controversy in the post-war, conservative reaction to modernism's humanistic materialism. The conservative group therefore embraced Calvinism's stress on man's hopelessness and God's sovereignty. This

> Calvinistic-Fundamental movement follows quite largely the program of holiness and Pentecostalism. It thrives on the alleged errors of churches and ministers and a continual stream of emotionalism. The leaders of the movement use certain carefully selected proof texts which are constantly repeated. Their method of Biblical interpretation is to spiritualize and to resort to extreme dispensationalism. Since God does all, baptism is not essential to salvation and water in connection with "born of the water and of the Spirit" does not mean literal water.[142]

Both I. D. Bowman and Claud Studebaker testified of their long-time feeling (1920 and twelve years respectively) that the Fundamentalist group had definite designs to guide the church in the direction of "so-called fundamental theology."[143]

One of the more intriguing analyses of the controversy was that by George T. Ronk in his four-part series, "The Anti-nomian Controversy in the Brethren Church" (though his argumentative, technical style tended to blunt the force of his insights). In his first article in the series, Ronk gave his own historical-theological interpretation of the conflict. He observed that two distinct periods could be identified in the history of Fundamentalism. The first, 1900–1925, was epitomized in *The Fundamentals* and was an orthodox, nondenominational response to the attacks of the Higher Critics on such doctrines of historic Christianity as the inspiration of Scripture, the virgin birth, the blood atonement, etc. He held that this original movement began to disintegrate after 1925 "into numerous cults, many claiming the light of special 'inspiration.'" The railing, criticism, and slander engaged in by this latter form of Fundamentalism caused many conservative theologians to repudiate the designation. Further, about 1925 the movement and its attendant Bible schools were largely captured by a radical form of Calvinism which distorted historic orthodoxy by means of an extreme dispensationalism and the neutralizing of ethical teaching. Ronk viewed the violent, militant, aggressive spirit of the Fundamentalist Brethren as typical of the post-1925 development and held that the "Pietistic group" of the Brethren "stands for a conservative theology represented by the spirit and teaching of the early Fundamentalism, of about the date 1916." He maintained that the conflict in the church involved "two irreconcilable schools of thought" and therefore demanded an immediate choice.[144] Though Ronk is inaccurate in holding that Calvinism played a key part in Fundamentalism only after 1925 and though it may be questioned whether his own aggressive spirit was consistent with the Pietistic spirit he extolled, yet the major outlines of the development of Fundamentalism, as he perceives them, are quite similar to those found in several recent works on the movement.[145]

The Grace group's response to these historical-theological treatments was typically to deny that doctrinal innovations were the crucial problem. For most, the real issue was posed by liberalism and an incipient modernism.[146] Martin's analysis of this point is quite correct: "They [the Grace side] rarely openly accused the Brethrenists of modernism, though they were quite certain the evil had invaded Ashland College and, having gained a foothold, would spread into the denomination."[147] McClain, for example,

denied Bell's contention that doctrinal innovations from Calvinistic schools and the Bible institutes were the source of the conflict. He admitted that many Grace leaders had received education at such institutions but he noted that leaders on the Ashland side had also attended Calvinistic seminaries. Even more importantly for McClain, seven members of the Ashland College faculty had attended the University of Chicago and others had been educated at "other similar institutions, practically all of them hotbeds of modernism and unbelief." He emphasized that "the real root of the trouble" was the "liberal tendencies and opposition to complete orthodoxy in Christian faith and life" at Ashland College.[148]

Louis S. Bauman, in responding to a number of issues raised in Ronk's series of articles, held that many of these issues possessed no critical significance as causative factors: the view of the Sermon on the Mount, eternal security, modernism in the churches (Bauman held that the church as such was free of modernism), legalism, antinomianism, historic Brethrenism, disloyalty to the institutions of the Brethren Church, and the R. Paul Miller case. For him the sources of the division included modernism at Ashland College (he brings a series of charges against former presidents), freemasonry in the college, and personal animosities.[149]

In addition to these interpretations written at the time of the split, three other accounts of the division have appeared. Homer A. Kent, a historian for the Grace Brethren, has noted that a number of issues were involved in the controversy: the essentiality of baptism, the place of obedience in Christianity, eternal security, the significance of the Sermon on the Mount, congregational government, and unorthodox teaching at Ashland College. However, in a departure from the original Grace position, he sees the major issue as doctrinal, relating to the attitude which the two groups had "toward the grace of God and all its implications." Thus, "while the Grace Seminary group laid great stress upon the grace of God and its place in man's salvation, the Ashland College group tended toward a legalistic view."[150]

Albert Ronk, a historian for the Ashland Brethren, has viewed the controversy itself as primarily a personality conflict which had behind it "a power struggle to determine the emphasis in theology and the control of General Conference and church institutions." However, he also traces the roots of the controversy back to the liberal controversy of the teens when an extreme Calvinism was introduced into the church.[151]

By far the most comprehensive discussion of the division is that by Dennis Martin. With many of his findings, this study is in complete agreement. He states:

> We find the Brethren Church of the early twentieth century choosing for its heroes evangelists and home mission pastors who knew the secrets of building a thriving church. As these enthusiastic pastors and evangelists fell more and more under the influence of Calvinistic fundamentalism, as their churches outstripped the rural and declining traditionalist Brethren congregations, as aspersions were cast on the spirituality of those whose churches stagnated, and as spirituality and a successful Christian life came to be equated with adherence to a set of doctrinal precepts and a rising growth rate for the congregation, those who felt unable to join the fundamentalist frenetics, those who felt strongly about their ties to the non-theological, ordinance-bound faith of their fathers, saw their way of life under attack. Tension developed over Home Missionary Board policy, *Brethren Evangelist* editorial policy, and especially over Ashland College. When the Ashland College administration and faculty, who were defending their concepts of education more than any theological position, resisted McClain's efforts to dominate Ashland College policy, those within the denomination whose religious lifestyle was most threatened by fundamentalist innovations, lined up in support of Ashland College.
>
> Thus it was not a conflict between fundamentalism and modernism that divided the Brethren Church, as in the mainline Protestant denominations in the 1930s, but a conflict between fundamentalism and Brethrenism, between fundamentalism and the remnants of a way of life which, although Henry Holsinger did not realize it, had been rejected at Dayton in 1883 in favor of late nineteenth century evangelistic Christianity, a way of life which had, in spite of that, not altogether disappeared by 1930.[152]

Martin's analysis of the dynamics of the division is generally quite thorough. He has included the basic elements that caused the division: theological/methodological differences, the catalytic nature of the college controversy, and a power struggle for the church's institutions. He has suggested that the Ashland side was actually a coalition of two groups: (1) the rank-and-file of the church, both laity and clergy, who saw the traditional emphases of "Brethrenism" threatened by the interloper, Fundamentalism and (2) a more educated group which, though not as steeped in traditional Brethren ways as the other group, shared a similar aversion to the rigidity of the Fundamentalist Brethren. Most importantly, he has observed that the basic conflict was between Fundamentalism and Brethrenism. This fact was also recognized by George and Albert Ronk and Robert Porte and was intimated in the contention by Homer Kent that the basic difference between the two

groups involved their respective attitudes towards God's work in salvation.

This chapter and preceding ones have documented the origin and development of Fundamentalism in the church. From a theological standpoint, Fundamentalism, like liberalism, had certain features that were especially appealing to the Brethren. Herbert Hogan, in discussing the influence of Fundamentalism on the Church of the Brethren has observed: "Nineteenth century Brethren theology, when divorced from its distinctive ordinances and its pietistic heritage, was essentially 'orthodox' or 'fundamental.'"[153] Besides being basically compatible with Brethren doctrine, Fundamentalism was deemed by men like Bauman and McClain a powerful ally when liberalism threatened to shift the Brethren Church from its firm Biblical moorings. Given the traditional Brethren concern for evangelism and commitment to premillennialism, the coalescence of Fundamentalism, dispensationalism, and revivalism by 1920 also provided a very appealing package, especially to those Brethren separated from direct interaction with the main body of the church (the West Coast especially).

Several features of Martin's model are weak, nevertheless. First, his depiction of the traditional Brethren as non-theological fails to explain why theology played such an important part in the controversy, even before the conflict broke into the open in 1936. This fact alone should indicate that the Brethrenists were not theologically indifferent. Second, Martin apparently identifies "Brethrenism" solely with a "special lifestyle" which he holds was gradually lost as the Brethren moved into the mainstream of American life.[154] However, such a supposition breaks down when one realizes that some of the most staunch defenders of Brethrenism were men who had fully transferred from "the Brethren subculture" to the American mainstream. Thus, George T. Ronk was a successful businessman who was "worldly wise" when it came to matters of corporate and legal affairs. Charles A. Bame was a candidate for governor of Ohio in 1935. Willis Ronk, Robert Porte, and M. A. Stuckey were likewise very much aware of modern religious trends. Certainly, Brethrenism had a more substantial content then merely the peculiar lifestyle of the nineteenth century Brethren subculture.

The strong reaction by Bowman, Studebaker, Willis and George Ronk, and others in the latter 1930s can be seen as an attempt to preserve the historic Brethren Biblical theological and dialectic approach to crucial issues. George Ronk probably recognized this point more clearly than most of the Brethren leaders. In 1935 he stated:

> They [Brethren leaders] have traditionally maintained a median position [on conflicting issues] allowing for ELECTION AND FREE-WILL, MEDIATION AND ATONEMENT, FAITH AND WORKS, ETHICS AND PIETY, CHRISTIAN RESPONSIBILITY AND SAINTHOOD, REPENTANCE AND REGENERATION: all apparent conflicts being reconciled and resolved in the INSCRUTABLE WISDOM for those who obey Christ's commands and "walk in His steps."

> Again I say, Brethren must hold to their historic position, midway between Calvinism and Arminianism, leaving the reconciliation of doctrines beyond our finite comprehension to the Inscrutable Wisdom, implicitly obeying Him, in whose Cross is sole merit, but as God's imperatives, God's sanctions for His Covenant of Grace.[155]

Whether conscious or unconscious, this concern for a middle position explains the tenacity with which the Ashland group maintained certain theological positions. For example, they perceived that the dispensationalism of Bauman and others was weakening their traditional Christocentric motivation for leading a Christ-like life, i.e., obedience to Christ's commands and examples. They rebelled against McClain's strong emphasis on God's sovereignty, feeling that its concomitants—eternal security and a salvation "by grace through faith plus nothing"—depreciated and neutralized the Biblical truth of human responsibility. The Fundamentalist use of statements of faith grated against the traditional Brethren conviction that fixed statements limit the Holy Spirit's ability to shed new light on the living Word in response to changing cultural and religious environments. (It also gave dramatic evidence to the Brethren conviction that binding creeds were inherently divisive.) The Brethrenists balked at the strong prophetic emphasis in the Grace group because they felt that the Christian's first priority must be to live a life which, to ever greater degrees, is conformable to Christ's example. Only against this background can the stiff resistance of the Brethrenists to Fundamentalist Brethren theological propositions be understood.

Chapter 16

READJUSTMENT AND REVITALIZATION (1940-1987)

Introduction

The division affected the Ashland Brethren far more adversely than it did the Grace Brethren. Those elements that added vitality and zeal to the church—an aggressive home mission program, a successful foreign mission program, nearly all the young ministerial recruits—were inherited by the Grace group. This fact, coupled with the difficult and painful task of reorganizing the local churches, created a period of depression and defeatism in the church which lasted until the late 1950s. However, a revitalized youth program, better organization at the national level, a renewed home and foreign missions program, and a revived interest in the Brethren heritage have given the church a fresh optimism and perception of purpose since the early 1960s. It was with a new sense of urgency that the church entered the decade of the 80s.

The Organizational Life of the Church

Following the 1939 division a number of the national auxiliaries of the church remained, for the most part, intact—the Woman's Missionary Society, the Sisterhood and Brotherhood, the National Laymen's Organization, the National Ministerial Association, the National Sunday School Association, and the Benevolent Board (Brethren Home). Nevertheless, several other auxiliaries and Conference Boards suffered severely from the split: the National Christian Endeavor, the Home Mission Board, and the Publication Board.

As noted earlier (p. 225), the Publication Board moved immediately in September, 1939, to secure the publishing interests for the Ashland Brethren. Dyoll Belote's service as office editor during the transition period following the split lasted about a year. Subsequent editors have been Fred Vanator

(1941-1952), W. St. Clair Benshoff (1953-1963), Spencer Gentle (1963-1970), George Schuster (the first layman to serve as editor, 1970-1975), Ronald Waters (1976-1978), and Richard Winfield (1978 to the present). A problem that has continued to plague the *Evangelist*, due to a limited readership, is its yearly deficit. Several changes in the format and frequency of issue of the *Evangelist* have been instituted to try to rectify this problem. In 1962 the various church papers once more unified with the *Evangelist* (though again unification proved unsatisfactory), in 1966 the *Evangelist* became a biweekly publication, and in 1976 a monthly. Continued financial problems caused the 1979 General Conference "to establish a revolving gift [endowment] fund so that the interest could be used to help finance Brethren publications."[1] Though the *Evangelist* continues to be published at a loss, its importance to the denomination is such that the Publication Board uses other sources of income to meet the shortfall.

At the time of the division, the denominational Christian Endeavor leadership was dominated by the Grace group. In addition, the Christian Endeavor program in the local churches had been languishing. With a deep concern about the lack of an organization for Brethren young people, three young men, Archie Martin, Woodrow Brant, and Gilbert Dodds (a one-time holder of the world's indoor mile record), dedicated themselves to revitalizing the youth program. In 1946 their efforts bore fruit when the first Brethren Youth Conference met and a Youth Board was created during General Conference. So enthusiastic was the response of the youth to the new program that a need for central direction was recognized. In 1948 Charles Munson was chosen as the first National Director of Brethren Youth. No small credit goes to the Brethren Youth in revitalizing the church in the traumatic years following the division. Ronk pays a well-deserved tribute to the youth program when he attests: "It is sufficient to say that their contribution to the recovery of the Church in its readjustment is surpassed by no other agency of the denomination."[2] In 1966 the Youth Board and Sunday School Board merged and a Board of Christian Education was formed.

Probably the area of denominational work most affected by the division was the missions program, both home and foreign. With the Foreign Missionary Society's alignment with the Grace group, the Ashland Brethren were forced to begin from scratch. In 1940 the Missionary Board (the former Home Mission Board) was authorized to engage in foreign mission work. In 1940 C. F. Yoder came out of retirement and returned to his second home, Argentina, to found a new Brethren mission. Beginning in 1948 a number of Brethren missionaries worked in Nigeria in conjunction with the Church of the Brethren's missions program (this work became autonomous in 1972). New fields have also been opened up in India (1969), Colombia (1974), Malaysia (1975), Mexico and the Hispanic community of Southern California (1979), and Paraguay (1987; this mission field is being spearheaded by the Argentina Brethren Church). The Sarasota, Florida, Brethren Church also has a Hispanic work which it began in 1980.

The home mission program of the Ashland group also faced serious problems. Most of the home mission works which were under the care of the Home Mission Board during R. Paul Miller's tenure went with the Grace Brethren.[3] Even more critical, much of the young ministerial leadership departed with the Grace Brethren, leaving a number of the existing churches without pastors.[4] World War II only prolonged the shortage of young ministers. Much of the time of the Missionary Board's field secretary, J. Ray Klingensmith (appointed in 1940), was necessarily spent in ministering to the spiritual and psychological needs of the existing congregations and the church at large. Somewhat desperately, he called the church to her missions task in 1943 and, in the process, reflected the mood of the church at the time.

> None of us for the past few years have been satisfied with our total ministry as a denomination. With a great shortage of pastors to take care of our organized churches it has seemed without reason to attempt to build new churches and start new points. But God will never use us if we stop there. It is ours to get more men and to get more points and churches.[5]

It was not until the mid-1950s, however, that the church recaptured its old zeal for church extension.

Whereas only two new works were started in the 1940s, eight were initiated in the 1950s, twelve in the 1960s, eleven in the 1970s, and nine thus far in the 1980s (not all these church starts have survived, however). Two entirely new districts, Florida and Southwest (Arizona), have resulted from this extension work.

The overall location of Brethren churches has not changed significantly during the last nearly fifty years. At the time of the 1939 division, "Ashland" congregations were overwhelmingly rural. 73% of the congregations were in towns of less than 2000 population and only 5% were in cities with populations above 50,000.[6] In 1987, 41% of the congregations were in towns with less than 2000 population while only 17% of the churches were in population centers of 50,000 or more.

The membership statistics for 1940 to 1986 show a gradual increase in membership until the late 1950s followed by an opposite trend.[7] No doubt, the continuing rural complexion of the church is partially to blame for this trend as are the perennial problems of insufficient numbers of ministers and the limited resources of a small denomination. Nevertheless, a commitment to build new churches in larger metropolitan areas and a steady stream of ministerial candidates from the seminary in recent years have led to a slight rise in membership figures since 1985.

The Spiritual Temper of the Church
THE CRISIS OF CONFIDENCE (1940–1960)

Ronk testifies to the general feeling following the division that the church had become sidetracked from its "historic emphasis of Brethrenism."[8] Representative of the frequent calls for greater immersion in the traditional emphases of the church is one of A. B. Cover's suggestions for the agenda of the 1940 General Conference:

> . . . we need to emphasize our Historical and Doctrinal position. There has been in years gone by, too little emphasis upon our particular position, so that it became easy for members of the Brethren Church to say, "one church is as good as another; we are all working to go to the same place." We need not be *narrow*, but we have a right to define our position. Addresses and sermons should be spiced with the purpose for The Brethren Church, and a reason for our practices.[9]

Materials designed to reindoctrinate the membership of the Brethren Church in the church's historic teachings formed an important part of the church literature during the early 1940s. In 1940 the National

Sunday School Association published an edition of Alexander Mack's writings (it was edited by M. A. Stuckey) and the *Evangelist* reprinted a series of doctrinal statements penned by the late J. Allen Miller. This same year C. F. Yoder wrote a four part series explicating the Brethren creed, "The Bible, the whole Bible, and nothing but the Bible" as well as the "slogan" which the Progressives had adopted at the time of the controversy in the 1880s: "In essentials unity, in nonessentials liberty, and in all things charity."[10] In 1941 the Ohio District Conference memorialized General Conference to create a committee "to make plans for the promotion of intensive denominational instruction among the churches of the brotherhood."[11] The appointed committee consequently prepared a six-week Brethren Emphasis program and distributed 2500 copies to the Brotherhood for use in Sunday Schools or other study groups.

In spite of these attempts to gain a renewed sense of direction, the deep emotional scars left by the division, the shortage of ministerial recruits (which was compounded by the war), and the resulting discouragement in the local churches led to a period of "defeatism, lethargy, gloom."[12] There were a number of men who called the church to focus its attention on its mission rather than its problems. John Locke in his 1944 Moderator's address challenged the denomination to forget about the division and "forge ahead. . . . Let us concern ourselves with *the State of the Brethren Church NOW*."[13] Charles Munson admonished the church in 1947: "We have been crying, a lot of us, but don't you see it's not in what we do not have, but in the way we use what we do have."[14] In his 1952 Moderator's address W. C. Berkshire got to the heart of the problem:

> We are defeated people, a fearful, apprehensive people. We are bound by some of the unfortunate turns in our church history. The "chance theory" has dominated our thinking and shrouded us in pessimism. But it is choice and not chance that determines destiny. If we have appeared destined to die as a church, it is because we have waited for accomplishments to be dumped into our lap. It is because our choices have been negative and not positive—aggressive, God-willed. And our choices have been negative because we have been fearful. But why have we been fearful? Because we have not put our whole dependence upon God.[15]

Indicative of this defeatism was a lengthy history of passing resolutions at General Conference without making any attempt to implement them.[16] In 1955 Moderator Woodrow Brant rehearsed this unbecoming history. He noted that in 1945 Moderator N. V. Leatherman had recommended a "new life" program

which included a "Council of Boards." The Conference later approved the plan to create "a Council whose duty it shall be to promote united cooperative work on the part of all Boards, the said Council to become a standing committee of Conference."[17] Though it met during the Conference, there is no mention of this council in subsequent Conferences. A similar fate was accorded Leatherman's proposal to revise the "Manual of Procedure" (no revision had occurred since its passage in 1915). Moderators in 1949, 1950, and 1951 decried the lack of coordination and efficiency in the national work of the church.[18] Yet, it was not until 1955 when Brant indicted the church for its procrastination that this problem was rectified.

At the Conference the ten year old "Council of Boards" was reactivated and named the Coordinating and Planning Committee. In 1956 it was given standing status and designated The Central Planning and Coordinating Committee. The rather cumbersome title was changed to Central Council in 1963. This council kept close watch over the denomination's spirit, doctrine, and polity and served as a refining agent for resolutions before they were brought to General Conference. It soon became apparent that a full-time Field Secretary, responsible for communicating the program of the church to the local and district levels, was needed for the coordination of the Council program. John W. Porte was therefore hired in 1959 to fill this position. (In 1968, when Smith Rose replaced Porte, the position was designated Executive Secretary of Central Council to reflect the more comprehensive coordinating functions of the office.) The activity of Central Council, together with the enthusiastic youth program and the revitalized home and foreign mission works of the church began to foster a new mood in the church. The fifteen year period during which the church "marked time" was drawing to a close as a new generation of leaders took over the reins of the church.[19]

The story of the college and seminary forms a noteworthy part of the history of this period. Enrollment at the college dropped to 100 during World War II but rose to 600 in the late 1940s and peaked at 2570 in the undergraduate program in 1970/71 (due in large part to the post-war baby-boom generation and the college deferment program during the Vietnam War era). During this boom period, President Glenn L. Clayton (1948–1977) pioneered a bold building program which increasingly depended on funding outside the denomination. As a result the college developed more of a strictly liberal-arts college philosophy. However, under Presidents Arthur

Schultz (1977–1979) and Joseph Shultz (1979 to the present), a policy of increasing sensitivity to the church has evolved.

The college was adversely affected by the sharp decrease in student enrollment that nearly all colleges and universities experienced beginning in 1973. Enrollment at the undergraduate level dropped rapidly from this point, bottoming out in 1982 at 1196. As a result, major cutbacks were needed to arrive at balanced budgets especially during the latter 1970s. However, under Joseph Shultz's leadership, the college has made significant progress. With the addition of a number of new degree programs, especially at the master's level, as well as the opening of several new extensions, enrollment has increased to a record 3813 (in undergraduate and graduate programs) in 1986 (compare this with a total of 2135 in both programs in 1976). An aggressive financial campaign has also resulted in major increases in the endowment fund and decreases in indebtedness.

Under Deans Willis E. Ronk (1937–1940), M. A. Stuckey (1943–1951), and Delbert Flora (Faculty Chairman, 1951–1953; Dean, 1953–1963), Ashland Theological Seminary continued its training of a predominantly Brethren student body. Enrollment remained quite small (between ten and twenty) throughout this period. In 1958 the seminary was moved off the college campus to a new location several blocks away though no administrative changes were involved. This move was deemed advantageous by both college and seminary personnel. Under Dean/Vice President Joseph R. Shultz (1963–1980) the seminary entered upon a bold expansion program that took the school from the smallest such institution in Ohio (22 students in 1963) to the largest (378 students in 1980; enrollment peaked in 1983 at 464). Keys to this rapid growth have been extension programs in Akron, Cleveland, and Detroit and a solid evangelical reputation that has drawn students from fifty different denominations. Dean Charles Munson (1980–1982) and Vice President Frederick Finks (1982 to the present) have continued to build upon this foundation. The seminary has retained an eclectic theological position which reflects its heritage with professors from American Baptist, Independent Baptist, Presbyterian, Free Methodist, United Methodist, Plymouth Brethren, and Brethren in Christ backgrounds in addition to the seven full-time Brethren professors and administrators.

REVITALIZATION (1960–1987)

The aforementioned developments during the latter 1950s led to a markedly different spirit throughout the church by the early 1960s. In 1960 John W. Porte reflected upon the progress made during General Conference: "there was a feeling of fellowship, of accomplishment. There is a feeling of purpose and urgency."[20] J. D. Hamel concluded his 1961 Moderator's address with the following observations:

> 1. For one thing, in the last few years, a major change has taken place in the character of this denomination. It is a change for the better. About ten years ago we began a new venture. We started making serious consistent efforts to reach people in the new community. In church extension we no longer look for people with a Brethren background, but we have gone out into new housing developments or suburban areas of our cities . . .
>
> 2. My second general observation is that there is evidence of a new spirit in the Church. There have been times when we adopted a defeatist attitude. We almost apologized for our existence. We were self-conscious about our size. We must learn that size is not the first criteria of the usefulness and effectiveness of a Church of Jesus Christ. . . .
>
> 3. My third general observation is that there are evidences of spiritual life and renewal in this denomination.[21]

Several developments have contributed to the fostering of a healthier, more optimistic perspective in the church since the 1960s. One facet has been a continuing interest in the heritage of the church. This interest has manifested itself in a number of significant ways: the preparation in 1960 of a manual of instruction, *Our Faith*, for new members; Conference's authorization of a major study of Brethren history by Albert Ronk, *History of the Brethren Church*, 1968; the attendance by Joseph Shultz and Owen Alderfer (church history professor at the seminary) at the 1968 Louisville Conference on the concept of the Believers' Church; the publication of a more popular work on Brethren history and doctrine, *The Brethren: Growth in Life and Thought*, by the Board of Christian Education in 1975; the participation of many in the Brethren Church in writing and financing *The Brethren Encyclopedia*, 1983–1984; and the publication in 1984 of *A Centennial Statement* of faith, a pamphlet explicating the basic beliefs of the church in honor of its centenary in 1983. In addition, the study of Brethren heritage has assumed a more prominent place in the teaching at the seminary and in the local churches.

Denominational polity has also been evolving during this period in an effort to effect greater concert of action among the denominational boards. Though an informal "Board Group" had been functioning throughout much of the 1970s, more definite structural organization was deemed necessary. Prior to the 1976 General Conference, Frederick Burkey had prepared a major study paper with recommendations for reorganization at the denominational level. The paper called for the restructuring of the church's existing ministries into five departments, each with an executive. These executives were to be responsible to a Director of Denominational Ministries who was, in turn, to be responsible to a Board of Brethren Church Ministries elected by General Conference. The 1976 Conference referred the matter to the Church Polity Committee for thorough study. In 1977, General Conference revealed hesitancy to accept such a centralized structure and referred the matter back to committee. The following year General Conference accepted a proposal brought jointly by the Polity Committee and Central Council. It called for the dissolving of Central Council (which had 31 members) and the Conference Planning Executive Committee (which had 27 members) and their replacement by a nine member Executive Committee of General Conference. This committee, composed of the elected officers of General Conference and the past moderator, assumed the planning, coordinating, and office functions of Central Council and the General Conference week program planning of the old Executive Committee. This General Conference Executive Council was expanded to a potential nineteen members by the 1987 General Conference to provide greater involvement by the conference boards and greater representation from the various districts.

Another significant step in restructuring occurred in 1979 when Conference approved the first phase of a plan for denominational reorganization. The total plan involved the selection of three denominational "directors" by the new Executive Council. The Director of Pastoral Ministries was to work in the area of pastor-church relations, serve as a counselor to pastors, and assist churches which were seeking new pastors. The Director of Denominational Business would coordinate the business interests of the denomination. The Director of Denominational Ministries would serve as a coordinator of the various ministries of the denomination. The 1979 General Conference voted to accept the report for the proposed denominational reorganization and to implement the first phase with the employment of a director of pastoral ministries. Though none of the existing structure was done away with in this reorganization plan, it represented an attempt to provide greater efficiency and coordination at the denominational level.[22] The first Director of Pastoral Ministries, William Kerner (1980–1987), gave excellent leadership to the church in his role. He has been followed by David Cooksey. The second phase of the reorganization was implemented in 1982 with the hiring of Ronald W. Waters as the Director of Denominational Business. He was succeeded by Sterling Ward in 1984. However, finan-

cial considerations have led at least to a temporary termination of this position in 1987 and have delayed the implementation of the third phase.

Though this entire process has not gone as quickly or as far as some had hoped, it does indicate that the Brethren will adopt changes when they are made aware of the existing problems and given the opportunity for full and free discussion of an issue. The reorganization also represents an implicit recognition that the church needs greater unity of action and accountability at all levels of its activity. For all too long the fears of "Standing Committee" from the 1880s and the lethargy following the 1939 division stymied any efforts at developing an effective organization at the national level.

Besides the revival of interest in Brethren heritage, the progress made in more effective denominational organization, and the burgeoning seminary program, other factors have contributed to the reawakened sense of mission in the church. The Crusader Program, renewed in 1970 (there was a similar program in the 1950s) by Fred Burkey, the Director of the Board of Christian Education (1967–1978), has been the means for several hundred young people to gain experience and serve the church in a variety of forms of Christian outreach during the summer. Through widespread participation in such evangelism programs as Explo 72, Key 73, Here's Life, America, and the Church Growth movement, the Brethren have retained a firm commitment to community outreach. Another expression of this concern for evangelism was the creation of an Evangelism Committee by the 1983 General Conference to aid local congregations in carrying out this work. In addition, during the last half of the 1970s, a renewed sense of urgency concerning church planting has resulted in an ongoing commitment by the church to start new churches.

During the 1980s, the prevailing mood in the church can be described as one of critical self-evaluation of its strengths and weaknesses. Unlike the score of years following 1939, however, the church has sought to overcome its deficiencies through concerted, coordinated efforts. Though membership continued to slip in the first part of the decade, this trend seems to have reversed. There is great optimism that the church is turning the corner. It possesses greater certitude about its distinctive priorities and mission, a characteristic which had been lacking in the church for nearly sixty years.

Relationship to other Christian Bodies

The Brethren Church's relationship with other Christian groups during the period 1940–1987 mirrors its dramatic shift in moods. During the early and mid-1940s the church had cooperated with the Church of the Brethren in its peace witness and war-time agencies and in its missionary and relief programs. By 1946 the Fraternal Relations Committee of the church felt that the time was ripe for serious talk about union[23] and it apparently presented a report at the 1947 General Conference recommending steps toward reunification. However, as in 1936 (see p. 223), the church balked at the recommendation.[24] It was the general feeling that cooperation should be continued but fears were expressed both at the motive for the desired union and the effects. George Ronk suggested that part of the motivation for calling for organic union was due to the inferiority complex felt by the church at the time. In his usual pointed style, he rebuked

> the cabals of little men maneuvering themselves into places of power, then not knowing what to do with responsibilities when they acquire them; alibi-ing themselves by abusing the smallness of the church, and planning some betrayal to a larger interest to cover up their own lack of vision and real leadership![25]

He further warned against union with the Church of the Brethren because of what he viewed as tendencies toward liberalism, postmillennialism, a Presbyterian form of polity, and a loose view of inspiration, and its association with the Federal Council of Churches.[26] James E. Ault summarized in 1950 the attitude which probably predominated among the Brethren toward the question of ecumenism in general. He criticized union when it was sought merely for the sake of convenience or expediency, yet he felt greater cooperation could lead to increased self-understanding and the more efficient use of resources.[27]

With the church's better self-perception in the late 1950s and early 1960s, the conviction arose that the denomination needed to tap into some larger framework in which it could acquire new methods and resources and exchange ideas with like-minded conservatives. These pragmatic, methodological, and theological concerns therefore have led the church to develop closer association with evangelicals in general and the National Association of Evangelicals (NAE) in particular (even though at the time the NAE still had a heavy representation of holiness and Pentecostal groups).[28] As a result, the *Evangelist* in 1960 began carrying items from the Evangelical Press Association; the church in 1961 adopted the graded Sunday School curriculum of Gospel Light Publications; by 1966 the Missionary Board and Conference Peace Committee had become members of the cor-

responding agencies of the NAE; in 1967 General Conference voted to establish regular participating membership in the NAE and urged individuals and congregations to do likewise; and in 1971 General Conference adopted a goal for local churches that they become annual members of the NAE.[29] In addition, many leading evangelicals have spoken at General Conference and at Ashland Theological Seminary.

Though this relationship is generally viewed as healthy, caution has also been expressed lest the church's faith be circumscribed by evangelicalism. The Brethren Church still retains a distinctive heritage and message which give it reason for continued existence.[30]

Doctrinal Development and Interaction

INTRODUCTORY OBSERVATIONS

The thought life of the Brethren since the 1940s, as mirrored in the *Evangelist*, shows general continuity with traditional concerns of the Brethren. Devotional literature, news from the churches, and articles focusing on evangelism and missions continue to dominate the pages of the church organ. When doctrinal articles do appear, they generally deal with the distinctive practices of the church (though by the later 1960s a reaction to viewing the ordinances as *the* Brethren distinctive sets in). Nevertheless, the Brethren have continued to uphold a conservative, evangelical form of faith. It is noteworthy that during the 1930s when the liberal/fundamentalist dichotomy left a no-man's-land in between, the Brethrenists disavowed the label "modernist" or "liberal" outright but generally avoided the self-designation "fundamentalist" as well. They preferred to use terms which emphasized their conservatism but which did not force them into a theological mold. Thus, one finds the common use of the self-designations "conservative," "evangelical," "orthodox," and "fundamental."[31] This preference has lasted to the present, though since the 1960s "evangelical" has come more into vogue. Also of note is that the term "Brethrenism" gradually fell into disuse by the mid-1940s and that the "whole Gospel" plea met a similar fate by the late 1950s. Both of these developments point to a continued weakening of the exclusivism which typified such traditional Brethren leaders as Bame, Bowman, and Studebaker.

The Brethren have continued to reaffirm their commitment to a Christ-centered and Word-centered faith. Their fidelity to traditional Brethren sources of authority and a conservative Protestant conception of the doctrines of God, Christ, man, and sin has likewise remained firm. But a comparison of the doctrinal position of the Brethren Church following 1940 to that of the church prior to this date reveals several points of development. Some changes represent further departure from the Brethren heritage; others, however, represent a return to a position more in keeping with the original genius of the church.

THE VIEW OF
SALVATION AND THE CHRISTIAN LIFE

Brethren doctrinal writings in the *Evangelist* and the manual, *Our Faith*, present traditional discussions of the doctrine of salvation. Repentance, faith, and obedience (or obedient faith) are seen as conditions or stages in the process of salvation; such an obedient faith will gladly submit to the rites of public confession, baptism, and confirmation; to a repentant faith God grants the gracious, spiritual effects of forgiveness, the gift of the Spirit, justification, adoption, and regeneration; sanctification is a continuous process, depending on the Spirit's constant empowering, which has personal holiness for its ultimate goal.[32]

The trend away from the traditional Anabaptist/Pietist ethic that began in the Brethren Church following the split in the 1880s was all but complete by the 1940s. The great themes of the nineteenth century Brethren—self-denial, nonconformity, simplicity, discipleship to Christ—are almost entirely absent from Brethren literature by 1940. The former ethic is replaced by the negative marks of the Christian life peculiar to Fundamentalism (no drinking, smoking, dancing, card-playing, etc.) and, more recently, by the more open, middle-class ethic of evangelicalism. The theological foundation for the Anabaptist/Pietist ethic—the believer belongs to a spiritual kingdom and walks in the present world as a pilgrim and a stranger to the customs of the world—has generally been undermined by an ethic tied more closely to American culture.[33] There are signs, however, that the Brethren are searching for a life style defined by Scripture and by their commitment to Christ rather than contemporary Christian culture. Thus, recent writers have begun to emphasize the point that Brethren doctrine expresses itself in a life of obedient discipleship to Christ.[34]

Paralleling the demise of the traditional piety (and, indeed, integrally linked to it) was the continuing loss of the Christ-mysticism that was so strong in the early Brethren. This cultivation of a sense of Christ's presence through prayer, Bible study, and meditation, which, in turn, became the impetus for the

Christ-like life suffered greatly from the externalism of the nineteenth century and the doctrinal battles of the twentieth. Men like J. Allen Miller, George Baer, and the three Ronk brothers kept this feature of the Brethren heritage alive, but there have been few who have come on the scene recently to carry on this element of the traditional faith.[35]

This loss of a strong devotional/mystical element in Brethren faith together with the already discussed weakening of the conviction that total surrender to Christ should be part of the initial salvation experience (not something that may occur as a "second blessing" later—see pp. 175-176) has created a void in the Brethren faith. It is therefore not surprising that the charismatic movement has had some impact (though not a great one) on the Brethren Church. In an article in the *Woman's Outlook* in 1973 which Randal Best has described as "unique in all of Brethren history,"[36] Ruth Barber described her personal experience with what she referred to as the baptism of the Holy Spirit and the gift of tongues. Though, under the influence of dispensationalism between the 1920s and 1940s, the validity of such an experience would have been questioned by many Brethren,[37] Best observes that "toward the end of the period [1940 to 1976] a growing acceptance or at least toleration of these gifts [tongues, healing, and other charismatic gifts] seems apparent, at least on the literary surface of Brethren history."[38] Best's conclusion is borne out by the passage of a motion at the 1977 General Conference relative to the charismatic movement. It did not condemn the movement but called the "charismatic Brethren" to rethink the theological implications of their position in the light of Scripture and the Brethren heritage.[39]

The Doctrine of the Church

Developments during the 1970s and 80s have revealed that a new concern for recovering the original genius of the church as a covenanted Brotherhood is awakening. These developments involve important changes in the conception of baptism and of the church itself.

It has already been noted that the rigidly objective view of baptism as a means of grace and an initiatory rite which predominated during the nineteenth and early twentieth centuries was being weakened from several different directions—the emphasis on the spiritual meaning of the ordinances championed by Gillin and Yoder, J. Allen Miller's return to a position more like that of the early Brethren, and the impact of fundamentalist theology. It was being replaced in both the seminary and the church literature by a view which stressed the spiritual significance and symbolic nature of the rite. An excellent example of this view is an article by Delbert Flora. In summarizing one section of his article, he writes:

> . . . recall that I said, first that baptism is an outward symbol of an inward change over against circumcision of the old covenant; and that as circumcision pointed forward to the birth of Christ, that rite which should supersede circumcision must point back to the end of His work, i.e.: His death, burial, and resurrection. . . . Next, I said that as circumcision is a sign of separation from sin and the world, so baptism is a sign of separation from the flesh, consequently from the old life and the world. . . . In the third place, I said that baptism symbolizes the burial of the old man and the resurrection into newness of life. . . . Then I connected baptism with the washing away of sins in the blood of the Lamb.[40]

This new emphasis did not come in without some protest from a Brethrenist like Charles A. Bame.[41] Yet, the theological influence of the staunch Brethrenists, who by this time were retired or out of leadership positions, was greatly weakened as the somewhat younger, college and seminary trained men assumed leadership positions. By the 1950s the view of baptism espoused by these men was ascendant. This view represented a conception of baptism which was closer to Mack's view, for it perceived baptism as an outward sign or symbol of an inward grace. The emphasis was thereby shifted from viewing baptism as a condition for what followed to perceiving it as an outward act of obedience which in some sense participates in the spiritual change which has taken place and is taking place in the believer's life.[42]

Undoubtedly connected to this change in the perception of the meaning of baptism was a change in practice. By 1834 the strong objective view of baptism, the conviction that trine immersion was the apostolic form of the rite, and the emphasis on baptism as an initiatory rite had led the German Baptist Brethren to call for the rebaptism of all those joining the church who had been baptized by some mode other than trine immersion. This practice was not seriously questioned in the Brethren Church until the 1960s. In 1969, however, the Central District sent a memorial to General Conference urging "that The Brethren Church accept into membership persons who have confessed Jesus Christ as personal Lord and Savior, and have been baptized by Believers' Immersion, and who evidence a personal faith in their lives."[43] Reflecting the ferment in the church about the question of rebaptism, Richard Allison

asserted in his moderator's address at the 1969 General Conference (citing a statement by Fred Burkey):

> we have become "so preoccupied with defending particular modes of administering the ordinances that the original attitude of openness of new 'light' in the context of Christian brotherhood and mutual acceptance was lost. These distinctive modes soon became, and to some extent continue to be thought of as tests of fellowship and fidelity rather than expressions of faith and obedience. . . ."
> . . . Our men are no longer willing to perpetuate rites and ordinances as the genius of Brethrenism.[44]

Central Council was assigned the task of considering the memorial. It pursued its task in a thorough, unhurried manner and sought to incorporate the best of the Brethren heritage into the entire process. Thus, the theological and historical significance of baptism was carefully researched in nine major study papers; the major findings of this research were disseminated throughout the Brotherhood; each congregation was encouraged to study the findings in the light of Scripture and, under the guidance of the Spirit, arrive at a consensus. This study process continued until 1974. Votes were taken on the memorial in 1974 and 1977 but both times the required two-thirds vote was not achieved (54% and 63% approval respectively). It was finally passed, however, in 1978 (73% in favor). Though there continues to be some opposition to the change (the acceptance, without rebaptism, of members previously baptized by believers' immersion was made optional), the nearly ten year procedure is a dramatic testimony to how a potentially divisive question can be dealt with when all parties exercise forbearance while they together seek to discern the will of God through the guidance of the Word and Spirit. The process also demonstrates that the church is becoming aware of another significant fact: its genius does not rest predominately in the outward ordinances but in the inner spiritual realities which give to the ordinances their fundamental meaning.

Paralleling this dramatic demonstration of the Brethren corporate decision-making process has been a concern that the denomination relearn what it means to be a *Brotherhood*. In 1968 Richard Allison shared his feelings with General Conference about the essence of what it means to be "Brethren."

> Our uniqueness is a style of life characterized by openness and freedom based on Jesus' words concerning the abundant life. In the 1880's we received the label of "Progressive Brethren." It is my judgment that we lost this designation in the twenties and thirties as we became defenders of God, protectors of God's Word, biblicists. We lost the essence of what it means to be *Brethren*, brothers in the Lord dwelling

together in love and openness. . . .

　　Yes, the essence of the Brethren Church is found in brotherliness. Defensive and divisive action destroy brotherliness. The Brethren Church cannot go on without brotherliness because brotherliness is our essence.[45]

Other articles have appeared as well which have challenged the church to become a sharing, caring fellowship which seeks to remain open, under the Spirit's guidance, to new methods and new ideas; which have called the church to become a hermeneutic community, discerning God's will for itself through humble dependence upon the Word and Spirit; which have confronted the Brotherhood with its historic principles of nonconformity and separation from the world.[46] These articles reflect the church's desire to rediscover its heritage and apply it in a way that is responsive to the needs of the contemporary setting.

An aspect of Brethren heritage which has continued to be weakened in the church is its peace witness. Though the Conscientious Objector status and noncombatant positions were made available to the Brethren during World War II through the efforts of the historic peace churches (Quakers, Mennonites, and Church of the Brethren), it does not appear that many Brethren availed themselves of these options.[47] Throughout the war Charles A. Bame reminded the Brethren of their historic stance, but the peace position claimed very few other vocal supporters, especially among the younger pastors. Bame, no doubt, touched on the basic reason for the weakening of the peace position when he warned the Brethren and other Christians "to stop pretending they are the guardians of the national policy in a secular world."[48] (Note that in World War I a liberal theology of the destiny of America had weakened the peace position while in World War II a conservative-fundamentalist theology in which patriotism was important yielded the same result.)

In the years immediately following the war, little was said about the peace position of the church. However, Phil Lersch, who had worked with the Church of the Brethren's post-war Brethren Service program, has reiterated the historic stance of the church on numerous occasions since 1957.[49] What N. V. Leatherman said about the peace question in 1959 seems quite to the point: "Our declared position in conferences on this subject, often seems more like an appeasement of our own minds than a declaration of principle and position to serve as a guide for those who need the guidance."[50] In view of the situation where the majority of members in the church may

hold a more militaristic (as opposed to pacifistic or nonresistant) perspective,[51] the challenge raised in 1967 by Richard Allison is quite relevant:

　　At this juncture in history, we are in danger of losing it [the peace position] by neglect. Perhaps it should be discarded. However, let us never be guilty of allowing any historic position to fall by the wayside out of neglect. If the position is not worthy of Christ and His teachings, let us be bold enough to point this out. Never let us be guilty of prattling about pragmatic considerations. Practical considerations are hardly a fit place to commence a discussion of Christian doctrine. And if in our pursuit of understanding we find the peace position true to the life of Jesus Christ and to His teachings, let us pray for the courage of Jeremiah to actively support the peace position.[52]

Eschatology

Though there remained a moderate amount of interest in eschatological topics immediately following the division (C. F. Yoder regularly discussed prophetic questions), the number of articles by no means compares with the number prior to the split. Following the war, however, the number of articles decreases to only a few a year.[53] Interestingly, every discussion of eschatology between 1940 and 1963 follows the dispensational ordering of the events of the end times. These articles generally avoid any speculation about "the signs of the times," preferring to emphasize the certainty of Christ's return. In 1963, however, the first non-dispensational interpretations of eschatology appear. Jerry Flora upheld a post-tribulation view of premillennialism while George Solomon advocated a mid-tribulation view.[54] It would appear today that the church continues to be solidly premillennial but that there is no unanimity (nor is it felt to be necessary) on the relation of Christ's return to the tribulation period.

Concluding Observations

Following nearly a score of years dominated by a feeling of defeatism, the Brethren Church is demonstrating some noteworthy signs of progress. Yet, the rediscovery of the church's theological and practical heritage is necessarily a process that will take time and will, no doubt, involve some resistance. Certain areas of the church's present thought and practice, however, are in need of further analysis. First, much of the church has adopted a revivalistic/fundamentalistic view of salvation that tends not only to view faith as merely a confession of Christ as Savior (*assensus*) but also to see salvation as connected primarily with this confession of faith. This conception of salvation is completely foreign to the original Brethren view which perceived faith as *assensus*, repentance (a radical change in one's heart and mind which necessarily leads to a change in life), and faith as *fiducia* (commitment of one's life to Christ in discipleship) as indispensable conditions to salvation. In this view there is no room for "cheap grace" but the believer by the very nature of his response to God's grace is expected to live a life of total surrender to Christ. Second, the church needs to fill the void left by the loss of the traditional mystical/devotional piety. From many sides of Christianity today there are calls coming for a reawakening of spirituality in the church. It would seem ironic if the Brethren Church, with a rich heritage of a Christ-centered piety, had to rely solely on other contemporary guides to regain a stronger spiritual sense. Third, the Brethren Church has inherited a Christian ethic from fundamentalist and evangelical Christianity which tends to identify a number of outward marks which delimit what a Christian should or should not do. There seems to be no integral relationship between this ethic and the initial aspects of salvation. The traditional Brethren conception of the Christian life, however, viewed the salvation process as issuing in a life that conformed more and more completely to the perfection that is in Christ. Thus, the complete surrender and unqualified commitment to Christ found in repentance and faith, the conception of baptism as a covenant before God and His people to live the new Christ-like life, the experience of regeneration which provided the foundation and enabling power for the new life, and the experience of communion with God which manifested itself in a will conformed to God's own will, became powerful catalysts for desiring to live an obedient life.

Fourth, if the church is to take seriously its traditional principles of nonconformity, simplicity of life, nonresistance, and self-denial, it must be ready to divorce itself more completely from the current popular conceptions of Christianity and found its faith solely on the Word of God. Progressivism means advancement toward the ideal of Scripture, not acceptance of current theological fads. Fifth, the church must regain a sense of brotherhood. For too long individualism (both with regard to church leadership and inter-congregational relations) has reigned in the church, blunting the total effectiveness of the denomination. Sixth, accountability must be restored in all levels of the church. The concept of a *covenanted* community, founded upon the individual's commitment to a body of believers as a part of his baptismal vows, needs to be revived. What Franklin Littell has said about Free Churches concerning their lack of discipline is apropos: "That the Free Churches, whose original complaint against the establishments was precisely that they practiced no true Christian discipline, should have succumbed to such a degree is a scandal twice compounded."[55] (The present practice of roll revision as an "innocuous" form of discipline is a travesty!)

If the church truly desires to rediscover its heritage and identity, these practical/theological distortions of its original genius need to be addressed. The continued commitment of the Brethren to God's Word is commendable, but, as Mack and the early Brethren did, the church must be willing to judge every form of Christian faith (including its own) by the touchstone of Scripture.

CONCLUSION

"AS THEIR FAITH IS, SO SHALL BE THEIR OUTCOME"

Introduction

The above words, penned by Alexander Mack, Sr., when asked to speculate about the future of the young Brotherhood, are a sober reminder to every generation of the Brethren that the possession of a vital heritage does not lead inevitably to an assured outcome. Each generation bears a responsibility to discern and then actualize the truth to which it is led by the guidance of the Word and Spirit.

It has not been the purpose of this work to develop a systematic statement of Brethren thought and practice. As should be clear by now, there has been a process of change and modification in Brethren thought throughout the history of the church. In addition, to *fix* a theological *standard* of belief would be contrary to the basic genius of the denomination which has sought to avoid the creation of any external barrier which would limit the enlightening activity of the Holy Spirit. What can be done, however, is to note the method by which the Brethren arrived at theological truth and the theological parameters or limits which are inherent in this methodology.

The Brethren Theological Method

Comparison of the thought of the three men (Mack, Nead, and Miller) who have generally been recognized as the theological leaders of their respective generations reveals several important observations. These men utilized theological insights from all different traditions; they searched for truth wherever it was to be found (the title of Albert Ronk's autobiography, *A Search for Truth*, is reflective of this Brethren trait). Yet, in the case of all three, a winnowing process was operative which helped them to separate the kernel from the shell (to use Pietistic imagery). It is the interpretative tools used by these men which gave distinctive form to their theological structure.

By comparing the sources of authority recognized by Mack, Nead, and Miller, it can be seen that there is a great deal of unanimity in their quest for discerning God's will. A synthesis of their three approaches to the theological task must include the following elements: God's sovereign purpose in history is to form a people for Himself; Jesus Christ has given to man a perfect, living example of God's will for His people; a perfect record of God's will for man is to be found in the New Testament; the Holy Spirit not only inspired this perfect record but is the One who leads believers into an understanding of its content; the life of the early church provides a valuable commentary on the ideal life set forth in the Word; believers are directed to the church as the place where God's will is to be worked out in and through them; Nead and, to a lesser extent, Miller would also hold that the Brethren heritage provides definite guidelines for how the Christian life is to be lived; Miller, in turn, would see enlightened reason as an aid in perceiving God's purposes for man.

On the basis of these sources of authorities, it can be seen that the primary focus in Brethren thought will be the creation of a God-like character and *life* in a people committed to their Father. This life is exemplified in Christ and made possible through His atoning death; it is delimited in Scripture and formed in believers by the power of the Holy Spirit; though necessarily beginning individually, its ultimate fulfillment is attained in *community*. Other sources of authority—the example of the early church, the testimony of Brethren heritage, reason—realize their purpose in the actualization of this life.

The Parameters of Brethren Thought

The above interpretative or hermeneutical presuppositions act as the standard against which truth is measured in the Brethren tradition. To this standard the Brethren have traditionally added one important corollary—truth is not to be found in extremes but in the union of elements which, though seemingly contradictory, are equally valid and necessary. Whether the inner-outer dialectic of the early Brethren, the equipoise of C. H. Balsbaugh, the concept of mediation of George Ronk, or the "mystic-minded moderates" of Albert Ronk,[1] this principle has remained as a plumb line for discerning truth throughout Brethren history. It is a fair question to inquire where the source of this principle is to be found. Though having historical roots in Pietism, the Brethren felt, no doubt (see p. 156), that the principle of a middle way derives ultimately from the very nature of the Christian life and faith. Our faith rests in a Savior who is fully God and Man; our Scriptures are the compilation of works inspired by the Holy Spirit but penned by human writers; as Luther noted, we are at the same time saints and sinners; we remain in the world but not of the world; we are a pilgrim people who are living between the times. These truths give a dialectical quality to the Christian life which has ramifications for many aspects of our present existence.[2]

When the above sources of authority and the corollary of mediation are applied to the various facets of doctrinal and practical theology, definite limits are set on Brethren thought. The interworking of these two elements needs to be explored in four key areas: the search for truth, the individual Christian life, the corporate life of the church, and life in the world.

THE SEARCH FOR TRUTH

Traditionally, the Brethren search for truth has been delimited by the dialectical concept of the inner Word (Spirit) and outer Word (Scripture). Because the Brethren viewed the New Testament as the perfect, final, and complete revelation of God through Jesus Christ, their faith necessarily looked to the Word as the final authority on all questions of faith and practice. The believer was expected to approach Scripture in a humble, straightforward manner and to seek to apply obediently the truths contained therein to his life. No other source of human authority was to mediate the Word's authority to the individual or church. It was at this juncture that George Ronk and the fundamentalist Brethren sensed the grave danger posed by liberalism to the Brethren faith. Reason and/or experience were elevated to such a position that they became the final interpreters of the Word, thereby undermining the authority of Scripture. In the Brethren heritage the

people of God are ever a community *under* the authority of God's Word.

Just as important, however, is the realization that the ultimate purpose of the Word is the creation of a new Christ-like life in the believer; it is this goal which necessitates the work of the Spirit in illuminating the meaning of Scripture and actualizing the intent of Scripture in the life of the Christian. This illuminating power of the Holy Spirit keeps the Word from becoming a "dead letter" and likewise prevents obedience to the Word from becoming a slavish, legalistic endeavor. It has been a traditional conviction of the Brethren that the enlightening activity of the Spirit must not be impeded by fixed outward forms. This conviction explains the antipathy of the Brethren to binding creeds and the revolt of the Progressive Brethren against the assumption that faithfulness to a prescribed order of dress is the hallmark of the spiritual qualities of simplicity and holiness.

Two observations should be made with regard to the inner-outer Word dialectic. First, the unreserved commitment to Scripture typical of the early Brethren leaves no room for an indifferent attitude toward doctrine. Though individual opinions were allowed on subjects not fully developed in Scripture, the Brethren have not countenanced beliefs that were contrary to the clear intent of the Word. For example, when universalism and, later, liberalism strayed from the standards of revealed truth, stiff opposition ensued. Unfortunately, however, the extreme openness of the Progressives in the late nineteenth century, coupled with the twentieth century supposition that the Brethren possess a non-theological tradition, opened the church to every theological movement that has come upon the American scene. This situation has had two unfortunate results. (1) Controversy resulted when one group of Brethren whose faith was determined by the perspective of a contemporary theological movement (liberalism in one case, fundamentalism in the other) sought to steer the church in the direction of that theological movement. (2) The Brethren Church has been left with an incongruous set of practices and theologies (see pp. 240–241) which, in some cases, bear little resemblance to its original heritage. If the church had realized that there is a vital link between theology and practice and between doctrine and life this situation would not have arise. *The best way to preserve the practical heritage of the church (especially the ordinances) is not to institutionalize its contemporary expression but to have a thorough understanding of the theological, spiritual truths to which it bears testimony.*

Second, the Brethren dialectic of the Word and Spirit can speak to the contemporary debate in evangelical circles concerning the nature of Scripture. It is true that propositional truth has been inscripturated through the direction of the Holy Spirit. It must be borne in mind, however, that this truth points our faith to the living Word, Jesus Christ, and has as its ultimate purpose the recreation of man into God's image. It realizes this purpose and takes on the character of a living Word when, under the Holy Spirit's power, the truth is actualized in the life of the believer.[3] The emphasis is entirely misplaced (especially if all parties are "evangelical") if we "stake our faith on a rationalistic demand for a proof of logical perfection or scientific inerrancy."[4] The vital union between the written Word and the dynamic, spiritual intent of that Word must not be divorced.

Given the sources of authority recognized by the Brethren and the principle of mediation, definite guidelines can be laid down for the community's search for truth. The Brethren have recognized the right of every individual to study Scripture and to seek to discern its import for himself under the Spirit's guidance. Yet, because the Christian life is to be lived out in community, the individual's right of interpretation is not absolute. Rather, the ideal is that all believers strive for a unity of mind and purpose in their Christian faith. A group of believers is settling for something far less than the ideal if, under the umbrella of "doctrinal pluralism," they are content to let every person believe as he wishes.[5]

Because in the new covenant God's Spirit is given to every believer, the covenanted body of believers shares the responsibility as a "hermeneutic community" to discern the will of God concerning any given problem. This demands of every member of the body a knowledge of God's Word and a commitment to the process of discernment. By being a part of the decision-making process, he shares in the responsibility for implementing or accepting the final decision.

What is the spirit with which believers are to proceed in their quest to resolve doctrinal or practical differences? First, it must be emphasized that unreserved commitment to the authority of God's Word and an open mind to the leading of the Spirit are indispensable presuppositions for the resolution of any difference. Without these elements, there can be no unanimity. Second, the entire process must be ruled by a spirit of brotherly love and forbearance which will not allow individual differences on the question at hand to rend the body. It is a Pyrrhic victory if, in the effort to resolve a problem, antagonism, dissension, and bitterness result.[6] Third, the

deliberations concerning a given issue must be entirely transparent. Behind the scenes politics and scheming are the surest way to destroy the unity of the faith (as seen during the 1930s). Only when all of God's people are allowed to explore every facet of the problem in open, frank discussion will a Spirit-directed consensus be able to develop. Fourth, a lengthy period of time may ensue before a consensus is reached. But, as Miller noted (p. 172), it is better to *wait* for a consensus to develop than to try to push a decision through against a large minority.[7] Fifth, once a decision is reached, it is not to be forced on the minority party. Such an action would only destroy the bonds of fellowship. Rather, the minority should receive the decision of the body in a spirit of submissive love (see p. 271, n. 37).

THE INDIVIDUAL CHRISTIAN LIFE

The studies of the thought of Mack, Nead, and Miller reveal a general continuity of thought on the question of salvation and the Christian life. Basically, five principles have governed the Brethren conception of salvation: (1) acceptance of the Bible "as it reads" (the Brethren generally have not sought to work out in fine detail the interrelationships of the various parts of the salvation process); (2) the inner-outer dialectic which perceives the outward ordinances as testimonies or symbols and seals of an inward grace and faith (though Nead reversed the emphasis, viewing the outward as a condition for reception of the inward); (3) the conviction that God has desired to fashion a people for Himself who will reflect His character in the world; (4) recognition of both divine sovereignty and human responsibility in the salvation process; (5) the conviction that salvation is both an event and a process.

These governing principles give to the Brethren view of salvation and the Christian life their characteristic features: (1) enlightenment by the Word and Spirit as a necessary precondition to the salvation process; (2) repentance as a change of heart and mind which will bring forth fruits—a changed life; (3) faith as both confession of belief in Christ and commitment and surrender of one's life to Him; (4) obedience as a quality inherent in saving faith; (5) baptism as an integral part of the salvation process which looks both backward as a response of obedient faith to the gracious work of God and forward as a symbol of the new life (in both its individual and corporate aspects) to which the baptizand dedicates himself; (6) God's gracious gifts to the repentant believer of forgiveness of sins, the

Holy Spirit, justification, and adoption; (7) regeneration as the divine work of creating a new being in the believer; (8) union with Christ and communion with God as a relational experience which acts as a catalyst for godly living; (9) the new life, denoted by obedient faith, as a loving response to a gracious Father; (10) sanctification as the progressive change of the believer into the character of Christ and the divine nature. It should be emphasized again that the goal of the Brethren view of salvation is the new life in Christ. Every aspect of the salvation process can be seen as pointing to this end.

THE CORPORATE LIFE OF THE CHURCH

An aspect of the Brethren heritage that has been severely weakened by adoption of practices and theologies foreign to its genius has been its sense of brotherhood.[8] Traditionally, the Brethren have seen the community of believers as *the* context in which the individual's new life in Christ is to be molded. The new life is a life of fellowship with both God and the brotherhood. This conviction led to a strong sense of responsibility for the spiritual growth of each member within the community of believers. Discipline not only was for the sake of the purity of the fellowship but also was an expression of concern and love for the life of the individual. Even the early Brethren strictures against marriage outside the Brotherhood are to be seen in this light. Because all are united in Christ there can be no room for the notion that "what I do will affect only me." The attitudes and associated practices of brotherly love, mutual admonition and submission, forbearance, and aid to needy members can be viewed as an outgrowth of the belief that God's purpose for man is realized in the formation of a people bearing His image.

The Brethren Church has resolved the question of inter-congregational relationships with the dialectic concept of limited congregationalism. Though the local congregation bears the right and responsibility for ordering its own life and affairs, the uniting of congregations for the purpose of work beyond their resources is effective only within the context of a shared doctrinal and practical faith. Likewise, when a congregation, through its representatives, takes part in the formation of denominational policy, that congregation becomes responsible for implementing the policy. This "participatory accountability", i.e., the right to participate leads to the responsibility to implement decisions, has been a key aspect of the periods in the history of the church when spiritual and numerical growth was most pronounced. Though the district conferences and General Conference may refuse to seat the delegates from a church which is unwilling to abide by conference decisions, this has rarely occurred. Indeed in Brethren polity mutual submission in love to the denominational consensus is the most effective means by which government can be maintained. Thus, commitment to the unity, purpose, and goals of the brotherhood must be the foundation upon which all action rests.

LIFE IN THE WORLD

Throughout the history of the Brethren, the question of the relationship of the community of faith to the outside world, both secular and religious, has not found easy answers. In the Brethren Church little has been written about nonconformity to the world since the 1880s. There is little demarcation (as one would have among the Old Order Brethren) in outward matters between the church and cultural trends beyond the taboos of the fundamentalist ethic. One would suspect that the principles which undergirded the idea of a separate people—a sharp distinction between the people of God and the world, simplicity in life—have also been severely weakened. This aspect of the Brethren heritage along with its concomitants—nonresistance, nonlitigation, not taking the oath—are casualties of the Progressives' drive to minister to the modern world. The Brethren Church needs to face several difficult questions on this point: Is nonconformity Biblical? If so, how can it be creatively expressed today? How can we maintain nonconformity and at the same time minister in the modern world? Are these two ideals (nonconformity and missions) antithetical?[9]

In its relationship to other Christian groups, the Brethren Church has adopted the dialectic concept of what might be termed "cooperative separatism."[10] In essence, it means that the church should feel free to cooperate with any movement whose basic ideals it shares, but it must ever be cautious that its own mission and uniqueness not become replaced by that of another group (this was the basic problem faced by the church in the liberal and fundamentalist controversies and it is a concern some leaders have expressed with regard to evangelicalism).

The concept of cooperative separatism leads to several other derivative principles which likewise are dialectic in character. By its very nature, the Brethren Church is both progressive and conservative. Its progressivism is rooted in the realization that believers must be open to the Spirit's leading if their faith is to address the vital issues of the contemporary setting (see p. 213). Its conservatism is based upon its unreserved commitment to Scripture as God's unchanging Word. Note J. Allen Miller's formulation of this dialectic: "Ours is an UNCHANGING CREDAL STANDARD, perfect and complete in every detail, whose eternal spiritual and social principles await interpretation in every age in the terms of the life and experience of that day."[11] Dangers lurk, however, at both extremes of the dialectic. The church must never be so conservative that it fails to address God's Word to the culture in forms that will speak to its age. But the church must also beware becoming so progressive that it blunts the radicalness of God's truth by adopting the world's ways.

Another dialectic which defines the church's relationship to other Christian bodies is Miller's conviction that the Brethren are Protestant yet also unique (see p. 213). The church shares with Protestantism a common faith on such doctrines as God, Christ, the Holy Spirit, man, sin, and the atonement. Yet its uniqueness is found in its acceptance of certain doctrines and practices relating to salvation and ecclesiology which have given it a distinctive style of life. The acceptance of these truths and practices, many of which are considered adiaphorous by Protestantism, gave rise to the "Whole Gospel plea" around the beginning of the twentieth century.

A final dialectic regarding the church's stance vis-a-vis its contemporary religious setting is that it must be both traditional and contemporary. The church possesses a rich heritage of truth which has evolved as generations of Brethren have struggled with God's will for their lives in their day. To sell out the Brethren birth right in order to be "contemporary" would be to disown a set of truths which the modern world itself needs to hear (note that many traditional Brethren emphases—the importance of community, spirituality, discipleship—are being rediscovered in Christian circles today). At the same time, however, the church must not be so tied down to culturally defined aspects of its Christian life (dress, for example) that it avoids interaction with the movements and issues of its day and thereby fails to offer a message for society's pressing needs. This commitment to both tradition and contemporary mission can be balanced only by comparing *both* with the standard of Scripture and by being sensitive to the leading of the Spirit.

The Character of "Brethrenism"

When properly functioning the Brethren approach to the theological task issues in some distinctive features. (1) The Brethren Church must ever emphasize the teaching of the Word. Only when every member of the community of faith is immersed in the Brethren "creed" can the church realize its distinctive mission. R. R. Teeter (the editor of the *Evangelist* between 1915 and 1918) put the matter quite bluntly:

> We are distinctively a Bible Church. We seek to build our faith not upon human documents, but upon the inspired Word of God. For the Brethren church to become weak on the teaching side is nothing less than ecclesiastical suicide.[12]

(2) The church is ever built upon the concept of renewal (see p. 150). Because a "Believers' Church" is always one generation away from extinction,[13] great responsibility is placed upon *every* generation to rediscover for itself the genius of its Word-centered and Spirit-led faith. This fact likewise necessitates the continued restatement of the Brethren faith in both *word and deed*. The new life in Christ is something that must be both caught and taught.

(3) The goal of the Brethren faith is above all a Christocentric faith and life. It harbors great optimism at what the Word and Spirit can do in the life of an individual and a community which is dedicated wholly to the Living Word. Though frustration, tribulation, and occasional failures continue to be a part of the believer's present pilgrimage, the renewing power of the Holy Spirit is continuing to fashion the church into a people of God who will bear the message and life of Christ to the world.

What, then, can be said is the genius of "Brethrenism?" The best definition of the Brethren genius is that it is a life which is founded upon a distinctive approach to the theological task of discerning God's will. Brethrenism is necessarily *doctrinal* (or Biblical theological) and *practical*. J. Allen Miller furnishes a fitting conclusion to this work in one of the most penetrating analyses of the Brethren genius extant.

> . . . I find myself held by a controlling principle among our people. It is *the method of approach to the Word of God when we seek its meaning and its message to the heart* [italics mine]. Being indited by the Spirit of the living God we hold with St. Paul that only the spiritually minded can ascertain its divine import. Its interpretation is not an intellectual feat. Upon the other hand, it is not a privilege of a select few nor is it necessarily mystical. A man born of the Spirit of God and led by the same Holy Spirit has a necessary qualification in the understanding of the Spirit's message in the Book. Consider now what this will involve. In the first place it gives the humblest and the least of the disciples of Jesus the *high right of approaching the Word of God* and receiving the message it brings him. In the next place it compels every one to hear the message the Spirit brings in its totality. There can be and dare be no limitation

upon nor false nor partial division of the eternal truth of God expressed in precept and command. Neither the right of private judgment, the decrees of kings or councils, the opinions of priest or parson, nor the preferences of the individual can set aside the eternal truth of God revealed through His word to his child. . . . this principle holds every man to the full surrender in obedience to every teaching of the Gospel without any let or gainsaying. There is not a command taught in the New Testament that a member of the Brethren church has not the high privilege of obeying. There is not a solitary principle of life, not a teaching that can not be heartily accepted and as heartily incorporated in life. This may result in various differences of opinions on multitudes of minor beliefs, but it allows great spiritual freedom in Christ Jesus. On the great fundamental ordinances of the Christian church, on the fundamental Christian principles the [Brethren] church is a marvelous unit. No elimination of either has ever occurred under this guiding principle. The greatest brotherly love and the strongest ties of Christian fellowship bind us together under this interpretative principle. I hold it [the interpretative principle] FUNDAMENTAL and VITAL to the fullest development of the individual life and THE ONLY WAY OF APPROACH to the Word of God by an honest soul.[14]

NOTES

INTRODUCTION

[1] Throughout their history the German Baptist Brethren have preferred the simple self-designation, "Brethren." In both Europe and America, however, their distinctive form of baptism, trine immersion, gave rise to several more popular names. In German sources they were referred to as *Täufer* (Baptists), *Neu-Täufer* (new Baptists to differentiate them from the "old" Baptists, the Anabaptists), *Tunck-Täufer* ("Dippers"), or *Täuf-gesinnte* (Baptist-minded). In Dutch materials the term *Dompelaars* ("Dippers" or "Baptists") appears. In America they were commonly called "Dunkers" or "Tunkers," names which often became vulgarized into "Dunkards" and "Tunkards." These terms were all anglicizations of the German word *tunken*, to dip. For official purposes the church adopted the name "Fraternity of German Baptist" in 1836. In 1871 this name was changed to "German Baptist Brethren."

Today five main branches of the Brethren exist. Three of these bodies resulted from divisions in the early 1880s: the Old German Baptist Brethren (popularly called the "Old Order Brethren"), The Brethren Church (the "Progressive Brethren"), and the main body of the church, the German Baptist Brethren (known as the "Conservatives" at the time of the split), which changed its name in 1908 to the Church of the Brethren. A fourth group, the Dunkard Brethren, withdrew from the Church of the Brethren in 1926, while the fifth group, the National Fellowship of Grace Brethren Churches, resulted from a rupture in The Brethren Church in 1939. This group was popularly called the "Grace Brethren" because of its support of the newly founded Grace Theological Seminary. The faction which was committed to the existing institutions of Ashland College and Theological Seminary acquired the designation "Ashland Brethren."

Two smaller groups sharing the German Baptist Brethren heritage have continued to be active during this century: the (New Dunkard) Church of God, which disbanded in 1962, and the German Seventh Day Baptists, who are the spiritual offspring of Conrad Beissel's Ephrata Community (see pp. 87–88).

In this study, the term "Brethren" will be used to designate the Brethren movement in general. The use of official or popular names will reflect the historical record as much as possible. Thus "German Baptist Brethren" will refer strictly to the pre-1880 body (there has been a tendency among writers from the various branches to use anachronistically the name of their particular body to refer to the pre-division history).

[2] Fitting the Brethren into the larger historical and theological context in America is a definite need in Brethren studies. Donald Durnbaugh's recent call for relating "the Brethren much more to the general historical movements of the time" in order to arrive at a more adequate interpretation of Brethren history is likewise applicable to the study of Brethren theology. See Donald F. Durnbaugh, "A Study of Brethren Historiography," *Ashland Theological Bulletin* (hereafter *ATB*) 8 (Spring 1975):16.

[3] Of special significance for the study of German Baptist Brethren history is the Brethren Source Book Series consisting of Donald F. Durnbaugh, comp. and ed., *European Origins of the Brethren* (Elgin, Illinois: The Brethren Press, 1958); Donald F. Durnbaugh, comp. and ed., *The Brethren in Colonial America* (Elgin, Illinois: The Brethren Press, 1967); Roger E. Sappington, comp. and ed., *The Brethren in the New Nation . . . 1785–1865* (Elgin, Illinois: The Brethren Press, 1976); and Roger E. Sappington, comp. and ed., *The Brethren in Industrial America . . . 1865–1915* (Elgin, Illinois: Brethren Press, 1985).

A number of historical surveys have been written. Three older works are: Martin Grove Brumbaugh, *A History of the German Baptist Brethren in Europe and America* (Mount Morris, Illinois: Brethren Publishing House, 1899; reprint ed. L. W. Shultz and Carl A. Wagoner, 1961 and 1969), a standard history which utilizes primary sources and focuses on the eighteenth century development of the Brethren in Europe and America; George N. Falkenstein, *History of the German Baptist Brethren Church* (Lancaster, Pennsylvania: The New Era Printing Company, 1901), a general history with emphasis on the Germantown congregation; and Henry R. Holsinger, *Holsinger's History of the Tunkers and The Brethren Church* (Oakland, California: Pacific Press Publishing Company, 1901; reprint ed., North Manchester, Indiana: L. W. Shultz, 1962), a comprehensive history with special importance for the history of the divisions in the early 1880s and its numerous biographical and congregational sketches.

More recent denominationally oriented histories include: (Church of the Brethren) Otho Winger, *History and Doctrines of the Church of the Brethren* (Elgin, Illinois: Brethren Publishing House, 1919) and Floyd E. Mallott, *Studies in Brethren History* (Elgin, Illinois: Brethren Publishing House, 1954); (Old German Baptist Brethren) John M. Kimmel, *Chronicles of the Brethren* (Berne, Indiana: The Economy Printing Concern, 1972) and Marcus Miller, *"Roots by the River"* (Piqua, Ohio: Hammer Graphics, Inc., 1973); (Ashland Brethren) Albert T. Ronk, *History of The Brethren Church* (Ashland, Ohio: Brethren Publishing Company, 1968); and (Grace Brethren) Homer A. Kent, Sr., *Conquering Frontiers* (Winona Lake, Indiana: BMH Books, 1958, rev. ed. 1972). Numerous district and congregational histories, especially for the Church of the Brethren, are also available.

[4] Ernest R. Sandeen, *The Origins of Fundamentalism: Toward a Historical Interpretation*, Facet Books: Historical Series, no. 10 (Philadelphia: Fortress Press, 1968), p. 24.

[5] Several significant elements have contributed to this renaissance. The source book series edited by Durnbaugh and Sappington (see p. 249, n. 3) is of inestimable value for historical and theological research. An exciting recent development has been the series of Brethren assemblies which began as the special vision of M. R. Zigler, elder statesman of the Church of the Brethren, former executive of the Brethren Service Commission in the United States and Europe, and representative of his church to the Federal and World Council of Churches. These assemblies commenced with the gathering of representatives from the major Brethren groups at Tunker House, Broadway, Virginia, on June 12 and 13, 1973. This initial meeting gave birth to a series of conferences of Brethren historians.

The agenda for most of the conferences has been the consideration of a significant period in Brethren history or a significant aspect of Brethren thought and practice. The first conference, held at Ashland Theological Seminary on April 19 and 20, 1975, dealt with the Brethren between 1785 and 1860. Study papers from the conference were published in the *Ashland Theological Bulletin* in the Spring of 1975. The second conference gathered at Bethany Theological Seminary (Church of the Brethren) on May 13 to 15, 1976. Under consideration were the Brethren during the Revolutionary War. Conference papers appeared in the Winter 1977 issue of *Brethren Life and Thought*. The fourth conference was held at Bridgewater College (Church of the Brethren) on April 28 and 29, 1978, and considered the Brethren between 1865 and 1900 (focusing on the divisions of the 1880s). Papers from this gathering were published in the Summer 1979 issue of *Brethren Life and Thought*. The fifth conference gathered at Covington, Ohio (hosted by the Old Order Brethren) on June 14 and 15, 1985, and discussed the Brethren plain dress. Presentations at this conference were published in the Summer 1986 issue of *Brethren Life and Thought*. The most recent conference was held at Ashland College and Seminary on March 27 and 28, 1987. The concern of this meeting was the concept of mission among the various Brethren groups. Conference papers appeared in the Spring 1988 issue of *Old Order Notes*.

At the second conference M. R. Zigler proposed a momentous project: the compilation of a Brethren encyclopedia. The third conference, held at Covington, Ohio, on October 21 and 22, 1977, devoted its time to planning for this project. Work on the encyclopedia was completed in 1984. Its appearance has represented a significant step in Brethren historical and doctrinal studies. See *The Brethren Encyclopedia*, 3 volumes.

[6] Robert Fowler Porte, "The Pietistic Tradition in the Brethren Church" (Th.D. dissertation, Drew University, 1933).

[7] C. David Ensign, "Radical German Pietism (c.1675-c.1760)" (Ph.D. dissertation, Boston University Graduate School, 1955); William G. Willoughby, "The Beliefs of the Early Brethren" (Ph.D. dissertation, Boston University Graduate School, 1951); Donald F. Durnbaugh, "The Genius of the Brethren," *Brethren Life and Thought* (hereafter *BLT*) 4 (Winter/Spring 1959):4-34/4-18; Vernard Eller, "On Epitomizing the Brethren," *BLT* 6 (Autumn 1961):47-52.

[8] Dale W. Brown, "The Developing Thought and Theology of the Brethren—1785-1860," *ATB* 8 (Spring 1975):61-74.

[9] Kerby Lauderdale, "Division among the German Baptist Brethren" (M.Div. Independent Study, Bethany Theological Seminary, 1968).

[10] Herbert Hogan, "The Intellectual Impact of the Twentieth Century on the Church of the Brethren" (Ph.D. dissertation, The

Claremont Graduate School, 1958).

[11] Dennis Martin, "Law and Grace" (Independent Study, Wheaton College, 1973), p. vi.

[12] J. L. Gillin, "Christian Freedom," *The Brethren Evangelist* (hereafter *BE*) 36 (October 14, 1914):3-4. Gillin received his graduate education at Union Theological Seminary and Columbia University, completing his Ph.D. in 1906 at Columbia. He was a leading figure in the Brethren Church during the first two decades of this century.

[13] Idem, "Our Denominational Position," *BE* 33 (August 30, 1911):6-7.

[14] See, for example, Ronk, *Brethren Church*, p. 367; Martin, "Law and Grace," p. 8; Hogan, "Intellectual Impact," pp. 10, 371.

[15] Philip Jacob Spener, *Pia Desideria*, trans. and ed. Theodore G. Tappert (Philadelphia: Fortress Press, 1964), pp. 49-56, 104-107; Dale W. Brown, *Understanding Pietism* (Grand Rapids, Michigan: William B. Eerdmans Publishing Company, 1978), pp. 24-25, 85; F. Ernest Stoeffler, *German Pietism during the Eighteenth Century* (Leiden: E. J. Brill, 1973), p. 45; and Egon W. Gerdes, "Theological Tenets of Pietism," *The Covenant Quarterly* 34 (February/May 1976):26-27.

[16] Of the 188 titles listed for the period 1713-1865 (a breakdown of this extended period would reveal fairly consistent figures for each time segment) in the "Brethren Bibliography," 100 were of a devotional character (primarily hymnbooks, but also sermons, edifying discourses, and collections of poems), 62 were doctrinal in nature, and 26 (24%) were miscellaneous in nature (periodicals, political broadsides, historical works, and polemical treatises). Between 1866 and 1880 the percentages change significantly. Of the 101 titles, 16 are devotional (16%), 42 are doctrinal (42%), and 43 are miscellaneous in nature (43%). The noticeable shift in the percentages of the miscellaneous materials during these two periods is due to the flood of periodicals that appeared as tensions built up toward the divisions in the early 1880s. Though primarily devotional in nature, the periodicals became more doctrinal and polemical as they neared 1880. For an annotated list of Brethren works see Donald F. Durnbaugh and Lawrence W. Shultz, "A Brethren Bibliography, 1713-1963," *BLT* 9 (Winter/Spring 1964).

[17] Vernard Eller, *Kierkegaard and Radical Discipleship: A New Perspective* (Princeton, New Jersey: Princeton University Press, 1968), p. 137.

[18] Adolph Harnack viewed dogma as an element foreign to the Gospel. In his famous definition, Harnack calls dogma "a work of the Greek spirit on the soil of the Gospel." He acknowledges that dogma is a product of theology but posits a gradual development of dogma to the point that it limits and criticizes the work of theology itself. The great danger of dogmatic Christianity is that "as knowledge it may supplant religious faith, or connect it with a doctrine of religion, *instead of with God and a living experience* [italics mine]." See Adolph Harnack, *History of Dogma*, 7 vols., trans. Neil Buchanan (London: Williams & Norgate, 1894), I:9, 16-17. Significantly, in discussing the dogmatism of Protestant Scholasticism, Gillin includes the following footnote: "See especially, Harnack, *History of Dogma*, Eng. trans. 7:168f. I have received the most help on this subject from the unpublished lectures of Prof. A. C. McGiffert of Union Theological Seminary, of New York." John Lewis Gillin, *The Dunkers: A Sociological Interpretation* (New York: n.p., 1906), p. 18. Harnack's implicit emphasis on experience in the above quote finds explicit elaboration in an article written by Gillin. He discerns only four possible bases for the Christian faith: an infallible creed, an infallible church, an infallible Bible, and an infallible experience. Utilizing *ad hominem* argumentation, he maintains that the judgment of those who have

sought an infallible authority during the course of church history has been decidedly against the infallible character of creed, church, and "book." He concludes: "Therefore they have found a basis for faith in Christ in the infallible experience which, after all, throughout the ages has been the fundamental thing." Gillin, "The Bases of Christian Faith (In Three Parts—Part I)," *BE* 37 (October 6, 1915):4.

[19] Hogan, "Intellectual Impact," p. 377 notes that the non-credal emphasis of the Brethren formed a foundation for liberalism in the Church of the Brethren also.

[20] These traits are exemplified in a speech which Gillin delivered at the 1915 General Conference of the Brethren Church.

In its [the Brethren Church's] essence and nature it is pietistic, having to do with life rather than doctrine, using that term in the theological sense. The church was not concerned

with such theological questions as predestination, virgin birth, relation of the three persons of the Trinity, definition of the exact relation of man to God, or any of the other historic theological doctrines and controversies. . . .

. . . A person may be a member of the Brethren church and be a Millenial Dawnist, and he may be a member of the church and not believe in that theory at all. He may be a member of the church and be an Athanasian on the subject of the nature of the person of Christ, or on the other hand he may be an Arian and still be a good member of the church. These things are of minor importance.

See J. L. Gillin, "The Conservation of Our Denominational Resources," in *Minutes of the Twenty-seventh General Conference of the Brethren Church . . . 1915* (Ashland, Ohio: The Brethren Publishing Company, n.d.), pp. 32–33.

PART I: THE HISTORICAL AND THEOLOGICAL ROOTS OF BRETHREN THOUGHT
CHAPTER 1: PIETISM

[1] For further details concerning these controversies see Otto W. Heick, *A History of Christian Thought*, 2 vols. (Philadelphia: Fortress Press, 1965), 1:447–466.

[2] Williston Walker, *A History of the Christian Church* (New York: Charles Scribner's Sons, 1959), pp. 390–391.

[3] Ibid., p. 396.

[4] For citation of books connected with this discussion see Allen C. Deeter, "An Historical and Theological Introduction to Philipp Jakob Spener's *Pia Desideria*: A Study in Early German Pietism" (Ph.D. dissertation, Princeton University, 1963), pp. 2–5. The problem involves the proper interpretation of the propogandistic reports of the suffering and loss during the Thirty Years' War.

[5] C. V. Wedgwood, *The Thirty Years War* (Garden City, New York: Anchor Books, 1961), pp. 497, 505–506.

[6] F. Ernest Stoeffler, *The Rise of Evangelical Pietism*, Studies in the History of Religions, no. 9 (Leiden: E. J. Brill, 1971), p. 112.

[7] Ibid., p. 114.

[8] A clear strain of piety can be found in Calvin's writings. Especially noteworthy is his booklet, *De Vita Hominis Christiani*, which was originally part of the *Institutes* but was published separately in Latin and French in 1550. The titles of the five chapters in this brief work reveal themes that constantly reappear in Pietistic literature: Humble Obedience, the True Imitation of Christ; Self-denial; Patience in Crossbearing; Hopefulness in the Next World; The Right Use of the Present Life. See John Calvin, *Golden Booklet of the True Christian Life*, trans. Henry J. Van Andel (Grand Rapids, Michigan: Baker Book House, 1952). The young Luther exhibited a strong inclination towards a piety of a more mystical nature than Calvin's. He showed special interest in Tauler and the *German Theology*. His writings from the period between 1516 and 1520 contain concepts which clearly have their roots in mystical piety: union with Christ, Christ as the bridegroom of the soul, love for God, and the necessity of crossbearing through the negation of self-will. Stoeffler draws the following conclusion from these facts: "While it is true that Luther expressed his divergence by making union with Christ the result of justification by faith he did prepare the ground for mystical piety among his own followers . . ." *Evangelical Pietism*, p. 192.

[9] Stoeffler, *Evangelical Pietism*, p. 116. Because Stoeffler's two volumes on Pietism are the only general survey of the movement available in English, much of the discussion, especially with regard to Reformed Pietism, comes from his works.

[10] Ibid.

[11] Ibid., pp. 117–118. Stoeffler details the considerable impact that Pietistic Puritanism had on Reformed Pietism. See also James Tanis "Reformed Pietism in Colonial America," in *Continental Pietism and Early American Christianity* (hereafter *Continental Pietism*), ed. F. Ernest Stoeffler (Grand Rapids, Michigan: William B. Eerdmans Publishing Company, 1976), pp. 35–36.

[12] Tanis, "Reformed Pietism," pp. 39–40.

[13] Stoeffler, *Evangelical Pietism*, p. 123.

[14] Ibid., p. 125.

[15] Ibid., pp. 125–126.

[16] Ibid., pp. 127–133.

[17] Ibid., p. 133. Stoeffler finds support for this designation in the title of a book on Ames by K. Reuter.

[18] Ibid., pp. 133–141.

[19] The incongruity that exists between the ethos of Scholasticism and that of Pietism may explain Stoeffler's omission of any extended discussion of Voetius. It should be remembered, however, that piety and doctrinal purity had existed side by side in the Reformed tradition from the start. Voetius' concern for both doctrine and piety certainly justifies his inclusion. Likewise the precisionist strain of Dutch Reformed piety would seem to be quite amenable to a more scholastic mentality.

[20] Tanis, "Reformed Pietism," pp. 34–35. Note the names of three of his writings cited by Tanis: *The Test of the Power of Godliness* (1628), *Exercitia et Bibliotheca Studiosi Theologiae* (1644), and *Exercitia Pietatis* (1664). See also Ensign, "Radical German Pietism," pp. 58–59.

[21] Stoeffler, *Evangelical Pietism*, pp. 141–148.

[22] Ibid., pp. 148–151. Tanis, "Reformed Pietism," p. 50 applies the appropriate term "spiritual precisionism" to Brakel's piety.

[23] Stoeffler, *Evangelical Pietism*, pp. 151–157 and Tanis, "Reformed Pietism," pp. 50–51.

[24] *The Mennonite Encyclopedia*, s.v. "Collegiants," by N. van der Zijpp.

[25] Ibid.

[26] Stoeffler, *Evangelical Pietism*, p. 177. In the latter part of the seventeenth century, German Radical Pietists came to share many of these beliefs, though no direct borrowing by the German Radicals from the Collegiants seems to have taken place.

[27] Ibid., pp. 162–169.

[28] Ibid., pp. 169–172.

[29] Ibid., pp. 172–174.

[30] Durnbaugh, *European Origins*, pp. 30–31 notes that between 1550 and 1700 the official religion of the Palatinate had changed eight times. From 1685 until the end of the eighteenth century the rulers of the Palatinate were more or less committed to Roman Catholicism.

[31] Stoeffler, *German Pietism*, pp. 218–219.

[32] Idem, *Evangelical Pietism*, pp. 175–176.

[33] Heinz Renkewitz, *Hochmann von Hochenau (1670–1721)*, Quellenstudien zur Geschichte des Pietismus, no. 5 (Witten: Luther-Verlag, 1969), pp. 194–195.

[34] Stoeffler, *Evangelical Pietism*, pp. 193–196.

[35] Ibid., pp. 196–200.

[36] Theosophy or nature mysticism is a speculative form of theology in which nature is appreciated as the macrocosm of divine wisdom and truth while man is viewed as the microcosm or concentration of the universe. Knowledge of divine truth "must be found in 'the heart of God,' [i.e., in mystical union with God] from whence nature proceeds, and only the pure in heart can see God. Hence it requires a strenuous spiritual discipline." Ensign, "Radical German Pietism," pp. 30–31. The inevitable result of such a system is to spiritualize the church and Scripture.

[37] Stoeffler, *Evangelical Pietism*, pp. 200–202.

[38] His principal writings include *Wahres Christentum* (*True Christianity*) and *Paradiesgärtlein* (*The Little Garden Of Paradise*). Heick, *Christian Thought*, 1:471 calls *True Christianity* the most widely read devotional book in Lutheranism.

[39] Stoeffler, *Evangelical Pietism*, pp. 202–210 and Ensign, "Radical German Pietism," pp. 53–55.

[40] Deeter, "Spener's *Pia Desideria*," p. 30.

[41] Ibid., p. 31; Stoeffler, *Evangelical Pietism*, p. 217; and Tappert, "Introduction" in Spener, *Pia Desideria*, pp. 6–7.

[42] For a more explicit discussion see Ensign, "Radical German Pietism," pp. 55–56.

[43] Stoeffler, *Evangelical Pietism*, pp. 218–227.

[44] Deeter, "Spener's *Pia Desideria*," p. 29.

[45] Ibid., pp. 44–45, 89–127 and Stoeffler, *Evangelical Pietism*, pp. 228–229.

[46] Deeter, "Spener's *Pia Desideria*," p. x.

[47] Spener, *Pia Desideria*, pp. 39–75.

[48] Ibid., pp. 76–86.

[49] Ibid., pp. 87–122.

[50] Stoeffler, *German Pietism*, p. 39.

[51] Ibid., p. 23.

[52] Ibid., pp. 25–28.

[53] For a discussion of the problems posed in a discussion of the "theology of Pietism" see Gerdes, "Theological Tenets," pp. 26–27.

[54] Three different approaches to the ordering of the various features of Pietism can be seen in Stoeffler, *Evangelical Pietism*, pp. 13–23; Brown, *Understanding Pietism*, pp. 27–28; and Gerdes, "Theological Tenets," pp. 28–53.

[55] Both Spener and Francke can be seen as following in the tradition of Johann Arndt. Since Arndt's thought has already been summarized, however, attention in this discussion will be focused on the views of Spener and Francke.

[56] Brown, *Understanding Pietism*, pp. 88–89.

[57] Stoeffler, *German Pietism*, p. 15.

[58] The orthodox *ordo salutis* of Spener's day consisted of divine calling, illumination, repentance, saving faith, justification, and sanctification. The first four items of the process were sometimes subsumed under the terms conversion or regeneration (frequently used interchangeably). Special emphasis was placed on justification. Stoeffler, *Evangelical Pietism*, pp. 240–241. Though Spener and Francke followed the general order of this scheme, the new birth or regeneration received the major attention following repentance and faith with justification being discussed more briefly in connection with faith. This shifting of emphasis in the *ordo salutis* from justification to regeneration had important ramifications. As in the discussion below, the Pietists frequently viewed forgiveness of sins as an aspect of the new birth whereas the Orthodox connected it with justification. The new righteous standing before God highlighted by the Reformation view of justification tended to be overshadowed by the new relationship to God effected in the new birth and expressed in terms of psychological or volitional union. In addition, the Reformers derived their doctrine of assurance from forgiveness of sins which they rooted in justification. Pietists, however, generally connected assurance with regeneration and sanctification. Thus, assurance for the Reformers was a purely divine gift of grace and forensically valid. For Pietists assurance was realized in the divine-human cooperation which characterized sanctification. Assurance therefore possessed an essential inward spiritual character—the new relationship to God effected in the new birth—which expressed itself in a new being characterized by outward visible marks—obedience, good works, active faith, love, etc.

[59] Brown, *Understanding Pietism*, p. 91. See also Stoeffler, *German Pietism*, pp. 16–17.

[60] Stoeffler, *Evangelical Pietism*, p. 242. See also Stoeffler, *German Pietism*, p. 17.

[61] An important question is raised at this juncture: What role does mysticism play in the piety of Spener and Francke? Most scholars would agree with Eric Seeberg's contention that "there is a streak of mysticism in all Pietism." Eric Seeberg, *Mystik, Spiritualismus und die Anfänge des Pietismus im Luthertum* (Giessen: Alfred Töpelmann, 1926), p. 2, quoted in Brown, *Understanding Pietism*, p. 18. Even though Spener and Francke felt mystical literature could be edifying, they also recognized its weaknesses. Spener, for example, commends Tauler for his emphasis on Christ as the foundation for our salvation but admits that Tauler has also placed the wood and stubble of papist errors and superstitions on this good foundation. Spener is also discriminating in his recommendation of mystical literature, generally endorsing only Arndt, à Kempis, Tauler, and the *German Theology*. Such mysticism tended to be practical, affective, Christ-centered, and active as opposed to other current forms (Boehmism, Quietism) which were speculative, ascetic, and passive. It is true that Francke translated the works of the quietist, Molinos, from Italian into Latin and appreciated his emphasis on humility, Christ-centeredness, and the trials associated with Christian experience. Yet scholars are generally agreed that Quietism had no profound effect on Francke's theology. Stoeffler, *German Pietism*, pp. 5, 9. What Deeter has concluded about Spener is applicable to Spener-Halle Pietism in general. "His Christianity is too sober, practical and duty-bound for high-flown allegories of the progress of the soul toward union with God, for contemplative inactivity and doctrinal indifference." "Spener's *Pia Desideria*," p. 48.

[62] Stoeffler, *German Pietism*, p. 18 and Gerdes, "Theological Tenets," p. 29.

[63] Stoeffler, *Evangelical Pietism*, p. 241; Brown, *Understanding Pietism*, pp. 94–97; and Deeter, "Spener's *Pia Desideria*," p. 178.

[64] Brown, *Understanding Pietism*, pp. 97–98 and Deeter, "Spener's *Pia Desideria*," pp. 70, 181–182.

[65] Stoeffler, *German Pietism*, pp. 19–20.

[66] Brown, *Understanding Pietism*, pp. 69–72; Stoeffler, *Evangelical Pietism*, p. 240; and Deeter, "Spener's *Pia Desideria*," p. 187.

[67] Unlike Orthodoxy, which maintained that there were no adiaphorous doctrines in theology (a central issue in the Calixtine

controversy; see Heick, *Christian Thought*, 2:50-53), Spener distinguished between esoteric and exoteric doctrines and again between primary and secondary matters of faith. Esoteric doctrines were privately held opinions which should not be exposed for public consideration; exoteric doctrines were the essential truths of the Christian faith which demanded constant reiteration. Spener differed little from Calixtus in differentiating between primary, essential truths and secondary, non-essential ones. His basic position was summarized in the saying: "in necessary things, unity; in things not necessary, liberty; in all things, love." Brown, *Understanding Pietism*, pp. 39-43. It is significant from the standpoint of emphasis that Spener-Halle Pietism sought freedom in dogmatic non-essentials while opposing the existence of ethical *adiaphora*; in contrast Orthodoxy maintained there were no theological *adiaphora* but in personal ethics recognized adiaphoristic practices. See Stoeffler, *German Pietism*, p. 70. Generally speaking, Spener and Francke sought a middle way between dogmatic inflexibility and dogmatic indifference.

[68] Brown, *Understanding Pietism*, pp. 78-79.

[69] F. Ernest Stoeffler, "Pietism: Its Message, Early Manifestation, and Significance," *The Covenant Quarterly* 34 (February/May 1967):13.

[70] Spener, *Pia Desideria*, pp. 76-86 and Gerdes, "Theological Tenets," pp. 43-45.

CHAPTER 2: RADICAL PIETISM

[1] Stoeffler, *German Pietism*, pp. 168-169, n. 2.

[2] Idem, *Evangelical Pietism*, pp. 212-217.

[3] Heick, *Christian Thought*, 2:28.

[4] Nils Thune, *The Behmenists and the Philadelphians: A Contribution to the Study of English Mysticism in the 17th and 18th Centuries* (Uppsala: Almqvist & Wiksells Boktryckeri AB, 1948), p. 20.

[5] The Radicals' strong aversion to marriage derives from their acceptance of the Boehmist view that sexuality is a post-fall phenomenon. Gichtel's further development of Sophia teaching gave added impulse for celibacy among separatists. Interestingly, Boehme was married and had no children.

[6] In Boehme's view of the virgin birth, there are definite intimations of the celestial flesh theory held by Anabaptists (Hofmann, Menno, the Philips brothers) and Spiritualists (Schwenckfeld) during the Reformation. See Heick, *Christian Thought*, 2:29. Ensign, "Radical German Pietism," pp. 122, 407 indicates that the concept of the "heavenly God-Manhood of Christ" was mediated to Radical Pietist circles by Boehme and Weigel.

[7] Ensign, "Radical German Pietism," pp. 37-43 and Heick, *Christian Thought*, 2:28-29.

[8] Stoeffler, *German Pietism*, pp. 169-170.

[9] Ibid., pp. 170-171. The use of the words "spiritualism" and "mysticism" in this chapter reflect the above Boehmist emphases. Thus spiritualism refers primarily to the spiritual interpretation or rejection of that which is outward, objective, and institutional. The contemporary, internal work of the Holy Spirit is viewed as superior to any historic, outward record of its work, be it in the church, the clergy, or, even in some cases, the Bible. Mysticism designates the desire to cultivate an affective union with God (this type of mysticism is shared by Boehmist and Arndtian Pietists). Here union is thought of not in terms of metaphysical substance but of "affection and will 'with the focus on the sentiment of the heart and on love as the way of being, feeling, knowing.'" Dale Weaver Brown, "The Problem of Subjectivism in Pietism" (Ph.D. dissertation, Northwestern University, 1962), p. 162. The impulse for separation from the established church was strengthened by viewing all the established churches, including the Lutheran church, as Babel. The term "Babel" became an important part of Radical Pietism's arsenal. In German it meant not only "Babel" but also "Babylon." Therefore the connotations of the term were manifold. "It means the confusion of the tower of Babel, the captivity of the children of Israel in a strange land, the mother of harlots and abominations of Revelation 17:5, and the great, wicked and luxurious city of Revelation 18, which God judged so severely." Ensign, "Radical German Pietism," p. 47.

[10] Ensign, "Radical German Pietism," p. 75 and Stoeffler, *German Pietism*, p. 171.

[11] The basic work on this movement is Thune, *Behmenists and Philadelphians*. The seventeenth century English followers of Boehme were called Behmenists as a result of a corruption of Boehme's name.

[12] Stoeffler, *German Pietism*, p. 209.

[13] Ibid., pp. 208-209 and Ensign, "Radical German Pietism," pp. 194-195.

[14] Ensign, "Radical German Pietism," p. 195 and Thune, *Behmenists and Philadelphians*, p. 78.

[15] Though Boehme taught that God had both the "light" and "dark" principles in Himself, he maintained that God was essentially love. Yet his voluntarism kept him from being a universalist. Thus, those who experienced God's "dark" side or wrath did so as the inevitable result of their own willful turning away from Him.

[16] Pordage's *Theologia Mystica* was translated in 1698, his *Sophia* in 1699 (Ensign, "Radical German Pietism," p. 191, n. 3 observes that "the similarity of Arnold's *Sophia* [1700] can scarcely be coincidental"), and his *Vier tractätlein* in 1704. Baron Knyphausen, the German patron of the Petersens (see below), sponsored the publication of Mrs. Leade's works in German by the publisher, Loth Fischer of Utrecht (two works appeared in 1694-95). Bromley's *The Way to the Sabbath of Rest* appeared in German in 1685 and was highly praised by Arnold. It was also published by the German presses in America run by the Ephrata Cloister and Christopher Sauer II (see pp. 87-88). Ensign, "Radical German Pietism," pp. 191-193.

[17] Thune, *Behmenists and Philadelphians*, p. 113.

[18] Ibid., pp. 125-126 and Ensign, "Radical German Pietism," pp. 203-204.

[19] Ensign, "Radical German Pietism," pp. 204-207.

[20] One is reminded of the phenomena accompanying the Cane Ridge revival during the Second Great Awakening in America.

[21] R. A. Knox, *Enthusiasm: A Chapter in the History of Religion* (London: Oxford University Press, 1950), p. 350.

[22] Ensign, "Radical German Pietism," pp. 229, 232. See also Erich Seeberg, *Gottfried Arnold: Die Wissenschaft und die Mystik Seiner Zeit*, Studien zur Historiographie und zur Mystik (Darmstadt: Wissenschaftliche Buchgesellschaft, 1964) pp. 43-47.

[23] Stoeffler, *German Pietism*, pp. 5, 171-172.

[24] Ensign, "Radical German Pietism," pp. 223-228.

[25] Arnold's prefaces were attached to German editions of Molinos' *Guida spirituale* (1699), Guyon's two treatises, "Les torrens" and "Moyen court pour faire l'oraison" (1701), and various letters by Petrucci (1702).

[26] Ensign's thesis that Boehmism represents Radical Pietism's "most significant doctrinal principle of unity" is made quite tenuous by the impact which Quietism came to have on the

movement. It is true that the distinctive character of the Babel-storming period is clearly Boehmist. It is likewise true that Boehmist elements continue to be present even after the flames of excitement had been quenched by Quietism. The Boehmist view of the creation, fall, and restoration of the divine image with the corollary emphases on Sophia mysticism and celibacy continued to be held by eighteenth century Radical Pietists as did his critical view of the "sects." However, the type of mysticism that controlled the character of Radical Pietism during the eighteenth century was Quietism. Ensign's attempt ("Radical German Pietism," p. 231) to down play the basic incompatibility of the characters of Boehmism and Quietism by noting that "the two strains are found quite peaceably side by side in Arnold, and in the Berleburg Bible" is not convincing. In Arnold's case (as will be detailed later) a theological struggle, evidenced by a new perspective toward marriage and the church, occurred in which he forsook a Boehmist-determined piety for one controlled by Quietism. Even in the Berleburg Bible the emphasis is on inwardness, *Gelassenheit*, and pure, disinterested love, though this emphasis frequently is clothed in Boehmist categories. Even Radical Pietists of the eighteenth century recognized the difference between the two systems and tended to depreciate the Babel-storming period. For example, see Ensign, "German Radical Pietism," p. 345. Significantly, Ensign also admits that "in Marsay and Tersteegen quietism may have supplanted Boehmism as the chief *motiv*" (p. 231). For details of Ensign's view, see "German Radical Pietism," pp. 21–22, 230–231, 409–410.

[27] Ibid., pp. 131, 222.

[28] For a fuller discussion of both these Radical Pietist literary productions, see Ensign, "Radical German Pietism," pp. 324–355.

[29] The individualism and resulting animosity which occasionally surfaced among the Radicals is attested to by the founder of the Ephrata Community in Pennsylvania, Conrad Beissel. Reflecting on conditions among the Radicals in Wittgenstein, Beissel testified that

> he beheld a worse Babel among the pious who had come out from Babel than he had seen in Babel itself; for while in the latter one religion strove against the other, here persons were opposed one to the other. Each one lived for himself, and regulated his conduct according to his own inclinations . . .

Lamech and Agrippa [pseud.], *Chronicon Ephratense: A History of the Community of Seventh Day Baptists of Ephrata, Lancaster County, Penn'a*, trans. J. Max Hark (Lancaster, Pennsylvania: S. H. Zahm and Co., 1899; reprint ed., New York: Burt Franklin, 1972), p. 9.

[30] It is a reflection on Spener's conciliatory nature that, though he was pleased with Arnold's *Abbildung*, he never read the *Ketzerhistorie*. When he heard reports of the contents of the *Ketzerhistorie*, Spener determined not to read it. In this way he avoided the obligation of passing judgment on the work (and thereby on Arnold), even though Arnold urged him to read it. See Ensign, "Radical German Pietism," p. 94.

[31] Jürgen Büchsel, *Gottfried Arnold: Sein Verständnis von Kirche und Wiedergeburt*, Arbeiten zur Geschichte des Pietismus, no. 8 (Witten: Luther-Verlag, 1970), pp. 26–27.

[32] Quoted in *The Mennonite Encyclopedia*, s.v. "Arnold, Gottfried," by Robert Friedmann. As a general principle this statement is true though Arnold also noted the shortcomings of the heretics and held that God had his true witnesses in the confessional churches as well.

[33] Seeberg, *Wissenschaft und Mystik*, pp. 174–175.

[34] The reason why Arnold and other Radicals had such scruples against taking communion was because they considered the Lutheran observance of the sacrament profaned by the admission of the unregenerate and unrepentant to the Lord's table. See Albrecht Ritschl, *Geschichte des Pietismus*, vol. 2: *Der Pietismus in der lutherischen Kirchen des 17. und 18. Jahrhunderts* (Bonn: Adolph Marcus, 1884), p. 314.

[35] Stoeffler, *German Pietism*, p. 177. The classical expression of the Radical Pietist schematization of marriage is found in an appendage to Hochmann's *Glaubensbekenntnis*, written as a condition for his release from the Detmold prison. He distinguished five types of marriages: (1) The completely beastly marriage occurs when men take wives like dumb beasts, purely for sexual motives. (2) In the honorable and moral, yet heathenish marriage, all legal requirements are observed. Yet, it is pagan because the partners do not stand in a covenant with God, and they enter into marriage for worldly considerations. (3) The Christian marriage takes place when two people, made holy by the blood of Christ, unite in married, Christlike love. (4) The *Jungfräuliche* marriage occurs when two people, who are already consecrated to God, unite for the purpose of helping each other to a fuller holiness (sexual abstinence is observed). (5) In the marriage of the soul to the Lamb, a believer takes Christ for "Mann" or "Braut" and thereby attains the highest degree of glory in the Kingdom of God. In this formulation Arnold had indeed "fallen," first by taking a wife and second by having children. Ensign, "Radical German Pietism," pp. 174–176.

[36] Büchsel, *Kirche und Wiedergeburt*, pp. 153–156.

[37] For a discussion of writings detailing Arnold's changed perspective, see Büchsel, *Kirche und Wiedergeburt*, pp. 110–121. See also Seeberg, *Wissenschaft und Mystik*, pp. 8–10.

[38] Some writers have interpreted Arnold's new perspective as a rejection of radicalism and a return to churchly Pietism (they simply equate radicalism with separatism). See, for example, Büchsel, *Kirche und Wiedergeburt*, pp. 106, 198–204; Seeberg, *Wissenschaft und Mystik*, p. 1; and Erich Seeberg, ed., *Gottfried Arnold; in Auswahl Herausgegeben*, Mystiker des Abendlandes (München: Albert Langen-Georg Müller Verlag, 1934), p. 4. To equate radicalism with separatism rather than with a mystical-spiritualist piety (as this discussion does) seems inappropriate for three reasons. (1) Separatism itself was a by-product of a mysticism and spiritualism derived from Boehme. (2) Although Arnold's mysticism underwent a basic change when he came under the influence of Quietism (see below), nevertheless, his piety continued to be expressed through this medium. (3) Arnold never fully shared the basic goals and emphases of church-related Pietism. Unlike churchly Pietists he refused to pledge allegiance to the Formula of Concord throughout his years of service to the Lutheran Church. Also Spener-Halle Pietism took a reserved view of mysticism (see p. 252, n. 61). For a similar judgment concerning the general continuity of Arnold's radical position, see Hermann Dörries, *Geist und Geschichte bei Gottfried Arnold* (Göttingen: Vandenhoeck & Ruprecht, 1963), pp. 99–102, 108–111, n. 118 and Ensign, "Radical German Pietism," pp. 146–147. Positing a rejection of radicalism and a return to churchly Pietism by Arnold likewise forces one to dispute Arnold's own contention that even in his later life he remained true to the basic insights of his radical period (cf. Büchsel, *Kirche und Wiedergeburt*, pp. 190–194). The attempts in this direction have not been convincing. Seeberg, *Auswahl Herausgegeben*, p. 11 admits that Boehmism contributed the distinctive color (*Grundfarbe*) to Arnold's thought throughout his life (this conclusion was derived from the fact that Arnold's

last writing, *Theologia Experimentalis*, manifests Sophia mysticism). Additionally, if it is correct to postulate mysticism and spiritualism as the modes of expression for the Radicals' piety, then Büchsel's admission that Arnold never forsook either his belief in the fall of the church or his appreciation for mysticism (see *Kirche und Wiedergeburt*, p. 202) would add further support to the position advocated in this chapter. Those changes which did occur in Arnold's thought can be traced to quietistic influences and by no means represent a rejection of a mystical-spiritualist understanding of the Christian life and church. Admittedly, separatism was a key element in Radical Pietism. (Radical Pietists in general would share Alexander Mack's lament that some separatists had hardly "left the great Babel several years before than they voluntarily returned to it." See Alexander Mack, "Basic Questions," in Durnbaugh, *European Origins*, p. 343.) Yet the truly constitutive element of Radical Pietism was its mystical-spiritualistic piety which, for Arnold at least, could still find expression within the context of the fallen church.

[39] Seeberg, *Wissenschaft und Mystik*, pp. 43–44.

[40] Ensign, "Radical German Pietism," p. 130.

[41] Ibid., p. 139.

[42] Seeberg, *Auswahl Herausgegeben*, pp. 393–394.

[43] As this discussion intimates, Arnold considers the three stages of mystical theology to be purity, illumination, and unity. Ibid., p. 392.

[44] Ibid., p. 12.

[45] Büchsel, *Kirche und Wiedergeburt*, p. 123.

[46] Ibid., p. 202.

[47] The full title is *Die Erste Liebe Der Gemeinen Jesu Christi, Das ist, Wahre Abbildung Der Ersten Christen, Nach Ihrem Lebendigen Glauben Und Heiligen Leben, Aus der ältesten und bewährtesten Kirchen-Scribenten eigenen Zeugnissen, Exempeln und Reden, Nach der Wahrheit der Ersten Eigenen Christlichen Religion, allen Liebhabern der Historischen Wahrheit, und sonderlich der Antiquität, als in einer nützlichen Kirchen-Historie, Treulich und unpartheyisch entworffen, worinnen zugleich des Herrn William Cave Erstes Christenthum Nach Nothdurfft erläutert wird, Von Gottfried Arnold.* (Franckfurt am Mayn: Gottlieb Friedeburgs Buchhandlung, 1696).

[48] Ibid., Zuschrift, pp. 1–2.

[49] Ibid., 8, 21, 1, p. 408 (the notations refer to book, chapter, paragraph, and page respectively).

[50] Ibid., Vorrede 1, pp. 1–2 and Vorrede 3, p. 3.

[51] Büchsel, *Kirche und Wiedergeburt*, p. 33. He cites the *Abbildung*, 5, 5, 5, p. 100: "Sie [the early Christians] 'giengen die Mittel-Strasse zwischen einer schädlichen Unwissenheit und einer falschen Weißheit und sündlichen Neugierigkeit.'" Though the quote refers to the first Christians, Büchsel is correct, no doubt, in extending its application.

[52] Arnold, *Abbildung*, Vorrede 4, p. 4 and Vorrede 5, p. 4.

[53] Ibid., Zuschrift, p. 2.

[54] Büchsel, *Kirche und Wiedergeburt*, p. 34. An example of this principle can be seen in Arnold, *Abbildung*, Vorrede 6, p. 5.

[55] Arnold uses this word infrequently in his work (Büchsel cites eight appearances) and he does not explicitly define the term. See Büchsel, *Kirche und Wiedergeburt*, p. 34, n. 16.

[56] Martin Schmidt, "Gottfried Arnold (1666–1715)," in *Das Zeitalter des Pietismus*, Martin Schmidt and Wilhelm Jannasch, eds. (Bremen: Carl Schünemann Verlag, 1965), p. 143.

[57] Seeberg, *Wissenschaft und Mystik*, p. 230.

[58] Of the 135 Christian authors listed by Arnold in his "Zeit-Register der vornehmsten Kirchen-Scribenten" (a two page introductory section), only twenty-six lived in the first three centuries,

while twenty-one lived in the fourth century; thus only about one-third lived in the period described by Arnold. In addition, twenty-eight are later than 1000 A.D. Compare with Büchsel, *Kirche und Wiedergeburt*, p. 38.

[59] Arnold, *Abbildung*, Vorrede 11, p. 8; see also Büchsel, *Kirche und Wiedergeburt*, p. 38.

[60] Büchsel, *Kirche und Wiedergeburt*, pp. 38–40. See also Dörries, *Geist und Geschichte*, pp. 148–193.

[61] Seeberg, *Auswahl Herausgegeben*, p. 16.

[62] Idem, *Wissenschaft und Mystik*, p. 69 observes that the *Abbildung* can be rightly called Arnold's "Dogmatik." This work delimits Arnold's view of what the church should be (though he must "idealize" the early church in the process).

[63] Büchsel, *Kirche und Wiedergeburt*, pp. 43–44.

[64] For further details on the above points, see Arnold, *Abbildung*, 8, 2, 14, p. 207; 8, 1, 1, p. 190; 8, 4, 20, p. 233.

[65] Büchsel, *Kirche und Wiedergeburt*, pp. 44–45.

[66] Arnold, *Abbildung*, Zuschrift, p. 1.

[67] Büchsel, *Kirche und Wiedergeburt*, p. 44.

[68] Seeberg, *Wissenschaft und Mystik*, p. 219 fittingly describes Arnold's conception of the heretics as the ἀνακεφαλαίωσις (recapitulation) of his thought.

[69] Arnold, *Abbildung*, 8, 21, 16, p. 416.

[70] Ibid., 8, 22, 13, p. 425. Arnold preferred the "lenient" term, "error" (*Irrthum*), to that "detested" word, "heresy." Ibid., 8, 21, 7, p. 412.

[71] Ibid.

[72] Ibid., 8, 21, 8, p. 412.

[73] Ibid., 8, 21, 9, p. 413. In this passage some of Arnold's characteristic vocabulary for the fall is to be found. The "Clerisey" bore the major responsibility for the fall. The most serious evils of the fall were "Menschen-Satzungen," "Gewissenszwang," "Heucherlei," and "opus operatum."

[74] See his criticism in ibid., 8, 17–20.

[75] Ibid., 8, 23, 6, p. 429.

[76] Ibid., 8, 23, 8, pp. 430–431. As examples of "witnesses of the truth," Arnold cites such men as Origen, Pelagius, Raymond Lull, Vigilantius, Eutyches, and Nestorius. Arnold does not make a simple equation between the heretics and the representatives of the true church. Frequently, he will use a qualifying word or phrase to show he has only some heretics in mind. For instance, note this statement which precedes the above quotation: "Ich müste hievon ein sehr longes Register derer jenigen machen, welche allein um ihrer Gottseligkeit Willen von der bösen Welt verketzert worden . . ."

[77] Ibid., see also Büchsel, *Kirche und Wiedergeburt*, p. 46.

[78] Cf. Büchsel, *Kirche und Wiedergeburt*, p. 47 and Seeberg, *Wissenschaft und Mystik*, p. 145.

[79] Arnold, *Abbildung*, 1, 1, 1, p. 1.

[80] Ibid., 1, 1, 1–8, pp. 1–4.

[81] Ibid., 1, 1, 13–18, pp. 6–9.

[82] Ibid., 1, 3, 1–20, pp. 18–30.

[83] Ibid., 1, 4, 3–4, pp. 33–34.

[84] Ibid., 1, 4, 15, p. 39. Arnold cites Tatian, Irenaeus, and Tertullian in this regard.

[85] Ibid., 1, 19, 2, p. 132.

[86] Ibid., 1, 4, 9, p. 36.

[87] Ibid., 1, 4, 15, p. 39; 1, 5, 1, p. 40.

[88] Ibid., 1, 4, 6, p. 34.

[89] Ibid., 1, 4, 6–14, pp. 34–39.

[90] Ibid., 1, 11, 3–7, pp. 81–82. Note the similarity between Arnold's view of intentional sin and that of Wesley.

[91] Ibid., 1, 12, 1–9, pp. 85–88.

[92] Büchsel, *Kirche und Wiedergeburt*, p. 52.

[93] Arnold, *Abbildung*, 1, 13, 3-7, pp. 90-92. This emphasis on fulfilling God's law, which was quite prominent in Reformed Pietism, was likewise important for both Spener-Halle Pietism and Radical Pietism.

[94] Ibid., 1, 13, 10-11, p. 93. Note for example the following citation from Macarius: "Er ward davon überwogen und gleichsam truncken gemacht, ja verschlungen und gefangen genommen in eine andere Welt, gleich als ob er seine Natur nicht mehr empfünde. . . . Deswegen begehrten sie die Liebe dieses Himmels-Königes, und hatten ihr nun allein in ihren Verlangen vor Augen, durch ihn befreyten sie sich von aller Liebe der Welt, und entrissen sich den Banden der irrdischen Eitelkeiten, damit sie diese Begierden allein in ihren Hertzen hegen konten."

[95] Ibid., 1, 20, 2-6, pp. 136-138.

[96] Ibid., 1, 6, 1-12, pp. 47-52.

[97] Ibid., 1, 6, 13, p. 52; 1, 6, 15, p. 54. These are Arnold's three unfailing marks of true faith.

[98] Ibid., 1, 10, 1-5, pp. 74-76; 1, 9, 8, p. 72.

[99] Ibid., 1, 18, 10-12, pp. 129-131.

[100] Ibid., 1, 18, 10, p. 129, citing Augustine: "Wir nennen uns auch außerwehlte Jünger Christi, und Kinder Gottes: Weil man die so nennen muß, welche wiedergebohren sind, und gottselig leben."

[101] Ibid., 4, 1, 18, p. 464; 4, 2, 13, p. 471.

[102] Ibid., 4, 2, 10-17, pp. 470-473.

[103] Ibid., 1, 8, 11-14, pp. 67-69.

[104] Ibid., 3, 2, 1, p. 348; 1, 1, 11, p. 59.

[105] Ibid., 4, 7, 1-3, pp. 516-517.

[106] Ibid., 4, 3, 3, p. 478; 4, 3, 8, p. 480. The concept of a middle way (*Mittelstraße*), which becomes important to Arnold later in life, is employed several times in the *Abbildung*. The concept appears in his discussions of moderation, the place of reason and knowledge (2, 5, 5, p. 100; see p. 26), and the balance between boldness and doubt concerning our attainment of heaven (1, 14, 9, p. 97). See Büchsel, *Kirche und Wiedergeburt*, p. 56, n. 77 and Seeberg, *Wissenschaft und Mystik*, pp. 160-161.

[107] Büchsel, *Kirche und Wiedergeburt*, p. 57.

[108] Arnold, *Abbildung*, 3, 1, 1-3, pp. 337-338; 3, 1, 6, p. 339; 3, 1, 9, p. 341.

[109] Ibid., 2, 3, 17, p. 177. "Die Gemeine . . . bestehet nicht in Wänden, sondern in der Menge der Frommen. . . . Wir nennen die Gemeine nicht den Ort, sondern die Versammlung der Außerwehlten."

[110] Büchsel, *Kirche und Wiedergeburt*, p. 58.

[111] Arnold, *Abbildung*, 3, 1, 13-18, pp. 343-345; 3, 7, 1, p. 392; 3, 8, 1, p. 406; 3, 6, 12-13, p. 388; 8, 19, 7, p. 389.

[112] Ibid., 8, 22, 1, p. 419; 4, 3, 10, p. 481; 2, 5, 11, p. 201.

[113] Büchsel, *Kirche und Wiedergeburt*, p. 60.

[114] Arnold, *Abbildung*, 8, 1, 2, pp. 190-191.

[115] Ibid., 2, 1, 1, p. 415.

[116] Ibid., 2, 3, 4-10, pp. 171-173. Arnold is not averse to buildings per se but condemns them only when they serve to localize worship or become ostentatious.

[117] Ibid., 2, 4, 1-3, pp. 183-184.

[118] Ibid., 2, 1, 3, p. 146; 2, 1, 6, p. 149; 2, 2, 4, p. 160; 2, 12, 4, p. 276.

[119] Ibid., 2, 1, 6, p. 148; 2, 1, 9, p. 150; 2, 2, 11, p. 165; 2, 12, 12, p. 281.

[120] Ibid., 2, 1, 12, p. 152; 2, 2, 6-9, pp. 161-164; 2, 12, 8-9, pp. 277-279; 2, 12, 20, p. 287.

[121] Ibid., 2, 14, 1, p. 303. Arnold notes that sacrament is a Latin word which originally meant a secret, hidden matter

(=μυστήριον). It then came to mean, under Augustine's influence, "a sign of holy and divine things." Büchsel, *Kirche und Wiedergeburt*, p. 65, makes the plausible conjecture that Arnold utilizes this historical overview of the word sacrament to relativize the dogmatic position of his opponents and thereby to create freedom for his own interpretation.

[122] Arnold, *Abbildung*, 2, 14, 1, p. 303. Interestingly, Arnold makes little reference to the term sacrament following this initial background study. Rather his basic concern regarding baptism and the Lord's Supper is to set forth those practices which the Lord or His disciples have ordained by their words or example. See for instance 2, 14, 3-4, pp. 304-306; 2, 15, 9-13, pp. 330a-331a.

[123] Ibid., 1, 2, 6-15, pp. 14-16; 2, 14, 18, p. 314.

[124] Corresponding to this position, Arnold holds that the Holy Spirit is received prior to baptism. Ibid., 2, 14, 19, p. 315.

[125] Ibid., 2, 14, 18, p. 315. Pietists in general viewed an *ex opere operato* interpretation of the sacraments as destructive to active faith. See for example Spener, *Pia Desideria*, pp. 65-67.

[126] Arnold, *Abbildung*, 2, 14, 8, p. 308.

[127] Ibid., 2, 15, 4, p. 327; 2, 15, 11-19, pp. 331-334; 2, 15, 25, p. 335.

[128] Büchsel, *Kirche und Wiedergeburt*, p. 67.

[129] Arnold, *Abbildung*, 2, 15, 20-22, p. 334; 2, 15, 9, p. 330; 2, 15, 14, p. 332.

[130] Ibid., 3, 7, 1, p. 392; 3, 7, 18, p. 403.

[131] Ibid., 3, 7, 6-7, pp. 397-398.

[132] Ibid., 3, 7, 15-16, pp. 402-403.

[133] Arnold employs the word teacher as an inclusive term for all offices in the early church—apostle, elder, bishop, overseer, deacon. He even perceives no great distinction among these latter terms. See 2, 11, 1, p. 261; 2, 11, 8-9, p. 266. This usage reflects Arnold's contention that all members of the early church shared equal power in and responsibility for the church. The leaders possessed no titles and formed no special class which might lead to divisions of power and a hierarchy. Instead, they bore names that designated their function (teacher, deacon, overseer, evangelist) and that could be interchanged (elder and teacher could be substituted for any of the others; bishop, elder, and servant [*Diener*] were synonymous).

[134] Ibid., 2, 5, 14-16, pp. 203-204.

[135] Ibid., 2, 8, 16, p. 233.

[136] Ibid., 2, 5, 19, p. 206: " . . . wer nach der Politischen Art davon reden will, der weiset, wie in der Kirche keine Monarchische Regierungs-Art sondern eine Aristocratische oder vielmehr Democratische gewesen sey, da man nichts ohne des Volcks Gutachten gethan." Büchsel, *Kirche und Wiedergeburt*, p. 69, n. 109 notes that Arnold's use of "democratic" in a positive light is quite astonishing. Though the concept "democracy" had come into use in German as a Latin loanword by the mid-seventeenth century, the first use of the adjective in a positive valuation is listed by etymological dictionaries as 1741. That Arnold should use this word to describe church polity is thus remarkable. Büchsel feels that Arnold probably borrowed the word from English Puritan literature.

[137] Ibid., 2, 5, 16, p. 204; 2, 8, 16, p. 233.

[138] Ibid., 2, 8, 10-12, pp. 229-231.

[139] Ibid., 2, 11, 1, p. 261.

[140] Ibid., 2, 11, 1, p. 261; 2, 11, 14, p. 270. Arnold maintains that the term "Geistliche" originally applied to every Christian, since they all had received the Spirit; see 1, 5, 8, pp. 43-44.

[141] Ibid., 2, 11, 3-11, pp. 262-268.

[142] Büchsel, *Kirche und Wiedergeburt*, p. 72.

[143] Arnold, *Abbildung*, 8, 8-19, pp. 267-398.

[144] Büchsel, *Kirche und Wiedergeburt*, p. 72.

[145] Arnold, *Abbildung*, 8, 11, 9, p. 306; see also 2, 10, 7, p. 235.

[146] Büchsel, *Kirche und Wiedergeburt*, p. 73.

[147] Arnold, *Abbildung*, 5, 2, 4, p. 21.

[148] Ibid., 8, 8, 2, p. 268; 2, 12, 8, p. 278.

[149] Büchsel, *Kirche und Wiedergeburt*, p. 61.

[150] Arnold, *Abbildung*, 7, 4, 19, p. 156. For Arnold the miracle-gifts include casting out demons, healing the sick through the laying on of hands, raising the dead, speaking in different tongues, and the reception of prophesies, divine dreams, and visions.

[151] Ibid., 8, 5, 15, p. 241.

[152] Ibid., 8, 5, 18, p. 243; 8, 19, 3, p. 387.

[153] Ibid., 2, 4, 11, p. 188; see Büchsel, *Kirche und Wiedergeburt*, p. 62.

[154] Büchsel, *Kirche und Wiedergeburt*, p. 74.

[155] Hochmann's concern for Jewish evangelism, like that of Spener and some other Pietists, was motivated by the conviction that the conversion of the Jews would precede the coming of God's kingdom. The eschatological fervor among Radical Pietists, especially around 1700, gave added zeal to Hochmann's efforts at Jewish evangelism. Significantly, Hochmann published an *Exhortation to the Jews* in 1699. See Renkewitz, *Hochmann*, p. 51 and Stoeffler, *German Pietism*, p. 203.

[156] Renkewitz, *Hochmann*, p. 2. Because so few primary sources are available (ibid., pp. 418-426 presents a list), this discussion will rely heavily on Renkewitz's fine biography of Hochmann.

[157] Ibid., pp. 25-27.

[158] Ibid., pp. 26-29.

[159] Ibid., pp. vii, 98, 356.

[160] Ibid., p. 98.

[161] Ibid., pp. 41-43.

[162] There is some disagreement as to when Hochmann first met Arnold. It is thought by some that one of the "two companions" who is reported to have been present with Dippel at Giessen in 1697 was Hochmann. For the different views see Stoeffler, *German Pietism*, p. 203; Ensign, "Radical German Pietism," p. 150; Renkewitz, *Hochmann*, p. 43; and Ritschl, *Pietismus in der lutherischen Kirchen*, p. 323.

[163] For a list of Hochmann's citations of these works, see Renkewitz, *Hochmann*, p. 357, n. 47.

[164] Ibid., p. 357.

[165] Ibid., pp. 87, 123.

[166] Hochmann's own immediate call to this priesthood had occurred during a brief period of solitude at the castle at Biesterfeld in March, 1700. Biesterfeld became a spiritual retreat for Hochmann during a period of frequent preaching tours from August, 1700, to the beginning of 1703.

[167] Ibid., pp. 95-97.

[168] In America the confession was reprinted by the Sauer press (1743), the Ephrata press (n.d.), and Peter Leibert's press (1787). Since all three presses published works by the German sectarians and separatists, it is not certain whether the Brethren were sponsors for any of the publications. Durnbaugh, "Genius" (Winter 1959): 10-11 has rightly questioned the traditional Brethren assumption that Hochmann's creed was cherished by the early Brethren as an unofficial expression of their beliefs. As will be seen later, the Brethren were eclectic in their theological development, but they subjected every tradition—Reformed, Lutheran, Radical Pietist, and Anabaptist—to a critical evaluation in the light of Scripture. Ensign, "Radical German Pietism," pp. 290-291 especially has overstated the Brethren dependence on Hochmann's and Arnold's thought:

Certain it is that the Brethren came from a Radical background. Is it likely that they honored Hochmann's *Glaubensbekenntnis* but rejected its supplement on the five types of marriage? That they were his disciples without agreeing with his mysticism? That they followed Arnold's history, but rejected his Boehmism? The early Brethren cannot be fully explained apart from the radical Pietist movement.

Though his conclusion warrants careful consideration, Ensign's rhetorical questions presuppose an uncritical identification by the early Brethren with Radical Pietism which does not find substantive support in the historical record. (See Durnbaugh's article for an analysis of Ensign's supposition of a close connection between Brethren and Radical Pietist thought.) Though the early Brethren would certainly have recognized Hochmann as a "witness of the truth" and thus held his confession in special regard, they would still have measured this writing by the plumb line of Scripture.

[169] The confession received wide circulation among the Radicals. It first was circulated in handwritten form but several printed editions quickly appeared. During this process some slight variations crept into the text. For a list of handwritten copies and printed editions of the confession together with the full German text with notations of textual variants, see Renkewitz, *Hochmann*, pp. 401-412, 418. A reproduction of the first seven articles of the German text along with an English translation appears in Brumbaugh, *German Baptist Brethren*, pp. 75-88. Brumbaugh's text is followed in this discussion.

[170] For details of this fringe group of Radical Pietism, see Ensign, "Radical German Pietism," pp. 233-240. Essentially, they took the Sophia mysticism of the Radicals and gave it fleshly meaning. Eva was the "new Eve." Through union, i.e., sexual intercourse, with her, one could become pure and holy and his sinful lust could be quenched for all time.

[171] Renkewitz, *Hochmann*, p. 172.

[172] Ibid., pp. 184-187. Renkewitz poses the interesting question of why Hochmann felt a need to organize a new society after forming the Melchizedek priesthood in 1700 (interest in this spiritual fellowship had gradually diminished along with the Berleburg enthusiasm). Renkewitz postulates that Hochmann felt that the latter group was too widely distributed and that a more compact, fully prepared community was needed in view of various signs pointing to the impending judgment (p. 189).

[173] The fact that the "deteriorated condition" of the churches was the motivating factor for Hochmann's cry for separation finds confirmation in Alexander Mack, Jr.'s reflections in 1774 on the awakening of the first leaders of the Brethren (many of them were Reformed and some responded to Hochmann's message on his first trip to the lower Rhine). Mack writes that "many were aroused from the sleep and death of sin . . . [and came] to see with sorrowful eyes the great decay [*Verfall*, the word used by Arnold to designate the fall] almost in every place." Alexander Mack, Jr., "Second Preface or Introduction" to *A Short and Plain View of the Outward, Yet Sacred Rites and Ordinances of the House of God . . .* by Alexander Mack (Ashland, Ohio: National Sunday School Association of the Brethren Church, 1939), p. 13.

[174] Renkewitz, *Hochmann*, pp. 243-244, 257, 360-361.

[175] Ibid., pp. 244-246.

[176] Ibid., pp. 214, 237, 248.

[177] Ibid., pp. 342, 357-358. Renkewitz (p. 358) lists a number of mystics whom Hochmann refers to: the Spanish quietist, Theresa of Avila; the German medieval mystics, Tauler and Gertrude the Great; Catherine of Genoa; and Angelus Silesius. He notes that

Hochmann owed to the mystics three concepts: Christ must be formed in us; He will unite Himself with us if we surrender ourselves to Him; we should follow Christ in our lives. This Christ-mysticism appears in Hochmann's thought much more frequently than the Boehmist-inspired Sophia speculation.

[178] Ibid., pp. 276, 285, 294.

[179] Ibid., p. 209.

[180] Ibid., pp. 298-314.

[181] Ibid., pp. 362-365, 375.

[182] Ibid., p. 152.

[183] This biblical literalism brought on Hochmann the criticism of Gichtel, who viewed Hochmann's act as an external undertaking with counter productive results. Such fasting is actually a cunning temptation by Satan to think highly of oneself. Otherwise, why should the fourth petition in the Lord's Prayer be offered up? Ibid., p. 166.

[184] Ibid., pp. 263-264.

[185] Ibid., pp. 257, 260, 267-268, 360. Several years after the founding of the Brethren, however, Hochmann changed his position. In a letter to a friend at Krefeld, he held that baptism was not necessary for a person baptized as an infant. His own desire was that God would baptize him each day with His Holy Spirit. Durnbaugh, *European Origins*, pp. 206-207.

[186] Renkewitz, *Hochmann*, pp. 269, 358.

[187] Though Hochmann and the Brethren shared the desire for the establishment of a visible community, their motivations for this desire had little in common. Hochmann's Spirit-impelled, eschatological fellowship belonged literally to a different world from the Brethren *Gemeinde* based on a desire to fulfill the New Testament commands and examples for baptism, communion, and discipline.

[188] Renkewitz, *Hochmann*, pp. 300, 351, 382.

[189] Ibid., p. 389.

[190] Ensign, "Radical German Pietism," p. 177.

CHAPTER 3: ANABAPTISM

[1] It is true that representatives of a second branch of Anabaptism, the Swiss Brethren, were to be found in the Palatinate where Mack was raised. These Swiss Brethren had come to the Palatinate during the second half of the seventeenth century due to continuing persecution in Zürich and Bern, the two cantons where Swiss Anabaptism still survived at the time. The Swiss Brethren, however, had produced no significant literature during the seventeenth century and relied on Dutch and Hamburg Mennonite literature. This indebtedness to the Mennonites for doctrinal and edificatory writings tended to level the differences between the Swiss and Dutch Anabaptists. See Robert Friedmann, *Mennonite Piety through the Centuries: Its Genius and its Literature* (Goshen, Indiana: The Mennonite Historical Society, 1949), pp. 35-36, 105, 162. It should also be borne in mind, however, that the Swiss and South German Anabaptists had already agreed at the Council of Schleitheim (see p. 45) on the essentials which the Mennonites came to adopt under the guidance of Dirk Philips and Menno Simons and which the German Baptist Brethren took over nearly two centuries later.

[2] Walter Klaassen, Anabaptism: *Neither Catholic nor Protestant* (Waterloo, Ontario: Conrad Press, 1973), p. 2.

[3] A. J. F. Zieglschmid, *Die älteste Chronik der Hutterischen Brüder* (New York: Carl Schurz Memorial Foundation, 1943), p. 47, quoted in William R. Estep, *The Anabaptist Story* (Nashville, Tennessee: Broadman Press, 1963), pp. 9-10.

[4] John H. Yoder, "Anabaptist Origins in Switzerland," in *An Introduction to Mennonite History* (hereafter *Mennonite History*), ed. Cornelius J. Dyck (Scottdale, Pennsylvania: Herald Press, 1967), p. 34.

[5] George Huntston Williams, *The Radical Reformation* (Philadelphia: The Westminster Press, 1962), p. 144.

[6] Ibid., p. 181. The seven articles in the confession dealt with baptism, excommunication, communion, separation from the world, the pastoral office, nonresistance, and the oath.

[7] The Amish came into being as a result of a split of the Swiss Brethren between the supporters of Jacob Ammann and those of Hans Reist. Ammann advocated the avoidance of excommunicated persons, the practice of feetwashing, and the wearing of both plain clothes and, for men, a beard. Reist took the traditional Swiss Brethren view that excommunication was not to be accompanied by avoidance. See Ernst Crous, "Mennonites in Europe 1648-1815," and J. C. Wenger, "The Amish," in *Mennonite History*, pp. 144, 181.

[8] J. C. Wenger, *The Mennonite Church in America* (Scottdale, Pennsylvania: Herald Press, 1966), pp. 39, 44-51, 67.

[9] John Oyer, "Central German and Moravian Anabaptism," in *Mennonite History*, p. 46.

[10] The claim is made by several writers that Hut made "more converts during the two years of his ministry than all of the other Anabaptist missioners together." Ibid., p. 48. See also Klaassen, *Neither Catholic nor Protestant*, p. 86.

[11] Walter Klaassen, "Pilgram Marpeck and South German Anabaptism," in *Mennonite History*, pp. 72-73.

[12] Robert Friedmann, "The Hutterian Brethren," in *Hutterite Studies*, ed. Harold S. Bender (Goshen, Indiana: Mennonite Historical Society, 1961), p. 41.

[13] Williams, *Radical Reformation*, p. 422.

[14] Harold S. Bender and C. Henry Smith, *Mennonites and Their Heritage* (Scottdale, Pennsylvania: Herald Press, 1964), pp. 55-56. Impetus for the move to Canada came from persecution during World War I stemming from their pacifistic views.

[15] Estep, *Story*, pp. 108, 118.

[16] Menno, like Melchior Hofmann and Dirk Philips, held an unorthodox view of Christ's incarnation. Menno "insisted that Jesus was conceived of the Holy Spirit, not begotten of Mary (Menno thought that women produced no seed), and that He became a human being in Mary (but not of Mary)." John Christian Wenger, "Introduction" to "Brief and Clear Confession" in *The Complete Writings of Menno Simons c.1496-1561* (hereafter *CW*), trans. Leonard Verduin and ed. John Christian Wenger (Scottdale, Pennsylvania: Herald Press, 1956), p. 420.

[17] William Keeney, "Anabaptists-Mennonites in Northern Europe, 1550-1650," in *Mennonite History*, pp. 96-97.

[18] *The Mennonite Encyclopedia*, s.v. "Netherlands," by N. van der Zijpp.

[19] The name *Doopsgezinde* (Baptist-minded), first adopted by the Waterlanders, is the name used by all Dutch Mennonites today.

[20] Wenger, *Mennonite Church*, pp. 37-41, 124-125.

[21] *The Mennonite Encyclopedia*, s.v. "Waterlanders," by N. van der Zijpp.

[22] The Dordrecht Confession was drawn up by Adriaan Cornelisz, a Flemish elder, and accepted in 1632 by fifty-one Flemish

and Frisian preachers as a basis for union. It was later adopted by Mennonites in the Palatinate and North Germany and found general usage among American Mennonites.

23 Quoted in Friedmann, *Mennonite Piety*, p. 120.

24 Ibid., pp. 101–103.

25 *The Mennonite Encyclopedia*, s.v. "Pietersz, Pieter," by Christian Neff and N. van der Zijpp.

26 Friedmann, *Mennonite Piety*, p. 114.

27 Renkewitz, *Hochmann*, pp. 195, 208, 283.

28 Friedmann, *Mennonite Piety*, p. 125.

29 Martin H. Schrag, "The Impact of Pietism upon the Mennonites in Early American Christianity," in *Continental Pietism*, p. 75.

30 Ibid., p. 76.

31 Ibid., pp. 76–77.

32 Friedmann, *Mennonite Piety*, p. 9.

33 Renkewitz, *Hochmann*, p. 283.

34 A leading Brethren minister, Christian Liebe, was arrested at Bern and told authorities he had come to "visit the local brethren to teach, to solace, and to baptize someone if the occasion arose." Durnbaugh is quite certain Liebe's "local brethren" were the Bernese Anabaptists. Liebe was sentenced as a galley slave along with four Swiss Brethren leaders. Donald F. Durnbaugh, "Relationships of the Brethren with the Mennonites and Quakers, 1708–1865," *Church History* 35 (1966):37. Given the fact that the Brethren generally worked in areas which had been responsive to Radical Pietist activity, especially that of Hochmann, it would seem a sound inference that Radicals had worked among the Mennonites at Bern.

35 Friedmann, *Mennonite Piety*, p. 157.

36 Ibid., pp. 157–166.

37 Ibid., p. 114.

38 Ibid., p. 214.

39 The connection between Radical Pietism and Dutch and especially German Mennonitism noted in the historical and literary discussions of this section will be explored at the end of this chapter. Friedmann's thesis of "a hidden connection between Anabaptism and Pietism" which helped to bring about a substantial change in the character of Anabaptism would have been enhanced if he had discerned that the type of Pietism he was describing was quietistic Radical Pietism. His generalized definitions of Pietism combine elements of quietistic Radical Pietism and Spener-Halle Pietism into a mixture that represents neither form of Pietism adequately. Note his definition of Pietism:

> Pietism in the larger sense is a quiet conventicle-Christianity which is primarily concerned with the inner experience of salvation and only secondarily with the expression of love toward the brotherhood, and not at all in a radical world transformation.

Ibid., p. 11. The individualism of Radical Pietism, though having quietistic qualities, prevented conventicles from having the place they did in Reformed and Lutheran Pietism. Spener-Halle Pietism, however, avoided a quietistic form of piety and was very active, through its institutions, in directing its piety toward the neighbor and the world. Cf. the criticism by Durnbaugh, "Genius" (Winter 1959):5 that Friedmann "tends to compare *early* Anabaptism with later Pietism, and does not seem to take into account the difference between *radical* Pietism and *churchly* Pietism."

40 The stated purpose of these latter two works was not only to promote a revival of the old uncompromising Anabaptist spirit by reprinting exemplary Christian and/or Anabaptist testimonies of the past but also to warn their readers of the deceptive allure posed by the "better, quieter and more comfortable" conditions of their present setting. See Thieleman J. van Bragt, *The Bloody Theater or Martyrs Mirror of the Defenseless Christians . . .*, 10th ed., trans. Joseph F. Solm (Scottdale, Pennsylvania: Herald Press, 1957), p. 8 and Friedmann, *Mennonite Piety*, pp. 159, 164.

41 Dietrich Philip [sic], "The Church of God," in *Enchiridion or Hand Book of the Christian Doctrine and Religion . . .*, trans. A. B. Kolb (Aylmer, Ontario: Pathway Publishing Corporation, 1966), p. 369. See also Simons, "Reply to Gellius Faber," in *CW*, p. 735 and van Bragt, *Martyrs Mirror*, p. 21.

42 Philip, "Church of God," p. 371.

43 Van Bragt, *Martyrs Mirror*, p. 21.

44 Ibid., pp. 22, 26. *Martyrs Mirror* actually is divided into two studies, each one proceeding by centuries. The first study traces the transmission of the doctrine of baptism from the apostolic church while the second is the catalogue of Christian martyrs.

45 This book represents the perspective of the Dompelaar movement, a division from the Mennonites of Hamburg-Altona which emphasized immersion as the correct form of baptism. Mehrning sought to promote immersion baptism by demonstrating its antiquity and by tracing, by centuries, how the original baptismal order of Christ was corrupted by the church. The work is actually the translation and enlargement of a Dutch book by Herman Montanus, a Calvinist turned Socinian. Friedmann, *Mennonite Piety*, p. 123 notes that Mehrning's work was utilized by "wellnigh all studies in Mennonite history in the seventeenth and eighteenth centuries." It has a twofold importance for Mennonites: it provided "a veritable historical arsenal on the 'baptism ordinance of Christ'" and, dependent on the lead of Montanus, it derived Anabaptism from the Waldensian movement, a theory which served as an effective counterargument to the allegation of a Münsterite origin. *The Mennonite Encyclopedia*, s.v. "Mehrning, Jakob," by Otto Schowalter and Friedmann, *Mennonite Piety*, p. 123. Mehrning's work was also utilized in two other works of importance to the early Brethren: Jeremias Felbinger's *Christian Handbook* and Gottfried Arnold's *Ketzerhistorie*.

46 Van Bragt, *Martyrs Mirror*, p. 278.

47 Ibid., p. 154.

48 Ibid., p. 25. This idea of "the church in the wilderness" has been a popular theme not only among all Anabaptist groups but also throughout the history of the church. For a discussion of this motif, see George Huntston Williams, "The Wilderness and Paradise in the History of the Church," *Church History* 28 (1959):3–24 and idem, *Wilderness and Paradise in Christian Thought* (New York: Harper & Brothers, 1962). Connected with van Bragt's discussion of the the church in the wilderness is another complex of ideas drawn from the Song of Songs. Here the church is likened to a rose that has blossomed among the thorns (2:2), a dove that was hidden in the clefts of the rock (2:14), and a well-enclosed garden (4:12). Williams notes that the connection of the Revelation passage with the "beloved" in the Song of Songs was common among the Anabaptists.

> Especially interesting was the eschatology which saw in the woman seeking refuge in the wilderness of Rev. 12:6, the true church identical with the beloved of the Bridegroom coming up out of the wilderness in Canticles 8:5. Proponents of this eschatology found solace in the cultivation of their remnant church as a provisional paradise precariously maintained pending the advent of the millennium.

Idem, *Radical Reformation*, p. 858. The eschatological hope of the Mennonites was not in the millennium (as a reaction to the Münster debacle, the Mennonites were characteristically amillennial) but in the return of Christ with the attendant resurrection of all men for the final judgment. Note that the Mennonites interpreted the bride in the Song of Songs as the church, unlike the Radical Pietists who saw her as the individual soul.

[49] Van Braght, *Martyrs Mirror*, p. 27.

[50] Philip, "Church of God," p. 374.

[51] Ibid., p. 369.

[52] Simons, "The Spiritual Resurrection," in *CW*, p. 54.

[53] Idem, "Confession of the Distressed Christians," in *CW*, p. 506.

[54] Philips sees "the keeping of all his [Christ's] commandments" as one of the marks of the true church while Menno's list of marks includes obedience to the Word. Philip, "Church of God," p. 394 and Simons, "Reply to Gellius Faber," in *CW*, p. 743. Philips' total list includes (1) pure doctrine, (2) scriptural use of the sacraments of baptism and the Supper, (3) the feet washing of the saints, (4) evangelical separation, (5) Christ's command of brotherly love, (6) the keeping of all Christ's commandments, and (7) suffering and persecution. Philip, "Church of God," pp. 383-398. Menno's marks include (1) pure doctrine, (2) scriptural use of the sacraments of baptism and the Lord's Supper, (3) a holy life derived from obedience to the Word, (4) unfeigned brotherly love, (5) open confession of Christ, and (6) suffering for the sake of Christ and His Word. Simons, "Reply to Gellius Faber," in *CW*, pp. 739-741, 743.

[55] Simons, "Reply to Gellius Faber," p. 749.

[56] Idem, "Foundation of Christian Doctrine," in *CW*, p. 159.

[57] Van Braght, *Martyrs Mirror*, p. 40.

[58] Simons, "Distressed Christians," p. 518 and "Reply to Martin Micron," in *CW*, p. 909; see also Philip, "Spiritual Restitution," in *Enchiridion*, p. 325.

[59] Simons, "Christian Doctrine," p. 214.

[60] The simple, uncritical approach of the Mennonites toward Scripture led to a high regard for the Old Testament Apocrypha among Anabaptists and Mennonites. Menno, in fact, quoted from the Apocrypha as if it were inspired. John C. Wenger, "Introduction" in *CW*, p. vii.

[61] Idem, "Instruction on Excommunication," in *CW*, p. 965.

[62] Philip, "A Very Beautiful and True Explanation and Interpretation of the Tabernacle of Moses . . . ," in *Enchiridion*, p. 256. Cf. "Confession of our Faith," in *Enchiridion*, p. 13.

[63] Simons, "Instruction on Excommunication," p. 990.

[64] See the discussion of the problem in *The Mennonite Encyclopedia*, s.v. "Restitution," by Robert Friedmann and John Howard Yoder, "The Recovery of the Anabaptist Vision," *Concern* 18 (July 1971):18.

[65] Yoder, "Anabaptist Vision," p. 18.

[66] *The Mennonite Encyclopedia*, s.v. "Restitution," by Friedmann.

[67] The two attributes of holiness and righteousness are emphasized frequently as being the key attributes of God's character. See van Braght, *Martyrs Mirror*, pp. 34, 39, 40 and Simons, "The Incarnation of Our Lord," in *CW*, p. 816 (Menno adds a third quality, piety).

[68] Van Braght, *Martyrs Mirror*, p. 39. Both Menno and Philips accept the doctrine of original sin. See Simons, "Christian Doctrine," p. 130 and "Christian Baptism," in *CW*, p. 244 and Philip, "Our Confession of the Creation, Redemption and Salvation of Man," in *Enchiridion*, pp. 14-15.

[69] Simons, "Incarnation," p. 817 and van Braght, *Martyrs Mirror*, p. 39.

[70] Simons, "Incarnation," p. 817 and van Braght, *Martyrs Mirror*, pp. 34, 39. The Mennonites would have upheld the importance of both Christ's active and passive obedience, though they would not have used these technical theological terms.

[71] Simons, "Christian Doctrine," p. 145.

[72] Ibid., p. 130; "Meditation on the Twenty-fifth Psalm," in *CW*, p. 29; "True Christian Faith," in *CW*, pp. 396-397; and "Distressed Christians," pp. 504-505.

[73] Idem, "New Birth," p. 92; see also Philip, "Church of God," p. 376.

[74] Simons, "Christian Doctrine," p. 110. As the quote suggests, Menno intensifies the seriousness of the call with an eschatological note.

[75] Ibid., p. 110.

[76] Ibid., p. 111.

[77] Ibid., p. 115.

[78] Ibid.

[79] Ibid., p. 116.

[80] Ibid., p. 124.

[81] Ibid., p. 123.

[82] Idem, "New Birth," p. 92.

[83] Van Braght, *Martyrs Mirror*, pp. 40-41.

[84] Simons, "Christian Doctrine," pp. 126-142 and "Reply to Gellius Faber," pp. 684-716. See also Philip, "Of the Baptism of Our Lord Jesus Christ," in *Enchiridion*, pp. 32-65. The Mennonite view of the state of children is quite well summarized by Philip, "Christian Baptism," p. 45.

Hence we conclude with the apostles and the entire holy scripture, that original sin has been paid and taken away by Jesus Christ, and that therefore children are not to be judged and damned on account of Adam's transgression (Gen. 6:5; 8:21). That the tendency of the child's nature is toward evil, does not damn them (Gen. 6:5; 8:21); yea, by the grace of God it is not accounted as sin unto them, but so long as they are simple and without the knowledge of good and evil, they are pleasing and acceptable to God through Jesus Christ. . . . It is true and indubitable that children as well as adults—the children by their simplicity, the adults by their faith—are saved by the grace of our Lord Jesus Christ (Acts 15:11).

[85] Simons, "Christian Doctrine," pp. 124-125. Menno denies, however, that baptism is a sign of grace, for Christ is the only true sign and means of grace (pp. 125, 131).

[86] Ibid., pp. 124-125.

[87] Ibid., p. 124.

[88] Ibid., pp. 123-125, 130-131 and "Christian Baptism," pp. 244-245.

[89] Idem, "Why I Do not Cease Teaching and Writing," in *CW*, p. 302.

[90] Idem, "Christian Faith," p. 396.

[91] Idem, "New Birth," p. 99.

[92] Idem, "Christian Baptism," p. 245.

[93] Idem, "Christian Faith," p. 329 and van Braght, *Martyrs Mirror*, pp. 30, 37.

[94] Simons, "Reply to Gellius Faber," p. 734.

[95] Van Braght, *Martyrs Mirror*, p. 42.

[96] Simons, "Christian Baptism," p. 234.

[97] Idem, "Reply to Gellius Faber," p. 747.

[98] Robert Friedmann, *The Theology of Anabaptism*, Studies in Anabaptist and Mennonite History, no. 15 (Scottdale, Pennsylvania: Herald Press, 1973), p. 117.

[99] Philip, "Church of God," p. 400.

[100] Van Braght, *Martyrs Mirror*, p. 42.

[101] Simons, "Distressed Christians," p. 520.

[102] See p. 260, n. 54.

[103] Simons, "Spiritual Resurrection," p. 55.

[104] Van Braght, *Martyrs Mirror*, p. 41.

[105] Ibid. and *The Mennonite Encyclopedia*, s.v. "Church," by Harold S. Bender and "Elder," by Cornelius Krahn.

[106] Simons, "Teaching and Writing," p. 302 and Philip, "Church of God," p. 386.

[107] Van Braght, *Martyrs Mirror*, p. 42.

[108] Ibid.; cf. Philip, "A Loving Admonition or Epistle to the Church of God," in *Enchiridion*, p. 454.

[109] Philip, "A Plain Presentation of the Evangelical Ban and Shunning," in *Enchiridion*, p. 521.

[110] Simons, "Instruction on Discipline to the Church at Emden," in *CW*, p. 1051.

[111] Idem, "A Clear Account of Excommunication," in *CW*, p. 480.

[112] Ibid., pp. 458-476 and idem, "Instruction in Excommunication," pp. 988-993; Philip, "Evangelical Ban," pp. 520-521.

[113] *The Mennonite Encyclopedia*, s.v. "Excommunication," by Harold S. Bender.

[114] Simons, "Account of Excommunication," pp. 478-479 and "Instructions on Excommunication," pp. 968-972; Philip, "Evangelical Ban," pp. 524-528.

[115] Simons, "A Kind Admonition on Church Discipline," in *CW*, p. 413.

[116] Idem, "Instruction on Excommunication," pp. 979, 981 and "Final Instruction on Marital Avoidance," in *CW*, p. 1062.

[117] Van Braght, *Martyrs Mirror*, p. 42.

[118] *The Mennonite Encyclopedia*, s.v. "Footwashing," by Harold S. Bender.

[119] Renkewitz, *Hochmann*, pp. 283-284.

[120] The contention is made in Friedmann, *Mennonite Piety*, p. 217. The impact of Radical Pietism on the Mennonites was undoubtedly far greater than the reverse impact. Arnold does show a good deal of interest in the Anabaptists, for he devotes about 250 pages in his *Ketzerhistorie* to them. See Gottfried Arnold, *Unparteyische Kirchen- und Ketzer-Historie . . .*, 3 vols. (Schaffhausen: Emanuel and Benedict Hurter, 1740), 1:856-899, 1299-1310, 1313-1500; 2:159-167, 1059-1065. Significantly, 218 of these pages are devoted to the mystical-spiritualist, David Joris. If Arnold can be said to be "partial" to the Anabaptists, it is to the spiritualist wing of the movement. Note also his use of Joris to critique the Mennonites. Ibid., 2:2, 16, 20, 39, p. 874 (the notations refer to volume, part, book, chapter, section, and page respectively).

[121] Ibid., 1:2, 16, 21, 6-10, pp. 859-861. It is noteworthy that Arnold quotes passages from such Mennonite works as Menno's "Reply to Gellius Faber," the Dordrecht Confession, and van Sittert's *Christliches Glaubensbekenntnus*, which contained the Dordrecht Confession (Arnold, in fact, cites the passage quoted from van Sittert above, p. 48, to show the impartiality of the seventeenth century Mennonites). See *Ketzerhistorie*, 2:2, 17, 12, 10, p. 162.) He also cites Mehrning's baptismal history.

[122] Arnold, *Ketzerhistorie*, 1:2, 16, 21, 7, p. 859; 1:2, 16, 21, 39, p. 874; 2:2, 17, 12, 31, p. 167.

CHAPTER 4: JEREMIAS FELBINGER AND THE POLISH BRETHREN

[1] Morgan Edwards, *Materials toward a History of the American Baptists*, 2 vols. (Philadelphia: Joseph Crukshank and Isaac Collins, 1770; xerographed, Ann Arbor, Michigan: Xerox University Microfilms, 1976), 2:66.

[2] Brumbaugh, *German Baptist Brethren*, p. 68.

[3] The above evidence is drawn from Donald F. Durnbaugh, "The Descent of Dissent: Some Interpretations of Brethren Origins," *BLT* 19 (Spring 1974):130-131.

[4] Alexander Mack, "Rights and Ordinances," in Durnbaugh, *European Origins*, p. 358.

[5] Jeremias Felbinger, *Christliches Hand-Büchlein*, 3d ed. (Baltimore: Samuel Saur, 1799), pp. 37-38.

[6] This biographical information is gleaned from *The Mennonite Encyclopedia*, s.v. "Felbinger, Jeremias," by Christian Neff; Stanislas Kot, *Socinianism in Poland: The Social and Political Ideas of the Polish Anti-trinitarians in the Sixteenth and Seventeenth Centuries* (Boston: Starr King Press, 1957), p. 205; Earl Morse Wilbur, *A History of Unitarianism: Socinianism and its Antecedents* (Boston: Beacon Press, 1945), p. 573; and Arnold, *Ketzerhistorie*, 2:2, 27, 13, 24, p. 176.

[7] Arnold, *Ketzerhistorie*, 2:2, 27, 13, 24, p. 176. There is a discrepancy in the dating of the *Christian Handbook*. In Felbinger's forward in the American edition of 1799 and presumably that of 1822, 1651 is given as the date of publication, whereas all available secondary literature states that the work appeared in 1661. Clearly 1661 is the correct date since Felbinger notes (p. 109) that his discussion on communion is borrowed from a work written in 1656.

[8] Felbinger, *Hand-Büchlein*, Vorrede, p. 1.

[9] Ibid., p. 17.

[10] Ibid., pp. 11-15.

[11] Ibid., pp. 1-2.

[12] Ibid., pp. 3-4.

[13] Ibid., pp. 6-7.

[14] Ibid., p. 23.

[15] In the next section Felbinger indicates that man's part in this salvation process is to abandon the unbelief and disobedience of the first Adam and turn himself to the faith and obedience of the second Adam, Christ. Ibid., p. 36. Felbinger sees a basic continuity throughout Scripture in the way that man should come to God. Those who lived both before and after the giving of the law were accepted by God by believing the measure of truth revealed to them. In this faith, then, they performed works which they knew would please God. Ibid., p. 17.

[16] Ibid., pp. 19-20, 36. Felbinger borrows this Adam-Christ comparison from a work by the aforementioned Courcelles.

[17] Ibid., pp. 15, 36.

[18] Ibid., pp. 3-6. Felbinger is a bit inconsistent here. Though he contends that God does not render condemnation to innocent children for the sin of Adam, yet earlier he admits that the mortal nature passed on by Adam to his race was part of God's judgment on Adam's sin. His attempt to explain away the incongruity by calling death "a natural condition" is by no means convincing.

[19] Ibid., pp. 22-24, 26-27, 30-31. When Felbinger discusses the salvation of children, he turns to a view of the atonement which stresses the power of Christ's death, shed blood, and sacrifice far more than does the Socinian "example theory." Once again Felbinger shows some inconsistency: he implies that there is something inherent even in children for which only Christ's death and shed blood (not merely his perfect obedience) can atone. He

seems to be wavering between a Socinian view of the atonement and the older satisfaction theory. The Socinian "example theory," as generally formulated, denied that Christ's death was necessary as a satisfaction for sins. Since there is no retributive justice in God, He can pardon sin without demanding satisfaction. See Louis Berkhof, *Systematic Theology*, 4th rev. and enl. ed. (Grand Rapids, Michigan: William B. Eerdmans Publishing Co., 1939), pp. 387–388.

[20] Felbinger, *Hand-Büchlein*, pp. 25–26, 32–34.

[21] Ibid., pp. 29–30.

[22] Ibid., p. 37. "Taufen und eintauchen ist einerley . . ."

[23] Ibid., pp. 37–44. Christ's example involved His baptism at John's hands "to fulfill all righteousness."

[24] Ibid., pp. 43–46.

[25] Ibid., pp. 59–65. Felbinger dates Tertullian around the year 250.

[26] Felbinger's reference (p. 56) to "die grosse Tauf-Historia, im Jahr 1646 und 1647 zu Dortmund gedruckt" is clearly Mehrning's work. Felbinger notes that his following discussion (which includes pp. 56–97) is taken from this work "als ein summarischer Auszug."

[27] Ibid., p. 67.

[28] Ibid., p. 55.

[29] Ibid., pp. 98–100.

[30] Ibid., pp. 106, 108–109.

[31] Ibid., pp. 110–113.

[32] Ibid., pp. 113–127.

PART II: ALEXANDER MACK AND THE EARLY BRETHREN (1708–1785)
CHAPTER 5: ALEXANDER MACK'S LIFE AND THOUGHT

[1] For further details about Alexander Mack's family and life, see Donald Floyd Durnbaugh, "Brethren Beginnings: The Origins of the Church of the Brethren in Early Eighteenth-Century Europe" (Ph.D. dissertation, University of Pennsylvania, 1960) and William G. Willoughby, *Counting the Cost: The Life of Alexander Mack, 1679-1735* (Elgin, Illinois: The Brethren Press, 1979).

[2] Durnbaugh, *European Origins*, p. 52.

[3] Hermann Brunn, "Alexander Mack, the Founder, 1679-1735," in *Schwarzenau Yesterday and Today*, updated ed., ed. Lawrence W. Shultz (Winona Lake, Indiana: Light and Life Press, 1977), p. 40.

[4] Durnbaugh, "Brethren Beginnings," p. 21.

[5] Ibid., pp. 16-19. Traut and Bossert later joined the Brethren movement.

[6] Idem, *European Origins*, pp. 38-51.

[7] Ibid., pp. 107-109.

[8] Mack, Jr., "Second Preface," p. 15. Though the younger Mack identifies the person who visited the Mennonites only as "a leader, and speaker of the word in their meetings," it is generally agreed that he is referring to his father.

[9] This is especially true when Hochmann's thought is viewed from the perspective of his Detmold confession.

[10] The question of obeying Christ's example and command of water baptism had been seriously raised among Hochmann's followers in 1703 and again in 1706. See Willoughby, *Counting the Cost*, pp. 48-49.

[11] See Durnbaugh's well reasoned arguments in "Descent of Dissent," pp. 129-131.

[12] Idem, *European Origins*, pp. 110-115.

[13] Willoughby, *Counting the Cost*, p. 56. Baptism was viewed in the letter as the outward cleansing testifying to the inward cleansing "through the blood of Jesus Christ in faith." See Durnbaugh, *European Origins*, pp. 118-119. Willoughby is not reflecting the main thrust of the letter, however, when he maintains that "it allowed for that person, 'grounded in God,' who did not consider water baptism necessary, to live conscientiously 'according to his or her own calling.'" The letter very clearly indicates that the writer was convinced that anyone who examined "the teachings of Christ and His apostles out of the freedom of conscience which each one has" would come to the same conclusions concerning the need for baptism. See Durnbaugh, *European Origins*, p. 119.

[14] Mack, Jr., "Introduction," in Durnbaugh, *European Origins*, p. 121.

[15] On the basis of his research, Willoughby has placed the date of the baptisms between August 5 and 8. *Counting the Cost*, p. 58. Because the early Brethren sought to avoid any glorification of their leaders, neither the date nor the name of the person who baptized Mack is recorded. This trait is also the reason why there is a paucity of documents from the eighteenth century concerning the Brethren.

[16] Durnbaugh, *European Origins*, pp. 133-134.

[17] Ibid., p. 129. Concerning their praying Gichtel wrote: "They yell so loud that one's ears hurt. They were incited therein by K. and H. [probably König and Hochmann]."

[18] Idem, "Brethren Beginnings," p. 67.

[19] Ibid., p. 65.

[20] Though there is no extant evidence to indicate whether or not the Brethren practiced ordination by the laying on of hands during the German development of the movement, sources are available as early as the 1750s demonstrating that at least the elders and deacons were installed with the imposition of hands (see p. 268, n. 27). This fact would strongly suggest that the rite of the laying on of hands was observed from the beginning. This practice should not be viewed, however, in a sacerdotal sense whereby the clergy, by virtue of their office, were perceived as possessing special spiritual privileges superseding those of the laity. Rather, the early Brethren viewed the laying on of hands as a rite which set the individual apart for a special function within the body. Ordination was therefore functional and involved no inherent clergy/laity distinction.

[21] Idem, *European Origins*, p. 73. The latter part is no doubt emphasized for the sake of the authorities.

[22] This literary device is found in other Pietistic literature. It was used by Theodore à Brakel (see p. 9) in his work, *Steps of the Christian Life*. See Stoeffler, *Evangelical Pietism*, pp. 149-150. The more general dialogue format was popular in devotional literature of the seventeenth century. Note the works of the Mennonites Pieter Pietersz and Johann Schabalie (see p. 48) and Bunyan's *Pilgrim's Progress*.

[23] Durnbaugh, "Brethren Beginnings," pp. 152-155.

[24] Willoughby, *Counting the Cost*, pp. 114-116.

[25] Details concerning the development of the church in America will be found in later chapters.

[26] Mack's writings were reprinted in 1774, 1799, 1822, 1860, 1888, 1901 (in H. R. Holsinger's history), 1939, 1954, 1958, and 1975. All present day groups except the Grace Brethren have made reprint editions available.

[27] Mack, "Rights and Ordinances," p. 348.

[28] Most of the early Brethren were from the Reformed Church and were taught the Heidelberg Catechism. Six of the eight original Brethren at Schwarzenau were Reformed; the others were Lutheran. Willoughby, *Counting the Cost*, p. 58. Likewise, all the centers of Brethren activity in Europe were Reformed.

[29] Durnbaugh, *European Origins*, p. 324.

[30] Stoeffler, *Evangelical Pietism*, p. 184. These tracts are devoid, however, of the rancor found in polemical writings of Protestant Orthodoxy.

[31] Durnbaugh, *European Origins*, p. 161.

[32] Mack, "Basic Questions," p. 329.

[33] Idem, "Rights and Ordinances," pp. 345, 347.

[34] Ibid., p. 347.

[35] Brethren indebtedness to the Reformed for "preciseness" is confirmed in an eighteenth century account of the Brethren by the American Quaker, Samuel Smith (1720-1776). He observes that the Calvinistic training of many of the early Brethren who were taught "out of the Heidelberg Confession had given them high notions of the purity that ought to be in those who were converted to God, with the sense of their own evil condition." Durnbaugh, *Colonial America*, p. 16.

[36] For an Anabaptist model see the first confession cited by van Braght, *Martyrs Mirror*, p. 30 and for a Radical Pietist model see the younger Hochmann (above, p. 41).

[37] Mack, "Basic Questions," p. 329.

[38] The Radical Pietists believed that a special awakening or direct calling by the Spirit was necessary before outward baptism could be practiced. In a letter to Christian Liebe, Hochmann wrote, "If, however, this [inward baptism by fire and spirit] has happened, and the person wishes to have himself baptized outwardly, then I will not oppose it, although one must inwardly take care that one is impelled to do this by the Divine Spirit." See Durnbaugh, *European Origins*, p. 127. Note also the Inspirationist criticism that the Brethren had not waited "for the correct time, which God had planned, to gather and prepare a congregation from among the sinners through His prophetic Spirit." Ibid., p. 149.

[39] Mack, "Basic Questions," p. 329.

[40] Martin Schrag, "The Early Brethren Concept of Authority," *BLT* 9 (Autumn 1964):121.

[41] Mack, "Rights and Ordinances," pp. 345-347. Parallel arguments can be found in Mennonite, Radical Pietist, and Polish Brethren (Felbinger's) writings.

[42] Ibid., p. 364.

[43] Ibid., p. 355. This passage is aimed at those who rejected the necessity of water baptism, i.e., the Radical Pietists.

[44] Schrag, "Authority," p. 112 and "Mennonites in Early American Christianity," p. 98.

[45] Cf. the letter to the Palatine Pietists in Durnbaugh, *European Origins*, pp. 116-119.

[46] Mack, "Basic Questions," p. 342.

[47] Ibid., p. 327. Mack clearly is following the lead of Felbinger, van Braght, and Mehrning in seeing baptism as an essential part of the teaching maintained continually by faithful witnesses. Of course Arnold also insisted that "witnesses of the truth" throughout the history of the church had preserved the doctrine of Christ by true teaching and pure lives, though he did not place special significance on baptism.

[48] Schrag, "Authority," p. 121.

[49] Chalmer E. Faw, "The Brethren and the Book of Books," in *The Adventurous Future*, comp. and ed. Paul W. Bowman (Elgin, Illinois: The Brethren Press, 1959), p. 112.

[50] Mack, "Rights and Ordinances," p. 380.

[51] Schrag, "Authority," p. 124. Another indication that Mack sees a basic continuity between the two covenants is his assumption, along with his querist, Gruber, that Israel represented the church in the Old Covenant. Mack, "Basic Questions," p. 326. This conviction also has Mennonite support.

[52] Mack, "Basic Questions," pp. 342-343 and Letter from Alexander Mack to Count Charles August, in Durnbaugh, *European Origins*, p. 163.

[53] Schrag, "Authority," p. 124.

[54] Mack, "Rights and Ordinances," p. 355.

[55] Eller, *Radical Discipleship*, p. 421.

[56] Willoughby, *Counting the Cost*, p. 65.

[57] Mack, "Rights and Ordinances," pp. 345-347.

[58] Durnbaugh, "Genius" (Spring 1959):9.

[59] Mack, "Rights and Ordinances," pp. 349, 352, 368-369.

[60] Bernard Ramm, who would be representative of current evangelical views on hermeneutics, notes that two elements should be present if a type is valid. First, "in a type there must be a genuine resemblance in form or idea between the Old Testament reference and the New Testament counterpart." Second, "this resemblance must be designated. . . . A type is properly designated when either it is so stated to be one in the New Testament, or wherein the New Testament states a whole as typical." See Bernard Ramm, *Protestant Biblical Interpretation*, 2d ed. (Grand Rapids, Michigan: Baker Book House, 1970), p. 228.

[61] Ibid., p. 54.

[62] Mack, "Rights and Ordinances," p. 397.

[63] Hans Volz, "Continental Versions to c. 1600: German Versions," in *The Cambridge History of the Bible: The West from the Reformation to the Present Day*, ed. S. L. Greenslade (Cambridge: Cambridge University Press, 1963), p. 100.

[64] Mack, "Rights and Ordinances," p. 386.

[65] Ibid. This hermeneutical principle of the coincidence of the inner and outer words is prominent in Anabaptist thought.

[66] Schrag, "Authority," p. 116.

[67] Mack, "Rights and Ordinances," p. 386.

[68] Durnbaugh, "Brethren and the Authority of the Scripture," *BLT* 13 (Summer 1968):173. This tenet was probably emphasized more by the Radical and church-related Pietists than by the other theological traditions. One of their basic presuppositions was that a regenerating *experience* with God *must precede* any true *knowledge* of divine matters.

[69] Mack, "Rights and Ordinances," p. 384.

[70] Ibid., p. 385.

[71] Ibid.

[72] Schrag, "Authority," p. 122.

[73] Mack, "Basic Questions," p. 341.

[74] Idem, "Rights and Ordinances," pp. 356-357.

[75] Durnbaugh, "Genius" (Spring 1959):5.

[76] Mack, "Rights and Ordinances," p. 361.

[77] Mack, Jr., "Introduction," in Durnbaugh, *European Origins*, p. 121.

[78] For a study of the historical sources used by Mack, see pp. 85-86.

[79] Scriptural evidence for the threefold action has traditionally been found by the Brethren in the Trinitarian formula of the Great Commission. It has been held that the formula of Matthew 28:19 is elliptical in construction and therefore supports an action for each of the three names.

[80] Faw, "Book of Books," pp. 108-109.

[81] Mack, "Rights and Ordinances," p. 347.

[82] Idem, "Basic Questions," p. 337.

[83] Durnbaugh, *European Origins*, pp. 62, 71, 249.

[84] Cf. ibid., pp. 249–250. The Brethren difficulty with the sixtieth question on justification by faith did not arise from the doctrine per se. Rather, it resulted from a rigidly objective and forensic interpretation of justification which left no room for that life of piety and obedience which Pietists and Brethren alike believed should issue from faith.

[85] Mack, "Basic Questions," p. 338; cf. "Rights and Ordinances," p. 366.

[86] Idem, "Rights and Ordinances," pp. 404–405.

[87] Letter from Alexander Mack to Count Charles August, p. 163; see also Mack, "Rights and Ordinances," p. 385. That the concept of grace was not foreign to Mack, especially in a non-polemical setting, is indicated by one of Mack's notations in his personal Bible. Note the thoroughly evangelical formulation of the gracious work of God and Christ in the believer's life (it is reminiscent of Arnold's discussion of conversion).

> The first operation of grace in the soul is a true awakening from the carefree slumber in sin and separation from God, and a recognition of our poverty and revelation of the divine life. Out of this arises in the soul the hunger and desire for help, sanctification, forgiveness of sins, and righteousness. Then grace shows how sanctification and forgiveness, indeed everything, can be received from Jesus alone. Then grace effects obedience to Jesus and, prior to this, the true faith out of which obedience issues.

Cf. Durnbaugh, *Colonial America*, p. 426.

[88] Mack, "Rights and Ordinances," p. 400.

[89] Idem, "Basic Questions," p. 331 and "Rights and Ordinances," p. 384.

[90] Idem, "Basic Questions," p. 335. As with the Pietists in general, Mack is preoccupied with the new existence rather than the new standing of the believer.

[91] Ibid., p. 331.

[92] Ibid., p. 335.

[93] Idem, "Rights and Ordinances," p. 353.

[94] Idem, "Basic Questions," pp. 335–336.

[95] Ibid., p. 335.

[96] Ibid., pp. 335–336.

[97] Ibid., pp. 326, 331.

[98] Ibid., p. 332.

[99] Ibid., p. 335.

[100] Ibid.

[101] Ibid., p. 331.

[102] Ibid., p. 338.

[103] Ibid.

[104] Ibid., pp. 338–339. Mack and the early Brethren followed the Mennonites, for the most part (see p. 53), in this formulation. Such a formulation could express most aptly the Brethren penchant for the coincidence of inner and outer aspects of the faith. Thus spiritual rebirth occurs in (but not through) the "washing of water [baptism] with the word [grasped by faith]" (Eph. 5:26). The only difference between the Brethren and Mennonite treatments is that Mack tended to link rebirth with remission of sins or cleansing while the Mennonites placed rebirth or regeneration prior to baptism but generally connected remission of sins more closely with baptism.

This understanding of the relation between baptism and regeneration differed from the Pietist view at two related points. First, Radical Pietists in particular would understand baptism as a sign of an already commenced rebirth (Arnold)—hence Gruber's

pointed question: "Could not a person be truly reborn even before he is baptized . . . ?" Second, the above Brethren view resulted in applicants being baptized simply on confession of faith and the pledge to lead a Christ-like life. This drew the Radical Pietist criticism that failure to test applicants prior to baptism for a godly life (which should have been present if regeneration had already occurred) forced the Brethren to place recently baptized converts under the ban. See Durnbaugh, *European Origins*, pp. 210, 212, 376–377. Significantly, both of these differences arise again in the late eighteenth century in America between the Brethren and the River Brethren (Brethren in Christ), a group composed especially of former Mennonites who had been strongly influenced by revivalistic Pietism. The differences were symbolized in the Brethren practice of laying hands on the baptisand while in the water whereas the River Brethren omitted the practice. (Because Menno tended to dissociate regeneration and remission of sins, both the Brethren and River Brethren could find support for their respective views in his works.) With the exception of these dissimilarities, both groups are nearly alike.

The end result of these differences is to shift the emphasis to the more objective faith-obedience-baptism-discipleship for the Brethren as compared with the more "pentecostal" penitential struggle-new birth-baptism-discipleship typified by the River Brethren. See Schrag, "Mennonites in Early American Christianity," pp. 96–98 and Roger E. Sappington, "How the Brethren Were Influencing the Development of Other Denominations between 1785 and 1860," *ATB* 8 (Spring 1975):77. This shift is likewise evidenced in the following exchange between Gruber and Mack:

> [Gruber]: Is not the true brotherhood of Christians founded much rather upon rebirth than upon water baptism?
> [Mack]: The true brotherhood of Christians has always been founded upon true faith and obedience to Jesus Christ and His gospel.

Mack, "Basic Questions," p. 339.

[105] Mack, "Basic Questions," p. 339. Here Mack differs with the Pietists in emphasis. Whereas the Pietists derived assurance equally from the new birth and the new being of active faith, Mack, though acknowledging that assurance begins in the new relationship with God (Rom. 5:1–2), shifts the emphasis to the new life of obedience and faithfulness to Christ. Ibid., p. 342. Such a formulation is similar to that of the Mennonites.

[106] Mack, "Rights and Ordinances," p. 379.

[107] Hochmann, for instance, spiritualized the ban by claiming that no person could place him in the ban except himself. Cf. Durnbaugh, *European Origins*, p. 208.

[108] Mack, "Rights and Ordinances," pp. 380–381.

[109] Cf. Stoeffler, *Evangelical Pietism*, p. 237. Stoeffler notes that Spener's conventicles (*collegia pietatis*) were often criticized for their tendency to pervert the doctrine of the priesthood of all believers by making it reflexive. Spener sought to alleviate this danger by stressing that these conventicles should become *ecclesiolae in ecclesia*, i.e., small groups of dedicated Christians who should seek to lead the larger congregation to a reformation of life. This emphasis differs essentially from the Anabaptist view of the church as a visible community. Here each believer commits himself to the body. Together the body, in every one of its individual parts, seeks to become more Christ-like (discipleship) through mutual aid and admonition, corporate observance of the ordinances (baptism and the Lord's Supper), community worship and Bible study, and a common Christian life style.

[110] Mack, "Rights and Ordinances," p. 380; cf. "Basic Questions," p. 341. Mack is undoubtedly responding here to the frequent Radical Pietist criticism that the Brethren did not exhibit "impartial love." Cf. Lamech and Agrippa, *Chronicon Ephratense*, p. 247 and statements by Hochmann in Durnbaugh, *European Origins*, p. 126.

[111] Mack, "Rights and Ordinances," p. 350.

[112] Ibid., pp. 367–368.

[113] In the less polemical setting of the letter addressed to separatists prior to the initial act of baptism in 1708, the anonymous writer does give the following elaboration:

> This [baptism] is then the covenant of a good conscience with God [a common Anabaptist view of baptism], as Peter writes in First Peter 3:21 and explains very clearly that as the great flood cleansed the first world, so . . . all of the old sins and uncleanliness shall be washed away through baptism. For as a person is cleansed outwardly through water, so is the inner person cleansed through the blood of Jesus Christ in faith. The Holy Spirit gives His testimony thereto.

Cf. Durnbaugh, *European Origins*, pp. 118–119.

[114] The amount of attention given to each of the three issues is a fair indication of Mack's audience (and of the groups he wished to proselytize). The least attention is given to infant baptism (the established churches), a moderate amount is focused on immersion as the proper mode (the Mennonites), and the greatest portion is placed upon the necessity of obedience to Christ's command of baptism (the Radical Pietists). Of his two writings, *Basic Questions* is geared almost entirely toward the Radical Pietists (five pages) with about one-and-a-half pages addressing the issue of infant baptism. *Rights and Ordinances* devotes nearly two pages to infant baptism, three to the necessity of outward baptism, and four to immersion. Because the most complete discussion of infant baptism and immersion comes from *Rights and Ordinances*, the following presentations are based on the arguments from this document.

[115] Mack, "Rights and Ordinances," p. 351.

[116] Ibid., pp. 351–352.

[117] Ibid., pp. 352–353.

[118] Ibid., p. 352.

[119] Ibid.

[120] Philip, "Baptism of Our Lord Jesus Christ," p. 59.

[121] By his use of various non-literal interpretive devices—allegory, typology, concordance—to show that different Old Testament events correspond to New Testament practices, Mack reveals an indebtedness to Anabaptist hermeneutics. See Williams, *Radical Reformation*, pp. 830–832. Interestingly, Mack seeks to provide New Testament evidence for his first three types: 1 Peter 3:20-21; Hebrews 3; and 1 Corinthians 10:2 respectively.

[122] Mack, "Rights and Ordinances," pp. 348–350.

[123] Ibid., p. 358. Note that Felbinger had stressed this point.

[124] Ibid.

[125] Ibid., pp. 358–360.

[126] Ibid., pp. 361–362.

[127] Mack, "Rights and Ordinances," p. 364.

[128] Possible sources for the Brethren observance of feetwashing as part of the communion service are Felbinger, Arnold, and some Mennonite groups. Felbinger's emphasis on its observance before communion has already been observed. Arnold also mentions in his *Ketzerhistorie*, 2:2, 17, 12, 13, p. 162, during his discussion of the seventeenth century Mennonites, that both the love feast and feetwashing were celebrated by a group led by Matthaeus Servatius, called the "Apostolicos" or "footwashers." The Biblical evidence for the observance of feetwashing with communion was obtained by conflating John 13 with the Synoptic pericopes of the Last Supper. Alexander Mack, Jr., after reflecting upon the reasoning utilized by the Schwarzenau Brethren for this harmonization, revealed the hermeneutical basis for the reasoning: "All of which [process] evolves into a glorious harmony for a believing soul and gives testimony at the same time of how the Holy Spirit has avoided in [the writings of] the holy evangelists all unnecessary repetition of words." Durnbaugh, *Colonial America*, p. 235.

[129] Mack, "Rights and Ordinances," pp. 363–365.

[130] Note Mack's statement in *Basic Questions*: "There can be no church of Christ without the ban. . . . They [true believers] have used it as a firm wall around the church of the Lord." Idem, "Basic Questions," p. 336.

[131] Idem, "Rights and Ordinances," pp. 365–367.

[132] Ibid., pp. 368, 379.

[133] Ibid., pp. 368–370.

[134] Ibid., pp. 393–394.

[135] Ibid., p. 370.

[136] Ibid., p. 394; cf. "Basic Questions," p. 336.

[137] Idem, "Rights and Ordinances," p. 372.

[138] Ibid., pp. 372–373.

[139] Ibid. Arnold, *Abbildung*, 3, 7, 6-7, pp. 397–398 twice warns that Christians must be free of blame themselves before taking part in discipline.

[140] Mack, "Rights and Ordinances," pp. 376–379.

[141] Ibid., p. 376.

[142] Ibid.

[143] See Durnbaugh, *European Origins*, pp. 159–172. This episode brings into consideration a concept that has played a key role in the interpretation of Brethren thought during this century. Ever since Brumbaugh, *German Baptist Brethren*, p. 3, maintained that "'no exercise of force in religion' was fundamental in the belief and practice of the Taufers or German Baptist Church," early Brethren thought has been viewed through this filter. The following men have followed Brumbaugh in giving "no force in religion" a major place in the understanding of the early Brethren: Frederick Denton Dove, *Cultural Changes in the Church of the Brethren* (Elgin, Illinois: Brethren Publishing House, 1932), p. 45; Rufus D. Bowman, *The Church of the Brethren and War, 1708-1941* (Elgin, Illinois: Brethren Publishing House, 1944), p. 33; Ronk, *Brethren Church*, p. 51; and Willoughby, *Counting the Cost*, p. 97.

Brumbaugh's expansion of the principle of "no force in religion" gives clues to its theological source. He held the following ideals were derived from it.

> (1) To compel anyone to join the church of Christ [e.g., through infant baptism] is an exercise of force. . . .
> (2) To compel by law an individual to take an oath is not only contrary to the teaching of Jesus, but it is a violation of the sacred rights of a people whose religious tenets decry all force. . . .
> (3) War is a violent interference with the rights of others. . . .
> (4) The injunction of Christ is one thing, the power of prince or ecclesiastic another. The might of the state has no right to interfere with the religious belief of the individual. . . .
> (5) In matters of faith each individual is free to follow his own convictions.

German Baptist Brethren, p. 4. These ideals, as formulated by Brumbaugh, are supported more from the perspective of the inherent dignity of man than from the conception of the believer owing his fundamental obedience to God. As such they are given an Enlightenment or classical liberal slant which is not characteristic of the thought of the Anabaptists, Radical Pietists, or early Brethren. These latter three groups based their arguments for freedom of conscience, nonresistance, and nonswearing on the more fundamental belief that only a free-willing, uncoerced faith and obedience is pleasing to God. When Brethren thought is interpreted in light of "no force in religion" (rather than the primary element of uncompromising commitment to Christ), the entire corpus of Brethren doctrine is skewed in a fashion which does not find support from the sources. In recent literature the idea of "no force in religion" has been used to question concerted evangelism and the practice of discipline and to defend doctrinal pluralism. Significantly, Willoughby, "Early Brethren," pp. 15-16 notes that Brumbaugh gives no documentary evidence for his thesis and that the term "no force in religion" does not even appear in Mack's writings. In fact, this phrase is of modern pedigree, becoming current only since the latter part of the nineteenth century.

[144] According to Lamech and Agrippa, *Chronicon Ephratense,* p. 2, the Brethren observed continence for seven years. Recent writers have challenged the length of this period of continence based on extant records of births in the Schwarzenau fellowship. Willoughby, *Counting the Cost,* p. 72, holds that the period could not have exceeded two and one-half years. See also Durnbaugh, "Genius" (Winter 1959):12-13. The possibility that the chronicler was reckoning the period from the time Mack first appeared in Schwarzenau (or possibly even some earlier point), rather than from the founding of the movement, has not been suggested. This would add about two years to Willoughby's figure. Note in this latter regard Stephen Koch's comment that the Brethren "brought matrimony into high favor, and finally cast off the estate of virginity [their views toward virginity and continence in marriage would have been linked], which *before* [italics mine] their baptism they had rated so high." Durnbaugh, *Colonial America,* p. 91.

[145] Mack, "Rights and Ordinances," p. 390.

[146] Ibid.

[147] Ibid.

[148] Ibid., p. 392.

[149] Ibid., pp. 392-393. Mack bases the forbidding of sexual relationships on Deuteronomy 24:3, 4. Since the adulterer had made himself unclean by his relationship with another person, further sexual relationships with the spouse would defile the innocent spouse as well.

[150] Willoughby, "Beliefs," p. 171.

[151] Mack, "Rights and Ordinances," pp. 398-399.

[152] Ibid., p. 399. This concept should not be identified with universalism as it is customarily defined. Mack had a vivid sense of God's judgment and of unbelievers' punishment. The admittedly fine distinction Mack is making is between *ever*lasting vs. *long*-lasting punishment. This belief is derived from Romans 5:18; 1 Corinthians 15:22, 26; Philippians 2:9-11; 1 Peter 3:19; 4:6; Revelation 5:12-13.

[153] Ibid.

[154] Durnbaugh, "Genius" (Winter 1959):5. For Durnbaugh's most recent formulation, which has been reshaped by the interchange noted below, see Durnbaugh, "The Brethren in Early American Church Life," in *Continental Pietism,* pp. 222-265.

[155] Ensign, "Radical German Pietism"; Willoughby, "Beliefs"; Durnbaugh, "Genius"; Eller, "Epitomizing the Brethren." Eller's

proposal was seconded by Allan C. Deeter, "Membership in the Body of Christ as Interpreted by Classical Pietism," *BLT* 9 (Autumn 1964):30-49 and Dale W. Brown, "Membership in the Body of Christ as Interpreted by the Heritage of the Brethren," *BLT* 9 (Autumn 1964): 63-77.

[156] Durnbaugh, "Early American Church Life," p. 226.

[157] Eller, "Epitomizing the Brethren," p. 49. Cf. p. 73 above.

[158] Ibid., pp. 50-51.

[159] Mack also gave a new foundation to other Radical Pietist emphases such as brotherly love, community, and the work of the Holy Spirit. Whereas these emphases were given an eschatological or spiritualist foundation in Radical circles, Mack concreted them in the life of the visible community. This preoccupation with giving visible expression to Jesus' teachings tended generally to weaken interest in eschatology.

[160] The related idea of the middle way, found sparingly in Arnold's early thought and more often in his later works, was also a characteristic of Spener's thought. See Brown, "Subjectivism in Pietism," p. 191.

[161] In a certain sense Mack combined his Radical Pietist presuppositions with the results of Arnold's analysis of the early church in a more consistent way than did Arnold himself. Arnold had shown the importance the early church placed upon community, corporate discipline, and the observance of the ordinances. The solution for Mack, given the Radical Pietist principle that all current expressions of the church were fallen and Arnold's picture of the ideal early church, was to form a *Gemeinde* truly fashioned after the early church. This option apparently was never a live one for Arnold. He was convinced by his findings in the *Ketzerhistorie* that no church or sect could escape the fall. Yet he was not satisfied with total separation either. Ultimately, his pastoral concern for his weaker brethren led him back into service within the fallen church.

[162] This may explain Mack's failure to discuss in any detail the Radical Pietist emphasis on the Spirit's work in regeneration, perfection, and restoring God's lost image. Likewise, Mack's depreciation of such mystics as Tauler and à Kempis (Mack, "Rights and Ordinances," p. 395) is atypical of Radical Pietists and points to greater interest in the objective Word rather than human "testimony" of any form. Mack also criticizes the medieval mystics because they "remained within the great Babel."

[163] The Radical Pietist periodical, the *Geistliche Fama,* noted in 1733 that the Brethren argument for the necessity of baptism persuaded many among the separatists. Cf. Durnbaugh, *European Origins,* p. 300.

[164] Mack, like Arnold, felt the Mennonites had deteriorated or fallen away (*verfallen;* Arnold's word for the fall) in their "doctrine and life" from the original Anabaptists. Mack, "Basic Questions," p. 340. For this reason, Mack probably never seriously considered joining the Mennonites.

[165] Ibid., pp. 342-343.

[166] Influence which Arnold may have had upon the early Brethren view of personal salvation, corporate worship, and ethics has been noted by a Church of the Brethren researcher, Donald E. Miller, "The Influence of Gottfried Arnold upon the Church of the Brethren," *BLT* 5 (Summer 1960): 39-50. In the area of salvation, Miller observes a common stress upon repentance, enlightenment by God's Spirit, the inner baptism of the Spirit, active faith, obedience to Christ, denial of the world, humble service, and God-likeness. Common features in their concept of worship include emphasis on earnest prayer, simplicity in singing, the use of plain meeting houses rather than church buildings, the priesthood of all believers, elected preachers who serve as examples,

the recognition of the place of women, the exercise of discipline in connection with communion. Similarities with regard to their respective views of ethics include a high regard for community, shared material goods, brotherly unity, humility, and love, caring for the poor, hospitality which included feetwashing, denial of self and the world, love of one's enemies, abhorrence of war, and a faith expressed at home and in the world as well as within the *Gemeinde.*

[167] Durnbaugh, *European Origins*, pp. 352, 389. The first reference cites Arnold's work as evidence that infant baptism was not practiced until the end of the second century. Mack cites the *Abbildung* the second time, not with reference to baptism, but, curiously, to bolster his brief argument against eating the blood of animals. Ensign, "Radical German Pietism," p. 375 observes that this prohibition was common among the Radical Pietists. It may be directed at the German practice of making "blood pudding." Willoughby, "Early Brethren," p. 134, n. 4.

[168] Durnbaugh, "Genius" (Winter 1959):10.

[169] Willoughby, "Early Brethren," p. 77 has observed that Mack used a Dutch, rather than a German, version of this writing (it could have been either the first Dutch edition of 1660 or the second of 1685). Mack refers to the work as "blutigen *Tonel*"; the "*Tonel*" indicates use of a Dutch version. This same conclusion is deduced from the fact that the first German translation was that done for American Mennonites by the Ephrata Cloister between 1748 and 1751. A German reprint of the American edition did not appear in Germany until 1780.

[170] Willoughby further implies that the quotations from Wallfried Strabo and Tertullian come from *Martyrs Mirror*, but these quotations probably are from Felbinger's *Christian Handbook* (see below). Willoughby does concede, however, that "other works, current in Mack's lifetime . . . may have had the same information." "Early Brethren," p. 78. Willoughby claims that Mack also used the Dordrecht Confession, perhaps unconsciously, as a pattern for his *Rights and Ordinances*. He notes that confession appears in the martyrology (it is also found in *Golden Apples in Silver Bowls*). See "Early Brethren," pp. 78–79 and, more recently, *Counting the Cost*, p. 95. Though both contain sections on Scripture, baptism, communion, marriage, the state, swearing

of oaths, discipline, and the ban, they show little similarity in ordering these subjects. Both also add a number of discussions not found in the other. These are subjects which any Anabaptist confession or church handbook (like Felbinger's) would have included. Cf. Durnbaugh, "Genius" (Winter 1959):25.

[171] Mack, "Rights and Ordinances," pp. 359–360.

[172] Mack alludes to two different sections of the "Gospel." The first deals with the testimony of Karinus and Lentzius, the two sons of Simeon (cf. Luke 2:25–35), who arose after Jesus' resurrection and appeared in Jerusalem. Their testimony is found at the end of Nicodemus' report proper. The second comes from the apocryphal story of how Emperor Tiberius sent a great prince, Wolusin, to Jerusalem in order to bring Jesus back to Rome to heal him (Tiberius). Of course, the plan was spoiled by Jesus' crucifixion by Pilate. The story is one of the "official" reports and histories following Nicodemus' testimony. See Johann George Homan, ed., *Das Evangelium Nicodemus oder Gewißer Bericht Von dem Leben, Leiden und Sterben, Unsers Heilands Jesu Christi . . .* (Reading, Pennsylvania: C. A. Bruckman, 1819), pp. 61–62, 70–84.

[173] Berthold Altaner, *Patrology*, trans. Hilda C. Graef (New York: Herder and Herder, 1960), p. 70.

[174] *Mennonite Encyclopedia*, s.v. "Nicodemus, Gospel of," by William Klassen.

[175] Mack, "Rights and Ordinances," p. 359.

[176] Ibid., p. 360.

[177] Quoted in Durnbaugh, *European Origins*, p. 360. The work by Renan mentioned in the Imbrioch quotation is from *Tertulliani Opera*, ed. Beatus Rhenanus (Basil, 1528), p. 451. Cf. Rollin Stely Armour, *Anabaptist Baptism: A Representative Study*, Studies in Anabaptist and Mennonite History, no. 11 (Scottdale, Pennsylvania: Herald Press, 1966), p. 184, n. 113.

[178] Durnbaugh, "Genius" (Winter 1959):27.

[179] Julius Friedrich Sachse, *The German Sectarians of Pennsylvania*, vol. 2: *1742–1800: A Critical and Legendary History of the Ephrata Cloister and the Dunkers* (Philadelphia: Printed for the author, 1900; reprint ed., New York: AMS Press, 1971), pp. 234–236, 244–252.

[180] Durnbaugh, "Descent of Dissent," p. 131.

CHAPTER 6: THE CRYSTALLIZATION OF THOUGHT AND PRACTICE IN AMERICA

[1] Durnbaugh, *European Origins*, p. 319. Details about the congregation which remained at Krefeld and its association with Tersteegen can be found in Friedrich Nieper, *Die ersten deutschen Auswanderer von Krefeld nach Pennsylvanien* (Neukirchen, Kreis Moers: Buchhandlung des Erziehungsvereins, 1940). Though Nieper provides valuable historical material on the Brethren, his interpretation of their thought is colored by identifying them too closely with the spiritualism of men like Hochmann and of groups like the Ephrata Cloister and the Quakers. See pp. 247–249, 262–263.

[2] Durnbaugh, *Colonial America*, p. 61.

[3] The Radical Pietist framework of the thought and practice of Beissel and his Ephrata Community is evident from the *Chronicon Ephratense*, which chronicled the history of the cloister from its own viewpoint. Besides the characteristics named above, the Ephrata Community utilized the Melchizedekan priesthood concept with its practice of assuming a new name, the Philadelphian understanding of church history and eschatology, and Sophia mysticism. See Lamech and Agrippa, *Chronicon Ephratense*, pp. 113, 134, 285.

[4] Durnbaugh, *Colonial America*, pp. 112–140. Even Voltaire heard of them and declared them to be the "most inimitable Christians" current.

[5] See the testimony of the *Geistliche Fama*, idem, *European Origins*, p. 300, and Stephen Koch, idem, *Colonial America*, p. 91.

[6] For a complete list of those who made up the "exodus," see The Committee appointed by District Conference, *History of the Church of the Brethren of the Eastern District of Pennsylvania* (Lancaster, Pennsylvania: The New Era Printing Company, 1915; reprint ed., Knightstown, Indiana: The Bookmark, 1977), p. 70. Two older ministers, Peter Becker and John Naas, opposed the revival because they saw in it the enthusiastic, mystical spirit of Ephrata.

[7] Lamech and Agrippa, *Chronicon Ephratense*, p. 50.

[8] See, for example, the criticism of two men at Ephrata, Stephen Koch and George Adam Martin, and of the *Geistliche Fama*, found respectively in Lamech and Agrippa, *Chronicon Ephratense*, pp. 95–96, 246–247 and Durnbaugh, *European Origins*, pp. 299–301.

[9] Note the reports by Lutheran and Reformed pastors of Brethren activity among their respective people in Durnbaugh, *Colonial America*, pp. 125-136.

[10] Durnbaugh, *Colonial America*, pp. 172-191 and "Early History," in *The Church of the Brethren Past and Present*, ed. Donald F. Durnbaugh (Elgin, Illinois: The Brethren Press, 1971), p. 16.

[11] Idem, *Colonial America*, p. 353.

[12] The best discussion of the influence of Pietism on the Colonial Brethren is idem, "Early American Church Life," pp. 222-265.

[13] Lamech and Agrippa, *Chronicon Ephratense*, pp. 98-99.

[14] John J. Stoudt, *Pennsylvania German Poetry, 1685-1830* (Norristown, Pennsylvania: Pennsylvania German Folklore Society, 1956).

[15] Durnbaugh, *Colonial America*, pp. 548-596.

[16] Ibid., pp. 252, 457, 561.

[17] Ibid., pp. 127, 204, 562, 237, 468.

[18] Ibid., pp. 243, 249, 252, 257; cf. Renkewitz, *Hochmann*, p. 113.

[19] Mack, Jr., "Second Preface," p. 12.

[20] Durnbaugh, *Colonial America*, p. 265. It seems there was some reason to question Catherine's moral integrity. When she was in her trances, no one was allowed in her presence except one young man whom she later married. After the wedding, the visions abruptly ceased. Mallott, *Studies*, p. 77 notes she was subsequently disciplined by the Brotherhood.

[21] It is noteworthy that two hymns by Mack, Jr., were appended to an edition of *Der Kleine Kempis* (1795). Apparently, the Brethren also read mystical works from the Boehmist and Quietist traditions. An anonymous Lutheran observed in 1814 that the Brethren "read all writings of the mystics—Bernier, Madame Gayon, Tauler, John of the Cross, Bertot, Molino, Arnold, etc. and even the writings of Jacob Boehme—mornings and evenings for their home worship, and this as regularly as their bibles." "Gestalt des Reiches Gottes unter den Deutschen in Amerika," *Evangelisches Magazin* 3 (1814):130-132 quoted in Durnbaugh, "Early American Church Life," p. 235. The above "recreational" devotional reading was typical of the Mennonites as well.

[22] Traditionally, Brethren historians have looked to the literary achievements of the Brethren (through the Sauer press especially) as representing a cultural high point of the early movement. Durnbaugh, "Brethren Historiography," pp. 8-9, 13-15 has challenged the idealized picture of these achievements. He points out that the Sauer press was an entirely private venture and in no way directly connected to the church. Sauer I was not even a member of the Brethren, while the disciplining of Sauer II by the Brethren for his printing of the Heidelberg Catechism (it contained the commandments of men—especially infant baptism and the swearing of oaths) was based on a concern about his reputation for honesty. In addition to these points, it should be observed that the Ephrata and Sauer presses actually *prolonged* the cultural and religious isolation of the Brethren. They provided the Brethren with devotional literature in their native language which continued to foster a piety like that of their forefathers. As will be seen, pietistic themes and concepts continued well into the next century due, no doubt, to the immersion of the Brethren in this literature.

[23] What Friedmann has observed about Mennonite fascination with these apocryphal writings is also true of the Brethren: "It was, so to speak, their recreational reading, their fiction, fairy tales, legends, and so on, adapted to replace secular imaginative literature which was almost unknown in Mennonite homes." *Mennonite Piety*, p. 222.

[24] For an excellent treatment of the folk-religion of the Pennsylvania Germans, see Richard E. Wentz, "The American Character and the American Revolution: A Pennsylvania German Sampler," *Journal of the American Academy of Religion* 44 (March 1976): 115-131.

[25] Durnbaugh, *Colonial Brethren*, p. 79.

[26] Ibid., pp. 243, 249, 252, 257, 448-459.

[27] Ibid., pp. 174-175, 221; Holsinger, *Tunkers*, pp. 782, 808; Brumbaugh, *German Baptist Brethren*, pp. 175-176, 219, 226, 391.

[28] Durnbaugh, *Colonial America*, p. 186.

[29] Ibid., pp. 123-124.

[30] Singing has always been a significant part of Brethren public and private worship. Between 1708 and 1867, the Brethren put out six different hymnbooks, most of which went through numerous editions. As the editor of one of these hymnbooks stated, "The relation that the Hymn Book stands in to singing in the Church, is such, that gives it a place next in importance to the Bible, among Christians." Sappington, *New Nation*, p. 415. The first Brethren hymnbook printed in America, *Das Kleine Davidische Psalterspiel*, appeared in 1744.

[31] From the time of the first baptism in Germany, the passage in Luke 14:25-33 about counting the cost of discipleship had been read (this practice was inspired by Hochmann's advice). In 1737 George Adam Martin (1715-1794), who had joined the Brethren in 1735, induced them to read the Matthew 18 passage. The very able, but disputatious, Martin became a Brethren minister but joined the Ephrata group in 1762 following a dispute involving, among other things, discipline. See Lamech and Agrippa, *Chronicon Ephratense*, p. 244.

[32] This description of a Brethren baptism comes primarily from Peter C. Erb, "The Brethren in the Early Eighteenth Century: An Unpublished Contemporary Account," *BLT* 22 (Spring 1977):107 (the baptismal account comes from 1734); see also Lamech and Agrippa, *Chronicon Ephratense*, p. 244 and Brumbaugh, *German Baptist Brethren*, pp. 526-549.

[33] This observation is based upon records from the Germantown church in Brumbaugh, *German Baptist Brethren*, p. 514.

[34] See the letter from A. G. Spangenberg to the Congregation at Herrnhut in Durnbaugh, *Colonial Brethren*, p. 272.

[35] William Knepper, "The Testament of William Knepper," in Durnbaugh, *Colonial Brethren*, p. 568.

[36] Durnbaugh, *Colonial Brethren*, p. 467. Johann Heinrich Reitz (1655-1720), a Reformed theologian and linguist, served as a church official in the Palatinate in the late seventeenth century. He joined the Radical Pietist movement during the Babel-storming period but later returned to the established church, ending his life as a teacher of a Latin school at Wesel. He is best known in Pietist circles for his compilation of edifying biographies, *Historie der Wiedergebohrnen* (1717).

[37] Ibid., p. 200.

[38] For Martin's narrative of these difficulties, see Lamech and Agrippa, *Chronicon Ephratense*, pp. 249-252. Though Martin's testimony must be taken with a grain of salt, this reservation extends not so much to the larger details of his narrative as to his interpretation of the details.

[39] Durnbaugh, "Early History," p. 16.

[40] The "final straw" for the Brethren occurred when some Indian converts were baptized by a mode other than immersion. They feared that the ecumenical gatherings were in fact a means devised by Zinzendorf for increasing the membership of the Moravian church (a suspicion which was not altogether false). Idem, *Colonial America*, pp. 278-285 and "Early American Church Life," p. 246.

[41] Idem, *Colonial America*, p. 287.

[42] Edwards, *History of the Baptists*, 1:94.

[43] Durnbaugh, "Early American Church Life," p. 237.

[44] Idem, *Colonial America*, p. 286.

[45] Ibid., p. 430.

[46] Ibid., p. 431.

[47] Ibid., p. 430; cf. p. 519.

[48] Ibid., p. 468.

[49] Ibid., p. 464. That the colonial Brethren were not always successful in this regard is revealed by George Adam Martin. He noted that the institution of yearly meetings allowed the Brethren to come together to discuss various matters. He continues in an acrimonious and haughty tenor (apparently this was part of his problem):

> since most of the Baptists who had laid the foundation of their Congregation in Schwarzenau, were uneducated arch-idiots and ignoramuses, their followers, of course, brought their absurd notions also to this meeting, always appealing to their predecessors, saying the old Brethren in Germany did so, and we must not depart from their ways.
>
> When I heard this I contradicted them, which occasionally gave rise to disputes, in which I always had P. B. and M. U. [Peter Becker and Martin Urner] and most of the common people on my side.

Lamech and Agrippa, *Chronicon Ephratense*, pp. 245–246.

[50] Durnbaugh, *Colonial Brethren*, pp. 463–464.

[51] Ibid., p. 243.

[52] Ibid., pp. 467–468.

[53] Hogan, "Intellectual Impact," pp. 4–5 suggests that the roots of Brethren anti-intellectualism lie, to a great degree, in the events of the Revolution, particularly the destruction of the Sauer press. However, the Brethren critique of reason precedes these events, for it is derived from the Pietist and Radical Pietist aversion to Scholasticism. It is not true that the early Brethren were averse to learning per se. Mack, Sr., like Arnold, felt that "ignorance causes great damage to the soul." The point of contention was the *foundation* of knowledge. Autonomous reason cannot be trusted and needs to be subservient to faith. Note the counsel of Mack, Sr.: "If people would just follow after Him [Jesus] in the obedience of faith, taking reason captive in obedience to the Lord Jesus, they would not be led astray by the high-sounding talk of men." Mack, "Rights and Ordinances," pp. 372, 395.

[54] Durnbaugh, *Colonial America*, p. 520; cf. pp. 523, 567, 585–586.

[55] Lamech and Agrippa, *Chronicon-Ephratense*, p. 246. Knowing that Frantz came from Switzerland and that he was a vocal advocate of both avoidance and the celestial flesh idea might indicate that he was originally Amish. Dubois was Reformed according to Morgan Edwards. See Durnbaugh, *European Origins*, pp. 178, 180.

[56] Lamech and Agrippa, *Chronicon-Ephratense*, pp. 246–247.

[57] Michael Frantz, *Einfältige Lehr-Betrachtungen, und Kurzgefaßtes Glaubens-Bekäntniß*... (Germantown: Christoph Saur, 1770), p. 13. The German text is:

163. Sein Leib nicht irrdisch sundlich ist,
      Auch nicht verweßlich sagt die Schrifft,
      Verwesung hat ihn nicht berührt,
      Sein'n Leib er mit gen himel führt. . . .

165. Also will ich auch glauben nicht
      Dann nur wie sagt gantz klar die Schrifft,
      Daß Jesus von dem Himmel kam,
      Von Menschen Sam er nichts.

[58] Durnbaugh, *Colonial Brethren*, pp. 238, 553, 561, 566, 587, 589, 591.

[59] Ibid., pp. 563, 565.

[60] See Morgan Edward's comment that the Brethren believed in general redemption. Ibid., p. 174; cf. p. 497.

[61] Ibid., p. 431.

[62] Ibid., p. 433.

[63] Ibid., p. 449.

[64] Ibid.

[65] Ibid., p. 453.

[66] Ibid., pp. 248, 251, 237, 454 and Brumbaugh, *German Baptist Brethren*, pp. 128, 210, 237, 435.

[67] In Reformed Pietism, an entire book was written by William A. Saldenus (1627-1694) to address the problem of why earnest Christians often felt no spiritual elation. See Stoeffler, *Evangelical Pietism*, p. 157.

[68] Durnbaugh, *Colonial America*, p. 249. This quietistic approach to inner spiritual struggles would have been tempting to the Brethren since it was typical of eighteenth-century Radical Pietists.

[69] Ibid., p. 237; cf. pp. 249, 253, 256.

[70] Ibid., pp. 445–446.

[71] Ibid., pp. 532–533.

[72] Ibid., pp. 434–436.

[73] Ibid., pp. 502, 491.

[74] Ibid., pp. 508, 503.

[75] Ibid., pp. 521–522.

[76] Mack pointedly states: "Whoever can laugh about original sin is vain and not thoroughly converted." Ibid., p. 497; cf. pp. 264, 619.

[77] Ibid., p. 497.

[78] Ibid., pp. 477–478.

[79] Ibid., pp. 571, 579–582, 594–596.

[80] Ibid., pp. 360–361, 363.

[81] Ibid., p. 562 and Lamech and Agrippa, *Chronicon Ephratense*, p. 134. In the next century, an Adventist schema held that there were to be six millennia of human history followed by the millennium of the Great Sabbath.

[82] Frantz may hold the doctrine of universal restoration. For him as for other Brethren, however, this doctrine is a matter of personal opinion and therefore should not lead to controversy. Note the following stanza:

491. The thousand year reign of Christ,
      The restoration of every branch,
      Not everyone agrees upon,
      Therefore one should not quarrel thereabout.

The German is:

491. Das Tausendjährig Christi Reich,
      Die wiederbrigung [sic] aller Zweig,
      Nicht jedermann fällt ins Gesicht,
      Drum soll man darum Zancken nicht.

Lehr-Betrachtungen, p. 34.

[83] Durnbaugh, *Colonial America*, p. 338.

[84] George Klein-Nicolai [Paul Siegvolck], *The Everlasting Gospel Commanded to be Preached by Jesus Christ, Judge of the Living and the Dead, Unto All Creatures*..., trans. John S. [Price] (Germantown: Christopher Sower, 1753), pp. 4–5.

[85] Ibid., p. 4.

[86] M. K., *The Fatal Consequences of the Unscriptural Doctrine of Predestination and Reprobation; With a Caution Against It,*

translated an [sic] Desire (Germantown: Christopher Sowr, 1753), pp. 3, 6. Though there is no indication that this definitely was translated by the Brethren, Durnbaugh sees a possible connection due to its being bound with *The Everlasting Gospel.* Durnbaugh and Shultz, "Brethren Bibliography," p. 14.

[87] M. K., *Fatal Consequences*, p. 7.

[88] Durnbaugh, *Colonial America*, p. 321.

[89] Frantz, *Lehr-Betrachtungen*, p. 15, stanzas 201-203; p. 17, stanza 228.

[90] Ibid., p. 14. The German text is:

187.   Der Ehestand von Gott eingesetzt,
       Noch vor dem Fall, gantz unverletzt:

Dann Adam war verführet nicht
Wie Paulus klar das selber spricht.

Frantz also cites the principle utilized by Arnold in justifying his marriage: to the pure all things are pure. See p. 16, stanzas 214 and 215.

[91] Ibid., pp. 28-30.

[92] Ibid., p. 10. The German is:

126.   Das Aeußre auf das Inre geht
       Sonst ists der Buchstab der nur tödt,
       Das Aeußre das hat nur gezeigt,
       Daß sich hernach der Mensch so beugt.

PART III: EXPANSION AND CONSOLIDATION (1785-1865)
CHAPTER 7: HISTORICAL, PRACTICAL, AND DOCTRINAL DEVELOPMENTS

[1] See, for example, the articles by Durnbaugh, "Brethren Historiography" and Brown, "Developing Thought."

[2] The Kentucky Brethren, along with those in southern Indiana, were won over *en masse* to the Disciples movement of Alexander Campbell and Barton Stone. The story of this defection is recounted in David Barry Eller, "The Brethren in the Western Ohio Valley, 1790-1850: German Baptist Settlement and Frontier Accommodation" (Ph.D. dissertation, Miami University, 1976).

[3] Durnbaugh, "Early History," p. 22.

[4] Idem, "Brethren Historiography," pp. 11-12.

[5] Sappington, *New Nation*, p. 333.

[6] Ibid., pp. 339-372, 398-399.

[7] Ibid., pp. 255-262.

[8] Benjamin Funk, comp., *Life and Labors of Elder John Kline, the Missionary Martyr* (Elgin, Illinois: Brethren Publishing House, 1900; reprint ed., Elgin, Illinois: The Brethren Press, 1964), p. 213; cf. p. 382.

[9] Because hymnbooks were often scarce (it was up to members to supply their own), Brethren, like the Mennonites and other frontier churches, always lined their hymns. In this practice the leader or *Vorsinger* (usually a deacon) would first set the tune (known by all through oral tradition) and pitch and then read two lines of a hymn from the hymnbook. The congregation would sing these lines, after which two more would be read and the pattern repeated until the song was completed. The hymnbooks contained no notes and singing in parts was frowned upon until the latter part of the nineteenth century.

[10] When a number of ministers were present, they sat in order of seniority behind the table. The senior elder, the overseer or housekeeper, had the first opportunity to speak. Frequently, he gave "liberty" to the minister next in seniority to speak. That minister could either preach or pass the "liberty" to the next minister. If a minister did preach, he passed the liberty on at the end of his remarks.

[11] Some examples of evangelistic preaching from the period can be found in Funk, *John Kline*, pp. 18, 63, 88, 115-116, 194-195, 322-325, 412-413. These sermons must be used with caution because they were expanded by Funk (p. 99). (It is uncertain what happened to the Kline diary after Funk completed his work; it has never been located.) Yet, the salient ideas found in these edited sermons are certainly from Kline's own briefer entries.

[12] The General Mission Board, *Minutes of the Annual Meetings of the Church of the Brethren, Containing all Available Minutes from 1778 to 1909* (Elgin, Illinois: Brethren Publishing House, 1909), Art. 3, p. 97.

[13] Winger, *History and Doctrines*, p. 206.

[14] Brown, "Developing Thought," p. 66.

[15] The Brethren did not like to use the terms ban, anathema, excommunication, and expulsion to refer to this practice. Expulsion implied the use of physical force which was felt to be "contrary to the spirit and law of Christ." The Jewish words "ban" and "anathema" and the "Roman" word "excommunication" were foreign terms which had acquired meanings different from "the letter and spirit of the gospel." Avoidance had the advantage of being "a simple plain word in our language" which had scriptural roots. Henry Kurtz, *The Brethren's Encyclopedia . . .* (Columbiana, Ohio: By the author, 1867), p. 26.

[16] General Mission Board, *Minutes*, 1842, Art. 1, pp. 74-75; 1850, Art. 5, pp. 78-79.

[17] The explicit office of deaconess had been discontinued by this time. Henry Kurtz, a leading Brethren elder from Ohio, noted, however, that the wives and widows of ministers or deacons "were considered as occupying the place of those called 'deaconesses' in the primitive or apostolic church." [Henry Kurtz], "Answer" to a Query, *The Monthly Gospel Visitor* (hereafter *MGV*) 14 (April 1864):123.

[18] In 1848 Philip Boyle, an elder from Maryland, described only three levels of leadership in the local church: deacon, preacher (or teacher), and elder (or bishop). Sappington, *New Nation*, pp. 199-200.

This depiction follows the traditional Brethren order of ministry. Yet, in Kline's diary in 1848 the new threefold order first becomes apparent. In prior entries Kline mentioned only the speaker or minister of the Word and elder. But in April, 1848, he clearly distinguishes the speaker, advancement to the second degree or grade of the ministry of the Word, and establishment in the ministry (eldership). Funk, *John Kline*, p. 218.

How three degrees of ministry developed is somewhat puzzling. A possible explanation is that the office of deacon was originally considered the first step in ministry, followed by the offices of speaker and elder. As confirmation of such a possibility see Kline's statement in 1841 that "two brethren were advanced from the deaconship to the ministry of the Word" (p. 131). See also Peter Nead's description of three "grades" of officers with (1) bishops and overseers, (2) teachers, ministers, or preachers, and (3) deacons. Peter Nead, *The Wisdom and Power of God as Displayed in Creation and Redemption* (Cincinnati: E. Morgan & Sons, 1866), p. 268. The next step in the development was a sharp distinction between deacons and ministers of the Word. (This distinction, based on the claim that the officers in Acts 6 were not deacons but ministers in the second degree, was instrumental in ending the practice of ordaining deacons; see Holsinger, *Tunkers*, p. 477.) This position was advocated by George Hoke, an influential elder from Ohio, and Kline. See Funk, *John Kline*, pp. 26-28; "Manuscript Notes on Different Subjects by our Departed Brother George Hoke," *MGV* 14 (June 1864):180-182; and John Kline, "Notes of Br. John Kline on the Letter from Br. George Hoke, as Published in last No.," *MGV* 14 (August 1, 1864):225-227. The final step was the retention of three degrees in the ministry, each with greater responsibility, while the office of deacon was distinguished from the ministry per se. (The second degree corresponded to the traditional office of trial elder while the third degree was the ordained elder.) This step had certainly occurred by 1848 in some places, but queries to Annual Meeting in 1864 (Art. 32) and 1865 (Art. 52) as well as Kline's article in the *Gospel Visitor* indicate the new practice was still not fully accepted. Kline supported the three-degree ministry by appealing to the various steps in Jesus' authorization of the apostles: the calling of the twelve disciples, the sending out of disciples two by two, and the final commissioning in Matthew 28. Kline, "Notes," p. 227.

Dale Brown has also observed that the Brethren were shifting from a functional to an institutional understanding of the ministry (paralleling other changes in the church toward greater form and structure). Thus the earlier task-oriented nomenclature for ministers (minister of the Word, housekeeper) gradually gave way to more formal titles (elder, bishop, degrees of ministry). Brown, "Developing Thought," p. 67.

[19] Holsinger, *Tunkers*, pp. 233-238 and James H. Lehman, *The Old Brethren* (Elgin, Illinois: The Brethren Press, 1976), pp. 154-158.

[20] Durnbaugh, "Brethren Historiography," p. 12.

[21] Marcus Miller, "Roots by the River," *ATB* 8 (Spring 1975):52. In some literature (ibid., p. 52 and Brumbaugh, *German Baptist Brethren*, pp. 504-505) a meeting held at Germantown in 1791 is cited as the first recorded instance of a committee being called in to settle a problem. Yet, the description of this meeting ("a large meeting took place in Germantown, where many brethren from near and far came together") and the fact that the gathering occurred on Pentecost, the traditional time for holding Annual Meeting, would suggest this was, in fact, a Yearly Meeting.

[22] Sappington, *New Nation*, pp. 203-204.

[23] Ibid., p. 206.

[24] An indication of the swelling load of business handled by Annual Meeting is given by the following figures. In the decade from 1830 to 1839, Annual Meeting considered 92 articles of business; from 1840 to 1849, 185 articles; from 1850 to 1859, 378 articles; from 1860 to 1869, 372 articles; and from 1870 to 1879, 292 articles. The leveling off and drop in the number of queries in the 1860s and 1870s respectively reflects the organization and growing efficiency of district meetings.

[25] Sappington, *New Nation*, p. 209.

[26] Brown, "Developing Thought," p. 64.

[27] Durnbaugh, "Early History," p. 18.

[28] Henry Kurtz listed the "gospel principles" according to which Annual Meeting made its decisions as:

> . . . 1, Simplicity; 2, Liberty; 3, Order; 4, Subordination of our reason to the word of God in its letter and spirit in all matters of difference; 5, A due regard to the conclusions of former Yearly Meetings; 6, A sincere love of the brethren consistent with the love of God, and Truth and Righteousness; 7, A constant aim for union in the body of Christ, the church . . .

Sappington, *New Nation*, p. 210. This list forms an excellent summary of the values which undergirded Brethren thought and practice.

[29] The first two examples where a query was answered by referring the questioner to a previous minute are found in 1842, Article 1 and 1844, Article 1, both of which include support from Scripture as well. In 1845, Articles 1, 9, 10, and 12 present the past minutes alone. Significantly, in 1857 Annual Meeting was asked whether it would not be better in deciding questions "to refer first to the word of God, instead of first referring to the old minutes." Annual Meeting concurred but continued its practice of referring to past minutes alone the very next year.

[30] Ronk, *Brethren Church*, p. 80. See also the 1828 Annual Meeting, Art. 7.

[31] General Mission Board, *Minutes*, Art. 44, p. 177.

[32] Ibid., 1858, Art. 4, p. 174; 1859, Art. 11, p. 184; Art. 22, p. 186; 1860, Art. 6, p. 196; Art. 11, p. 198. Cf. also the occasional use prior to 1858 of the dual authorities of the gospel and the "profession" of our brotherhood: 1851, Art. 14, p. 125; 1853, Art. 4, p. 134.

[33] Ibid., Art. 1, p. 195.

[34] Ibid., Art. 34, pp. 239-240.

[35] Brown, "Developing Thought," p. 63. In another discussion of this same issue, Kurtz observes that the questions brought to Annual Meeting were those which were normally divisive. Yet the decisions, made as much as possible "according to the pure sense and spirit of the word," were conducive to unity when accepted in obedience to the "word, 'Be subject one to another.'" [Henry Kurtz] Editor. Note to "Old Letters," *MGV* 9 (June 1859):169.

[36] Brown, "Developing Thought," p. 63.

[37] Confirmation that such a view was held among the early Brethren comes from Mack, Jr. (see p. 92). Also, if it is correct to assume that the 1791 "large meeting" held at Germantown was a Yearly Meeting, Mack, Jr.'s comments about the Germantown congregation's attitude toward the decision of the gathered elders takes on great significance.

> After careful deliberation the visiting brethren gave us, in the fear of the Lord, an advice [!] to which they signed their names. We Germantown brethren also have signed in the name of the entire congregation, to bear witness that we have received their advice in submissive love and are willing to submit to the same loving advice, in the fear of the Lord . . .

Brumbaugh, *German Baptist Brethren*, p. 505.

[38] Brown, "Developing Thought," p. 69.

[39] Ibid.

[40] I. D. Parker, "Church Polity," in *Two Centuries of the Church of the Brethren*, ed. D. L. Miller (Elgin, Illinois: Brethren Publishing House, 1908), p. 161. (Interestingly, Gottfried Arnold chose the term "democratic" to describe the type of church government he felt was found in the early church.)

[41] Peter Nead, one of these men who came from a non-Brethren (Lutheran) background, will be given special attention in the next chapter.

[42] For further details about Kurtz's life and contributions to the Brethren, see Donald F. Durnbaugh, "Henry Kurtz: Man of the Book," *BLT* 16 (Spring 1971):103-121 and Roger E. Sappington, *Courageous Prophet: Chapters from the Life of John Kline* (Elgin, Illinois: The Brethren Press, 1964).

[43] It needs to be remembered that the pietistic faith of this period was derived from Radical Pietism and classical Pietism and not American revivalism.

[44] For the few poetic publications that followed Stoll's work during the period, see Durnbaugh and Shultz, "Brethren Bibliography," numbers 108, 136, 160, 161, 162 (some of these publications contain works belonging to the previous century).

[45] Friedmann, *Mennonite Piety*, pp. 106-109, 207-208.

[46] Durnbaugh and Shultz, "Brethren Bibliography," p. 27.

[47] For a brief depiction of devotions in a "Tunker" family around the beginning of the nineteenth century, see Eller, "Western Ohio Valley," p. 87.

[48] Durnbaugh, "Henry Kurtz," p. 107.

[49] [Heinrich Kurtz, trans.], *Zeugnisse der Wahrheit, oder: Menno Symons sämtliche Schriften. . . . Des zweyten Theiles Erster Band.* (Osnaburg, Ohio: Heinrich Kurtz, 1833), pp. i, ii.

[50] Henry Kurtz, "The Church in the Wilderness . . . ," *MGV* 1 (June 1851):33 quoted in Durnbaugh, "Descent of Dissent," p. 126.

[51] Henry Kurtz, "Remarks" to a Query, *MGV* 6 (January 1856):24.

[52] Peter Nead, "The Land of Promise," *The Vindicator* 1 (March 1, 1870):8.

[53] Henry Kurtz, "Annual Meeting," excerpt from *Brethren's Encyclopedia* in Sappington, *New Nation*, p. 210.

[54] Christian Longenecker, "On the True Conversion and New Birth," trans. Vernard Eller, *BLT* 7 (Spring 1962):25.

[55] Ibid., pp. 23-28.

[56] Sappington, *New Nation*, pp. 134-135. Bowman's treatise, *A Testimony on Baptism . . .* , was written first in German in 1817 and translated into English in 1831.

[57] General Mission Board, *Minutes*, p. 38.

[58] Ibid., see also 1820, Art. 2, p. 44.

[59] Peter Nead, *Theological Writings on Various Subjects; or a Vindication of Primitive Christianity as Recorded in the Word Of God. . . .* (Dayton, Ohio: B. F. Ells, 1850), p. 90. Nead's work was composed of three previous writings combined with some new material. The first part of the work, *Primitive Christianity . . .* , was printed originally in 1834. For another quite objective presentation of the correct order of salvation, see General Mission Board, *Minutes*, 1835, Art. 21, pp. 61-62.

[60] Sydney E. Ahlstrom, *A Religious History of the American People* (New Haven: Yale University Press, 1972), p. 450. Scott's five step approach, arrived at in 1827, included faith, repentance, baptism, the remission of sins, and the gift of the Holy Spirit (note the similarity to the Brethren order).

[61] General Mission Board, *Minutes*, Art. 7, p. 83.

[62] The relationship between the two elements did create some discussion in 1866. See David Kimmel, "The First Principles," *The Christian Family Companion* (hereafter *CFC*) 2 (June 12, 1866):181 and E. Umbaugh, "Faith and Repentance—Their Relation to each Other," *CFC* 2 (August 7, 1866):243. The generally acceptive attitude toward either simplified order is illustrated in Nead's writings. In his earliest writing, *Primitive Christianity* (1834), Nead formulates the order as repentance-faith; in a work published in 1845 which forms the second part of his *Theological Writings*, the order is reversed to faith-repentance; in his final major work, *Wisdom and Power of God* (1866), and in his periodical articles written in the 1870s, the order returns to a repentance-faith schema.

[63] See Peter Bowman, *A Testimony on Baptism as Practised by the Primitive Christians, from the Time of the Apostles . . .* (Baltimore: Benjamin Edes, 1831), p. 12 and Funk, *John Kline*, pp. 130, 259, 330, 409.

[64] This argumentation can be discerned in Bowman, *Testimony*, pp. 13, 47, though he is careful to observe that baptism is a means of salvation in the sense that it tests our faith and obedience. It is on the basis of this testing process that the remission of sins is

promised. It is Peter Nead, however, who makes some of the earliest and most direct statements about the connection of baptism and salvation. See Nead, *Theological Writings*, pp. 45-46, 90, 250, 294.

[65] E. S., "Expository.—1 Tim. 4:16," *MGV* 8 (April 1858):103.

[66] S. H. Bashor, "Objections Reviewed," *The Brethren at Work* (hereafter *BAW*) 3 (January 3, 1878):5.

[67] J. W. Beer, "Baptism for the Remission of Sins," *The Christian Family Companion and Gospel Visitor* (hereafter *CFC & GV*) n.s. 1 (March 24, 1874):187.

[68] Bowman, *Testimony*, p. 47; cf. Sappington, *New Nation*, p. 240.

[69] James Quinter, "Means of Grace," *CFC & GV* n.s. 2 (January 26, 1875):58.

[70] C. F. Yoder, *God's Means of Grace* (Elgin, Illinois: Brethren Publishing House, 1908). See pp. 174-175 for a discussion of Yoder's work.

[71] Sappington, *New Nation*, pp. 167-168.

[72] The predominant theme of Brethren doctrinal literature during the period from 1785 to 1865 was baptism. This contention is borne out by analyzing the 155 titles in the "Brethren Bibliography" for the period. Of these, 84 were of a devotional character, 16 were of a miscellaneous nature (periodicals, historical works, Annual Meeting minutes, etc.), and 54 were doctrinal in nature. Of these 54 doctrinal writings, 13 dealt almost exclusively with baptism while another 17 gave substantial treatment to the rite. Of the remaining 24, 7 dealt with eschatology, 3 with nonresistance, 2 each with discipline and conversion, and the rest with a variety of other subjects. Durnbaugh and Shultz, "Brethren Bibliography," pp. 18-38.

[73] Peter Bowman, for example, sought to support the forward action in baptism by referring to the motion of the children of Israel as they walked through the Red Sea. John Kline argued for a kneeling position from Jesus' baptism of suffering in the garden of Gethsemane. Brown, "Developing Thought," p. 66.

[74] Nead, *Theological Writings*, pp. 39, 110.

[75] Ibid., p. 409.

[76] Ibid.

[77] Funk, *John Kline*, p. 34 and I. S. M., "Election," *MGV* 8 (October 1858):303.

[78] Funk, *John Kline*, pp. 326-327.

[79] The eclectic theology that has typified the Brethren throughout their history makes it almost impossible to pigeon-hole the Brethren. This point is illustrated by Brethren observations about Calvinism and Arminianism. One Brethren writer, for example, noted that some Brethren believed in a Calvinistic view of election. See D. Dierdorff, "Who Are God's Chosen People," *CFC* 2 (May 15, 1866):157. In a different vein Benjamin F. Moomaw, an elder from Virginia, reacted against the popular current expressions of Arminianism (Methodism, revivalism) which placed so much emphasis on "the emotions of the mind." Benjamin F. Moomaw, *Discussion on Trine Immersion . . .* (Singer's Glen, Virginia: Joseph Funk's Sons, 1867), pp. 217-218.

[80] [Henry Kurtz], "Answer" to "A Request," *MGV* 4 (October 1854):114 and Nead, *Theological Writings*, p. 47.

[81] Nead, *Theological Writings*, pp. 59, 395.

[82] Ibid., pp. 182, 303, 395 and Moomaw, *Trine Immersion*, p. 198.

[83] Nead, *Theological Writings*, p. 249.

[84] An Occasional Contributor, "A Dialogue," *MGV* 4 (September 1854):82.

[85] Funk, *John Kline*, p. 344.

[86] Ibid., p. 334.

[87] Ibid., p. 243; cf. pp. 268, 317.

[88] Ibid., p. 286.

[89] Ibid., p. 242.

[90] They were reacting to the teaching of an elder from North Carolina, John Ham, who believed that (1) there was no other heaven or hell but that in man, (2) God has no form or shape (Annual Meeting regarded this as an aspersion against the incarnation), (3) God is not wrathful and would punish no one, and (4) the dead would not rise. Durnbaugh, *Colonial America*, pp. 327–328.

[91] General Mission Board, *Minutes*, 1849, Art. 30, p. 110.

[92] James Quinter, "'Who Are the Dunkards?,'" *MGV* 8 (August 1858):241.

[93] Obed, "The New System," *MGV* 6 (July 1856):173–175 and E. S., "Expository.—1 Tim. 4:16," *MGV* 8 (April 1858):103.

[94] Sappington, *New Nation*, pp. 133–134.

[95] Nead, *Theological Writings*, pp. 223–226.

[96] See Durnbaugh and Shultz, "Brethren Bibliography," p. 26; Nead, *Theological Writings*, pp. 203–238; and [Henry Kurtz], "The Second Advent of Christ," *MGV* 4 (December 1854):145–150.

[97] Funk, *John Kline*, pp. 274–275.

[98] Note that the Brethren hymnals of the period contained a section on Christ's return and His kingdom. Sappington, *New Nation*, pp. 407–409, 411.

[99] Funk, *John Kline*, p. 299.

[100] J. C. Wenger, *Introduction to Theology* (Scottdale, Pennsylvania: Herald Press, 1954), p. vii.

CHAPTER 8: PETER NEAD'S LIFE AND THOUGHT

[1] Ronk, *Brethren Church*, p. 80.

[2] Loren Bowman, "The Life and Work of Peter Nead," *Schwarzenau* 1 (January 1940):10.

[3] Fred W. Benedict, "The Life and Work of Elder Peter Nead," *BLT* 19 (Winter 1974):64.

[4] Donald F. Durnbaugh, "Vindicator of Primitive Christianity: The Life and Diary of Peter Nead," *BLT* 14 (Autumn 1969):198.

[5] Ibid.

[6] Roger E. Sappington, *The Brethren in Virginia: The History of the Church of the Brethren in Virginia* (Harrisonburg, Virginia: Park View Press, 1973), p. 56.

[7] J. H. Moore, *Some Brethren Pathfinders* (Elgin, Illinois: Brethren Publishing House, 1929), p. 187.

[8] Sappington, *Brethren in Virginia*, p. 56.

[9] Durnbaugh, "Vindicator," p. 200.

[10] For instances of Nead's self-denying spirit toward the counsel of the church, see Benedict, "Elder Peter Nead," p. 70.

[11] Moore, *Pathfinders*, p. 185. Brethren writers did not generally cite their use of previous Brethren works though they did provide copious citations from non-Brethren sources. In Nead's major works, the only cited Brethren source is one quote from Alexander Mack. See Nead, *Theological Writings*, p. 358. There may be several reasons for this characteristic. Since most Brethren doctrinal works were apologetic during the eighteenth and nineteenth centuries and were therefore directed as much to the "sects" as to the church, evidence from Brethren sources was kept to a minimum. Also, this trait may be an indication that each new generation of Brethren, though acquainting itself thoroughly with the thought of its forefathers, sought to contemporize Brethren thought by applying it afresh to its own cultural and religious setting.

[12] Nead, *Wisdom and Power*, p. 95 and *Theological Writings*, p. 18.

[13] Idem, *Theological Writings*, p. 272; see also pp. 356, 370, 381.

[14] Ibid., p. 370.

[15] Ibid., p. 31.

[16] Ibid., p. vi.

[17] Ibid., p. 405 and *Wisdom and Power*, pp. 164, 254.

[18] Idem, "The School of Christ. No. 3," *The Vindicator* 1 (July 1870):34. The phrase "School of Christ" has a long history in sectarian circles. The imagery is suggestive of a group of co-disciples who learn all the necessary lessons for life from a common master. The learning that takes place in this school is frequently set in juxtaposition with that which occurs in the schools of society. Like Arnold's "mystical theology," the "School of Christ" conveys the idea that the wisdom of God is radically different from the wisdom of man. For examples of the use of this imagery by Brethren writers, see Durnbaugh, *Colonial America*, p. 98 (Stephen Koch) and Nead, "The School of Christ. No. 1," *Vindicator* 1 (March 1, 1870):2–3. See also a brief discussion of the phrase by George Huntston Williams, "A People in Community: Historical Background," in *The Concept of the Believers' Church*, ed. James Leo Garrett, Jr. (Scottdale, Pennsylvania: Herald Press, 1969), pp. 121–122.

[19] Peter Nead, "The Restoration of Primitive Christianity. No. 28," *Vindicator* 4 (February 1873):50.

[20] Idem, *Theological Writings*, p. 37.

[21] Ibid. and *Wisdom and Power*, p. 65.

[22] Idem, *Theological Writings*, p. 361.

[23] Ibid., p. 356.

[24] Ibid., pp. 259–260.

[25] Ibid., p. 21.

[26] Idem, "Restoration. No. 21," *Vindicator* 3 (June 15, 1872):89.

[27] Idem, *Theological Writings*, p. 37.

[28] Ibid., pp. 318–319.

[29] Ibid., p. 36.

[30] Ibid., pp. 50, 195 and *Wisdom and Power*, pp. 101, 104.

[31] Idem, *Theological Writings*, p. 96.

[32] Idem, *Wisdom and Power*, p. 164.

[33] Idem, *Theological Writings*, p. 324.

[34] Idem, "Restoration. No. 16," *Vindicator* 3 (February 1, 1872): 17–18.

[35] Idem, *Theological Writings*, p. 51.

[36] Ibid., p. 427.

[37] Idem, "Restoration. No. 37," *Vindicator* 5 (October 1874):145.

[38] Idem, *Theological Writings*, p. 152.

[39] Idem, "Restoration. No. 9," *Vindicator* 2 (June 1 & 15, 1871): 81–82.

[40] Idem, *Theological Writings*, p. 196.

[41] Ibid.

[42] Ibid., p. 108.

[43] Idem, "Restoration. No. 21," *Vindicator* 3 (June 15, 1872):89.

[44] Idem, "Restoration. No. 1," *Vindicator* 1 (April 1870):9.

[45] C. G. Lint, "Apostolical Succession," *CFC* 8 (July 30, 1872):465.

[46] Nead, "Restoration. No. 42," *Vindicator* 6 (October 1875):147.

[47] Idem, "Restoration. No. 43," *Vindicator* 7 (January 1876):2.

[48] This quote comes from the motto adopted by Samuel Kinsey for the *Vindicator*.

[49] Nead, "Restoration. No. 2," *Vindicator* 1 (June 1870):25.

[50] Idem, "Restoration. No. 43," *Vindicator* 7 (January 1876):2–3 and "School of Christ. No. 14," *Vindicator* 3 (January 1, 1872):2.

[51] Idem, "Restoration. No. 2," *Vindicator* 1 (June 1870):26-27. Regularly in the *Vindicator* the church of forty or fifty years prior is idolized for its plain and self-denying order. See, for example, John Harshbarger, "The Evidences of an Humble Heart," *Vindicator* 3 (December 1 & 15, 1872):187 and Nead, "Restoration. No. 39," *Vindicator* 6 (February 1875):20. It should be remembered that simplicity was one of the important principles inherited from both Radical Pietism and Anabaptism and also that the 1830s is the period when a number of changes begin to be noticed as the Brethren start interacting with the surrounding culture: the gradual loss of the old piety, the shift from German to English, the developing formalism in church practice, a more objective view of salvation, the increasing centralization of power in Annual Meeting.

[52] Nead, "Restoration. No. 48," *Vindicator* 7 (August 1876):228.

[53] Idem, "School of Christ. No. 14," *Vindicator* 3 (January 1, 1872):2.

[54] Idem, *Wisdom and Power*, p. 7.

[55] Ibid., pp. 8-9.

[56] Ibid., p. 16.

[57] Ibid., p. 17.

[58] Ibid., pp. 17-23.

[59] Ibid., p. 22. He may be reacting to a still existent bias, derived from Radical Pietism, against the term.

[60] Ibid., p. 23.

[61] Ibid., p. 98.

[62] Ibid., p. 67.

[63] Ibid., p. 70.

[64] Ibid., p. 73.

[65] Nead sees only two parts to creation: heaven (consisting of three parts) and earth. Since hell cannot be in heaven, it must be on earth.

[66] Ibid., p. 72.

[67] Ibid., p. 92.

[68] Ibid., pp. 93, 99. Note that Anabaptists singled out righteousness and holiness as the key attributes of God's image in man.

[69] Idem, *Theological Writings*, pp. 9-10.

[70] Ibid., p. 10.

[71] Ibid., pp. 409-410.

[72] Ibid., p. 10.

[73] Idem, *Wisdom and Power*, pp. 148-149.

[74] Idem, *Theological Writings*, p. 14.

[75] Idem, *Wisdom and Power*, p. 114. Nead holds that fallen man retains the natural image of God (p. 98).

[76] Ibid., p. 217.

[77] Idem, *Theological Writings*, p. 10.

[78] Ibid., p. 16. Nead explicitly rejects the Pelagian notion that wickedness originates in bad examples. *Wisdom and Power*, p. 137.

[79] Idem, *Wisdom and Power*, p. 138.

[80] Ibid., pp. 24, 156.

[81] Ibid., pp. 26, 150-153.

[82] Idem, *Theological Writings*, p. 26.

[83] Ibid., pp. 26-27.

[84] Ibid., pp. 27-29.

[85] Ibid., p. 30.

[86] Idem, *Wisdom and Power*, pp. 169-170. The use of the theological categories "preceptive" and "penal" is not typical of the early Brethren but is definitely representative of a trend toward greater theological acumen among some of the Brethren leaders by the 1860s.

[87] Idem, *Theological Writings*, p. 31.

[88] Ibid., pp. 19-21.

[89] Ibid., p. 21.

[90] Idem, *Wisdom and Power*, p. 177.

[91] Ibid., p. 202.

[92] Ibid., p. 207.

[93] Ibid., pp. 210-211 and *Theological Writings*, p. 32. Nead holds that this aspect of the atonement has special ramifications for those who die in infancy. Though children still have a depraved nature, all those who die before reaching the years of maturity will be saved through Christ's atonement.

[94] Idem, *Theological Writings*, p. 210.

[95] Ibid., p. 92.

[96] Ibid., pp. 47, 90-93, 247-250.

[97] Ibid., p. 38. Nead's principle of free will with respect to salvation is thus delimited by receptivity to the divine action of the Word and Spirit. He acknowledges that "if sinners make no resistance against the word and spirit of God, their situation will be plainly revealed unto them."

[98] Idem, *Wisdom and Power*, pp. 224-227.

[99] Ibid., p. 241.

[100] Ibid., p. 230.

[101] Ibid., pp. 228-230, 237.

[102] Ibid., p. 234 and *Theological Writings*, p. 310.

[103] Idem, *Wisdom and Power*, p. 236.

[104] Idem, *Theological Writings*, p. 273.

[105] Ibid., pp. 90-93, 274-275.

[106] Ibid., p. 394. The use of God-appointed means becomes an effective counter argument to man's "new measures" (see pp. 109-111). Here again the reaction to revivalism may account for the expanding use and application of the term "means of grace."

[107] Reflective of Nead's shifting of the emphasis from the internal and subjective to the external and objective is his interpretation of 1 Peter 3:21. Whereas previous Brethren writers called for the observance of baptism because it represented "the answer of a good conscience toward God," Nead places the emphasis fully on the rite itself: "Here we have the type and the anti-type, the ark and baptism—both appointed for salvation. The ark prefigured our salvation by baptism. . . . Baptism saved the soul from sin—the ark saved the bodies of Noah and his family from death." Ibid., p. 283.

[108] Nead does not distinguish between the sign and seal language of the Baptists and Presbyterians and his own position. In his later years, however, he does make the distinction, criticizing the view that baptism "is only an outward work, and a *sign* of the remission of sins." Idem, "Restoration. No. 38," *Vindicator* 5 (December 1874):179. Nead, *Theological Writings*, p. 289 seeks support for his position in Calvin's statement that those who regard baptism as

> nothing more than a mark or sign by which we profess our religion before men . . . have not considered that which was the principal thing in baptism, which is that we might so receive it with this promise—"He that believeth, and is baptized shall be saved."

Cf. John Calvin, *Institutes of the Christian Religion*, trans. Ford Lewis Battles, The Library of Christian Classics, no. 21 (Philadelphia: The Westminster Press, 1960), 4, 15, 1, p. 1304. Some of Nead's strongest evidence (pp. 291-294) comes from Luther, however. Noteworthy is Luther's assertion (drawn from a polemical passage that is not altogether representative of his thought):

> Internally he [God] acts with us by the Holy Spirit, faith, and other gifts. But all this in such order, that the outward means must precede, and the inward must arise through the

outward, and succeed them; for thus he has concluded not to give to any person these internal things but by the externals; . . .

Cf. Martin Luther, "Against the Heavenly Prophets in the Matter of Images and Sacraments," trans. Conrad Bergendoff in *Luther's Works*, gen. ed. Helmut T. Lehman, vol. 40: *Church and Ministry II*, ed. Conrad Bergendoff (Philadelphia: Muhlenberg Press, 1958), p. 146.

[109] Nead, *Theological Writings*, pp. 285–307.

[110] Ibid., p. 256.

[111] Ibid., pp. 52, 283, 318.

[112] Ibid., pp. 316–317.

[113] Idem, *Wisdom and Power*, p. 246.

[114] Idem, *Theological Writings*, p. 318.

[115] Ibid., pp. 91–92.

[116] Ibid., pp. 247, 256, 279.

[117] Ibid., pp. 256, 318 and *Wisdom and Power*, p. 213.

[118] Idem, *Wisdom and Power*, pp. 248, 252.

[119] Idem, *Theological Writings*, pp. 192–193, 196, 199, 400.

[120] Ibid., p. 54.

[121] Idem, "Restoration. No. 2," *Vindicator* 1 (June 1870):25.

[122] Idem, *Theological Writings*, p. 122.

[123] Ibid., p. 123.

[124] Benedict, "Elder Peter Nead," p. 72.

[125] Nead, *Theological Writings*, p. 102.

[126] Ibid., pp. 111, 155, 192.

[127] Ibid., pp. 103–104, 108–109.

[128] Ibid., p. 256.

[129] Ibid., p. 356.

[130] Ibid., pp. 356–358.

[131] Ibid., pp. 63–64, 171, 354–355, 357, 420.

[132] Quoted in Benedict, "Elder Peter Nead," p. 74.

[133] Nead, *Theological Writings*, pp. 256–257.

[134] Nead devotes 139 of the 472 pages in his *Theological Writings* to baptism and mentions it frequently in other connections.

[135] Ibid., p. 64.

[136] Ibid., p. 260.

[137] Ibid., p. 65.

[138] Ibid., pp. 66–73.

[139] Ibid., p. 73.

[140] Ibid., pp. 75–78.

[141] Ibid., p. 82.

[142] Ibid., pp. 83–85. Nead introduces for the first time in the Brethren apologetic for trine immersion the practice of the Greek church. During the course of the nineteenth century, this argument takes on added importance. Probably the most extreme use of the argument is found in Stephen H. Bashor, *The Brethren Church* (Waterloo, Iowa: Brethren Publishing Co., [1893]), p. 3. He contends, on the basis of vague and undocumented evidence, that "the Brethren Church is a lineal descendant of the Greek Church."

[143] Ibid., p. 86.

[144] Ibid., p. 87.

[145] Ibid., p. 127.

[146] Ibid., pp. 131–133.

[147] Ibid., p. 376.

[148] Ibid., p. 378.

[149] Ibid., pp. 144–145.

[150] Ibid., pp. 158, 379–380. An entire series of articles was written on the subject for the *Christian Family Companion* by Joseph W. Beer in 1871 and later appeared as a book. See Joseph W. Beer, *The Jewish Passover and the Lord's Supper* (Lancaster,

Pennsylvania: Inquirer Printing and Publishing Co., 1874). The Brethren held that the Last Supper was eaten the day before the legal Passover and that Jesus was crucified when the Passover lamb was slain.

[151] Nead, *Theological Writings*, p. 153.

[152] Ibid., p. 379.

[153] Ibid., pp. 155–157.

[154] Ibid., pp. 135–136, 371.

[155] Ibid., pp. 161–162.

[156] Idem, *Wisdom and Power*, pp. 277, 284–285.

[157] Ibid., pp. 278–286.

[158] Nead differs from the usual Anabaptist view of the state when he distinguishes between good and corrupt governments. He maintains that God has not ordained those governments which are corrupt because, if this was true, "then you must also admit, that it was the powers of God which put Jesus Christ, the apostles, and all the holy martyrs to death." Ibid., p. 118. The Anabaptists, with their sharp dualism between the church and the world, held no illusions about the character of the state; because the state was part of the kingdom of the world, it, like the citizens of the world, came in all shades of moral integrity. Obedience was to be given to all as long as the dictates of the state did not violate the law of Christ. If suffering was the inevitable result of such a position, it was to be accepted and became, in effect, a witness against that government. Nead, however, apparently had a more optimistic opinion about the state's ability to mirror Christian values. This higher estimate may derive from the American experience of a "republican government" (p. 119) and may also explain Nead's controversial advocacy of voting in political elections (which he later retracted). See Benedict, "Elder Peter Nead," p. 70. Nead does not indicate how the Christian should relate to a corrupt government.

[159] Nead, *Theological Writings*, pp. 116–122.

[160] Ibid., pp. 423.

[161] Idem, *Wisdom and Power*, p. 331.

[162] Ibid., p. 341.

[163] Ibid., pp. 335–341.

[164] Idem, *Theological Writings*, pp. 203–209.

[165] Nead does not elaborate on the time relationship between the events surrounding the church and those regarding Israel. His only pertinent comment is:

I shall, therefore, hasten to call the attention of the reader to those great events which shall now be accomplished by our Lord Jesus Christ—though not all in an hour, or so short a period as many would have us to believe. No, it will require some time for the accomplishment of these events . . .

Ibid., p. 211. However, Nead does not see two phases to Christ's return (as in dispensationalism), one for the church and one for Israel (he has stated that *all* people will see Christ at His return). See also idem, "Restoration. No. 50," *Vindicator* 7 (November 1876):322–323 and "Restoration. No. 51," *Vindicator* 7 (December 1876):354.

[166] Idem, *Theological Writings*, pp. 211–230.

[167] Ibid., p. 233. Nead further describes the righteous as those "who are not outwardly in covenant with God, but who do love the children of God." He cites Matthew 25:31–46. Ibid., pp. 234–235. Given the exclusivism of the Brethren at this time, the category of the righteous may be Nead's way of "opening" heaven to non-Brethren.

168 Ibid., pp. 232-235 and *Wisdom and Power*, p. 350.

169 Idem, *Wisdom and Power*, p. 352.

170 Idem, *Theological Writings*, pp. 236, 245.

171 Jesse O. Garst, et al., *History of the Church of the Brethren of the Southern District of Ohio* (Dayton, Ohio: The Otterbein Press, 1920), pp. 526-527.

172 Nead, *Wisdom and Power*, p. 314.

173 Idem, *Theological Writings*, p. 223.

174 Ibid., pp. 361, 441.

175 Idem, *Wisdom and Power*, p. 320.

176 Idem, *Theological Writings*, p. 225.

177 Idem, "Restoration. No. 6," *Vindicator* 2 (February 1, 1871):18.

178 Idem, "Restoration. No. 23," *Vindicator* 3 (August 1, 1872):113.

179 Idem, "Restoration. No. 32," *Vindicator* 4 (November 1873):169 and "Restoration. No. 35," *Vindicator* 5 (May 1874):65.

180 Idem, "Restoration. No. 37," *Vindicator* 5 (October 1874):146.

181 Idem, "Restoration. No. 39," *Vindicator* 6 (February 1875):20.

182 Idem, "Restoration. No. 40," *Vindicator* 6 (April 1875):56 and "Restoration. No. 49," *Vindicator* 7 (October 1876):290.

183 Moore, *Pathfinders*, p. 189.

PART IV: CONTROVERSY, DIVISION, AND CHANGE (1865-1883)
CHAPTER 9: ISSUES CONTRIBUTING TO THE SCHISM

1 Henry Holsinger, the leader of the Progressives (see p. 249, n. 1 for the common names given to the three factions), calls the period between 1850 and 1880 "transitional" and states, "With the appearance of the *Visitor* was ushered in the progressive era in the Tunker Church." Holsinger, *Tunkers*, p. 470.

2 Kurtz could argue in the second issue for the paper's continued existence on the "principle of liberty": "For the Yearly Meeting now to forbid its publication . . . would appear so contrary to that principle of liberty, which we profess, and grant too at every meeting for worship, and which was enjoyed even with regard to printing, as the books of Br. Alexander Mack, sen. and jun., of Br. Benjamin Bowman, of Br. Philip Boyle, and last, but not least of Br. Peter Nead—testify." Yet he was also willing, as he states in the third issue, to cease publication if the *Visitor* had "to be sacrificed on the altar of brotherly love as a peace-offering." Sappington, *New Nation*, pp. 426, 427.

3 Ibid., pp. 422-423.

4 Martin, "Law and Grace," p. 30.

5 Ronk, *Brethren Church*, p. 87.

6 Holsinger, *Tunkers*, p. 473.

7 Idem, "Introductory," *The Progressive Christian* (hereafter *PC*) 1 (January 3, 1879):2.

8 Even though Quinter did retain a progressive viewpoint and the open forum format in the paper, he was not forceful enough for Holsinger who wished that Quinter had used his editorial position in a more aggressive manner. Idem, *Tunkers*, p. 480.

9 Idem, "Introductory," p. 2. Between 1874 and 1878 Holsinger served as a solicitor for the proposed Berlin College (1874), traveled extensively through the Midwest (1875), and worked as a job printer and commission merchant for farm produce in Chicago (1876-1877). He returned to Berlin, Pennsylvania, in the latter part of 1877 to minister to the Brethren there.

10 Samuel Kinsey, "Our Prospectus," *Vindicator* 1 (March 1, 1870):2.

11 Sappington, *New Nation*, pp. 288-294.

12 Miller, "Roots," pp. 56-57.

13 Sappington, *New Nation*, pp. 294-297.

14 Ibid., p. 297.

15 S. Z. Sharp, *The Educational History of the Church of the Brethren* (Elgin, Illinois: Brethren Publishing House, 1923), pp. 59-71.

16 Holsinger, *Tunkers*, pp. 473-474. Donald F. Durnbaugh, "Henry R. Holsinger: A Church of the Brethren Perspective," *BLT* 24 (Summer 1979): 142-143 has astutely observed how frequently the word "intelligence" appears in the writings of Holsinger and the Progressives. Intelligence was viewed as a kind of key that could admit the Brethren into the wider circles of American

society; it also became a critiquing tool (as above) in the hands of the Progressives. It was this optimistic conception of education and intelligence which opened the Progressives to the influence of liberalism.

17 Ibid., p. 475. Brethren elders were expected to have long hair (down to the collar in back) and wear full beards.

18 Kent, *Conquering Frontiers*, p. 130.

19 Note, however, the reasoning given by the early Brethren to Morgan Edwards for not having a paid ministry. "They pay not their ministers unless it be in a way of presents, though they admit their right to pay; neither do the ministers assert the right, esteeming it *more blessed to give than to receive.*" Durnbaugh, *Colonial America*, p. 175. The early Brethren were not opposed to the *principle* of paying ministers.

20 General Mission Board, *Minutes*, p. 156.

21 Ibid., p. 194.

22 Ibid., p. 203.

23 Funk, *John Kline*, pp. 185-186. See also Miller, "Roots," p. 56.

24 J. W. Beer, "Ministerial Support," *CFC* 2 (July 32 [sic] 1866):235. Beer worked as an assistant editor of the *Christian Family Companion* and *Primitive Christian* and was a partner with Holsinger on the *Progressive Christian*. Significantly, Beer had penned a similar article for the *Gospel Visitor* the year before. This was one of the first articles (if not *the* first one) to address this issue specifically in any of the papers. See J. W. B. [Beer], "Ministerial Support," *MGV* 15 (June 1865):169-171.

25 Sappington, *New Nation*, p. 246.

26 Ibid.

27 General Mission Board, *Minutes*, Art. 17, p. 319.

28 Ibid., pp. 192-194; see also 1856, Art. 22, pp. 158-159 and Funk, *John Kline*, p. 366.

29 General Mission Board, *Minutes*, 1874, Art. 18, p. 319.

30 Ibid., 1879, Art. 17, pp. 368-369; 1880, Art. 3, pp. 372-373.

31 Ronk, *Brethren Church*, pp. 103-104.

32 Ibid., pp. 104-106.

33 General Mission Board, *Minutes*, p. 276.

34 Samuel Kinsey, "Editorial," *Vindicator* 1 (July 1870):38 and idem, "Neglect Not the After Care," *Vindicator* 8 (February 1877):59. See also General Mission Board, *Minutes*, p. 379.

35 Samuel Murray, George V. Siler, and Samuel Kinsey, "The Brethren's Reasons," in *Minutes of the Annual Meetings of the Old German Baptist Brethren from 1778 to 1955*, Publishing Committee (Covington, Ohio: The Little Printing Company, 1956), p. 36.

36 Sappington, *New Nation*, pp. 247-248. The 1857 decision showed a willingness to be open to adiaphorous questions: "we know of no scripture which condemns Sabbath-Schools . . ."

[37] James Quinter, "Sabbath Schools," *MGV* 8 (September 1858):261; cf. idem, "Parental Responsibility," *MGV* 9 (August 1859):242.

[38] Idem, "Sabbath Schools," p. 259.

[39] Ibid., p. 260.

[40] Ibid., p. 261.

[41] General Mission Board, *Minutes*, pp. 379–380.

[42] John Wampler, "Sabbath Schools," *Vindicator* 9 (October 1878):305–306 and Peter Nead, "Restoration. No. 30," *Vindicator* 4 (September 1873):130.

[43] Adam Frantz, "Sunday Schools," *Primitive Christian* (hereafter *Prim. C.*) 1 (August 8, 1876):501.

[44] General Mission Board, *Minutes*, Art. 22, p. 413.

[45] The increasing casuistry of these rulings is highlighted by the fact that between 1800 and 1850 only sixteen articles in the Annual Meeting minutes dealt with questions of dress. Between 1851 and 1880 there were forty-seven! See Esther Fern Rupel, "An Investigation of the Origin, Significance, and Demise of the Prescribed Dress Worn by Members of the Church of the Brethren" (Ph.D. dissertation, University of Minnesota, 1971), pp. 340–341.

[46] See especially the articles by John Harshey, "Explanatory and Suggestive," *Vindicator* 8 (May 1877):132–137 and "Dress and Holiness," *Vindicator* 9 (March 1878):73–77. Cf. A. Kinzie, "Is the Outward Appearance of a Christian Essential to his Profession or Not?" *Vindicator* 8 (March 1877):76–77 and Alex. W. Reese, "The Moral Significance of Dress," *Vindicator* 8 (August 1877):225–232.

[47] Henry R. Holsinger and Stephen H. Bashor, "The Issue," *PC* 3 (October 14, 1881):1. Note the special emphasis on the inward.

[48] See J. H. Moore, "Close of Volume I," *BAW* 1 (December 21, 1876):2. The *Brethren At Work* was a leading mouthpiece for Conservative viewpoints in the Midwest. It was published in Lanark, Illinois.

[49] James Quinter, "Christian Apparel and Non-Conformity to the World," *MGV* 15 (November 1865):326.

[50] R. H. Miller, "Is the Brotherhood Right?" *BAW* 7 (January 5, 1881):4.

[51] Idem, "On the Dress Question Still," *PC* 1 (July 18, 1879):1.

[52] Holsinger, *Tunkers*, p. 417 writes: "In all the controversies that ever disturbed the Tunker fraternity, none was so prolific in the propagation of bad feelings, harsh sayings, and unholy conduct as was that upon the mode of feet-washing."

[53] It has generally been held that the roots of the Far Western Brethren can be traced to Germantown. See Eller, "Western Ohio Valley," p. 140.

[54] General Mission Board, *Minutes*, pp. 277–279; see also Sappington, *New Nation*, p. 88.

[55] William C. Thurman, *The Ordinance of Feet Washing, As Instituted by Christ, Defended and Restored to its Original Purity* (Philadelphia: John Goodyear, 1864), pp. 96–97. Thurman, a Brethren minister from Virginia, was disfellowshipped by the 1865 Annual Meeting more for his controversial stance on feetwashing than for his Adventist views. This conjecture is substantiated by his reinstatement to office by the 1866 Annual Meeting upon the condition that he did not preach on the doctrine of feetwashing. He did not abide by his pledge and was expelled by his home church, the Green Mount church, in November, 1867.

[56] General Mission Board, *Minutes*, pp. 277–279.

[57] For the exchange between Kinsey and Cassel, see Abraham H. Cassel, "Original Sketch of the Early History of the Brethren," *CFC* 4 (September 1, 1868):328–330; Samuel Kinsey, "It Is Desired," *CFC* 4 (September 29, 1868):351; Abram H. Cassel, "Reply to Samuel Kinsey," *CFC* 4 (October 27, 1868):438–439; and Samuel Kinsey, "To A. H. Cassel," *CFC* 4 (December 1, 1868):530.

For Holsinger's intervention see H. R. Holsinger, "Feetwashing," *CFC* 5 (April 27, 1869):253.

[58] General Mission Board, *Minutes*, p. 300.

[59] A report of the findings, signed only by Sayler, did not appear until March 30, 1881, in the periodical, *The Brethren's Advocate*. Kimmel, *Chronicles*, pp. 186–188 provides a part of the report. In it Sayler argued that the Germantown church should not be considered a mother church since other churches were organized "nearly simultaneously." Therefore, Germantown need not be followed in its practice of the single mode. Cassel prepared a point by point rebuttal for the *Brethren At Work* but his rejoinder was never published in the paper. It did appear, however, as a separately published tract in 1881. See Durnbaugh and Shultz, "Brethren Bibliography," pp. 55–56, nos. 297, 298. Cassel's reply also appears in Holsinger, *Tunkers*, pp. 219–226.

[60] Abram H. Cassel, "On Feet-Washing," *CFC* 8 (April 9, 1872):228–231.

[61] General Mission Board, *Minutes*, Art. 17, p. 304.

[62] Ibid., Art. 24, p. 352.

[63] Marcus Miller, "Leaders of the Old Order Movement, 1865 to 1900," *BLT* 24 (Summer 1979):147, 149.

[64] Murray, "Brethren's Reasons," p. 15.

[65] The question whether Annual Meeting decisions are obligatory until repealed or merely advisory (especially regarding modern practices) has never been definitively settled by the Old Orders. Though there has always been a strong emphasis upon unity in faith and practice (unity for the Old Orders has the connotation of uniformity), the Old Order Brethren have also shown a willingness to accept a minority who are "ahead-of-their-time" in using modern inventions and practices not yet sanctioned by Annual Meeting. See Fred W. Benedict, "The Old Orders and Schism," *BLT* 18 (Winter 1973):27.

[66] Publishing Committee, *Minutes of the Old German Baptist Brethren*, pp. 502–503. When the Old Order Brethren use the term "district," it is applied in its original Brethren connotation. All the Brethren living within the boundaries of a given "district" were considered members of a single congregation, even though the district might include several preaching points.

[67] Holsinger, *Tunkers*, pp. 531–533. These points are taken from a document prepared immediately following the expulsion of Holsinger and other Progressives from the church in 1882. It is interesting that the Progressives, in criticizing the Conservatives in this document, used terminology similar to that which the Old Orders had used during the preceding decade in attacking the Progressive elements in the church. For example, the Progressives declared their "independence from all innovations and additions" introduced by the Conservatives regarding church polity and decried the "continued departures from the primitive simplicity of the Christian faith in almost every essential feature of gospel liberty and church rule." Of course the innovations and departures for the Progressives were defined in terms of the principle of "gospel liberty," while for the Old Orders they were defined in terms of the principle of continuity with the "ancient order of the Brethren."

[68] J. W. Beer, "The Old and Sure Foundation," *PC* 3 (November 11, 1881): 1 and P. H. Beaver, "Wild Shots," *PC* 3 (July 1, 1881):4.

[69] Henry R. Holsinger and Stephen H. Bashor, "Progressive Unity—Our Principles Defined," *PC* 3 (October 7, 1881):2.

[70] Holsinger, *Tunkers*, p. 534. Holsinger's most infamous attack against the Standing Committee occurred in an article in which he compared it to a secret organization (the Brethren strictly forbade participation in such societies) with (1) a room to itself, (2) a doorkeeper, (3) sessions held with closed doors, (4) exclusion of the

press, (5) exclusion of all but the third degree ministry, and (6) secrets which are not to be revealed. H. R. Holsinger, "Is the Standing Committee a Secret Organization?" *PC* 1 (June 27, 1879):2.

[71] General Mission Board, *Minutes*, Art. 5, p. 406. D. P. Sayler was the moving force behind this "mandatory clause."

[72] Ibid., p. 421.

[73] R. H. Miller, "Liberties," *BAW* 7 (January 12, 1882), quoted in Lauderdale, "Division," p. 83.

[74] Peter Nead, "Restoration. No. 43," *Vindicator* 7 (January 1876):2.

[75] Samuel Kinsey, "Business Thoughts for Annual Meeting," *Vindicator* 9 (June 1878): 183–184.

[76] Henry R. Holsinger, "What Is the General Order?" *PC* 3 (January 28, 1881):2. The Progressive position was well summarized in the often cited adage: "In essentials unity, in nonessentials liberty, and in all things charity."

[77] Idem, *Tunkers*, p. 486.

[78] Ibid., p. 535. The historiography of the Old Orders and Progressives is noteworthy. Whereas the Old Orders idealized the Brethren of the 1820s and 30s (see p. 274, n. 51), the Progressives idealized their conception of the eighteenth century Brethren (before the development of the "order of the Brethren").

[79] J. H. Moore, "Due Respect to Our Fathers," *BAW* 7 (June 20, 1882):4.

[80] The difference between the Conservatives and Progressives on this point is one of degree only. The degrees of difference between the three groups can be illustrated by noting the concern of each group regarding the availability of the minutes of past Annual Meetings. The Old Orders not only print the minutes for each Annual Meeting following the gathering, but they make available as needed (editions in 1917, 1944, 1955 and 1971) a single volume containing all the extant minutes of Annual Meetings (beginning in 1778). The Church of the Brethren also prints minutes following each Annual Meeting, but only the minutes from 1945 on are still in print. The last complete edition of the minutes was published in 1909 "for historical value." The Brethren Church (Progressives) publish only the year by year proceedings of their Annual Conference. They have *never* published a collection of past minutes.

[81] Quoted in Ronk, *Brethren Church*, pp. 90–91.

[82] J. H. Moore, "Our Reflector," *BAW* 6 (October 18, 1881):633.

CHAPTER 10: THE DIVISION AND AN ANALYSIS

[1] Kimmel, *Chronicles*, p. 171.

[2] Murray, "Brethren's Reasons," p. 14. For details of the petition, see p. 142.

[3] Ibid., p. 16.

[4] General Mission Board, *Minutes*, Art. 1, p. 276.

[5] Murray, "Brethren's Reasons," p. 23.

[6] Ibid.

[7] Ibid., p. 27.

[8] Ibid., p. 28.

[9] Ibid., p. 29.

[10] Lauderdale, "Division," p. 14.

[11] Murray, "Brethren's Reasons," p. 30.

[12] Ibid., p. 31. This quote underscores the polarization taking place among the Brethren, for "liberty of conscience" was indeed a basic Brethren principle which, however, was always balanced with a reciprocal respect for the consensus of the body.

[13] Ibid., p. 31.

[14] Ibid., p. 32.

[15] Kimmel, *Chronicles*, p. 220.

[16] Lauderdale, "Division," p. 19.

[17] Kimmel, *Chronicles*, p. 233.

[18] Murray, "Brethren's Reasons," p. 37.

[19] Ibid., pp. 37–40.

[20] Kimmel, *Chronicles*, p. 244. Marcus Miller indicates, however, that it is unclear whether this meeting "was intended to be a decisive break or an interim move to be followed by a wait-and-see attitude." Miller, "Leaders," p. 155.

[21] Murray, "Brethren's Reasons," p. 46.

[22] Ibid., p. 45.

[23] Ibid.

[24] Ronk, *Brethren Church*, pp. 132–133.

[25] Lauderdale, "Division," p. 34.

[26] Holsinger, *Tunkers*, p. 495.

[27] General Mission Board, *Minutes*, p. 368.

[28] Holsinger, *Tunkers*, p. 495.

[29] Note the comments by Samuel Kinsey, "Editorial," *Vindicator* 12 (February 1881):59: "Brother Holsinger is by no means the most dangerous man that ever lived. His *principle* is commendable even if his *course* is not. . . . He does not half hide, but comes out square, that all may know where he stands, and no one need be deceived."

[30] Ronk, *Brethren Church*, pp. 95–96.

[31] General Mission Board, *Minutes*, pp. 393–394.

[32] Holsinger, *Tunkers*, pp. 499–501.

[33] Throughout Holsinger's disputes with the Brotherhood and Annual Meeting in particular, Holsinger continued to have the support of his home church in Berlin, Pennsylvania. In fact, he was ordained to the eldership in 1880, just as his difficulties with Annual Meeting were intensifying.

[34] Holsinger, *Tunkers*, pp. 503–506.

[35] General Mission Board, *Minutes*, p. 404.

[36] Holsinger, *Tunkers*, p. 508.

[37] Ibid., pp. 509, 512. Miller sided with the Conservatives in the split after he had a falling out with the Progressives over the spirit they manifested in the controversy. He criticized the Progressives for their depreciation of the fraternal spirit, their stance on the dress question and the paid ministry, and their lack of appreciation for the traditions of the church. See Howard Miller, "To S. H. Bashor," *PC* 4 (February 3, 1882):1 and idem, "To Brother Peck," *PC* 4 (April 14, 1882):1.

[38] Holsinger, *Tunkers*, p. 516.

[39] Ibid., p. 535.

[40] Ibid., p. 526.

[41] Ronk, *Brethren Church*, p. 365 has sought to trace the source of this motto to a pamphlet written by the Anglican, William Chillingworth, in 1635. Chillingworth affirms: "The Bible, the Bible, I say, the Bible only, is the Religion of Protestants." Though the sentiment is similar, the source is far too removed from the thought world of the Brethren. Much more likely is the possibility that this motto was borrowed from the Disciples of Christ. This motto appears frequently in their early literature as a principal tenet of their thought. See for example Alexander Campbell, "Incidents on a Tour to the South. No. 4," *The Millennial Harbinger* n.s. 3 (April 1839):188 and idem, "Union of Christians. No. 3," *The Millennial Harbinger* n.s. 3 (August 1839):344.

[42] Holsinger, *Tunkers*, p. 536.

[43] Ibid., p. 538. By taking this course of action, the Progressives also felt that the responsibility for the division would rest upon

Annual Meeting. Idem, "Why the Convention Should Be Held after Annual Meeting," *PC* 5 (March 7, 1883):2.

[44] Idem, "A Review," *PC* 5 (May 23, 1883):3.

[45] Idem, *Tunkers*, p. 544.

[46] Gillin, *Dunkers*, p. 227.

[47] Ibid., p. 228.

[48] Ibid., pp. 231-232.

[49] Ibid., pp. 161-199.

[50] Ibid., pp. 198, 199.

[51] Representative of some of these tendencies is the following quote:

> The spirit of these organizations [the Progressives and Conservatives] is slowly becoming more liberal, the idea that the individual exists for the church is gradually being displaced by the conception that the church exists for the welfare of the individual.... Even more dominant is becoming the idea that the only reason for the existence of the church is its ability and purpose to contribute to the welfare of man; first, by contributing to the welfare of the individual member of the denomination; secondly, by contributing to the welfare of society at large by the kind of men it is able to make of its members and send out into the larger society, the nation and the world.

Ibid., pp. 224-225.

[52] Mallott, *Studies*, pp. 151-152.

[53] Durnbaugh, "Recent History," in *Church of the Brethren Past and Present*, p. 24.

[54] Ronk, *Brethren Church*, p. 502.

[55] Ibid.

[56] Ibid., p. 111.

[57] Ibid., pp. 502-503.

[58] For example, Ronk quotes at length from two articles which develop that inner-outer dialectic which is at the heart of much early Brethren thought: inner piety must find outward expression, but external forms are meaningless unless animated by inner holiness. Yet he fails to identify this basic Brethren conviction and can exclaim only:

> What sentiment is here spoken! This is Conservative-Progressivism in its most lucid expression. This is the very soul of true Dunkardism harking all the way back to Alexander Mack; and whatever has wavered from its pivotal center, in whatever branch of the church, casts a shadow of shame upon the deposit of truth vouchsafed to the children of its heritage.

Ibid., p. 144.

[59] Lauderdale, "Division," pp. 2, 76-77, 92. This interpretation of the split had been suggested first by Dale Brown, "Membership in the Body of Christ," pp. 69-70. It was Lauderdale, however, who presented the documentation for this thesis.

[60] Lauderdale, "Division," pp. 76-77.

[61] Fred Benedict indicates that the Old Order Brethren have adopted a moderate view toward the use of modern inventions: "some inventions should be forbidden when they cause offense but may be accepted if and when offense is not present." Besides accepting some modern developments the Old Orders even bear with a minority "fast" element (progressives?) who hold that since "modern inventions are not mentioned in Scripture, Annual Meeting decisions on such matters should be optional." Benedict notes that these "fast" brethren are "affectionately referred to by the moderates as 'ahead-of-their-time,' for often the very things they advocate are later adopted by the general brotherhood." "Old

Orders and Schism," p. 27. This picture of the Old German Baptist Brethren church is intriguing, for the main body of the church finds itself in exactly the same position as did the Conservatives at the time of the division in the 1880s with traditionalists and a "fast" element on either side! The positions of each of these groups is also remarkably similar to those of their counterparts in the 1870s and 80s. (Benedict indicates this configuration of parties had appeared at least by 1900.)

The situation in the Brethren Church is only a little different. Though the Brethren Church has never really had an "Old Order" group, the controversies which have arisen among the former Progressives can be viewed as struggles between a traditional Brethren element and a group which had been more thoroughly influenced by a modern theological trend (liberalism or fundamentalism-dispensationalism). Lauderdale's claim that the Progressives maintained absolute congregationalism, depreciated the significance of community, and sought neither separation nor uniformity in practice is not entirely borne out by the facts. Though the Progressives would continue to wrestle with the question of church government for the next thirty years, none of their official statements on polity proposed absolute congregationalism. They recognized the need for cooperation at the national level and maintained that there must be unity in "doctrinal practices and tenets" (see p. 142). It is true that the fraternal spirit, especially at the national level, was weakened among the Progressives. See especially the testimonies of A. D. Gnagey, "The National Conference of 1901 as It Impressed Us," *BE* 23 (October 10, 1901):3 and J. Allen Miller, "A Characteristic Note," *BE* 36 (October 21, 1914):1. The bitter memories of the actions of the Standing Committee and of Annual Meeting's interference in local church affairs caused the Progressives to discontinue the practice of yearly conferences until 1892. Yet the fraternal void thus created was filled by active and warm fellowship at the district level, a fact to which Ronk personally testifies. Ronk, *Brethren Church*, p. 255. Finally, the Progressive polemic against uniformity was aimed against *coerced* uniformity. They recognized the need for unity in doctrinal practices (above) and sought a uniformity in non-essentials (dress) and a separation from the world which arose from a common understanding of and adherence to Scripture (see p. 142). Note in this latter regard a resolution passed at the 1882 Ashland Convention:

> RESOLVED, That we recommend our ministers and members everywhere to labor earnestly for the maintenance of simplicity and modesty of life and dress, and that the teachings of the Gospel upon this subject, as upon all positive Gospel precepts, be strictly adhered to by all congregations throughout the church.

Report of Progressive Convention, Held at Ashland, Ohio. Commencing June 29, 1882 (n.p., n.d.), p. 30.

[62] Martin, "Law and Grace," p. 42.

[63] Ibid., pp. 42-43.

[64] Lauderdale, "Division," p. 94.

[65] See p. 148; John Harshey, "For the Vindicator, Primitive Christian, and the other Periodicals," *Vindicator* 10 (May 1879): 135-136; Howard Miller, "Conservators, Middle-men, Church Bats," *PC* 1 (May 23, 1879):1; and David L. Williams, "Consistency," *PC* 2 (April 30, 1880):1.

[66] J. S. Mohler, "Principle and Form," *The Primitive Christian and The Pilgrim* (hereafter *PC & P*) 2 (August 6, 1878):484, 485, 486.

[67] Charles H. Balsbaugh, "Pressing Toward the Mark," *Prim. C.* 20 (April 4, 1882):214, 215.

CHAPTER 11: DOCTRINAL DEVELOPMENT AND INTERACTION

[1] F. P. L., "An Extract from a Letter," *MGV* 8 (September 1858):286.

[2] J. T. Meyers, "Theology—What It Is—a Science—Necessity of System," *Prim. C.* 1 (January 18, 1876):33. In what may be a veiled response to Meyers' statements, Silas Thomas penned for the *Vindicator* an article which took sharp exception to viewing theology as a science. He observed that such a view implies the necessity of an education for the understanding of "science-theology." Thomas even directs his attack against the word "theology," noting that until very recently it was "a stranger to the vocabulary of the brethren." Its source, in fact, is "in the same 'great apostasy' [sic] with a collegiate, hireling, caste clergy . . ." Silas Thomas, "Theology," *Vindicator* 7 (May 1876):140-141.

[3] Noah Longenecker, "'God in Christ'" *Prim. C.* 1 (January 25, 1876): 53 and C. H. Balsbaugh, "God in Christ," *Prim. C.* 1 (February 29, 1876):134. Balsbaugh (1831-1909) was a much respected writer in the church. An invalid much of his life, he earned his livelihood by his pen. Beginning in the mid-1860s he carried on an extensive ministry through letters to those seeking spiritual guidance in the church. Many of these epistles appeared in the Brethren periodicals. His writing was thoroughly Christological in emphasis. He maintained that the Christian faith was founded upon Christ's incarnation and that the Christian life of the believer was firmly rooted in the indwelling of and the transformation into the divine nature (character) of Christ through the power of the Holy Spirit. Throughout his writing there is a definite mystical thread which has many affinities to the Christ-mysticism of the early Brethren and their Radical Pietist contemporaries. His epistles also constantly manifest the inner-outer dialectic of the earlier period that based the outward expression upon the inner reality of the divine life.

[4] Mary N. Quinter, *Life and Sermons of Elder James Quinter* (Mt. Morris, Illinois: Brethren Publishing Company, 1891), p. 190.

[5] Sidney E. Mead, *The Lively Experiment: The Shaping of Christianity in America* (New York: Harper & Row, Publishers, 1963), p. 125.

[6] The helpful distinction between the two forms of revivalism—one characteristic of the holiness tradition and the other based in the more Reformed tradition of the Baptists, Congregationalists, and Presbyterians—is found in C. Norman Kraus, "Evangelicalism: The Great Coalition," in *Evangelicalism and Anabaptism*, ed. C. Norman Kraus (Scottdale, Pennsylvania: Herald Press, 1979), p. 46.

[7] See Timothy L. Smith, *Revivalism and Social Reform: American Protestantism on the Eve of the Civil War* (Gloucester, Massachusetts: Peter Smith, 1976) pp. 148-162.

[8] The mercurial nature of pietism, when loosed from the stabilizing factor of the formal church, has been observed by Sidney Mead: "For pietism, cut off from the forms of a traditional church and by itself made the guiding genius of a denomination, has successively lent itself to whatever live movement seemed to give structure to current problems and their solutions." Mead, *Lively Experiment*, p. 128.

[9] Moomaw, *Trine Immersion*, p. 5. His treatise on the new birth in this work is the first detailed discussion of the subject in Brethren literature.

[10] See, for example, Zelotes [pseud.], "On Regeneration," *MGV* 5 (February and March 1855):28-29, 63-64; Moomaw, *Trine Immersion*, pp. 191-192; J. W. Stein and D. B. Ray, *The Stein Ray Debate, A Church Discussion between the Brethren and Baptist* (Mt. Morris, Illinois: Western Book Exchange, 1881), pp. 265-266.

[11] Moomaw, *Trine Immersion*, p. 187.

[12] Ibid., pp. 192-193.

[13] Ibid., p. 199.

[14] Ibid., p. 185.

[15] Ibid., p. 194.

[16] Ibid., pp. 205-206, 214.

[17] Funk, *John Kline*, pp. 226, 379. The source of the phrase "professing sanctification" is probably Phoebe Palmer who was conducting Methodist camp meetings and revivals in the eastern United States beginning in about 1850. Smith, *Revivalism*, p. 123.

[18] C. H. Balsbaugh, "Winning and Losing," *CFC* 3 (March 26, 1867):114 and Samuel Kinsey, "Answer" to a Query, *Vindicator* 8 (November 1877):346.

[19] James Quinter, "Growth in Grace," *MGV* 3 (March 1859):69.

[20] Kinsey, "Answer," p. 346.

[21] See H. R. Holsinger, "Avoidance, What It Is," *CFC* 1 (February 21, 1865):59 and Grabill Myers, "On Avoidance," *CFC* 1 (April 11, 1865):114.

[22] In his debate with D. B. Stein, the editor of the *Baptist Battle-Flag*, J. W. Stein cited evidence that both Henry Kurtz and A. H. Cassel believed Mack was a *Waldensian*. See Stein and Ray, *Debate*, pp. 178-179.

[23] B. F. Moomaw, "A Responsive Letter," *CFC & GV* n.s. 1 (August 11, 1874):501.

[24] William C. Thurman, *The Sealed Book of Daniel Opened; Or A Book of Reference for those who Wish to Examine the "Sure Word of Prophecy"* (Philadelphia: John Goodyear, 1864), pp. 5-6.

[25] Ibid., p. 5.

[26] See William C. Thurman, *To the Disappointed and Tried* (n.p., [1868]), pp. 1-2; William C. Thurman, *The Answer to Dr. Thurman's Epistle* (n.p., [c. 1868]); James Quinter, "Another Error in W. C. Thurman's Prophetical Calculations," *CFC & GV* n.s. 2 (April 27, 1875):266; and James Quinter, "William C. Thurman on Definite Time Again," *Prim. C.* 1 (May 2, 1876):282. Sappington cites sources which indicate he may have also set two other dates: July 10, 1868 (somewhat doubtful), and sometime in June, 1875. Sappington, *Brethren in Virginia*, p. 91.

[27] Quoted in Quinter, "Definite Time Again," p. 282.

[28] John S. Flory, *Flashlights from History* (Elgin, Illinois: Brethren Publishing House, 1932), pp. 61-62.

[29] J. H. Moore, "The Thurman and Grant Discussion," *BAW* 3 (January 31, 1878):4. Out of this debate a Trine Immersion Adventist movement was born. J. C. Cassel, a nephew of A. H. Cassel and significant figure in the Brethren Church, attended a convention of this group in 1902. J. C. Cassel, "Maine Notes," *BE* 24 (April 30, 1902):4.

[30] H. R. Holsinger, "Editorial Correspondence," *BE* 8 (September 15, 1886):4.

[31] Sappington, *Brethren In Virginia*, p. 191.

[32] See P. Deardorf, "The Time of the End," *MGV* 18 (July 1868):211 and O. L. Baer, "On the Advent of Our Saviour," *MGV* 18 (September 1868):274.

[33] Samuel Kinsey, "Christ's Second Coming," *CFC* 3 (November 5, 1867):373.

[34] William G. Schrock, "Answer to Query in No. 18, Vol. 4," *CFC* 4 (June 2, 1868):169; Baer, "Advent of Our Saviour," p. 273; Leah Cronce, "Thy Kingdom Come:—A Reply to Brother Spicher on the Lord's Prayer," *CFC* 8 (February 13, 1872):97.

[35] General Mission Board, *Minutes*, Art. 48, p. 177; M. M. Esheiman, *Sabbatism. The Law and the Gospel Contrasted* (Lanark, Illinois: Hay and Lowis, Printers, 1875); R. H. Miller, "The Seventh Day," *Prim. C.* 1 (April 25, 1876):260-263, 267 and *Vindicator* 7 (May and June 1876): 151-154, 172-178. One wonders

whether the sharp distinction made between the law and gospel in defense of Sunday worship did not prepare the way for dispensational thinking in the church and in America generally (see pp. 284-285, n. 109).

[36] I. J. Rosenberger, "A Knowledge of the Sciences Tends to Mould the Mind in Favor of Christianity," *CFC* 4 (October 27, 1868):444-445. See also A. D., "Correspondence," *MGV* 10 (October 1860):317.

[37] Arthur M. Schlesinger, Sr., *A Critical Period in American Religion, 1875-1900*, Facet Books, Historical Series, no. 7 (Philadelphia: Fortress Press, 1967), p. 2 and Ahlstrom, *Religious History*, p. 770. Cf. H. R. Holsinger, "The Problem of Human Life," *PC* 2 (December 17, 1880):2.

[38] S. H. Sprogle, "Odds and Ends," *Prim C.* 1 (November 14, 1876):723.

[39] Ibid. and Howard Miller, "Science and Religion," *PC & P* 1 (May 1, 1877):262.

[40] Lewis O. Hummer, "Theological Science vs. Materialistic Science.—No. 1," *PC & P* 1 (June 26, 1877):389.

[41] Alex W. Reese, "Human Philosophy Versus Religion," *PC & P* 1 (November 20, 1877):716, 717.

[42] H. R. Holsinger, "The Problem of Human Life," *PC* 2 (December 17, 1880):2 and J. A. Miller, "Beecher, Evolution, Science and the Bible," *PC* 5 (December 12, 1883):1.

[43] S. B. Furry, "Answer to brother Sharp's Query," *CFC* 3 (January 22, 1867):39; H. M. Lichty, "Science and the Bible," *PC* 1 (August 22, 1879):1; Noah Longanecker, "Time," *CFC & GV* n.s. 1 (March 17, 1874):161-162; and Noah Longenecker, "Formation of the Earth," *The Gospel Preacher* (hereafter *GP*) 4 (March 21, 1882):4.

[44] J. Keim, "Reply to 'The Formation of the Earth,'" *GP* 4 (February 7, 1882):3. J. Keim was probably Jacob Keim, the Natural Sciences professor at Ashland College, though a Josiah Keim was a trustee of the college.

[45] J. B. Brumbaugh, "Communism," *PC & P* 2 (June 11, 1878):361.

[46] E. Nosam, "Why Not Go into the Cities," *PC* 5 (May 16, 1883):1 and J. H. Worst, "*Keep My Commandments*" (n.p., [c. 1882]), p. 3.

[47] General Mission Board, *Minutes*, 1867, Art. 13, p. 262.

[48] James A. Sell, "License or No License," *CFC* 9 (February 4, 1873):65 and H. R. Holsinger, "No License," *CFC* 9 (February 4, 1873):74.

[49] Fred W. Benedict, "The Moderate Principle," *BLT* 24 (Summer 1979):185.

[50] James Quinter, "A Few Thoughts Submitted," *Prim. C.* (July 18, 1876):458.

PART V: THE WINDS OF DOCTRINE (1883-1987)
CHAPTER 12: DENOMINATIONAL REORGANIZATION AND CULTURAL INTERACTION (1883-1915)

[1] Holsinger, for example, felt that he had to jolt the Brethren Church into the realization that "there is no longer any use of pretending union with the German Baptists." H. R. Holsinger, "Our Relation to the German Baptist Church," *BE* 6 (January 9, 1884):1.

[2] Albert Ronk seems justified in his contention that the 1887 gathering completed the organization of the denomination, for it was at this convention that the Articles of Incorporation were accepted. See Ronk, *Brethren Church*, pp. 220-221.

[3] Martin, "Law and Grace," p. 45. Though the Convention recommended purchase of the *Progressive Christian*, it continued to be published privately until 1892.

[4] *Proceedings of the Dayton Convention* . . . (Dayton, Ohio: Daily Journal, 1883), p. 75.

[5] Ronk, *Brethren Church*, p. 220.

[6] John Duke McFadden, "Some Things in Particular," *BE* 8 (May 5, 1886):1 and A. L. Garber, "Convention," *BE* 8 (August 11, 1886):4.

[7] Edward Mason, *Proceedings of the General Convention of the Brethren Church,* . . . *September 21, 22 and 23, 1887* (Ashland, Ohio: The Brethren Publishing House, 1887), p. 20.

[8] H. M. Lichty, "How Often Hold National Conferences. 1892—1893—1894—?—," *BE* 16 (May 30, 1894):338 and idem, "The Ashland '95 Convention," *BE* 17 (July 31, 1895):4.

[9] B. C. Moomaw, "How Often Should We Have a National Conference?," *BE* 15 (August 9, 1893):8.

[10] Ronk, *Brethren Church*, pp. 180-185, 262-264.

[11] Holsinger's figure of 2900 members in 1896 is based on a report that notes that its "figures are evidently far below the actual number." See Holsinger, *Tunkers*, p. 548 and *The Brethren Annual* . . . *for* . . . *1897* (Ashland, Ohio: Brethren Publication Board, n.d.), p. 9.

[12] In 1895 there were 146 Sunday Schools reported in 138 congregations, though regular worship was held in 206 locations. *The Brethren Almanac for* . . . *1896* (Ashland, Ohio: Brethren Book and Tract Committee, n.d.), p. 15.

[13] The Brethren Tract Society had begun as a private venture in 1886 with John Duke McFadden playing the principal role in its organization. The Tract Society came under the aegis of the denomination at the 1887 Ashland Convention. See J. D. McFadden, "The Brethren Tract Society," *BE* 8 (June 2, 1886):1 and Mason, *Proceedings of 1887*, p. 51.

[14] E. E. Jacobs, "A Brief History of Ashland College," *Ashland College Bulletin* 6 (November 1932):9-10.

[15] Note that the *Progressive Christian* was renamed the *Brethren's Evangelist* in 1883.

[16] J. H. Swihart was clearly one of the most active evangelists in the field. In 1887, Swihart reported that he had organized eleven churches and in 1890, as Indiana State evangelist, he reported the organization of six more churches. See *Proceedings of 1887*, p. 10 and *The Brethren Annual for* . . . *1891* . . . (Waterloo, Iowa: H. R. Holsinger, n.d.), p. 24.

[17] *The Brethren Annual for* . . . *1893* (Waterloo, Iowa: The Brethren Publishing House, n.d.), p. 49.

[18] Note the comments regarding city missions made by E. E. Haskins, "Our Work in the Cities," *BE* 27 (October 4, 1905):3.

> I remember when it was talked in this [National] conference, that the city was no place for the Brethren church, and then the city member was looked upon as an unnatural member of the Brethren. In not over 15 years this has all been changed and the city brethren have an active place in the spread of the gospel with us, and over one-half of the additions to the Brethren church is in the cities.

See also Louis S. Bauman, "Quaker City Notes," *BE* 28 (July 18, 1906):15. Intermittent admonitions of caution with relation to foreign endeavors came from the pen of J. L. Gillin. Yet his warnings were occasioned more by concern over the church's inadequate preparation for foreign activity than opposition to foreign missions per se. See J. L. Gillin, "Necessary Preparation for Successful Foreign Mission Work," *BE* 24 (August 27, 1902):11.

[19] George H. Jones, "A Rural Church Survey," *BE* 36 (March 4, 1914):5. Jones objected to the priority given to urban mission work.

[20] Jacob C. Cassel attended and enthusiastically reported on the New York Ecumenical Council for Missions held in 1900 for missionary leaders from all over the world. See Jacob C. Cassel, "Ecumenical Echoes," *BE* 22 (May 3, 1900):10; (May 10, 1900):9, and (May 17, 1900):10. In 1896 Cassel had attended another missionary convention at which Dean Peck of the Methodist Episcopal Seminary in Denver had spoken. Cassel was so impressed with Peck that he personally paid his expenses to come to speak at the 1896 General Conference. One of Peck's "converts" to the missions cause was L. S. Bauman (see further). Cf. Isaac D. Bowman, "As I Recall," *BE* 68 (January 26, 1946):6 and Louis S. Bauman, "What First Interested Me in Missions," *BE* 30 (August 26, 1908):15. Bauman's dating of Peck's Conference speech in 1896 is to be preferred to Bowman's (1900) because of the temporal proximity of Bauman's article to the event.

[21] Martin, "Law and Grace," p. 68.

[22] Ibid., p. 70.

[23] Actual reported membership was 5381 but because 41 congregations did not provide statistics, the average membership of those churches reporting was used by this writer to project the above figure.

[24] The decrease in congregations and membership is reflective of a trend that continued into the 20s. Many weak, rural congregations disappeared while the strong urban and town congregations tended to make up much of the loss. Martin, "Law and Grace," pp. 83-84 suggests that growth was hampered in the late teens by the repercussions of World War I and the flu epidemic of 1918-1919 which forced the cancellation of many church and revival services. In addition, he speculates (p. 88) that economic hardships in rural America during the 20s were especially trying for rural congregations which were unable to support a full-time pastor.

[25] *Brethren Almanac for 1896*, p. 15. In the 1889 report three men were serving three congregations apiece while one was serving four. See *The Brethren's Annual, for . . . 1890* (Waterloo, Iowa: Holsinger & Hildebrand, n.d.), pp. 38-42. Martin, "Law and Grace," p. 56 observes that many ministers were still serving multiple congregations between 1914 and 1920.

[26] Ronk, *Brethren Church*, pp. 170-171.

[27] In the 1883 Convention an "Intelligence Bureau" was established to "assist in bringing congregations and ministers into contact with each other." It is not known whether this committee ever functioned. Ibid., p. 172. That the problem continued to exist (until the 1960s!) is underscored by Ronk. Ibid.

[28] S. H. Bashor, "The Sound of the Trumpet," *BE* 6 (March 12, 1884):3.

[29] Ibid.

[30] *Brethren Annual for 1893*, pp. 23-24.

[31] See the papers read at the 1892 Conference by Holsinger and I. D. Bowman. Ibid., pp. 17-31.

[32] See Ronk, *Brethren Church*, p. 239 and Clara W. Miller, "Deaconesses," *BE* 24 (May 28, 1902):12-13.

[33] See above pp. 270-271, n. 18. See also Christian Shank, "From Brother C. Shank," *BE* 6 (April 16, 1884):6; *The Brethren Annual, for . . . 1894* (Ashland, Ohio: The Brethren Publishing House, n.d.), p. 37; and *The Brethren Annual, for . . . 1895* (Ashland, Ohio: The Brethren Publishing House, n.d.), p. 12.

[34] *Brethren Annual for 1893*, p. 28; *Brethren Annual for 1895*, p. 12; and Ronk, *Brethren Church*, p. 236.

[35] Cf. . . . *Minutes of the Forty-sixth General Conference of the Brethren Church . . . 1934* (n.p., n.d.), p. 38. There is some indication that the preparation received by ministerial students at Ashland College and similar institutions was deemed as a preliminary step to ordination (though a college education has never been considered a prerequisite). Note the following statement in the Manual of Procedure: "A candidate for the ministry may preach the gospel while pursuing his course of preparation at such times and places as he may have opportunity." Ronk, *Brethren Church*, p. 341.

[36] Martin, "Law and Grace," p. 56.

[37] The early Brethren apparently elected at least one woman elder, the wife of Jacob Schneider. Alexander Mack, Jr.'s list of dead "brothers and sisters" notes that "after her husband's death she lived and served the [Schwarzenau] congregation for seven years." Durnbaugh, *Colonial America*, p. 597. See also pp. 600, 601 entries #121, 172, 173. By the nineteenth century, it had become contrary to the Brethren order for a woman to preach, not to mention be elected to the ministry. Yet, Sarah Righter Major (1804-1884) broadened the minds of many Brethren during the nineteenth century on the preaching question. Converted under the preaching ministry of Harriet Livermore (who is immortalized in John Greenleaf Whittier's "Snowbound"), Sarah overcame official opposition by her exemplary Christian life and her tactful and respectful bearing. See Donald F. Durnbaugh, "She Kept on Preaching," *Messenger* 124 (April 1975):18-21 and Sappington, *New Nation*, pp. 228-239.

[38] *Brethren Annual for 1892*, p. 23. See also *Brethren Annual for 1891*, p. 26 and *Brethren Annual for 1893*, p. 130.

[39] *Brethren Annual for 1893*, p. 43.

[40] A. D. Gnagey, "Women and the Apostle," *BE* 21 (October 4, 1899):1.

[41] Note the statement by Editor Gnagey: "Women ministers are distinctly a product of the advanced period of the nineteenth century." Idem, "Women as Ministers," *BE* 17 (February 27, 1895):11.

[42] G. [A. L. Garber], "Response to Bro. Harrison's Farewell," *BE* 16 (October 3, 1894):603.

[43] Grossnickle wrote a sixteen page pamphlet around 1893 for the Brethren tract series entitled "Woman's Divine Right to Preach the Gospel" (the only known copy is in the Ashland College archives) and presented an address to the 1892 Conference on "Woman's Work in the Church." See *Brethren Annual for 1893*, pp. 38-43. For more information on Grossnickle, as well as a historical survey of women in ministry in the Brethren Church, see the paper by Jerry R. Flora, "Ordination of Women in The Brethren Church: A Case Study from the Anabaptist-Pietist Tradition" to be published in Volume 30, No. 4 of the *Journal of the Evangelical Theological Society*.

[44] Ibid., p. 31. For Moomaw's paper, see pp. 76-93.

[45] *Brethren Annual for 1896*, p. 19.

[46] *Brethren Annual for 1897*, p. 39.

[47] G. W. Rench, "That Committee on Government," *BE* 18 (February 5, 1896):5.

[48] B. C. Moomaw, "The Convention," *BE* 17 (September 4, 1895):4.

[49] W. H. Miller, "Centralization," *BE* 20 (August 10, 1898):5.

[50] For the text see Ronk, *Brethren Church*, pp. 234-242.

[51] G. W. Rench, "Governmental Expediency," *BE* 20 (February 9, 1898):3.

[52] Ronk, *Brethren Church*, pp. 244-246.

[53] *The Brethren Annual . . . for . . . 1902* (Ashland, Ohio: Brethren Publication Board, n.d.), p. 15.

54 Ronk, *Brethren Church*, p. 329.

55 C. F. Yoder, *Gospel Church Government* (n.p., n.d. [1906]). A copy of the undated work at Ashland Theological Seminary bears the notation on the inside cover "Christmas, 1906." This thorough study of polity includes major sections on the organization of the church, the work of the pastor, the conduct of religious services, and church leadership.

56 J. Allen Miller, "A General Mission Board," *BE* 28 (August 8, 1906):12.

57 Ronk, *Brethren Church*, p. 334.

58 Ibid., p. 343. For the complete text, see pp. 337–346.

59 The minutes which report the appointment of the Commission of Ten further state: "The present condition of affairs, so far as government is concerned, is evidence that there has not been a proper application of Gospel principles." *Brethren Almanac for 1896*, p. 19.

60 J. Allen Miller, "The General Conference," *BE* 40 (August 7, 1918):1.

61 W. J. H. Bauman, "To What Extent May the Brethren Consistently Co-Operate with Other Christian Sects?," *BE* 6 (January 2, 1884):6.

62 Holsinger and Beer pledged themselves to total abstinence in the Berlin, Pennsylvania, Christian Temperance Union in 1879. See H. R. Holsinger, "B.C.T.U.," *PC* 1 (May 9, 1879):2.

63 Ronk, *Brethren Church*, p. 186. Band of Hope organizations were apparently a ministry of the WCTU.

64 J. C. Cassel, "Convention Thoughts," *BE* 16 (July 18, 1894):451; C. F. Yoder, "Christian Endeavor and King's Children," *BE* 16 (October 3, 1894):529; and idem, "Federation and Ordinances," *BE* 28 (January 24, 1906):9.

65 C. F. Yoder, "More about the Denver Convention," *BE* 25 (July 22, 1903):11.

66 Ibid. The Sunday Schools were acting as an ecumenical force among the Brethren because not only did the Brethren have a number of union Sunday Schools (27 out of 170 in 1905) but they also were attending interdenominational Sunday School conventions. William H. Beachler in fact served as the president of the Iowa State Sunday School Association in 1915 and 1916.

67 A. H. Lichty, "Our Editor," *BE* 25 (July 8, 1903):1.

68 For Yoder's brush with liberalism, see I. D. Bowman, "Campbell, Michigan," *BE* 37 (December 22, 1915):14. Bowman notes that Yoder had confessed to being "side-tracked by destructive criticism" but had "got back again to accept the old Book as 'given by inspiration of God.'" Also of special interest is the fact that, upon graduating from the University of Chicago, he was offered a teaching fellowship in the University with the opportunity of becoming professor of Church History. "This offer he declined to accept the call of the church to be editor of its stated publications and professor in Ashland College." Dyoll Belote, "The Contributing Editor's Page," *BE* 61 (December 9, 1939):8.

69 Alma Leslie, "The Y.W.C.A.," *The Purple and Gold* (hereafter *P & G*) 3 (November 1902):8.

70 Enrollment during the first week of classes at Ashland in 1902 was 105; the YMCA had 34 men enrolled, the YWCA had 25 women enrolled, and the CE meeting had an attendance of about 60. See George C. Carpenter, "Ashland College," *BE* 24 (September 17, 1902):13.

71 Vianna Detwiler, "The Students Volunteer Band," *P & G* 1 (January 1901):12.

72 A. D. Gnagey, "Laymen's Missionary Convention," *BE* 34 (November 6, 1912):1 and idem, "The Whole World for Jesus Christ," *BE* 37 (January 20, 1915):3–4.

73 The last significant example of this apologetic is S. H. Bashor's, *The Brethren Church* (see p. 275, n. 142). Bashor (p. 3) argued that the Brethren Church was a "lineal descendent of the Greek Church; or at farthest a modified branch of the Waldensians." Bashor denied the authenticity of the introductory material by Mack, Jr., which was appended to the editions of Mack, Sr.'s writings beginning with the 1774 edition. (The introductory account was merely signed "Abend-Mahl"; as was the frequent custom, the two large case letters are the initials of the author. Bashor apparently was unaware of this practice.) He did this to discredit the idea that the first eight Brethren baptized themselves and to open the way for his contention that "the Swartzenau [sic] administrator was a Greek missionary" who would have baptized the group by trine immersion.

74 Holsinger, *Tunkers*, 33–34 uses this apologetic. He notes that "the church of Christ is a principle as well as an organization [note the inner-outer dialectic]. . . . The gospel of Christ is the embodiment of that principle, and those who hear or read the gospel, and imbibe its teachings, become subjects of Christ's spiritual kingdom; and the association of a number of such sectaries will constitute the visible body or kingdom of Christ." It is this conception of the church that Ronk utilizes in his understanding of "Brethrenism" (see p. 153).

75 See, for example, Yoder's questioning of the "old idea" that "literal obedience" is a "ticket to heaven." He prefers instead the contention that obedience to the whole Gospel leads to a larger measure of life. C. F. Yoder, "Federation and Ordinances," *BE* 28 (January 24, 1906):9.

76 A. D. Gnagey, "Why We Exist as a Church," *BE* 17 (February 13, 1895):8.

77 Idem, "Our National Conference," *BE* 29 (August 3, 1898):13.

78 Yoder's copious citation of Biblical, theological, historical, and patristic evidence has made this work a standard defense of Brethren practice. In 1979 it was republished by the Grace Brethren.

79 Yoder, *Means of Grace*, p. 13. The premise underlying this philosophy of the ordinances, i.e., that God's revealed truth as found in Scripture is reasonable and meets man's greatest needs, is probably derived from liberalism. Yoder, who was trained in theology at the University of Chicago, seems to be reflecting an anthropocentric pragmatism, derived principally from Albrecht Ritschl, which was having a considerable impact in American liberal and social gospel circles. Cf. Ahlstrom, *Religious History*, pp. 789, 936 and Emil Brunner, *The Mediator: A Study of the Central Doctrine of the Christian Faith*, trans. Olive Wyon (Philadelphia: The Westminster Press, 1947), p. 408.

80 J. L. Gillin, "Our Denominational Position," *BE* 23 (August 30, 1911):6.

81 Idem, "The Philosophy of the Ordinances," *BE* 18 (April 1, 1896):4–5.

82 Idem, "Denominational Plea," p. 6.

83 Holsinger, *Tunkers*, pp. 811–812.

84 H. L. Goughnour, "Philosophy of Child Conversion," *BE* 31 (June 23, 1909):10.

85 The Keswick movement began in England in 1875 but its initial impetus came from several American figures—William Boardman, Robert Pearsall Smith and his wife, Hannah Whitall Smith, and the American revival team, Moody and Sankey. Keswick teaching was brought to America in the 1890s by F. B. Meyer, who spoke at Moody's Northfield conferences. Other British Keswick teachers followed Meyer to America, notably Andrew Murray, H. W. Webb-Peploe, and G. Campbell Morgan. Keswick doctrine won acceptance in America among non-holiness

evangelicals who might be termed "mild Calvinists"—A. J. Gordon, C. I. Scofield, A. B. Simpson (the founder of the Christian and Missionary Alliance), R. A. Torrey, J. Wilbur Chapman, and Robert Speer (note the dispensationalist connections). Keswick teaching understands

> sanctification as a threefold activity: gift, crisis, and process. The gift of sanctification is that position or standing which was wrought by Christ on the cross for every believer. The crisis is an experience which is usually but not necessarily subsequent to conversion in which the believer by faith surrenders his life fully to the control of Christ. The process of sanctification is the gradual development of the believer by the Holy Spirit toward the likeness of Christ.

C. Mel Loucks, "Keswick Teaching and Consecration," (Unpublished paper, Fuller Theological Seminary, n.d.), pp. 14-15.

[86] A. D. Gnagey, "Concentrated Effort," *BE* 17 (May 1, 1895), p. 8. Consecration is the characteristic Keswick term for the idea of total surrender while the "victorious life" is one of Keswick's distinguishing phrases.

[87] J. C. Cassel, "Foreign Missions—Continued," *BE* 20 (September 28, 1898):13 and idem, "The Mission of the Holy Spirit," *BE* 18 (January 1, 1896):3.

[88] Idem, "A Reply," *BE* 17 (July 10, 1895):2. It should be remembered that at this period of time the great outbreak of speaking in tongues had not yet occurred; therefore the term "baptism of the Holy Spirit," as used by Cassel, should not be confused with its later connotations.

[89] Idem, "The Two Baptisms," *BE* 20 (February 2, 1898):7. I. D. Bowman, Cassel's pastor at Philadelphia, caused some stir at the 1897 Conference when he claimed he was wholly sanctified. See D. C. Moomaw, "The Johnstown Conference," *BE* 19 (September 15, 1897):11. Bowman held a view of sanctification similar to that of Cassel.

[90] Cassel, "Foreign Missions," p. 13.

[91] For a study of the details of the extended Cassel-Wampler exchange and an overview of Brethren thought concerning the Holy Spirit since 1864, see Randal A. Best, "The Mind of the Brethren Church on the Baptism of the Holy Spirit and Related Topics" (M.Div. project, Ashland Theological Seminary, 1976).

[92] J. B. Wampler, "A Reply to Brother Cassel," *BE* 17 (August 21, 1895):2.

[93] J. Allen Miller, "The Gospel Teaching concerning the Holy Spirit," *BE* 17 (October 16, 1895):7.

[94] C. F. Yoder, "Holy Living," *BE* 28 (August 29, 1906):9.

[95] Idem, "Information Bureau," *BE* 27 (October 4, 1905):12.

[96] Idem, "Holy Living," *BE* 26 (September 7, 1904):11. Yoder also observes that the circles in which "entire consecration" is discussed use a variety of terms to refer to the experience: sanctification, second blessing, baptism with the Holy Spirit. This point explains the variation of expressions used by Cassel above.

[97] Some background on the Bible Conference is to be found in Vincent H. Gaddis and Jasper A. Huffman, *The Story of Winona Lake: A Memory and A Vision* (Winona Lake, Indiana: Winona Lake Christian Assembly, 1960). The Winona Bible Conference was the prototype of a phenomenon which became an important part of the Fundamentalist movement.

[98] C. F. Yoder, "Work and Workers," *BE* 25 (September 2, 1903):10-11 and idem, "The Bible Conference," *BE* 26 (September 7, 1904):10. In 1903 Yoder observed that he had attended every conference from its inception. An intriguing claim is also made by Yoder's brother in a tribute written at Charles' death. It was stated that Charles "with another Warsaw pastor, organized what later developed into the Winona Bible Conference." Frank B. Yoder, "Charles F. Yoder," *BE* 77 (April 16, 1955):9.

[99] A Keswick conception of the Christian life remained strong in Bauman's circle at Long Beach. The Long Beach church hosted Victorious Life conferences in 1920 and 1921. Two men within Bauman's aura of influence, R. Paul Miller and Alva J. McClain, reflect Keswick viewpoints. See R. Paul Miller, "The Greatest Need of the Church—The Baptism of the Holy Spirit," *BE* 42 (January 14, 1920):8-9 and Alan S. Pearce, "18th Annual Brethren Conference of Southern California," *BE* 51 (August 31, 1929):15. McClain also spoke at the Canadian Keswick in 1931.

[100] Best, "Baptism of the Spirit," pp. 86-88.

[101] About the only man to call this new emphasis into question during the 1920s was the "old timer" G. W. Rench (1864-1949). He was alarmed by those claiming that we are saved by faith alone and that "our salvation is secured for us the moment we believe."

> We are now told that instead of conversion ("turned," see R. V.) being a process, it is a single act taking place instantly; that instead of finding a place for all scriptures having "shall be saved" in them, that we need but one, "He who believes is saved." "You can be saved while walking down this aisle," we now hear in Brethren churches. . . . And if he is saved, how can he be "MORE SAVED," whatever may be required after that belief.

G. W. Rench, "What Saves Men from Their Sins," *BE* 46 (February 13, 1924):5. Rench further asks whether such men are not more familiar with the works of Spurgeon, Moody, and Torrey than they are with those of Bashor and Holsinger. The crucial contrast highlighted by Rench is between the newer punctiliar view of salvation (derived from revivalism and typical of fundamentalism) and the traditional Brethren view of salvation as both an event and a process. The clash between these concepts of salvation becomes intense during the late 1930s.

[102] H. R. Holsinger, "Holsinger Correspondence," *BE* 16 (January 17, 1894):43 and G. W. Rench, "The Lord's Supper," *BE* 20 (October 12, 1898):5.

[103] A, "Souls not Immortal," *BE* 7 (April 1, 1885):1.

[104] E. Mason, "'Souls not Immortal,'" *BE* 7 (May 13, 1885):6.

[105] J. H. Swihart, *The Immortality of the Soul or Death and the Resurrection* (Ashland, Ohio: The Brethren Publishing House, 1889).

[106] A. L. Garber, "The Soul Question," *BE* 11 (May 1, 1889):4-5, 8. The Brethren Church extended the domain of individual opinion much further than the German Baptists at this time. Thus the traditional Brethren convictions that Jesus did not eat the Passover in the upper room and that the baptism of John was essentially the same as Christian baptism were openly questioned. However, the best known private opinion among the German Baptists—restorationism—though having at least one active supporter among the Progressives, James A. Ridenour, seems to have generally succumbed to more evangelical views of eschatology.

[107] A. D. Gnagey, "Endowing a Doctrine," *BE* 21 (September 27, 1899):1.

[108] Ronk, *Brethren Church*, p. 211.

[109] H. E. Wolfe, "California State Conference," *BE* 16 (May 16, 1894):312. Sabbatarianism apparently continued to be a problem in California, for in 1896 a paper was presented at the state conference which contended that the Christian Sabbath was Sunday. See C. E. Doty, "Does the Observation of the Seventh Day Sabbath Obtain in the Christian Dispensation?," *BE* 18 (September 23, 1896):4-7. This paper is even more important, however, because it represents the first full blown use of dispensationalist argumentation in Brethren literature. Note Doty's introductory remarks: "I wish to notice the mutability of God's law or dealings with man, in the several dispensations from Adam to

Christ inclusive." He then pursues his investigation by considering the relevant material in the Adamic, Noachic, Abrahamic, Mosaic, and Christian dispensations.

[110] Geo. A. Copp, "A Statement," *BE* 17 (August 28, 1895):12.

[111] "Report of Board of Elders of Ohio," *BE* 27 (April 26, 1900):2.

[112] C. F. Yoder, "Work and Workers," *BE* 29 (October 2, 1907):8.

[113] The most comprehensive study of Dowie and his utopian city, Zion, is by Philip Lee Cook, "Zion City, Illinois: Twentieth Century Utopia" (Ph.D. dissertation, University of Colorado, 1965).

[114] S. J. Harrison, "More about Divine Healing," *BE* 16 (May 9, 1895):296. Cf. Ronk, *Brethren Church*, p. 202.

[115] See *BE* 16 (July 4, 1894). The consensus that emerged from this issue was that divine healing was Biblical but opinions regarding Dowie ranged from complete skepticism to complete approbation. Holsinger (p. 421) reflected a cautious Brethren response: "Now I am no healer; I'm an anointer. The Lord does the healing."

[116] Ronk, *Brethren Church*, p. 207.

[117] C. F. Yoder, "Work and Workers," *BE* 28 (September 19, 1906):8. Piper was from the Philadelphia church where J. C. Cassel had initially been a vocal supporter of Dowie.

[118] Ronk, *Brethren Church*, pp. 202-203.

[119] For an exposition of these themes, see A. B. Simpson, *The Four-Fold Gospel* (Harrisburg, Pennsylvania: Christian Publications, Inc., n.d.).

[120] S. B. Furry, "An 'Alliance' Meeting," *BE* 16 (June 6, 1894):363.

[121] In underscoring the positive effect that concerted evangelistic and missionary activity would have on the growth of the church, Cassel pointed to the examples of D. L. Moody, C. I. Scofield, and the Christian and Missionary Alliance. Jacob C. Cassel, "How May We Extend the Borders of the Brethren Church?," *BE* 21 (July 5, 1899):4.

[122] J. C. Cassel, "Divine Healing," *BE* 22 (May 3, 1900):4.

[123] In 1898 in defending his premillennial position, Cassel states: "Finally let me say that I hold those views because I believe them with all my heart to be the clear, plain teaching of the gospel of Christ, and not in any sense because they are taught by what is known as the Christian and Missionary Alliance." Jacob C. Cassel, "A Criticism," *BE* 20 (October 26, 1898):4.

[124] Jacob C. Cassel, "Philadelphia Items," *BE* 20 (October 5, 1898):14 and Louis S. Bauman, "What First Interested Me in Missions," *BE* 30 (August 26, 1908):10.

[125] Cassel, "A Criticism," p. 4.

[126] John Duke McFadden, "Some Western Ideas: The Christian Alliance," *BE* 21 (September 13, 1899):13 and B. C. Moomaw, "The Christian and Missionary Alliance," *BE* 21 (September 27, 1899):5.

[127] J. L. Gillin, "Christian Freedom," *BE* 36 (October 14, 1914):3 and H. L. Goughnour, "Another Protest," *BE* 37 (December 15, 1915):3.

[128] Besides spurring the closer definition of limited congregationalism by the denomination as a whole, the difficulties raised in the church by the impact of outside groups motivated the formation of two other organizations. In 1891 the Illiokota district recommended the organization of a ministerial association (realized in 1892) "for the protection of the churches from the piracy of designing and unscrupulous imposters." *Brethren Annual for 1892*, p. 26. In 1899 the Virginia and Maryland conference created a district board for the examination of candidates for ordination who had already been approved by their respective congregations. This procedure was adopted to correct "the loose method we have been pursuing in permitting weak and unqualified men to slip into our ministry." J. C. Mackey, "'The Entering in of the Wedge,'" *BE* 21 (August 16, 1899):4. This action was viewed by some, however, as the entrance of "the little edge of the wedge" which would ultimately lead to the loss of congregationalism. See V. M. Reichard, "The Entering in of the Wedge," *BE* 21 (July 12, 1899):6. Gradually, most districts realized the need for such Ministerial Examining Boards.

CHAPTER 13: THE LIBERAL CONTROVERSY (1913-1921)

[1] Kenneth Cauthen, *The Impact of American Religious Liberalism* (New York: Harper & Row, Publishers, 1962), p. 28.

[2] Ahlstrom, *Religious History*, pp. 782-783.

[3] C. Norman Kraus, *Dispensationalism in America: Its Rise and Development* (Richmond, Virginia: John Knox Press, 1959), p. 82.

[4] This point causes Sandeen to observe that "the 1878 Premillennial Conference marks the beginning of a long period of dispensationalist cooperation with Princeton-oriented Calvinists." Ernest R. Sandeen, *Origins of Fundamentalism*, p. 11.

[5] Ernest R. Sandeen, *The Roots of Fundamentalism: British and American Millenarianism, 1800-1930* (Chicago: The University of Chicago Press, 1970), pp. 172-186.

[6] Ahlstrom, *Religious History*, p. 816.

[7] Sandeen, *Origins of Fundamentalism*, p. 22.

[8] The willingness of the old leaders to work for the premillennial cause in general is demonstrated by the fact that William G. Moorehead, a post-tribulationist, was one of the "consulting editors" for the Scofield Bible. A most illuminating forty-four page manuscript from Moorehead to Scofield (undated) is to be found in the Moorehead files at Pittsburgh Theological Seminary. It reveals that Moorehead had very serious reservations about Scofield's interpretation of the kingdom and church and his view of law and grace.

[9] The "postponement of the kingdom" thesis held that Jesus had offered the kingdom to the Jews at His first coming. When the Jews rejected the kingdom, its establishment was postponed and the "Church age" or "time of the Gentiles" was parenthetically instituted. At the end of the Church age Christ will return to remove the Church by rapture and the prophetic timetable will again be in effect. Following the tribulation, Christ will again return, this time to establish His millennial kingdom. This dispensational approach treats the kingdom primarily as a Jewish phenomenon.

[10] Sandeen, *Roots of Fundamentalism*, pp. 208-226.

[11] The word "Fundamentalist" was apparently coined in 1920 by Curtis Lee Laws, the Baptist editor of the *Watchman-Examiner*. Ibid., p. 246.

[12] A noteworthy work written from the perspective of "militant Fundamentalism" is George W. Dollar, *A History of Fundamentalism in America* (Greenville, South Carolina: Bob Jones University Press, 1973). For the cleavage which developed between the Fundamentalism of the 20s and 30s and both the Keswick and Calvinistic/seminary groups, see Sandeen, *Origins of Fundamentalism*, pp. 22-24; Dollar, *History of Fundamentalism*, pp. 181-183; and George Marsden, "Fundamentalism as an American

Phenomenon, A Comparison with English Evangelicalism," *Church History* 46 (June 1977): 220-221.

[13] For background material on Gillin, see p. 151.

[14] C. Orville Witter, "The Message of Science in the Twentieth Century," *BE* 23 (January 3, 1901):8. At about the same time, one of Witter's students, Emily B. Gnagey, penned these sentiments which probably reflect Witter's own position:

> Evolution does not explain development in Nature. That is, it does not clear away the mysteries of life. But it is at once a beautiful and a reasonable theory as to how the worlds were made, as to how the ends in Nature were and are still reached. Some one has prettily said that "Evolution is God's way of doing things." That way is growth.

Emily B. Gnagey, "What is Evolution?," *P & G* 1 (November 1900):14. The source for Witter's views may have been the works of the American geologist, Joseph LeConte, who sought to build a bridge between the theory of evolution and religious belief in his book, *Evolution and its Relation to Religious Thought* (1888). Witter used another work by LeConte, *Compend of Geology*, in a correspondence course at Ashland College in 1900.

[15] C. Orville Witter, "Does the Doctrine of Descent Depreciate Our Conception of God?," *BE* 31 (June 23, 1909):3. Witter also feels the idea of divine intervention at crucial periods of evolution is an outmoded belief.

[16] H. L. Goughnour, "The Things that Jesus Didn't Say Plainly to His Disciples but which the Holy Spirit Has Declared [note the article title]," *BE* 38 (June 28, 1916):7. It should be observed that J. Allen Miller at all times desired an educated faith that could deal with critical issues from a knowledgeable perspective rather than an emotional, reactionary one. He avoided theological controversy, feeling that it obscured the more important issues. Note his perspective in a message delivered in 1916 (this is a secretary's synopsis): "Don't quibble about where we came from or how we came, but consider that we are here and make the most and best of it. The world is meaningful, not meaningless. Everything goes in this world by the direction of God, not by chance." "Minutes of the Conference of Ohio Churches . . . ," *BE* 38 (July 19, 1916):16. (Miller would, no doubt, have rejected the deterministic, materialistic view of Witter.) Miller's own position on evolution apparently was that the lower forms of life were the result of evolution (he accepted the gap theory of creation) but that man was, in some unique sense, God's special creation. See J. Allen Miller, *Christian Doctrine—Lectures and Sermons* (Ashland, Ohio: The Brethren Publishing Company, 1946), pp. 13, 177.

[17] Albert T. Ronk, *A Search for Truth* (Ashland, Ohio: Brethren Publishing Company, 1973), p. 83. During the Fundamentalist controversy in the Brethren Church in the late 1930s, A. L. DeLozier, "More Inside History," *BE* 61 (August 12, 1939):15 revealed the authors of some of the books utilized by Gillin: Marcus Dods, John W. Chadwick, Samuel Henry Kellogg, (?) Watson, William R. Harper, William Garden Blaikie, and Frederick W. Farrar.

[18] W. D. Furry, "The End of Creation," *BE* 23 (August 15, 1901):6.

[19] Idem, "The Message of the Higher Criticism," *BE* 25 (May 20, 1903):9.

[20] Idem, "Our Father," *BE* 25 (June 24, 1903):3. See also idem, "The Education of a Minister," *BE* 26 (August 3, 1904):3.

[21] Idem, "One-ness with God," *BE* 28 (August 29, 1906):2. In this article Furry cites such men as Matthew Arnold and the German liberals, Julius Kaftan and Hermann Lotze.

[22] Idem, "The Church and Education," *BE* 33 (June 21, 1911):3.

[23] Idem, "The Brethren Spirit," *BE* 33 (August 30, 1911):3. Cf. idem, "Are We a Militant Church? A Reply with a Reason," *BE* 35

(April 16, 1913):1. Interestingly, in both these articles Furry cites Shailer Mathews in a positive light.

[24] By 1915 John R. Mott's vision of a new world arising through America's missionary efforts had captured Furry's attention. He wrote:

> Are we putting the Christ into this new and strategic era that has opened itself to us? Precisely here we are to find the task of the Church today. To Christianize America and Americanize the world—this is our supreme task and our transcendent opportunity. THIS IS THE CHALLENGE OF THE NEW WORLD.

Idem, "The Challenge of the New World," *BE* 37 (September 22, 1915):10. This article later appeared in tract form. Though Furry's perception of America as "God's chosen people" would not have been a general conviction among the Brethren, the better educated and liberal members (like Gillin and Goughnour) were very conscious of their responsibilities to American society (both advocated support of the war effort in 1917).

[25] G. T. Ronk, "The Issue Challenged," *BE* 37 (December 29, 1915):6.

[26] J. B. Lambert, "A Voice from the 'To Be'—A Protest," *BE* 37 (December 1, 1915):6.

[27] G. T. Ronk, "The Present Issue (V): Authority or Experience," *BE* 37 (November 3, 1915):3.

[28] Holsinger, *Tunkers*, pp. 613-618.

[29] J. C. Cassel, "Maine Notes," *BE* 24 (April 30, 1902):4-5. This date precedes the Azusa street revival by four years! See also Bauman's experience with this group: Louis S. Bauman, *The Modern Tongues Movement* (n.p., 1930).

[30] Isaac D. Bowman, "Philadelphia, Pa.," *BE* 23 (November 21, 1901):11.

[31] Idem, "A Short Reply to Brother Rench," *BE* 21 (August 16, 1899):12.

[32] Louis S. Bauman, "What First Interested Me in Missions," *BE* 30 (August 26, 1908):10. I. D. Bowman may have also played a role in Bauman's "conversion" to premillennialism. During the controversy surrounding Ashland College in 1937-1939, I. D. Bowman wrote an apparently unpublished manuscript, "A Statement by One of the Organizers of Ashland College." (It can be found in the Ronk files, Ashland Theological Seminary, Ashland, Ohio.) In this manuscript Bowman claimed that he "saved him [Bauman] from Post Millenialism [sic] nearly forty years ago."

[33] Louis S. Bauman, "Prophecy, the Gibraltar of the Book," *BE* 59 (September 25, 1937):10.

[34] Alan S. Pearce, "Summary of Dr. Bauman's Life," *The Brethren Missionary Herald* 13 (January 6, 1951):3.

[35] Interview with Charles Mayes, retired pastor of the Long Beach First (Grace) Brethren Church, Long Beach, California, April 11, 1978. Bauman was greatly impressed by the 1906 Torrey-Alexander revival that lasted for three months in Philadelphia. See Louis S. Bauman, "The Torrey-Alexander Mission," *BE* 28 (March 7, 1906):15.

[36] The Philadelphia church did retain its fundamentalist character, however, through a succession of pastors having close ties with Bauman: Alva J. McClain (1918-1923), R. Paul Miller (1923-1929), and Arthur V. Kimmel (commencing in 1930).

[37] Louis S. Bauman, "The Brethren Church of Long Beach," *BE* 35 (August 6, 1913):14.

[38] Martin, "Law and Grace," p. 67.

[39] Men from Long Beach who studied at Xenia (between 1915 and 1926) include Alva J. McClain, Stewart P. McLennan (who built the Hollywood Presbyterian Church into a congregation of national prominence), Francis Reagan, Homer A. Kent, Herbert Tay, Harold Fry, Floyd Taber, Kenneth M. Monroe, and Miles Taber.

[40] Though Moorehead died in 1914, before any of the Brethren men had arrived, his influence lived on at Xenia as is demonstrated by the fact that McClain cited him frequently in his class lectures at Ashland and Grace Seminaries. See the interview with Delbert B. Flora, retired professor and dean at Ashland Theological Seminary, Ashland, Ohio, April 2, 1979, and Martin, "Law and Grace," p. 72, n. 2. The theological textbook used while McClain was at Xenia was A. A. Hodge's *Outlines of Theology*. See *The Annual Catalogue of the United Presbyterian Theological Seminary of Xenia, Ohio 1916* (Xenia, Ohio: Smith Advertising Co., 1916), p. 12.

[41] Interview with Charles Mayes.

[42] Quiet Observer, [no title], *BE* 23 (January 3, 1901):23.

[43] J. C. Cassel, "A Twentieth Century Forecast," *BE* 23 (January 3, 1901):6.

[44] Furry, "End of Creation," p. 5. See also G. W. Rench, *Power and the Word* (Ashland, Ohio: Brethren Publication Board, 1900), pp. 18-19 and J. L. Gillin, *Jesus and Society* (Ashland, Ohio: Brethren Publishing Board, 1900), p. 18.

[45] *Progressive Convention*, p. 25.

[46] J. C. Cassel, "A Sermon," *BE* 23 (July 18, 1901):4.

[47] A. D. Gnagey, "A Criticism," *BE* 20 (October 5, 1898):3 and Jacob C. Cassel, "A Criticism," *BE* 20 (October 26, 1898):4.

[48] I. D. Bowman, "Neglected Bible Truth," *BE* 22 (October 11, 1900):6 and Louis S. Bauman, "III. Thy Kingdom Come," *BE* 24 (August 27, 1902):5. Bauman wrote a series of prophetic articles in 1902.

[49] Louis S. Bauman, "God's Plan for the Present Age," *BE* 24 (April 2, 1902):7. Cf. J. C. Cassel, "Criticisms Nos. 1, 2 & 3," *BE* 24 (April 16, 1902):7. Cassel further distinguishes the kingdom of heaven from the kingdom of God. He holds the former is a flesh and blood kingdom while the latter, according to 1 Corinthians 15:50, is a spiritual kingdom.

[50] B. C. Moomaw, "Optimism vs. Pessimism," *BE* 24 (March 26, 1902):4-5. In this article Moomaw uses the parables of the mustard seed and leaven (Luke 13:18-21) to respond to a challenge by Cassel for the optimist "to cite one clear cut, well sustained passage of New Testament in proof of his optimistic views . . ." See J. C. Cassel, "Optimism vs. Pessimism," *BE* 24 (March 12, 1902):6. In a follow-up article Moomaw denied he was a postmillennialist. He confessed that he had become disillusioned with premillennialism through the emphasis of some on absolute dates (being from Virginia, he probably had Thurman in mind) and described himself now as "a seeker after light." B. C. Moomaw, "Let there Be Light," *BE* 24 (May 7, 1902):2. See also C. F. Yoder, "The Success of the Kingdom," *BE* 24 (March 26, 1902):2-3. Cassel's challenge to optimists was prompted by comments in C. F. Yoder's booklet, *Some Significant Tendencies of the Times* (Ashland, Ohio: Brethren Publication Board, 1900). Yoder had said in part (p. 53):

> Less and less the church sits as a bride adorned for her husband, thanking God that it is not as the wicked world around it, and waiting for the establishment of the kingdom by a miracle at the sudden re-appearance of our Lord, and more and more she goes about doing good, wearing the garment of praise and seeking to help the kingdom to come by causing God's will to be done on earth more as it is done in heaven.

In *God's Means of Grace*, pp. 591-593, Yoder combined an optimistic view of the Kingdom's growth with a very mild premillennial, non-dispensational position. Paralleling this position is his contention in 1906 that evolutionary and revolutionary views of God's kingdom need not be contradictory. Even in the "operation of evolutionary forces" there are "'breaks' or periods of transition." C. F. Yoder, "Evolution or Revolution," *BE* 28 (October 3, 1906):9.

[51] Moomaw, "Let there Be Light," p. 3. Moomaw held the day-age theory of creation.

[52] Louis S. Bauman, "Literalization, versus, Spiritualization," *BE* 24 (June 4, 1902):5. Cf. P. J. Brown, "Let there Be Light," *BE* 24 (May 14, 1902):2-3.

[53] B. C. Moomaw, "New Testament Hyperbole," *BE* 26 (November 30, 1904):3.

[54] Jacob C. Cassel, "A Criticism," *BE* 26 (December 14, 1904):12; C. F. Yoder, "John 13:14 not a Hyperbole," *BE* 26 (December 21, 1904):11; and D. C. Moomaw, "Idealism versus Legalism" *BE* 26 (December 21, 1904):12.

[55] J. C. Cassel, "Apocalypses," *BE* 31 (August 18, 1909):2.

[56] J. Allen Miller, "Apocalypses. (A Review)," *BE* 31 (August 18, 1909):2.

[57] J. L. Gillin, "Religion and Modern Education," *P & G* 2 (June 1902):26. Cf. Furry's statements above (p. 183).

[58] Louis S. Bauman, "The Message of Highest Criticism," *BE* 25 (July 8, 1903):12, 13. Bauman's article was in response to Furry's comments on Scripture (see p. 286, n. 19). Verbal inspiration and the literal interpretation of Scripture are especially important for dispensationalists. Thus, neither the Old Testament prophecies nor the millennial reign of Christ in Revelation 20 is to be spiritualized and, because every word of Scripture bears special significance, it is important to discern the radical distinction between "kingdom of heaven" and "kingdom of God" and between Israel and the church.

[59] Cassel, "Apocalypses," p. 2.

[60] C. F. Yoder, "Business," *BE* 25 (May 20, 1903):10.

[61] Miller, "Apocalypses. (A Review)," p. 3.

[62] J. C. Cassel, "The Old Religion and the New (II)," *BE* 36 (February 4, 1914):3.

[63] C. E. Weidner, "What Is Gospel Preaching," *BE* 33 (October 18, 1911):5.

[64] A. D. Gnagey, "Theological and Sociological," *BE* 34 (April 10, 1912):1.

[65] Louis S. Bauman, Moderator and Alva E. Bowman, Secretary, "Minutes of the Annual Conference of the Brethren Churches in the District of Southern California," *BE* 36 (June 24, 1914):14.

[66] W. H. Beachler, Moderator and Dyoll Belote, Secretary, "Minutes of the Annual Conference of the Brethren Church." *BE* 36 (September 16, 1914):10.

[67] J. L. Gillin, "Christian Freedom," p. 3. For another quotation from this article, see pp. 2-3 above.

[68] H. L. Goughnour, "Relation of the Ministry to Social Problems," *BE* 36 (October 28, 1914):2.

[69] Both Ronk, *Brethren Church*, p. 305 and Martin, "Law and Grace," p. 78 (following Ronk) hold that McClain is answering Goughnour, but the excerpts cited by McClain are taken from Gillin's article.

[70] Alva J. McClain, "Theological Dogma," *BE* 36 (December 9, 1914):4.

[71] G. T. Ronk, "The Present Issue. (I): Right of Perpetuity: Its Relation to Liberty of Interpretation," *BE* 37 (August 11, 1915):13.

[72] Ibid.

[73] Idem, "The Present Issue. (II): The Method of the Kingdom," *BE* 37 (August 18, 1915):11; idem, "The Present Issue. (III): Was Christ Mistaken?," *BE* 37 (August 25, 1915):11; and idem, "The Present Issue. (III) [IV]: The Church and the Kingdom," *BE* 37 (September 15, 1915):10-11. Ronk's eschatological views were still not completely parallel to those of dispensationalism (though they were later) for he shows uncertainty about the relation of the rapture to Christ's final return: "The connection of this consummation of the activities of the church [i.e., the translation of living

saints] with the descent of the Lord gives strong force to the expectancy of the restored kingdom about the same time . . ." "Church and Kingdom," p. 11.

[74] Idem, "Authority or Experience," pp. 3, 4.

[75] J. L. Gillin, "The Brethren Church—A Factor," *BE* 37 (September 1, 1915):10.

[76] Idem, "Conservation of Our Denominational Resources," p. 32. Cf. p. 251, n. 20 above for another excerpt from Gillin's conference speech.

[77] Idem, "What Most Impressed Me at the Late Conference," *BE* 37 (September 29, 1915):6.

[78] Idem, "The Bases of Christian Faith. (In Three Parts—Part I)," *BE* 37 (October 6, 1915):4.

[79] Idem, "The Bases of Christian Faith. (In Three Parts—Part II)," *BE* 37 (October 13, 1915):4.

[80] Idem, "The Bases of Christian Faith. (In Three Parts—Part III)," *BE* 37 (October 20, 1915):3.

[81] Alva J. McClain, "A Revaluation of 'Verbal Inspiration' and 'Literal Interpretation': Their Importance to the Brethren Church," *BE* 37 (October 27, 1915):3-4.

[82] W. S. Bell, "A Pre-Millennialist," *BE* 38 (January 26, 1916):4.

[83] E. M. Cobb, "Symposiums," *BE* 38 (January 26, 1916):6. Cobb is responding to Goughnour's contention that the "eschatological scheme" propounded by the advocates of the "blessed hope" was "never heard in any wide sense until after certain of our preachers began to attend Christian alliance conventions." See H. L. Goughnour, "Another Protest," *BE* 37 (December 15, 1915):3.

[84] George A. Copp, "Northern California Notes," *BE* 38 (January 26, 1916):15.

[85] *Minutes of the Twenty-eighth General Conference of The Brethren Church . . . 1916* (Ashland, Ohio: The Brethren Publishing Company, n.d.), p. 36.

[86] Ibid., p. 56. McClain, one of the members of the committee which drafted the resolution, included the following qualification with his signature: "To me the Resolution is indefinite and evasive." He, no doubt, wanted the term "verbal inspiration" to appear in the document.

[87] Ronk, *Brethren Church*, p. 312. For charts detailing the goals see R. R. Teeter, "Four Year Program for the Brethren Church," *BE* 38 (September 13, 1916):1 and "Four Year Program of the Brethren Churches, 1916-1920," *BE* (September 12, 1917):8-9.

[88] Ronk, *Brethren Church*, p. 268.

[89] A major study of the movement has been done by Ernst Eldon Gilbert, "The Interchurch World Movement of North America 1919-1920" (Ph.D. dissertation, Yale University, 1968).

[90] Ibid., pp. 73-98. George S. Baer, the editor of the *Evangelist* between 1919 and 1935, reflects the concerns of post-war Protestantism:

> The churches are coming to see that just as the allied nations, by a co-operation that did not lose them their individuality and sovereignty, won the world war against Prussianism, so they can co-operate to take possession of the unoccupied fields, and hasten the coming of the Kingdom of God through the earth.

George S. Baer, "The Coming Awakening and Moving," *BE* 41 (December 10, 1918):3.

[91] George S. Baer, "A Practical Phase of the Interchurch Movement," *BE* 41 (November 5, 1919):6.

[92] J. A. Garber, "Significant Meeting at Ashland," *BE* 42 (January 14, 1920):13.

[93] Louis S. Bauman, "Mirages of the Great War," *BE* 42 (February 25, 1920):8.

[94] Idem, "Long Beach, California," *BE* 42 (March 31, 1920):15. McClain's position regarding the IWM was similar to Bauman's though McClain characteristically focused on the doctrinal defects of the movement and its leaders. See Alva J. McClain, *The Interchurch World Movement* (n.p., n.d. [1920]). This tract was a reprint of an article in *Serving and Waiting*, the publication of the Philadelphia School of the Bible.

[95] G. W. Rench, "The Plea of Our Fathers—Does It Need Revision," *BE* 43 (June 8, 1921):6.

[96] B. T. Burnworth, "Bigger Than a Creed," *BE* 43 (July 6, 1921):2-3.

[97] E. D. Burnworth, "Another View of Creeds," *BE* 43 (August 24, 1921):5.

[98] Alva J. McClain, "Intolerance," *BE* 43 (August 24, 1921):10.

[99] Idem, "The Christian Faith of Dr. J. Allen Miller," *BE* 57 (May 4, 1935):2. Kent, *Conquering Frontiers*, p. 132 has incorrectly ascribed the preparation of the "original form" of the "Message" to McClain. McClain notes Miller contributed the preamble and part of the article on Biblical Inspiration (which bears Miller's characteristic emphases—see p. 193).

[100] *Minutes of the Thirty-Third General Conference of the Brethren Church . . . 1921* (n.p., n.d.), p. 16.

[101] Note that the statement on Scripture is almost exactly the same (with only insignificant changes) as that adopted by the 1916 General Conference. Oddly, McClain seems to have registered no complaints about this statement in 1921 as he did in 1916.

[102] J. L. Gillin, "Here and There in Red Cross," *BE* 43 (November 23, 1921):14.

[103] *Minutes of 1921*, p. 16.

[104] Ronk, *Brethren Church*, pp. 15, 368. Delbert Flora indicates some of the young liberals also joined the Methodist Church. See the interview with Delbert Flora, April 2, 1979.

[105] Ronk, *Brethren Church*, p. 446.

[106] Notice has already been made of Bauman's role in the development of the 1916 General Conference "testimony" concerning Scripture (see p. 190). The Long Beach church had accepted a statement of faith (which, in addition to the Brethren distinctives, placed special prominence on premillennialism and the "distinctives" of Fundamentalism) in 1915 and other churches which were within the Bauman circle of influence, Sunnyside, Washington, and Dayton, Ohio, followed suit. Cf. A. D. Gnagey, "Review of the Thought and Work of the Church," *BE* 37 (January 6, 1915):8-9. Bauman also let it be known at the 1915 General Conference that "pastors who do not emphasize 'the blessed hope' are not wanted in the Brethren churches of the Pacific coast." See H. L. Goughnour, "Another Protest," *BE* 37 (December 15, 1915):3. As early as 1919 Bauman began pushing for a statement of faith at Ashland College, though the Board of Trustees of the College did adopt a doctrinal statement as the basis of teaching at the seminary at the 1919 Conference. See L. S. Bauman, "The Problem of the Christian College," *BE* 41 (October 1, 1919):10 and Edwin E. Jacobs, "Learning and Religion," *BE* 41 (October 1, 1919):5.

[107] See A. D. Gnagey, "The Fundamentals: A Testimony," *BE* 32 (April 20, 1910):7 and the interview with Kenneth Monroe, retired professor at Westmont College, Santa Barbara, California, November 7, 1979.

[108] Representative of this open attitude is J. Allen Miller, who cited in his writings such conservative scholars as James Orr, A. T. Pierson, and G. Campbell Morgan and more liberal men like William Newton Clarke, William Adams Brown, and James Moffatt. Miller also made use of textbooks by both liberals and conservatives in his courses at the seminary. Cf. the interview with Charles Mayes, Long Beach, California, April 11, 1978. Likewise, C. F. Yoder could recommend for Christian workers the writings

of conservatives A. J. Gordon, R. A. Torrey, and John A. Broadus and liberals William Newton Clarke, Henry Churchill King, Shailer Mathews, and Washington Gladden. See Yoder, *Gospel Church Government*, pp. 82-83.

[109] See Martin, "Law and Grace," p. 76, n. 2; Samuel Kiehl, "Controversy, Protest, or the Bread and Water of Life," *BE* 38 (March 22, 1916):6; and Miles J. Snyder, "Some General Conference Impressions,"*BE* 38 (September 20, 1916):3-4.

CHAPTER 14: THE LIFE AND THOUGHT OF J. ALLEN MILLER

[1] Martin Shively, "Some Brethren Church Leaders of Yesterday As I Knew Them. Number 38. J. Allen Miller," *BE* 57 (August 17, 1935):5.

[2] Ibid., p. 6.

[3] William D. Furry, "Introductory Note of Appreciation" in *Christian Doctrine*, p. xiv.

[4] Shively, "J. Allen Miller," p. 6.

[5] L. L. Garber, "Among His Fellow Workers," *Ashland College Bulletin* 8 (May 1935):8-9.

[6] Charles A. Bame, "Dr. Miller as a Bible Teacher," *BE* 57 (April 27, 1935):5.

[7] J. Allen Miller, "The Sure Foundation," *BE* 50 (December 29, 1928):3. As an example of this concern, Ronk relates how Miller took him and other divinity students through a course of liberal, destructive criticism to acquaint them with its methods and dangers. See Ronk, *Brethren Church*, p. 408.

[8] W. H. Beachler, "An Early Student's Estimate of Dr. Miller as a Teacher," *BE* 57 (April 27, 1935):9.

[9] J. Allen Miller, "The Brethren Church: Why?," *BE* 35 (July 30, 1913):1.

[10] Idem, *Christian Doctrine*, pp. 166-167, 208-209. Miller, for apologetic purposes, can also reverse his logic. Noting that an intelligent, reasoned view of the universe reveals it to be orderly and harmonious and therefore purposeful, he argues that the ground for such a universe can be only a personal God. Ibid., pp. xv-xvi, 312.

[11] Ibid., p. 167.

[12] Ibid., p. 215.

[13] Idem, "The New Testament An All-Sufficient Creed. (I)," *BE* 32 (June 15, 1910):7.

[14] Idem, *Christian Doctrine*, p. 169.

[15] Ibid., p. 215.

[16] Ibid., p. 207.

[17] Idem, "Baptism,—Is It Immersion?," *BE* 18 (August 9, 1896):10.

[18] Idem, "Sure Foundation," p. 3.

[19] Idem, "New Testament," p. 7.

[20] Ibid., p. 6.

[21] Ibid., p. 7.

[22] Idem, *Christian Doctrine*, p. 118.

[23] Ibid., p. 125.

[24] Ibid., pp. 126-127.

[25] Ibid., p. 130.

[26] Ibid., pp. 128-219. It is enlightening to compare Alva J. McClain's view of inspiration with Miller's. Although McClain did not deny a human aspect (he preferred the words "aspect" or "touch" to "element") in Scripture, he maintained that divine inspiration extended beyond the thoughts and ideas expressed "down even to the choice of their [the writers'] words." McClain averred: "An inspired Bible apart from inspired words is an unthinkable, absurd proposition. There is but one kind of Biblical inspiration, and that is *verbal* inspiration. . . . The Bible is a Book of words! Take away the words and you have nothing left but the paper." Alva J. McClain, "The Inspiration of the Bible," in *Winona Echoes: Notable Addresses Delivered at the Thirty-Eighth Annual Bible Conference. Winona Lake, Indiana, August 1932* (n.p.: Victor M. Hatfield, Publisher, n.d.), p. 206. Whereas Miller advocated a view of inspiration which would make adequate allowance for the distinctive style of each writer and thereby a balance between the divine and human aspects of Scripture, McClain emphasized the verbal inspiration of Scripture and thereby the divine control of the message.

[27] Miller, *Christian Doctrine*, pp. 137-139.

[28] Ibid., p. 139.

[29] Ibid., pp. 140-148.

[30] Idem, "Sure Foundation," p. 3.

[31] Idem, *Christian Doctrine*, p. 137.

[32] Ibid., p. 99.

[33] Idem, "Steps in the Way of Salvation," *BE* 32 (August 31, 1910):7. Cf. idem, "Baptism," pp. 13-15.

[34] Idem, *Christian Doctrine*, p. 313.

[35] Ibid., p. 250; idem, "Questions and Answers," *BE* 51 (October 26, 1929):2; and idem, "Some Points of Emphasis," *BE* 39 (August 1, 1917):1.

[36] Idem, *Christian Doctrine*, pp. 116-117, 130-134, 158-162.

[37] Ibid., p. 280.

[38] Ibid., p. 117.

[39] Ibid., p. 2.

[40] Ibid., pp. 2-3. Interestingly, the highlighting of the qualities of holiness and love may be seen as a blending of the emphases of Anabaptism and Radical Pietism, though it is doubtful that Miller had this point consciously in mind.

[41] Ibid., pp. 3-5.

[42] Ibid., p. 6.

[43] Ibid., p. 7.

[44] Ibid., pp. 8-10.

[45] Ibid., p. 17.

[46] As is typical of Miller, he does not speculate about the origin of evil but simply sets forth "the self-evident facts"—sin is in the world, neither moral nor physical evil can be charged to God. Miller does indicate, however, that evil is primarily a matter of "a rebellious will against God and God's order." Ibid., p. 18. A fuller discussion of Miller's view of sin follows.

[47] There are definite tinges of the liberal, developmental view of God's kingdom in Miller's thought here, but he differs with liberalism by viewing the end assured because of God's work in Christ, not because of man's ethical and religious improvement.

[48] Ibid., p. 18.

[49] Ibid., p. 13.

[50] Ibid., pp. 13-14.

[51] Ibid., pp. 14-15.

[52] Ibid., pp. 15-16.

[53] Ibid., p. 16.

[54] In another writing Miller does refer to the fall account, but he simply recounts the basic principles which he feels are taught by the passage: (1) "sin is a subtle, insidious and malignant invader into the Garden of God; (2) . . . God is set against sin and has planned to destroy it through One born of woman." Idem, *Doctrinal Statements* (Ashland, Ohio: The Brethren Publishing Company, n.d.), 3, 1 (notations refer to part and section).

[55] Idem, *Christian Doctrine*, pp. 19–20.

[56] What is implied here, that death was part of God's creation plan, is explicitly stated elsewhere by Miller. He believed that Paul probably held that, had sin never entered into the world, men would "have passed through a change corresponding to what is called death, i.e., a dissolution of the material body." Miller argues in this fashion because of Paul's statement (1 Cor. 15:20) that fleshly bodies cannot inherit a future spiritual kingdom. That aspect of death which is depicted as a penalty for sin "is not to be regarded so much as the dissolution of the body, as the train of evils that accompany it—sickness, pain, separation from loved ones, and doubt as to the future because of sin." Ibid., p. 237.

[57] Ibid., p. 19.

[58] Idem, "Sin and Human Need. (IV)," *BE* 32 (July 27, 1910):7.

[59] Ibid.

[60] Miller underscores this point by emphasizing that man can remove neither the legal difficulties involved in self-redemption (he cannot effect atonement for even the least violation of God's law) nor the moral impediment to self-redemption (consciousness of moral uncleanness and guilt incurred by sin). Idem, *Christian Doctrine*, p. 21.

[61] Ibid., pp. 21–22.

[62] Idem, "The Divine Savior—Continued. (III)," *BE* 32 (July 13, 1910):7.

[63] Idem, *Christian Doctrine*, pp. 23–25.

[64] Ibid., p. 26.

[65] Ibid., pp. 25–28.

[66] Ibid., pp. 28–30.

[67] Ibid., p. 30.

[68] Ibid., p. 32.

[69] Ibid., pp. 32–34.

[70] Ibid., p. 35.

[71] Ibid., pp. 35–38.

[72] Ibid., p. 39.

[73] Ibid., pp. 39–40. Miller's view of the atonement has affinities with the governmental theory, especially when he asserts that God did not demand strict satisfaction of the penalty of man's guilt and that Christ's death met the ends of God's moral government. Cf. Berkhof, *Systematic Theology*, p. 388. The only writer Miller cites in this discussion is George Barker Stevens (professor of Systematic Theology at Yale). Stevens does make many of the points emphasized by Miller. See George Barker Stevens, *The Theology of the New Testament*, International Theological Library (New York: Charles Scribner's Sons, 1925), pp. 403–416.

[74] Miller, *Christian Doctrine*, pp. 40–41.

[75] Ibid., pp. 42–43.

[76] Ibid.

[77] Ibid., pp. 45–46.

[78] Ibid., pp. 46–49.

[79] Ibid., pp. 49–50.

[80] Ibid., pp. 51–52.

[81] Ibid., pp. 52–55.

[82] Ibid., pp. 56–58.

[83] Ibid., p. 59. Interestingly, while Miller considers faith before repentance in his *Christian Doctrine*, the order is reversed in his two other doctrinal series.

[84] Ibid., pp. 60–63.

[85] Ibid., p. 64.

[86] Ibid., pp. 64–66.

[87] Ibid., p. 66.

[88] Ibid.

[89] Miller uses the term in his doctrinal series in 1910 to refer to such practices as Bible study, prayer, church attendance, and observance of the ordinances (he is following the broad application of the term epitomized in Yoder's *God's Means of Grace*). Yet Miller emphasizes the inner attitude which must accompany these practices (especially in discussing prayer) as much as he does the benefits that will accrue from their observance. See J. Allen Miller, "The Christian's Triumphant Life. (I)," *BE* 32 (October 12, 1910):7 and "Duties along the Way. (Church Duties)," *BE* 32 (December 28, 1910):7. A similar non-technical use of "means of grace" appears in his 1922 doctrinal statements. However, Miller does not utilize the term in his class lectures on doctrine.

[90] Idem, "Steps in the Way of Salvation. (VII)," *BE* 32 (August 31, 1910):7.

[91] Idem, "Confirmation and the Gift of the Holy Spirit. (VII [VIII])," *BE* 32 (September 21, 1910):12.

[92] Idem, *Christian Doctrine*, p. 67.

[93] Ibid.

[94] Ibid., p. 68.

[95] Ibid.

[96] Ibid.

[97] Miller rejects the idea that guilt belongs to all by descent (note his rejection of the contention that man's guilt was transferred to Christ in the atonement). As already noted (p. 201), Miller held that man inherited a predisposition to sin.

[98] Ibid., pp. 70–71.

[99] Ibid., p. 74.

[100] Ibid., pp. 75–77.

[101] Ibid., p. 79.

[102] Ibid.

[103] Ibid., p. 80.

[104] Ibid., pp. 80–81.

[105] Ibid., pp. 82–85.

[106] Ibid., p. 85.

[107] Ibid., pp. 87–88.

[108] Ibid., p. 89.

[109] Ibid., pp. 90–95.

[110] Ibid., p. 96.

[111] Ibid., pp. 95–99.

[112] Ibid., pp. 92–102.

[113] Ibid., p. 103.

[114] Ibid., p. 249.

[115] Idem, *Doctrinal Statements*, 4, 4.

[116] Idem, *Christian Doctrine*, p. 104.

[117] Ibid., pp. 105–106. Miller holds firmly to the principle, when discussing church offices, "of discriminating between office and function, or as in some instances an extraordinary work, as well as between what is temporary and local and what is permanent and universal."

[118] Ibid., p. 106. Miller maintains that there is no essential difference in the terms elder, bishop, pastor, teacher, and evangelist. Whereas the terms elder and bishop express both official position and function, the words pastor, teacher, and evangelist emphasize function.

[119] Ibid., p. 315.

[120] Ibid., p. 106.

[121] Idem, *Doctrinal Statements*, 4, 6.

[122] Idem, "Baptism," pp. 10–15.

[123] Idem, *Doctrinal Statements*, 4, 6.

[124] Idem, *Christian Doctrine*, p. 255.

[125] Idem, *Doctrinal Statements*, 4, 8 and 10.

[126] Idem, *Christian Doctrine*, pp. 255–258.

[127] Ibid., pp. 258–260.

[128] Idem, *Doctrinal Statements*, 4, 11.

[129] Idem, *Christian Doctrine*, pp. 106–107.

[130] Idem, "Triumphant Life. (I)," p. 7.

[131] Idem, "Duties along the Way. (Family)," *BE* 32 (December 21, 1910):7.

[132] For an elaboration of Miller's views on war, see *Christian Doctrine*, pp. 333–344.

[133] Idem, *Doctrinal Statements*, 4, 12.

[134] Idem, "The Christian's Death," *BE* 33 (January 4, 1911):7.

[135] Idem, *Christian Doctrine*, pp. 204, 239–241.

[136] Ibid., p. 204.

[137] Ibid., pp. 203, 241.

[138] Ibid., pp. 241–242, 293.

[139] Ibid., pp. 295–296, 300.

[140] Ibid., p. 206. On the basis of the first two principles, Miller gives preference to the didactic and narrative portions of the New Testament rather than the apocalyptic passages.

[141] Ibid., p. 163.

[142] Ibid., pp. 213–214, 217.

[143] Ibid., pp. 220–226.

[144] Ibid., pp. 226, 228, 242.

[145] Ibid., pp. 230–231.

[146] Ibid., p. 231.

[147] Ibid., p. 299.

[148] Furry, "Note of Appreciation," pp. xiii–xiv.

[149] J. Allen Miller, "Some Points of Emphasis," *BE* 39 (August 1, 1917):1.

[150] Idem, "The Forward Look," *BE* 39 (July 4, 1917):1.

[151] In this latter regard, Miller had stated in 1914:

> Our Interpretative Standard is that revealed by the New Testament itself. . . . How shall we approach the Word of God and find its message to the heart? By the same HOLY SPIRIT that INSPIRES the Word and BEGETS the child of God.

Idem, "The Brethren Church: A Challenge," *BE* 36 (September 2, 1914):3.

[152] Idem, "Does It Matter What A Man Believes?," *BE* 40 (October 16, 1918):1.

[153] Ibid.

[154] Idem, "The Origin and Spirit of the Brethren People," *BE* 37 (August 18, 1915):3.

CHAPTER 15: THE BACKGROUND AND COURSE OF THE BRETHRENIST-FUNDAMENTIST CONTROVERSY (1920–1939)

[1] Following the formation of Grace Theological Seminary by the Fundamentalist Brethren in 1937, the labels "Grace Brethren" or "Grace group," i.e., supporters of Grace Seminary, and "Ashland Brethren" or "Ashland group," i.e., backers of Ashland College and Seminary, gradually came into vogue (especially by 1939).

[2] Ronk, *Brethren Church*, p. 264.

[3] George S. Baer, "General Conference and Some Things It Did," *BE* 55 (September 9, 1933):4, 8.

[4] J. A. Garber, "Young People's Summer Camp, Shipshewana Lake, Indiana," *BE* 49 (August 6, 1927):15.

[5] George S. Baer, "Editorial Review," *BE* 49 (September 10, 1927):3.

[6] Ronk, *Brethren Church*, pp. 264–266.

[7] Ibid., pp. 268–269, 315–316.

[8] George S. Baer, "The General Conference of 1923," *BE* 45 (September 12, 1923):14.

[9] The League, as originally set forth in the preamble of its constitution, was a response by Fundamentalist Brethren to German "destructive criticism" and the "age of apostasy." The major signs of apostasy were identified as (1) a mutilation of the Word of God, (2) the denial of the fundamentals of the Christian faith, (3) the breaking down of all obstacles to the unification of all faiths in preparation for one supreme ecclesiastical head, and (4) the demands for a New Theology. See J. C. Beal, "The Evangelistic and Bible Study League—The Need and the Objective," *BE* 41 (September 17, 1919):6–7.

[10] See W. S. Bell, "Field Report of the Evangelistic League," *BE* 41 (November 26, 1919):14.

[11] The evangelists connected with the League during the 1920s were W. S. Bell, Charles H. Ashman, I. D. Bowman, R. Paul Miller, A. V. Kimmel, A. E. Thomas, A. T. Ronk, F. G. Coleman, C. E. Kolb, G. W. Kinzie, J. C. Beal, and Charles A. Bame.

[12] The statistics for annual baptisms between 1928 and 1939 are as follows:

1928	1415	1934	1811
1929	1344	1935	1645
1930	1369	1936	1500
1931	1868	1937	1096
1932	2053	1938	1909
1933	1775	1939	2240

Martin, "Law and Grace," p. 90, n. 1 interprets the 1938–1939 spurt as indicating a desire by the two factions "to prove the correctness of their positions by evidencing growth" (no idea of falsification of reports need be implied, though both sides may have been more conscientious about sending in their reports).

[13] Note the figures for congregations reporting during the period (using five year intervals where available):

Year	Churches Reporting	Membership
1920	171	21,848
1927	159	22,682
1930	148	25,826
1935	145	27,520
1939	152	29,389

The trend noted earlier (p. 282, n. 24) of the loss of weaker, rural congregations being offset in terms of membership by large urban congregations continues through the mid-30s. (Martin, "Law and Grace," p. 89, n. 1 observes that about sixty congregations apparently disbanded between 1900 and 1930.) Comparing these statistics with the accessions by baptism, it is clear that roll revision (the lopping off of inactive members [a "painless" form of discipline?]) was taking its toll on denominational growth.

[14] In 1927 the *Evangelist* cited a Department of Commerce report which analyzed various facets of the 174 Brethren Churches making information available in 1926. 53 of these churches were located in urban areas (defined as incorporated places of 2500 inhabitants or more) and 121 were in rural areas. Of the total membership, 12,089 were in the urban churches and 13,937 were in the rural churches. George S. Baer, "Statistics Come Home to Us," *BE* 49 (October 8, 1927):3. Though 70% of the churches was in rural areas, only 54% of the membership was in these churches. Although the ratio between urban and rural churches had not changed much since 1914 (see p. 167), one would suspect the membership ratio had.

[15] Note the remarkable record of giving between 1901 and 1939.

1901	$ 403.94	1920	$29,787.70
1905	$ 459.39	1925	$34,568.73
1910	$3,836.27	1930	$45,003.01
1915	$3,939.84	1935	$42,228.38
		1939	$50,818.06

16 George S. Baer, "The Proclamation," *BE* 41 (February 19, 1919):3.

17 Martin, "Law and Grace," p. 84.

18 Quinter M. Lyon, "Orthodox Temperance Thinking," *BE* 50 (October 13, 1928):7–9 and George S. Baer, "Why and How to Vote," *BE* 54 (November 5, 1932):3–4.

19 George S. Baer, "First Fruits of Prohibition Repeal," *BE* 56 (April 21, 1934):3.

20 H. L. Goughnour and J. L. Gillin especially upheld the responsibilities of "Christian patriots" in the war effort. Typical of the liberal viewpoint was Gillin's address to the 1917 graduating class at Ashland College. He stressed that the Christian patriot has

> a challenge and an opportunity. He will see a challenge to rethink his positions and readjust his actions in the light of a world movement for democracy, of which he is a part. He will judge of his positions, with reference not only to the world movement, but with reference to the fundamental thing in all his thinking, the kingdom of God. He will see in them, also, an opportunity to serve his God by loving service to his fellowmen in his day and generation by active participation in efforts to establish the kingdom of God here and now.

J. L. Gillin, "The Meaning and Opportunity of Christian Citizenship," *BE* 39 (July 11, 1917):5.

21 Landis R. Bradfield, "The Brethren Church in Relation to War," *BE* 48 (April 28, 1926):6. This article and one by H. F. Stuckman, "What Can We Do about War," *BE* 56 (November 3, 1934):5–6 castigated the Brethren for selling "out body and soul to the militarist" during World War I.

22 Martin, "Law and Grace," p. 83 and W. D. Furry, "Ashland College," *BE* 40 (September 11, 1918):12.

23 George S. Baer, "The Time to Oppose Military Training," *BE* 42 (February 11, 1920):2 and Louis S. Bauman, "Important Notice," *BE* 43 (November 2, 1921):16.

24 George S. Baer, "The Proposal to Renounce War," *BE* 50 (November 24, 1928):2–3, 7. Some dispensationalists among the Brethren, however, saw the pact portending something quite other than world peace. Herbert H. Tay, "A Workable Plan for World Peace," *BE* 59 (November 3, 1928):16 admonished: "The whole world is acclaiming the Kellogg treaty as the harbinger of world peace. But Jesus said, 'When men shall be saying "Peace and safety," then sudden destruction cometh upon them.' Beloved, lift up your heads, for your redemption draweth nigh."

25 George S. Baer, "Have We Any Left?," *BE* 46 (August 6, 1924):3.

26 Mrs. A. L. Cloyd, " 'Have We Any Left?,' " *BE* 46 (August 27, 1924):5.

27 Cf. Martin, "Law and Grace," pp. 96–97, n. 2; 104, 105, n. 1.

28 Ibid., p. 96, n. 2.

29 Edwin E. Jacobs, "Christian Education and the Study of Biology," *BE* 49 (June 4, 1927):5. In 1931 Jacobs further stated:

> . . . A Christian college ought to be in the very vanguard of intellectuality. . . . Personally I have no patience with schools which advertise that they are "safe" simply because they are intellectually asleep. Nor is there any need of that, for as it is well known, Christianity lends itself to a very high degree of intellectuality.

Edwin E. Jacobs, "The Christian College," *BE* 53 (July 18, 1931):5. Jacobs did, however, possess a more critical perspective than

Miller. In the late 1920s he became upset with Kenneth Monroe's strong emphasis on blood atonement. See the interview with Kenneth Monroe, October 22, 1979. (Following the departure of McClain and J. A. Garber from the seminary department in 1927, Kenneth Monroe and M. A. Stuckey were hired.)

30 Edwin E. Jacobs, "News of the College," *BE* 52 (October 18, 1930):14.

31 Martin, "Law and Grace," p. 105.

32 See the suspicion with which R. I. Humberd was regarded for attending Moody Bible Institute (1919–1921) rather than Ashland. Ibid., p. 92. Humberd sought to silence such criticism by attending Ashland from 1924 to 1926.

33 Goughnour, "Another Protest," p. 5. Goughnour clearly has Bauman in mind.

34 J. L. Gillin, "My Apologia," *BE* 41 (June 4, 1919):6. Gillin aims his comments at "the Torrey brand of so-called orthodoxy."

35 Bauman, "Christian College," p. 10. Cf. p. 288, n. 106. Note that the Board of Trustees had accepted a doctrinal statement for the Seminary in 1919. It is quite significant that Gillin's complaint and Bauman's call occurred shortly after the Philadelphia meeting (in May 1919) of the World Conference on Christian Fundamentals (see pp. 181–182). In the report of the Committee on Correlation of Colleges, Seminaries, and Academies at the Conference, two resolutions stand out that are of particular importance in the light of Bauman's statements above and of future developments regarding the college.

> Resolved, That in this day, when infidelity, atheism, anti-Christianity are making such inroads on the higher and professional education of our time, it is the duty of all Christian preachers and parents and young people to know definitely what the teaching of the schools in which they are interested is. Unfortunately, most schools of these classes profess to be Christian, but they teach doctrines respecting the Word of God, the person and work of Christ and the origin of the human race which are contrary to the teaching of the Bible and destructive to Christian faith and morals.

> Resolved, That Christian people should positively refuse to support with money or send their children to institutions which teach the anti-Christian, atheistic and irrational doctrines to which reference is made above.

Bible Conference Committee, *God Hath Spoken* (Philadelphia: Bible Conference Committee, 1919), p. 19. Remember also that the Evangelistic and Bible Study League (see p. 215) was formed about this same time.

36 E. G. Mason, "From a Layman's View Point," *BE* 45 (April 4, 1923):7.

37 Edwin E. Jacobs, President of Ashland College, to Milton Puterbaugh, July 20, 1922, Ronk Files, Ashland Theological Seminary, Ashland, Ohio. It is noteworthy that these general policies remained consistent through the bitter disputes of the 1930s. For other evidence of conflict between Jacobs and Bauman by 1921 or 1922, see Martin, "Law and Grace," p. 93.

38 J. L. Gillin, "Gifts to Colleges with Conditions Attached," *BE* 45 (February 7, 1923):6; Mason, "Layman's View Point," pp. 6–7; G. T. Ronk, "Conditional Gifts to Colleges,—Query," *BE* 45 (February 28, 1923): 7; and Louis S. Bauman, "A Preacher's View Point of 'A Layman's View Point,' " *BE* (June 6, 1923):5–6.

39 Martin, "Law and Grace," p. 92.

40 Edwin E. Jacobs, "News of the College," *BE* 49 (June 25, 1927):14 and Alva J. McClain, "Santa Monica, California," *BE* 49 (October 1, 1927):12.

[41] Alva J. McClain, "The Background and Origin of Grace Theological Seminary," in *Charis* (the Grace Seminary yearbook), 1951, p. 12.

[42] In a discussion of Christian education in 1922, McClain had distinguished between a "religious education" and a Christian one. The deciding difference was theological; one could receive a religious education at Harvard, the University of Chicago, or Princeton, even though these schools denied the virgin birth, the deity of Christ, and the inspiration of Scripture. Martin, "Law and Grace," p. 94.

[43] Alva J. McClain, "Christian Education," in *Minutes of the Thirty Seventh General Conference of the Brethren Church . . . 1925* (n.p., n.d.), pp. 61–62.

[44] See the interview with Delbert Flora, April 2, 1979.

[45] Alva J. McClain, *The Greatness of the Kingdom* (Winona Lake, Indiana: BMH Books, 1974), pp. 22–36, 41, 304–384. For a briefer treatment of the salient features of McClain's view, see the contribution of Herman Hoyt, "Dispensational Premillennialism," in *The Meaning of the Millennium: Four Views*, ed. Robert G. Clouse (Downers Grove, Illinois: Inter-Varsity Press, 1977), pp. 63–92.

[46] Illustrative of McClain's attempt to combine Reformed and dispensational thought is his use of Emery H. Bancroft's *Christian Theology* in his theology classes at Ashland Theological Seminary. See the interview with Delbert Flora, April 2, 1979. This systematic theology followed the outline developed by A. H. Strong very closely (in fact, Bancroft got into copyright difficulties because of this) but incorporated a dispensational view of eschatology. Other scholars frequently cited by McClain in his lectures were William G. Moorehead, Charles Hodge, and Sir Robert Anderson (*The Coming Prince*). This combination of Reformed theology and dispensationalism in McClain's thought has interesting implications for Sandeen's thesis that Fundamentalism was comprised of an alliance between dispensationalists and Princeton-oriented Calvinists which maintained a united front against Modernism until about 1918. Sandeen, *Origins of Fundamentalism*, p. 24. McClain added the first theologically consistent Calvinistic element to the Fundamentalist Brethren. Significantly, his Calvinism was gained at Xenia, a premillennial Calvinist school. Thus, there was not a great disparity between what he learned at Xenia and what the more dispensational oriented Fundamentalist Brethren held. Whereas the Calvinistic and dispensational groups gradually separated in the Baptist and Presbyterian denominations, McClain's integrating ability kept these two elements together, though in the process he modified both.

[47] Martin, "Law and Grace," p. 95 and interview with Delbert Flora, April 2, 1979.

[48] Martin, "Law and Grace, p. 109 (cf. p. 107, n. 2) rightly emphasizes the incompatibility between McClain's dogmatic view of truth and the open, less restricted model inherent in liberal arts education: "His [McClain's] concept of truth and his firm belief that the truth dare not be 'compromised' left little room for the questioning and probing methods of the scientific or liberal arts approach to truth."

[49] McClain, "Origin of Grace Seminary," p. 13. See also Ronk, *Brethren Church*, p. 408 and the interviews with Kenneth Monroe, November 7, 1979, and Delbert Flora, April 2, 1979.

[50] McClain, "Origin of Grace Seminary," p. 14.

[51] This provision probably was added to insure the retention of Kenneth Monroe and M. A. Stuckey (along with Miller). Both had had disagreements with Jacobs about conditions on the college campus. See the interview with Kenneth Monroe, October 22, 1979.

[52] McClain, "Origin of Grace Seminary," p. 17.

[53] George T. Ronk, "The Ten-Year Forward Program for Ashland College," *BE* 52 (May 31, 1930):2, 15.

[54] In 1905 George Drushal and his wife began a life-long ministry to the people living in the Allegheny mountains in eastern Kentucky. Besides establishing several preaching points, they organized the Riverside Institute, which provided both grade and high school education.

[55] Martin, "Law and Grace," p. 99, n. 1.

[56] See the "Transcript of the Proceedings against H. C. Marlin by the National Ministerial Association of the Brethren Church . . . 1932," Ronk Files, Ashland Theological Seminary, Ashland, Ohio, p. 19.

[57] For further excerpts from the *Postscript*, see *Minutes of the Forty-fourth General Conference of the Brethren Church . . . 1932* (n.p., n.d.), pp. 42–44.

[58] Note especially his publicizing of the Paul Lorah incident. H. C. Marlin, "Bame's Old Story Failed to Work So Lorah is Out," *The Postscript* 2 (January 1, 1933):4. Lorah was an Ashland College student pastor who was removed from the Middlebranch, Ohio, church for his attacks against the college.

[59] Ronk, *Brethren Church*, p. 406.

[60] Edwin E. Jacobs, "The Teaching of Evolution in Ashland College," *BE* 55 (February 25, 1933):6. Jacobs, in an earlier article on evolution, had explored the evidence for evolution. Speaking as a biologist, he concluded that "the whole evolutionary scheme is only a theory" and, more importantly, that the unsolved problems in the theory throw "us back upon a theistic interpretation of the world and of life." Idem, "The Problem of Evolution," *BE* 51 (October 12, 1929):6. Significantly, the outline Jacobs used in this latter article follows *exactly* the notes actually utilized by Jacobs in his classroom lectures (he points this out in the article), which are now in the possession of Delbert Flora.

[61] Another facet of the problem about what was being taught at the college was the cat-and-mouse games engaged in by both pre-seminary students and college professors. Ronk, *Brethren Church*, p. 407 places the burden of blame on the students who would bait and heckle their professors and, when the professors retaliated, draw "the wrong conclusion" and hasten "to report with embellishments." Nevertheless, Dr. Jacobs had a special reputation as one who knew how to play the "game." At times he would throw out a question in his science courses to the pre-seminary students just to stir them up. When they began to debate the subject, Jacobs would raise other questions with which they could not deal. Then they would go away with "evidence" that Jacobs believed, for example, in the evolution of man. See the interview with Delbert B. Flora, April 2, 1979.

[62] Interview with Delbert B. Flora, April 2, 1979.

[63] This issue of the impact of the arts faculty on future ministers again forced Jacobs into print in the *Evangelist*. In July, 1933, Jacobs reassured the readership: "A typical Christian arts college, such as Ashland, it would seem, ought to have a Christian faculty, with a high degree of intellectual training, many of whom represent the denomination, although not necessarily all, and none of whom would purposely set spiritual pitfalls in the way of any student, theological or otherwise." Edwin E. Jacobs, "The Influence of the Arts College in the Training of Ministers," *BE* 55 (July 29, 1933):5.

[64] McClain, "Origin of Grace Seminary," p. 21.

[65] The irreconcilable philosophical/theological positions of the college and seminary were underscored in McClain's 1934 Moderator's address at General Conference. He observed that there were only three paths of progress for a church college: modern liberalism, Christian faith, and compromise. He concluded:

> Of these three alternate ways, the only possible road to harmony and success for our own college is the road of unreserved Christian Faith. To take either the way of compromise or the way of undisguised infidelity will mean the doom of the institution.

Alva J. McClain, "'Hold That Fast Which Thou Hast, That No Man Take Thy Crown,'" *BE* (September 29, 1934):8. The critical analysis of the full range of scientific theories espoused by Jacobs and even the interaction with liberal and conservative theologies exemplified by Miller (which were fundamental to the liberal arts approach marked out by the Board and administration) belong to a different world view from McClain's.

[66] Interview with Delbert Flora, April 2, 1979.

[67] Fall enrollment in 1932 stood at 272 and in 1936 it was down to 251. The seminary, however, was booming. From 4 seminary students in 1930, the seminary had grown to 19 seminary and 19 pre-seminary students in the 1934–1935 academic year and 18 and 34 respectively the following year. Martin, "Law and Grace," p. 114. For the financial difficulties see Edwin E. Jacobs, "News of the College," *BE* 54 (October 8, 1932):12. Tensions between the college and seminary were heightened in this period of tight finances because of the liberal financial policies in the seminary. Seminary students were not charged tuition and $100 of college tuition (for those who attended Ashland) was returned for each year of seminary attendance. See Martin, "Law and Grace," p. 114, n. 1 and the interview with Herman A. Hoyt, retired professor and president of Grace College and Seminary, Winona Lake, Indiana, June 15, 1979.

[68] McClain, "Origin of Grace Seminary," p. 22 and Louis S. Bauman, "Ashland College—Her Vision and Her Purpose," *BE* 57 (June 1, 1935):2, 18.

[69] McClain, "Origin of Grace Seminary," p. 22. Martin, "Law and Grace," pp. 115–116 observes that it is possible that neither McClain nor Anspach had an intimate knowledge of the Wheaton College that was flourishing under J. Oliver Buswell's leadership. (Bauman was acquainted with the president prior to Buswell, Charles Blanchard.) Therefore, the mutual commitment of McClain and Anspach to a Wheaton model could have been based on quite divergent perceptions of the ideal.

[70] C. L. Anspach, "A Statement of Policy," *BE* 57 (June 1, 1935):6.

[71] The separated life, with certain distinctive marks, had become a very important part of the Fundamentalist ethic. In the 1935 Board meeting which called Anspach to the presidency, McClain lashed out against the college's toleration of fraternities, smoking, card playing, movie attendance, dancing, and drinking. He saw worldliness as a problem not only among the students but also among the faculty. McClain, "Origin of Grace Seminary," p. 23.

[72] Ibid., pp. 24–25.

[73] C. L. Anspach, "A Statement Relative to Ashland College," *BE* 58 (June 27, 1936):14. The original 36 positions remained as they were before: 33 members from the various districts of the church and 3 members (increased to 6) from Ashland.

[74] It came as quite a shock the following year to Bauman and others to learn that the church legally had no direct control over the college. See Louis S. Bauman, "Who Owns and Controls Ashland College?," *BE* 59 (June 19, 1937):12–14. Martin, "Law and Grace," p. 119, n. 1 summarizes the legal technicality that created this situation:

> On 10 July 1888 the college was . . . reincorporated, with the result that the election of trustees, indeed all functions of the college, were vested in the Board of Trustees itself by default, since the charter made no mention of qualifications for membership in the non-profit corporation, the Brethren Church was not mentioned, and, under Ohio law, "where the charter and regulations do not expressly provide for membership in a corporation not for profit, the Board of Trustees shall from time to time constitute the membership."

[75] Anspach, "A Statement," p. 14.

[76] The Ministerial Board of Southern California to Charles L. Anspach, June 16, 1936, Archives, Ashland Theological Seminary, Ashland, Ohio.

[77] Ronk, *Brethren Church*, p. 419. Anspach had also suggested such a conference at the 1936 Board meeting.

[78] Ibid., p. 420.

[79] McClain, "Origin of Grace Seminary," p. 26.

[80] "The New Constitution of Ashland College," *BE* 59 (June 26, 1937):2, 20 and "Further Report of the Meeting of the Board of Trustees of Ashland College," *BE* 59 (July 31, 1937):16–17.

[81] This change in staff represented on the one hand a desire to bring the seminary into a greater harmony with the philosophy of the college and on the other the commitment to a thoroughly conservative theology. Stuckey had been at the seminary since 1927. Even though he had originally backed the policies of McClain (he allegedly played a key role in the distribution of the "Open Letter" in 1936), he chose to remain at Ashland Seminary (much to the consternation of McClain and Bauman). Lindower was a graduate of Ashland College and Dallas Theological Seminary. Willis Ronk, a brother of George and Albert, was an alumnus of Xenia Theological Seminary. These men gave to Ashland Seminary a mildly Reformed, dispensational perspective which was, nevertheless, open to other theological traditions.

[82] It was the original intention of this association to present the plans for the new institution to the 1937 General Conference for approval, but this course of action failed to materialize. Apparently, the association was fearful that their plans would be rejected by Conference, so they organized the Seminary outside the structure of Conference, following the model used in the creation of the Foreign Missionary Board. See "Compromise," *Ashland College Bulletin* 11 (August 1938):4 and McClain, "Origin of Grace Seminary," p. 33.

[83] *Report of the National Conference Committee on Investigation of Ashland College*, by W. H. Schaffer, [Secretary].

[84] Ronk, *Brethren Church*, p. 421.

[85] Though the close vote (275 to 263) on the motion was made immaterial by the invoking of the little used "two-thirds rule" by the Ashland supporters (according to the "Manual of Procedure" any conference delegate could call for a two-thirds vote on a given question), there is disagreement as to which group had the majority. The confusion is based upon the motion's negative wording (*not* to accept the report). Even McClain's attempted clarification of the issue only confuses the problem: "Those who were *for* the report [i.e., the Grace group], and therefore *against* the motion, called for a two-thirds majority vote to pass the motion [!]. . . . Thus the motion to reject the report failed." McClain, "The Origin of Grace Seminary," p. 31. See also Ronk, *Brethren Church*, p. 422 and Kent, *Conquering Frontiers*, p. 149.

86 Martin, "Law and Grace," p. 117.

87 Ibid., p. 125.

88 This report apparently never reached the conference floor because of the evident move toward greater centralization in government. The motivation for this report was the National Home Mission Board's desire to have greater oversight of location, building, and financing of new churches. See Ronk, *Brethren Church*, pp. 409–411. In the light of the later Grace Brethren emphasis of strict congregationalism, it should be pointed out that the majority of members on this committee were Fundamentalist Brethren.

89 George S. Baer, "General Conference and Some Things It Did," *BE* 55 (September 9, 1933):3 and idem, "Editorial Review," *BE* 56 (February 3, 1934):4.

90 This conjecture is not only borne out by statements made later in the decade as the controversy in the denomination heated up, e.g., Ronk, *Brethren Church*, pp. 416–417 and I. D. Bowman, "Article II: The Peace Committee," *BE* 61 (April 22, 1939):17, but also by several oblique references to dissension in the church at the time. For instance, shortly before the originally announced changes were to take effect, Editor Baer encouraged an exchange of ideas on some controversial theological issues and some churches had threatened either to cut back or cut off support for foreign missions. See George S. Baer, "Editorial Review," *BE* 56 (March 3, 1934):4, 8 and Charles H. Ashman, "An Emergency Call," *BE* 56 (March 24, 1934):5.

91 Cf. Russell D. Barnard, "A Statement of Policy," *BE* 59 (December 18, 1937):4 and Charles Mayes, "Our Policy," *BE* 60 (July 30, 1938):3. Mayes notes that at the Publication Board meeting at the 1937 Conference it was unanimously decided to print no articles of a controversial nature. An editorial committee was appointed to determine whether an article was controversial, but Mayes observes that the committee itself was divided.

92 Martin, "Law and Grace," pp. 138–139.

93 Charles Mayes, "Not Neutral," *BE* 61 (March 11, 1939):3.

94 Martin, "Law and Grace," p. 133.

95 Ibid., p. 135. In the ensuing controversy the Grace group was very careful not to say that they were forming a separate or new organization. They claimed that they were part of the same body that, in its articles of incorporation, had upheld the rights of "congregational control and government." The implications of this policy for any future litigation are obvious.

96 M. A. Stuckey, "The Brethren Loyalty Association of the Brethren Church," *Ashland College Bulletin* 11 (August 1938):2.

97 Louis S. Bauman, "Retrospective and Prospective," *BE* 61 (January 7, 1939):3.

98 Martin, "Law and Grace," pp. 168–169.

99 Ibid., p. 172.

100 Ronk, *Brethren Church*, p. 431. The credential committee at General Conference cited a precedent in this procedure. In 1921 the credentials of delegates from the Los Angeles First Brethren Church were rejected because the church was out of fellowship with the Southern California District. See *Minutes of the Thirty-Third General Conference of the Brethren Church . . . 1921* (n.p., n.d.), p. 6.

101 A. L. DeLozier, "The Contents of Our Church Paper," *BE* 62 (January 13, 1940):5 and E. G. Mason, "Loyalty to the Brethren Publishing Company," *BE* 62 (January 13, 1940):7.

102 The irony in these court cases was that the Brethrenists resorted to litigation, a traditional prohibition (it should be noted though that such court action could have been prevented in some cases by a mutual willingness to seek a fair settlement with the minority party), while the Grace Brethren resorted to stressing both "sovereign congregational rights" (they had desired greater district control in 1934, see above, n. 88) and the non-credal heritage of the Brethren which thereby made it impossible to define "Brethren" (they had always fought for strict statements of faith). Cf. Martin, "Law and Grace," pp. 184–185.

103 Charles W. Mayes, "Advantages, Dangers, Needs and Opportunities," *BE* 53 (October 31, 1931):6.

104 Note, for example, McClain's chastising of I. D. Bowman, a leading Brethrenist, for Bowman's contention: "The sinner hates sin and loves God with all his heart *before* he is saved, as conditions of salvation" (the traditional Brethren definition of repentance). Alva J. McClain, "Baptism, Obedience and Salvation," *BE* 61 (September 2, 1939):5–7, 14. McClain contends that such a view is "religious legalism, which in the last analysis leads directly to paganism."

105 Claud Studebaker, "'Legalism,'" *BE* 57 (December 28, 1935):20.

106 Alva J. McClain, "Signs of the Times," *BE* 56 (February 10, 1934):2.

107 Idem, *Law and Grace* (Winona Lake, Indiana: BMH Books, 1954), p. 53. This position has more in common with revivalistic theology than it does with Calvin's theology. Though Calvin recognized the need to distinguish justification and sanctification (which is an integral part of the entire issue) for theological purposes, he maintained that in Christ they are conjoined. The one whom Christ justifies, He also sanctifies. "Thus it is clear . . . that we are justified not without works yet not through works." Calvin, *Institutes*, 3, 16, 1, p. 798.

108 See, for example, George S. Baer, "The Wonder of the Grace of God," *BE* 56 (July 28, 1934):3–4 and idem, "The Story of God's Saving Grace," *BE* 56 (September 1, 1934):3–4, 9.

109 I. D. Bowman, "Progressive Unfolding of God's Plan of Salvation," *BE* 57 (December 14, 1935):2.

110 Charles Mayes provides a dramatic example of the clash of these two perspectives. He relates that he and J. A. Garber were together at the Winona Bible Conference in 1924 when J. Gresham Machen made the statement that salvation is an absolute, one time crisis event. Garber became livid and, turning to Mayes, said: "He can't prove that, that is absolutely impossible!" (Mayes would agree with Machen.) Interview with Mayes.

111 See Bowman, "God's Plan of Salvation," p. 11; Claud Studebaker, "The Importance of Christian Baptism," *BE* 56 (August 11, 1934):8; and interview with Kenneth Monroe, November 7, 1979.

112 Louis S. Bauman, "Christian Baptism," *BE* 50 (December 29, 1928):4.

113 Bowman, "God's Plan of Salvation," p. 12.

114 Claud Studebaker, "Why A Brethren Church?," *BE* 61 (October 14, 1939):4.

115 L. S. Bauman, "The Grace that 'Bringeth Salvation'; the Salvation that Bringeth 'Good Works,'" *BE* 60 (September 3, 1938):4.

116 The charge is noted by N. V. Leatherman, "Was Alexander Mack a Legalist?," *BE* 57 (November 2, 1935):5. See also I. D. Bowman, "A Defensive Plea," *BE* 61 (April 8, 1939):13.

117 Studebaker, "'Legalism,'" p. 2.

118 George T. Ronk, "The Antinomian Controversy in the Brethren Church," *BE* 61 (April 15, 1939):10.

119 Alva J. McClain, "'Eternal Security' and the Brethren Church," *BE* 61 (April 15, 1939):15.

120 Claud Studebaker, "Brethren History and Doctrine—Can Be Defined?," *BE* 61 (July 15, 1939):4.

[121] Idem, "Sovereignty of God and the Free will of Man," *BE* 56 (February 10, 1934):5. Cf. Clarence Y. Gilmer, "The Kind of Security the Scriptures Teach," *BE* 61 (June 3, 1939):18-20. It is interesting that Bauman and J. C. Beal did not accept the doctrine of eternal security until relatively late in their careers while L. E. Lindower, an Ashland supporter and graduate of Dallas Theological Seminary, held the doctrine through much of the 1930s before finally modifying his position. See the interview with Delbert Flora, May 26, 1979.

[122] Claud Studebaker, "Preaching the Second Coming," *BE* 61 (May 20, 1939):3.

[123] W. S. Bell, "A Separatist Movement," *BE* (March 18, 1939):6.

[124] See the interviews with Kenneth Monroe, November 7, 1979, and Delbert Flora, May 26, 1979.

[125] Martin, "Law and Grace," p. 144 notes that of the 49 Bible and prophecy conferences mentioned in the *Evangelist* between 1936 and 1939, 40 were in Grace-oriented congregations, 5 in Ashland congregations, and 4 in congregations which were evenly divided.

[126] Ibid., p. 144. Bauman had speculated by the mid-1920s that Mussolini would be the anti-christ and, somewhat later, that Russia was the "Gog" and Germany the "Gomer" of Ezekiel 38:1-6.

[127] Studebaker, "Second Coming," p. 3.

[128] Martin, "Law and Grace," pp. 145-146.

[129] Louis S. Bauman, "An Open Letter to Charles A. Bame," in *Open Letters*, p. 18. Pamphlet in Ronk Files, Ashland Theological Seminary. Note also Bauman's reservations about praying the Lord's Prayer unless the words, "And this we ask in the name of our Lord and Savior Jesus Christ," were added.

[130] Charles H. Ashman, "The Prevailing Church," *BE* 59 (July 31, 1937):14.

[131] George T. Ronk, "Freedom—Mediation—Sainthood," *BE* 57 (December 21, 1935):2 and idem, "Antinomian Controversy," p. 9.

[132] Ibid., p. 9.

[133] Ashman, "Prevailing Church," p. 13. Note that the Brethren distinctives are added almost as an afterthought.

[134] Louis S. Bauman, "Creed and Character," *BE* 45(July 25, 1923):2.

[135] McClain, "Origin of Grace Seminary," p. 25.

[136] Bowman, "Defensive Plea," p. 13. The motion was defeated but lost apologetic value because Bauman even voted against it.

[137] George S. Baer, "We Agree on Two Points," *BE* 52 (August 16, 1930):3.

[138] Charles Mayes, "A Strong Point of Brethrenism," *BE* 60 (October 8, 1938):3.

[139] George T. Ronk, "The Antinomian Controversy in the Brethren Church, II," *BE* 61 (May 20, 1939):7.

[140] W. S. Bell, "Ways of Peace vs. Ways of Separation," *BE* 61 (February 4, 1939):12 and idem, "Reply to Editorial Statement and Proposed Peace Committee," *BE* 61 (March 11, 1939):15.

[141] Idem, "Separatist Movement," p. 5.

[142] Robert F. Porte, "Theology and Theologians," *BE* 61 (March 18, 1939):8. In his critique of Porte's analysis, Martin, "Law and Grace," pp. 155-156 rightly calls into question Porte's confusion of the "literalism of dispensationalism and the spiritualization of the baptism issue." Yet, his criticism that Porte "lacked a clear understanding of the role of Pentecostalism in the Fundamentalist movement" misses Porte's point. There seems to be some validity to the contention that both movements shared a "program" that tended to be emotionally charged and reactionary.

[143] Bowman, "Defensive Plea," p. 12 and Claud Studebaker, "Standards of Faith," *BE* 61 (February 18, 1939):4.

[144] Ronk, "Antinomian Controversy," pp. 8-10.

[145] See, for example, the accounts in Sandeen, *Roots of Fundamentalism* and *Origins of Fundamentalism*, and Marsden, "Fundamentalism as an American Phenomenon."

[146] See Charles H. Ashman, "The Real Issue in the Brethren Church," *BE* 61 (March 11, 1939):16; Charles W. Mayes, "Why Slight Eddy?," *BE* 61 (January 28, 1939):4; McClain, "Eternal Security," p. 14; and Louis S. Bauman, "What Has Divided the Brethren Church?," *BE* 61 (September 2, 1939):15-21.

[147] Martin, "Law and Grace," p. 157.

[148] McClain, "Eternal Security," pp. 14-15.

[149] Bauman, "What Has Divided the Church?," pp. 15-21.

[150] Kent, *Conquering Frontiers*, pp. 163, 170.

[151] Ronk, *Brethren Church*, pp. 387, 390, 426.

[152] Martin, "Law and Grace," pp. 202-203.

[153] Herbert Hogan, "Fundamentalism in the Church of the Brethren," *BLT* 5 (Winter 1960):26. Cf. George Ronk's confirmation of this point (p. 229).

[154] Martin, "Law and Grace," pp. 50, 203, 204.

[155] Ronk, "Freedom—Mediation—Sainthood," *BE* 57 (December 21, 1935):20 and (December 28, 1935):14. Cf. I. D. Bowman, "Grace and Obedience," *BE* 60 (April 30, 1938):17-18.

CHAPTER 16: READJUSTMENT AND REVITALIZATION

[1] *1979 General Conference Annual* (n.p., n.d.), p. 17. Interestingly, this very same proposal was made in 1934 by R. R. Teeter, "Self-Supporting Christian Institutions," *BE* 56 (January 20, 1934):6.

[2] Ronk, *Brethren Church*, p. 484.

[3] Of the 27 churches listed in the Home Mission Board annual reports between 1930 and 1938, 18 went with the Grace Brethren and 10 with the Ashland Brethren (the Uniontown, Pennsylvania, church split). All of the works (9) in the Northwest, Southern California, and Southeast districts went with the Grace Brethren. 2 of the mission works that stayed with the Ashland group were connected with the older Kentucky mission field (Krypton, Lost Creek); others were centered in the Midwest, Indiana, and Pennsylvania districts.

[4] Analysis of the active ministerial list in 1950 gives graphic evidence of the shortage of young leadership during the 1940s.

Definite or approximate birth dates could be obtained on 77 of the 81 active ministers (there were 109 churches!). In 1950, 29 active ministers were above 55 years of age; 28 were between the ages of 55 and 35, and 20 were younger than 35 years of age. However, in the middle bracket 10 men had joined the church from other denominations during the 1940s while among the younger ministers at least four had served in World War II. Though some of the older ministers who had retired by 1950 did fill in a number of the gaps during the 1940s, it is still evident that throughout much of the 1940s a critical shortage of younger men existed.

[5] J. Ray Klingensmith, "If We Fail in Greatness Now, What?," *BE* 65 (November 20, 1943):3. Klingensmith felt it necessary for his own sake to resign his position in 1945 due to continued frustrations in working with the churches.

[6] Martin, "Law and Grace," p. 164. In contrast, 23% of Grace congregations were in cities of more than 100,000 population, 34%

were in town above 50,000 population, and 34% were in rural communities.

[7] The available figures at five year intervals are (the years represent the year of the statistician's report so that the figures are for the previous year):

Year	Churches reporting	Membership
1940	(see below)	17,282
1945	100	17,512
1950	110	18,403
1955	99	18,672
1960	110	18,207
1965	118	17,830
1970	116	17,327
1975	119	16,900
1980	119	15,170
1985	122	14,229
1987	124	14,965

The statistician's report for 1940 did not provide the number of churches reporting but there would have been around 100. (Grace Brethren churches were still being included in the church list.) Due to the irregular practice of roll revision, the statistics should be viewed as giving only an approximate figure for membership. Yet, the downward trend is clearly discernible after 1955.

[8] Ronk, *Brethren Church*, p. 449.

[9] A. B. Cover, "What Objectives Should Motivate Our Conference of 1940?," *BE* 62 (August 17, 1940):16.

[10] C. F. Yoder, "The Brethren Slogan (I)," *BE* 62 (April 13 and 20, 1940):8-9/8; "The Brethren Slogan II. In Non-Essentials, Liberty," *BE* 62 (April 27, 1940):8-9; and "The Brethren Slogan III. In All Things Charity," *BE* 62 (May 4, 1940):11-12.

[11] Ronk, *Brethren Church*, p. 449.

[12] Ibid., p. 450.

[13] *The 1944 Conference Minutes* ... (Ashland, Ohio: The Brethren Publishing Company, 1944), p. 3.

[14] Charles Munson, "'You Can't See the Sun When You're Crying,'" *BE* 69 (July 12, 1947):5.

[15] *The 1952 Conference Minutes* ... (Ashland, Ohio: The Brethren Publishing Company, 1952), p. 3.

[16] This problem is not a new one but is an inherent danger in the cooperative nature of the Brethren denominational structure. In 1894 H. R. Holsinger chastened the Brethren for their lack of accountability for conference decisions:

> There is one thing among us which must be removed or we will disintegrate: and that is selfishness or insubordination. We go together in state and national conferences and resolve and promise to do, and then go home and obstinately refuse to do or even afford an opportunity to obey the decisions we helped to make.

H. R. Holsinger, "Holsinger Correspondence," *BE* 16 (March 14, 1894):173.

[17] Ronk, *Brethren Church*, p. 454.

[18] See excerpts from Brant's address in ibid., pp. 454-458. A revised edition of the "Manual of Procedure" eventually appeared in 1957.

[19] Ibid., pp. 451, 452.

[20] John W. Porte, "Having Eyes, See Ye Not? ... Mark 8:18," *BE* 82 (September 10, 1960):8.

[21] *The 1961 Conference Minutes* ... (Ashland, Ohio: The Brethren Publishing Company, 1961), p. 13.

[22] See Fred Burkey, "Organizing for Growth," Ashland, Ohio, May 1976. (Xeroxed); *Report of the Polity Committee*, by Arden Gilmer, Chairman (Ashland, Ohio: n.p., 1977); "Conference Approves Denominational Reorganization," *BE* 100 (September 1978):8; and "Conference Approves First Phase of Proposed Denominational Organization," *BE* 101 (September 1979):15.

[23] See the articles by Claud Studebaker, Charles A. Bame, I. D. Bowman, and R. F. Porte in the January 25, 1947, issue of the *Evangelist*.

[24] The initial reaction of the Conference was the proposal of a substitute motion "that the report of the Fraternal Relations Committee be withdrawn from the records and the committee be discharged." However, final deliberation on this substitute motion was deferred until the following day when a new and more moderate substitute motion was accepted (it desired continued cooperation with the possibility of future union). See *The 1947 Conference Minutes* ... (Ashland, Ohio: The Brethren Publishing Company, 1947), pp. 13-15.

[25] George T. Ronk, "The History and Destiny of the Brethren Church," *BE* 70 (August 21, 1948):8.

[26] Ibid., p. 9.

[27] James E. Ault, "The Call to the Church," *BE* 72 (August 5, 1950):5.

[28] See the interviews with Delbert Flora, May 26, 1979, and Joseph R. Shultz, Vice President of Ashland Theological Seminary, Ashland, Ohio, May 23, 1979.

[29] *1961 Conference Minutes*, p. 17; Spencer Gentle, "Is Our Denomination a Member?" *BE* 98 (June 4, 1966):3; *The 1967 Conference Minutes* ... (Ashland, Ohio: The Brethren Publishing Company, 1968), p. 17; and *Conference Annual, 1971* (Ashland, Ohio: The Brethren Publishing Company, 1971), p. 25.

[30] See the interviews with Delbert Flora, May 26, 1979, and Joseph R. Shultz.

[31] Cf. I. D. Bowman, "A Message to the Brethren Ministry," *BE* 59 (December 25, 1937):9; idem, "A Defensive Plea," p. 13; A. L. Garber, "The Church and College," *BE* 61 (August 5, 1939):28; and A. L. DeLozier, "More Inside History," *BE* 61 (August 12, 1939):16.

[32] See, for example, General Conference Committee on Indoctrination Materials, *Our Faith* (Ashland, Ohio: The A. L. Garber Co., 1960), pp. 24-32, 81-84; Delbert B. Flora, "Brethren and the Doctrine of the New Birth," *BE* 66 (April 15, 1944):5-6; Albert T. Ronk, "Inherent Theology in Brethren Rites: The Public Confession," *BE* 80 (March 29, 1958):4-7; and L. O. McCartneysmith, "New Testament Doctrines: The Doctrine of Sanctification," *BE* 75 (May 2, 1953):4-6.

[33] See a criticism of evangelicalism for its cultural ties in Albert T. Ronk, "Inherent Theology in Brethren Rites: The Theology of Baptism, Part One," *BE* 80 (April 26, 1958):5.

[34] Note especially Jerry Flora, "Doctrine: Brethren Theology—Believers' Lifestyle," *BE* 97 (June 28, 1975):16-17 and idem, "Why a Church Called Brethren," *BE* 99 (October 1977):4-5, 28-29.

[35] A single recent exception has been the article by Julia Flora, "Roots of Brethren Devotion," *BE* 100 (November 1978):4-5. For a survey of the Pietistic origins of Brethren devotion as well as a critique of the reigning theologies for their lack of appreciation for mysticism, see Albert T. Ronk, "The Elements of Mysticism in the Faith," *BE* 83 (September 9 and 16, 1961):16-18/12-13.

[36] Best, "Baptism of the Spirit," p. 116. For the article see Ruth Barber, "Praise the Lord—for a Giving God," *Woman's Outlook* 62 (November and December, 1973).

[37] Typical of the dispensational arguments against the gift of tongues is that of Louis S. Bauman, *Tongues Movement*, pp. 18–19. He cites several errors of the movement, the first of which is:

> . . . The error of making the great prophecy of the day of Pentecost a prophecy for a *continuing* fulfillment. It is true that because of the Jews' rejection of Christ as their king, the prophecy had only a partial fulfillment on the day of Pentecost; and, that the complete fulfillment will be toward the close of the Great Tribulation . . . But, the teaching that "Pentecost" is an experience which God's children may expect today is a gross error. Pentecost was an experience through which the Jews were to pass at a most *definitely fixed time* . . . Fifty days . . . after the resurrection, the Holy Spirit came from above to abide with the church during this dispensation.

Best, "Baptism of the Spirit," p. 87 notes, however, that even the dispensationalists were generally unwilling to condemn totally

> the gift of tongues "per se," due to their respect for the sovereignty of the Holy Spirit and their concern not to be found in opposition to what just might be God's working in an extremely complex and controversial subject.

Exemplifying this caution is Bauman's statement (p. 32):

> If ever the Holy Ghost again imparts this gift to men, then let us open our hearts to receive it. The writer will be the first to welcome it when it comes with the Scriptural earmarks of the Holy Ghost, fully tested by the sure and unchangeable Word of God.

[38] Best, "Baptism of the Spirit," p. 120.

[39] *1977 General Conference Annual*, p. 26. The full motion, brought by Clarence Stogsdill, states:

> I move that this Conference go on record as re-affirming the *Brethren theology of the Holy Spirit* as being totally adequate; that we endeavor in love to "keep the unity of the spirit in the bond of peace" (Eph. 4:3); that we encourage all brethren to study prayerfully the full meaning of SALVATION and SANCTIFICATION, ONE STAGE CHRISTIANITY with many experiences of the Spirit as spiritual growth and crises of life enable us. We encourage all Brethren to "stir up the gift of God that is within," and that they "seek to walk by the Spirit, and not by the flesh." We urge charismatic Brethren to take a second look at the TWO STAGE approach of "baptism of the Spirit" as it is taught by the leaders of the charismatic movement—a practice which is at the base of the division of evangelical Christians, placing the saints of God in two categories and on two separate levels. In doing this—keeping the walk in the Spirit one continuous experience—we can remove the "wall of separation" between the growing factions and allow the GIFTS OF THE SPIRIT to become FRUITS OF THE SPIRIT. There is but ONE SALVATION, but there are unnumbered spiritual blessings attainable through many crises as we develop our individual gifts and talents. Let us "in honor prefer one another," rejoicing in the Lord always. "There is ONE BODY, ONE HOPE OF (our) CALLING, ONE LORD, ONE FAITH, *ONE BAPTISM*, one God and Father of us all, who is above all, through all and in (us) all." Brethren, this is our faith and our sanctification.

[40] Delbert B. Flora, "The Spiritual Significance of Triune Immersion," *BE* 62 (August 24, 1940):12.

[41] See Charles A. Bame, "Travel Flashes," *BE* 69 (April 12, 1947):14 and Charles A. Bame to [Willis E.] Ronk, May 12, 1943, Ronk Files. According to the contents of the letter, an article (attached to the letter) by Bame which upheld the essential nature of baptism was being rejected by the Publication Board because of concern about adverse reaction.

[42] Brethren writers have continued to see baptism as an integral part of the process of salvation and regeneration; therefore, baptism is more than a "naked" symbol. Note the following statements:

> Baptism enters into the work of Regeneration. [1 Cor. 6:11; Gal. 3:27; Tit. 3:5 are cited.] No, this would not be a so-called 'Baptismal Regeneration,' but baptism as an essential part in Regeneration, if Regeneration is a continuing process.

Albert T. Ronk, "Inherent Theology in Brethren Rites: The Theology of Baptism, Part Two," *BE* 80 (May 31, 1958):6.

> The outward obedience in baptism is therefore symbolical of the inward work of grace and allied with it, for Peter said "baptism doth now save us." This is not salvation by water baptism but baptism as a part of the Believer's obedience.

Committee on Indoctrination Materials, *Our Faith*, p. 29.

[43] *Conference Annual 1969* (Ashland, Ohio: The Brethren Publishing Company, 1970), p. 8.

[44] Ibid., pp. 5, 8.

[45] Richard Allison, "Let God's Love Prevail," *BE* 91 (March 15, 1969):20.

[46] Kent Bennett, "What It Means to Be Brethren," *BE* 92 (November 21, 1970):21–23; idem, "The Rediscovery of the Hermeneutic Community," *BE* 93 (February 13, 1971):13–14; M. W. Dodds, "The Christian in the World," *BE* 94 (June 17, 1972):28–30; and Charles Munson, "Progressive Brethren," *BE* 97 (June 28, 1975):17–18.

[47] Interview with Delbert Flora, May 26, 1979.

[48] Charles A. Bame, "The Brethren and the War," *BE* 64 (January 5, 1942):9.

[49] During the decade of the 1970s, Phil Lersch devoted his attention to the promotion of World Relief (the relief agency of the National Association of Evangelicals) in the denomination. Though this is another area which is entirely consistent with the Brethren heritage, it is actually the stirring of interest in social concerns within evangelicalism which has led the church to reconsider the importance of this ministry.

[50] N. Victor Leatherman, "The Christian and War," *BE* 81 (October 24, 1959):6.

[51] This observation is based on an informal survey taken at the 1973 General Conference. See John Shultz, "National Conference and Peace," *BE* 95 (October 22, 1973):9.

[52] Richard E. Allison, "Resources for a Remedy," *BE* 89 (October 28, 1967):8. In defining the Brethren peace position, one should avoid the temptation of equating pacifism and nonresistance. The distinction to be borne in mind is the *principle* motivating the position. Many Christian pacifists work with the same assumption as do the militarists in the Christian community: the church is

responsible for the actions of the state. This assumption has no basis in the Brethren/Mennonite tradition. Nonresistance is based on Christ's own character and example of defenseless love which is "eminently *non*political in character." See the development of the distinction in Vernard Eller, *King Jesus' Manual of Arms for the 'Armless* (Nashville: Abingdon Press, 1973), pp. 193–205.

[53] Delbert Flora observes that many pastors backed away from eschatology following the division because they felt it was in some sense connected with the dissension which led to the split. See the interview on May 26, 1979.

[54] Jerry Flora, "An Outline of Prophecy," *BE* 85 (July 20, 1963): 12–14 and George W. Solomon, "The Rapture: Part I/II," *BE* 85 (August 17 and 31, 1963):10–11/16–17.

[55] Franklin Hamlin Littell, *The Free Church* (Boston: Starr King Press, 1957), p. 116.

CONCLUSION

[1] Ronk, *Brethren Church*, pp. 244–245 applies this term to those discerning men who "steered the Church through many dangerous waters in all of her history."

[2] A number of recent New Testament theologians have recognized the importance and ramifications of the concept that Christians are living "between the times" of Christ's resurrection and parousia. It is the inherent dialectical tension between already having experienced some of the powers of the age to come and not yet receiving these powers in their fullness that gives to this age its distinctive quality. See, for example, George Eldon Ladd, *A Theology of the New Testament* (Grand Rapids, Michigan: William B. Eerdmans Publishing Company, 1974), pp. 369–373, 524–525.

[3] Note Peter Nead's statement (p. 118) that Scripture, separated from the work of the Spirit, is not all-sufficient for the illumination and conversion of the sinner.

[4] Harold S. Bender, *Biblical Revelation and Inspiration*, Focal Pamphlet no. 4 (Scottdale, Pennsylvania: Herald Press, 1959), p. 17.

[5] Alexander Mack, Sr., chastened the Radical Pietists for this very attitude. He described as "pernicious hypocritical love" the notion: "Leave me alone in my own will, opinion, and actions, and I will leave you alone in yours; we will love each other and be brethren." Mack, "Basic Questions," p. 341.

[6] Note in this regard G. W. Rench's criticism of the spirit with which the "Message of the Brethren Ministry" was adopted:

> Were the midnight session of ministers, in which "The Message of the Brethren Ministry" was adopted, characterized by the fruits of the Spirit . . . ? Every impartial observer knows that just the opposite is true, and subsequent events have only widened the breach among the ministers.

G. W. Rench, "The Fundamentals of the Brethren Church," *BE* 50 (June 30, 1928):7.

[7] J. Ray Klingensmith has observed that the slowness of the working of the Brethren machinery is really a blessing in disguise.

> Of its denominational life the Brethren are often accused of the common failing today "too little and too late," but nevertheless this very disposition of our people has been our strength in the past few years. Not that we are to be excused wherein we hesitated through indifference, but that the Pied Pipers of our present evil world, some of whom are dressed in the garbs of prophetic priests and others in the very modern robes of worldly philosophy, have failed to charm the Brethren ear. And thus we face whatever is ahead of us as the same solid conservative Brethren people that to some is our fault but to ourselves is our strength.

J. Ray Klingensmith, "What the Brethren Face Now," *BE* 64 (September 19, 1942):4.

[8] Revivalism's emphasis on the individual's experience of salvation and periodic spiritual "highs" bears a good deal of the blame here (cf. pp. 158–159). No doubt, cultural trends which have led to less of a church-oriented society and more of a school, job, and club-centered culture have also played a part.

[9] In the Brethren experience it would appear that these two emphases have militated against each other. The Old Order Brethren, who maintain the principle of nonconformity quite vigorously, have disavowed foreign mission (and derivatively the importance of evangelism) on the basis of the argument that the Great Commission was given to and fulfilled by the apostles. See The Vindicator Committee, *Doctrinal Treatise*, 3d ed. (Covington, Ohio: The Vindicator, 1970), pp. 57–60. The Progressive Brethren, on the other hand, quickly lost their distinctive life style in their desire to carry the gospel to America and the world.

[10] This term was coined by Franklin Littell in *From State Church to Pluralism*. Littell utilizes it as a call "for the energetic and vigorous testimony of the churches in the public sphere . . . without seeking to capture and control the political machinery of the nation." See Ross Thomas Bender, *The People of God* (Scottdale, Pennsylvania: Herald Press, 1971), p. 38.

[11] J. Allen Miller, "The Brethren Church: Why?," *BE* 35 (July 30, 1913):1.

[12] R. R. Teeter, "The First Bible Institute. Will You Be There?," *BE* 38 (February 16, 1916):9.

[13] Note J. K. Zeman's sobering observation about Believers' Churches.

> A denomination which is constituted on the principle of "mixed membership" and on infant baptism can predict its numerical growth on the basis of national vital statistics. By way of contrast, a believers' church is only one generation away from extinction. Unless God the Spirit continues His gracious work of regeneration, such a church is doomed to death.

J. K. Zeman, Response to the address by Warren F. Groff, in *Concept of the Believers' Church*, p. 60.

[14] Miller, "The Brethren Church: Why?," p. 1.

BIBLIOGRAPHY

I. Sources for the
Background of Early Brethren Thought

A. Works on Anabaptism

Articles

Crous, Ernst. "Mennonites in Europe 1648-1815." In *An Introduction to Mennonite History*, pp. 112-125. Edited by Cornelius J. Dyck. Scottdale, Pennsylvania: Herald Press, 1967.

Durnbaugh, Donald F. "The Descent of Dissent: Some Interpretations of Brethren Origins." *Brethren Life and Thought* 19 (Spring 1974):125-133.

———. "Relationships of the Brethren with the Mennonites and Quakers, 1709-1865." *Church History* 35 (1966): 35-59.

Friedmann, Robert. "The Hutterian Brethren." In *Hutterite Studies*, pp. 41-49. Edited by Harold S. Bender. Goshen, Indiana: Mennonite Historical Society, 1961.

Keeney, William. "Anabaptists-Mennonites in Northern Europe, 1550-1650." In *An Introduction to Mennonite History*, pp. 89-102. Edited by Cornelius J. Dyck. Scottdale, Pennsylvania: Herald Press, 1967.

Klaassen, Walter. "Pilgram Marpeck and South German Anabaptism." In *An Introduction to Mennonite History*, pp. 61-73. Edited by Cornelius J. Dyck. Scottdale, Pennsylvania: Herald Press, 1967.

Oyer, John. "Central German and Moravian Anabaptism." In *An Introduction to Mennonite History*, pp. 44-60. Edited by Cornelius J. Dyck. Scottdale, Pennsylvania: Herald Press, 1967.

Schrag, Martin H. "The Impact of Pietism upon the Mennonites in Early American Christianity." In *Continental Pietism and Early American Christianity*, pp. 74-122. Edited by F. Ernest Stoeffler. Grand Rapids, Michigan: William B. Eerdmans Publishing Company, 1976.

Wenger, J. C. "The Amish." In *An Introduction to Mennonite History*, pp. 181-191. Edited by Cornelius J. Dyck. Scottdale, Pennsylvania: Herald Press, 1967.

Williams, George Huntston. "The Wilderness and Paradise in the History of the Church." *Church History* 28 (1959): 3-24.

Yoder, John H. "Anabaptist Origins in Switzerland." In *An Introduction to Mennonite History*, pp. 26-35. Edited by Cornelius J. Dyck. Scottdale, Pennsylvania: Herald Press, 1967.

———. "The Recovery of the Anabaptist Vision." *Concern* 18 (July 1971):5-23.

Books

Bender, Harold S., and Smith, C. Henry. *Mennonites and Their Heritage*. Scottdale, Pennsylvania: Herald Press, 1964.

Estep, William R. *The Anabaptist Story*. Nashville, Tennessee: Broadman Press, 1963.

Felbinger, Jeremias. *Christliches Hand-Büchlein*. 3d ed. Baltimore: Samuel Sauer, 1799.

Friedmann, Robert. *Mennonite Piety through the Centuries: Its Genius and its Literature*. Goshen, Indiana: The Mennonite Historical Society, 1949.

———. *The Theology of Anabaptism*. Studies in Anabaptist and Mennonite History, no. 15. Scottdale, Pennsylvania: Herald Press, 1973.

Klaassen, Walter. *Anabaptism: Neither Catholic Nor Protestant*. Waterloo, Ontario: Conrad Press, 1973.

Kot, Stanislas. *Socinianism in Poland: The Social and Political Ideas of the Polish Anti-trinitarians in the Sixteenth and Seventeenth Centuries*. Boston: Starr King Press, 1957.

Philip, Dietrich. *Enchiridion or Hand Book of the Christian Doctrine and Religion . . .* Translated by A. B. Kolb. Alymer, Ontario: Pathway Publishing Corporation, 1966.

Simons, Menno. *The Complete Writings of Menno Simons c.1496-1561*. Translated by Leonard Verduin and edited by John Christian Wenger. Scottdale, Pennsylvania: Herald Press, 1956.

van Braght, Thieleman J. *The Bloody Theater or Martyrs Mirror of the Defenseless Christians . . .* Translated by Joseph F. Solm. Scottdale, Pennsylvania: Herald Press, 1975.

Wenger, J. C. *The Mennonite Church in America*. Scottdale, Pennsylvania: Herald Press, 1966.

Wilbur, Earl Morse. *A History of Unitarianism: Socinianism and its Antecedents*. Boston: Beacon Press, 1945.

Williams, George Huntston. *The Radical Reformation*. Philadelphia: The Westminster Press, 1962.

————. *Wilderness and Paradise in Christian Thought*. New York: Harper & Brothers, 1962.

Reference Works

The Mennonite Encyclopedia. 4 volumes.

B. Works on Pietism

Articles

Gerdes, Egon W. "Theological Tenets of Pietism." *The Covenant Quarterly* 34 (February/May 1976):25-60.

Miller, Donald E. "The Influence of Gottfried Arnold upon the Church of the Brethren." *Brethren Life and Thought* 5 (Summer 1960):39-50.

Schmidt, Martin. "Gottfried Arnold (1666-1715)." In *Das Zeitalter des Pietismus*, pp. 142-189. Edited by Martin Schmidt and Wilhelm Jannasch. Bremen: Carl Schünemann Verlag, 1965.

Stoeffler, F. Ernest. "Pietism: Its Message, Early Manifestation, and Significance." *The Covenant Quarterly* 34 (February/May 1976):3-24.

Tanis, James. "Reformed Pietism in Colonial America." In *Continental Pietism and Early American Christianity*, pp. 34-73. Edited by F. Ernest Stoeffler. Grand Rapids, Michigan: William B. Eerdmans Publishing Company, 1976.

Books

Arnold, Gottfried. *Die Erste Liebe Der Gemeinen Jesu Christi, Das ist, Wahre Abbildung Der Ersten Christen . . .* Franckfurt am Mayn: Gottlieb Friedeburgs Buchhandlung, 1696.

————. *Unparteyische Kirchen- und Ketzer-historie . . .* 3 vols. Schaffhausen: Emanuel and Benedict Hurter, 1740.

Brown, Dale. *Understanding Pietism*. Grand Rapids, Michigan: William B. Eerdmans Publishing Company, 1978.

Büchsel, Jürgen. *Gottfried Arnold: Sein Verständnis von Kirche und Wiedergeburt*. Arbeiten zur Geschichte des Pietismus, no. 8. Witten: Luther-Verlag, 1970.

Calvin, John. *Golden Booklet of the True Christian Life*. Translated by Henry J. Van Andel. Grand Rapids, Michigan: Baker Book House, 1952.

Dörries, Hermann. *Geist und Geschichte bei Gottfried Arnold*. Göttingen: Vandenhoeck & Ruprecht, 1963.

Knox, R. A. *Enthusiasm: A Chapter in the History of Religion*. London: Oxford University Press, 1950.

Renkewitz, Heinz. *Hochmann von Hochenau (1670-1721)*. Quellenstudien zur Geschichte des Pietismus, no. 5. Witten: Luther-Verlag, 1969.

Ritschl, Albrecht. *Geschichte des Pietismus*. Vol. 2: *Der Pietismus in der lutherischen Kirchen des 17. und 18. Jahrhunderts*. Bonn: Adolph Marcus, 1884.

Seeberg, Erich. *Gottfried Arnold: Die Wissenschaft und die Mystik Seiner Zeit*. Studien zur Historiographie und zur Mystik. Darmstadt: Wissenschaftliche Buchgesellschaft, 1964.

————, ed. *Gottfried Arnold: in Auswahl Herausgegeben*. Mystiker des Abendlandes. München: Albert Langen-Georg Müller Verlag, 1934.

Spener, Philip Jacob. *Pia Desideria*. Translated and edited by Theodore G. Tappert. Philadelphia: Fortress Press, 1964.

Stoeffler, F. Ernest. *German Pietism during the Eighteenth Century*. Studies in the History of Religions, no. 24. Leiden: E. J. Brill. 1973.

————. *The Rise of Evangelical Pietism*. Studies in the History of Religions, no. 9. Leiden: E. J. Brill, 1971.

Thune, Nils. *The Behmenists and the Philadelphians: A Contribution to the Study of English Mysticism in the 17th and 18th Centuries*. Uppsala: Almqvist & Wiksells Boktryckeri AB, 1948.

Dissertations

Brown, Dale. "The Problem of Subjectivism in Pietism." Ph.D. dissertation, Northwestern University, 1962.

Deeter, Allen C. "An Historical and Theological Introduction to Phillip Jakob Spener's *Pia Desideria*: A Study in Early German Pietism." Ph.D. dissertation, Princeton University, 1963.

Ensign, C. David. "Radical German Pietism (c.1675-c.1760)." Ph.D. dissertation, Boston University Graduate School, 1955.

II. Sources for the
History and Thought of the Brethren

A. General Works

Articles

Durnbaugh, Donald F. "A Study of Brethren Historiography." *Ashland Theological Bulletin* 8 (Spring 1975): 3-18.

———— and Shultz, Lawrence W. "A Brethren Bibliography." *Brethren Life and Thought* 9 (Winter/Spring 1964):1-177.

Books

Bowman, Rufus D. *The Church of the Brethren and War, 1708-1941*. Elgin, Illinois: Brethren Publishing House, 1944.

The Committee appointed by District Conference. *History of the Church of the Brethren of the Eastern District of Pennsylvania*. Lancaster, Pennsylvania: The New Era Printing Company, 1915; reprint ed., Knightstown, Indiana: The Bookmark, 1977.

Dove, Frederick Denton. *Cultural Changes in the Church of the Brethren.* Elgin, Illinois: Brethren Publishing House, 1932.

Falkenstein, George N. *History of the German Baptist Brethren Church.* Lancaster, Pennsylvania: The New Era Printing Company, 1901.

Holsinger, Henry R. *Holsinger's History of the Tunkers and The Brethren Church.* Oakland, California: Pacific Press Publishing Company, 1901; reprint ed. North Manchester, Indiana: L. W. Shultz, 1962.

Kent, Homer A., Sr. *Conquering Frontiers.* Winona Lake, Indiana: BMH Books, 1958; rev. ed. 1972.

Kimmel, John M. *Chronicles of the Brethren.* Berne, Indiana: The Economy Printing Concern, 1972.

Mallott, Floyd E. *Studies in Brethren History.* Elgin, Illinois: Brethren Publishing House, 1954.

Miller, Marcus. *"Roots by the River."* Piqua, Ohio: Hammer Graphics, Inc., 1973.

Ronk, Albert T. *History of The Brethren Church.* Ashland, Ohio: Brethren Publishing Company, 1968.

Winger, Otho. *History and Doctrines of the Church of the Brethren.* Elgin, Illinois: Brethren Publishing House, 1919.

Reference Works

The Brethren Encyclopedia. 3 vols.

B. The Early Brethren (1708–1785)

1. Brethren Works

Articles

Brown, Dale W. "Membership in the Body of Christ as Interpreted by the Heritage of the Brethren." *Brethren Life and Thought* 9 (Autumn 1964):63–77.

Brunn, Hermann. "Alexander Mack, the Founder, 1679–1735." In *Schwarzenau Yesterday and Today*, pp. 37–43. Updated ed. Edited by Lawrence W. Shultz. Winona Lake, Indiana: Light and Life Press, 1977.

Deeter, Allen C. "Membership in the Body of Christ as Interpreted by Classical Pietism." *Brethren Life and Thought* 13 (Autumn 1964):30–49.

Durnbaugh, Donald F. "Brethren and the Authority of the Scriptures." *Brethren Life and Thought* 13 (Summer 1968):170–183.

————. "The Brethren in Early American Church Life." In *Continental Pietism and Early American Christianity*, pp. 222–265. Edited by F. Ernest Stoeffler. Grand Rapids, Michigan: William B. Eerdmans Publishing Company, 1976.

————. "Early History." In *The Church of the Brethren Past and Present*, pp. 9–22. Edited by Donald F. Durnbaugh. Elgin, Illinois: The Brethren Press, 1971.

————. "The Genius of the Brethren." *Brethren Life and Thought* 4 (Winter/Spring 1959):4–34/4–18.

Eller, Vernard. "On Epitomizing the Brethren." *Brethren Life and Thought* 6 (Autumn 1961):47–52.

Faw, Chalmer E. "The Brethren and the Book of Books." In *The Adventurous Future*, pp. 103–116. Compiled and edited by Paul W. Bowman. Elgin, Illinois: The Brethren Press, 1959.

Schrag, Martin. "The Early Brethren Concept of Authority." *Brethren Life and Thought* 9 (Autumn 1964): 109–126.

Books

Brumbaugh, Martin Grove. *A History of the German Baptist Brethren in Europe and America.* Mount Morris, Illinois: Brethren Publishing House, 1899; reprint ed. L. W. Shultz and Carl A. Wagoner, 1969.

Durnbaugh, Donald F., comp. and ed. *The Brethren in Colonial America.* Elgin, Illinois: The Brethren Press, 1967.

————, comp. and ed. *European Origins of the Brethren.* Elgin, Illinois: The Brethren Press, 1958.

Eller, Vernard. *Kierkegaard and Radical Discipleship: A New Perspective.* Princeton, New Jersey: Princeton University Press, 1968.

Frantz, Michael. *Einfältige Lehr-Betrachtungen, und Kurzgefaßtes Glaubens-Bekäntniß . . .* Germantown: Christoph Saur, 1770.

K., M. *The Fatal Consequences of the Unscriptural Doctrine of Predestination and Reprobation; With a Caution against It.* Translated an [sic] Desire. Germantown: Christopher Sower, 1753.

Klein-Nicolai, George [Paul Siegvolck]. *The Everlasting Gospel, Commanded to be Preached by Jesus Christ, Judge of the Living and the Dead, Unto All Creatures . . .* Translated by John S. [Price]. Germantown: Christopher Sower, 1753.

Lamech and Agrippa [pseud.]. *Chronicon Ephratense: A History of the Community of Seventh Day Baptists of Ephrata, Lancaster County, Penn'a.* Translated by J. Max Hark. Lancaster, Pennsylvania: S. H. Zahm and Co., 1899; reprint ed., New York: Burt Franklin, 1972.

Mack, Alexander. *A Short and Plain View of the Outward Yet Sacred Rites and Ordinances of the House of God . . .* Ashland, Ohio: [National Sunday School Association of the Brethren Church], 1939.

Willoughby, William G. *Counting the Cost: The Life of Alexander Mack, 1679–1735.* Elgin, Illinois: The Brethren Press, 1979.

Dissertations

Durnbaugh, Donald Floyd. "Brethren Beginnings: The Origins of the Church of the Brethren in Early Eighteenth-Century Europe." Ph.D. dissertation, University of Pennsylvania, 1960.

Porte, Robert Fowler. "The Pietistic Tradition in the Brethren Church." Th.D. dissertation, Drew University, 1933.

Willoughby, William G. "The Beliefs of the Early Brethren." Ph.D. dissertation, Boston University Graduate School, 1951.

2. Non-Brethren Works

Articles

Volz, Hans. "Continental Versions to c.1600: German Versions." In *The Cambridge History of the Bible: The West from the Reformation to the Present Day*, pp. 94–109. Edited by S. L. Greenslade. Cambridge: Cambridge University Press, 1963.

Wentz, Richard E. "The American Character and the American Revolution: A Pennsylvania German Sampler." *Journal of the American Academy of Religion* 44 (March 1976):115–131.

Books

Altaner, Berthold. *Patrology*. Translated by Hilda C. Graef. New York: Herder and Herder, 1960.

Armour, Rollin Stely. *Anabaptist Baptism: A Representative Study*. Studies in Anabaptist and Mennonite History, no. 11. Scottdale, Pennsylvania: Herald Press, 1966.

Edwards, Morgan. *Materials toward a History of the American Baptists*. 2 vols. Philadelphia: Joseph Crukshank and Isaac Collins, 1770; xerographed, Ann Arbor, Michigan: Xerox University Microfilms, 1976.

Homan, Johann George, ed. *Das Evangelium Nicodemus oder Gewißer Bericht Von dem Leben, Leiden und Sterben, Unsers Heilands Jesu Christi* . . . Reading, Pennsylvania: C. A. Bruckman, 1819.

Nieper, Friedrich. *Die ersten deutschen Auswanderer von Krefeld nach Pennsylvanien*. Neukirchen, Kreis Moers: Buchhandlung des Erziehungsvereins, 1940.

Sachse, Julius Friedrich. *The German Sectarians of Pennsylvania*. Vol. 2: *1742–1800: A Critical and Legendary History of the Ephrata Cloister and the Dunkers*. Philadelphia: Printed for the author, 1900; reprint ed., New York: AMS Press, 1971.

Stoudt, John J. *Pennsylvania German Poetry, 1685–1830*. Norristown, Pennsylvania: Pennsylvania German Folklore Society, 1956.

C. The German Baptist Brethren (1785–1883)

1. Brethren Works

Articles

Benedict, Fred W. "The Life and Work of Elder Peter Nead." *Brethren Life and Thought* 19 (Winter 1974): 63–79.

———. "The Moderate Principle." *Brethren Life and Thought* 24 (Summer 1979):181–187.

———. "The Old Orders and Schism." *Brethren Life and Thought* 18 (Winter 1973):25–32.

Bowman, Loren. "The Life and Work of Peter Nead." *Schwarzenau* 1 (January 1940):9–22.

Brown, Dale W. "The Developing Thought and Theology of the Brethren—1785–1860." *Ashland Theological Bulletin* 8 (Spring 1975):61–74.

Durnbaugh, Donald F. "Henry Kurtz: Man of the Book." *Brethren Life and Thought* 16 (Spring 1971):103–121.

———. "Henry R. Holsinger: A Church of the Brethren Perspective." *Brethren Life and Thought* 24 (Summer 1979):142–146.

———. "Recent History." In *Church of the Brethren Past and Present*, pp. 23–38. Edited by Donald F. Durnbaugh. Elgin, Illinois: The Brethren Press, 1971.

———. "She Kept on Preaching." *Messenger* 124 (April 1975):18–21.

———. "Vindicator of Primitive Christianity: The Life and Diary of Peter Nead." *Brethren Life and Thought* 14 (Autumn 1969):196–223.

Longenecker, Christian. "On the True Conversion and New Birth." Translated by Vernard Eller. *Brethren Life and Thought* 7 (Spring 1962):23–34.

Miller, Marcus. "Leaders of the Old Order Movement, 1865 to 1900." *Brethren Life and Thought* 24 (Summer 1979):147–161.

———. "Roots by the River." *Ashland Theological Bulletin* 8 (Spring 1975):47–60.

Murray, Samuel; Siler, George V.; and Kinsey, Samuel. "The Brethren's Reasons." In *Minutes of the Annual Meetings of the Old German Baptist Brethren from 1778 to 1955*, Appendix, pp. 3–53. Publishing Committee. Covington, Ohio: The Little Printing Company, 1956.

Parker, I. D. "Church Polity." In *Two Centuries of the Church of the Brethren*, pp. 153–169. Edited by D. L. Miller. Elgin, Illinois: Brethren Publishing House, 1908.

Sappington, Roger E. "How the Brethren Were Influencing the Development of Other Denominations between 1785 and 1860." *Ashland Theological Bulletin* 8 (Spring 1975): 75–86.

Books

Beer, Joseph W. *The Jewish Passover and the Lord's Supper*. Lancaster, Pennsylvania: Inquirer Printing and Publishing Co., 1874.

Bowman, Peter. *A Testimony on Baptism as Practised by the Primitive Christians, from the Time of the Apostles* . . . Baltimore: Benjamin Edes, 1831.

Flory, John S. *Flashlights from History*. Elgin, Illinois: Brethren Publishing House, 1932.

Funk, Benjamin, comp. *Life and Labors of Elder John Kline, the Missionary Martyr*. Elgin, Illinois: Brethren Publishing House, 1900; reprint ed., Elgin, Illinois: The Brethren Press, 1964.

Garst, Jesse O., et al. *History of the Church of the Brethren of the Southern District of Ohio*. Dayton, Ohio: The Otterbein Press, 1920.

The General Mission Board. *Minutes of the Annual Meetings of the Church of the Brethren, Containing all Available Minutes from 1778 to 1909.* Elgin, Illinois: Brethren Publishing House, 1909.

Gillin, John Lewis. *The Dunkers: A Sociological Interpretation.* New York: n.p., 1906.

Kurtz, Henry. *The Brethren's Encyclopedia . . .* Columbiana, Ohio: By the author, 1867.

[Kurtz, Heinrich, trans.]. *Zeugnisse der Wahrheit, oder: Menno Symons sämtliche Schriften. . . . Des zweyten Theiles Erster Band.* Osnaburg, Ohio: Heinrich Kurtz, 1833.

Lehman, James H. *The Old Brethren.* Elgin, Illinois: The Brethren Press, 1976.

Moomaw, Benjamin F. *Discussions on Trine Immersion . . .* Singer's Glen, Virginia: Joseph Funk's Sons, 1867.

Moore, J. H. *Some Brethren Pathfinders.* Elgin, Illinois: Brethren Publishing House, 1929.

Nead, Peter. *Theological Writings on Various Subjects; or a Vindication of Primitive Christianity as Recorded in the Word of God. . . .* Dayton, Ohio: B. F. Ells, 1850.

_____. *The Wisdom and Power of God as Displayed in Creation and Redemption.* Cincinnati: E. Morgan & Sons, 1866.

Quinter, Mary N. *Life and Sermons of Elder James Quinter.* Mt. Morris, Illinois: Brethren Publishing Company, 1891.

Sappington, Roger E. *The Brethren in Virginia: The History of the Church of the Brethren in Virginia.* Harrisonburg, Virginia: Park View Press, 1973.

_____. *Courageous Prophet: Chapters from the Life of John Kline.* Elgin, Illinois: The Brethren Press, 1964.

_____, comp. and ed. *The Brethren in Industrial America, A Source Book on the Development of the Church of the Brethren, 1865-1915.* Elgin, Illinois: Brethren Press, 1985.

_____, comp. and ed. *The Brethren in the New Nation, A Source Book on the Development of the Church of the Brethren, 1785-1865.* Elgin, Illinois: The Brethren Press, 1976.

Sharp, S. Z. *The Educational History of the Church of the Brethren.* Elgin, Illinois: Brethren Publishing House, 1923.

Stein, J. W., and Ray, D. B. *The Stein and Ray Debate, A Church Discussion between the Brethren and Baptist.* Mt. Morris, Illinois: Western Book Exchange, 1881.

Thurman, William C. *The Ordinance of Feet Washing, As Instituted by Christ, Defended and Restored to its Original Purity.* Philadelphia: John Goodyear, 1864.

_____. *The Sealed Book of Daniel Opened; Or A Book of Reference for those who Wish to Examine the "Sure Word of Prophecy."* Philadelphia: John Goodyear, 1864.

Dissertations and Projects

Eller, David Barry. "The Brethren in the Western Ohio Valley, 1790-1850: German Baptist Settlement and Frontier Accommodation." Ph.D. dissertation, Miami University, 1976.

Lauderdale, Kerby. "Division among the German Baptist Brethren." M.Div. Independent Study, Bethany Theological Seminary, 1968.

Rupel, Esther Fern. "An Investigation of the Origin, Significance, and Demise of the Prescribed Dress Worn by Members of the Church of the Brethren." Ph.D. dissertation, University of Minnesota, 1971.

Pamphlets

Bashor, Stephen H. *The Brethren Church.* Waterloo, Iowa: Brethren Publishing Company, [1893].

Eshelman, M. M. *Sabbatism. The Law and the Gospel Contrasted.* Lanark, Illinois: Hay and Lowis, Printers, 1875.

Report of Progressive Convention, Held at Ashland, Ohio. Commencing June 29, 1882. N.p., n.d.

Thurman, William C. *The Answer to Dr. Thurman's Epistle.* N.p., [c. 1868].

_____. *To the Disappointed and Tried.* N.p., [1868].

Worst, J. H. *"Keep My Commandments."* N.p., [c.1882].

Periodicals

The Brethren at Work, vols. 1-3, 6-7 (1876-1878, 1881-1882).

The Christian Family Companion, vols. 1-9 (1865-1873).

The Christian Family Companion and Gospel Visitor, vols. 1-2 (1874-1875).

The Gospel Preacher, vol. 4 (1882).

The Monthly Gospel Visitor, vols. 4-10, 13-16, 18, 21-23 (1854-1860, 1863-1866, 1868, 1871-1873).

The Primitive Christian, vol. 1 (1876).

The Primitive Christian and The Pilgrim, vols. 1-3 (1876-1878).

The Progressive Christian, vols. 1-5 (1879-1883).

The Vindicator, vols. 1-13 (1870-1882).

2. Non-Brethren Works

Articles

Kraus, C. Norman. "Evangelicalism: The Great Coalition." In *Evangelicalism and Anabaptism,* pp. 39-61. Edited by C. Norman Kraus. Scottdale, Pennsylvania: Herald Press, 1979.

Williams, George Huntston. "A People in Community: Historical Background." In *The Concept of the Believers' Church,* pp. 100-142. Edited by James Leo Garrett, Jr. Scottdale, Pennsylvania: Herald Press, 1969.

Books

Mead, Sidney E. *The Lively Experiment: The Shaping of Christianity in America.* New York: Harper & Row, Publishers, 1963.

Schlesinger, Arthur M., Sr. *A Critical Period in American Religion, 1875-1900.* Facet Books, Historical Series, no. 7. Philadelphia: Fortress Press, 1967.

Smith, Timothy L. *Revivalism and Social Reform: American Protestantism on the Eve of the Civil War.* Gloucester, Massachusetts: Peter Smith, 1976.

D. The Brethren Church (1883-1987)

1. Brethren Works

Articles

"Compromise." *Ashland College Bulletin* 11 (August 1938): 4-8.

Garber, L. L. "Among his Fellow Workers." *Ashland College Bulletin* 8 (May 1935):7-11.

Hogan, Herbert. "Fundamentalism in the Church of the Brethren." *Brethren Life and Thought* 5 (Winter 1960): 25-36.

Hoyt, Herman. "Dispensational Premillennialism." In *The Meaning of the Millennium: Four Views*, pp. 63-92. Edited by Robert G. Clouse. Downers Grove, Illinois: Inter-Varsity Press, 1977.

Jacobs, E. E. "A Brief History of Ashland College." *Ashland College Bulletin* 6 (November 1932):1-20.

Marlin, H. C. "Bame's Old Story Failed to Work So Lorah Is Out." *The Postscript* 2 (January 1, 1933):4.

McClain, Alva J. "The Background and Origin of Grace Theological Seminary." In *Charis*, pp. 9-39. Edited by John Whitcomb. N.p., 1951.

———. "The Inspiration of the Bible." In *Winona Echoes: Notable Addresses Delivered at the Thirty-Eighth Annual Bible Conference. Winona Lake, Indiana, August 1932*, pp. 199-208. N.p.: Victor M. Hatfield, Publisher, n.d.

Pearce, Alan S. "Summary of Dr. Bauman's Life." *The Brethren Missionary Herald* 13 (January 6, 1951):3-5.

Stuckey, M. A. "The Brethren Loyalty Association of the Brethren Church." *Ashland College Bulletin* 11 (August 1938):2-4.

Books

Eller, Vernard. *King Jesus' Manual of Arms for the 'Armless.* Nashville: Abingdon Press, 1973.

General Conference Committee on Indoctrination Materials. *Our Faith.* Ashland, Ohio: The A. L. Garber Co., 1960.

McClain, Alva J. *The Greatness of the Kingdom.* Winona Lake, Indiana: BMH Books, 1974.

———. *Law and Grace.* Winona Lake, Indiana: BMH Books, 1954.

Miller, J. Allen. *Christian Doctrine—Lectures and Sermons.* Ashland, Ohio: The Brethren Publishing Company, 1946.

Ronk, Albert T. *A Search for Truth.* Ashland, Ohio: Brethren Publishing Company, 1973.

Yoder, C. F. *Gospel Church Government.* N.p., n.d. [1906].

Dissertations and Projects

Best, Randal A. "The Mind of the Brethren Church on the Baptism of the Holy Spirit and Related Topics." M.Div. project, Ashland Theological Seminary, 1976.

Hogan, Herbert. "The Intellectual Impact of the Twentieth Century on the Church of the Brethren." Ph.D. dissertation, The Claremont Graduate School, 1958.

Martin, Dennis. "Law and Grace." Independent Study, Wheaton College, 1973.

Interviews

Flora, Delbert B. Ashland, Ohio. April 2, 1979, and May 26, 1979.

Hoyt, Herman. Winona Lake, Indiana. June 15, 1979.

Mayes, Charles. Long Beach, California. April 11, 1978.

Monroe, Kenneth. Santa Barbara, California. October 22, 1979, and November 7, 1979.

Shultz, Joseph R. Ashland, Ohio. May 23, 1979.

Manuscript Collections

[William G.] Moorehead Papers, Pittsburgh Theological Seminary, Pittsburgh, Pennsylvania.

[Albert T.] Ronk Files, Ashland Theological Seminary, Ashland, Ohio.

Pamphlets and Printed Reports

Bauman, Louis S. *The Modern Tongues Movement.* N.p., 1930.

———. "An Open Letter to Charles A. Bame." In *Open Letters*, pp. 17-27. N.p., n.d.

Gillin, J. L. *Jesus and Society.* Ashland, Ohio: Brethren Publishing Board, 1900.

Mason, Edward. *Proceedings of the General Convention of the Brethren Church, . . . September 21, 22 and 23, 1887.* Ashland, Ohio: The Brethren Publishing House, 1887.

McClain, Alva J. *The Interchurch World Movement.* N.p., n.d. [1920].

Miller, J. Allen. *Doctrinal Statements.* Ashland, Ohio: The Brethren Publishing Company, n.d.

The Ministerial Board of Southern California to Charles L. Anspach. June 16, 1936.

Proceedings of the Dayton Convention . . . Dayton, Ohio: Daily Journal, 1883.

Rench, G. W. *Power and the Word.* Ashland, Ohio: Brethren Publication Board, 1900.

Report of the National Conference Committee on Investigation of Ashland College. By W. H. Schaffer, [Secretary].

Report of the Polity Committee. By Arden Gilmer, Chairman. Ashland, Ohio: n.p., 1977.

Swihart, J. H. *The Immortality of the Soul or Death and the Resurrection*. Ashland, Ohio: The Brethren Publishing House, 1889.

The Vindicator Committee. *Doctrinal Treatise*. 3d ed. Covington, Ohio: The Vindicator, 1970.

Yoder, C. F. *Some Significant Tendencies of the Times*. Ashland, Ohio: Brethren Publication Board, 1900.

Periodicals

The Brethren Annual/General Conference Minutes (1890–1986).

The Brethren Evangelist, vols. 5–11, 16–109 (1883–1889, 1894–1987).

The Purple and Gold, vols. 1–11 (1900–1911).

Unpublished Papers

Burkey, Fred. "Organizing for Growth." Ashland, Ohio, May 1976 (Xeroxed.)

2. Non-Brethren Works

Articles

Campbell, Alexander. "Incidents on a Tour to the South. No. 4." *The Millennial Harbinger* n.s. 3 (April 1839): 185–192.

_____. "Union of Christians. No. 3." *The Millennial Harbinger* n.s. 3 (August 1939):344–345.

Marsden, George. "Fundamentalism as an American Phenomenon, A Comparison with English Evangelicalism." *Church History* 46 (June 1977):215–232.

Zeman, J. K. Response to the address by Warren F. Groff. In *The Concept of the Believers' Church*, pp. 59–60. Edited by James Leo Garrett, Jr. Scottdale, Pennsylvania: Herald Press, 1969.

Books

The Annual Catalogue of the United Presbyterian Theological Seminary of Xenia, Ohio, 1916. Xenia, Ohio: Smith Advertising Co., 1916.

Bender, Harold S. *Biblical Revelation and Inspiration*. Focal Pamphlet no. 4. Scottdale, Pennsylvania: Herald Press, 1959.

Bender, Ross Thomas. *The People of God*. Scottdale, Pennsylvania: Herald Press, 1971.

Bible Conference Committee. *God Hath Spoken*. Philadelphia: Bible Conference Committee, 1919.

Brunner, Emil. *The Mediator: A Study of the Central Doctrine of the Christian Faith*. Translated by Olive Wyon. Philadelphia: The Westminster Press, 1947.

Cauthen, Kenneth. *The Impact of American Religious Liberalism*. New York: Harper & Row, Publishers, 1962.

Dollar, George W. *A History of Fundamentalism in America*. Greenville, South Carolina: Bob Jones University Press, 1973.

Gaddis, Vincent H., and Huffman, Jasper A. *The Story of Winona Lake: A Memory and a Vision*. Winona Lake, Indiana: Winona Lake Christian Assembly, 1960.

Kraus, C. Norman. *Dispensationalism in America: Its Rise and Development*. Richmond, Virginia: John Knox Press, 1958.

Ladd, George Eldon. *A Theology of the New Testament*. Grand Rapids, Michigan: William B. Eerdmans Publishing Company, 1974.

Littell, Franklin Hamlin. *The Free Church*. Boston: Starr King Press, 1957.

Sandeen, Ernest R. *The Origins of Fundamentalism: Toward a Historical Interpretation*. Facet Books: Historical Series, no. 10. Philadelphia: Fortress Press, 1968.

_____. *The Roots of Fundamentalism: British and American Millenarianism, 1800–1930*. Chicago: The University of Chicago Press, 1970.

Simpson, A. B. *The Four-Fold Gospel*. Harrisburg, Pennsylvania: Christian Publications, Inc., n.d.

Stevens, George Barker. *The Theology of the New Testament*. International Theological Library. New York: Charles Scribner's Sons, 1925.

Dissertations and Projects

Cook, Philip Lee. "Zion City, Illinois: Twentieth Century Utopia." Ph.D. dissertation, University of Colorado, 1965.

Gilbert, Ernst Eldon. "The Interchurch World Movement of North America 1919–1920." Ph.D. dissertation, Yale University, 1968.

Loucks, C. Mel. "Keswick Teaching and Consecration." Unpublished paper, Fuller Theological Seminary, n.d.

INDEX OF SCRIPTURE REFERENCES

INDEX OF PERSONS, PLACES, AND INSTITUTIONS

INDEX OF THEOLOGICAL SUBJECTS

317